THE SOLDIER'S SERVICE DICTIONARY

OF

English and French Terms

THE SOLDIER'S SERVICE DICTIONARY

OF

English and French Terms

Embracing 10,000 Military, Naval, Aeronautical, Aviation, and Conversational Words and Phrases Used by the Belgian, British, and French Armies

With Their French Equivalents Carefully Pronounced, the Whole Arranged in One Alphabetical Order

Designed Especially for Instant Use in the United States Service

With the Pronunciations Indicated by the Continental System of Vowel Values-One Symbol for Each Sound Throughout the Alphabet -Used in "Funk & Wagnalls New Standard Dictionary."

Edited by

FRANK H. VIZETELLY, Litt.D., LL.D.

Managing Editor of "The New Standard Dictionary," Member of the Royal Society of Arts, London, etc.

Illustrated with Topographical Symbols Used in Official Charts

KALPAZ

ISBN: 978-93-5128-855-8(HB)

First Published in 1917
Indian Reprint in 2017

Published by

Kalpaz Publications
C-30, Satyawati Nagar,
Delhi – 110052
E-mail: kalpaz@hotmail.com
Website: kalpazpublications.com
Ph.: +91-9212142040

Cataloging in Publication Data—DK
Courtesy: D.K. Agencies (P) Ltd. <docinfo@dkagencies.com>

The soldier's service dictionary of English and French terms : embracing 10,000 military, naval, aeronautical, aviation, and conversational words and phrases used by the Belgian, British, and French armies, with their French equivalents carefully pronounced, the whole arranged in one alphabetical order, designed especially for instant use in the United States service ... / edited by Frank H. Vizetelly.

pages cm
English and French.
"First published in 1917"—Title page verso.
ISBN 9789351288558

1. French language—Conversation and phrase books (for soldiers, etc.) 2. English language—Dictionaries—French. 3. French language—Dictionaries—English. 4. Military art and science—Dictionaries. I. Vizetelly, Frank H., 1864-1938, editor.

PC2120.S7V5 2017 DDC 448.3421 23

TO THE READER.

In the preparation of the Soldier's Service Dictionary of terms and phrases, with their French equivalents, the endeavor has been to provide a key to the military and conversational terms used in the Belgian, British, and French armies that shall instantly serve any one who consults it, and thus measure up to the maxim "*prompt* service is *true* service."

It is assumed that the person likely to consult this book speaks and understands English; that he knows in English what he wishes to say in French, and that he wants to know how to say it, and say it promptly so that he can be understood. For example, suppose he wished to ask in French: "Where is the enemy?" he would look up these English words in their vocabulary places, thus obtaining the French equivalents "Où (*where*) est (*is*) l'ennemi (*the enemy*)?" or, as indicated phonetically, ū ē len″‿nə-mī′, which form the sentence required. As many phrases are given under the important word, this should always be *looked up first*, to save time. For instance, if he wished to say in French: "Bring up the horses!" by turning to the word *horse* in the vocabulary he will find the French phrase in full: "Faites venir les chevaux!" with its pronunciation. If he wanted to say "Give me some breakfast, please," he would turn to *breakfast* and there find the needed phrase.

Instead of following the beaten track by grouping the terms in this book under several heads, divided and subdivided, as has been done by compilers of other works that aim to cover the subjects of which this treats, the entire contents, which total more than ten thousand terms, are presented in one alphabetical order, and, as explained above, *the related phrases are grouped under the most important word in the phrase.*

As will be seen by consulting the key to the symbols used for indicating the pronunciations of the various terms the guide contains, the plan followed throughout is to give the chief vowel sounds the same values that they have on the continent of Europe: — *a* as in *art*; *e* as in *prey*; *i* as in *police*; *o* as in *go*, and *u* as in *rule*. Variations are indicated by different letters — one, *and one only*, for each sound throughout the alphabet (see page xii). The Editor invites the cooperation of all persons who are interested in making this the most complete and most serviceable book of its kind to those for whose use it has been designed and compiled.

To simplify the study of the positions of the different parts of speech and the inflections and irregularities of French verbs brief explanations are included together with a concise table of verbs in an Appendix to the main vocabulary.

NEW YORK, September, 1917. F. H. V.

PRONUNCIATION

OF FRENCH VOWELS, DIPHTHONGS, AND CONSONANTS.

In most of the languages of Continental Europe the vowels have Latin values: ɑ as in "ɑrt"; ē as in "prey"; ī as in "machine"; ō as in "go"; and ū as in "rule." Persons who speak English need to be cautioned against pronouncing foreign long vowels as diphthongs. In English long ē with most speakers ends with a light i resonance (that is, as a diphthong, ē^{i}); long ō is generally turned into ō^{u}; long ū into ū^{u}. But in German, French, and European languages generally, these vowels are to be pronounced without the i or u element at their close. Foreign vowels are generally tenser than English vowels.

Vowel Modifications.

In French the vowel-sounds, as we know them in English, are modified in two ways, by "rounding" and by becoming "nasalized."

"Rounding" is the effect on a speech-sound of pursing the lips till the orifice is roundish, as in sounding English ū (*boot*). In English only back vowels are rounded; in some other languages certain front vowels are thus modified.

(1). Rounded ī. To make it, say ī (as in *see, machine*), at the same time pursing the lips as for ū (in *rule*). The symbol used in this guide is ü.

(2). Rounded ē. Say ē (as in *fate*), at the same time pursing the lips. This is the sound heard in French (*eu*), German (long *ö*), etc.

(3). Rounded e or a (really a sound between e and a). Make such a sound, at the same time pursing the lips. The sound is heard in French (*eu*), German (short *ö*), etc.

The English sound nearest to these last two is the ū of *burn* (būrn), and hence the symbol here used for these two rounded vowels is ū. But the foreign sounds are not exactly ū.

(4). In French are heard "nasal" vowels, that is, vowels to which a nasal quality is imparted from the fact that, while they are being sounded, the passage through the nose is open as well as that through the mouth. Hence part of the voiced breath escapes through the nose and reverberates in the nasal cavities. The nasal vowels are not vowels *followed* by n or ŋ, but simply vowels that receive their quality or *timbre* from resonance in both mouth and nose instead of in mouth alone. In this dictionary nasality in a vowel is indicated by adding to the symbol of that vowel the symbol ṅ; whence ɑṅ = nasal ɑ, aṅ = nasal a, etc. Many Americans, in their normal speech, unconsciously pronounce some or all of their vowels with a nasal quality; hence they are in danger of making the foreign vowels too strongly nasal, a practise which should be guarded against with all possible care.

In the following table the components of each diphthong are shown:

Diphthong. *French sounds.*

ia = ī + ɑ (ī as in *police* + ā as in *art*), as French *viande* (vī″ānd′).

iai = ī + è (ī as in *police* + ā as in *fare*), as French *liaison* (lī″ā″zeṅ′).

ié = ī + é (ī as in *police* + ē as in *prey*), as French *prié* (prī″‿yē′).

iè = ī + è (ī as in *police* + ā as in *fare*), as French *pièce* (pī″‿yās′).

In the following the division occurs after the *i*, and each diphthong represents two sounds. The nasal sound is added in some cases:

io as in French *idiot* (ī″dī″‿yō′).

ian as in French *expédiant* (eks″pē″dī″‿yāṅ′).

iau as in French *miauler* (mī″ō″lē′).

ien as in French *bien* (bī″‿yaṅ′).

ient as in French *patient* (pɑ″sī″‿yɑṅ′).

ieu as in French *lieu* (lī″‿yū′).

ion as in French *portion* (pōr″sī″‿yoṅ′).

oi = o + a (o as in *obey* + ā as in *art*).

Preceded by a consonant *oi* sounds like *wa;* as in French *foi* (fō-ā *or* fwā).

Diphthong. *French sounds.*

oin = o + in (o as in *obey* + a as in *at*): as in French *loin* (lwaṅ).

oua = ou + ā (ū as in *rule* + ā as in *art*): as in French *secoua* (se″kū″ā′).

oui = ou + ī (ū as in *rule* + ī as in *police*): as in French *Louis* (lū″ī′).

ua = u + ā (ü as in French *dune* + ā as in *art*): as in French *nuage* (nü″āʒ′).*

ui = u + ī (ü as in French *dune* + ī as in *police*): as in French *pluie* (plwī).

uin = u + in (ü as in French *dune* + a as in *at*): as in French *Juin* (ʒwaṅ).

Consonant Modifications.

Consonants in foreign languages (with some exceptions) are more carefully, and often more firmly or energetically, enunciated than in English.

(5). What one may call "palatalized" consonants are made by combining the sound y with the normal consonants. Palatalized l, for example, is not l followed by y (as one hears it in *brilliant*), but l and y merged into one—an l made by raising not the tip of the tongue to the upper gums, but the front of the tongue to the front part of the palate above it. Palatalized n is made by raising the front of the tongue just as for y, but further, until it is pressed against the front palate. After such a palatalized consonant there will almost unavoidably be a more or less distinct y heard as a glide to a following vowel; and the symbol used in this book for these consonants is a combination of the appropriate consonant symbol with the symbol y (ny, ly, etc.). But such a symbol as ny is not to be interpreted as n followed by y, but as an n made at the same place in the mouth as y is made. It should be noted that the so-called *l-mouillé*

* The symbol ʒ = zh. See Number 9, page xi.

in French (spelled *-il*, *-ill*) has in the best standard pronunciation ceased to be an l and is pronounced simply as y.

(6). Two r's are heard in French. (*a*) In French, German, etc., a trilled r is heard. It is made by raising the tip of the tongue almost to the upper gums and setting the tip to vibrating or fluttering against the gums. (*b*) The "uvular" r, made by raising the back of the tongue close to the soft palate and by means of the stream of breath setting the uvula to flapping in the narrow passage. In Continental (European) languages the uvular r is frequent.

(7). Strictly native words in French, Italian, Spanish, and some other European languages, do not use the letter *w*, which appears, in the main, only in borrowed words. In some native words, however, a sound like w is heard, represented by other letters. In French, for example, there are two w's, one represented by *u* (as in *nuit*), the other by *ou* (as in *oui*). They differ in that the first (that represented by *u*) begins with the tongue and lips approximately in position for "rounded" ī [see Vowel Modifications (1)], and the second begins with a position similar to that for ū—is, in fact, about the normal English w. The sound of French *ui* would, then, be more nearly represented by üi; but to avoid multiplying symbols the one symbol w is used in this dictionary to represent both the normal w sound (which begins with ū) and this other w (which begins with ü).

(8). English f and v are made by placing the lower lip against the upper teeth. In some other languages, as Spanish and Latin (Roman method), similar consonants are *bilabial*, that is, made between the two lips. Such a v is like an English w, except that the lips are not pursed into a roundish opening, but are spread, the voice escaping, not all at the center, but between the lips along their total length. When the lips separate, they do so all at once, not with the gradual widening that marks the English w.

In French words no one syllable has a decided accent, but nearly all syllables are uttered with equal stress of voice. To an English ear a chief stress seems to fall on the final syllable; hence, in this guide, the primary accent (′) has been placed over the last syllable of most French words, and the secondary accent (″) on the other syllables (except over obscure *e*), to indicate a careful enunciation of all the unaccented syllables.

Vowel and Consonant Sounds.

1. *a* represents sometimes ā, but generally a sound between a and a: (1) *a* = ā, in the endings *-as*, *-az* (when the *s* or *z* is pronounced, and often when *s* is silent), *-ase*, *-azon*, *-aille*; and when circumflexed (â); (2) *a* (in most other cases), *à*, and *á* are pronounced with a sound near that of a, but not so "flat" as this English vowel. French *a* approaches the sound a especially before the final sounds b, d, g, l, m, n, ny (that is, the letters *b*, *d*, *g*, *l*, *m*, *n*, *gn* when these are pronounced), and before final *-ve*, *-ge*. *oi* = wā when following *r*, and in the ending *-oie*; in most other cases *oi* = wa (with a not so "flat" as the English a).

2. (1) *e* before a pronounced consonant, before final silent *t*, *ts*, and final silent *s* in monosyllables; *ei*, *ai* (except the verbal ending *gai*); *è*, *ê*; *ay*, *ey*—all are pronounced as e (really a sound between e and a). (2) *é*; *e* followed by a silent final consonant (other than *t*); *ai* (when it is a verbal ending)—all are pronounced as ē.

3. (1) *o* when it is the final sound in a syllable (that is, it may be followed by silent consonants), and *o* in the endings *-ose* (and generally before an *s* which has the value of z), *-me* and *-ne*; *ô*, *aô*, *au*, *eau*—all are pronounced as ō. (2) *o* not as above, and *au* before *r*, = e.

4. *eu*, *œu*, not followed in the same syllable by a pronounced consonant, or in a closed syllable ending with the sound of z or t (*-euse*, *-eute*, *-eutre*), *eû* = "rounded" ē [see Vowel Modifications (2)]: otherwise, *eu*, *œu*, and always *ue*, *œ* before *-il*, *-ille* (= y), = "rounded" e [see Vowel Modifications (3)].

5. For pronunciation of *u*, *û* = ü, see Vowel Modifications (1).

6. *e* when final in unstressed syllables = ə; at the end of a word it is usually silent (as in English).

7. Final *d*, *g*, *n*, *p*, *s*, *t*, *x*, and *z* are usually silent. But when the following word begins with a vowel, "liaison" may occur. These consonants (not in all cases; no rule can be given) are then pronounced as if beginning the following word, *d* being sounded as t, *g* as k, *s* and *x* as z. *r* is silent in the final syllables *-er* and *-ier*. *h* is in most words silent.

8. *c* before *a*, *o*, *u* = k; before *e*, *i*, *y* = s; *ç* = s. *ch* = sh; but when final or before a consonant = k. *q* and *qu* generally = k.

9. *g* before *a*, *o*, *u* = g; before *e*, *i* (*y*) = ʒ; *ge* before *a*, *o*, *u* also = ʒ. The sound of *j* is indicated by ʒ (= zh).

10. *gn* = "palatal" n [see Consonant Modifications (5)].

11. *il* after a vowel = y; *ill* = ly [see Consonant Modifications (5)]; also *i* before a vowel = y, unless a *group* of consonants precedes. By y is here meant the *initial* stage of the sound, not its consummation.

12. *m*, *n*, final or before a consonant, other than *m*, *n*, are silent, but impart to the preceding vowel a nasal quality. In such conditions, *am*, *an*, *em*, *en*, = ań (but final *en* preceded by the sound y = ań, not ań); *aim*, *ain*, *eim*, *ein*, *im*, *in*, *ym*, *yn* = ań; *om*, *on* = eń; *oin* = wań; and *um*, *un* = uń (or əń). [See Vowel Modifications (4)].

13. *s* between vowels = z.

14. *-ti-* = -si-, or -ty-; a rule cannot be stated.

15. French has the letter *w* only in some foreign words; but the sound is heard in French words, spelled *ou* (as in *oui*); and it is, further, the first element in the sound represented by *oi* (= wa or wa), and by *oin* (= wań). A similar sound is spelled with *u* (as in *nuit*, *nuage*); but the sound of *u* in these words is not exactly w; it differs from w in that it begins with the organs in position for ü, not for ū [see Consonant Modifications (8)].

16. *x* between vowels generally = z. Otherwise, *x* = ks.

EXPLANATION OF SYMBOLS USED TO INDICATE PRONUNCIATION.

The pronunciations given are indicated by the alphabet used in the *Funk & Wagnalls New Standard Dictionary*.

a as in *a*rtistic.
ā as in *a*rt.
a as in f*a*t.
ā as in f*a*re.
e as in g*e*t.
ē as in pr*ey*.
i as in h*i*t.
ī as in pol*i*ce.
o as in *o*bey.
ō as in g*o*.
e as in n*o*t.
ē as in *o*r.
u as in f*u*ll.
ū as in r*u*le.
v as in b*u*t.
ū as in b*u*rn.

ai as in *ai*sle.
au as in sa*u*erkra*u*t.
iu as in d*u*ration.
iū as in f*eu*d.
ei as in *oi*l.
k as in *k*in, *c*at, *q*uit.
g as in *g*o.
ŋ as in si*ng*.
th as in *th*in.
th as in *th*is.
s as in *s*o, *c*ent.
z as in *z*est, wa*s*.
ch as in *ch*ur*ch*.
sh as in *sh*ip, o*c*ean, fun*c*tion, ma*ch*ine.

j as in *j*et.
ʒ as in a*z*ure, lei*s*ure, vi*s*ion.
a as in *a*sk.
ə (unstressed) as in sof*a*, ov*e*r, arb*o*r, gutt*u*ral, mart*y*rd*o*m.
ɪ (unstressed) as in hab*i*t, sen*a*te, surf*ei*t, bisc*ui*t, min'*u*te, privil*e*ge, v a l l *e y*, Sund*a*y, cit*i*es, ren*e*w.

The Consonants and Semivowels are: b, d, f, g, ŋ, h, j, ch, k, l, m, n, p, r, s, sh, t, th, th, v, w, y, z, ʒ. Of these, b, d, f, h, k, p, t, v, z have the familiar and unmistakable sounds heard in *be*, *do*, *fee*, *he*, *key*, *pea*, *tea*, *vow*, *zest;* g sounds always as in *get*, never as in *gem*, and s always as in *sit*, never as in *rose* or in *sugar*.

H as in lo*ch* (Scotch), a*ch*, mi*ch* (German). ñ as in bo*n* (French), indicating a nasal quality. ü as in L*u*beck (German), D*u*mas (French).

The single accent (′) indicates the primary or chief stress; the double accent (″) indicates the secondary stress. The ligature (‿) when used in connecting two consonants indicates that the sound of the first consonant is carried over to the second, as in *accommodement:* ak″‿kem″‿mō″də-mañ′. When connecting two vowels, as in *position:* pō″zi″si″‿yoñ′, it indicates a rapid utterance, almost obliterating the syllable division. The double dagger (‡) indicates a variant form.

ABBREVIATIONS USED IN THIS BOOK.

a. = adjective.
adv. = adverb.
conj. = conjunction.
f. = feminine.
Fr. = French.
int. = interjection.
m. = masculine.
n. = noun.
naut. = nautical.
neu. = neuter.
pa. = participle.
pl. = plural.
pp. = present participle.
pron. = pronoun.
sing. = singular.
v. = verb.

SPECIAL NOTE. In French nouns are masculine or feminine and the definite article that precedes them should be of the same gender —*the* in French is *le*, *la* or *l'* according to the following rules. *Le* masculine, *la* feminine, *l'* masculine or feminine whenever the word that follows begins with a vowel. One should say *le fusil* (lə fü″si′) for the rifle; *la cartouche* (la kar″tūsh′) for the cartridge; *l'officier* (lof″fi″si″‿yē′), the officer; *l'armée* (lar″mē′), the army.

Likewise the indefinite articles *a* and *an* are indicated in French by the words *un* for the masculine and *une* for the feminine. Thus, a rifle is *un fusil;* a cartridge is *une cartouche;* an officer is *un officier*, and an army is *une armée*. For more detailed information, see Appendix.

A SERVICE DICTIONARY

A

a, an. **1.** Un (*m.*): aṅ. **2.** Une (*f.*): ün.
Aachen, ā'Hen, *n.* German name for AIX-LA-CHAPELLE.
abaft or **aft,** *a.* *Naut.* A l'arrière: a lar"rī"‿yār'.
abandon, *v.* Abandonner: a"baṅ"deṅ"‿nē'.—**abandon the position.** Abandonner la position: a"baṅ"deṅ"‿nē' la pō"zī"-sī"‿yeṅ'.
abatis. Abatis (*n. m.*): a"ba"tī'.—**form an abatis.** Formez un abatis: fēr"mēz'‿aṅ a"ba"tī'.
abattoir. Abattoir (*n. m.*): a"bat"‿twār'.
abbey. Abbaye (*n. f.*): ab"bē'. On maps abbreviated *Abbe.*
abeam, *a. & adv.* Par le travers: pār lə tra"vār'.
about, *adv.* Environ: en"vī"reṅ'.—**about face** or **about turn.** Volte-face: velt"-fās'.—**left about.** Demi-tour à gauche: də-mī'tūr a gōsh.—**right about.** Demi-tour à droite: də-mī'tūr a drwāt.
above, *prep.* Au-dessus: ō-də-sü'.
abreast, *adv.* De front: də freṅ.
abrupt. **1.** Escarpé (*a.*): es"kar"pē' (*steep*). **2.** Brusque (*a.*): brüsk (*rough* or *rude*).
abscess. Abcès (*n. m.*): ab"sē'.
absent, *a.* Absent: ab"saṅ'.—**absent oneself.** S'absenter: sab"saṅ"tē'.—**absenting oneself without leave.** S'absentir sans permission: sab"saṅ"tīr' saṅ pār"mīs"‿yeṅ'.
absorbent. Absorbant (*n. m.*): ab"sēr"bāṅ'.—**absorbent cotton.** Coton hydrophile: kō"teṅ' ī"drō"fīl'.—**absorbent cotton-wool.** Ouate hydrophile: ū"āt'‿ī"drō"fīl'.
abutment (*of a bridge*). Culée de point: kü"lē' də pwaṅ.
accent. Accent (*n. m.*): aks"sāṅ'.
access. Accès (*n. m.*): ak"sē'.—**difficult of access.** D'un accès difficile: daṅ ak"sē' dī"fī"sīl'.—**means of access.** Moyens d'accès: mwa"yaṅ' dak"sē'.
accommodation, *n.* **1.** Accommodement (*m.*): a"kem"‿mō"-də-maṅ'. **2.** Logement (*m.*): leʒ"maṅ'. **3.** Billet (*m.*): bī"yē'.
accomplice. Complice (*a. & n., m. & f.*): keṅ"plīs'.
accordance. Accord (*n. m.*): a"kēr'.—**in accordance with.** **1.** Conformément à: keṅ"fēr"mē"maṅ' ā. **2.** En conformité: aṅ keṅ"fēr"mī"tē'.—**accordingly,** *adv.* En conséquence: aṅ kaṅ"-sē"kāṅs'.—**according to your orders.** **1.** Suivant vos ordres: swī"vaṅ' vōz‿ēr'‿drə. **2.** En conséquence de vos ordres: aṅ kaṅ"sē"kāṅs' də vōz‿ēr'‿drə.
account, *n.* **1.** Compte (*m.*): kēṅt. **2.** Récit (*m.*): rē"sī'. **3.** Conte (*m.*): kēṅt (*story*).—**fancy account.** Conte de fantaisie: kēṅt də faṅ"tē"zī'. Called also **fairy story:** conte des fées: kēṅt dē fē.—**on account of.** En raison de: aṅ rē"zeṅ' də.—**on no account.** Sous aucun prétexte: sūz‿ō-kan' prē'tekst.
accouter, *v.* Équiper: ē"kī"pē'.—**accoutered.** Équipé: ē"kī"pē'.—**accouterment,** *n.* Équipement: ē"kīp"maṅ'.
accuracy. **1.** Précision (*n. f.*): prē"sī"zī"yeṅ'. **2.** Exactitude (*n. f.*): egz"ak"tī"tüd'.—**accurate,** *a.* Exact (*m.*): egz"akt'; exacte (*f.*): egz"akt'.—**accurate fire.** Justesse de tir: ʒüs"tes' də tīr.—**accurate information.** Renseignement juste: raṅ"-sēn"yə-māṅ' ʒüst.

---

artistic; ārt; fat; fāre; fast; get; prēy; hit; polīce; obey; gō; net; ēr; full; rūle; but; būrn; ə = final; ı = habit; aisle; au = *out*; eil; iū = feud; dūne; ćhin; go; ŋ = si*ng*; ŝhip; ŧhin; ŧħis.

accusation. Accusation (*n. f.*): a″kü″za″sī″‿yeṅ′.

accuse or **charge,** *v.* Accuser: a″kü″zē′.—**accused, the.** L'accusé: la″kü″zē′.

acetic acid, crystallizable or **glacial.** Acide acétique, cristallisable ou glacial: a″sīd″a″sē″tīk′, krīs″ta″lī″zā′‿blə ū gla″sī″āl′.

aching. Douleur: dū″lūr′.

acknowledge, *v.* **1.** Reconnaître: rə-keṅ″‿nê′tr. **2.** Accuser reception de (*acknowledge the receipt of*: said of letters): a″kü″zē′ rē″sep″sī″‿yeṅ′ də.—**acknowledge the facts.** Avouer les faits: a″vū″ē′ lē fē.

acquainted with, be. **1.** Connaître (*v.*): keṅ″nē′trə. **2.** Se mettre au courant de: sə mēt′trə ō kū″raṅ′ də.—**get acquainted with.** Faire la connaissance de: fār la keṅ″nēs″sāṅz′ də.

across. **1.** À travers: a tra″vār′. **2.** Au travers de: ō tra″vār′ də. **3.** Le long de: lə leṅ də.—**across country.** À travers champs: a tra″vār′ shāṅ.

act, *n.* Fait (*n. m.*): fē.—**act of war.** Fait de guerre: fē də gār.—**in the act.** Sur le fait: sür lə fē.—**in the act of.** En train de: aṅ traṅ də.—**taken in the act.** Pris sur le fait: prī sür lə fē.—**the act will be regarded as plundering.** L'action sera considérée un acte de pillage: lak″sī″‿yeṅ′ sə-rā′ keṅ″sī″dē″rē′ aṅ akt də pī″yāz′.

act, *v.* Agir: a″ʒīr′.—**act on one's own initiative.** Agir d'après sa propre initiative: a″ʒīr′ da″prē′ sa pre′prə ī″nī″sī″ā″tīv′.—**he acts.** Il agit: īl a″ʒī′.

action. **1.** Action (*n. f.*): ak″sī″‿yeṅ′. **2.** Combat: keṅ″bā′.—**action after the capture of works.** Conduite après la prise de travaux: keṅ″dwīt′ a″prē′ la prīz də tra″vō′. See WORKS.—**action front.** Feu en avant: fū aṅ‿a″vāṅ′.—**action rear.** Feu en arrière: fū aṅ‿ar″‿rī″yār′.—**before action.** Avant le combat: a″vāṅ′ lə keṅ″bā′.—**in** or **into action.** **1.** En batterie: aṅ bat″‿tə-rī′. **2.** Engagez: aṅ″ga″zē′.—**rear action.** Attaque en queue: a″tāk′‿aṅ ku.—**to begin the action.** Engager le combat: aṅ″ga″ʒē′ lə keṅ″bā′.—**to clear** (the decks) **for action.** Faire le branle-bas de combat: fār lə bran″lə-bā′ də keṅ″bā′.—**to go into action.** S'engager au combat: saṅ″ga″ʒē′ ō keṅ″bā′.

active, *a.* Actif (*m.*): ak″tīf′; active (*f.*): ak″tīv′.—**be on the active list.** Etre de service actif: ē″trə də sār″vīs′ ak″tīf′.

addition. En plus: aṅ plü.—**in addition to.** Outre: ū′trə.

address. Adresse: a″dres′.—**what address.** Quelle adresse: kel a″dres′.—**what is the address.** Quelle est l'adresse: kel ē lad″dres′.—**addressee,** *n.* Destinataire: des″tī″na″tār′.

adequate, *a.* **1.** Suffisant (*m.*): süf″‿fī″sāṅ′; suffisante (*f.*): süf″‿fī″saṅt′. **2.** Proportioné (*m.*); proportionée (*f.*): prō″pēr″-sī″‿yen″nē′—**ascertain that adequate reserve is maintained.** S'assurer de l'entretien d'une réserve suffisante: sa″-sü″rē′ də laṅ″trə-tī″‿yaṅ′ dün rē″zārv′ süf″fī″zāṅt′.

adjust, *v.* Régler: rē″glē′.

adjutant, *n.* Adjudant: a″ʒü″dāṅ′.—**adjutant-general.** Chef d'état-major: shef dē′tā′ma″ʒōr′.—**adjutant-major.** Adjudant-major: a″ʒü″dāṅ′-ma″ʒōr′.

administration. **1.** Administration (*n. f.*): ad″mī″nīs″tra″-sī″‿yeṅ′. **2.** Gouvernement (*n. m.*): gū″vār″nə-maṅ′.—**administrative,** *a.* Administratif: ad″mī″nīs″tra″tīf′.—**administrative district.** Préfecture (*n. f.*): prē″fek″tür′.—**administrative officer.** Officier d'administration: of″fī″sī″‿yē′ dad″mī″-nīs″tra″sī″‿yeṅ′.—**administrative service.** **1.** Administration (*n. f.*): ad″mī″nīs″trā″sī″‿yeṅ′. **2.** Services administratifs: sār″vīs′ ad″mī″nīs″tra″tīf′.

admiral. Amiral (*n. m.*): a″mī″rāl′.—**admiralty.** Amirauté (*n. f.*): a″mī″rō″tē′.

advance. **I.** *n.* Avance (*n. f.*): a″vāṅs′. **II.** *v.* **1.** Marcher en avant: mar″shē′ aṅ a″vāṅ′. **2.** Avancer: a″vaṅ″sē′. **3.** Se porter en avant: sə pōr″tē′ aṅ a″vāṅ′. See FORWARD.—**advance and give the countersign.** Avancez au ralliement: a″vāṅ″sēz′‿ō ral″lī″maṅ′.—**advance and give the counterword.** Avancez à l'ordre: a″vaṅ″sē′ a lōr′drə.—**advance by column.** Avancez par colonne: a″vaṅ″sē′ pār kə″lōṅ′.—**advance guard.** Avant garde: a″vāṅ′ gārd.—**advance in extended order.** En avant, à la débandade: aṅ a″vāṅ′ a la dē″baṅ″dād′.—**in advance.** D'avance: da″vāṅs′.—**sound the advance.** Sonnez l'avance: səṅ″nē′ la″vāṅs′.—**advanced,** *pa.* Avancé: a″vāṅ″sē′.—**advanced dressing-station.** Poste de secours divisionnaire: pōst də sē″kūr′ dī″vī″zī″‿yəṅ″‿nār′.

advice, *n.* **1.** Avis (*m.*): a″vī′. **2.** Conseil (*m.*): kəṅ″sē′‿yə.—**his advice was not followed.** On n'a pas suivi son conseil: əṅ nā pā swī″vī′ səṅ kəṅ″sē′‿yə.—**advisable.** Bon de: bōṅ də.—**advisable to do.** Bon de faire: bəṅ də fār.—**advise.** Aviser: a″vī″zē′.

aerial, *a.* Aérien (*m.*): a″ē″rī″aṅ′; aérienne (*f.*): a″ē″rī″yeṅ′‿nə. —**aerial torpedo.** Torpille aérienne: tōr″pī′‿yə a″ē″rī″yeṅ′‿nə.

aerodrome. Aérodrome (*n. m.*): a″ē″rō″drōm′ (*course where aeroplanes are tried out*).

aerogram. Aérogramme (*n. m.*): a″ē″rō″grām′.

aeronaut. Aéronaute (*n. m. & f.*): a″ē″rō″nōt′.—**aeronautics.** Aérostation (*n. f.*): a″ē″rō″stā″sī″‿yeṅ′.

aeroplane. **1.** Aéroplane (*n. m.*): a″ē″rō″plā′‿nə. **2.** Avion (*n. m.*): a″vī″əṅ′. Compare HYDRAVION.—**aeroplane squadron.** Escadrille (*n. f.*), d'aéroplanes: es″ka″drī′yə dā″ē″rō″plā′‿nə.

affray. **1.** Échauffourée (*n. f.*): ē″shōf″fū″rē′. **2.** Émeute (*n. f.*): ē″mūt′. See RIOT, SKIRMISH.

afraid of, be. Avoir peur de: a″vwār′ pūr də.—**do not be afraid of.** N'ayez pas peur de: nē″yē′ pa pūr də.

after, *adv.* Après: a″prē′.

afternoon, *n.* Après-midi (*n. f.*): a″prē′-mī″dī′.

age. Âge (*n. m.*): āʒ.—**age limit.** La limite d'âge: la lī″mīt′ dāʒ.

again, *adv.* Encore: aṅ″kōr′.

agent. Agent (*n. m.*): a″ʒāṅ′.

aggravating. Aggravante (*a.*): a″gra″vāṅt′.—**aggravating circumstances.** Circonstances aggravantes: sīr″kōṅ″stāṅs′ a″gra″vāṅt′.

agricultural, *a.* Agricole: a″grī″kōl′. On maps abbreviated *Agr[le].*

ahead. En avant: aṅ a″vāṅ′.—**go ahead.** **1.** Allez-y: al″-lē″‿zī′. **2.** En avant: aṅ a″vāṅ′.—**send ahead.** Envoyer en avant: aṅ″vwa″yē′ aṅ a″vāṅ′.—**they are ahead of.** Ils sont en avant de: īl səṅ aṅ a″vāṅ′ də.

aid. **1.** Aide (*n. m.*): ēd. **2.** Secours (*n. m.*): sə-kūr′ (*help; relief*).—**first aid.** Premier secours: prə-mī″yē′ sə-kūr′.

aide-de-camp. Aide-de-camp (*n. m.*): ēd″‿də‿kāṅ′.

aileron, ē″lə-rəṅ′ (*n. m.*). A wing-tip or surface for maintaining the balance of an aeroplane.

aim. **I.** *n. f.* Point de mire: pwaṅ də mīr. **II.** *interj.* Joue, ʒū (contraction of *en joue!* aṅ ʒū). See TO AIM AT. **III.** *v.* Viser: vī″zē′.—**bad aim.** Mauvaise mire *or* visée (*f.*): mō″vēz′ mīr *or* vī″zē′.—**correct aim.** Justesse de tir: ʒūs″tes′ də tīr.—**good aim.** Bonne mire *or* visée (*f.*): bən mīr *or* vī″zē′.—**the object to be aimed at.** **1.** Le point de mire: lə pwaṅ də mīr. **2.** L'objectif à viser: ləb″jek″tīf′ a vī″zē′.—**to aim at.** **1.** Viser (*v.*): vī″zē′. **2.** Mettre ou coucher, en joue: mētrū kū″shē′, aṅ ʒū.

aiming. Pointage (*n. m.*): pwaṅ″tāʒ′.

air. Air (*n. m.*): ār.

air-base. **1.** Avionnerie (*n. f.*): a″vī″əṅ″nə-rī′. **2.** Port d'attache (*n. m.*): pōr da″tash′.

aircraft. 1. Aérostat (*n. m.*): a″ē″rō″stā′ (*balloons of all types*). 2. Avion (*n. m.*): a″vī″oṅ′ (*military aeroplanes of all types*).—**aircraft-arrow.** Flèche d'aéro: flāsh da″ē″rō′ (*spiked weapon dropped from aeroplanes*).

air-eddy. Remous (*n. m.*): rə-mū′.

airman. Aviateur (*n. m.*): a″vī″a″tūr′. See AVIATOR.

air-pocket. Trou d'air (*n. m.*): trū dār.

air-pump. Pompe pneumatique (*n. f.*): peṅp nū″ma″tīk′.

airship or **dirigible balloon.** Dirigeable (*n. m.*): dī″rī″jā′‿blə.

Aisne. ēn. A river in France.

Aix-la-Chapelle, ā″la″sha″pel′. A Prussian city and air-base.

alarm. Alerte (*n. f.*): a″lārt′.—**beat the alarm.** Battre la générale: bā″tr la ʒē″nē″rāl′.—**false alarm.** Fausse alerte: fōs a″lārt′.—**in case of alarm.** En cas d'alarme: aṅ kā da″lārm′.—**Is it an alarm?** C'est-il une alarme? sē‿tīl ün a″lārm′.—**It is an alarm.** C'est une alarme: sē‿tün a″lārm′.—**sound the alarm.** Sonner la générale: sen″‿nē le ʒē″nē″rāl′.—**alarm-gun.** Canon d'alarme (*n. m.*): ka″nen′ da″lārm′.—**alarm-post.** 1. Poste d'alarme (*n. m.*): pōst da″lārm′. 2. Le point de ralliement et de rassemblement: lə pwaṅ də ral″‿lī″maṅ′ ē də rās″‿saṅ″-blə-maṅ′.

Albino. Albinos (*n. m. & f.*): āl″bī″nōs′ (persons with milky-white skin, whitish hair, and pink eyes: used in identification).

alcoholic, *a.* Alcoolique: al″kō″līk′.

alibi. Alibi (*n. m.*): a″lī″bī′.

alight, *a.* Allumé: əl″lü″mē′.

alighting. Atterrissage (*n. m.*): a″tār″‿rīs″‿sāʒ′.

alinement. Alignement (*n. m.*): a″līn″‿yə-maṅ′.

alive. Vivant (*n. m.*): vī″vāṅ′.—**look alive!** 1. Vivement: vīv″maṅ′. 2. Dépêchez-vous: dē″pē″shē″vū′.

all around traverse. Un volant: aṅ vō″laṅ′. A machine gun mounted on a swivel so that it can be fired in any direction. Une (ün) mitrailleuse (mī″tra″yūz′) à (a) volant (vō″laṅ′) de (də) pointage (pwaṅ″tāʒ′) en (aṅ) direction (dī″rek″sī″‿yeṅ′) et (ē) hauteur (ō″tūr′).

Allies. Alliés (*n. m.*): al″‿lyē′.

allot, *v.* 1. Départir: dē″pār″tīr′. 2. Désigner: dē″zī″nyē′. 3. Répartir: rē″pār″tīr′. 4. Distribuer: dīs″trī″bü″ē′.—**allotment.** Répartition (*n. f.*): rē″pār″tī″sī″‿yeṅ′.

allow, *v.* 1. Permettre: pār″met′‿trə. 2. Accorder: a″kōr″dē′.—**allow of easy communication.** Permettre une communication facile: pār″met′‿trə ün kem″‿mü″nī″ka″sī″‿yoṅ′ fa″sīl′.

allowance. Indemnité (*n. f.*): aṅ″dem″nī″tē′.—**draw an allowance.** Toucher une indemnité: tū″shē′ ün aṅ″dem′nī″tē′.—**extra food allowance.** Indemnité supplémentaire de vivres: aṅ″dem″nī″tē′ sü″plē″maṅ″tār′ də vī′vrə.—**field allowance.** Indemnité de campagne: aṅ″dem″nī″tē′ də kaṅ″pā′nyə.—**horse allowance.** Indemnité de monture: aṅ″dem″nī″tē′ də mon″-tūr′.—**lodging allowance.** Indemnité de logement: aṅ″dem″-nī″tē′ də lō″ʒə-maṅ′.—**on allowance.** À la ration: a la ra″sī″‿yoṅ′.—**ration allowance.** Indemnité de vivres: aṅ″dem″nī″-tē′ də vīv′‿rə.—**traveling allowance.** Indemnité de route: aṅ″dem″nī″tē′ də rūt.

ally, *n.* Allié (*m.*), alliée (*f.*): a″lī″‿yē′.

almond-eyed. Yeux en amande (*n. m.*): Yū aṅ a″mānd′ (*used in describing physical characteristics of individuals*).

alone, *a.* Seul (*m.*); seule (*f.*): sūl.

along, *adv.* Le long: lə loṅ.—**all along.** Tout le long de: tū lə loṅ də.—**all along the road.** Tout le long du chemin: tū lə loṅ dü shə-maṅ′.—**along the road.** Sur la route: sür la rūt.—**come along.** Venez donc: və-nē′ doṅ.

alongside, *adv.* 1. A côté: a kō″tē′. 2. A bord: a bōr.—**alongside dock, quai, or wharf.** À quai: a kē.—**alongside**

ship. Donner à la bande: den″nē′ a la bānd.—**to come alongside.** Accoster (*v.*): a″kes″tē′.
already, *adv.* Déja: dē″ʒā′.
Alsace, *n.* al″zās′. A crown territory of Germany.
also, *adv.* Aussi: o″sī′.
alteration. Modification (*n. f.*): mō″dī″fī″kā″sī″‿yeṅ′.
altimeter. Altimètre: (*n. m.*): al″tī″mā′‿trə.
altitude. Altitude (*n. f.*): al″tī″tüd′.
alum. Alun (*n. m.*): a″laṅ′.
aluminum. Alumine (*n. f.*): a″lü″mīn′‿ə.
always, *adv.* Toujours: tū″jūr′.
am I. Suis-je: swī′ʒə.—**I am.** Je suis: ʒə swī.
ambulance. Ambulance (*n. f.*): aṅ″bü″lāns′.—**ambulance car.** Ambulance automobile. aṅ″bü″lāns′ ō″tō″mō″bīl′.—**ambulance wagon.** Wagon ambulance (*n. m.*): va″geṅ′ aṅ″bü″lāns′.—**field ambulance.** 1. Ambulance de campagne (*n. f.*): aṅ″bü″lāns′ də kāṅ″pā′nyə. 2. Ambulance divisionnaire (*n. f.*): āṅ″bü″lāns′ dī″vī″zī″‿yeṅ″‿nār′.—**motor ambulance.** Ambulance automobile: aṅ″bü″lāns′ ē″tō″mō″bīl′.
ambush, ambuscade. 1. Embûche (*n. f.*): aṅ″büsh′. 2. Embuscade (*n. f.*): aṅ″büs″kād′.—**fall into an ambush.** Tomber dans une anbuscade: ten″bē′ dān‿zün aṅ″büs″kād′.—**lay an ambush.** Dresser une embûche: drē″sē′ ün aṅ″büsh′.—**lie in ambush.** Se tenir en embuscade: sə tə-nīr′ aṅ aṅ″büs″kād′.
America. Amérique (*n. f.*): a″mār″ īk′.—**American.** 1. Américain (*a.* & *n. m.*): ā″mār″ī″kaṅ′. 2. Americaine (*n. f.*): ā″mār″ī″kēn′.
amidships, *adv.* Par le travers: par lə tra″vār′.
Amiens, *n.* a″mī″aṅ′. Fr. city.
ammo, am′o. Contraction of AMMUNITION.
ammonal (Eng.). am′o-nəl; (Fr.) am″mō″nāl′, *n.* An explosive with which Mills bombs are charged.
ammunition. Munitions (*n. f. pl.*): mü″nī″sī″‿yeṅ′. In full, *munitions de guerre* (mü″nī″sī″‿yeṅ′ də gār) to distinguish them from military or naval stores, that are also designated *munitions*.—**ammunition bread.** Pain de munition: paṅ də mü″nī″sī″‿yeṅ′.—**ammunition chest.** Caisson (*n. m.*): kē″seṅ′.—**ammunition clip.** Chargeur de fusil: shar″ʒūr′ də fü″zī′.—**ammunition column.** Section de munitions (*n. f.*): sek″sī″‿yeṅ′ də mü″nī″sī″‿yēṅ′.—**ammunition supply.** Approvisionnement de munitions: ap″prō″vī″zī″‿yeṅ″maṅ′ də mü″nī″sī″‿yeṅ′.—**ammunition wagon.** Caisson (*n. m.*): kē″seṅ′.—**expended ammunition.** Munitions consommée: mü″nī″sī″‿yeṅ′ keṅ″sem″‿mē′.—**use up all available ammunition.** Epuiser toutes les munitions disponibles: ē″pwī″zē′ tūt lē mü″nī″sī″‿yeṅ′ dīs″pō″nī′‿blə.
amnesty. Amnistie (*n. f.*): am″nīs″tī′.
among, *prep.* 1. Entre: aṅ′trə. 2. Parmi: par″mī′.—**among ourselves.** Entre-nous: aṅ′trə nū.
amount. 1. Montant (*n. m.*): meṅ″taṅ′ (*said of a bill*). 2. Quantit (*n. f.*): kaṅ″tī″tē′. 3. Somme (*n. f.*): sōm.
ampulea. Ampoule (*n. f.*): aṅ″pūl′.
amputate, *v.* Amputer: aṅ″pü″tē′.
anarchy. Anarchie (*n. f.*): a″nār″shī′.
anchor. Ancre (*n. f.*): āṅ′krə.—**cast** or **drop anchor.** Jeter l'ancre: ʒhe″tē′ laṅ′krə.—**come to anchor.** Venir au mouillage: və-nīr′ ō mwī″yāʒ′.
anchorage. Mouillage (*n. m.*): mū″ī″‿yāʒ′.
ancient, *a.* Ancien (*m.*): aṅ″sī″‿aṅ′; ancienne (*f.*): aṅ″sī″‿yen′‿nə. Abbreviated *Ancn.* on maps.
and. Et: ē. Compare IS.
anemometer. Anémomètre (*n. m.*): a″nē″mō″mā′trə.

anesthetic. Anesthisique (*n. f.*): a″nes″tī″zīk′.
angle. Angle (*n. m.*): āṅ′glə.—**angle of descent.** Angle de chute (*n.m.*): aṅ′glə də shüt′‿ə.—**angle of elevation.** Angle d'élévation (*n. m.*): aṅ′glə dē″lē″vā″sī″‿yoṅ′ (*the angle between the axis of a gun and the line of aim*).—**angle of sight or vision.** Angle de site (*n. m.*): aṅ′glə də sīt (*the angle between the line of sight and the line of fire*).—**dead angle.** Angle mort (*n. m.*): aṅ′glə mōr.—**defilading angle.** Angle de défilement (*n. m.*): aṅ′glə də dē″fī″lə-māṅ′.—**reentering angle.** Angle rentrant (*n. m.*): aṅ′glə raṅ″trāṅ′.—**salient angle.** Angle saillant (*n. m.*): aṅ′glə sa″ī″-yāṅ′; but frequently contracted to *sailliant*.
animal. Animal (*n. m.*): a″nī″māl′. Pronounced the same way when used as an adjective and spelt *animal* (*m.*) or *animale* (*f.*).
ankle. Cheville (*n. f.*): she″vī′‿yə.
annihilate, *v.* Anéantir: a″nē″aṅ″tīr′.
announcement. Communiqué (*n. m.*): kom″‿mü″nī″kē′.
answer. **I.** *n.* Réponse (*f.*): rē″poṅs′. **II.** *v.* Répondre: rē″-poṅ′‿drə.
antenna. Antenne (*n. f.*): aṅ″teṅ′‿nə (*wireless telegraphy*).
anti-aircraft gun. Canon contre-avion (*n. m.*): ka″noṅ′ koṅ′tr‿a″vī″‿yoṅ′.
anticipate, *v.* **1.** Devancer: də-vaṅ″sē′. **2.** Prévenir: prē″və-nīr′.—**anticipate orders.** Prévoir les ordres: prē″vwār′ lēz ōr′‿drə.—**anticipation.** **1.** Anticipation (*n. f.*): aṅ″tī″sī″pā″-sī″‿yoṅ′. **2.** Prévision (*n. f.*): prē″vī″zī″‿yoṅ′.
antiseptic. Antiseptique (*a.* & *n. m.*): aṅ″tī″sep″tīk′.—**antiseptic cotton-wool.** Ouate antiseptique: ū″āt′ aṅ″tī″sep″tīk′.—**a. surgical bandage.** Bande de pansement antiseptique: baṅd də paṅs″māṅ′ aṅ″tī″sep″tīk′.
antitetanic serum. Sérum antitétanique (*n. m.*): sē″rum′ aṅ″tī″tē″ta″nīk′.
Antwerp, ant′wərp, *n.* A city of Belgium: in French, **Anvers:** aṅ″vār′.
Anzac (Eng.). an′zak; (Fr.) aṅ″zāk′, *n.* A soldier of the Australian or New Zealand Army Corps.
apartment, lodging. Logement (*n. m.*): lō″zə-māṅ′.
A. P. M. Assistant Provost Marshal. **Aide Prévôt:** ēd prē″vō′.
apparatus. Appareil (*n. m. pl.*): ap″pa″rē′‿yə.—**apparatus for asphyxiating or suffocating gas.** Engins asphyxiants ou suffocants: aṅ″zaṅ′ zas″fīks″‿yāṅ′ ū sü″fō″kāṅ′.
appetite. Appétit (*n. m.*): ap″‿pē″tī′.—**appetizer.** **1.** Apéritif (*n. m.*): a″pē″rī″tīf′ (liquid). **2.** Hors d'œuvre (*n. m.*): hōr dū′‿vrə (*solid*).
appliance, *n.* Machine (*n. f.*): ma″shīn′.
apply to. **1.** S'adresser à *or* au: sad″dres″‿sē′ a *or* ō. **2.** S'appliquer à *or* au: sap″plī″kē′ a *or* ō.—**apply to the captain.** S'adresser au capitaine: sad″‿dres″‿sē′ ō ka″pī″tān′.
appoint, *v.* **1.** Nommer: nom″mē′ (*select for some position*). **2.** Monter: moṅ″tē′ (*equip*).—**ill appointed.** **1.** Mal monté: mal moṅ″tē′. **2.** Mal équipé: mal ē″kī″pē′.—**to be appointed.** Être nommé: ā′trə nom″mē′.
appointment, *n.* **1.** Nomination (*f.*): nom″ī″na″sī″‿yoṅ′. **2.** Rendez-vous (*m.*): raṅ″dē″-vū′. **3.** Etablissement (*m.*): ē″tā″-blīs″‿sə-maṅ′. **4.** Emploi (*m.*): aṅ″plwā′.—**special appointment.** Emploi spéciale: aṅ″plwā′ spē″sī″‿yāl′.
approach, *n.* **1.** Approche (*f.*): a″prosh′. **2.** Rampe d'accès (*f.*): raṅ′p dak″sē′.—**approaches.** Ouvrages d'approche: ū″-vrā′zə dap″‿prōsh′.
approximate, *v.* **1.** Rapprocher: ra″prō″shē′. **2.** Approximer: ap″‿prok″sī″mē′.
April. Avril (*n. m.*): a″vrīl′.
aqueduct. Aquéduc (*n. m.*): a″kē″dük′. In French official

maps abbreviated *Aquc.*—**aqueduct bridge.** Pont aquéduc: peṅ a″kē″dük′.
aquiline. Aquilin: a″kī″laṅ′: said of noses in describing personal characteristics.
arbalest. Arbalète (*n. f.*): ar″ba″lēt′‿ə (*weapon for shooting bombs, bolts, etc.*).
arbitration. Arbitrage (*n. m.*): ar″bī″trāʒ′.
arch. Arche (*n. f.*): arsh.—**arched,** *a.* **1.** Arqué: ar″kē′. **2.** Busqué: büs″kē′.
are. Être: ā′trə. See also AM, BE, IS. When used interrogatively, as, *are they? are we? are you?*, transpose the French words in the following phrases.—**they are.** Ils sont: īl seṅ.—**we are.** Nous sommes: nū sōm′—**you are.** Vous êtes: vūz‿ēt.
are there? Y a-t'il? ī a tīl.
area. **1.** Terrain (*n. m.*): tār″‿raṅ′. **2.** Zone (*n. f.*): zōn.—**area of concentration.** Zone de concentration (*n. f.*): zōn də keṅ″saṅ″trā″sī″‿yeṅ′.—**area of the ground.** Étendue du terrain: ē″taṅ″dü′ dü tār″raṅ′.—**billeting area.** Lieu de cantonnement: lī″‿yū′ də kan″ten″māṅ′.—**brigade a.** Emplacement de brigade (*n. m.*): aṅ″plas″maṅ′ də brī″gād′.—**grazing a.** Pâturage (*n. m.*): pā″tü″rāʒ′.—**requisitioning a.** Circonscription pour réquisitions: sīr″keṅ″skrīp″sī″‿yeṅ pūr rē″kī″zī″sī″‿yeṅ′.
arm. **1.** Bras (*n. m.*): brā (*limb*). **2.** Arme (*n. f.*): ārm (*a weapon*). See ARMS.
armament. Armement (*n. m.*): ar″mə-maṅ′.
armed seaman. Fusilier=marin (*n. m.*): fü″zī″lī″‿yē′=ma″raṅ′.
Armentières, ar″maṅ″tyār′, *n.* French northern town.
armistice. Armistice (*n. f.*): ar″mīs″tīs′.
armlet. Brassard (*n. m.*): bras″‿sār′.
armored, *a.* **1.** Cuirassé: kwī″ra″sē′. **2.** Blindé: blaṅ″dē′.—**armored battleship.** Cuirassé (*n. m.*): kwī′ras″‿sē′.—**armored train.** Train blindé (*n. m.*): traṅ blaṅ″dē′.—**a. car.** Automobile blindée: ō″tō″mō″bīl′ blaṅ″dē′.—**a. observation station.** Observatoire cuirassé (*n. m.*): eb″zār″va″twār′ kwī″ras″‿sē′.—**a. cruiser.** Croiseur=cuirassé (*n. m.*): krwā″zūr′= kwī″ras″‿sē′.—**armorer.** Armurier (*n. m.*): ar″mü″rī″‿yē′.
armory. **1.** Arsenal (*n. m.*): ar″sə-nāl′. **2.** Salle d'armes (*n. f.*): sal dārm.
arms, *n. pl.* **1.** Armes (*f.*): ārm (*weapon*). **2.** Bras (*m.*): brā (*limb*).—**ground arms** or **order arms!** **1.** Reposez vos armes! rə-pō″zē′ vōs‿ārm. **2.** Descendez armes! dēs″‿saṅ″dēz′‿ārm.—**inspection of a.** Inspection d'armes: aṅ″spek″sī″‿yeṅ′ dārm.—**order=a.!** Same as GROUND ARMS!—**pile a.!** Formez les faisceaux! fōr″mē′ lē fē″sō′.—**present a.!** Présentez armes! prē″zaṅ″tēz′‿ārm.—**shoulder a.!** Portez armes! pōr″tēz′‿ārm.—**side=a.** Armes blanches: ārm blaṅsh.—**slope a.!** Armes à l'épaule! ārmz‿ā lē″pōl′.—**small a.** Armes portatives: ārm pōr″ta″tīv′.—**stand to a.!** Aux armes! ōz‿ārm.—**unpile a.!** Rompez les faisceaux! reṅ″pē′ lē fēs″sō′.—**under a.** Sous les armes: sū lēz‿ārm.
army. Armée (*n. f.*): ar″mē′.—**army agent.** Agent (a″ʒaṅ′) qui (kī) tient (tī″‿yaṅ′) le (lə) solde (seld) des (dē) officiers(ef″‿fī″sī″‿yē′) et (ē) fait (fē) tous (tūz) actes (akt) de (də) banque (baṅk) à (a) leur (lūr) égard (ē″gār′).—**a. corps.** Corps d'armée (*n. m.*): kōr dār″mē′.—**a. council.** Conseil de l'armée (*n. m.*): keṅ″sē′‿yə də lār″mē′.—**a. headquarters.** Quartier général de l'armée: kar″tī″‿yē′ ʒē″nē″ral′ də lār″mē′.—**a. list.** Annuaire militaire: an″‿nü″ār′ mī″lī″tār′.—**A. Medical Board.** Conseil de santé de l'armée: keṅ″sē′‿yə də saṅ″tē′ də lār″mē′. (*Abbreviated* **A. M. B.**)—**a. orders.** Ordres de l'armée: ērd′‿rə də lār″mē′.—**A. Ordnance Corps.** Corps de Munitions, Matériel et Fourniture: kōr də mü″nī″sī″‿yeṅ′, ma″tē″rī″el′ ē fūr″nī″tūr′. (*Abbreviated* **A. O. C.**)—**A. Organization Act.** Loi organique de l'armée: lwa ēr″ga″nīk′ də lār″mē′.—**A. Service Corps.** In-

tendance Militaire: añ"tañ"dāñs' mī"lī"tār'. *Commonly abbreviated* **A. S. C.** See ARMY ORDNANCE CORPS.—**A. S. C. General Officer.** Intendant-général (*n. m.*): añ"tañ"dāñ' ʒē"nē"rāl'.—**A. S. C. Officer in charge.** Commandant (*n. m.*): kəm"mañ"dāñ'. —**A. S. C. Officer in charge of supplies.** Intendant de l'armée (*n. m.*): añ"tañ"dāñ' də lar"mē'.—**A. S. C. Officer in charge of first line transport.** Commandant de distribution au premier train régim-ntaire (*n. m.*): kəm"mañ"dāñ' də dīs"trī"bü"sī"‿yəñ' ō prə-mī"‿yē' trañ rē"ʒī"mañ"tār'.—**A. S. C. Officer in charge of railhead.** Commandant de gare origine d'étapes (*n. m.*): kəm"mañ"dāñ' də gār ō"rī"ʒīn' dē"tā'‿pə.—**A. S. C. Officer in charge of roadhead.** Commandant de tête d'étapes (*n. m.*): kəm"mañ"dāñ' də tēt dē"tā'‿pə.

around, *prep.* Autour: ō"tūr'.

arrangement. Disposition (*n. f.*): dīs"pō"zī"sī"yəñ'.—**ascertain arrangements.** S'assurer des dispositions: sas"‿sü"rē' dē dīs"pō"zī"sī"‿yəñ'.—**make a. for.** Prendre des dispositions pour: prañ'drə dē dīs"pō"zī"sī"‿yəñ' pūr.

arrest. Arrêts (*m. pl.*): ār"‿rē'.—**close arrest. 1.** Arrêts forcés: ār"‿rē' fōr"sē'. **2.** Arrêts de rigueur: ār"‿rē' də rī"gūr'.—**I arrest you.** Je vous arrête: ʒə vūz‿ār"‿rēt'ə.—**open a.** Arrêts simples: ār"‿rē' sañ'pl.—**put under a.** Mettre aux arrêts: met'trə ōz‿ār"‿rē'.—**under arrest.** Aux arrêts: ōz‿ār"‿rē'.

arrival. Arrivée (*n. f.*): ar"‿rī"vē'.

arrive, *v.* Arriver: ār"‿rī"vē'.—**arrive at the time set.** Arriver à l'heure fixée: ār"‿rī"vē' a lūr fīk"sē'.—**when shall we a. at —?** Quand arriverons nous à —? kañ ār"rī"‿və-roñ' nū a.—**he has just arrived.** Il vient d'arriver: īl vī"‿añ' dar"‿rī"vē'.

arsenal, *n.* Arsenal: ar"sə-nal'.

artesian, *a.* Artésien (*m.*): ar"tē"zī"añ'; artésienne (*f.*): ar"tē"zī"en'. In maps abbreviated *Artn.*

articles. Objets (*n. m.*): ob"ʒē'.—**articles of equipment.** Objets d'équipement: ob"ʒē' dē"kīp"māñ'. See KIT.

artificial, *a.* Artificiel: ar"tī"fī"sī"el'.

artillery. Artillerie (*n. f.*): ār"tī"‿yə-rī'.—**artillery banquette** (*platform*). Banquette d'artillerie (*n. f.*): bañ"ket' dār"tī"‿yə-rī'.—**a. butts, proving- or practise-grounds.** Polygone (*n. m.*): po"lī"gōñ'. In maps abbreviated *Polyg.*—**battery of a.** Batterie d'artillerie (*n. f.*): bat"‿tə-rī' dār"tī"‿yə-rī'.—**divisional a.** Artillerie divisionnaire: ār"tī"‿yə-rī' dī"vī"zī"yəñ"‿nār'.—**field a.** Artillerie de campagne: ār"tī"‿yə-rī' də kañ"pā'nyə.—**garrison a.** Artillerie de forteresse: ār"tī"‿yə-rī' də fōr"tə-res'.—**heavy a.** grosse artillerie (*n. f.*): grōs‿ār"tī"‿yə-rī'.—**heavy field a.** Artillerie lourde de campagne: ār"tī"‿yə-rī' lūrd də kañ"pā'nyə.—**horse a.** Artillerie à cheval: ār"tī"‿yə-rī' a shə-vāl'.—**marine a.** Artillerie de marine: ār"tī"‿yə-rī' də ma"rīn'.—**mountain a.** Artillerie de montagne: ār"tī"‿yə-rī' də moñ"tā'nyə.—**siege a.** Artillerie de siège: ār"tī"‿yə-rī' də sī"āʒ'.—**the a. is firing.** L'artillerie tire: lār"tī"‿yə-rī' tīr.—**the a. must resume firing.** L'artillerie doit ouvrir le feu de nouveau: lār"tī"‿yə-rī' dwāt‿ū"vrīr' lə fū də nū"vō'.—**artilleryman.** Artilleur (*n. m.*): ar"tī"yūr'.

artisan, *n.* Ouvrier (*m.*): ū"vrī"yē'; ouvrière (*f.*): ū"vrī"yār'.

artist. Artiste (*n. m.*): ar"tīst'.

as, *adv. & conj.* Comme: kəm.

asbestos. Amiante (*n. f.*): a"mī"ānt'ə (*a variety of white asbestos*).

ascend, *v.* Monter: moñ"tē'.

ascent. L'ascension (*n. f.*): la"sañ"sī"‿yoñ' (*of a balloon*).

ascertain, *v.* S'assurer de: sas"‿sü"rē' də.—**ascertain that.** S'assurer que: sas"‿sü"rē' kə.—**ascertain the disposition (of troops, etc.).** Reconnaître les dispositions: rə-koñ"‿nē'trə lē dīs"pō"zī"sī"‿yoñ'.—**a. or establish the facts.** Constater les faits: koñ"sta"tē' lē fē.

ashes. Cendre (*n. f.*): sañ′drə.—**reduce to ashes.** Réduire en cendre: rē″dwī′rə añ sañ′drə.
ashy pale. Pâle comme la cendre: pāl kəm la sañ′‿drə.
ask, *v.* Demander: də-mañ″dē′.
asphyxia. Asphyxie (*n. f.*): as″fīk″zī′.
asphyxiate, *v.* Asphyxier: as″fīk″sī″‿yē′.—**asphyxiating gas.** Asphyxiant (*n. m.*): as″fīks″yāñ′.—**asphyxiating shell.** Obus asphyxiant (*n. m.*): ō″büs′ as″fīks″yāñ′.
assailant. Assaillant (*n. m.*): as″sa″yāñ′.
assault, attack, onset, storming. Assaut (*n. m.*): as″‿sō′.—**a successful assault, attack,** etc. Un assaut heureux: añ as″‿sō′ ūr″ūz′.—**at the time set for the assault, attack,** etc. Au moment de l'assaut: ō mə″māñ′ də las″‿sō′.—**if the a.** or **attack fails.** Si l'assaut échoue: sī las″‿sō′ ē″shū′.—**repel an a., attack,** etc. Repousser un assaut: rə-pus″‿sē′ añ as″‿sō′.—**to make an a.** Livrer un assaut: lī″vrē′ añ as″‿sō′.—**to take by a.** or **storm.** Prendre d'assaut: prañ′drə das″‿sō′.
assemble, *v.* **1.** Assembler: as″sañ″blē′. **2.** Rassembler: ras″-sañ″blē′.
assembly, *n.* Rassemblement (*m.*): ras″‿sañ″blə-māñ′.—**place of assembly.** Lieu de rassemblement: lī″yu′ də ras″sañ″-blə-māñ′.
assign, *v.* Assigner: as″‿sī″nyē′. Compare ALLOT.
assist, *v.* **1.** Assister: as″‿sīs″tē′. **2.** Aider: ā″dē′.—**assist in any way.** Rendre aucun service: rāñ′drə ō″kañ′ sār″vīs′.
assistance, *n.* **1.** Aide (*f.*): ād. **2.** Secours (*m.*): se″kūr′.—**substantial assistance.** Secours matériels: se″kūr′ ma″tē″rī″el′.—**assistant.** Adjoint (*n. m.*): a″ʒwañ′.—**assistant director.** Directeur adjoint: dī″rek″tūr′ a″ʒwañ′.—**intelligent assistant.** Aide intelligent: ād añ″tel″lī″ʒāñ′.—**technical assistant.** Adjoint téchnique: a″ʒwañ′ tēk″nīk′.
assume, *v.* **1.** Prendre: prāñ′drə. **2.** Assumer: as″sü″mē′.—**assume any and every rôle.** Remplir tous les rôles: rañ″plīr′ tū lē rōl.—**a. command.** Prendre le commandement: prāñ′drə lə kəm″mañ″də-māñ′.—**to a.** or **take the offensive.** Prendre l'offensive: prāñ′drə ləf″‿fañ″sīv′.
astray, *a.* & *adv.* Égaré: ē″ga″rē′.—**to go astray.** S'égarer: sē″ga″rē′.
asylum, *n.* **1.** Hospice (*m.*): os″pīs′ (*refuge*). Abbreviated *Hosp.* on maps. **2.** Asile (*m.*): a″zīl′ (*for the insane*). Abbreviated *Ase* on maps.
as you were! Revenez! rə-və-nē′! (*a command*).
at, *prep.* **1.** À: a, as in "à Paris" (a pa″rī′), at Paris. **2.** En: añ, as in "en liberté" (añ lī″bār″tē′), at liberty. **3.** Chez: shē, as in "chez moi" (shē mwā), at my home.—**all at once.** Tout de suite: tū də swīt.—**at first.** D'abord: da″bōr′.—**at last.** Enfin: añ″fañ′.—**at least.** Au moins: ō mwañ.—**at most.** Au plus: ō plüs.—**at once.** De suite: də swīt.—**at the home** or **house of.** Chez: shē.
attach, *v.* Attacher: at″‿ta″shē′.
attaché. Attaché (*n. m.*): at″‿ta″shē′.—**foreign military attaché.** Attaché militaire à l'étranger: at″‿ta″shē′ mī″lī″tār′ a lē″trañ″ʒē′.
attack, *n.* & *v.* Attaque: at″‿tāk′.—**attack pushed home.** Attaque poussée à fond: at″‿tāk′ pūs″‿sē′ a foñ.—**counter-a.** Contre-attaque: koñ′tr‿at″‿tāk′.—**decisive a.** Attaque décisive: at″‿tāk′ dē″sī″sīv′.—**false a.** Attaque fausse: at″‿tāk′ fōs.—**flank a.** Attaque de flanc: at″‿tāk′ də flāñ.—**frontal a.** Attaque de face: at″‿tāk′ də fās.—**fruitless a.** Attaque infructueuse: at″‿tāk′‿añ″frük″tü″yūz′.—**ill-timed a.** Attaque intempestive: at″‿tāk‿añ″tam″pes″tīv′.—**rear a.** Attaque par derrière: at″‿tāk′ pār dē″rī″‿yār′.—**renewed a.** Attaque renouvelée: at″‿tāk′ rə-nū″və-lē′.—**threatened a.** Attaque

imminente: at″‿tä·k′‿ï.n″mï″nänt′.—**attacker.** Assaillant (*n. m.*): as″‿sai″‿yäṅ′.—**attacking columns.** Colonnes d'assaut: ko″lōn′ das″sō′.—**attacking troops.** Troupes d'assaut: trūp das″sō′.

attain, *v.* Atteindre: at″‿taṅ′‿drə.—**attainment. 1.** Acquisition (*n. f.*): a″kï″zï″sï‿yeṅ′. **2.** Portée (*n. f.*): pōr″tē′.

attempt, *v.* Essayer: es″‿sē″yē′.

attempt, *n.* Tentative (*f.*): taṅ″ta″tïv′.—**to forestall all attempts.** Prévenir toutes tentatives: prē″və-nïr′ tūt taṅ″-ta″tïv′.

attention! Garde à vous: gārd‿ā vū.

attract. Attirer (*v.*): at″‿tï″rē′.

auburn, *a.* Châtain (*m.*): sha″taṅ′; châtaine (*f.*): sha″tān′. Said of hair, and used for identification.

August. Août (*n. m.*): ū.

Australia. l'Australie (*n. f.*): lō″stra″lï′.—**the Australians.** Les Australiens (*n. m.*): lēz‿ōs″tra″lï″yaṅ′.

Austria. l'Autriche (*n. f.*): lō″trïsh′.—**the Austrians.** Les Autrichiens (*n. m.*): lēz‿ō″trï″shï″yaṅ′.

authority. Autorité (*n. f.*): ō″tōr″ï″tē′.—**he exerts his authority over.** Il exerce son autorité sur: ïl ex″ārs″ soṅ ō″tōr″ï″tē′ sür.—**authorized,** *a.* Réglementaire: rēg″lə-maṅ″tār′.

automobile. Automobile (*n. m.*): ō″tō″mō″bïl′.

autumn. L'automne (*n. m. & f.*): lō″təṅ′.

available, *a.* Disponible: dïs″pō″nï′blə.

avalanche. Avalanche (*n. f.*): a″va″lāṅsh′.

avenue. Avenue (*n. f.*): a″və-nü′. In maps abbreviated *Avue.*

average, *a.* Moyen (*m.*): mwa″‿yaṅ′; moyenne (*f.*): mwa″‿yeṅ′.—**an average march.** Une marche de longueur moyenne: ün mārsh də loṅ″gūr′ mwa″yeṅ′.—**a. powers.** Facultés moyennes: fa″kül″tē′ mwa″yeṅ′.

aviation. Aviation (*n. f.*): a″vï″a″sï″‿yeṅ′.—**aviation station.** Port d'attache: pōr dat″‿tāsh′.

aviator. Aviateur (*n. m.*): a″vï″a″tūr′.

avion, *n.* Aéroplane militaire: a″ē″re″plāṅ′ mï″lï″tār′.

avocation. Profession (*n. f.*): prō″fes″sï″‿yeṅ′.

avoid. Éviter (*v.*): ē″vï″tē′.—**avoid an engagement.** Refuser le combat: rə-fü″sē′ lə keṅ″bā′.

await. Attendre (*v.*): at″‿tāṅ′drə.

awake. Eveillé (*pa.*): ē″vē″yē′.

axe. Hache (*n. f.*): āsh.—**felling axe.** Grande hache: grānd‿āsh.

axle. Essieu (*n. m.*): es″‿sï″‿yū′.—**front axle.** Essieu-avant: es″‿sï″‿yū′ a″vāṅ′.—**rear or back a.** Pont-arrière: peṅt‿ar″‿rï″‿yār′.—**set a. to a.** Rangés essieu contre essieu: raṅ″ʒē′ es″‿sï″‿yū′ koṅ′tr‿es″sï″yū′.

B

back. Dos (*n. m.*): dō.—**back to back.** Dos à dos: dōz‿a dō.—**in the back.** Au dos: ō dō.

back. Reculer (*v.*): rə-kü″lē′.—**back her.** En arrière: aṅ ar″‿rï″‿yār′ (*a command on shipboard*, etc.).

background, *n.* **1.** Terrain en arrière: tār″‿raṅ′ aṅ ar″‿rï″‿yār′. **2.** Arrière-plan (*n. m.*): ar″rï″‿yār″-plāṅ′.—**to assimilate with the background.** Se confondre avec le terrain en arrière: sə koṅ″foṅ′drə a″vek′ lə ter″‿raṅ′ aṅ‿ar″‿rï″‿yār′.

back-sight, *n.* Cran de mire (*m.*): kraṅ də mïr.

bacon. Lard (*n. m.*): lār.

bad, *a.* Mauvais (*m.*): mō″vā′; mauvaise (*f.*): mō″vāz′.

badge. 1. Écusson (*n. m.*): ē″küs″‿soṅ. **2.** Brassard (*n. m.*): bras″sār′ (*armlet*).—**collar-badge.** Écusson de col: ē″küs″‿soṅ′

də kel.—**neutrality badge.** Insigne de neutralité: añ"sī'yə də nü"tra"lī"tē'.

bag. Sac (*n. m.*): sāk.—**kit-bag.** Havresac: ha"vrə-sāk'. Compare KIT.—**sand-bag.** Sac à terre: sāk a tār.—**section-b.** Sac de distribution: sāk də dīs"trī"bü"sī"‿yeñ'.—**sleeping-bag.** Sac de couchage: sāk də kū"shāʒ'. Colloquially termed *flea-bag*: sac à puce: sāk a püs.

baggage, luggage. Bagage (*n. m.*): ba"gāʒ'.—**baggage car.** Wagon de bagage: va"gəñ' də ba"gāʒ'.

bailer. Écope (*n. f.*): ē"kō'‿pə.

baker. Boulanger (*n. m.*): bū"lañ"ʒē'.

bakery. Boulangerie (*n. f.*): bū"lañ"ʒə-rī'.—**field-bakery,** *n.* Boulangerie de campagne: bū"lañ"ʒə-rī' də kam"pā'‿nyə.—**baking.** La cuisson (*n. f.*): lā kwīs"‿səñ'.

balance of power. Balance politique: ba"lāns' pəl"ī"tīk'.

balancing tip. Aileron (*n. m.*): ā"lə-rəñ'.

bald, *a.* Chauve: shōv.—**baldness.** Calvitie (*n. f.*): kal"vī"sī'.

baler, *n.* **1.** Louche à puiser: lūsh a pwī"zē'. **2.** Écope (*n. f.*): ē"kōp'.

balk. Poutrelle (*n. f.*): pū"trel'.—**claw-balk,** *n.* Poutrelle à griffes: pū"trel'‿a grīf.—**false b.** Fausse poutrelle de guindage: fōs pū"trel' də gañ"dāʒ'.—**hinged b.** Poutrelle à charnière: pū"trel' a shār"nī"‿yār'.—**jointed b.** Poutrelle articulée: pū"trel' ar"tī"kü"lē'.—**planked truss-b.** Poutrelle en planches: pū"trel' añ plāñsh.—**shore-b,** *n.* Poutrelle de culée: pū"trel' də kü"lē'.—**short b.** Poutrelle courte: pū"trel' kūrt.—**truss-b. made of chesses.** Poutrelle en madriers: pū"trel' añ ma"drī"‿yē'.

ball. **1.** Balle (*n. f.*): bal (*bullet; shot*). **2.** Bille (*n. f.*): bī'yə (*billiard-ball*).—**ball-bearing,** *n.* **1.** Coussinet à billes: kūs"sī"nē' a bī'‿yə. **2.** Roulement à billes: rū"lə"māñ a bī'‿yə.

ballast. Lest (*n. m.*): lest.

ballista. Baliste (*n. f.*): bā"līst'.

balloon, *n.* **1.** Aérostat (*m.*): a"ē"rōs"tā'. **2.** Ballon (*m.*): bal"‿ləñ'.—**balloon companies.** Compagnies d'aérostiers: kəñ"pa"-nyī da"ē"res"tī"yē'.—**b. reconnaissance.** Reconnaissance par ballon: rē"ken"nē"sāns' pār bal"‿ləñ'.—**captive b.** Ballon captif: bal"‿ləñ' kap"tīf'.—**dirigible b.** Ballon dirigeable: bal"‿ləñ' dī"rī"ʒāb'‿lə.—**free balloon.** Ballon libre: bal"‿ləñ' lī'‿brə.—**inflate a b.** Gonfler un ballon: gañ"flē' añ bal"‿ləñ'.—**kite b.** Ballon aux cerfs-volants: bal"‿ləñ' ō sērf vō"lāñ'.—**observations from b.** Observations faites en ballon: əb"zār"va"sī"‿yeñ' fāt añ bal"‿ləñ'.—**pilot b.** Ballon pilote: bal"‿ləñ' pī"lō'.—**test b. or feeler.** Ballon d'essai: bal"‿ləñ des"‿sā'.

balloonist, *n.* Aérostier: a"ē"res"tī"‿yē'.—**balloonists' section.** Section d'aérostiers: sek"sī"‿yeñ' da"ē"res"tī"‿yē'.

band, *n.* **1.** Bandeau (*m.*): ban"dō'. **2.** Musique (*f.*): mü"zīk'.—**bandmaster.** Chef de musique: shef de mü"zīk'.—**dressing-band.** Bandage (*n. m.*): bañ"dāʒ'.—**military b.** Musique militaire: mü"zīk' mī"lī"tār'.—**the band.** La musique: la mü"zīk'.—**white arm b.** Brassard blanc: bras"sār' blañ.—**bandsman.** Musicien (*n. m.*): mü"zī"sī"‿yañ'.

bandage. Bandage (*n. m.*): bañ"dāʒ'.—**circular b.** Bandage circulaire: bañ"dāʒ' sīr"kü"lār'.—**double T b.** Bandage en T double: bañ"dāʒ' añ tē dū'blə.—**many-tailed b.** Bandage de frondes: bañ"dāʒ' də frond.—**my bandage is untied.** Mon bandage est délié: mañ bañ"dāʒ' ē dē"lī"‿yē'.—**oblique b.** Bandage circulaire oblique: bañ"dāʒ' sīr"kü"lār' ō"blīk'.—**reverse spiral b.** Bandage renversé: bañ"dāʒ' rañ"vār"sē'.—**roller b.** Bande (*n. f.*): bānd.—**simple spiral b.** Bandage spiral ou roulé: bañ"dāʒ' spī"rāl'‿ū rū"lē'.—**square b.** Bandage carré: bañ"dāʒ' kar"‿rē'.—**triangular b.** Bandage triangulaire: bañ"dāʒ' trī"-

an″gū″lär′.—**T-shaped b.** Bandage en T simple: bañ″dā3′ añ tē sañ′plə.

bank[1] (*Slope or ridge*). **1.** Berge (*n. f.*): bār3. **2.** Rive (*n. f.*): rīv.—**character of banks and ground.** Caractère des rives et du terrain: ka″rak″tār′ dē rīv ē dü ter″rañ′.

bank[2] (*Depository for money*). Banque (*n. f.*): bāñk.—**I wish to go to the bank.** Je veux aller à la banque: 3ə vū al″‿lē′ a la bāñk.

bank, *v.* (*Aviation*). Pencher: pañ″shē′ (*incline: said of driving an aeroplane*).

banquette. Banquette (*n. f.*): bañ″ket′ (*firing-bank or -platform*).—**infantry banquette.** Banquette d'infanterie: bañ″ket′ dañ″fañ″tə-rī′.

Bantam, *n.* Bantam: bañ″tāñ′ (*English infantryman below 5 ft. 3 in. in height*).

barbed wire. Fil-de-fer barbelé: fīl″-də-fār′ bar″bə-lē′.

barber. Coiffeur (*n. m.*): kwaf″‿fũr′.

barbette. Barbette (*n. f.*): bār″bet′ (*firing-platform for cannon*).—**barbette gun.** Pièce en barbette: pī″yās′‿añ bār″bet′.

bareback, *a. & adv.* À poil: a pwāl.

barefoot, *a. & adv.* Nu pieds: nü pī″‿yē′.

barge. **1.** Chaland (*n. m.*): sha″lāñ′. **2.** Mahonne (*n. f.*): ma″-ōn′.—**bargeman.** Batelier (*n. m.*): ba″tə-lī″‿yē′.

bark. **I.** *n.* Aboiement: a″bwa″māñ′. **II.** *v.* Aboyer: a″bwa″‿yē′.—**barking of dogs.** L'aboiement des chiens: la″bwa″māñ′ dē shī″‿yañ′.

barley. Orge (*n. f.*): ōr3.—**barley-corn,** *n.* Grains d'orge: grañ dōr3.—**b.-meal,** *n.* Farine d'orge: fa″rīn′ dōr3.

barn. Grange (*n. f.*): grañ3. On maps abbreviated *Gge.*—**barn-floor,** *n.* Aire de la grange: ār də la grāñ3.

barndook, barn″dūk′, *n.* [Soldiers' slang.] A rifle.

barracks. Caserne (*n. f.*): ka″zārn′. Sometimes abbreviated *Casne.*—**barrack accommodation.** Casernement: ka″zār″nə-māñ′.—**b. warden.** Casernier (*n. m.*): ka″zār″nī″‿yē′.

barrage. Barrage (*n. m.*): bar″rā3′. (*Shell-fire concentrated, as along a given line.*) Compare CURTAIN OF FIRE under CURTAIN.

barrel (for water), *n.* Baril: ba″rī′.—**barrel of a rifle.** Canon d'un fusil: ka″noñ′ dañ fü″zī′.—**barrel-casing,** *n.* Enveloppe du canon: añ″və‿lōp′ dü ka″noñ′.

barricade. Barricade (*n. f.*): bār″‿rī″kād′.

barrier. Barrière (*n. f.*): bār″rī″‿yār′. Sometimes abbreviated *Bre.*

base, *n.* Base (*f.*): bāz.—**advanced base.** La base avancée: la bāz‿a″vañ″sē′.—**base of support.** Point d'appui: pwañ dap″pwī′.

base, *v.* **1.** Établir: ē″ta″blīr′. **2.** Baser: ba″zē′.

basement. Sous-sol (*n. m.*): sū″sol′.

basin. **1.** Bassin (*n. m.*): bas″sañ′ (*of a river*). On maps abbreviated *Bin.* **2.** Cuvette: kü″vet′ (*wash-basin*).

basket. Panier (*n. m.*): pa″nī″‿yē′.

bastion. Bastion (*n. m.*): bas″tī″‿yoñ′.

bath (cold, hot). Bain froid (*n. m.*): bañ frwā; bain chaud (*n. m.*): bañ shō.

bathe, *v.* Se baigner: sə bā″nyē′.

batman. Ordonnance d'un officier (*n. m.*): ōr″doñ″‿nāñs′ dañ of″‿fī″sī″‿yē′ (*a military servant*).

battalion. Bataillon (*n. m.*): ba″tai″‿yoñ′.

batten, *n.* **1.** Latte (*f.*): lāt′‿tə. **2.** Lattis (*m.*): lat″‿tī′.

battery (artillery). Batterie (*n. f.*): bat″‿tə-rī′. On maps abbreviated *Batie.*—**field battery.** Batterie de campagne: bat″‿tə-rī′ də kañ″pā′‿nyə.—**fighting b.** Batterie de tir: bat″‿tə-rī′ də tīr.—**screened b.** Batterie défilée: bat″‿tə-rī′ dē″fī″lē′.—**siege**

b. Batterie de siège: bat'‿tə-rī' də sī"‿yĕʒ.'—**to move a b.** Déplacer une batterie: dē"pla"sē' ün bat"‿tə-rī'.

battle. Bataille (*n. f.*): ba"tai'.—**battle array.** Ordre de bataille: ēr'drə də ba"tai'.—**battle=front,** *n.* See FRONT.—**pitched b.** Bataille rangée: ba"tai' ran"ʒē'.—**protracted b.** Une bataille prolongée: ün ba"tai' prō"lən"ʒē'.

battle=cruiser, *n.* Croiseur de bataille: krwa"zūr' də ba"tai'.

battle=field, *n.* Champ de bataille (*n. m.*): shān də ba"tai'.

battle=ship, *n.* Cuirassé (*n. m.*): kü"ra"sē'.

bay[1], *a.* Bai (*m.*), baie (*f.*): bē (*reddish=brown, as the coat of a horse*). For variations see the following.—**blood=bay.** Bai cerise: bē se"rīz'.—**brown bay.** Bai brun: bē brun.—**light b.** Bai clair: bē klār.

bay[2], *n.* **1.** Baie (*n. f.*): bā (*inlet*). On maps abbreviated *B.* **2.** (*Arch.*) Travée: tra"vē'. **3.** Intervalle: an"tār"val'.—**bay** or **bow window.** Fenêtre rotonde: fə-nā'trə rō"tənd'.

bayonet. Baïonnette (*n. f.*): bai"‿yən"‿net'.—**bayonet=belt,** *n.* Porte=baïonnette (*n. f.*): pērt bai"‿yən"‿net'.—**bayonet=charge,** *n.* Charge à la baïonnette (*n. f.*): shārʒ a la bai"‿yən"‿net'.—**b.=frog,** *n.* Porte=baïonnette (*n. m.*): pērt bai"‿yən"‿net'.—**b.=practise,** *n.* Escrime à la baïonnette: es"krīm' a la bai"‿yən"‿net'.—**b.=stop.** Arrêtoir de baïonnette: ar"‿rā"twār' də bai"‿yən"‿net'.—**b.=wound,** *n.* Blessure de baïonnette: bles"sūr' də bai"‿yən"‿net'.—**fix bayonets.** Baïonnette au canon: bai"‿yən"‿net' ō ka"nən'.—**trench=b.,** *n.* Baïonnette courte de tranchée: bai"‿yən"‿net' kūrt də tran"shē'.—**the bayonet only is to be used.** On ne se servira que de la baïonnette: ən nə sə sār"vī"rā' kə də la bai"‿yən"‿net'.—**with fixed b.** Baïonnette au canon: bai"‿yən"‿net' ō ka"nən'.

be. Être (*v.*): ē'trə. (For parts of this verb see Appendix. For interrogatives the positions of pronoun and verb are reversed: as, *suis-je?* Am I? *sommes nous?* Are we?)

beach. Plage (*n. f.*): plāʒ.

beacon. 1. (*Light* or *fire.*) Feu (*n. m.*): fū. **2.** (*Landmark* or *sea=mark.*) (1) Amer: a"mār'. (2) Balise: ba"līz'. **3.** Phare: fār.

beam. 1. (*Of a house.*) Poutre (*n. f.*): pū'trə. **2.** (*Of a ship.*) Bau (*n. m.*): bō.—**cross=beam.** Traverse (*n. f.*): tra"vārs'.—**main beam (of a ship).** Maître bau: mā'trə bō.

bean. Haricot (*n. m.*): a"rī"kō'.

bear, *v.* **1.** (*Carry.*) Porter: pōr"tē'. **2.** (*Aim.*) Tirer sur: tī"rē' sūr.—**artillery was brought to bear on . . .** L'artillerie fut amenée à tirer sur. . . : lār"tī"‿yə-rī' fū a"mə-nē' a tī"rē' sūr.—**to b. in mind. 1.** Ne pas oublier: nə pās‿ū"blī"yē'. **2.** Se mettre dans l'esprit: sə met'trə dan lē"sprī'.—**to b. the brunt of the attack.** Supporter le fort de l'attaque: sup"pēr"tē' lə fēr də lat"‿tāk'.

beard. Barbe (*n. f.*): bārb.—**beard beginning to grow.** Barbe naissante: bārb nās"‿sant'.—**pointed b.** Barbe en pointe: bārb an pwant.

bearer, *n.* **1.** Porteur (*n. m.*): per"tūr'; porteuse (*n. f.*): pēr"tūz'. **2.** Brancardier (*n. m.*): bran"kar"dī"‿yē'.—**bearer division.** Section de brancardiers (*n. f.*): sek"sī"‿yən' də bran"kar"dī"‿yē'.—**b. of a letter.** Porteur d'une lettre: per"tūr' dün lēt'‿trə.—**b. of a flag of truce.** Parlementaire (*n. m.*): par"lə-man"tār'.—**color=b.** Porte=drapeau (*n. m.*): pērt dra"pō'.—**guidon=b. (of cavalry).** Porte=guidon (*n. m.*): pērt gī"dən'.—**standard=b. (of infantry).** Porte=étendard (*n. m.*): pērt"‿ē"tan"dār'.—**bearers' company.** Compagnie de brancardiers: kən"pa"‿nyī' də bran"kar"dī"‿yē'.

bearing, *n.* **1.** (*Mechanical.*) (1) Coussinet: kūs"‿sī"nē'. (2) Roulement: rū"lə-mān'. **2.** (*Direction.*) Direction: dī"rek"sī"‿yən'.—**general bearing.** Direction générale: dī"rek"sī"‿yən' ʒē"nē"rāl'.—**find one's bearings.** S'orienter: sēr"ī"an"tē'.

beat. Battre (*v.*): bat'‿trə.—**beat the enemy with his**

own tactics. Battre l'ennemi en lui empruntant sa propre tactique: bat'trə lē"nə-mī' an lwī an"pran"tān' sū prō'prə tak"tīk'.—**to b. back the rushes.** Repousser les assauts: rē"pūs"‿sē' lēz‿as"‿sō'.

beautiful, *a.* Beau (*m.*): bō; belle (*f.*): bel.

beauty=spot, *n.* Grain de beauté (*n. m.*): gran də bō"tē'. Used in identification.

Beauvais, bō"vē', *n.* Town in northern France.

because, *conj.* Parce que: pār'sə-kə.

become, *v.* Devenir: dev"ə-nīr'.

bed, *n.* Lit (*n. m.*): lī.—**bed and board (food).** Lit et à manger: lī ē a man"ʒē'.—**can I have a b.?** Puis=je avoir un lit? pwī'‿ʒə‿a"vawār' an lī.—**put to b.** Mettre au lit: met'‿trə ō lī.

beech=tree, *n.* Hêtre (*n. m.*): hē'trə.

beef. Bœuf (*n. m.*): būrf; *or* viande de bœuf: vī"ānd' də būrf.—**canned** or **tinned beef.** Bœuf en boîte d'étain: būrf an bwāt' dē"tan'.—**preserved b.** Bœuf en conserve: būrf an kon"sārv'. See BULLY BEEF.

beer. Bière (*n. f.*): bī"‿yār'.

beetroot. Betterave (*n. f.*): bet"‿trāv'.

before, *adv.* Avant: a"vān'.

begin, *v.* Commencer: kom"‿man"sē'.

beginning. Commencement (*n. m.*): kom"‿man"sə-mān'.—**at the very beginning.** Tout au début: tūt‿ō dē"bü'.

behalf. Part (*n. f.*): pār.—**in behalf of.** Au nom de: ō non də.—**on behalf of.** De la part de: də la pār də.—**on behalf of the admiralty.** Au nom de l'amirauté: ō non də la"mī"rō"tē'.

behind, *prep.* **1.** Derrière: der"‿rī"yār'. **2.** Par derrière: par der"‿rī"‿yār'. **3.** En arrière: an ar"‿rī"‿yār'.

belfry, *n.* Same as BELL=TOWER.

Belgian, *a.* & *n.* Belge (*n. m.* & *f.*): belʒ.—**the Belgians.** Les Belges: lē belʒ.

Belgium, *n.* La Belgique (*n. f.*): lā bel"ʒīk'.

Belgrade, bel"grād', *n.* Capital of Serbia.

bell. Sonnette (*n. f.*): son"‿net'.—**bell=tower** or **belfry,** *n.* Clocher (*n. m.*): klə"shē'. On maps, *Cler.*

belligerent. Belligérant (*n. m.*): bel"‿lī"ʒē"rān'.

belly, *n.* Ventre (*n. m.*): vān'trə.—**belly=band,** *n.* Sous=ventrière: sū"van"trī"‿yār'.

belong. Appartenir (*v.*): ap"‿par"tə-nīr'.

below, *prep.* En bas: an bā.—**see below.** Voyez ci=dessous: vwa"‿yē' sī'-des"sū'.

belt, *n.* **1.** Ceinture (*n. f.*): san"tür'. **2.** Bande (*n. f.*): bānd.—**belt=plate.** Plaque de ceinturon (*f.*): plāk də san"tü"ron'.—**cholera=b.** Ceinture de flanelle: san"tür' də fla"nel'.—**"Sam Brown" b.** Ceinture et accessoires: san"tür' ē aks"‿ses"‿swār'—**sword=** or **waist=b.** Ceinturon (*n. m.*): san"tü"ron'.

bend or **hitch.** Noeud (*n. m.*): nū.

berm. **1.** Berme (*n. f.*): bārm (*ledge* or *bench*). **2.** Accotement (*n. m.*): ak"‿kō"tə-mān' (*narrow level at the outside foot of a parapet*).

berth (of a ship), 1. *n.* Poste d'amarrage (*n. m.*): pōst da"mar"‿rāʒ'. **2.** Cabine (*f.*): ka"bīn' (*aboard ship*).—**berthing (a ship),** *n.* Mise à quai (d'un navire): mīz‿a kē dan na"vīr'.

Besançon, be"zan"son', *n.* Town in eastern France.

besides, *adv.* **1.** Aussi: ōs"‿sī'. **2.** D'ailleurs: dai"‿yūr'.

besiege, *v.* **1.** Assiéger: as"‿sī"‿yē"ʒē'. **2.** Faire le siège: fār lə sī"‿yēʒ'.—**besieged,** *pa.* Assiégé: as"‿sī"‿yē"ʒē'.—**besieger.** Assiégeant (*n. m.*): as"‿sī"‿yē"ʒan'.—**besieging force.** Force assiégeante: fōrs‿as"‿sī"‿yē"ʒānt'.

betray, *v.* **1.** Trahir: tra"‿yīr'. **2.** Déceler: dē"sə-lē'.—**to betray oneself.** Se trahir: sə tra"‿yīr'.—**b. their positions.**

Déceler leurs positions: dē″sə-lē′ lūr po″zī″sī″‿yəṅ′.—**betrayer.** Traître (*n. m.*): trā′trə.

better, *adv.* Mieux: mī″‿yʊ′.—**I am better.** Je vais mieux: ʒə vē mī″yʊ′. See ALLER, in Appendix.—**I feel b.** Je me sens mieux: ʒə mə saṅ mī″yʊ′. See SENTIR, in Appendix.—**he is b.** Il va mieux: īl va mī″‿yʊ′. See ALLER, in Appendix.

between, *prep.* Entre: aṅ′trə.

beware, *v.* Prendre garde: praṅ′drə gārd.—**beware!** Prenez garde! pre″nē′ gārd!

beyond, *adv.* Au delà de: ō də-lā′ də.—**from beyond the seas.** D'outre-mer: dū′trə-mār′.

bias, *a.* Préjugé: prē″ʒü″ʒē′.—**biased,** *a.* Partial (*m.*), partiale (*f.*): par″sī″‿yāl′.—**biased mind.** Esprit prévenu: es″prī′ prē″və-nü′.

bicarbonate of soda. Bicarbonate de soude: bī″kar″bə″nāt′ də sūd.

bicycle, *n.* Bicyclette (*n. f.*): bī″sī″klet′.

big, *a.* **1.** Gros (*m.*): grō; grosse (*f.*): grōs. **2.** Grand (*m.*): graṅ; grande (*f.*): graṅd.—**big-boy,** *n.* [Soldiers' slang.] A gun having a bore of more than 8 inches.—**Big Willie.** The British soldiers' nickname for the German Emperor.—**the Big Push.** The battle of the Somme: British soldiers' name.

bill. **1.** Note (*n. f.*): nōt. **2.** Billet (*n. m.*): bī″‿yē′.

billet. **I.** *n.* **1.** Billet de logement: bī″‿yē′ də lōʒ″māṅ′. **2.** Cantonnement (*n. m.*): kaṅ″təṅ″‿nə″māṅ′. **II.** *v.* Loger: lō″ʒē′.—**billet-guard,** *n.* Garde de logement (*n. f.*): gārd də lōʒ″māṅ′ (*a guard posted to protect the billet of soldiers*).—**b. without subsistence or sustenance.** Billet de logement sans nourriture: bī″yē′ də lōʒ″‿māṅ′ saṅ nūr″‿rī″tür′.—**b. with subsistence or sustenance.** Billet de logement avec nourriture: bī″‿yē′ də lōʒ″māṅ′ a″vek′ nūr″‿rī″tür′.—**close b.** Cantonnements resserrés: kaṅ″təṅ″‿nə-māṅ′ rə-sār″rē′.—**ordinary b.** Cantonnements ordinaires: kaṅ″təṅ″‿nə-māṅz′‿ōr″dī″nār′.—**reserve b.** Cantonnement d'alerte: kaṅ″təṅ″‿nə-māṅ′ da″lārt′.—**to evacuate the b.** Quitter le cantonnement: kīt″tē′ lə kaṅ″təṅ″‿nə-māṅ′.—**to go into or occupy b.** Prendre possession du cantonnement: praṅ′drə pōs″‿ses″‿sī″‿yəṅ′ dü kaṅ″təṅ″‿nə-māṅ′.—**billeting,** *n.* Logement des troupes: lōʒ″māṅ′ dē trūp.—**billeting area.** **1.** Surface de cantonnement: sūr″fās′ də kaṅ″-təṅ″‿nə-māṅ′. **2.** Superficie couverte: sü″pār″fī″sī′ kū″vārt′.—**b. officer.** Officier de billets de logement: əf″‿fī″sī″‿yē′ də bī″‿yē′ də lōʒ″māṅ′.—**b. orders, b. paper.** Billets de logement: bī″yē′ də lōʒ″māṅ′.—**b. party.** Campement de cantonnement: kaṅp″māṅ′ də kaṅ″təṅ″‿nə-māṅ′.

billhook. Serpe (*n. f.*): sārp.

biplane. Biplan (*n. m.*): bī″plāṅ′.

bind, *v.* **1.** Lier: lī″‿yē′ (*tie*). **2.** Garroter: gar″‿rō″tē′ (*a prisoner*).

birch-tree. Bouleau (*n. m.*): bū″lō′.

bird. Oiseau (*n. m.*): wā″zō′.

birth, *n* Naissance (*f.*): nās″sāṅs′.—**birthday,** *n.* Jour de naissance: ʒūr də nās″sāṅs′.

biscuit, *n.* Biscuit (*n. m.*): bīs″kwī′.—**biscuit tins.** Caisses à biscuit en étain: kēs a bīs″kwī′ aṅ ē″taṅ′.—**b. and sugar.** De biscuit et du sucre: də bīs″kwī′ ē dü sü′krə.

bisected, *a.* Divisé en deux: dī″vī″zē′ aṅ dū.

bishop. Évêque (*n. m.*): ē″vēk′—**bishop's house.** Evêché (*n. m.*): ē″vē″shē′.

bit. **1.** Morceau (*n. m.*): mōr″sō′. **2.** Mors (*n. m.*): mōr. **3.** Frein (*n. m.*): fraṅ (*mouthpiece of a bridle*).

bite, *v.* Mordre: mōr′drə.

bitt. Bitte (*n. f.*): bīt.

bivouac. **1.** Bivouac (*n. m.*): bī″vū″āk′. **2.** Cantonnement (*n. m.*): kaṅ″təṅ″‿nə-māṅ′.

black, *a.* Noir (*m.*), noire (*f.*): nwār.

blacksmith. Forgeron (*n. m.*): fōr″‿ʒə-reṅ′.

blade. **1.** Lame (*n. f.*): lām (*of a sword*). **2.** Branche d'hélice: brāṅsh dē″lis′ (*of a propeller*).

blank, *a.* Faux (*m.*): fō; fausse (*f.*): fōs (*said of ammunition*).—**blank cartridge.** Cartouche à blanc: kar″tūsh′ a blaṅ.—**to fire with blank cartridge.** Tirer à blanc: tī″rē′ a blaṅ.

blanket. Couverture (*n. f.*): kū″vār″tür′.—**bring me a blanket.** Apportez-moi une couverture: ap″‿por″tē′ mwā üṅ kū″vār″tür′.—**soldier's b.** or **rug.** Couverture de campement: kū″vār″tür′ də kaṅp″ə-māṅ′.—**take no blankets.** Portez pas de couvertures: pōr″tē′ pā də kū″vār″tür′.

blast-furnace. Haut-fourneau (*n. m.*): ō″-fūr″nō′.

blaze, *v.* Marquer: mar″kē′ (*said of trees*).—**blaze the trees.** Marquez l'écorce des arbres: mar″kē′ lē″kōrs′ dēz‿ār′brə.

bleed, *v.* Saigner: sē″‿nyē′.—**bleeding.** Saignement (*n. m.*): sē″‿nyə-māṅ′.

"Blighty," *n.* [Soldiers' slang.] England. From the East Indian *Belait,* Europe.

blimp, *n.* [Soldiers' slang.] A small airship.

blind, *a.* Aveugle (*m. & f.*): a″vū′‿glə.—**blind alley.** **1.** Cul-de-sac: kūl″də-sāk′. **2.** Impasse (*n. f.*): aṅ″pās′.

blindfold, *v.* Bander les yeux: baṅ″dē′ lēz‿yū.

blinds. Blindes (*n. pl.*): blaṅd (*screen of wood* or *metal*).

blinking. **I.** *a.* Clignotant: klī″nyō″tāṅ′. **II.** *n. m.* Clignement: klī″nyə-māṅ′. Used in identification.

blister. Ampoule (*n. f.*): aṅ″pūl′.

block, *n.* **1.** Encombrement (*n. m.*): aṅ″keṅ″brə-māṅ′. **2.** Enchevêtrement (*n. m.*): aṅ″shə-vē″trə-māṅ′.

block, *v.* **1.** Fermer: fār″mē′. **2.** Barrer: bar″‿rē′. **3.** Bloquer: blo″kē′.—**to block a road or thoroughfare.** Fermer un chemin, ou une route: fār″mē′ aṅ shə-maṅ′, ū üṅ rūt.

blockade. **I.** *n.* Blocus (*m.*): blo″kü′. **II.** *v.* Faire le blocus de: fār lə blo″kü′ də.—**blockade-running,** *n.* Forcement de blocus: fōr″sə-māṅ′ də blo″kü′.—**raise the blockade.** Lever le blocus: lə-vē′ lə blo″kü′.

blocked, *a.* **1.** Barrée (*a. f.*): bar″‿rē′. **2.** Pas libre: pā lī′‿brə.

blockhouse. **1.** Bastide (*n. f.*): bas″tīd′. On maps *Bide.* **2.** Blockhaus (*n. m.*): blo″kōs′. On maps *Bl.*

blond, *a. & n.* Blond (*m.*): bleṅ; blonde (*f.*): bleṅd.

blood. Sang (*n. m.*): saṅ.—**bath of blood.** Bain de sang: baṅ də saṅ. (*German name for the battle of the Somme.*)—**check** or **stop the flow of b.** Arrêtez le saignement: ar″rē″tē′ lə sē″‿nyə-māṅ′.

blotting-paper. Papier buvard (*n. m.*): pa″pī″‿yē′ bū″vār′.

blouse. Blouse (*n. f.*): blūz′‿ə.

blow. **I.** (*n. m.*): Coup: kū. **II.** *v.* Souffler: sūf″‿flē′.—**the wind blows the smoke toward the defenders.** Le vent chasse la fumée vers les défenseurs: lə vaṅ shas la fü″mē′ vār lē dē″faṅ″sūr′.—**to blow up.** Faire sauter: fār sō″tē′.—**to b. up with petards.** Pétarder: pē″tar″dē′.—**to strike a crushing b. at the enemy.** Porter un coup écrasant à l'ennemi: pōr″tē′ aṅ kū ē″kra″sāṅt′‿a leṅ″‿nə-mī′.—**to strike a decisive b.** Porter un coup décisif: pōr″tē′ aṅ kū dē″sī″sīf′.

blue, *a.* bleu (*m.*); bleue (*f.*): blū.—**blue-jackets,** *n.* **1.** Marins de l'État: ma″raṅ′ də lē″tā′. **2.** Matelots de la marine de guerre: ma″tə-lō′ də lā ma″rīn′ də gār.

bluff. **I.** *a.* Brusque (*m. & f.*): brūsk. **II.** *n.* **1.** Berge (*f.*): bārʒ. **2.** Escarpement (*m.*): es″kar″‿pə-māṅ′.

B. M. G. C., *abbr.* Brigade Machine-Gun Company.

board, *n.* **1.** Planche (*f.*): plaṅsh (*plank*). **2.** Pension (*f.*): paṅ″sī″‿yeṅ′ (*food*). **3.** Conseil (*m.*): koṅ″sē′‿yə (*council*).—**board of reference.** Le conseil consultatif: lə koṅ″sē′‿yə keṅ″sül″ta″tīf′.

—**distribution b.** Tableau de distribution: tɑ̄b″lō′ də dīs″trī″bü″-sī″‿yeṅ′.—**on b. ship.** À bord d'un bateau: ɑ bōr daṅ bɑ″tō′.
boat, *n.* **1.** Bateau (*m.*): bɑ″tō′. On maps *Bat.* **2.** Nacelle (*f.*): nɑ″sel′ (*skiff* or *car of a balloon*). **3.** Canot (*m.*): kɑ″nō′ (*ship's cutter*). **4.** Embarkation (*f.*): aṅ″bɑr″kɑ″sī″‿yeṅ′ (*wherry*).—**collapsible boats.** Bateaux pliants (*n. m.*): bɑ″tō′ plī″āṅ′.—**I am going to the b.** Je m'en vais au bateau: ʒə maṅ vē ō bɑ″tō′.—**the boats were sunk.** Les bateaux furent coulés à fond: lē bɑ″tō′ für kü″lē′ ɑ feṅ.
boatswain, *n.* Maître d'équipage: mā′‿trə dē″kī″pāʒ′.
Boche (*n. m.*): bōsh (*French nickname for a German*).
body, *n.* **1.** Corps (*m.*): kōr. **2.** Gros (*m.*): grō (*main body of an army*). **3.** Caisse (*f.*): kēs (*of a vehicle*). **4.** Cadavre (*m.*): kɑ″dāv′‿rə (*corpse*).—**body-bandage,** *n.* Bandage plein: baṅ″-dāʒ′ plaṅ.—**the main b.** Le gros: lə grō.
bog, *n.* Tourbière (*f.*): tūr″bī″‿yār′.
bogie, *n.* Bogie (*f.*): bō″ʒī′ (*truck*).—**bogie-coach,** *n.* Wagon à bogies: vɑ″geṅ′‿ɑ bō″ʒī′.
boil, *v.* Bouillir: bū″yīr′.
boiler, *n.* Chaudière (*f.*): shō″dī″yār′.
bold, *a.* Hardi (*m.*), hardie (*f.*): ɑr″dī′.—**boldness.** Hardiesse (*n. f.*): ɑr″dī″‿yes′.—**to act with great boldness.** Agir avec grande hardiesse: ɑ″ʒīr′‿ɑ″vek′ grūnd‿ɑr″dī″‿yes′.
bollard or **warping-post.** Corps mort (*n. m.*): kōr mōr.
bolt, *n.* **1.** Goupille (*f.*): gū″pī′ (*pin*). **2.** Écrou (*m.*): ē″krū′ (*screw-nut*). **3.** Levier (*m.*): lə-vī″‿yē′ (*lever-bolt*).
bolt, *v.* **1.** Bourrer: būr″‿rē′. **2.** S'emporter: saṅ″pōr″tē′.
bomb, *n.* **1.** Bombe (*f.*): beṅ′‿bə. **2.** Obus (*m.*): ō″bü′ (*shell*).—**b.-proof,** *n.* À l'épreuve d'obus ou de bombe: ɑ lē″-prūv′ dō″bü′ ū də beṅ′‿bə.—**b.-proof cover.** Abri blindé: ɑ″brī′ blaṅ″dē′.—**incendiary-bomb,** *n.* Bombe incendiaire: beṅ′bə aṅ″saṅ″dī″yār′.—**to drop** or **throw a b. 1.** Jeter une bombe: ʒə-tē′ üṅ beṅ′bə. **2.** Lancer une bombe: laṅ″sē′ üṅ beṅ′bə.—**b.-thrower,** *n.* Lance-bombe (*m.*): laṅs beṅ′bə.
bombard, *v.* Bombarder: beṅ″bɑr″dē′.—**bombardment.** Bombardement (*n. m.*): beṅ″bɑr″də-māṅ′.—**bombardment-battery, counter-battery,** *n.* Batterie de bombardement ou contre batterie: bɑt″‿tə-rī′ də beṅ″bɑr″də-māṅ′ ū keṅ′trə bɑt″‿tə-rī′.—**protected against b.** À l'abri d'un bombardement: ɑ lɑ″brī′ d'aṅ beṅ″bɑr″də-māṅ′.
bombsight. Viseur (*n. m.*): vī″zūr′.
bona fide, *a.* De bonne foi (*m.* & *f.*): də beṅ′‿nə fwā.
bone, *n.* Os (*m.*): ō.
bonnet, *n.* **1.** Chapeau (*m.*): shɑ″pō′ (*of a woman*). **2.** Bonnet (*m.*): beṅ″‿nē′ (*of a Scotsman*).
book, *n.* Livre (*m.*): līv′‿rə.—**bookstall,** *n.* Bibliothèque des chemins de fer (*f.*): bī″blī″o″tēk′ dē shə-maṅ′ də fār.—**booking-office.** Guichet (*n. m.*): gī″shē′. **b.-clerk,** *n.* See TICKET-CLERK.
boom, *n.* **1.** Boute-hors (*m.*): būt″ōr′ (*of a ship*). **2.** Chaîne (*f.*): shēn (*of a harbor*).
boot, *n.* **1.** Soulier (*m.*): sū″lī″‿yē′. **2.** Botte (*f.*): bet′‿tə (*for a man*). **3.** Bottine (*f.*): bet″‿tīn′ (*for a woman*). **4.** Chaussure (*f.*): shōs″‿sūr′ (*footwear in general*). **5.** [Soldiers' slang.] Godillot (*m.*): gō″dī″yō′.—**boot-laces. 1.** Lacets (*m. pl.*): lɑ″sē′. **2.** Lacets de bottines (*m. pl.*): lɑ″sē′ də bet″‿tīn′.—**give me some b.-l.** Donnez-moi des lacets de bottines: deṅ″‿nē′ mwā dē lɑ″sē′ də bet″‿tīn′.
bootmaker, *n.* Cordonnier (*n. m.*): kor″deṅ″‿nī″‿yē′.
boots, *n. pl.* Bottes (*f.*) bet′‿tə. **ammunition boots.** Brodequins (*m. pl.*): brō″‿də-kaṅ′.—**high b.** Bottes à l'écuyère: bet′‿təs‿ɑ lē″kwī″yār′.—**mess-b.** Demi-bottes: də-mī′ bet′‿tə.—**riding-b.,** *n.* Bottes à l écuyère: bet′‿zɑ lē″kwī″yār′.—**rubber b.** Bottes en caoutchouc: bet′‿təs‿aṅ kɑ″ū″shū′.—**service-**

b. Brodequins (*m. pl.*): brō"də-kaṅ'.—**Wellington b.** Bottes molles: bot'‿tə mōl.

booty. Butin (*n. m.*): bü"taṅ'.

boracic, *a.* Borique (*m.* & *f.*): bō"rīk'.—**boracic acid.** Acide borique (*n. f.*): a"sīd' bō"rīk'.—**b. powder.** Poudre boriquée (*n. f.*): pū'‿drə bō"rī"kē'.—**b. vaseline.** Vaseline boriquée: va"sə-līn' bō"rī"kē'.

Bordeaux, bōr"dō', *n.* Town in southwestern France.

bore. Âme (*n. f.*): ām.—**bore=hole,** *n.* Same as BORING, 2.

boring, *n.* **1.** Forage (*m.*): fo"rāʒ'. **2.** Alésage (*m.*): a"lē"sāʒ'.—**boring=bar.** Barre à mine (*n. f.*): bār‿ā mīn.—**b.=bit.** Pistolet de mine (*n. m.*): pīs"to"lē' də mīn.—**b.=machine.** **1.** Perforatrice (*n. f.*): pār"fo"ra"trīs'. **2.** Perceuse (*n. f.*): pār"sūz'.

born, *n.* Né (*m.*); née (*f.*): nē.

borough, *n.* Bourg (*n. m.*): būrg. Abbreviated *Bg.*

Bosnia, *n.* Bosnie (*n. f.*): boz"nī' (*Austrian province*).

Bosporus, *n.* Bosphore (*n. m.*): bos"fōr' (*strait between Black Sea and Sea of Marmora*).

both, *a.* **1.** Tous les deux: tū lē dū. **2.** L'un et l'autre: laṅ‿ē lō'‿trə.

bottle, *n.* **1.** Bouteille (*f.*): bū"tē'‿yə. **2.** Carafe (*f.*): ka"rāf' (*decanter*).—**oil=bottle** or **=cruet,** *n.* Burette à l'huile: bū"ret'‿a lwīl.

bottom. Fond (*n. m.*): foṅ.—**kind of bottom.** Nature du fond: na"tūr' dü foṅ.—**muddy b.** Fond de vase: foṅ də vāz.—**rocky** or **stony b.** Fond de roche: foṅ də rō'‿shə.—**sandy b.** Fond de sable: foṅ də sā'‿blə.

bough, *n.* **1.** Branche (*f.*): brāṅsh (*large*). **2.** Rameau (*m.*): ra"mō' (*small*).

bound, boundary. Lisière (*n. f.*): lī"zī"ār'.—**boundary=stone.** Borne (*n. f.*): bōr‿nə. Abbreviated *Bne.*—**out of bounds.** Hors des limites: hōr dē lī"mīt'.

bow (of a ship). Avant (*n. m.*): a"vāṅ'.

bowels. **1.** Intestins (*n. m.*): aṅ"tes"taṅ'. **2.** Entrailles (*n. f. pl.*): aṅ"trai'‿yə.

box. Boîte (*n. f.*): bwāt.—**box=car.** Wagon=écurie (*n. m.*): va"goṅ' ē"kü"rī'.

boxing. La boxe (*n. f.*): la boks.

boy. Garçon (*n. m.*): gar"soṅ'.

Boy Scouts. Les Éclaireurs de France: lēz‿ē"klā"rūr' də Frāṅs'‿ə.

Brabant, bra"bāṅ', *n.* A province of Belgium.

bracelet. Bracelet (*n. m.*): bra"sə-lē'.

braces. **1.** Bretelles (*n. f. pl.*): bre"tel'. **2.** Bretelles de suspension du havresac: bre"tel' də süs"paṅ"sī"‿yoṅ' dü ha"vrə-sāk'.

bracket. **I.** *n.* Fourchette (*f.*): fūr"shet' (*gunnery term used in range=finding*). **II.** *v.* Encadrer: aṅ"ka"drē'.

brain, *n.* **1.** Cerveau (*m.*): sār"vō'. **2.** Cervelle (*f.*): sār"vel'.

brake, *n.* Frein (*m.*): fraṅ.—**air=brake,** *n.* Frein à air (*m.*): fraṅ a ār.—**emergency=b.,** *n.* Frein de secours: fraṅ də se"kūr'.—**put on the b.** Serrez le frein: ser"‿rē' lə fraṅ.—**vacuum=b.,** *n.* Frein à vide: fraṅ a vīd.

brakeman, *n.* Garde=frein (*m.*): gard"-fraṅ'.

bran. Son (*n. m.*): soṅ.

branch. **1.** (*Division.*) Branche (*n. f.*): brāṅsh. **2.** (*Bough.*) Rameau (*n. m.*): ra"mō'. In military mining a small gallery connecting with the main gallery.—**branch with supports** (*military mining*). Rameau de combat: ra"mō' də koṅ bā'.—**listening b.** (*military mining*). Rameau d'écoute: ra"mō' dē"kūt'.—**main b.** Grand rameau: graṅ ra"mō'.

brandy. **1.** Cognac: kō"nī"‿yāk'. **2.** Eau=de=vie: ō-də-vī'.

brass. Cuivre (*n. m.*): kwī'‿vrə.—**brass band.** **1.** Ceinture de cuivre: saṅ"tür'də kwī'vrə. 2. Musique d'instruments de cuivre: mü"zīk' dəṅ"strü"mäṅ' də kwī'‿vrə.—**brass wire.** See under WIRE.

brassard. Brassard (*n. m.*): bras"‿sär' (*armlet*).—**Geneva brassard.** Brassard de la Convention de Genève: bras"‿sär' də lä keṅ"vaṅ"sī"‿yeṅ' də ʒə-nēv'.

brave, *a.* 1. Courageux (*m.*): kū"ra"ʒū'. 2. Brave: bräv.—**bravery.** Bravoure (*n. f.*): bra"vūr'.

brazen, *a.* Impudent (*m.*): aṅ"pü"däṅ'; impudente (*f.*): aṅ"pü"däṅt'.

brazier. Seau à incendie (*n. m.*): sō a aṅ"saṅ"dī' (*fire=bucket*).

Brazil. Brésil (*n. m.*): brē"zīl'. A South=American Republic.

breach. Brèche (*n. f.*): brēsh.—**breach of trust.** Abus de confiance: ä"bü' də keṅ"fī"äṅs'.—**to make a b.** Culasser: kü"las"‿sē'.

bread (*n.*), or **a loaf of bread. 1.** Pain (*m.*): paṅ. **2.** Du pain: dü paṅ.—**give me some bread, please.** Donnez moi du pain, s'il vous plait: deṅ‿nē' mwä dü paṅ, sīl vū plē.—**some bread.** Du pain: dü paṅ.

bread=crum. 1. Miette (*n. f.*): mī"‿yet'. **2.** *pl.* Au gratin: ō gra"taṅ' (*dressed with bread=crums*).

break, *v.* **1.** Casser: kas"‿sē'. **2.** Briser: brī"zē'. **3.** Crever: krə-vē' (*burst, as a tire*).—**to break in a horse.** Dresser un cheval: dres"‿sē' aṅ shə-väl'.—**to b. into, rush into.** Faire irruption: fār īr"‿rüp"sī"‿yeṅ'.—**to b. into a trot.** Prendre le trot: präṅ'‿drə lə trō.—**to b. off the fight.** Rompre le combat: reṅ'‿prə lə keṅ"bä'.—**to b. out of custody.** s'Évader: sē"va"dē'.—**to b. step.** Rompre le pas: reṅ'‿prə lə pä.—**to b. through. 1.** Percer: pär"sē'. **2.** Enfoncer: aṅ"feṅ"sē'.—**to b. up.** Fractionner: frak"sī"‿yeṅ"‿nē'.—**to b. up a dashing attack.** Briser l'élan d'une attaque: brī"zē lē"läṅ' dün at"täk'.

breakdown. Panne (*n. f.*): paṅ'‿nə.

breakfast. Déjeuner (*n. m.*): dē"ʒʊ"nē'.—**breakfast is ready.** Le déjeuner est prêt: lə dē"ʒʊ"nē' ē prē.—**breakfast time.** L'heure du déjeuner: lūr dü dē"ʒʊ"ŋē'.—**give me some b., please.** Donnez moi à déjeuner, s'il vous plait: deṅ"‿nē' mwä a dē"ʒʊ"nē', sīl vū plē.—**is breakfast ready?** Le déjeuner est=il prêt: lə dē"ʒʊ"nē' ē"‿tīl' prē.—**I will take my b. at 8 o'clock.** Je prendrai mon déjeuner à huit heures: ʒə praṅ"drē' meṅ dē"ʒʊ"nē' a wīt hūr.

breast. Poitrine (*n. f.*): pwa"trīn'.—**breastwork,** *n.* **1.** Parapet (*m.*): par"a"pē'. **2.** Épaulement (*m.*): ē"pōl"mäṅ'. **3.** Masse couvrante (*f.*): mäs kū"vräṅt'.—**the b. is manned by infantry.** Le parapet est occupé par l'infanterie: lə par"a"pē' ēt‿ōk"‿kü"pē' pä laṅ"faṅ"tə-rī'.

breathe, *v.* Respirer: res"pī"rē'.

breech. Culasse (*n. f.*): kü"läs'. — **breech=block.** Culasse mobile: kü"läs' mə"bīl'.—**b.=lever.** Poignée de culasse: pwa"nyē' də kü"läs'.—**b.=loading.** Chargement par la culasse: shaʒ"mäṅ' pä la kü"läs'.—**b.=screw.** Vis de culasse: vī də kü"läs'.—**concentric groove breech=plug.** Culasse à filets concentriques: kü"läs'‿a fī"lē' keṅ"saṅ"-trīk'.

breeches. Culotte (*n. f.*): kü"lət'.

breeching. Reculement (*n. m.*): rə-kū"lə-mäṅ'.

brevet. Brevet (*n. m.*): brə-vē'.—**brevet rank.** Grade honorifique: gräd eṅ"ō"rī"fīk'.

Briand, Aristide, brī"äṅ', a"rī"stīd'. A French statesman.

bribe. I. *n.* Présent (*m.*): prē"säṅ'. **II.** *v.* Corrompre: kər"‿reṅ'prə.

briber. Suborneur (*n. f.*): sü"bōr"nūr'.

brick. Brique (*n. f.*): brīk.—**brickfield.** Briqueterie (*n. f.*): brīk"tə-rī'. Abbreviated *Briqie.*—**brick=kiln.** Four à briques (*n. m.*): fūr a brīk.

bridge. Pont (*n. m.*): peṅ. On maps *P.*—**barrel=bridge.**

Passerelle de tonneaux (*f.*): pas″‿sə-rel′ də ton″‿nō′.—**boom in, dismantle,** or **strip a b.** Démanteler un pont: dē″mañ″tə-lē′ añ peñ.—**boom out a b.** Jeter un pont traverse par traverse: ʒə-tē′ añ peñ tra″vārs′ pār tra″vārs′.—**b. a river.** Jeter un pont sur une rivière: ʒə-tē′ añ poñ sūr ün rī″vī″‿yār′.—**b.=building equipment.** Agrès et accessoires de pont: a″grē′ ē aks″‿ses″‿swā′ də peñ.—**b. by cuts, rafts, or swing=bays.** Jeter un pont par portières: ʒə-tē′ añ peñ pā pōr′tī″‿yār′.—**b. detachment.** Détachement de pontage (*m.*): dē″ta″shə-māñ′ də peñ″tāʒ′.—**build a b.** Jeter un pont: ʒə-tē′ añ peñ.—**canvas=bag b.** Passerelle de sacs d toile (*f.*): pas″‿sə-rel′ də sāk də twāl.—**destroy a b.** Détruire un pont: dē″trwīr′‿añ peñ.—**emergency b.** Pont de circonstance (*m.*): peñ də sīr″keñ″stāñs′.—**far side of a b.** Sortie d'un pont (*f.*): sēr″tī′ dañ peñ.—**floor of a b.** Platelage (*n. m.*): pla″tə-lāʒ′ —**leather=bag,** or **leathern=bottle b.** Passerelle d'outres (*f.*): pas″‿sə-rel′ dū′trə.—**near side of a b.** L'entrée d'un pont (*f.*): lañ″trē′ dañ peñ.—**oblique** or **skew b.** Pont obliquant: peñ ō″blī″kāñ′.—**roadway of a b.** Tablier d'un pont: ta″blī″yē′ dañ peñ.—**suspension b.** Pont suspendu: peñ sus″pañ″dü′.—**swing b.** Pont tournant: peñ tūr″nāñ′.—**tarpaulin b.** Passerelle de bâches: pas″sə-rel′ də bāsh.—**tilting b.** Pont à bascule: peñt‿a bas″kül′.—**the b. sways.** Le pont s'incline: lə peñ sañ″klīn′.—**to swing a b.** Jeter un pont par mouvement tournant: ʒə-tē′ añ peñ pā mū″‿və-māñ′ tūr″nāñ′.

bridging trains. Équipages de pont: ē″kī″pāʒ′ də peñ.

bridle, *n.* **I.** (1) Bride (*f.*): brīd. (2) Frein (*m.*): frāñ. **II.** *v.* Brider: brī″dē′.

brigade. Brigade (*n. f.*): brī″gād′.—**b.=major.** Major de brigade (*m.*): ma″ʒōr′ də brī″gād′.—**horse=b.** 1. Escadron: es″ka″droñ′. 2. Groupe à cheval (*f.*): grūp a sha-vāl′.—**b. staff=office.** Bureau de l'état=major de la brigade (*m.*): bü″rō′ də lē″tā′ ma″ʒēr′ də la brī″gād′.—**mounted b.** Groupe monté (*f.*): grūp meñ″tē′.

brigadier or **brigadier=general.** Général de brigade (*m.*): ʒē″nē″rāl′ də brī″gād′.

bring, *v.* **1.** Amener: a″mə-nē′ (*lead*). **2.** Apporter: ap″‿per″tē′ (*carry*). **3.** Ramener: ra″mə-nē′ (*bring back*).—**bring about,** *v.* Faire arriver: fār ar″‿rī″vē′.—**b. into action.** Engager dans le combat: añ″gā″ʒē′ dañ lə koñ″bā′.—**b. me.** Apportez=moi: ap″‿por′tē″ mwā.—**b.** or **shoot down an aeroplane.** Faire descendre ou abattre un aéroplane: fār de″sāñ′‿drə ū a″bāt′‿trə añ a″‿ē″rō″plān′.—**b. to the notice of commanders.** Attirer l'attention des commandants: a″tī″rē′ la″tañ″sī″‿yeñ′ dē kem″mañ″dāñ′.—**b. up the rear.** Fermer la marche: fār″mē′ lā mārsh.

British, *a.* **1.** Anglais: añ″glē′. **2.** Britannique: brī″tan″‿nīk′.—**British army.** L'armée anglaise: lar″mē′ añ″glēz′.—**British=warm.** Pardessus (*n. m.*): par″də-sü′.

broad, *a.* **1.** Large: lārʒ. **2.** Grand: grañ.

broadsword. Sabre (*n. m.*): sā′‿brə.

broken, *a.* Cassé: kas″‿sē′.—**broken=kneed,** *a.* Couronné: kū″roñ″‿nē′.

bronzed, *a.* Bronzé: broñ″zē′.

brook. Ruisseau: rwīs″‿sō′. On maps *Rau.*

broom. Balai (*n. m.*): ba″lē′.

broth. Bouillon (*n. m.*): bwī″‿yoñ′.

brother. Frère (*n. m.*): frār.—**brothers in arms.** Frères d'armes: frār dārm.

brown, *a.* Brun (*m.*): brun; brune (*f.*): brün.

Bruges, brūʒ′ə, *n.* A city in Belgium.

bruise. Contusion (*n. f.*): koñ″tü″sī″‿yoñ′.

brume, *n.* **1.** Brume (*f.*): brü′‿mə. **2.** Brouillard (*m.*): brwī″yār′. **3.** Nouage (*m.*): nū″āz′.

brush. Brosse (*n. f.*): brōs.—**brush aside.** Bousculer: būs″kü″lē′.

brushwood. Broussailles (*n. f. pl.*): brū"sai'. On maps *Br.*
Brussels. Bruxelles (*n.*): brü"sāl'. Capital of Belgium.
brutal, *a.* Brutal (*m.*): brutale (*f.*): brü"tāl'.
B. S. M., *abbrev.* Battalion Sergeant Major.
bucket. Seau (*n. m.*): sō.—**bucket-baler.** 1. Louche à pulser (*n. f.*): lūsh ā pwī"sē'. 2. Écope (*n. f.*): ē"kōp'.—**canvas-b.** Seau en toile: sō an twāl.—**rifle-b.** Étui de crosse: ē"twī' də krōs.—**watering-b.** Seau d'abreuvoir: sō da"brū"vwār'.
buckle. 1. Boucle (*n. f.*): bū'klə. 2. Plaque (*n. f.*): plāk.—**belt-buckle.** Plaque de ceinturon (*n. f.*): plāk də san"tü"ren'.
buckskin. Peau de daim (*n. f.*): pō də dan.
buckwheat. Sarrazin (*n. m.*): sar"‿ra"zan'.
buffer. 1. Frein (*n. m.*): fran (*brake; check*). 2. Tampon (*n. m.*): tan"pen' (*stopper*).
buffet. Buffet (*n. m.*): büf"‿fē'.—**where is the buffet?** Où est le buffet? ū ē lə büf"‿fē'.
bugle. Clairon (*n. m.*): klā"ren'.—**bugle-call,** *n.* Sonnerie de clairon (*f.*): sen"‿nə-rī' də klā"ren'.—**bugler,** *n.* Clairon (*m.*): klā"ren'.
build, *v.* Bâtir: ba"tīr'. See Appendix.—**to build up the firing line.** Installer la ligne de feu: an"stal"lē' lā lī'‿nyə də fū.
building, *n.* Bâtiment (*m.*): ba"tī"mān'. Abbreviated *Bment.*
built, *pa.* Bâti: ba"tī'.
Bukowina, *n.* Bukovine: bü"ko"vīn'. Department of northeastern Austria.
bulb, *n.* Filament à boucle (*m.*): fī"la"mān' ā bū'klə.
bulging, *a.* Bombé: ben"bē'.
bulk, *n.* 1. Gros (*m.*): grō. 2. Masse (*f.*): mās.—**in bulk.** En bloc: an blek.
bullet, *n.* 1. Balle (*f.*): bal (*of rifles, pistols, etc.*). 2. Boulet (*m.*): bū"lē' (*of cannon*).—**bullet-proof,** *a.* À l'épreuve des balles: ā lē"prūv' dē bal.
bull's-eye, *n.* Mouche (*f.*): mūsh (*of a target*).
bully-beef, *n.* Corned beef canned. Conserve de bœuf salé: ken"sārv' də būf sa"lē'.
Bundesrath, bun'des-rāt, *n.* The German federal council.
bundle, *n.* 1. Paquet (*m.*): pa"kē' (*package*). 2. Botte (*f.*): bet (*of hay*).
bunkers, *n. pl.* Soutes à charbon (*f. pl.*): sūt a shar"ben'.
buoy, *n.* 1. Balise (*f.*): ba"līz' (*beacon; sea-mark*). Abbreviated *Bse.* 2. Bouée (*f.*): bū"ē' (*floating buoy*).—**life-buoy,** *n.* Boué de sauvetage: bū"ē' də sōv"tāʒ'.—**mooring b.** Corps mort: kēr mēr.
burial, *n.* Enterrement (*m.*): an"tār"‿rə-mān'.—**burial of dead.** L'enterrement des morts: lan"tār"‿rə-mān' dē mēr.
burn, *v.* Brûler: brü"lē'.—**burning,** *pa.* En feu: an fū.—**burnt to ashes.** Réduit en cendre: rē"dwī' an san'drə.
burst. I. *v.* 1. Crever: krə-vē' (*break, split, or tear*). 2. Éclater: ē"kla"tē' (*crack, flash, or shiver into pieces*). II. *n. m.* Éclatement: ē"kla"‿tə-mān' (*of a motor-wheel tire*).—**sudden b. of fire.** Ouverture violente et subite du feu: ū"vār"tür' vī"o"lānt' ē su"bīt' dü fū.—**the burst of shells.** L'éclatement des projectiles: lē"kla"tə-mān' dē prō"jek"tīl'.
bury, *v.* Enterrer: an"tār"‿rē'.—**to bury the dead.** Enterrer les morts: an"tār"‿rē' lē mēr.
bus, bus, *n.* [Soldiers' slang.] A flying-machine.
bush, *n.* Buisson (*m.*): bwīs"‿sen'.—**bush-fighting,** *n.* Combat sous bois: ken"bā' sū bwā (*in colonial warfare*).—**in b.** 1. Dans la brousse: dan la brūs. 2. Sous bois: sū bwā.
business, *n.* Affaire (*f.*): af"‿fār'.
busy, *a.* Occupé: ek"‿kü"pē'.

but, *conj.* Mais: mē.
butcher, *n.* Boucher (*m.*): bū"shē'.
butt, *n.* **1.** Crosse (*f.*): kros (*of a rifle*). **2.** Cible (*f.*): sī'‿blə (*target*).—**small of the b.** Poignée: pwa"nī"‿yē'.—**with the butt-end.** A coups de crosse: a kū də kros.
butter. Beurre (*n. m.*): būr.—**please give me some butter.** Donnez moi du beurre, sil vous plaît: don"‿nē' mwa dü būr, sīl vū plē.
buttock, *n.* Fesse (*f.*): fes.
button, *n.* Bouton (*m.*): bū"toṅ'.—**some buttons are missing.** Des boutons me manquent: dē bū"toṅ' mə māṅk'ə.
buttress, *n.* Arc-boutant (*m.*): ārk"bū"tāṅ'.
buy, *v.* Acheter: a"shə-tē'.—**I want to buy.** **1.** Je voudrais acheter: ʒə vū"drē' a"shə-tē'. **2.** Je veux acheter: ʒə vū a"shə-tē'. —**can I b. some . . . ?** Puis-je acheter des . . . ? pwī‿ʒə a"shə-tē' dē . . . ? See Appendix.
by. **I.** *prep.* Par: pār. **II.** *prep.* & *adv.* Près: prē.

C

cab, *n.* **1.** Fiacre (*m.*): fī"āk'‿rə. **2.** Voiture de place (*f.*): vwa"tür' də plas.—**to call a cab.** Faire venir un fiacre: fār və-nīr' aṅ fī"āk'rə.
cabbage, *n.* Chou (*m.*): shū.
cabin, *n.* **1.** Cabine (*f.*): ka"bīn' (*of a ship*). **2.** Cabane (*f.*): ka"bāṅ' (*hut, cottage*).
cable, *n.* **1.** Câble (*m.*): kāb'‿lə. **2.** Cincinelle (*f.*): saṅ"-sī"nel'‿lə (*tow-line*).
cadet, *n.* Cadet (*m.*): ka"dē'.
cadre, *n.* Cadre (*m.*): kā'drə (*the nucleus or framework of a French regiment or corps*).
caisson, *n.* Caisson (*m.*): kēs"‿soṅ'.
cake, *n.* Gâteau (*m.*): gā"tō'.
Calais, kal'is (*Eng.*) *or* ka"lē' (*Fr.*), *n.* Town in northwestern France.
calendar, *n.* Almanach (*m.*): al"ma"nā', *or before a vowel*, al"ma"nāk'.
calf, *n.* **1.** Veau (*m.*): vō (*animal*). See VEAL. **2.** Mollet (*m.*): mol"‿lē' (*of the leg*).
caliber, *n.* Calibre (*m.*): ka"līb'‿rə.
calkin, *n.* Crampon (*m.*): kraṅ"poṅ' (*spur on a horseshoe*).
call. **I.** *n.* **1.** Appel: ap"pel'. **2.** Sonnerie (*f.*): soṅ"‿nə-rī' (*of a trumpet*). **II.** *v.* Appeler: ap"‿pə-lē'.—**call me early.** Appelez-moi de bonne heure: ap"pə-lē' mwā də bōn‿nūr.—**c. out, Halt!** Criez, Halte! krī"yē' alt.—**c. out reservists.** Convoquer les réservistes: kon"vō"kē' lē rē"zār"vīst'.—**c. the roll.** Faire l'appel: fār lap"pel'.—**c. to arms.** Alarme (*n. f.*): a"lārm'.—**regimental c.** Refrain du régiment (*m.*): rə-fraṅ' dü rē"ʒī"māṅ'.
called, *pa.* **1.** Appelé: ap"pə-lē'. **2.** Dit: dī (*named*).—**called to the colors.** Appelé au service: ap"‿pə-lē' ō sār"vīs'. —**infantry should be c. upon.** Il faut faire appel à l'infanterie: īl fō fār ap"‿pel' a laṅ"faṅ"tə-rī'.—**to be c. to assume a command.** Être appelé à exercer un commandement: ē'‿trə ap"‿pə-lē' a eks"ār"sē' aṅ kom"‿maṅ"də-māṅ'.
calm, *a.* Calme (*m.* & *f.*): kāl'‿mə.
Calvary. Calvaire (*n. f.*): kal"vār' (*wayside cross*). Abbreviated *Cre.*
camber. Cambrure (*n. f.*): kaṅ"brūr' (*a bend as in an arion wing* or *plane*).
Cambon, Pierre Paul, kaṅ"boṅ', pī"yār' pōl. French diplomat.

Camion, ka″mī″yeṅ′, *n.* [Fr]. A motor-lorry, truck, or wagon.
camouflage, ka″mū″flāʒ′, *n. m.* Deception of the enemy, as by artificial scenery, dummy cannon, etc.
camouflet, ka″mū″flē′, *n. m.* A small mine for use at close quarters and in galleries against sappers.
camp. I. (*n. m.*) Camp: kaṅ. **II.** *v.* Camper: kaṅ″pē′.—**camp-bed.** Lit de camp (*m.*): lī də kaṅ.—**c. boundaries.** Limites du camp: lī″mīt′ dü kaṅ.—**c. bestriding a river.** Camp à cheval: kaṅ a ʃhə-vūl′.—**c.-commandant.** Major du camp (*m.*): ma″ʒēr′ dü kaṅ.—**c.-duties.** Service de camp (*m.*): sār″vīs′ də kaṅ.—**c.-equipment.** Effets ou matériel de camp (*m.*): ef″fē′ ū ma″tē″rī″‿yel′ də kaṅ.—**c.-fever.** Maladie de camp (*f.*): ma″la″dī′ də kaṅ.—**c.-follower. 1.** Un civil autorisé à suivre l'armée (*m.*): aṅ sī″vīl′‿ō″tər″ī″zē′ a swīv′‿rə lar″mē′. **2.** Un goujat (*m.*): aṅ gū″ʒā′.—**c.-guard.** Garde de camp (*m.*): gārd də kaṅ.—**c.-head** or **-front.** Tête (*f.*), ou front (*m.*), de camp: tēt, ū freṅ də kaṅ.—**c.-kettle. 1.** Bidon (*m.*): bī″deṅ′. **2.** Marmite de campement (*f.*): mar″mīt′ də kaṅ″‿pə-māṅ′.—**c.-kitchen.** Cuisine (*f.*): kwī″zīn′.—**c.-lines.** Cordeaux (*n. pl.*): kēr″dō′.—**c.-measure (for water, etc.).** Pot de camp (*m.*): pō də kaṅ.—**c. ordinances.** Ordonnances (*f.*): ēr″deṅ″‿nāṅs′.—**c.-oven.** Four de campagne (*m.*): fūr də kaṅ″pāṅ′‿yə.—**c. quartermaster.** Fourrier de campement (*m.*): fūr″‿rī″‿yē′ də kaṅp″māṅ′.—**c. regulations.** Réglement du camp (*m.*): rē″glə-māṅ′ dü kaṅ.—**c. requisites.** Effets de campement (*n. pl.*): ef″‿fē′ də kaṅp″māṅ′.—**c.-robber. 1.** Maraudeur (*m.*): ma″rō″dūr′. **2.** Boulineur (*m.*): bū″lī″nūr′.—**c.-site.** Emplacement du camp: aṅ″plas″māṅ′ dü kaṅ.—**c.-stool.** Pliant (*m.*): plī″āṅ′.—**c.-street.** Ruelle (*f.*): rü″el′.—**c. without shelter-tents.** Bivouac (*m.*): bī″vū″‿āk′.—**commander of the c.** Commandant d'armes, ou du camp (*m.*): kem″‿maṅ″dāṅ′ dārm, ū dü kaṅ.—**concentration c.** Camp de concentration: kaṅ də keṅ″saṅ″tra″sī″‿yeṅ′.—**confinement to c.** Consigne au camp (*f.*): keṅ″sīn′‿yə ō kaṅ.—**convoy-c.** Camp de convois: kaṅ də keṅ″vwā′.—**entrenched c.** Camp retranché: kaṅ rə-traṅ″ʃhē′.—**fortified c.** Camp fortifié: kaṅ fēr″tī″fī″‿yē′.—**hut-camp. 1.** Camp de baraques: kaṅ də bar″āk′. **2.** Camp baraqué: kaṅ bar″a″kē′.—**permanent** or **standing c.** Camp fixe: kaṅ fīx.—**rest-c.** Camp de repos: kaṅ də rə-pō′.—**temporary c. 1.** Camp de séjour: kaṅ də sē″ʒūr′. **2.** Camp de marche: kaṅ də mārʃh.—**to break up the c.** Lever le camp: lə-vē′ lə kaṅ.—**to confine to c.** Consigner au camp: keṅ″sī″nyē′ ō kaṅ.—**to lay out a c.** Tracer, dresser un camp: tra″sē′, dres″‿sē′ aṅ kaṅ.—**to pitch c.** Asseoir un camp: as″‿swār′ aṅ kaṅ.—**to strike c.** Lever le camp: lə-vē′ lə kaṅ.
campaign. Campagne (*n. f.*): kaṅ″pa′‿nyə.
camping, *n.* Campement (*m.*): kaṅp″māṅ′.—**camping-ground,** *n.* Emplacement d'un camp (*m.*): aṅ″plas″māṅ′ daṅ kaṅ.
can, *n.* **1.** Bidon (*m.*): bī″deṅ′. **2.** Burette (*f.*): bü″ret′.
can, *v.* Pouvoir: pū″vwā′ (*to be able*). See verbs of 3d conjugation in the Appendix.—**can I?** Puis-je?: pwī′ʒə.—**can not.** Ne peut pas: nə pū pa.—**can you?** Pouvez-vous?: pū′vē′ vū?—**can you give me . . . ?** Pouvez-vous me donner . . . ? pū″ve′ vū mə den″‿nē′?
Canada. Le Canada (*n. m.*): kā″nā″dā′.
Canadians (the). Les Canadiens (*n. m.*): lē ka″na″dī″‿yaṅ′.
canal. Canal (*n. m.*): ka″nāl′. Pl. canaux: ka″nō′—**canal-lock.** Écluse (*n. f.*): ē″klüz′‿ə.—**irrigation c.** Canal d'irrigation: ka″nāl′ dīr″‿rī″ga″sī″‿yeṅ′.—**navigable c.** Canal navigable: ka″nāl′ na″vī″gā′‿blə.—**ship c.** Grand canal navigable (*m.*): grāṅ ka″nāl′ na″vī″gā′‿blə.
candle, *n.* **1.** Chandelle: ʃhaṅ″del′. **2.** Bougie (*f.*): bū″ʒī′.—**give me a candle.** Donnez-moi une chandelle: deṅ″‿nē′‿

mwā ün shan″del′.—**I want some candles.** Je voudrais des chandelles: ʒə vū″drē′ dē shan″del′.

canister, *n.* Boîte à balles (*f.*): bwāt a bāl.—**canister=shot,** *n.* Mitraille (*f.*): mī″trai′‿yə.

cannon, *n.* Canon (*m.*): ka″neṅ′.—**cannon=ball,** or **shot,** *n.* Boulet de canon: bū″lē′ də ka″neṅ′.—**cannon=bone,** *n.* Canon: ka″neṅ′ (*shank=bone of a horse*).

canteen, *n.* **1.** Cantine (*f.*): kaṅ″tīn′. **2.** Bidon (*m.*): bī″deṅ′. **3.** Gamelle (*f.*): ga″mel′.

canter. I. *n.* Petit galop: pə‿tī′ ga″lō′. **II.** *v.* Aller au petit galop: al″‿lē′ ō pə‿tī′ ga″lō′.

cantle (of a saddle). Troussequin (*n. m.*): trūs″‿sə-kaṅ′.

cantonment. Cantonnement (*n. m.*): kaṅ″teṅ″‿nə-māṅ′.

canvas. Toile de tente (*n. f.*): twal də taṅt.—**under canvas.** Sous tentes: sū tāṅt.

cap, *n.* **1.** képi (*f.*): kē″pī′. **2.** Casquette (*f.*): kas″ket′.—**cap=cover,** *n.* **1.** Couvre=képi (*m.*): kū′vrə kē″pī′. **2.** Manchon (*m.*): maṅ″sheṅ′.—**field=service** or **forage=c. 1.** Bonnet de police (*n. m.*): beṅ″‿nē′ də po″līs′. **2.** Casquette plate (*n. f.*): kas″ket′ plāt′ə (*in the English army*).—**night=c.** *n.* Bonnet de coton (*m.*): beṅ″‿nē′ də ke″teṅ′.

capability, *n.* Capacité (*f.*): ka″pa″sī″tē′.—**capabilities of defense.** Facilités pour la defensive (*n. pl.*): fa″sī″lī″tē′ pūr la dē″faṅ″sīv′.

cape, *n.* Pèlerine (*f.*): pā″lə-rīn′.

capitulate, *v.* Capituler: ka″pī″tü″lē′.

caponiere, *n.* Caponnière (*f.*): ka″peṅ″nī″‿yār′ (*small defensive work; blockhouse*).

capstan, *n.* Cabestan (*m.*): ka″bə-stāṅ′.

captain, *n.* Capitaine (*m.*): ka″pī″tēṅ′.—**let the captain know of an order.** Faire communiquer un ordre au capitaine: fār kem″‿mü″nī″kē′ ün ōr′drə ō ka″pī″tēn′.

captive, *a.* Captif (*m.*): kap″tīf′; captive (*f.*): kap″tīv′.

capture. I. *n.* **1.** Capture (*f.*): kap″tūr′. **2.** Prise (*f.*): prīz. **II.** *v.* **1.** Prendre: prāṅd′‿rə. **2.** Capturer: kap″tü″rē′.—**the capture of a fortress.** La prise d'une forteresse: la prīz dün fer″tə-res′.—**the position to be captured.** La position à enlever: la pō″zī″sī″‿yeṅ′ a aṅ″lə-vē′.

car, *n.* **1.** Voiture (*f.*): vwa″tūr′. **2.** Wagon (*m.*): va″geṅ′ (*of a train*). **3.** Nacelle (*f.*): na″sel′ (*of a balloon*).—**dining=car.** Wagon restaurant: va″geṅ′ res″tō″rāṅ′.—**parlor=car.** Wagon salon: va″geṅ′ sa″leṅ′.—**passenger=car.** Wagon de voyageurs: va″geṅ′ də voy″a″ʒūr′.—**sleeping=car.** Wagon lit: va″geṅ′ lī.

carbine, *n.* Carabine (*f.*): ka″ra″bīn′.

carbolic acid. Acide phénique (*f.*): a″sīd′ fē″nīk′.

carbureter, *n.* Carburateur (*m.*): kar″bü″ra″tūr′.

cardinal number. Nombre cardinal (*m.*): neṅ′brə kar″dī″-[nāl′.

care. Soin (*n. m.*): swaṅ.—**take care.** Same as BE CAREFUL.

careful, be. 1. Prendre garde (*inf.*): prāṅ′drə gārd. **2.** Prenez garde (*imper.*): prə-nē′ gārd.

carefully, *adv.* Soigneusement: swa″nyūz″māṅ′.—**carry him carefully.** Portez le avec soin: pōr″tē′ lə a″vek′ swaṅ.

carpenter, *n.* **1.** Charpentier (*m.*): shār″paṅ″tī″‿yē′. **2.** Menuisier (*m.*): mə-nwī″sī″‿yē′ (*joiner*).

carriage, *n.* **1.** Voiture (*f.*): vwa″tür′ (*vehicle*). **2.** Wagon (*m.*): va″geṅ′ (*of a train*). Compare CAR.

carrot, *n.* Carotte (*f.*): kar″‿ret′.

carry, *v.* **1.** Porter: pōr″tē′. **2.** Enlever: aṅ″‿lə-vē′.—**carry him.** Portez le: pōr″tē′ lə.—**c. off.** Enlever: aṅ″‿lə-vē′.—**c. on. 1.** Continuez: keṅ″tī″nü″ē′ (*keep on doing*). **2.** Poussez en avant: pūs″‿sēz′‿aṅ a″vāṅ′ (*go ahead*).—**c. out. 1.** Exécuter: eks″ē″kü″tē′. **2.** Développer: dē″vel″op″‿pē′.—**to**

c. at the point of or with the bayonet, or by cold steel. Enlever à la baïonnette: añ"‿lə-vē' a la bai"‿yəñ"‿net'.—**to c. out an attack.** Exécuter une attaque: eks"ē"kü"tē' ün at"‿tāk'.

cart, *n.* **1.** Fourgon: fūr"gəñ'. **2.** Charrette (*f.*): shar"‿ret'. **3.** Chariot (*m.*): sha"rī"‿yō'. **4.** Tombereau (*m.*): təñ"bə-rō'.—**dung-cart,** *n.* Tombereau à fumier (*m.*): təñ"bə-rō' a fü"mī"‿yē'.—**forage-c.** Fourragère (*f.*): fūr"ra"zār'.

cartel, *n.* Cartel (*m.*): kār"tel'.—**cartel of exchange (of prisoners).** Cartel d'échange (de prisonniers): kār"tel' dē"-shāñ'zə (də prī"zəñ"‿nyē').

cartridge, *n.* Cartouche (*f.*): kār"tū'‿shə.—**blank cartridge.** Cartouche à blanc: kār"tū'shə a blañ.—**c.-base.** Culot de cartouche (*m.*): kü"lō' də kār"tūsh'.—**c.-box.** Giberne (*n. f.*): zi"bārn'‿ə.—**c.-pouch.** Cartouchière (*f.*): kār"tū'shī"‿yār'.

case, *n.* Cas (*m.*): ka (*condition of affairs*).—**as the case may be.** Suivant le cas: swī"vāñ' lə ka.—**in c. of.** En cas de: añ ka də.—**in either c.** Dans l'un et l'autre cas: dañ lañ ē lō'‿trə ka.—**in such a c.** En pareil cas: añ pa"rē'‿yə ka.—**in that c.** Dans ce cas: dañ sə ka; or, en ce cas: añ sə ka.

casemate, *n.* Casemate (*f.*): kaz"māt'.

case-shot, *n.* Mitraille (*f.*): mī"trai'yə.

cash, *n.* **1.** Argent (*m.*): ar"zāñ'. **2.** Espèces (*f.*): es"pēs'.—**supply of cash.** Approvisionnement en numéraire: ap"‿prō"vī"sī"‿yəñ"‿nə-māñ' añ nü"mē"rār'.

cashier, *n.* **I.** (*m.*) Caissier: kē"sī"‿yē'. **II.** (*v.*) Casser: kas"‿sē' (*discharge in disgrace*).—**field-cashier.** Payeur d'armée (*m.*): pē"yūr' dar"mē'.—**to be cashiered.** Être cassé: ā'‿trə kas"‿sē'.

cast, *v.* Jeter: zə"tē'.—**cast aside.** Jeter à l'écart: zə"tē' a lē"kār'.—**to c. a shoe.** Se déferrer: sə dē"fār"‿rē'.—**to c. off moorings.** Rejeter l'amarre: rə-zə"tē' la"mār'.

casualty, *n.* Perte (*f.*): pārt. Plural **casualties.** Pertes: pārt.—**casualties from disease.** Pertes causées par les maladies: pārt kō"zē' pār lē ma"la"dī'.—**casualty-list, c.-returns.** État des pertes: ē"tā' dē pārt.—**notify parents of c.** Faire part des pertes aux parents: fār pār dē pārt ō pa"rāñ'.

catacombs. Catacombes (*n. f. pl.*): ka"ta"kōñ'bə.

catapult, *n.* Catapulte (*f.*): ka"ta"pült'.

caterpillar, *n.* In the British army, a pedrail tractor used for hauling heavy loads, etc., over rough ground.—**caterpillar tractor.** Tracteur en chenilles (*n. m.*): trak"tūr' añ shə-nī'‿yə.

cathedral. Cathédrale (*n. f.*): ka"tē"drāl'. Abbr. *Cathle.*

cattle. **1.** Bétail (*n. m.*): bē"tai'. **2.** Bestiaux (*n. m. pl.*): bēs"tī"ō'.—**c. on the hoof.** Viande sur pied: vī"ānd' sür pī"‿yē'.—**c.-train.** Convoi de bestiaux (*m.*): kəñ"vwā' də bes"tī"‿yō'.—**c.-truck.** Wagon étable: va"gəñ' ē"tā'blə.

cause, *v.* Causer: kō"zē'.

causeway. Chaussée (*n. f.*): shō"sē'.

caution, *n.* **1.** Précaution (*f.*): prē"kō"sī"‿yəñ'. **2.** Avis (*m.*): a"vī'.—**to act with caution.** Agir avec précaution: a"zīr' a"vek' prē"kō"sī"yəñ'.

cavalry. Cavalerie (*n. f.*): ka"va"‿lə-rī'.—**cavalry-charge,** *n.* Charge de cavalerie (*f.*): sharz də ka"va"‿lə-rī'.—**in the c.** De la cavalerie: də la ka"va"‿lə-rī'.

cease, *v.* Cesser: ses"‿sē'.—**cease-firing!** Cessez le feu!: sēs"‿sē' lə fū!—**when "cease-firing" is sounded.** Quand sonna cessez le feu! kān səñ"‿ñā' sēs"‿sē' lə fū.

cell. **1.** Cellule (*n. f.*): sel"‿lül'. **2.** Élément (*n. m.*): ē"lē"māñ' (*electricity*).

cellar, *n.* Cave (*f.*): kāv.

cement. Ciment (*n. m.*): sī"māñ'.

cemetery. Cimetière (*n. m.*): sīm"tī"‿yār'. Abbr. *Cimre.*

censor, *n.* Censeur (*m.*): san″sūr′.—**censorship. 1.** Fonctions de censeur: fonk″sī″‿yon′ də san″sūr′ (*functions of the censor*). **2.** Censure (*n. f.*): san″sür′ (*act of censoring*).—**censorship of the press.** Censure de la presse: san″sür′ də la pres.

cent. Cent. (*n. m.*): sān.—**ten per cent.** Dix pour cent: dī pūr san.

center, *n.* Centre (*m.*): sān′‿trə.

centimeter (.39 in.). Centimètre (*n. m.*): san″tī″mā′‿trə.

central depot of motor or **automobile service.** Magasin central du service automobile (*m.*): ma″ga″zan′ san″trāl′ dü sār″vīs′ ō″tō″mō″bīl′.

certain, *a.* Certain: sār″tān′.—**certainly,** *adv.* Certainement: sār″tān″mān′.

certificate. Certificat (*n. m.*): sār″tī″fī″kā′.—**birth certificate.** Acte de naissance: ākt də nēs″‿sāns′.—**examination c.** Certificat de visite: sār″tī″fī″kā′ də vī″zīt′.—**marriage c.** Acte de mariage: ākt də ma″rī″āʒ′.—**medical c.** Certificat médical: sār″tī″fī″kā′ mē″dī″kāl′.

cessation. Cessation (*n. f.*): ses″‿sa″sī″‿yon.—**cessation** or **ceasing of artillery-fire.** Cessation du feu d'artillerie: ses″‿sa″sī″‿yon dü fū dar″tī″‿yə-rī′.

chain, *n.* Chaîne (*f.*): shēn.—**chain-driven,** *a.* À chaîne: a shēn.—**curb-c.** Gourmette (*n. f.*): gūr″met′.

chair, *n.* Chaise (*f.*): shēʒ.

chalet. Chalet (*n.m.*): sha″lē′. Abbreviated *Chet.* See COTTAGE.

chalk. I. *n. f.* Craie: krē. **II.** *v.* Marquer à la craie: mar″kē′ ā lā krē.

challenge. I. *n. m.* Qui vive: kī vīv. **II.** *v.* **1.** Reconnaître: rə-kon″‿nā′‿trə. **2.** Crier "Qui vive" à: krī″‿yē′ kī vīv ā. **3.** Arrêter: ar″‿rē″tē′. **4.** Défier: dē″fī″ē′.—**to be challenged by the sentry.** Être arrêté par la sentinelle: ā′‿trə ar″‿rē″tē′ pār la san″tī″nel′.

Châlons, shā″lon′, *n.* City of eastern France.

chamber, *n.* Chambre (*f.*): shan′‿brə (*room*).—**chamber of commerce.** Chambre de commerce (*n. f.*): shan′‿brə də kom″‿mārs′.

chancellery. Chancellerie (*n. f.*): shan″sel″‿lə-rī′.

change, *n.* **1.** Monnaie d'une pièce (*f.*): mon″‿nē′ dün pī″‿yās′ (*money*). **2.** Changement (*m.*): shan″‿ʒə-man′ (*alteration*).—**can you change this twenty-franc piece?** Pouvez-vous me changer cette pièce de vingt francs?: pū″vē′-vū mə shan″ʒē′ set pī″‿yās′ də van fran.—**c. step!** Changez le pas. marche!: shan″ʒē′ lə pā, mārsh′.—**I have no c.** Je n'ai pas de monnaie: ʒə nē pa də mon″‿nē′.—**I want c. for this bank-note.** Il me faut changer ce billet de banque: īl mə fō shan″ʒē′ sə bī″‿yē′ də bank.—**please give me c. for this.** Changez-moi ça, s'il vous plaît: shan″ʒē′ mwa sa, sīl vū plē.—**the c. lacks, is short, or wanting (dix sous).** Il manque dix sous: īl mank dī sū.—**to c. money.** Pour changer de l'argent: pūr shan″ʒē′ də lar″ʒān′.—**where do I c. (trains, etc.) for . . .** Où dois-je changer (train, etc.) pour . . . ?: ū dwā′-ʒə shan″ʒē′ (tran, etc.) pūr.—**where can I get money changed?** Où pourrai-je faire changer de l'argent?: ū pūr″‿rē′‿ʒə fār shan″ʒē′ də lar″ʒān′.

channel, *n.* Canal (*m.*): ka″nāl′.—**the British Channel:** La Manche: lā man′‿shə.—**the official c.** La voie hiérarchique: lā vwā I″ē″rār″shik′.—**the St. George's C.** Le canal St. Georges: lə ka″nāl′ san ʒōr′‿ʒə.

Chantilly, shan″tī″‿yī′, *n.* French town.

chapel. Chapelle (*f.*): sha″pel′‿lə.

chaplain (the). Le chapelain (*n. m.*): lə sha″pə-lan′.—**get the chaplain.** Cherchez le chapelain: shār″shē′ lə sha″pə-lan′.

chapter-house. Chapitre (*n. m.*): sha″pī′trə. On maps *Ch'itre.*

character. Caractère (*n. m.*): ka″rak″tār′.
charcoal. Charbon de bois (*m.*): shār″boṅ′ də bwa.
charge, I. *n.* Charge (*f.*): shār′‿ʒə (*accusation, care, price*). **II.** *v.* **1.** Charger: shār″ʒē′. **2.** *Imperative.* Chargez! shār″ʒē′ (*order to attack*).—**bursting** or **exploding charge.** Charge d'explosif: shār′‿ʒə deks″plō″zīf′.—**charge magazine** (*load*)! Approvisionnez!: ap″‿prō″vī″zī″‿yoṅ″‿nē′.—**in the c. of.** Sous la garde de: sū lā gārd də.—**the officer in c.** L'officier commandant: lof″fī″si″‿yē′ kom″maṅ″daṅ′.—**under his c.** Sous son commandement: sū soṅ kom″‿maṅ″də‿maṅ′.
chargé d'affaires, shār″ʒē′ daf″‿fār′. A diplomatic agent or officer in the diplomatic service.
charger (*horse*): Cheval de bataille ou de guerre (*n. m.*): shə-val′ də ba″tāi′yə ū də gār.
charging, *n.* Chargement: shār″ʒə-maṅ′ (*filling, loading*).—**charging the mines.** Chargement des mines: shār″ʒə-maṅ′ dē mīn.
Charleroi. shar″lə-rwā′, *n.* Belgian town.
Charleville. shār″lə‿vīl′, *n.* French town.
chasseur. shas″‿sūr′, *n.* A light-armed French soldier of the infantry or cavalry.—**chasseurs d'Afrique,** shas″‿sūr′ da″frīk′. A body of Algerian mounted troops.
chassis. Châssis (*n. m.*): shās″‿sī′ (*base-frame or framework, as of barbette-gun or motor-car*).
château, sha″tō′, *n.* A castle or country mansion.
cheap. Bon marché: boṅ mar″shē′.
Chéchia. shē″shī″yā′, *n.* A cloth cap with a tassel, worn by [the Zouaves.
check, *n.* **1.** Échec (*m.*): ē″shek′ (*set-back*). **2.** Frein (*m.*): fraṅ (*curb; brake*). **3.** Chèque (*m.*): shāk (*written order for payment of money*).—**check-book.** Livre de mandats (*n. m.*): lī′vrə də maṅ″dā′.—**c.-roll.** Contre-appel (*n. m.*): koṅ′trə ap″‿pel′ (*muster-roll*).
check, *v.* **1.** Arrêter: ar″rē″tē′; enrayer: aṅ″rē″yē′. **2.** Faire éprouver un échec à: fār ē″prū″vē′ aṅ ē″shek′ a. **3.** Verifier: vār″ī″fī″‿yē′; enregistrer: aṅ″re″ʒīs″trē′.—**to check all attempts.** Arrêter toutes enterprises: ar″rē″tē′ tūt aṅ″trə‿prīz′.
checker. **1.** Contrôlleur (*n. m.*): koṅ″trōl″lūr′. **2.** *pl.* Dames (*f. pl.*): dām (*in England, draughts*).
cheek. Joue (*n. f.*): ʒū.
cheerful, *a.* Joyeux (*m.*): ʒwa″yū′; joyeuse (*f.*): ʒwā″yūz′.
cheese. Fromage (*n. m.*): fro″mā′‿ʒə.—**cheese factory.** Fromagerie (*n. f.*): fro″mā″ʒə‿rī′; buron (*n. m.*): bü″roṅ′.—**c. sandwich.** Sandwich au fromage: saṅ″dwītsh′ ō fro″maʒ′‿ə.
chemist. Pharmacien (*n. m.*): far″mā″sī″‿yaṅ′.
chess. Madrier (*n. m.*): ma″drī″‿yē′ (*cross-timber or plank as in a pontoon*).
chest, *n.* **1.** Poitrine (*f.*): pwa″trīn′ (*of man*). **2.** Poitrail (*m.*): pwa″trāl′ (*of a horse*).
chestnut, *n.* Châtaigne (*n. f.*): shā″tē′nyə.
chestnut, *a.* **1.** Châtain: shā″taṅ′ (*of color*). **2.** Alezan: a″lə‿zāṅ′ [(*of horses*).
chevaux-de-frise, shə-vō′-də-frīz′, *n.* A spiked obstruction to impede progress, as of cavalry.
chevron, *n.* **1.** Chevron (*m.*): shə-vroṅ′. **2.** Galon (*m.*): gā″loṅ′.
chicken. Poulet (*n. m.*): pū″lē′.
chief city. Capitale (*n. f.*): kā″pī″tāl′. Abbreviated *Caple.*
chief clerk. **1.** Commis chef (*m.*): kom″mī′ shef. **2.** Chef de bureau (*m.*): shef də bü″rō′.
chief of the staff. Chef d'état major (*m.*): shef dē″tā′ ma″ʒōr′.
child. L'enfant (*m. & f.*): laṅ″fāṅ′.—**childish,** *a.* **1.** Puéril (*m.*), puérile (*f.*): pü″ē″rīl′. **2.** Enfantin (*m.*): aṅ″faṅ″taṅ′; enfantine (*f.*): aṅ″faṅ″tīn′.—**children.** Enfants (*n. pl.*): aṅ″fāṅ′.

chill. Refroidissement (*n. m.*): rə-frwa″dīs″‿sə-mäṅ′.
chilly, *a.* **1.** Frileux (*m.*): frī″lū′; frileuse (*f.*): frī″lūz′. **2.** Froid (*m.*): frwä; froide (*f.*): frwäd.—**I am chilly** or **cold.** J'ai froid: ʒē frwä.—**it is chilly.** Il fait froid: il fē frwä.
chimney. Cheminée (*n. f.*): shə-mī″nē′. Abbreviated *Chnee.*—**chimney-pot.** Tuyau de cheminée (*n. m.*): twī″yō′ də shə-mī″nē′.
chin, *n.* Menton (*m.*): maṅ″toṅ′.—**chin-strap,** *n.* **1.** Jugulaire (*f.*): ʒü″gü″lär′. **2.** Fausse-gourmette (*f.*): fōs-gūr″met′. **3.** Mentonnière (*f.*): maṅ″toṅ″nī″‿yär′.
chisel, *n.* Ciseau (*m.*): sī″zō′.
chlorid of lime. Chlorure de chaux: klō″rür′ də shō.
chocolate. Chocolat (*n. m.*): shō″kō″lā′.
choose, *v.* Choisir: shwa″zīr′. See Appendix.
chop. I. *n. f.* Côtelette: kō″tə-let′. **II.** *v.* Hacher: hash″ē′.—**lamb-** or **mutton-chop,** *n.* Côtelette de mouton: kō″tə-let′ də mū″toṅ′.
church, *n.* Église (*f.*): ē″glī′zə. Abbreviated *Egse.*—**is there a church?** Y a-t-il une église? I ya″tīl′ ün ē″glī′zə.—**near a c.** Près d'une église: prä dün ē″glī′zə.
cider. Cidre (*m.*): sī′drə.
cinch (for a saddle girth), *n.* Large sangle (*f.*): lär′ʒə säṅ′glə.
cinch, *v.* Sangler: säṅ″glē′.
cipher, *n.* **1.** Chiffre (*m.*): shīf′‿frə. **2.** Zéro (*m.*): zē″rō′.—**in cipher. 1.** En chiffre: aṅ shīf′‿frə. **2.** En langage chiffré: aṅ laṅ″gāʒ′ shīf″‿frē′.—**the key to a c.** La clef de chiffre: la klē də shīf′frə.
circle. I. *n.* Cercle (*m.*): sär′‿klə. **II.** *v.* Entourer: aṅ″tū″rē′.
circuit, *n.* Circuit (*m.*): sīr″kwī′.
circumstances, *n. pl.* Circonstances (*f.*): sīr″koṅ″stäṅ′sə.—**extenuating circumstances.** Circonstances atténuantes: sīr″koṅ″stäṅ′‿sə at″‿tē″nü″äṅ′‿tə.—**under any c.** En tous cas: aṅ tū kä.—**under like c.** En pareille circonstance: aṅ par″ē′yə sīr″koṅ″stäṅ′‿sə.—**under no c.** Sous aucun prétexte: sūz‿ō″kaṅ′ prē″tekst′.
cistern. Citerne (*f.*): sī″tern′ (*well*). Abbreviated *Cite.*
citadel. Citadelle (*f.*): sī″ta″del′‿lə. Abbreviated *Cittle.*
cits (*civilian clothes*), **to be in.** Être en civil: ä‿′trə aṅ sī″vīl′.
civilian. Civil (*a. & n.*): sī″vīl′.—**civilian labor.** Main-d'œuvre civile (*f.*): maṅ″ dūv′‿rə sī″vīl′‿ə.—**civilians may be permitted to.** Les civils peuvent avoir la permission de: lē sī″vīl′ pūvt‿a″vwär′ la pär″mīs″‿sī″‿yoṅ′ də.—**have you seen any civilians?** Avez vous vu des civils? a″vē′ vū vü dē sī″vīl′.
clabber. klab′ər, *n.* [Soldiers' slang.] Underclothing.
claim. I. *n.* **1.** Prétention (*f.*): prē″taṅ″sī″‿yoṅ′. **2.** Droit (*m.*): drwä. **3.** Réclamation (*f.*): rē″kla″ma″sī″‿yoṅ′. **II.** *v.* **1.** Demander: də-maṅ″dē′. **2.** Réclamer: rē″kla″mē′.—**adjustment of claims.** Règlement des réclamations (*m.*): rā″glə-mäṅ′dē rē″-kla″ma″sī″‿yoṅ′.—**assessment of claims.** Recensement des indemnités (*f.*): rə-saṅs″maṅ′ dēz‿aṅ″dēm″nī″tē′.—**claims officer.** Officier chargé des réclamations: of″‿fī″sī″‿yē′ shar″ʒē′ dē rē″kla″ma″sī″‿yoṅ′.—**commission on claims.** Commission chargée d'examiner les réclamations (*f.*): kom″‿mīs″‿sī″‿yoṅ′ shar″ʒē′ degs″‿za″mī″nē′ lē rē″kla″ma″sī″‿yoṅ′.
claret, *n.* **1.** Vin ordinaire (*m.*): vaṅ ōr″dī″när′. **2.** Vin rouge (*m.*): vaṅ rūʒ′.
clasp (of a medal), *n.* Agrafe (*f.*) de médaille: a″gräf′ də mē″-dal′‿yə.
clasp-knife, *n.* Couteau pliant réglementaire (*m.*): kū″tō′ plī″äṅ′ rē″glə-maṅ″tär′.
clay, *n.* Argile (*f.*): ar″ʒīl′.—**clay-pit,** *n.* Marnière (*f.*): mar″nī″‿yär′. Abbreviated *Mar′e.*

artistic; ārt; fat; fāre; fast; get; prēy; hit; polīce; obey; gō; not; ōr; full; rūle; but; būrn; ə = final;

clean. **I.** *a.* Propre: prō′‿prə. **II.** *v.* **1.** Nettoyer: net″twa″‿yē′. **2.** Cirer: sī″rē′ (*of shoes*).—**clean my shoes.** Cirez mes chaussures: sī″rē′ mē chōs″‿sür′‿ə.

cleaner, *n.* Nettoyeur (*m.*): net″‿twa″‿yūr′.—**cleaner-out,** *n.* Nettoyeur (*m.*): net″‿twa″‿yūr′ (*one who routs out the enemy from his lair*).

cleanliness, *n.* Propreté (*f.*): prō″prə-tē′.

clear. **I.** *a.* **1.** Clair: klār′. **2.** Libre: lī′brə (*free*). **II.** *v.* **1.** Dégager: dē″ga″ʒē′ (*free from obstacles*). **2.** Franchir: frañ″shīr′ (*pass over*). **3.** Déblayer: dē″blē″‿yē′ (*said of ground, rubbish, etc.*)—**all is clear.** Tout est tranquille: tūt ē trañ″kīl′‿ə.—**c. firing range.** Un champ de tir dégagé: añ shañ də tīr dē″ga″ʒē′.—**c. the road.** Dégager la route: dē″ga″ʒē′ lā rūt′‿ə.—**till a passage is cleared.** Jusqu'à ce que le chemin soit déblayé: ʒüs″kā′‿sə kə lə shə-mañ′ swa dē″blē″yē′.—**till the clearing of camp.** Jusqu'à ce que le camp soit évacué: ʒüs″ka′‿sə kə lə kañ swā ē″va″kü″ē′.—**to clear away obstacles.** Déblayer, remuer les obstacles: dē″blē″yē′, rə-mü″ē′ lēs‿ob″stāk′‿lə.—**to keep c. of.** Se dégager de: sə dē″ga″ʒē′ də.

clearing, *n.* **1.** Dégagement (*m.*): dē″ga″ʒə-māñ′. **2.** Déblaiement: dē″blē″māñ′ (*of land*).

cleft, *a.* Fendu (*m.*): fendue (*f.*): fañ″dü′.

clerk, *n.* Commis (*m.*): kem″‿mī′.

click, klik, *v.* [Eng. soldiers' slang.] **1.** To get killed: with *it;* as, he *clicked it.* **2.** To be wounded: as, he was *clicked.*

cliff, *n.* Falaise (*f.*): fā″lēz′.

climate, *n.* Climat (*m.*): klī″mā′.

climb. **I.** *n.* Montée (*f.*): meñ″tē′. **II.** *v.* **1.** Grimper: grañ″-pē′. **2.** Escalader: es″ka″la″dē′.

clip, *n.* Chargeur (*m.*): shār″ʒūr′.

cloak, *n.* Manteau (*m.*): mañ″tō′.—**cloak-room.** Consigne (*n. f.*): keñ″sī′‿nyə (*of a railroad station*).

clock, *n.* **1.** Horloge (*f.*): ēr″lōʒ′ə. **2.** Pendule (*f.*): pañ″dül′.

clockwork. Mouvement d'horlogerie: mūv″māñ′ dēr″leʒ″‿ə-rī′.—**to be as regular as clockwork.** Être réglé comme une horloge: ā′‿trə rē″glē′ kem ün ēr″leʒ′.

clog. **I.** *n.* Billot (*m.*): bī″‿yō′. **II.** *v.* **1.** Encombrer: añ″-keñ″brē′. **2.** Embarrasser: añ″bār″ras″‿sē′.

close, *adv.* Auprès: ō″prē′.—**as close as possible.** Aussi près que possible: ōs″‿sī′ prē kə pes″‿sī′‿blə.—**c. at hand.** Tout près: tū prē.—**c. behind.** Juste derrière: ʒüst′‿ə dār″rī″yār′.—**c.-cropped,** *a.* Ras (*m.*): ra; rase (*f.*): raz.—**c. examination.** Interrogatoire serré: añ″tār″‿rō″ga″twār′ sār″rē′.—**c. order.** Ordre serré: ēr′drə sār″rē′.—**c. range.** *See* RANGE.—**c. to.** Près: prē.—**c. together.** L'un près de l'autre: lañ prē də lō′trə.

close, *v.* Approcher: ap″‿prō″shē′.—**close in!** Serrez les rangs! sār″‿rē′ lē rāñ.—**c. up!** Suivez! swī″vē′.—**to c. with the enemy.** En venir aux mains: añ və-nīr′ ō mañ.

closure, *n.* Clôture (*f.*): klō″tür′.

clot (of blood), *n.* Caillot de sang (*m.*): ka″yō′ də sāñ.

cloth. Drap (*n. m.*): drā.

clothes, *n. pl.*, **clothing,** *n.* **1.** Habillements (*m. pl.*): a″bī″‿yə-māñ′. **2.** Vêtements (*m. pl.*): vē″‿tə-māñ′.—**clothes-brush,** *n.* Brosse à habit: bres a a″bī′.—**in plain c.** En civile: añ sī″vīl′.

cloud, *n.* Un nuage (*m.*): añ nü″āʒ′.—**cloudy,** *a.* **1.** Nuageux (*m.*): nü″a″ʒū′; nuageuse (*f.*): nü″a″ʒūz′‿ə. **2.** Nébuleux (*m.*): nē″bü″lū′; nébuleuse (*f.*): nē″bü″lūz′‿ə.—**it is getting cloudy.** Le temps se couvre: lə tañ sə kūv′‿rə.

clover. Trèfle (*n. m.*): trē′flə.

clutch (*motor coupling-gear*). Embrayage (*n. m.*): añ″brē″yāʒ′ə.

coagulation. Coagulation (*n. f.*): kō″a″gü″la″sī″‿yeñ′.

coagulen, ko-ag′yu-len, *n.* A preparation for instantly checking the flow of blood.

ɪ = habit; aisle; au = *out;* oil; iū = feud; dūne; chin; go; ŋ = si*ng;* ship; thin; this.

artistic; ārt; fat; fāre; fast; get; prēy; hit; polīce;
obey; gō; not; ōr; full; rūle; but; būrn; ə = final;

coal, *n.* Charbon: shār″bəṅ′.—**cannel=c.** Charbon chandelle (*n. m.*): shār″bəṅ′ shaṅ″del′.—**coal=box,** *n.* Boîte à charbon: bwāt a shār″bəṅ′ (*a name given also to a German smoke-shell*).—**coalpit.** Houillère (*n. f.*): hū″‿ī″yār′.—**to coal.** Faire sa provision de charbon: fār sa pro″vīz″‿yoṅ′ də shār″bəṅ′.
coarse, *a.* Grossier (*m.*): grōs″‿sī″‿yē′; grossière (*f.*): gros″‿sī″‿yār′.
coast, *n.* Côte (*f.*): kōt.—**the coast is clear.** La voie est libre: lā vwā ē lī′‿brə.
coast=guard. Garde=côte (*n. m.*): gār′‿də kōt.
coat, *n.* **1.** Tunique (*f.*): tü″nīk′. **2.** Habit (*m.*): a″bī′. **3.** Robe (*f.*): rōb (*of some animals*). **4.** Fourrure (*f.*): fū″rür′‿ə (*fur=coat*).
cock, *n.* Chien (*m.*) shī″‿yaṅ′ (*of firearms*).
Cockneys of Paris. Division de Fer (39th Division): dī″vī″zī″‿yoṅ də fār.
cocoa, *n.* Cacao (*m.*): ka″ka″ō′.
cod. Cabillaud (*m.*): ka″bī″‿yō′ (*live codfish*).
coffee. Café (*n. m.*): ka″fē′.—**coffee=grinder.** Moulin à café (*n. m.*): mū″laṅ′ a ka″fē′.—**c.=house,** *n.* **1.** Café (*m.*): ka″fē′. **2.** Estaminet (*m.*): es″ta″mī″nē′.—**c.=pot.** Cafetière (*n. f.*): ka″fə-tī″ār′.—**c. with milk.** Café=au=lait (*n. m.*): ka″fē′=ō=lē.—**make c.** Faire le café: fār lə ka″fē′.
coil, *n.* Bobine (*f.*): bo″bīn′.—**induction coil.** Bobine d'induction: bo″bīn′ daṅ″dük″sī″‿yoṅ′.
coin, *n.* **1.** Pièce de monnaie (*f.*): pī″es′ də meṅ″‿nā′. **2.** Argent (*m.*): ār″ʒāṅ′. For values of coins, etc., see under MONEY.
cold, *a.* Froid (*m.*): frwā; froide (*f.*): frwād.—**cold storage depot.** **1.** Refroidisseur (*n. m.*): rə-frwa″dīs″sūr′. **2.** Dépôt de glace (*n. m.*): dē″pō′ də glās (see ICE=HOUSE).—**he is c.** Il a froid: īl a frwā.—**I am c.** J'ai froid: ʒā frwā.
cole, kōl, *n.* [English slang.] **1.** Money. **2.** A penny: soldiers' use.
colic, colics. Colique (*n. f.*): ko″līk′.
collapse, *n.* Affaissement (*m.*): af″‿fē″zə-māṅ′.
collar, *n.* **1.** Col (*m.*): kol (*of a shirt*). **2.** Collet (*m.*): kol″‿lē′ (*of a coat, etc.*). **3.** Collier (*m.*): kol″yē′.—**collar=bone.** Clavicule (*n. f.*): klav″ī″kül′.
collate, *v.* Réunir: rē″ü″nīr′.
collect, *v.* **1.** Rassembler: ras″‿saṅ″blē′. **2.** Se rassembler: sə ras″‿saṅ″blē′ (*assemble*).
collection. Réunion (*n. f.*): rē″‿yü″nī″‿yoṅ′.
college. Collège (*n. m.*): kol″‿lēʒ′. Abbreviated *Colge.*
colonel. Colonel (*n. m.*): kō″lō″nel′.
color, *n.* Couleur (*f.*): kū″lūr′.—**c.=guard.** Garde du drapeau (*n. f.*): gard dü dra″pō′.—**c.=sergeant.** Porte=drapeau (*n. m.*): pōr′tə dra″pō′.
colorless, *a.* Mat (*m.*); matte (*f.*): mat.
colors (of a regiment), the. Le drapeau (du régiment): lə dra″pō′ dü rē″ʒī″maṅ′.—**the colors (of a ship).** Le pavilion (de navire): lə pā″vī″yoṅ′ də na″vīr′.—**with the c.** Sous les drapeaux: sū lē dra″pō′.
colt. Poulain (*n. m.*): pū″laṅ′.
column. Colonne (*n. f.*): ko″loṅ′‿nə.—**column of fours.** Colonne par quatre (*n. f.*): ko″loṅ′‿nə pār kāt′‿rə.—**punitive c.** Colonne chargée d'infliger un châtiment (*n. f.*): ko″loṅ′nə shār″ʒē′ daṅ″flī″ʒē′ aṅ sha″tī″māṅ′.—**the attacking column.** La colonne de combat: la ko″loṅ′‿nə də koṅ″bā′.
comb. Peigne (*n. m.*): pē′‿nyə.
combat. Combat (*n. m.*): koṅ″bā′.—**combatant.** Combattant (*n. m.*): koṅ″bā″tāṅ′.
combine. Combiner (*v.*): koṅ″bī″nē′.—**combination.** Combinaison (*n.*): koṅ″bī″nā″‿zoṅ′.

come, *v.* Venir: və-nīr′.—**come** (*imp.*)! Venez: və-nē′.—**c. back!** Revenez: rə-və-nē′.—**c. here!** Venez ici: və-nēz′‿ī″sī′.—**c. in!** Entrez: aṅ″trē′.—**here they c.** Les voilà: lē vwa″lā′.—**may I c. in?** Puis=je entrer? pwī′‿ʒə aṅ″trē′.—**to c. into play.** Entrer en jeu: aṅ″trē′ aṅ ʒu.—**to c. to.** Revenir: rə-və-nīr′.—**before coming up with the enemy.** Avant d'aborder l'ennemi: a″vāṅ′ da″bōr″dē′ len″‿nə-mī′.—**in coming to a decision.** En prenant une décision: aṅ prə-nāṅ ün dē″sī″zī″‿yeṅ′.—**they are coming this way.** Ils viennent par ici: īl vī″‿en pār‿ī″sī′.

comfortable, *a.* Confortable (*m.* & *f.*): keṅ″fōr″tā′‿blə.

command. I. *n.* **1.** Commandement (*m.*): kem″‿maṅ″‿də-māṅ′. **2.** Unité (*f.*): ü″nī″tē′ (*a company of soldiers*). **3.** Vue sur hauteur de tranchée: vü sūr hō″tūr′ də traṅ″shē′ (*height of a work above ground*). **II.** *v.* Commander: kem″‿maṅ″dē′.—**assumption of command.** Prise de commandement: prī ‿ʒə də kem″‿maṅ″-də-māṅd′‿ə.—**c. of the sea.** Maîtrise de la mer: mā″trī′‿ʒə də la mēr.—**complete c.** Unité constituée: ü″nī″tē′ keṅ″stī″tü″ē′.—**he will move his c. to.** Il dirigera son unité vers: īl dī″rī″‿ʒə-rā′ seṅ ü″nī″tē′ vār.—**the heights which c. the line of march.** Hauteurs qui commandent la ligne de marche: hō″tūr′ kī kem″-māṅd′‿ə la lī′‿nyə də mār′‿shə.—**to place an officer in c. of a body of troops.** Placer un officier à la tête d'un corps de troupe: pla″sē′ aṅ of″‿fī″sī″‿yē′ a la tēt daṅ ker də trūp.—**words of c.** Commandements: kem″‿maṅ″də-māṅ′.

commandant, *n.* **1.** Chef le plus haut d'une unité (*m.*): shef lə plü hō dün ü″nī″tē′. **2.** Directeur (*m.*): dī″rek″tūr′.

commander. Chef (*n. m.*): shef.—**commander=in=chief.** Commandant=en=chef (*n. m.*): kem‿maṅ″dāṅ′ aṅ shef.—**commanding officer.** Officier commandant (*n. m.*): of″‿fī″sī″yē′ kem′-maṅ″dāṅ′.—**subordinate commanders.** Chefs en sous=ordre: shefs‿aṅ sūz‿er′‿drə.

commissariat, *n.* **1.** Commissariat (*m.*): kem″‿mī″sa″rī″ā′. **2.** Intendance (*f.*): aṅ″taṅ″dāṅs′. **3.** Ravitaillement (*m.*): ra″vī″-tai″māṅ′.

commission, *n.* **1.** Commission (*f.*): kem″‿mī″sī″‿yeṅ′. **2.** Brevet (*m.*): brə-vē′ (*of an officer*).—**commissioned,** *a.* Breveté (*m.*): brə-və-tē′.—**c. officer.** Officier breveté (*n. m.*): of″‿fī″sī″‿yē′ brə-və-tē′.

commit, *v.* **1.** Engager: aṅ″ga″ʒē′. **2.** S'engager: saṅ″ga″ʒē′.—**to commit oneself.** Se commettre: sə kem″met′‿trə.

common, *a.* **1.** Ordinaire (*m.* & *f.*): ōr″dī″nār′. **2.** Commun (*m.*): kem″‿muṅ′; commune (*f.*): kem″‿mün′‿ə.

commune. Commune (*n.f.*): kem″‿mün′‿ə. Abbr. *Com*[ne].

communicate, *v.* Communiquer: kem″‿mü″nī″kē′.—**communication,** *n.* **1.** Communication (*f.*): kem″‿mü′nī″ka″sī″‿yeṅ′. **2.** Communiqué (*m.*): kem″‿mü″nī″kē′ (*official*).—**to be in signaling communication.** Communiquer par signaux: kem″‿mü″nī″kē pār sī″‿nyō′.—**to enter into c. with.** Entrer en communication avec: aṅ″trē′ aṅ kem″‿mü″nī″ka″sī″‿yeṅ′ a″vek′.

companion. Camarade (*n. m.*): ka″ma″rād′.

company. Compagnie (*n. f.*): keṅ″pa″nyī′.—**company's agents.** Personnel technique: pār″seṅ″‿nel′ tek″nīk′‿ə.—**the company is scattered.** La compagnie est dispersée: la keṅ″pa″-nyī′ ē dīs″pār″sē′.

compartment. Compartiment (*n. m.*): kem″par″tī″māṅ′.—**first=class compartment.** Compartiment de première classe: kem″par″tī″māṅ′ də prə-mī″‿ār′ klās.—**second=class c.** Compartiment de deuxième classe: kem″par″tī″māṅ′ də dūz″‿ī″‿ām′ klās.—**third=class c.** Compartiment de troisième classe: kem″-par″tī″māṅ′ də trwāz″‿ī″‿ām′ klās.

compass. Boussole (*n. f.*): būs″‿sōl′.—**pair of compasses.** Compas (*n. m.*): kem″pā′.

compel, *v.* **1.** Forcer: fōr″sē′. **2.** Obliger: o″blī″ʒē′.—**to compel to surrender.** Forcer à se rendre: fōr″sē′ a sə rań′‿drə.
complaint. Plainte (*n. f.*): plańt.
complete. **I.** *a.* Complet (*m.*): kəń″plē′; complète (*f.*): kəń″plāt′. **II.** *v.* **1.** Accomplir: ak″‿kəń″plīr′. **2.** Achever: a″‿shəvē′.—**completed,** *pa.* Terminé (*m.*): terminée (*f.*): tār″mī″nē′.—**completion.** Achèvement (*n. m.*): ā″shāv″māń′.
complexion, *n.* **1.** Teint (*m.*): tań (*coloring*). **2.** Complexion (*f.*): kəń″plek″sī″yəń′ (*disposition, tendency*).
compliance, *n.* **1.** Acquiescement (*m.*): ak″‿kī″ās″māń′. **2.** Complaisance (*f.*): kəń″plā″zāńs′.
complicity. Complicité (*n. f.*): kəń″plī″sī″tē′.
compliment, *n.* **1.** Compliment (*m.*): kəń″plī″māń′. **2.** Honneur (*m.*): əń″‿nūr′.—**to pay compliments to.** Faire des compliments à: fār dē kəń″plī″māń′ a.
comply, *v.* **1.** Acquiescer à: ak″kī″ās″‿sē′ a. **2.** Se conformer à: sə kəń″fōr″mē′ a.
component, *a.* Constitutif (*m.*): kəń″stī″tü″tīf′; constitutive (*f.*): kəń″stī″tü″tīv′.—**component parts.** Éléments constitutifs: ē″lē″māń′ kəń″stī″tü″tīf′.
"compray," kəm″prē′ (*British soldiers' French for "do you understand?"*)
comrade. Camarade (*n. m.*): ka″ma″rād′.—**comradeship.** Camaraderie (*n. f.*): ka″ma″ra″‿də″rī′.
conceal, *v.* **1.** Cacher: ka″shē′. **2.** Céler: sē″lē′.—**concealment,** *n.* **1.** Recèlement (*m.*): rə-sāl″māń′. **2.** Dissimulation (*f.*): dīs″sīm″ü″la″sī″‿yəń′.
concentrate, *v.* **1.** Se concentrer: sə kəń″sań″trē′. **2.** Se réunir: sə rē″ü″nīr′.—**concentration.** Concentration (*n. f.*): kəń″sań″tra″sī″‿yəń′.
concert. Concert (*n. m.*): kəń″sār′.—**European concert.** Concert Européen: kəń″sār′ ū″rō″pē″āń′ (*agreement by the Powers to take only combined action in the Near East*).
concordat. Concordat (*n. m.*): kəń″kōr″ dā′ (*an agreement between the Papacy and a secular Power*).
concrete. Béton (*n. m.*): bē″təń′.
condemn, *v.* **1.** Condamner: kəń″da″nē′ (in morals). **2.** Réformer: rē″fōr″mē′ (*pronounce unfit for use, as equipment*).
condenser. Condensateur (*n. m.*): kəń″dań″sa″tūr′.
condition, *n.* **1.** Condition (*f.*): kəń″dī″sī″‿yəń′. **2.** État (*m.*): ē″tā′.—**conditional,** *a.* Conditionnel (*m.*): conditionnelle (*f.*): kəń″dī″sī″‿yəń″‿nel′.
conduct. Conduite (*n. f.*): kəń″dwī′‿tə.
conductor. Conducteur (*n. m.*): kəń″dük″tūr′.
cone. Cône (*n. m.*): kōn.—**cone of burst.** Gerbe d'éclatement (*n. f.*): ʒārb dē″kla″‿tə-māń′.—**cone of dispersion** or **spread.** Cône de dispersion: kōn də dīs″pār″sī″‿yəń′.—**coned breech-screw.** Culasse conique (*n. f.*): kü″lās′ kəń″īk′.
confer, *v.* Conférer: kəń″fē″rē′.—**conference,** *n.* **1.** Conférence (*f.*): kəń″fē″rāńs′. **2.** Critique (*f.*): krī″tīk′.
confess, *v.* **1.** Avouer: a″vū″ē′. **2.** Reconnaître: rə-kəń″nē′‿trə.
confidence. Confiance (*n. f.*): kəń″fī″āńs′.
configuration. Configuration (*n. f.*): kəń″fī″gü″ra″sī″‿yəń.
confine, *v.* Confiner: kəń″fī″nē′.—**confinement.** Confinement (*n. m.*): kəń″fī″‿nə-māń′.—**confinement to barracks.** Consigne au quartier (*n. f.*): kəń″sī′‿nyə ō kar″tī″‿yē′.
confiscation. Confiscation (*n. f.*): kəń″fīs″ka″sī″‿yəń′.
conflict. **I.** *n.* Lutte (*f.*): lüt. **II.** *v.* Lutter: lüt″‿tē′.
conform, *v.* **1.** Conformer: kəń″fōr″mē′. **2.** Suivre: swī′‿vrə.—**conform to orders.** Suivre les ordres: swī′‿vrə lēz‿ōr′‿drə.

confront, *v.* Confronter: keṅ"froṅ"tē'.
congestion. Amoncellement (*n. m.*): a"meṅ"sel"‿lə-māṅ'.
connect, *v.* Lier: lī"yē'.—**connected with.** Ce qui a trait à: sə kī a trāt‿a.—**connected by telephone.** Relié par le téléphone: rə-lī"yē' pär lə tē"lē"fōṅ'.—**connecting.** Qui unit: kī ü"nī'.—**connecting rod.** Bielle (*n. f.*): bī"‿yel'.—**connection.** Liaison (*n. f.*): lī"ā"zeṅ'.—**in this c.** À propos: a pre"pō'.—**to keep connection.** Assurer la liaison: as"‿sü"rē' la lī"ā"zeṅ'.—**to maintain c. with.** Maintenir la liaison avec: maṅ"‿tə-nīr' la lī"ā"zeṅ' a"vek'.
conquer, *v.* Vaincre: vaṅ'‿krə. [keṅ"skrīp"sī"‿yeṅ'.
conscript. Conscrit (*n. m.*): keṅ"skrī'.—**conscription** (*n. f.*):
consider. Considerer (*v.*): keṅ"sī"dē"rē".
consolidate, *v.* Consolider: keṅ"sel"ī"dē'.—**to consolidate the forces.** Consolider les troupes: keṅ"sel"ī"dē' lē trūp.
conspicuous, *a.* **1.** En vue: aṅ vü. **2.** En évidence: aṅ‿ē"vī"-dāṅs'.
constitution. Tempérament (*n. m.*): taṅ"pē"ra"māṅ' (*physical condition*).
construct, *v.* Construire: keṅ"strwīr'.—**under construction.** Ouverte (*a. f.*): ū"vārt' (*said of a road*).
consul. Consul (*n. m.*): keṅ"sül'.—**the American Consul.** Le consul américain: lə keṅ"sül a"mē"rī"kaṅ'.
consumption, *n.* **1.** Maladie de poitrine: ma"la"dī' də pwa"-trīn' (*the disease*). **2.** Phtisie (*f.*): tī"zī' (*the disease*). **3.** Consommation: keṅ"som"‿ma"sī"yeṅ' (*use of supplies, etc.*).
contact. Contact (*n. m.*): keṅ"täkt'.—**to come in contact with.** Prendre le contact avec: praṅ'‿drə lə keṅ"täkt' a"vek'.
content. **I.** *a.* Content (*m.*): keṅ"tāṅ'; contente (*f.*): keṅ"-tāṅt'. **II.** *n.* **1.** Contentement (*m.*): keṅ"taṅ"‿tə-māṅ' (*satisfaction*). **2.** Content (*m.*): keṅ"tāṅ' (*one's fill; contents*).
contraband of war. Contrebande de guerre (*n. f.*): keṅ"trə-bānd' də gār.—**conditional contraband.** Contrebande conditionnelle (*n. f.*): keṅ"trə-bāṅ'‿də keṅ"dī"sī"yeṅ"‿nel'.
contract, *v.* **1.** Traiter: trē"tē'. **2.** Entreprendre: aṅ"‿trə-prāṅ'‿drə.—**contractor,** *n.* **1.** Entrepreneur (*m.*): aṅ"‿trə-prə-nūr'. **2.** Fournisseur (*m.*): fūr"nīs"‿sūr'.
contribution. Contribution (*n. f.*): keṅ"trī"bü"sī"‿yeṅ'.—**to exact a contribution from a conquered country.** Mettre le pays conquis à contribution: met'‿trə lə pē"‿ī' keṅ"kī' a keṅ"-trī"bü"sī"yeṅ'.
control. **I.** *n.* **1.** Contrôle (*m.*): keṅ"trōl'. **2.** Surveillance (*f.*): sür"vē"‿yāṅs'. **II.** *v.* **1.** Contrôler: keṅ"trō"lē'. **2.** Réprimer: rē"prī"mē'.—**area under control.** Zone sous surveillance: zōn sū sür"vē"‿yāṅs.—**c. of fire.** Réglage du tir (*m.*): rē"glāʒ' dü tīr.—**traffic c.** Direction des mouvements: dī"rek"-sī"‿yeṅ' dē mūv"māṅ'.—**unity of c.** Unité de direction: ü"nī"tē' də dī"rek"sī"‿yeṅ'.
convalescent, *a.* Convalescent (*m.*): keṅ"va"lēs"‿sāṅ'; convalescente (*f.*): keṅ"va"lēs"‿sāṅt'.—**depot for convalescents and cripples.** Dépôt de convalescents et d'éclopés (*m.*): dē"pō' də keṅ"va"lēs"‿sāṅ' ē dē"klō"pē'.
convenient, *a.* Convenable (*m.* & *f.*): keṅ"və-nā'‿blə.—**when convenient.** Quand cela s'arrange: kāṅ sə-lā' sar"rāṅ'‿ʒə.
convent. Couvent (*n. m.*): kū"vāṅ'. Abbreviated *Covnt.*
conversation. Conversation (*n. f.*): keṅ"vār"sa"sī"‿yeṅ'.
convey, *v.* **1.** Porter: pēr"tē'. **2.** Transporter: traṅs"pēr"tē'.—**to convey information.** Transmettre des renseignements: traṅs"mēt'‿trə dē raṅ"sē"‿nyə-māṅ'.—**conveyance.** Transport (*n. m.*): traṅs"pēr'.
convoy. **I.** *n.* Convoi (*m.*): keṅ"vwā'. **II.** *v.* Convoyer: keṅ"vwa"yē'.—**commander of a convoy.** Chef de convoi: shef də keṅ"vwā'.—**motor c.** Convoi automobile: keṅ"vwā'

ō″to″mō″bīl′.—**to go on c.** Aller en convoi: al″‿lē′ an koṅ″vwā′.

cook. **I.** *n.* Cuisinier (*m.*): kwī″zī″nī″‿yē′. **II.** *v.* **1.** Cuire: kwīr. **2.** Préparer: prē″pa″rē′.—**cook a meal.** Préparer un repas: prē″pa″rē′ aṅ rə-pā′.—**cooking,** *n.* **1.** Cuisson (*m.*): kwīs″‿seṅ′. **2.** Cuisine (*f.*): kwī″zīn′.—**cooking=pot.** Marmite (*n. f.*): mar″mīt′.—**cooking=place.** Emplacement des cuisines (*m.*): aṅ″pla″‿sə-māṅ′ dē kwī″zīn′.—**we must do the cooking.** Il faut faire la cuisine: īl fō fār la kwī″zīn′.

cool, *a.* Frais (*m.*): frā; fraîche (*f.*): frāsh.

cooperate, *v.* Coopérer: kō″ō″pē″rē′.—**to cooperate in.** Contribuer à: koṅ″trī″bü″ē′ a.—**cooperation.** Coopération (*n. f.*): kō″ō″pē″ra″sī″‿yeṅ′.

cootie. Pou (*n. m.*): pū (*a louse: soldiers' slang*).

cope, *v.* Tenir tête à: tə-nīr′ tēt a.—**to cope with the enemy's fire.** Répondre au feu de l'ennemi: rē″peṅ′‿drə ō fū də len″‿ne-mī′.

copper, *n.* **1.** Sou (*m.*): sū (*small change*). **2.** Cuivre (*m.*): kwī′‿vrə (*the metal*).—**give me some coppers.** Donnez=moi des sous: doṅ″nē′ mwā dē sū.

copse. Taillis (*n. m.*): tai″yī′.

cord, *n.* **1.** Corde (*f.*): kōrd. **2.** Ficelle (*f.*): fī″sel′.

cordite. Cordite (*n. f.*): kōr″dīt′ (*a smokeless explosive compound*).

cork. Bouchon (*n. m.*): bū″sheṅ′.—**corkscrew.** Tire=bouchon (*n. m.*): tīr″bū″sheṅ′.

corn, *n.* **1.** Durillon (*m.*): dü″rī″yeṅ′ (*on the foot*). **2.** Cor (*m.*): kōr (*on the foot*). **3.** Maïs (*m.*): ma″‿ī′ (*maize*). **4.** Blé (*m.*): blē (*wheat*).—**corn=field,** *n.* Champ de blé: shaṅ də blē (*wheat=field*).—**corn sack.** Sac à avoine: sak a av″wān′.

corner. Coin (*n. m.*): kwaṅ.

coronet. Couronne (*n. f.*): kū″reṅ′‿nə.

corporal. Caporal (*n. m.*): kā″pə″rāl′.

corps. Corps (*n. m.*): kōr.—**picked corps.** Corps d'élite: kōr dē″līt′.

correct. **I.** *a.* Correct (*m.*); correcte (*f.*): ker″‿rekt′. **II.** *v.* Corriger: ker″‿rī″ʒē′.—**correct aim.** Justesse de tir: ʒüs″tes′ də tīr.—**to correct the dressing.** Rectifier l'alignement: rek″-tī″fī″yē′ la″lī″‿nyə-māṅ′ (*said of troops*).—**corrector.** Correcteur (*n. m.*): ker″‿rek″tūr′.

corslet. Plastron (*n. m.*): plas″treṅ′ (*steel breastplate worn by soldiers*).

Cossack. Cosaque (*n. m.*): ke″sāk′.—**Cossack post.** Groupe de vedettes (*f.*): grūp də və-det′.

cost. **I.** *n.* Prix (*m.*): prī. **II.** *v.* Coûter: kū″tē′.—**how much does it cost?** Combien coûte cela? koṅ″bī″‿yaṅ′ kūt sə-la′.—**obtain at the cost of.** Obtenir au prix de: ob″tə-nīr′‿ō prī də.—**this costs three francs.** Ceci coûte trois francs: sə-sī′ kūt trwā frāṅ.

cot. Lit de camp (*n. m.*): lī də kāṅ.

cottage, *n.* **1.** Chalet (*m.*): sha″lē′. **2.** Chaumière (*f.*): shō″-mī″yār′ (*peasant's dwelling*). **3.** Buron (*m.*): bü″reṅ′ (*shepherd's hut*).

counter=approach. Contre=approches (*n. f. pl.*): koṅ′‿trə ap″‿prō′‿shə.

counter=attack. **I.** *n.* Contre=attaque (*f.*): koṅ″‿trə-at″‿tāk′. **II.** *v.* Contre=attaquer: koṅ″‿trə-at″‿tak″ē′.—**to launch a counter=attack.** Lancer une contre=attaque: laṅ″sē′ ün koṅ″‿trə-at″‿tāk′.

counter=barrage. Contre=barrage (*n. m.*): koṅ″‿trə-bar″‿rāʒ′.

counter=mine. Contre=mine (*n. f.*): koṅ″‿trə-mīn′.

counterscarp. Contre=escarpe (*n. f.*): koṅ″‿trə-es″kārp′.

countersign, *n.* 1. Mot de ralliement (*m.*): mō də ral″‿lī″-māṅ′. 2. Mot d'ordre: mō dōr′‿drə.
country, *n.* 1. Pays (*m.*): pā″‿yī′ (*native land*). 2. Patrie (*f.*): pa″trī′ (*fatherland*). 3. Campagne (*f.*): kaṅ″pā′‿nyə (*as opposed to town*).—**difficult country.** Pays difficile: pā″‿yī′ dīf″‿fī″sīl′.—**enclosed, close c.** Pays couvert: pā″‿yī′ kū″vār′.—**intersected, broken c.** Pays coupé: pā″‿yī′ kū″pē′.—**level c.** Pays de plaine: pā″‿yī′ də plēn.—**mountainous c.** Pays montueux: pā″‿yī′ meṅ″tü″ū′.—**open c.** Pays exposé: pā″‿yī′ eks″pō″zē′.—**thick c.** Pays très couvert: pā″‿yī′ trē kū″vār′.
county, *n.* 1. Canton (*m.*): kaṅ″teṅ′. 2. Comté (*m.*): keṅ″tē′.
coupling, *n.* 1. Attelage (*m.*): at″tə-lāʒ′ (*in railroads*). 2. Accouplement (*m.*): ak″kū″‿plə-māṅ′ (*yoking together*).
courage, *n.* 1. Courage (*m.*): kū″rāʒ′. 2. Hardiesse (*f.*): har″dī″es′.
course. Cours (*n. m.*): kūr.—**in course of preparation.** En cours de préparation: aṅ kūr də prē″pa″ra″sī″‿yeṅ′.—**senior c.** Cours des officiers supérieurs: kūr dēz‿ef″fī″sī″‿yē′ sü″pē″rī″‿yūr′.—**such a c.** Une telle façon de faire: ün tel fa″seṅ′ də fār.
court. I. *n.* 1. Cour (*f.*): kūr (*in all senses*). 2. Tribunal (*m.*): trī″bü″nāl′ (*of justice*). II. *v.* 1. Faire la cour à: fār la kūr a. 2. Inviter: aṅ″vī″tē′.—**court battle.** Rechercher le combat: rə shār″shē′ lə keṅ″bā′.—**court of inquiry.** Conseil d'enquête (*m.*): keṅ″sē′‿yə daṅ″kē′‿tə.
court-martial, *n.* 1. Conseil de guerre (*m.*): keṅ″sē′‿yə də gār. 2. Cour martiale (*f.*): kūr mar″sī″‿yāl′.—**the c.-martial is convened.** Le conseil de guerre est convoqué: lə keṅ″sē′‿yə də gār ē keṅ″vō″kē′.—**to arraign a soldier before a c.-martial.** Traduire un soldat en conseil de guerre: tra″dwīr′ aṅ sōl″dā′ aṅ keṅ″sē′‿yə də gār.—**to be tried by c.-martial.** Être jugé par le conseil de guerre: ā′‿trə ʒü″ʒē′ pār lə keṅ″sē′‿yə də gār.
court-yard. Cour (*n. f.*): kūr.
cover. I. *n.* 1. Couvert (*m.*): kū″vār′. 2. Abri (*m.*): a″brī′ (*protection*). II. *v.* 1. Couvrir: kū″vrīr′. 2. Tenir en joue: tə-nīr′ aṅ ʒū (*aim at*).—**bombproof cover.** 1. Abri à l'épreuve des obus: a″brī′ a lē″prūv′ dēz‿ō″bü′. 2. Abri blindé à l'épreuve: a″brī′ blaṅ″dē′ a lē″prūv′.—**covering troops.** Troupes de couverture: trūp də kū″vār″tür′.—**overhead cover.** Abri contre le tir fusant: ā″brī′ keṅ′‿trə lə tīr fü″ʒāṅ′.—**to c. an area (with falling projectiles).** Garnir un terrain: gar″nīr′ aṅ tār″raṅ′.—**to c. or protect the train.** Couvrir le train: kū″vrīr′ lə traṅ.—**to get under c.** Défiler: dē″fī″lē′.—**to take c.** 1. Prendre abri: praṅ′‿drə a″brī′. 2. S'abriter: sa″brī″tē′.—**troops under c.** Des troupes abritées: dē trūpz‿a″brī″tē′.
covered, *a.* 1. Couvert (*m.*): kū″vār′; couverte (*f.*): kū″vārt′. 2. Boisé (*m.*), boisée (*f.*): bwā″zē′ (*wooded*).
cow. I. *n.* Vache (*f.*): vā′‿shə. II. *v.* 1. Effrayer: ef″‿frā″yē′. 2. Accabler: ak″‿ka″blē′.—**cow-house.** Vacherie (*n. f.*): vash″-ə-rī′. On maps *Vacie.*
coward. Lâche (*n. m.*): lāsh.
cradle. Berceau (*n. m.*): bār″sō′ (*in all senses*).
cramp. I. *n.* 1. Crampe (*f.*): krāṅp. 2. Crampon (*m.*): kraṅ″peṅ′ (*iron*). II. *v.* 1. Gêner: ʒē″nē′. 2. Resserrer: rə-ser″‿rē′.—**to cramp initiative.** Entraver l'initiative: aṅ″-tra″vē′ lī″nī″sī″‿a″tīv′.
crane, *n.* Grue (*f.*): grü (*in all senses*).
crank, *n.* 1. Manivelle (*f.*): ma″nī″vel′. 2. Cran (*m.*): kraṅ.—**to crank the machine.** Mettre le moteur en marche: met′‿trə lə mō″tūr′ aṅ mār″shə.
crankshaft. Vilebrequin (*n. m.*): vīl″brə-kaṅ′.
crater. Entonnoir (*n. m.*): aṅ″teṅ″‿war′ (*made by a shell*).
crawl, *v.* Se traîner: sə trā″nē′.—**crawling.** En rampant: aṅ raṅ″pāṅ′.

cream. Crème (*n. f.*): krēm.—**cream-colored,** *a.* Isabelle (*m. & f.*): ī″za″bel′ (*said of a horse*).
crest, *n.* **1.** Crête (*f.*): krē′‿tə (*summit*). **2.** Insigne (*m.*) aṅ″sī′‿nyə (*heraldic device or emblem*).—**crest line.** Ligne de crête (*f.*): lī′‿nyə də krē′tə.
crevice. Crevasse (*n. f.*): krə-vās′.
crew, *n.* **1.** Équipage (*m.*): ē″kī″pāʒ′. **2.** Troupe (*f.*): trūp. **3.** Personnel (*m.*): pār″səṅ″‿nel′.
cricket-ball, *n.* A ball-like bomb: soldiers' slang.
"crimed," *a.* Entered on the sergeant-major's "crime sheet" as an offender: said of a soldier.
cringe, *v.* Ramper: raṅ″pē′.—**cringing,** *a.* Servile (*m. & f.*): sar″vīl′.
cripple. **I.** *n.* **1.** Estropié (*m.*): es″trō″pī″‿yē′. **2.** Amputé (*m.*): aṅ″pü″tē′. **II.** *v.* Mettre hors de combat: met′‿trə ōr də keṅ″bā′.
crisis. Crise (*n. f.*): krī′‿zə.
crop, *n.* **1.** Culture (*f.*): kül″tür′ (*cultivation*). **2.** Récolte (*f.*): rē″kōlt′ (*harvest*).—**to gather crops.** Moissonner: mwa′səṅ″‿nē′.
cross. **I.** *n.* Croix (*f.*): krwā. **II.** *v.* **1.** Traverser: tra″vār″sē′. **2.** Croiser: krwa″zē′.—**crossed by water-courses.** Traversé par cours d'eau: tra″vār″sē′ pā kūr dō.—**to c. a river.** Traverser un fleuve: tra″vār″sē′ aṅ flūv.—**to cross one another.** Se croiser: sə krwa″zē′.—**wayside c.** Calvaire (*n. m.*): kal″vār′.
cross-bar. Palonnier (*n. m.*): pa″ləṅ″‿nī″‿yē′ (*swingletree*).—**front c.-bar.** Palonnier de frein: pa″ləṅ″‿nī″‿yē′ də fraṅ.—**rear c.-bar.** Palonnier d'appel: pa″ləṅ″‿nī″‿yē′ dap″pel′.
cross-examination. Contre-interrogatoire (*m.*): keṅ′‿trə aṅ″-tār″rə″ga″twār′.—**c.-examining a suspect.** Interrogatoire d'un individu suspect (*m.*): aṅ″tār″rə″ga″twār′ daṅ aṅ″dī″vī″dü süs″pē′.—**c.-eye.** Strabisme (*n. m.*): stra″bīsm′.
crossing, *n.* **1.** Croisement (*m.*): krwa″‿zə-māṅ′. **2.** Passage (*m.*): pas″‿sāʒ′.—**crossing below.** Passage en dessous (*m.*): pas″‿sāʒ′‿aṅ də-sū′.—**dangerous c.** Croisement dangereux (*m.*): krwa″‿zə-māṅ′ daṅ″‿ʒə-rū′.—**in c.** Pendant la traversée: paṅ″dāṅ′ la tra″vār″sē′.—**level c.** Passage à niveau: pas″‿sāʒ′‿a nī″vō′.—**overhead c.** Passage en dessus: pas″sāʒ′‿aṅ də-sü′.
cross-road, crossway. Carrefour (*n. m.*): car″‿rə-fūr′. Abbreviated *Carref*^r.
crouching, *a.* En rampant: aṅ raṅ″pāṅ′.
croup. Croupe (*n. f.*): krūp.
crow. Corbeau (*n. m.*): kēr″bō′.—**as the crow flies.** À vol d'oiseau: a vol dwa″zō′.—**crow's foot.** Chausse-trape (*n. f.*): shōs″trāp′ (*a caltrop*).
"crucifixion." Crucifixion (*n. f.*): crü″sī″fīk″sī″‿yeṅ′ (*being tied to the wheel of a limber: a military punishment*).
cruel, *a.* Cruel (*m.*): krü″el′; cruelle (*f.*): krü″el′‿lə.
cruiser. Croiseur (*n. m.*): krwa″zūr′.—**auxiliary cruiser.** Croiseur de deuxième classe: krwa″zūr′ də dū″zī″‿yām′ klās.—**cruising-squadron.** Croisière (*n. f.*): krwa″zī″‿yār′.
crupper. Bande de reculement: bāṅd də rə-kü″lə-māṅ′.
crush, *v.* **1.** Écraser: ē″kra″zē′. **2.** Moudre: mū′‿drə.
C. S. M. (*Company Sergeant-Major.*) Sergent major de compagnie (*n. m.*): sār″ʒāṅ′ ma″ʒōr′ də koṅ″pa″‿nyī′.
cuirassier. Cuirassier (*n. m.*): kwī″ras″‿sī″‿yē′.
cultivated, *a.* Cultivé (*m.*); cultivée (*f.*): kül″tī″vē′.
culvert. Ponceau (*n. m.*): poṅ″sō′. Abbreviated *Pceau.*
cummerbund. Ceinture (*n. f.*): saṅ″tür′ (*girdle worn by the Chasseurs d'Afrique*).
cunning, *a.* Rusé (*m.*); rusée (*f.*): rü″zē′.

cup, *n.* **1.** Tasse (*f.*): tās'‿sə (*for coffee, etc.*). **2.** Quart (*m.*): kār (*mug*).
cupola. Coupole (*n. f.*): kū"pōl'.
curb, *n.* **1.** Mors (*m.*): mōr (*of a bit*). **2.** Bordure (*f.*): bōr"dür' (*of a street*).—**curb-chain.** Gourmette (*n. f.*): gūr"met'.
current. Courant (*n. m.*): kū"rāṅ'.
curry-comb. Étrille (*n. f.*): ē"trī'‿yə.
curtain, *n.* **1.** Rideau (*m.*): rī"dō'. **2.** Courtine (*f.*): kūr"tīn' (*of a fort*).—**curtain of fire.** Rideau de feu: rī"dō' də fū (*shell-fire designed to prevent the advance of reinforcements*).
cushion. Bourrelet (*n. m.*): būr"‿rə-lē'.
"cushy." (*Soldiers' slang for comfortable.*)
custody. Garde (*n. f.*): gārd.—**custody of prisoners of war.** Garde des prisonniers de guerre: gārd dē prī"zəṅ"‿nī"‿yē' də gār.
custom-house. Douane (*n. f.*): dū"āṅ'. On maps *Dne.*—**customs officer.** Douanier (*n. m.*): dū"aṅ"‿yē'.
cut. **I.** *n. m.* Coup de taille: kū də tai'‿yə. **II.** *v.* **1.** Couper: kū"pē'. **2.** Tailler: tai"yē'.—**cut my hair.** Coupez moi les cheveux: kū"pē' mwa lē shə-vū'.—**cut short.** Court (*m.*): kūr; courte (*f.*): kūrt.—**to be cut off from the main body.** Être coupé du corps principal: ā'‿trə kū"pē' dü kōr praṅ"sī"pāl'.—**to cut short.** Raccourcir: rak"‿kūr"sīr'.—**to cut communications with the inside.** Couper les communications avec l'intérieur: kū"pē' lē kəm"‿mü"nī"ka"sī"‿yəṅ a"vek' laṅ"tē"rī"‿yūr'.—**to cut off.** Retrancher: rə-traṅ"shē'.—**to cut to pieces.** Écharper (*v.*): ē"shar"pē'.—**trees should not be cut down.** Il ne faut pas abattre les arbres: īl nə fō pāz‿a"bā'‿trə lēz‿ār'‿brə.
cutler. Coutelier (*n. m.*): kū"‿tə-lī"‿yē'.
cutting. Déblai (*m.*): dē"blē' (*of a railroad*).
cyclist. Cycliste (*n. m.*): sī"klīst'.
cylinder. Cylindre (*n. m.*): sī"laṅ'‿drə.
cymbal. Cymbale (*n. f.*): saṅ"bāl'.
Cyprus, *n.* Chypre: shīp'‿rə (*island in Mediterranean Sea*).
cyst. Kyste (*n. m.*): kīst.

D

D. A. C., *abbrev.* Divisional Ammunition Column.
daily. **I.** *a.* **1.** Quotidien (*m.*): kō"tīd"‿yaṅ'; quotidienne (*f.*): kō"tīd"‿yeṅ'‿nə. **2.** Journalier (*m.*): ʒūr"nal"‿yē'; journalière (*f.*): ʒūr"nal"‿yār'. **II.** *adv.* Tous les jours: tū lē ʒūr.—**daily rations.** Vivres d'ordinaire (*m.*): vīv'‿rə dər"dī"nār'‿ə.
dairy. Laiterie (*n. f.*): lā"tə-rī'.
dam. **I.** *n.* **1.** Digue (*f.*): dīg'‿ə. On maps *Dig.* **2.** Barrage (*m.*): bar"‿rāʒ'‿ə. On maps *Bge.* **II.** *v.* Faire un barrage: fār aṅ bar"‿rāʒ'‿ə.
damage. **I.** *n.* **1.** Dommage (*m.*): dəm"‿māʒ'‿ə. **2.** Dégât (*m.*): dē"gā'. **II.** *v.* Endommager: aṅ"dəm"‿ma"‿ʒē'.—**wanton damage.** Dommage volontaire: dəm"‿māʒ'‿ə vəl"əṅ"tār'‿ə.
damp. **I.** *n.* Humidité (*f.*): ü"mīd"ī"tē'. **II.** *a.* Humide (*m.* & *f.*): ü"mīd'‿ə.
dandy brush. Brosse à pansage (*f.*): brēs‿a paṅ"sāʒ'‿ə.
Dane, *n.* Danois (*m.*): da"nwā'; danoise (*f.*): da"nwāz'.
danger. Danger (*n. m.*): daṅ"ʒē'.—**dangerous,** *a.* Dangereux (*m.*): daṅ"ʒə-rū'; dangereuse (*f.*): daṅ"ʒə-rūz'.
dappled gray. Gris pommelé (*n.*): grī pəm"‿mə-lē' (*color of a horse*).
Dardanelles, dar"da"nel'‿lə, *f. pl.* Straits between the Sea of Marmora and the Ægean Sea.
daring. **I.** *n.* Audace (*f.*): ō"dās'‿ə. **II.** *a.* Audacieux (*m.*): ō"da"sī"‿yū'; audacieuse (*f.*): ō"da"sī"‿yūz'‿ə.

artistic; ärt; fat; fâre; fïrst; get; prēy; hit; polïce; obey; gō; net; ōr; full; rūle; but; būrn; ə = final;

dark. **I.** *n.* **1.** Obscurité (*f.*): ob″skü″rī″tē′. **2.** Nuit (*f.*): nwī (*night*). **II.** *a.* **1.** Noir (*m.*): noire (*f.*): nwār. **2.** Obscur (*m.*); obscure (*f.*): ob″skūr′. **3.** Sombre (*m.* & *f.*): soṅ′‿brə. **4.** Foncé (*m.*); foncée (*f.*): foṅ″sē′ (*in color*).—**before dark.** Avant la tombée de la nuit: a″vāṅ′ la tōṅ″bē′ də la nwī.—**in the d.** Dans l'obscurité: daṅ ləb″skü″rī″tē′.—**it is d.** Il fait nuit: il fē nwī.

dart. Flèche d'aéro (*n. f.*): flā′‿shə da″ē″rō′ (*to be dropped from an aeroplane*).

dash. **I.** *n. m.* Élan: ē″lāṅ′. **II.** *v.* **1.** Se précipiter: sə prē″-sī″pī″tē′. **2.** S'élancer: sē″laṅ″sē′.

data. **1.** Données (*f. pl.*): deṅ″‿nē′. **2.** Renseignements (*m. pl.*): raṅ″sē″‿nyə-māṅ′.

date. **I.** *n.* **1.** Date (*f.*): dāt (*day of year*). **2.** Datte (*f.*): dāt′‿tə (*fruit*). **II.** *v.* Dater: da″tē′.—**what is the date?** **1.** Quelle est la date? kel″‿ē la dāt. **2.** Quel jour sommes-nous? kel ʒūr som′‿mə nū.

daughter. Fille (*f.*): fī′‿yə.

dauntless, *a.* Indomptable (*m.* & *f.*): aṅ″deṅ″tā′‿blə.

dawn. Aube (*n. f.*): ō′‿bə.—**at dawn.** À l'aube: a lō′‿bə.

day, *n.* **1.** Jour (*m.*): ʒūr. **2.** Journée (*f.*): ʒūr″nē′ (*length of day*).—**by day.** **1.** De jour: də ʒūr. **2.** Pendant le jour: paṅ″daṅ′ lə ʒūr (*during the day*).—**day after to-morrow.** Après-demain: a″prē′ də-maṅ′.—**day before yesterday.** Avant-hier: a″vaṅ″tī″‿yēr′.—**day of month.** Jour du mois: ʒūr dü mwā.—**day of week.** Jour de la semaine: ʒūr də la sə-māṅ′.—**next day** (*n. m.*). Lendemain: laṅ″də-maṅ′.—**day's march.** Étape (*n. f.*): ē″tāp′‿ə.—**two days ago.** Il y a deux jours: īl ya du ʒūr.—**what day of the week is it?** Quel jour de la semaine sommes-nous? kel ʒūr də la sə-māṅ′ som′‿mə nū.—**what is the day of the month?** Quel jour du mois sommes-nous? kel ʒūr dü mwā som′‿mə nū.

daybreak, *n.* Point du jour: pwaṅ dü ʒūr.—**after daybreak.** Après le lever du jour: a″prē′ lə lə-vē′ dü ʒūr.—**at daybreak.** Au point du jour: ō pwaṅ dü ʒūr.

daylight, *n.* Jour (*m.*): ʒūr.—**before daylight.** Avant le jour: a″vaṅ′ lə ʒūr.—**broad d.** Grand jour: graṅ ʒūr.

dead, *a.* Mort (*m.*): mōr; morte (*f.*): mōrt.—**he is dead.** Il est mort: il ē mōr.—**to bury the d.** Enterrer les morts: aṅ″tār″‿rē′ lē mōr.

deaf, *a.* Sourd (*m.*): sūr; sourde (*f.*): sūrd.

deal. **I.** *n. m.* Sapin: sa″paṅ′ (*the wood*). **II.** *v.* Agir: a″ʒīr′.—**to deal with any violations.** Statuer sur toutes les infractions: sta″tü″ē′ sür tūt′‿ə lēz‿aṅ″frak″sī″‿yoṅ.—**to d. with the following points.** Mentionner les points suivants: maṅ″sī″‿yoṅ″‿nē′ lē pwaṅ swī″vāṅ′.

dear, *a.* Cher (*m.*); chère (*f.*): shār.—**it is dear.** C'est cher: sē shār.—**it is very d.** C'est très cher: sē trē shār.—**it is too d.** C'est trop cher: sē trō shār.—**not too d.** Pas trop cher: pā trō shār.

death. Mort (*n. f.*): mōr.

debark, *v.* Débarquer: dē″bar″kē′.

debt. Dette (*n. f.*): det′‿tə.

deceitful, *a.* Trompeur (*m.*): troṅ″pūr′; trompeuse (*f.*): troṅ″pūz′.

deceive, *v.* **1.** Tromper: troṅ″pē′. **2.** Décevoir: dē″sə-vwār′.

December. Décembre (*n. m.*): dē″sāṅ′‿brə.

decide, *v.* Décider: dē″sī″dē′.—**he has decided on offensive action.** Il s'est décidé pour l'offensive: il sē dē″sī″dē′ pūr lof″‿faṅ″sīv′.—**to decide on the number.** Fixer le nombre: fīk″‿sē′ lə noṅ′‿brə.

decimal. Décimale (*n. f.*): dē″sī″māl′.—**the decimal system** Le système décimal: lə sīs″tēm′ dē′sī″māl.

decision. Décision (*n. f.*): dē″sī″zī″‿yoṅ′.

ī = habit; aisle; au = *out*; oil; iū = feud; diine; chin; go; ŋ = si*ng*; ship; thin; this.

decisive, *a.* Décisif (*m.*): dē″sī″sīf′; décisive (*f.*): dē″sī″sīv′.—**to deliver the decisive attack.** Prononcer l'attaque décisive: pro″noṅ″sē′ lat″‿tāk′ dē″sī″sīv′.

deck. Pont (*n. m.*): poṅ.—**fore deck.** Gaillard d'avant (*m.*): gai″yār′ da″vāṅ′.—**lower d.** Entrepont (*m.*): aṅ″‿trə-poṅ′.—**main d.** Pont supérieur: poṅ sü″pē″rī″‿yūr′.—**quarter d.** Gaillard d'arrière (*m.*): gai″yār′ dar″‿rī″‿yār′.—**second d.** Pont inférieur: poṅ aṅ″fē″rī″‿yūr′.—**upper d.** Pont supérieur: poṅ sü″pē″rī″‿yūr′.

declaration. Déclaration (*n. f.*): dē″kla″ra″sī″‿yoṅ′.—**Declaration of London.** Déclaration de Londres: dē″kla″ra″sī″‿yoṅ′ də Loṅ′‿drə (agreement of the Great Powers as to blockades, contraband of war, etc., proposed in 1909).—**d. of war.** Déclaration de guerre: dē″kla″ra″sī″‿yoṅ də gār.

decline. **I.** *n. f.* Descente: des″‿sāṅt′. **II.** *v.* Décliner: dē″klī″nē′.—**steep decline.** Descente rapide: des″‿sāṅt′ ra″pīd′.—**tortuous d. with sharp turns.** Descente sinueuse avec mauvais virage: des″‿sāṅt′ sī″nü″ūz′ a″vek′ mō″vē′ vī″rāʒ′.

declivity, *n.* **1.** Descente (*f.*): des″saṅt′. **2.** Coteau (*m.*): ko″tō′. On maps *Cot.* **3.** Pente (*f.*): pāṅt. [*automobile term*).

declutch, *v.* Débrayer: dē″brā″yē′ (*to release the clutch of:*

decoration. Décoration (*n. f.*): dē″kōr″a″sī″‿yoṅ′.

deed, *n.* **1.** Action (*f.*): ak″sī″‿yoṅ′. **2.** Fait (*m.*): fē.

deep, *a.* Profond (*m.*): pro″foṅ′, profonde (*f.*): pro″foṅd′.—**deep-set,** *a.* Enfoncé (*m.*); enfoncée (*f.*): aṅ″foṅ″sē′ (*said of the eyes: a mark of identification*).

default, *v.* Faire défaut: fār dē″fō′.—**in default of.** A défaut de: a dē″fō′ də.—**defaulter,** *n.* **1.** Défaillant (*m.*): dē″fai″yāṅ′ (*one who has broken the law, civil or military*). **2.** Insoumis (*m.*): aṅ″sū″mī′ (*one who refuses to join the colors when called*).

defeat. Défaite (*n. f.*): dē″fāt′.—**a crushing defeat.** Une déroute: ün dē″rūt′.

defend, *v.* Défendre: dē″fāṅ′‿drə.—**we are to defend.** Nous allons défendre: nūz‿al″‿loṅ′ dē″fāṅ′‿drə.

defense. Défense (*n. f.*): dē″fāṅs′.—**accessory means of defense.** Défenses accessoires: dē″fāṅs′‿aks″‿ses″‿swār′.—**coast defenses.** Défenses côtières: dē″fāṅs′ kō″tī″yār′.—**inner d.** Défenses intérieures: dē″fāṅs′‿aṅ″tē″rī″‿yūr′.—**national d.** Défense nationale (*n. f.*): dē″fāṅs′ na″sī″‿yoṅ″āl′.—**permanent d.** Défenses permanentes: dē″fāṅs′ pār″ma″nāṅt′.—**provisional d.** Défenses provisoires: dē″fāṅs′ prō″vī″zwār′.—**system of general defense.** Système général de défense (*m.*): sīs″tēm′ ʒē″nē″rāl′ də dē″fāṅs′.—**to put in a state of d.** Mettre en état de défense: met′‿trə aṅ ē″tā′ də dē″fāṅs′.

defensive, *a.* Défensif (*m.*): dē″faṅ″sīf′; défensive (*f.*): dē″faṅ″sīv′.—**defensive works.** Travaux militaires: tra″vō′ mī″lī″tār′.—**on the d.** Sur la défensive: sür la dē″faṅ″sīv′.—**to occupy a d. position.** Occuper une position défensive: ok″kü″pē′ ün po″zī″sī″‿yoṅ′ dē″faṅ″sīv′.

deficiency. Manque (*n. m.*): māṅk; défaut (*m.*): dē″fō′.

defilade. Défiler (*v.*): dē″fī″le′ (*protect from enfilade*).

defile. **I.** *n.* Défilé (*m.*): dē″fī″lē′ (*a narrow pass*). On maps *Défé.* **II.** *v.* Défiler: dē″fī″lē′ (*march in single file*).—**command a defile.** Commander un défilé: kom″maṅ″dē′ aṅ dē″fī″lē′.—**to pass through a d.** Passer un défilé: pas″‿sē′ aṅ dē″fī″lē′.

deflate, *v.* Dégonfler: dē″goṅ″flē′.

deflection. Dérive (*n. f.*): dē″rīv′.

degree. Degré (*n. m.*): də-grē′.—**degree of education.** Degré d'instruction: də-grē′ daṅ″strük″sī″‿yoṅ′.

dejected, *a.* Abattu (*m.*), abattue (*f.*): a″bat″tü′.

dekko, dek′o, *n.* [Eng. soldiers' slang.] Look (at something). Regardez: rə-gar″dē′.

delay. **I.** *n.* **1.** Délai (*m.*): dē″lē′. **2.** Retard (*m.*): rə-tār′.

II. *v.* Retarder: rə-tar"dē'.—**with as little delay as possible.** Avec le moins de retard possible: a"vek' lə mwaṅ də rə-tār' pos"‿sī"‿blə.—**without d.** Sans retard: saṅ rə-tār'.—**the advance may be delayed.** La marche en avant peut être retardée: la mārsh aṅ a"vāṅ' pöt‿ā'‿trə rə-tar"dē'.

Delcassé, Theophile, del"kas"‿sē', tē"o"fil'. French statesman.

deliver, *v.* Distribuer: dis"trī"bü"ē'.—**to deliver** or **make an attack,** or **an assault.** Livrer une attaque, un assaut: lī"vrē' ün at"‿tāk', aṅ as"‿sō'.—**to d. up a fortress to the enemy.** Livrer une place à l'ennemi: lī"vrē' ün plas a len"nə-mī'.

delivery, *n.* **1.** Livraison (*f.*): lī"vrā"zoṅ'. **2.** Distribution (*f.*): dis"trī"bü"sī"‿yoṅ'.—**delivery of stores.** Distribution des approvisionnements: dis"trī"bü"sī"‿yoṅ' dēz‿ap"‿prō"vī"sī"‿yoṅ"‿nə-māṅ'.

dell, *n.* Creux (*m.*): krū; vallon (*m.*): val"‿loṅ'.

demand. I. *n. f.* Demande: də-māṅd'. **II.** *v.* **1.** Demander: də-maṅ"dē'. **2.** Réclamer: rē"kla"mē'.

démarche, dē"mārsh', *n. f.* A change in method of action or procedure.

demilune. Demilune (*n. f.*): də-mī"lün' (ravelin-like outwork).

demolish, *v.* Abattre: a"bat'trə.

denial. Dénégation (*n. f.*): dē"nē"ga"sī"‿yoṅ'.

denounce, *v.* Dénoncer: dē"noṅ"sē'.

dentist. Dentiste (*n. m.*): daṅ"tist'.

deny, *v.* **1.** Nier: nī"ē'. **2.** Dénier: dē"nī"ē'. **3.** Interdire à: aṅ"tār"dīr' a.

depart, *v.* Partir: par"tīr'.—**departure.** Départ (*n. m.*): dē"pār'.

department. Département (*n. m.*): dē"par"‿tə-māṅ'. Abbreviated *Dépt.*—**department of charities.** Département de bienfaisance: dē"par"tə-māṅ' də bī"‿yaṅ"fā"zaṅs'.

depend, *v.* Dépendre: dē"pāṅ'‿drə.—**depend on.** Compter sur: koṅ"tē' sür.—**that depends.** Cela dépend: sə-lā' dē"pāṅ'.

deploy, *v.* Se déployer: sə dē"plwa"yē'.

deploying. Déploiement (*n. m.*): dē"plwa"māṅ'.

depot. Dépôt (*n. m.*): dē"pō'. The term is used generally for a storehouse, recruiting-station, barracks, or base of supplies. In the French army there are in addition: **dépôts de convalescents** (dē"pō' də koṅ"va"les"āṅt); **dépôts de remonte** (dē"pō' də rə-moṅt'), for remounts; **dépôts de tranchées** (dē"pō' də traṅ"shē'), for tools and material used in siege operations.—**ordnance depot.** Dépôt de matériel de guerre: dē"pō' də ma"tē"rī"‿yel' də gār.—**regimental d. 1.** Dépôt de régiment: dē"pō' də rē"ʒī-māṅ'. **2.** Portion centrale (*f.*): pōr"sī"‿yoṅ' saṅ"trāl'.—**staff central motor d.** Dépôt de matériel automobile et personnel: dē"pō' də ma"tē"rī"‿yel' ō"tō"mō"bīl' ē pār"soṅ"‿nel'.

depth. Profondeur (*n. f.*): prō"foṅ"dūr'.

depute, *v.* **1.** Députer: dē"pü"tē'. **2.** Charger: shār"ʒē'.

deputy. 1. Adjoint (*m.*): a"ʒwaṅ'. **2.** Député (*m.*): dē"pü"tē'.

derrick. Mât de charge (*n. m.*): mā də shārʒ.—**to rig a derrick. 1.** Gréer un mât de charge: grē"ē' aṅ mā də shārʒ. **2.** Pousser une vergue en bataille: pūs"‿sē' ün vār"‿gə aṅ ba"tal'‿yə.

descend, *v.* Descendre: des"‿saṅ'‿drə.

description, *n.* **1.** Description (*f.*): des"krip"sī"‿yoṅ'. **2.** Signalement (*m.*): sī"nya"‿lə-māṅ' (*identification*).

desert, *v.* Déserter: dē"zār"tē'.—**deserter.** Déserteur (*n. m.*): dē"zār"tūr'.—**desertion, deserting.** Désertion (*n. f.*): dē"zār"sī"‿yoṅ'.

deserve, *v.* Mériter: mē"rī"tē'.

desire. I. *n. m.* Désir: dē″zīr′. II. *v.* Désirer: dē″zī″rē′.
despatch, *n.* & *v.* See DISPATCH.
destroy, *v.* **1.** Détruire: dē″trwīr′. **2.** Ruiner: rü″ī″nē′. **3.** Perdre: pār′‿drə.—**destroyer,** *n.* **1.** Destructeur (*m.*): des″trük″tūr′ (*one who destroys*). **2.** Croiseur-torpilleur (*m.*): krwa″zūr′ tōr″pī″yūr′ (*vessel of war*). [*fighting*).
desultory, *a.* Décousu (*m.*), décousue (*f.*): dē″kū″sü′ (*of*
detach. Détacher (*v.*): dē″ta″shē′.—**detached,** *pa.* Détaché (*m.*), détachée (*f.*): dē″ta″shē′.
detachment. Détachement (*n. m.*): dē″tash″mān′.
detail. I. *n. m.* Détail: dē″tai′‿yə. II. *v.* **1.** Détacher: dē″tash″ē′. **2.** Fournir: fūr″nīr′. **3.** Affecter: af″‿fek″tē′.—**in detail.** Minutieusement: mī″nü″sī″‿yūz″mān′.—**to enter** or **go into details.** Entrer dans les détails: an″trē′ dan lē dē″tai′.
detain, *v.* **1.** Arrêter: ar″‿rē″tē′. **2.** Retenir: rə-tə-nīr′.
detective. Agent de la police de sûreté (*n. m.*): a″ʒān′ də la pō″līs′ də sür″tē′.
detonator, *n.* **1.** Détonateur (*m.*): dē″tə″na″tūr′. **2.** Amorce fulminante (*f.*): a″mōrs′ fül″mī″nānt′.
detrainment, *n.* **1.** Débarquement (*m.*): dē″bar″‿kə-mān′. **2.** Descente du train (*f.*): dēs″sānt′ dü tran.—**detraining-station.** Gare de débarquement (*n. f.*): gār də dē″bar″‿kə-mān′.
devastate. Dévaster (*v.*): dē″vās″tē′.
develop. Développer (*v.*): dē″və-lōp″pē′.—**development.** Développement (*n. m.*): dē″və-lōp″‿pə-mān′.
diachylon, diachylum. Diachylon (*n. m.*): dī″ā″kī″lōn′ (*a plaster of lead-oxid, olive oil, and water*).
dial. Cadran (*n. m.*): ka″drān′.
dial-sight. Goniomètre (*n. m.*): gō″nī″ō″mē′‿trə.
diary. Journal (*n. m.*): ʒūr″nāl′.—**weekly diary.** Semainier: (*n. m.*): se″mē″nī″‿yē′.
dictionary. Dictionnaire (*n. m.*): dīk″sī″‿yən″‿nār′.
die, *v.* Mourir: mū″rīr′.—**to die bravely.** Mourir bravement: mū″rīr′ brav″mān′.—**to die hard.** Lutter contre la mort: lüt″‿tē′ kōn′‿trə la mōr.
difference. Différence (*n. f.*): dīf″fē″rāns′.—**to pay the difference.** Faire l'appoint: fār lap″pwan′.—**to split the difference.** Partager le différend: par″ta″ʒē′ lə dīf″‿fē″rān′.
different, *a.* Différent (*m.*): dīf″‿fē″rān′; différente (*f.*): dīf″‿fē″rānt′.
differential. Différentiel (*n. m.*): dīf″‿fē″ran″sī″‿yel′.
difficult, *a.* Difficile (*m.* & *f.*): dīf″‿fī″sīl′.—**difficulty,** *n.* **1.** Difficulté (*f.*): dīf″fī″kül″tē′. **2.** Peine (*f.*): pēn.—**to overcome a difficulty.** Sauter par-dessus une difficulté: sō″tē′ par-də-sü′ ün dīf″‿fī″kül″tē′.—**without difficulty.** Sans peine: san pēn.
dig. Creuser (*v.*): krū″ʒē′.—**to dig a trench.** Creuser une tranchée: krū″zē′ ün tran″shē′.—**to dig in.** Retrancher: rə-tran″shē′ (*intrench*).—**to dig open.** Ouvrir: ū″vrīr′.—**to dig out.** Déterrer: dē″tār″‿rē′.—**to dig through.** Percer: pār″sē′.
Dijon, dī″ʒōn′, *n.* French city.
dimple. Fossette (*n. f.*): fōs″‿sēt′. Used in identification.
dine. Dîner (*v.*): dī″nē′.—**dining-car.** Wagon-restaurant (*n. m.*): va″gōn′ res″tō″rān′.—**d.-room,** *n.* Salle à manger: sāl a man″ʒē′.—**dinner.** Dîner (*n. m.*): dī″nē′.—**dinner-halt,** *n.* Grand'-halte: grand″halt′.—**d.-time,** *n.* L'heure du dîner: lūr dü dī″nē′.—**d. is served.** Le dîner est prêt: lə dī″nē′ ē prē. In soldiers' slang, "*dinner up*."—**to sit down to d.** Se mettre à table: sə met′‿trə a tā′‿blə.
dip, *v.* Piquer: pī″kē′ (*with an aeroplane*).
direct, *v.* **1.** Diriger: dī″rī″ʒē′. **2.** Indiquer: an″dī″kē′.

direction. Direction (*n. f.*): dī"rek"sī"‿yoṅ'.—**in a direction toward.** Vers: vār.—**in all directions.** De tous côtés: də tū kō"tē'.
dirigible (*balloon*). Dirigeable (*n. m.*): dī"rī"ʒā'‿blə.
dirk, *n.* Poignard (*m.*): pwa"nyār'.
dirty, *a.* Sale (*m. & f.*): sāl.
disable, *v.* **1.** Rendre incapable: raṅ'‿drə aṅ"ka"pā'‿blə. **2.** Mettre hors de combat: met'‿trə hōr də koṅ"bā'.—**to disable a gun.** Démonter une piece: dē"moṅ"tē' ün pī"‿yēs'.
disappear, *v.* Disparaître: dīs"pa"rā'‿trə.—**disappearing carriage.** Affût disparaissant (*m.*): af"‿fü' dīs"par"ās"‿sāṅ'.
disarm, *v.* Désarmer: dē"zār"mē'.
disaster. **1.** Débâcle (*n. f.*): dē"bā'‿klə. **2.** Malheur (*n. m.*): ma"lūr'. **3.** Désastre (*n. f.*): dē"zās'‿trə.
disband, *v.* Se débander: sə dē"baṅ"dē'.
discharge. **I.** *n.* **1.** Décharge (*f.*): dē"shār'‿ʒə. **2.** Accomplissement (*m.*): ak"koṅ"plīs"sə-māṅ'. **II.** *v.* **1.** Réformer: rē"fōr"mē' (*to retire from the army as physically unfit*). **2.** Libérer: lī"bē"rē' (*to discharge on completion of military service*).—**in the discharge of his duties.** Dans l'exécution de son service: daṅ lēg"zē"kü"sī"‿yoṅ' də soṅ sār"vīs'.
discipline. Discipline (*n. f.*): dī"sī"plī'‿nə.—**discipline is a powerful aid.** La discipline est une aide puissante: la dī"sī"plīn' ēt‿ün‿ē'‿də pwīs"‿sāṅt'.
discourage, *v.* Décourager: dē"kū"ra"ʒē'.
disease. Maladie (*n. f.*): ma"la"dī'.—**infectious disease.** Maladie infectieuse: ma"la"dī' aṅ"fek"sī"‿yūz'.
disembark, *v.* Débarquer: dē"bar"kē'.—**disembarkation.** Débarquement (*n. m.*): dē"bar"‿kə-māṅ'.—**point of disembarkation.** Point de débarquement (*n. m.*): pwaṅ də dē"bar"‿kə-māṅ'.
disguise. **I.** *n. m.* Déguisement: dē"gī"zə-māṅ'. **II.** *v.* **1.** Déguiser: dē"gī"zē'. **2.** Cacher: ka"shē'.
dish. Plat (*n. m.*): plā.
disheartened, *a.* Découragé (*m.*); découragée (*f.*): dē"kū"ra"ʒē'.
disinfect, *v.* Désinfecter: dē"zaṅ"fek"tē'.—**disinfectant.** Désinfectant (*n. m.*): dē"zaṅ"fek"tāṅ'.—**disinfecting,** *a.* Désinfectan (*m.*): dē"zaṅ"fek"tāṅ'; désinfectante (*f.*): dē"zaṅ"fek"tāṅt'.—**disinfecting fluid.** Désinfectant (*n. m.*): dē"zaṅ"fek"tāṅ'.
disk, *n.* **1.** Disque (*m.*): dīsk. **2.** Plaque (*f.*): plāk'.—**identification or identity disk.** Plaque d'identité: plāk dī"daṅ"tī"tē'.—**signal-disk.** Disque signal (*n. m.*): dīsk sī"‿nyāl'.
dislocated, *a.* Disloqué (*m.*); disloquée (*f.*): dīs"lō"kē'.
dislodge, *v.* Débusquer: dē"büs"kē'.
dismantle, *v.* **1.** Démanteler: dē"maṅ"tə-lē'. **2.** Désarmer: dēz"ar"mē'. **3.** Écrêter: ē"krā"tē' (*with shot*).—**dismantlement.** Démantèlement (*n. m.*): dē"maṅ"tēl"māṅ'.
dismiss, *v.* **1.** Renvoyer: raṅ"vwa"yē'. **2.** Congédier: koṅ"ʒē"dī"‿yē'.—**dismiss!** Rompez! roṅ"pē' (*military command*).
dismount, *v.* Descendre de cheval: dē"sāṅ'‿drə də shə-vāl'.—**dismount!** Pied à terre! pī"yēd'‿a tār.
disorder. Désordre (*n. m.*): dē"ʒor'‿drə.
dispatch. **I.** *n.* **1.** Envoi (*m.*): aṅ"vwā'. **2.** Dépêche (*f.*): dē"pāsh'. **II.** *v.* **1.** Expédier: eks"pē"dī"‿yē'. **2.** Envoyer: aṅ"vwa"yē'.—**carry dispatches.** Porter des dépêches: pōr"tē' dē dē"pāsh.—**dispatch-rider,** *n.* Estafette (*f.*): es"ta"fet'.—**to d. a troop.** Expédier une troupe: eks"pē"dī"‿yē' ün trūp.—**with the utmost d.** Au plus vite possible: ō plü vīt pos"‿sī'‿blə.
disperse, *v.* Disperser: dīs"pār"sē'.
display, *n.* **1.** Étalage (*m.*): ē"tal"āʒ'. **2.** Déploiement (*m.*): dē"plwa"māṅ' (*of troops*).

disposal. Disposition (*n. f.*): dīs″pō″zī″sī″‿yeṅ′.—**at the disposal of.** À la disposition de: a la dīs″pō″zī″sī″‿yeṅ′ də.
dispose, *v.* **1.** Disposer: dīs″pō″zē′. **2.** Arranger: ar″‿raṅ″-ʒē′.—**to dispose of.** Se débarrasser de: sə dē″bar″‿ras″sē′ də.—**disposition,** *n.* **1.** Disposition (*f.*): dīs″pō″zī″sī″‿yeṅ′. **2.** Dispositif (*m.*): dīs″pō″zī″tīf′.—**detailed dispositions.** Dispositions de détail: dīs″pō″zī″sī″‿yeṅ′ də dē″tai′.
dispute. I. *n.* **1.** Dispute (*f.*): dīs″püt′. **2.** Débat (*m.*): dē″bā′. **II.** *v.* Disputer: dīs″pü″tē′.—**to dispute every inch of ground.** Disputer chaque pouce de terrain: dīs″pü″tē′ shāk pūs də tār″‿raṅ′.
distance, *n.* **1.** Distance (*f.*): dīs″tāṅ′‿sə. **2.** Éloignement (*m.*): ēl″wa″‿nyə-māṅ′.—**a long distance.** Une grande distance: ün graṅ′‿də dīs″tāṅ′‿sə.—**hearing d., speaking d.** À portée de la voix: a pēr″tē′ də la vwā.—**regulation d.** Distance réglementaire (*f.*): dīs″tāṅ′‿sə rē″‿glə-maṅ″tār′.—**short d.** Peu de distance: pu də dīs″tāṅ″‿sə.—**to be at a d.** Être à distance: ā′‿trə a dīs″tāṅ′‿sə.—**to come within striking d.** En venir à portée de: aṅ və-nīr′ a pēr″tē′ də—**to increase the d.** Augmenter la distance: ōg″maṅ″tē′ la dīs″tāṅ′‿sə.—**to keep the enemy at a d.** Tenir l'ennemi à distance: tə-nīr′ len″‿nə-mī′ a dīs″tāṅ′‿sə.
distillery. Distillerie (*n. f.*): dīs″tīl″‿lə-rī′. Abbrev. *Distie.*
distinctively, *adv.* Distinctivement: dīs″taṅk″tī″‿və-māṅ′.
distinguish, *v.* Distinguer: dīs″taṅ″gē′.—**distinguished,** *a.* Distingué (*m.*); distinguée (*f.*): dīs″taṅ″gē′.
distress, *n.* **1.** Détresse (*f.*): dē″tres′‿sə. **2.** Douleur (*f.*): dū″lūr′.
distribute, *v.* Distribuer: dīs″trī″bü″ē′.—**distribution.** Distribution (*n. f.*): dīs″trī″bü″sī″‿yeṅ′.—**distribution of fire.** Dispersion du tir: dīs″pār″sī″yeṅ′ dü tīr.—**d. of the garrison.** Répartition de la garnison: rē″par″tī″sī″yeṅ′ də la gar″nī″zeṅ′.
district. I. *a.* Cantonal (*m.*); cantonale (*f.*): kaṅ″teṅ″āl′. On maps *Cantal.* **II.** *n.* Canton (*m.*): kaṅ″teṅ′. .On maps *Cant.*
distrust, *v.* Se méfier de: sə mē″fī″‿yē′ də.
ditch. Fossé (*n. m.*): fes″‿sē′. Abbrev. *Fsé.*—**broad ditches.** Larges fossés: lar′‿ʒə fes″‿sē′.—**crossed by d.** Traversé par fossés: tra″vār″sē′ pār fes″‿sē′.
dive, *v.* **1.** Piquer: pī″kē′ (*aeronautical term*). **2.** Plonger: pleṅ″ʒē (*aeronautical term*).
divide, *v.* Diviser: dī″vī″zē′.—**division.** Division (*n. f.*): dī″vī″zī″‿yeṅ′.—**a division is formed of brigades.** Une division est formée de brigades: ün dī″vī″zī″‿yeṅ′ ē fēr″mē′ də brī″gād′‿ə.
dixie. Gamelle de campement (*f.*): ga″mel′‿lə də kaṅ″‿pə-māṅ′ (*a two-handled cooking-pot: soldiers' slang*).
do, *v.* Faire: fār.
dock. Bassin (*n. m.*): bas″‿saṅ′.—**dry dock. 1.** Bassin d'échouage: bas″‿saṅ′ dē″shū″āʒ′. **2.** Bassin de radoub: bas″‿saṅ′ də ra″dūb′.—**d.-master.** Directeur des bassins (*n. m.*): dī″rek″tūr′ dē bas″‿saṅ′.—**floating d.** Bassin à flot: bas″‿saṅ a flō.—**docker.** Ouvrier du port (*n. m.*): ū″vrī″‿yē′ dü pēr.
dockyard. L'arsenal maritime (*n.*): lar″sə-nāl′ ma″rī″tīm′.
doctor. Médecin (*n. m.*): mē″‿də-saṅ′.—**fetch the doctor.** Cherchez le médecin: shār″shē′ lə mē″‿də-saṅ′.—**send for the d.** Envoyez chercher le médecin: aṅ″vwa″‿yē′ shār″shē′ lə mē″‿də-saṅ′.
document. Document (*n. m.*): de″kü″maṅ′.—**forged document.** Faux en écriture (*n. m.*): fō aṅ ē″krī″tür′.
dog. Chien (*n. m.*): shī″‿yaṅ′.
done, *pa.* Fait (*m.*): fē; faite (*f.*): fēt.
donkey. Âne (*n. m.*): ā′‿nə.—**donkey-engine.** Pompe alimentaire (*n. f.*): peṅ′‿pə a″lī″maṅ″tār′.

don't you think so? 1. N'est ce pas? nē‿sə pā. 2. N'est-il pas vrai? nē til pā vrē.

door. Porte (*n. f.*): pōr'‿tə.—**at death's door.** Aux portes du tombeau: ō pōr'‿tə dü toṅ"bō'.—**front d.** Porte d'entrée: pōr'‿tə daṅ"trē'.—**next d.** 1. À côté: a kō"tē'. 2. Porte à porte: pōrt‿a pōr'‿tə.—**indoors,** *adv.* 1. À la maison: a la mē"zoṅ'. 2. Chez soi: shē swā.—**out of doors.** 1. Hors de la maison: hōr də la mē"zoṅ'. 2. Dehors: də‿hōr'.

doss. Sommeil (*n. m.*): som"‿mē'‿yə (*sleep: soldiers' slang*).

double. Double (*n. m.*): dū'‿blə.—**double time.** Pas de charge: pā də shārʒ'‿ə.—**to march at the double.** Marcher au pas redoublé: mar"shē' ō pā rə-dū"blē'.

doubt. Doute (*n. m.*): dūt'‿ə.

down, *adv.* En bas: aṅ bā.—**get down!** Descendez! dē"saṅ"dē'.—**downcast,** *a.* Abattu (*m.*); abattue (*f.*): a"bat"‿tü'.—**downhill.** En descendant: aṅ dē"saṅ"dāṅ'.—**down stream, down the stream.** En aval: aṅ‿a"vāl'.—**lower down the stream.** Plus bas en aval: plü bā aṅ‿a"vāl'.

down. Dune (*n. f.*): dü'‿nə (*grassy hill*).

downward, *adv.* Vers le bas: vār lə bā.

dozen. Douzaine (*n. f.*): dū"zēn'‿ə.

draft, *n.* 1. Conscription (*f.*): koṅ"skrīp"sī"yoṅ' (*the choosing by lot of men for army service*). 2. Détachement (*m.*): dē"tash"-māṅ' (*a group or body of men*). 3. Plan (*m.*): plaṅ (*a sketch, drawing*). 4. Courant d'air (*m.*): kū"rāṅ' dār (*current of air*). 5. Mandat (*m.*): maṅ"dā' (*check*).

draft, *v.* Rédiger: rē"dī"ʒē' (*to draw up, as a report*).

drag, drag-shoe. Sabot (*n. m.*): sa"bō'.

dragoon. Dragon (*n. m.*): dra"goṅ'.

drain. I. *n.* 1. Rigole (*f.*): rī"gōl'‿ə (*culvert*). 2. Tranchée (*f.*): traṅ"shē'. II. *v.* Assécher: as"‿sē"shē'.—**drainage.** Écoulement (*n. m.*): ē"kū"‿lə-māṅ'.

draper. Marchand de drap (*n. m.*): mar"shāṅ' də drā.

draw, *v.* 1. Tirer: tī"rē' (*in general sense*). 2. Dessiner: dēs"‿sī"nē' (*with a pencil*). 3. Porter: pōr"tē' (*of sails*).—**to d. near.** S'approcher de: sap"‿prō"shē' də.—**to d. the enemy's attention.** Attirer l'attention de l'ennemi: at"‿tī"rē' lat"‿taṅ"sī"yoṅ' də len"nə-mī'.—**to d. up.** Dresser (*v.*): dres"‿sē' (*as articles of agreement, etc.*).—**to d. up a plan of defense.** Établir un plan de défense: ē"tab"līr' aṅ plaṅ də dē"fāṅs'.

drawback, *n.* 1. Remise (*f.*): rə-mīz' (*delay*). 2. Désavantage (*m.*): dē"za"vaṅ"tāʒ'.

drawbridge, *n.* 1. Levis (*m.*): lə-vī'. Abbrev. *Lev.* 2. Pont-levis (*m.*): poṅ lə-vī'. 3. Pont à bascule: poṅ a bas"kül'.

drawers. Caleçon (*n. m.*): ka"lə-soṅ'.

drawn, *a.* Égal (*m.*): égale (*f.*): ē"gāl'.—**drawn battle.** Bataille indécise: ba"tai'‿yə aṅ"dē"sīz'.—**d. game.** Partie nulle (*n. f.*): par"tī' nül.

dread. I. *n.* 1. Crainte (*f.*): kraṅ'‿tə. 2. Effroi (*m.*): ef"‿frwā'. II. *v.* 1. Craindre: kraṅ'‿drə. 2. Redouter: rə-dū"tē'.

dreadful, *a.* 1. Terrible (*m. & f.*) ter"rī'blə. 2. Épouvantable (*m. & f.*): ē"pū"vaṅ"tāb'‿lə.

dreadnought. Cuirassé (*n. m.*): kwīr"as"‿sē'. The English word has, however, been taken over by the French, and is pronounced dred"nāt'. See *Larousse Mensuel*, 1911–13, p. 181.

dredge. I. *n.* Drague (*f.*): drāg'‿ə. II. *v.* Draguer: dra"gē'.—**dredger.** Drague (*n. f.*): drāg'‿ə.

dress. 1. Tenue (*n. f.*): tə"nü'. 2. Alignement: a"lī"‿nyə-māṅ'.—**in full dress.** En grande tenue: aṅ graṅd tə-nü'.—**in service d.** En tenue de campagne: aṅ tə-nü' də kaṅ"pa'‿nyə.

dress, *v.* 1. Habiller: a"bī"yē' (*of clothing*). 2. Panser: paṅ"sē' (*of a wound*).—**please dress my wound.** Pansez ma blessure, s'il vous plaît: paṅ"sē' ma bles"‿sür', sil vū plē.—**to d.**

a wound. Faire un pansement: fār aṅ paṅ″sə‿māṅ′.—**right, dress!** See under RIGHT.

dressing, *n.* **1.** Alignement d'une troupe: ɑ″lī″‿nyə-māṅ′ dün trūp (*of military ranks*). **2.** Pansement (*m.*): paṅ″sə‿māṅ′ (*of wounds*). **3.** Appareil (*m.*): ɑp″‿pɑ″rē′yə (*of wounds*). **4.** Toilette (*f.*): twɑ″let′ (*toilet*).—**field-dressing,** *n.* Pansement de campagne: paṅ″‿sə-māṅ′ də kaṅ″pɑ′‿nyə.

dressing-station, *n.* Poste de secours, de pansement: pōst də sə‿kūr′, də paṅ″‿sə-māṅ′.—**advanced dressing-station.** Ambulance divisionnaire: aṅ″bü″laṅs′ di″vīs″‿yeṅ″‿nār′.

drift, *n.* Dérive (*f.*): dē″rīv′.—**drift,** *v.* Déraper: dē″rā″pē′ (*of aeroplanes in the air*).

drill. **I.** *n.* Exercice (*m.*): eg″zār″sīs′. **II.** *v.* Exercer: eg″zār″sē′; faire l'exercice: fār leg″zār″sīs′.—**in drill order.** En tenue d'exercice: aṅ tə-nü′ deg″zār″sīs′.—**physical d.** Exercice d'assouplissement: eg″zār″sīs′ dɑs″‿sū″plīs″‿sə‿māṅ′ (*setting-up exercises*).—**to put through d.** Faire faire l'exercice: fār fār eg″zār″sīs′.

drink, *v.* Boire: bwɑr.—**is there time for a drink?** Y-a-t'il le temps à boire quelque chose?: ī ɑ-tīl lə taṅ ɑ bwār kel′kə shōz.—**let us d. a glass of wine.** Buvons un verre de vin: bü″veṅz′‿aṅ vār də vaṅ.—**please give me a d.** Donnez-moi à boire, s'il vous plaît: deṅ″nē′ mwɑ ɑ bwār, sīl vū plē.—**something to d.** Quelque chose à boire: kel′kə shōz ɑ bwār. Sometimes contracted to *à boire*.

drinking-water. Eau potable (*n. m.*): ō pō″tā′blə.

drive, *v.* **1.** Chasser: shɑs″sē′. **2.** Conduire: keṅ″dwīr′.——**to drive off or out.** Chasser hors de: shɑs″‿sē′ hōr də; renvoyer: raṅ″vwɑ″yē′.—**to d. back.** Repousser (*v.*): rə-pūs″‿sē′.

driven by. Actionné par: ɑk″sī″‿yeṅ″‿nē′ pār.

driver, *n.* **1.** Canonnier-conducteur (*m.*): kɑ″neṅ″‿nyē′ keṅ″dük″tūr′. Sometimes contracted to *conducteur*. **2.** Chauffeur (*m.*): shō″fūr′. **3.** Pilote (*m.*): pī″lōt′. **4.** Mécanicien (*m.*): mē″kɑ″nī″sī″aṅ′.

driving-band, *n.* Ceinture (*n. f.*): saṅ″tür′.

drop. **I.** *n.* **1.** Goutte (*f.*): gūt′‿ə. **2.** Chute (*f.*): shüt′‿ə (*fall*). **II.** *v.* **1.** Jeter: ʒə-tē′ (*throw down, as a bomb*). **2.** Laisser tomber: lēs″sē′ teṅ″bē′ (*let fall*). **3.** Tomber: teṅ″bē′ (*fall*).

drug. Drogue (*n. f.*): drōg′‿ə.—**druggist,** *n.* **1.** Pharmacien (*m.*): fɑr″mɑ″sī″‿yaṅ′. **2.** Droguiste (*m.*): drō″gīst′.—**where is the druggist's?** Où est le pharmacien? ū ē lə fɑr″mɑ″sī″‿yaṅ′.

drum. **I.** *n.* **1.** Tambour (*m.*): taṅ″būr′ (*musical instrument*). **2.** Tympan (*m.*): taṅ″paṅ′ (*of the ear*). **II.** *v.* **1.** Faire le tambour: fār lə taṅ″būr′. **2.** Battre le tambour: bɑt′‿trə lə taṅ″būr′.—**drum-major.** Tambour-major (*n. m.*): taṅ″būr′ mɑ″ʒōr′.—**drumstick.** Baguette de tambour (*f.*): bɑ″get′‿tə də taṅ″būr′.—**drummer.** Tambour (*n. m.*): taṅ″būr′.

drunk, *a.* Ivre: ī′‿vrə.—**drunk off duty.** Ivre en dehors du service: ī′‿vrə aṅ de″hōr′ dü sar″vīs′.—**d. on duty.** Ivre au service: ī′‿vrə ō sār″vīs′.—**drunkard.** Ivrogne (*n. m.*): ī″vrōṅ′‿yə.—**drunkenness.** Ivresse (*n. f.*): ī″vres′.

dry, *a.* Sec (*m.*): sek; sèche (*f.*): sēsh. [*leather straps, etc.*).

dubbing. Cirage gras (*n. m.*): sī″rāʒ′ə grɑ (*grease for shoes,*

duck[1], **I.** *n.* Plongeon (*m.*): pleṅ″ʒeṅ′. **II.** *v.* **1.** Plonger: pleṅ″ʒē′. **2.** Faire le plongeon: fār lə pleṅ″ʒeṅ′.

duck[2]. Canard (*n. m.*): kɑ″nār′ (*bird*).

duct. Conduite (*n. f.*): keṅ″dwit′ (*canal, pipe, tube*).

dud, dʊd, *n.* [Soldiers' slang.] A defective and unexploded enemy shell.

dugout, *n.* **1.** Abri de repos (*m.*): ɑ″brī′ də rə-pō′. **2.** Chambre de repos (*f.*): shaṅ′brə də rə-pō′. Called also *rest dugout*. **3.** Casemate-abri: kɑz″māt′ ɑ″brī′.—**deep dugout.** Abri-caverne: ɑ″brī′ kɑ″vārn′.

dumpy, *a.* Trapu (*m.*), trapue (*f.*): tra″pü′.
dung, *n.* **1.** Fumier (*m.*): fü″mī″‿yē′ (*manure*). **2.** Crottin (*m.*); krot″tañ′ (*of horses*). **3.** Fiente (*f.*): fī″yañt′ (*of cattle*).—**dung-pit.** Fosse à fumier (*n. f.*): fos a fü″mī″‿yē′.
duration. Durée (*n. f.*): dü″rē′.
during, *prep.* Pendant: pañ″dāñ′.—**during the journey,** or **transit.** Pendant le voyage, ou trajet: pañ″dāñ′ lə vwa″yā′‿ʒə, ū tra″ʒē′.
dusk, *n.* **1.** Brune (*f.*): brün. **2.** Crépuscule (*m.*): krē″püs″-kül′.—**at dusk.** Au crépuscule: ō krē″püs″kül′.—**in the d. of the evening.** À la brune: a la brün.—**dusky,** *a.* **1.** Sombre: soñ′‿brə. **2.** Brunâtre: brü″nā′‿trə (*brownish*).
dust, *n.* Poussière (*f.*): pūs″sī″‿yār′.
dusty, *a.* Poudreux (*m.*): pū″drū′; poudreuse (*f.*): pū″drūz′.
Dutch, *a.* Hollandais: hol″‿lan″dē′.—**a Dutchman.** Un Hollandais: añ‿ol″lan″dē′.
duty, *n.* **1.** Service (*m.*): sār″vīs′. **2.** Devoir (*m.*): də-vwār′.—**fatigue duty.** Corvée (*n. f.*): kōr″vē′.—**his duty is to . . . .** Son devoir est à . . . : soñ də-vwār′ ē a.—**off duty.** En dehors du service: añ də-ōr′ dü sār″vīs′.—**on d.** De service: də sār″vīs′.—**orderly d.** Service de jour: sār″vīs′ də ʒūr.—**the staff officer assigned to the d.** L'officier d'état-major détaché à cet effet: lof″‿fī″sī″‿yē′ dē″tā′ ma″ʒōr′ dē″ta″shē′ a set ef″‿fē′.
dwarf, *a.* & *n.* Nain (*m.*): nañ; naine (*f.*): nān.
dwelling. Habitation (*n. f.*): a″bī″ta″sī″‿yoñ′.—**dwelling-house,** *n.* **1.** Résidence (*f.*): rē″zī″dāñs′. **2.** Domicile (*m.*): dō″mī″sīl′.
dying, *a.* Mourant (*m.*): mū″rāñ′; mourante (*f.*): mū″rāñt′.—**he is dying.** Il est mourant: īl‿ē mū″rāñ′.
dyke. Digue (*n. f.*): dīg.
dynamite, *n.* Dynamite (*f.*): dī″na″mīt′.
dysentery. Dysenterie (*n. f.*): dī″sañ″tə-rī′.

E

each, *a.* & *pron.* Chaque: shak.—**each** or **each one.** Chacun (*m.*): sha″kañ′; chacune (*f.*): sha″kün′.—**e. other.** L'un l'autre: lañ lō′‿trə. *In the pl.* les uns les autres: lēz‿añ lēz‿ō′‿trə.—**for e. other.** L'un pour l'autre: lañ pūr lō′‿trə.—**of e. other.** L'un de l'autre: lañ də lō′‿trə.—**to e. other.** L'un à l'autre: lañ a lō′‿trə.
eagle. Aigle (*n. m.*): ē′‿glə.—**eaglet.** Aiglon (*n. m.*): ē″gloñ′.
ear. Oreille (*n. f.*): ō″rē′‿yə.—**earache.** Mal d'oreille: mal dō″rē′‿yə.—**e. protector, e.-flap.** Protège-oreilles (*n. f.*): pro″tē′‿ʒə o″rē′‿yə.—**e.-lobe.** Lobe (*n. m.*): lōb.
early, *adv.* **1.** De bonne heure: də bōn‿nūr. **2.** Tôt: tō.—**he gets up or rises early.** Il se lève de bonne heure: īl sə lāv də bōn‿nūr.—**I must get up or rise early to-morrow.** Il faut que je me lève de bon matin demain: īl fō kə ʒə mə lāv də boñ ma″tañ′ də-mañ′.
earth, *n.* **1.** Terre (*f.*): tār. **2.** Le monde (*m.*): moñd (*with the*).—**earthwork,** *n.* **1.** Terrasse (*f.*): tār″‿rās′; terrassement (*m.*): tār″ras″‿sə-māñ′. **2.** *pl.* Travaux en terre: tra″vō′ añ tār.—**to throw up earthworks.** Élever des ouvrages de terre: ē″lə-vē′ dēs‿ū″vrā′‿ʒə də tār.
ease, *n.* Repos (*m.*): rə-pō′; aise (*f.*): ēs.—**at ease.** A volonté: a vol′oñ″tē′.—**ease her.** Doucement: dū″sə-māñ′.
easily, *adv.* Facilement: fa″sīl″‿lə-māñ′.
east, the. L'est (*n. m.*): lest; l'orient: lōr″ī″‿yāñ′.—**eastward,** *adv.* Vers l'est: vār lest: vers l'orient: vār lōr″ī″‿yāñ′.
Easter, *n.* Pâques (*m.*): pā′‿kə.
easy, *a.* Facil (*m.* & *f.*): fa″sīl′; doux (*m.*): dū; douce (*f.*): dūs.
eat, *v.* Manger: mañ″ʒē′.—**give me something to eat.** Donnez-moi quelque chose à manger: doñ″nē′ mwa kel′kə shōs a mañ″ʒē′.—**let us eat.** Mangeons: mañ″ʒoñ′.

eating-house. Restaurant (*n. m.*): res″tō″rāñ′.—**eating-house keeper.** Restaurateur (*n. m.*): res″tō″ra″tūr′.
ecchymosis. Ecchymose (*n. f.*): ē″kī″mōz′ (*discoloration, as from a blow*).
economy. Économie (*n. f.*): ē″ken″o″mī′.—**interior economy.** Service intérieur: sār″vīs′ añ″tē″rī″‿yūr′.
eczema, *n.* Dartre (*f.*): dār′‿trə (*eruption of the skin*); eczéma (*m.*): ek″zē″mā′.
eddy, *n.* **1.** Contrecourant (*m.*): keñ″‿trə-kū″rāñ′ (*of water*). **2.** Tourbillon (*m.*): tūr″bī″‿yeñ′ (*of wind*).
edge, *n.* **1.** Bord (*m.*): bōr (*of a shore*, etc.). **2.** Lisière (*f.*): lī″zī″‿yār′ (*of a wood or forest*).—**edge of the wing.** Bord de l'aile: bōr də lēl (*of an aeroplane*).
education. Éducation (*n. f.*): ē″dü″ka″sī″‿yeñ′.
eel. Anguille (*n. f.*): añ″gīl′.
effect. Effet (*n. m.*): ef″‿fē′.—**to have a healthy effect.** Produire un effet salutaire: pro″dwīr′ añ‿ef″‿fē′ sa″lü″tār′.—**to the same effect.** À la même intention: a la mām añ″tañ″sī″‿yeñ′.—**effective.** Effectif (*n. m.*): ef″‿fek″tīf′.
efficacious, *a.* Efficace: ef″‿fī″kās′.
efficience, efficiency, *n.* **1.** Efficacité (*f.*): ef″‿fī″kas″ī″tē′. **2.** Bonne condition: bōn keñ″dī″sī″‿yeñ′ ("good condition": said of armies). **3.** Rendement (*m.*): rañ″də-māñ′ (*of machinery*).
efficient, *a.* Capable: ka″pā′‿blə.
egg, *n.* Œuf (*m.*): ūf.—**boiled eggs.** Œufs à la coque: ū a la kōk.—**fried e.** Œufs sur le plat: ū sür lə plā.—**new laid e.** Œufs frais: ū frā.—**poached e.** Œufs pochés: ū pō″shē′.—**scrambled e.** Œufs brouillés: ū brū″ī″‿yē′.—**some eggs.** Des œufs: dēz‿ū.
Egypt, ī′jipt, *n.* Égypte (*f.*): ē″ʒīpt′.—**Egyptian.** Égyptien: ē″ʒīp″sī″‿añ′.
eight, *a.* & *n.* Huit: hwīt.—**eighth.** Huitième (*a.* & *n. m.*): hwī″tī″‿yām′.—**eighteen,** *a.* & *n.* Dix-huit: dīz″hwīt′.—**eighteenth.** Dix-huitième (*a.* & *n.*): dīz″hwī″tī″‿yām′.—**eightieth.** Quatre-vingtième (*a.* & *n.*): kā″‿trə-vañ″tī″‿yām′.—**eighty.** Quatre-vingts (*a.* & *n.*): kā″‿trə-vañ′.
either, *pron.* **1.** Aucun (*m.*): ō″kañ′; aucune (*f.*): ō″kün′. **2.** L'un ou l'autre: lañ ū lō′‿trə. *In the plural*, "the ones or the others": les uns ou les autres (*m.*): lēz‿añ ū lēz‿ō′‿trə; les unes ou les autres (*f.*): lēz‿ün ū lēz‿ō′‿trə. **3.** Chacun (*m.*): sha″kañ′; chacune (*f.*): sha″kün′. **4.** L'un d'eux (*m.*): lañ dū; l'une d'elles (*f.*): lün del.
ejector, *n.* Éjecteur (*m.*): ē″ʒek″tūr′ (*in mechanics*).
elbow, *n.* Coude (*m.*): kūd.
electric, electrical. Électrique (*a.*): ē″lek″trīk′. Abbreviated *Elect.*—**electric battery.** Batterie électrique (*n. f.*): bat″‿tə-rī′ ē″lek″trīk′.—**e.-bell.** Sonnerie électrique (*n. f.*): sen″nə-rī′ ē″lek″trīk′ (*applying to the entire apparatus*). See BELL.—**e.-wire.** Fil électrique (*n. m.*): fīl ē″lek″trīk′.
electrician. Électricien (*n. m.*): ē″lek″trī″sī″‿yañ′.
electro-magnet. Electro-aimant: ē″lēk″trō ā″māñ′.
elevation, *n.* **1.** Hausse (*f.*): hōs. **2.** Élévation (*f.*): ē″lē″va″sī″‿yeñ′.—**point of elevation.** Point de pointage (*n. m.*): pwañ də pwañ″tāʒ′ (*of an objective or target*).
eleven, *a.* & *n.* Onze: ōñz.—**eleventh,** *a.* & *n.* Onzième: eñ″zī″‿yām′.
else, *a.* Autre: ō′‿trə.—**everybody else.** Tout autre: tūt ō′trə.—**everything e.** Tout le reste: tū lə rest.—**everywhere e.** Partout ailleurs: par″tūt′‿ai″yūr′.—**nobody e.** Aucun autre: ō″kañ′‿ō′trə.—**nothing e.** Pas autre chose: paz‿ō′‿trə shōs.—**what e.** Quoi de plus: kwa də plü.—**where e.** Où encore: ū añ″kōr′.—**who e.** Qui encore: kī añ″kōr′.
elsewhere, *adv.* Ailleurs: ai″‿yūr′.

artistic; ärt; fat; fāre; fast; get; prēy; hit; polīce;
obey; gō; not; ōr; full; rūle; but; būrn; ə = final;

embankment, *n.* **1.** Remblai (*m.*): raṅ″blē′. **2.** Levée de terre: lə-vē′ də tār.—**railway e.** Remblai de chemin de fer: raṅ″blē′ də sha-maṅ′ də fār.

embark, *v.* Embarquer: aṅ″bar″kē′.—**embarkation.** Embarquement (*n. m.*): aṅ″bar″‿kə-māṅ′.—**embarking.** Embarquement (*n. m.*): aṅ″bar″‿kə‿māṅ′.

embarrass, *v.* **1.** Gêner: ʒā″nē′. **2.** Embarraser: aṅ″bār″‿ras″‿sē′.

embassy. Ambassade (*n. f.*): aṅ″bas″‿sād′.

embody, *v.* **1.** Incorporer: aṅ″kōr″pō″rē′. **2.** Rassembler: ras″‿saṅ″blē′.

embrasure. Embrasure (*n. f.*): aṅ″bra″ʒür′.

emerge, *v.* Émerger: ē″mār″ʒē′.—**to emerge from.** Sortir de: sōr″tīr′ də.

emergency, *n.* **1.** Circonstance imprévue (*f.*): sīr″kəṅ″stāṅs′ aṅ″prē″vü′ (*unforeseen circumstance*). **2.** Cas urgent: ka ür″ʒāṅ′ (*urgent necessity*). **3.** Besoin: bə-zwāṅ′ (*need*).—**emergency rations.** Vivres du sac (*n. m.*): vīv′rə dü sak.—**e.-train.** En cas mobile (*n. m.*): aṅ kā mo″bīl′ (*of supplies, munitions*, etc.).

empennage, aṅ″pen″nā′‿ʒə, *n.* [Fr.]. Planes arranged about the tail of a dirigible balloon or an aeroplane to secure stability.

emplacement, *n.* Emplacement (*m.*): aṅ″pla″‿sə-māṅ′.

employ. **I.** *n.* **1.** Emploi (*m.*): aṅ″plwā′. **2.** Service (*m.*): sār-vīs′. **II.** *v.* Employer: aṅ″plwa″‿yē′.—**to employ oneself.** S'occuper à ou de: sok″‿kü″pē′ a ū də.—**employer.** Personne qui emploie (*f.*): pār″sōn′ kī aṅ″plwā′; patron (*m.*): pa″trəṅ′; patronne (*f.*): pa″trən″‿nə; maître (*m.*): mē′‿trə; maîtresse (*f.*): mā″tres′.—**employment,** *n.* Emploi (*m.*): aṅ″plwā′.

empower (to), *v.* **1.** Autoriser à: ō″tō″rī″zē′ a. **2.** Charger de: shar″ʒē′ də.

empty. **I.** *a.* Vide: vīd. **II.** *v.* Vider: vī″dē′.

enable, *v.* **1.** Rendre capable de: raṅ′‿drə ka″pā′‿blə də. **2.** Permettre de: pār″met′‿trə də.—**to be enabled to.** Être en état de: ā′‿trə aṅ ē″tā′ də; avoir le moyen de: a″vwār′ lə mwa″yaṅ′ də.

enact, *v.* **1.** Ordonner: ər″dən″‿nē′ (*establish by act of authority*). **2.** Arrêter: ar″‿rē″tē′ (*issue a decree*).

enactment. **1.** Loi (*n. f.*): lwā. **2.** Ordonnance (*n. f.*): ōr″dən″‿nāṅs′.

encampment. Camp (*n. m.*): kāṅ.—**field-battery encampment.** Camp de batterie: kaṅ də bat″‿tə-rī′.—**line of e.; line of front; or magistral line.** Front de bandière; ligne magistrale: frəṅ də baṅ″dī″‿yār′; lī′nyə ma″ʒīs″trāl′.

enceinte, *n.* Enceinte (*f.*): aṅ″saṅt′ (*the chief line of fortifications surrounding a place*).

encircle, *v.* Cerner: sār″nē′.

enclosure. Clôture (*n. f.*): klō″tür′.

encounter. **I.** *n.* **1.** Rencontre (*f.*): raṅ″kəṅ′‿trə. **2.** Mêlée (*f.*): mā″lē′. **II.** *v.* Rencontrer: raṅ″kəṅ″trē′.—**to encounter the enemy.** Engager le combat avec l'ennemi: aṅ″ga″ʒē′ lə kəṅ″bā′ a″vek′ len″‿nə-mī′.

encourage, *v.* Encourager: aṅ″kū″ra″ʒē′.

encumbrance. Encombrement (*n. m.*): aṅ″kəṅ″‿brə-māṅ′.

end. **I.** *n.* **1.** Fin (*f.*): faṅ. **2.** Extremité (*f.*): eks″trē″mī″tē′. **II.** *v.* **1.** Finir: fī″nīr′. **2.** Terminer: tār″mī″nē′.—**initial or free end.** Chef initial (*m.*): shef ī″nī″sī″‿yāl′ (*of a bandage*).—**terminal end.** Chef terminal (*m.*): shef tār″mī″nāl′ (*of a bandage*).—**to put an end to all resistance.** Amener la cessation de toute résistance: a″mə-nē′ la ses″‿sa″sī″‿yəṅ′ də tūt rē″zīs″tāṅs′.—**to this end.** À cet effet: a set ef″‿fē′.

endanger, *v.* **1.** Mettre en danger: met′‿trə aṅ daṅ″ʒē′. **2.** Exposer: eks″pō″zē′.

endeavor. **I.** *n.* **1.** Effort (*m.*): ef″‿fōr′. **2.** Tentative (*f.*):

tañ″ta″tīv′. **II.** *v.* **1.** Tâcher de: ta″shē′ də. **2.** S'efforcer de: sef″‿fēr″sē′ də.—**to use every endeavor.** Faire tous ses efforts pour: fār tū sēz‿ef″‿fər′ pūr.

enemy. Ennemi (*n. m.*): en″‿nə-mī′.

energy. Énergie (*n. f.*): ē″nār″ʒī′.

enfilade. **I.** *n.* Enfilade (*f.*): añ″fī″lād′‿ə. **II.** *v.* **1.** Prendre en enfilade: prañ′‿drə añ añ″fī″lād′‿ə. **2.** Enfiler: añ″fī″lē′.

enforce, *v.* Faire exécuter: fār eg″zē″kü″tē′.

engage, *v.* Engager: añ″ga″ʒē′.—**to be engaged with the enemy.** Etre aux prises avec l'ennemi: ā″‿trə ō prīz ā″vek′ len″‿nə-mī′.

engagement, *n.* **1.** Engagement (*m.*): añ″ga″ʒə-māñ′. **2.** Action (*f.*): ak″sī″‿yeñ′. **3.** Affaire (*f.*): af″‿fār′. **4.** Combat (*m.*): keñ″bā′.

engine, *n.* **1.** Locomotive (*f.*): lō″kō″mō″tī′‿və (*steam*). **2.** Moteur (*m.*): mō″tūr′ (*automobile*). **3.** Machine (*f.*): ma″shīn′‿ə. —**engine-room,** *n.* **1.** Chambre des machines: shāñ′‿brə dē ma″shīn′‿ə. **2.** Dépôt des machines: dē″pō′ dē ma″shīn′‿ə.—**e. trouble.** Panne de moteur: pān′‿nə də mō″tūr′.—**steam e.** Machine à vapeur: ma″shīn′‿a va″pūr′.—**start the e.** Mettez la machine en marche: met″tē′ la ma″shīn′ añ mārsh.

engineer, *n.* Soldat du génie: sōl″dā′ dü ʒē″nī′.—**engineer corps.** Corps du génie (*m.*): kēr dü ʒē″nī′.—**e. field troops.** Détachement du génie monté: dē″tash″‿ə-māñ′ dü ʒē″nī′ meñ″tē′.

engineers. Génies (*n. m. pl.*): ʒē″nī′.—**Royal Engineers' Field Signal Companies.** Service de Télégraphie Militaire: sār″vīs′ də tē″lē″gra″fī′ mī″lī″tār′.

England, *n.* Angleterre (*f.*): añ″‿glə-tār′.—**English,** *a.* Anglais (*m.*): añ″glē′; Anglaise (*f.*): añ″glēz′.—**English Channel.** La Manche (*n. f.*): la māñsh.—**do you speak English?** Parlez-vous anglais: par″lē′ vūz‿añ″glē′.—**is there anyone here who speaks English?** Y a-t-il quelqu'un ici qui parle anglais? ī″ya″-tīl′ kel″kañ′ ī″sī′ kī pārl añ″glē′.

enlist, *v.* **1.** S'enrôler: sañ″rō″lē′. **2.** S'engager: sañ″ga″ʒē′.—**enlistment,** *n.* **1.** Enrôlement (*m.*): añ″rō″‿lə-māñ′. **2.** Engagement (*m.*): añ″ga″‿ʒə-māñ′.

enormous, *a.* Énorme (*m. & f.*): ē″nərm′.

enough, *adv.* Assez: as″‿sē′.

ensign, *n.* **1.** Enseigne (*f.*): añ″sē′‿nyə. **2.** Drapeau (*m.*): dra″pō′ (*the colors*).

ensure. See INSURE.

entanglements (wire). Réseaux de fil de fer (*m.*): rē″zō′ də fīl də fār (*barbed wire barriers*).

entente. Entente (*n. f.*): añ″tāñt′ (*an informal understanding, as that between Great Britain, France, and Russia*).—**entente cordiale,** añ″tāñt′ kēr″dī″āl′ (*a cordial understanding*).

enter, *v.* **1.** Entrer: añ″trē′ (*go into*). **2.** Inscrire: añ″skrīr′ (*post in a book*).

enterprise, *n.* **1.** Entreprise (*f.*): añ″‿trə-prīz′ (*undertaking*). **2.** Hardiesse (*f.*): har″dī″es′ (*courage*).—**enterprising,** *a.* Entreprenant (*m.*): añ″‿trə-prə-nāñ′; entreprenante (*f.*): añ″‿trə-prə-nāñt′.

entire, *a.* Tout (*m.*): tū; toute (*f.*): tūt.

entrain, *v.* Embarquer: añ″bar″kē′.—**entraining station.** Gare d'embarquement: gār dañ″bar″‿kə-māñ′.—**entrainment.** Embarquement (*n. m.*): añ″bar″‿kə-māñ′.—**place of entrainment.** Lieu d'embarquement: lī″yū′ dañ″bar″‿kə-māñ′.

entrance. Entrée (*n. f.*): añ″trē′.

entrap, *v.* **1.** Attraper: at″‿tra″pē′. **2.** Prendre en piège: prañ′‿drə añ pī″ēʒ′.

entrench, *v.* Retrancher: rə-trañ″shē′. See INTRENCH.—**entrenching-tool.** Pelle-bêche (*n. f.*): pel′‿lə bēsh′‿ə (*spade-like implement used for digging*).—**entrenchment.** Retranchement (*n. m.*): rə-trañ″‿shə-māñ′.—**parts of an entrenchment.** Éléments d'un retranchement: ē″lē″māñ′ dañ rə-trañ″‿shə-māñ′.

entreating, *a.* Suppliant (*m.*): süp″‿plī″āṅ′; suppliante (*f.*): süp″‿plī″āṅt′.
entrust, *v.* Confier: kon″fī″‿yē′.
envelop. **I.** *n.* Enveloppe (*f.*): aṅ″‿və-lop′. **II.** *v.* Entourer: aṅ″tū″rē′.—**envelopment.** Enveloppement (*n. m.*): aṅ″‿və-lop″‿pə-māṅ′.
envious, *a.* Envieux (*m.*): aṅ″vī″‿yū′; envieuse (*f.*): aṅ″-vī″yūz′.
épaulette. Épaulette (*n. f.*): ē″pō″let′.
epaulement. Épaulement (*n. m.*): ē″pōl″‿ə-māṅ′ (a parapet or screen of earth in fortifications).—**rifle epaulement.** Emplacement de tir: aṅ″pla″‿sə-māṅ′ də tīr.
Épernay, ē″pār″nē′, *n.* Town in northern France.
Epsom salts. Sel Anglais (*m.*): sel aṅ″glē′.
equal, *a.* Égal (*m.*); égale (*f.*): ē″gāl′.
equip, *v.* Équiper: ē″kī″pē′.—**equipment,** *n.* **1.** (*m.*) Équipement: ē″kīp″māṅ′. **2.** Accoutrements (*n. pl.*): ak″‿kū″‿trə-māṅ′ (a soldier's arms, furnishings, etc.). **3.** Matériel (*m.*): ma″tē″rī″‿yel′; as, *veterinary equipment.* See VETERINARY.—**to remove the equipment.** Enlever l'équipement: aṅ″‿lə-vē′ lē″kīp″māṅ′.
equipped, *pa.* Équipé (*m.*); équipée (*f.*): ē″kī″pē′.—**lightly equipped.** Équipé à la légère: ē″kī″pē′ a la lē″ʒār′.
erect. **I.** *a.* **1.** Droit (*m.*): drwā; droite (*f.*): drwāt. **2.** Haut (*m.*): hō; haute (*f.*): hōt. **II.** *v.* Ériger: ē″rī″ʒē′.—**to stand erect.** Se tenir debout: sə tə-nīr′ də-bū′.
errand, *n.* **1.** Commission (*f.*): kom″‿mīs″‿sī″‿yeṅ′. **2.** Message (*m.*): mes″‿sāʒ′.
error, *n.* **1.** Erreur (*f.*): ēr″‿rūr′. **2.** Faute (*f.*): fōt.—**error in direction.** Écart en direction (*m.*): ē″kār′ aṅ dī″rek″sī″‿yeṅ′ [*aeroplanes*].
escadrille. Escadrille (*n. f.*): es″ka″drī′‿yə (*a squadron of*
escape, *v.* **1.** S'échapper: sē″shap″‿pē′. **2.** S'enfuir: saṅ″-fwīr′.—**any one attempting to e. will be fired on.** Toute personne qui tentera de s'échapper sera fusillée: tūt pār″son′‿nə kī taṅ″‿tə-rā′ də sē″shap″‿pē′ sə‿rā′ fū″zī″‿yē′.—**to escape observation.** Passer inaperçu: pas″sē′ in″a″pār″sü′.
escarpment. Escarpement (*n. m.*): ēs″kar″‿pə-māṅ′.
escort. **I.** *n.* Escorte (*f.*): es″kōrt′. **II.** *v.* Escorter: es″kōr″tē′.—**escort of prisoners.** Escorte des prisonniers: es″kōrt′ dē prī″-zon″‿nyē′.—**to provide an e.** Fournir une escorte: fūr″nīr′ ün es″kōrt′.—**under e.** Sous escorte: sūz‿es″kōrt′.
espionage. Espionnage (*n. m.*): es″pī″on″‿nāʒ′.
establishment. Établissement (*n. m.*): ē″tab″līs″‿sə-māṅ′. On maps, *Étabnt.*—**disciplinary establishment (military).** Pénitencier militaire: pē″nī″taṅ″sī″‿yē′ mī″lī″tār′.
estaminet, es″ta″mī″nē′, *n. m.* (*A French saloon or wine-shop.*)
estuary. Estuaire (*n. m.*): es″tü″ār′.
ether. Éther (*n. m.*): ē″tār′.
evacuate, *v.* Évacuer: ē″va″kü″ē′.—**evacuation.** Évacuation (*n. f.*): ē″va″kü″a″sī″‿yoṅ′.—**evacuation order.** Feuille d'évacuation: fu″ī′‿yə dē″va″kü″a″sī″‿yoṅ′.
evasive, *a.* **1.** Fuyant (*m.*): fwī″‿yāṅ′ (*fleeting*). **2.** Évasif (*m.*): ē″va″sīv′.
even. **I.** *a.* **1.** Égal (*m.*); égale (*f.*): ē″gāl′ (*equal, similar*). **2.** Pair (*m.*); paire (*f.*): pār (*of number*). **3.** Uni (*m.*); unie (*f.*): ü″nī′ (*smooth*). **II.** *adv.* Même: mām.
evening. Soir (*n. m.*): swār.—**this evening.** Ce soir: sə swār.
event, *n.* **1.** Événement (*m.*): ē″vē″‿nə-māṅ′ (*occurrence*). **2.** Cas (*m.*): kā (*case*).—**in the event.** En cas de: aṅ kā də.—**in the latter e.** Dans ce dernier cas: daṅ sə dār″nī″‿yē′ kā.—**in such an e.** En pareil cas: aṅ pa″rē″‿ī′ kā.
eventuality. Éventualité (*n. f.*): ē″vaṅ″tü″al″ī″tē′.

ever, *adv.* 1. Toujours: tū″ʒūr′. 2. Jamais: ʒa″mā′.
every, *a.* 1. Tout (*m.*): tū; toute (*f.*): tūt. 2. Chaque (*m.* & *f.*): shăk.—**everything.** Tout (*n. m.*): tū.—**everywhere,** *adv.* Partout: par″tū′.
exception. Exception (*n. f.*): ek″sep″sī″‿yeṅ′.
evidence. Témoignage (*n. m.*): tē″mwan″yăʒ′.—**e. for the defense** (or **for the prisoner**). Témoin à décharge (*m.*): tē″mwaṅ′ a dē″shărʒ′.—**e. for the prosecution** (or **against the prisoner**). Témoin à charge: tē″mwaṅ′ a shărʒ.—**to give evidence.** Faire une déposition: fār ün dē″pō″zī′sī′‿yeṅ′.
evident, *a.* Évident (*m.*): ē″vī″dăṅ′; évidente (*f.*): ē″vī″dăṅt′.
examine, *v.* Examiner: eg″za″mī″nē′.—**examination,** *n.* 1. Examen (*m.*): eg″za″maṅ′. 2. Interrogatoire (*m.*): aṅ″tăr″‿rə″ga″twăr′.—**examination of supplies.** Examen des marchés: eg″za″maṅ′ dē mar″shē′.—**entrance e.** Examen d'entrée: eg″za″maṅ′ daṅ″trē′.
example. Exemple (*n. m.*): eg″zăṅ′‿plə.—**for example.** Par exemple: par eg″zăṅ′‿plə.
excavate. 1. Creuser: krū″zē′ (*dig*). 2. Déblayer: dē″blā″‿yē′ (*clear away*).—**excavated.** En déblai: aṅ dē″blā′.—**excavator.** Excavateur (*n. m.*): eks″ka″va″tūr′ (*trench digging machine*).
excellent, *a.* 1. Excellent (*m.*): ek″sel″‿lăṅ′; excellente (*f.*): ek″sel″‿lăṅt′. 2. Parfait (*m.*): par″fā′; parfaite (*f.*): par″fāt′.
exchange, *v.* Échanger: ē″shaṅ″ʒē′.—**exchange of prisoners.** Échange de prisonniers: ē″shan′‿ʒə də prī″zen″‿nyē′.
execute, *v.* Exécuter: eg″zē″kü″tē′.
executive. I. *a.* Exécutif (*m.*): eg″zē″kü″tif′; exécutive (*f.*): eg″zē″kü″tīv′. II. (*n. m.*). Commandement: kom″‿maṅ″‿də-măṅ′ (*directing authority*).—**general functions of the executive.** Fonctions générales du commandement: fəṅk″sī″‿yeṅ′ ʒē″nē″răl′ dü kom″‿maṅ″‿də-măṅ′.
exercise, *v.* Exercer: eg″zăr″sē′.
exhaust. I. *v.* Épuiser: ē″pwī″zē′. II. *n. m.* Échappement: ē″shap″‿pə-măṅ′.—**exhaust box.** Pot d'échappement (*m.*): po dē″shap″‿pə-măṅ′.—**exhaust valve.** Soupape d'échappement (*f.*): sū″păp′‿ə dē″shap″‿pə-măṅ′.
exhaustion. Épuisement (*m.*): ē″pwī″‿zə-măṅ′.
exigencies of the situation. Exigences de la situation: eg″zī″ʒăṅs′ də la sī″tü″a″sī″‿yeṅ′.
exit, *n.* 1. Sortie (*f.*): sōr″tī′. 2. Débouché (*m.*): dē″bū″shē′.
expedition. Expédition (*n. f.*): eks″pē″dī″sī″yeṅ′.—**oversea expedition.** Expédition outre-mer: eks″pē″dī″sī″‿yeṅ′ ū′‿trə măr.
expel, *v.* Chasser: shas″‿sē′.
expend, *v.* Dépenser: dē″paṅ″sē′.—**expenditure.** 1. Dépense (*n. f.*): dē″păṅ′‿sə. 2. Consommation (*n. f.*): keṅ″səm″‿ma″sī″‿yeṅ′.
expense. Dépense (*n. f.*): dē″păn′‿sə.—**at the expense of.** 1. Au détriment de: ō dē″trī″măṅ′ də. 2. Au frais de: ō frē də.—**traveling expenses.** Frais de route: frā də rūt.
experience. Expérience (*n. f.*): eks″pē″rī″ăn′‿sə.—**experienced,** *a.* Expérimenté (*m.*); expérimentée (*f.*): eks″pē″rī″maṅ″tē′.
experiment. I. *n. f.* Expérience: eks″pē″rī″yăṅ′‿sə. II. *v.* Expérimenter: eks″pē″rī″maṅ″tē′.—**experimental,** *a.* Expérimental (*m.*); expérimentale (*f.*): eks″pē″rī″maṅ″tăl′.—**experimental officer.** L'officier chargé des expériences: lof″‿fī″sī″‿yē′ shăr″ʒē′ dēz‿eks″pē″rī″ăṅ′‿sə (*in artillery school*).—**experimentally,** *adv.* À titre d'essai: ă tī′‿trə dēs″‿sā′.
explain, *v.* Expliquer: eks″plī″kē′.
explode, *v.* Éclater: ē″kla″tē′.—**explosion.** Explosion (*n. f.*): eks″plō″zī″‿yeṅ′.—**premature explosion.** Éclatement prématuré: ē″kla″‿tə-măṅ′ prē″ma″tü″rē′.—**explosive,** *a.* Explosif (*m.*):

eks″plō″zīf′; explosive (*f.*): eks″plō″zīv′.—**high explosive.** Explosif brisant: eks″plō″zīf′ brī″zäṅ′.
explore, *v.* Explorer: eks″plō″rē′.
expose, *v.* **1.** Découvrir: dē″kū″vrīr′ (*uncover*). **2.** Exposer: eks″pō″zē′. **3.** Démasquer: dē″mas″kē′ (*unmask*).—**expose the enemy's plans.** Dévoiler les dispositions de l'ennemi: dē″vwa″lē′ lē dīs″po″zī″sī″‿yeṅ′ də len″nə-mī′.—**exposed places.** Espaces découverts: es″pās′‿ə dē″kū″vār′.—**to be exposed to heavy losses.** Être exposé à des grosses pertes: ā′‿trə eks″pō″sē′ a dē grōs′‿sə pārt.
express, *a.* Exprès (*m.*): eks″prā′; expresse (*f.*): eks″pres′‿sə.
express train. Train de grande vitesse: traṅ də grāṅ′‿də vī″tes′‿sə.
expression. Expression (*n. f.*): eks″prēs″‿sī″‿yeṅ′.
expulsion. Expulsion (*n. f.*): eks″pül″sī″‿yeṅ′.
extemporize, *v.* Improviser: aṅ″pro″vī″zē′.
extend, *v.* **1.** Étendre: ē″taṅ′‿drə. **2.** Allonger: al″leṅ″ʒē′.—**in extended formation.** En formation déployée: üṅ fēr″ma″sī″yeṅ′ dē″plwa″‿yē′.—**extension of leave.** Prolongation de congé: prō″leṅ″ga″sī″‿yeṅ′ də keṅ″ʒē′.—**extensive,** *a.* Étendu (*m.*); étendue (*f.*): ē″taṅ″dü′.
extent. Étendue (*n. f.*): ē″taṅ″dü′.—**possible extent of front.** Front possible à y déployer: freṅ pos″‿sī′‿blə a ī dē″plwa″‿yē′.—**a wide e.** Une large étendue: ün lārʒ ē″taṅ″dü′.—**to the fullest e.** À fond: a feṅ.
extra, *adv.* **1.** En sus: aṅ süs. **2.** De plus: də plü.
extract, *v.* Tirer: tī″rē′.—**extractor,** *n.* **1.** Tire-cartouche (*m.*): tīr″kar″tūsh′. **2.** Extracteur (*n. m.*): eks″trak″tūr′.
extraordinary, *a.* Extraordinaire (*m.* & *f.*): ek″stra″ōr″dī″nār′.
extreme. **I.** *a.* Extrême (*m.* & *f.*): ek″strām′‿ə. **II.** *n. f.* Extrémité: ek″strā″mī″tē′.
extricate, *v.* **1.** Dégager: dē″ga″ʒē′. **2.** Retirer: rə-tī″rē′.—**to extricate oneself from.** Se tirer de: sə tī″rē′ də.
eye. Œil (*n. m.*): ū″‿ī′; yeux (*pl.*): yū.—**eyebrow.** Sourcil (*n. m.*): sūr″sī′.—**eyelet.** Œillet (*n. m.*): ū″yē′.—**eyelid.** Paupière (*n. f.*): pō″pī″‿yār′.—**eyes front!** Fixe! fiks.—**eye-witness,** *n.* See under WITNESS.

F

face, **I.** *n.* **1.** Visage (*m.*): vī″zāʒ′. **2.** Face (*f.*): fās. **II.** *v.* Faire face: fār fās.—**face about!** Volte face! vōlt fās.—**facing away.** À dos tournéz: a dō tūr″nē′.—**facing in any direction.** Faire face en aucune direction: fār fās aṅ‿ō″kün′ dī″rek″sī″‿yoṅ′.
fact. Fait (*n. m.*): fā.
factor, *n.* **1.** Agent (*m.*): a″ʒāṅ′. **2.** Facteur (*m.*): fak″tūr′.
factory. Fabrique (*n. f.*): fa″brīk′. Abbreviated *Fab*[e].
fag, fag, *n.* [Slang Eng.] A cigarette.
fagot. Fagot (*n. m.*): fa″gō′.
fail, *v.* **1.** Échouer: ē″shū″ē′. **2.** Manquer: maṅ″kē′.—**failure,** *n.* **1.** Échec (*m.*): ē″shek′. **2.** Manquement (*m.*): maṅ″‿kə-māṅ′.
faint. Évanouir (*v.*): ē″va″nū″īr′.—**fainting.** Évanouissement (*n. m.*): ē″va″nū″īs″‿sə‿māṅ′.
fair. **I.** *n.* Blond (*m.*): bloṅ. **II.** *a.* Blond (*m.*): bloṅ; blonde (*f.*): bloṅd.
fairy. Fée (*n. f.*): fē.—**fairy story.** See FANCY ACCOUNT [under ACCOUNT.
fairway, *n.* Canal navigable (*m.*): ka″nāl′ na″vī″gā′‿blə.
faith. Foi (*n. f.*): fwa.—**bad faith.** Mauvaise foi (*n. f.*):

mō″vēz′ fwa.—**good faith.** Bonne foi: bōn′‿nə fwa.—**faithful,** *a.* Fidèle (*m.* or *f.*): fī″del′.

fall, I. *n.* **1.** Chute (*f.*): ŝhüt (*as of an aeroplane*). **2.** Éboulement (*m.*): ē″bū″‿lə-māṅ′ (*a landslide*). **3.** Baisse (*f.*): bās (*of prices*). **II.** *v.* **1.** Tomber: teṅ″bē′. **2.** Baisser: bās″‿sē′. **3.** Diminuer: dī″mī″nü″ē′.—**fall in! 1.** Rangez=vous! raṅ″ʒē′ vū. **2.** À vos rangs! a vō rāṅ.—**f. out! 1.** Rompez les rangs! reṅ″pē′ lē raṅ. **2.** Sortez des rangs: sōr″tē′ dē raṅ.—**to fall back upon. 1.** Se replier sur: sə rə‿plī″ē′ sür. **2.** Se retirer: sə rə‿tī″rē′.—**to f. in.** Se ranger: sə raṅ″ʒē′; s'aligner: sa″lī″‿nyē′.—**to f. into. 1.** Tomber dans: teṅ″bē′ daṅ. **2.** Tomber dedans: teṅ″bē′ də-daṅ′.—**to f. on, upon.** Tomber dessus: teṅ″bē′ də-sü′.

fallow. En friche (*n. m.*): aṅ frīŝh (of land).

false, *a.* **1.** Faux (*m.*): fō; fausse (*f.*): fōs. **2.** Fourbe: fūrb (*of character*). **3.** Postiche: pos″tīŝh′ (*of beard, hair, teeth*).—**false teeth.** Fausses dents (*n. f.*): fōs daṅ.

family. Famille (*n. f.*): fa″mī′‿yə.

famine. Famine (*n. f.*): fa″mīn′.

fan, *n.* **1.** Ventilateur (*m.*): vaṅ″tī″la″tūr′. **2.** Aile (*f.*): āl (*of a windmill*). **3.** Éventail (*m.*): ē″vaṅ″tai′ (*used by women*).

far, *a.* Éloigné: ē″lwaṅ″‿nyē′; lointain: lwaṅ″taṅ′.—**as far as.** Jusqu'à: ʒüs″ka′.—Loin (*adv.*): lwaṅ; au loin: ō lwaṅ.—**by far.** De beaucoup: də bō″kū′.—**far off.** Au loin: o lwaṅ.—**how far is it to . . . ?** Combien y a=t=il d'ici à . . . ? keṅ″-bī″‿yaṅ′ ī a-tīl′ dī″sī′ a.—**is it far to . . . ?** Est=ce loin à . . . ? ēs′‿ə lwaṅ a . . . .—**to be far apart.** Être éloigné: ā′‿trə ē″lwaṅ″nyē′.

fare. Prix (*n. m.*): prī (*price*).—**fare for the trip.** Prix de la course: prī də la kūrs.—**full fare.** Place entière: plās‿aṅ″tī″‿yār′.—**here is my fare.** Voici le prix de ma place: vwa″sī′ lə prī də ma plās.

farm, *n.* Ferme (*f.*): fārm. Abbreviated *Fme.*—**dairy=farm.** Métairie (*n. f.*): mē″tā″rī′.—**f.=yard.** Cour de ferme (*f.*): kūr də fārm. Basse=cour (*f.*): bās″kūr′ (*poultry=yard*).

farmer. Fermier (*n. m.*): fār″mī″‿yē′.

farmhouse, *n.* **1.** Ferme (*f.*): fārm. **2.** Métairie (*f.*): mē″tā″rī′.

farrier. Maréchal=ferrant (*n. m.*): ma″rē″ŝhāl′ fār″‿rāṅ′.—**farriery.** Maréchalerie (*n. f.*): ma″rē″ŝhal″rī′.

fascine. Fascine (*n. f.*): fas″‿sīn′.—**fascine=bands.** Harts (*n. f.*): hār.—**fascine work.** Clayonnage (*n. m.*): kla″‿yon″‿nāʒ′.

fast, *a.* **1.** Vite (*m.* & *f.*): vīt. **2.** Ferme: fārm (*fix*). **3.** En avance: aṅ‿a″vāṅs′ (*of watches, etc.*).—**to make fast. 1.** *v.* Amarrer: a″mar″‿rē′ (*of a ship*). **2.** Fermer (*v.*): fār″mē′ (*of doors, windows, etc.*). **3.** Attacher (*v.*): at″‿ta″ŝhē′ (*attach, fix*).

fasten. Attacher (*v.*): at″‿ta″ŝhē′.—**fastenings.** Attaches (*n. f.*): at″‿tāŝh′.

faster, *a.* Plus vite: plü vīt; plus fort: plü fōr.

fastness, *n.* **1.** Forteresse (*f.*): fōr″tres′ (*stronghold*). **2.** Place forte (*n. f.*): plās fōrt.

fat, *a.* Gras (*m.*): grā; grasse (*f.*): grās.

father, *n.* Père (*m.*): pār.

fatigue, *n.* Fatigue (*f.*): fa″tīg′.—**a fatigue=party.** Une corvée: ün kōr″vē′.—**fatigue=dress,** *n.* Tenue de corvée: tə‿nü′ də kōr″vē′.—**f.=duty.** La corvée (*n. f.*): la kōr″vē′.

fault. Faute (*n. f.*): fōt.

favor. Faveur (*n. f.*): fa″vūr′.

favorable, *a.* Favorable: fa″vō″rā′‿blə.—**favorable conditions.** Conditions favorables: kōṅ″dī″sī″‿yeṅ′ fa″vo″rā′‿blə.

February. Février (*n. m.*): fē″vrī″‿yē′.

fear, *n.* **1.** Peur (*f.*): pūr. **2.** Crainte (*f.*): kraṅt.—**fearless,** *a.*

Sans peur: sān pūr; intrépide: aṅ"trē"pīd'.—**fearless of.** Qui ne craint pas: kī nə kraṅ pā.

feat. Fait (*n. m.*): fā.—**feat of arms.** Fait d'armes: fā dārm.

feather, *n.* **1.** Plume (*f.*): plüm (*in general*). **2.** Plumet (*m.*): plü"mē'.

feature, *n.* **1.** Trait (*m.*): trā. **2.** Figure (*f.*): fī"gür'. **3.** Configuration (*f.*): koṅ"fī"gü"ra"sī"‿yoṅ' (*of ground*).

featured, *a.* Qui a des trait: kī a dē trā.—**hard featured.** Aux traits durs: ō trā dür.

fee, *n.* Honoraires (*m. pl.*): o"no"rār'.

feed, *n.* Fourrage (*m.*): fūr"‿rāʒ' (*stall-feed for cattle*).

feed, *v.* **1.** (1) Nourrir: nū"rīr'. (2) Entretenir: aṅ"trə-tə-nīr'. (3) Alimenter: a"lī"maṅ"tē'. **2.** Donner à manger à: don"‿nē' a maṅ"ʒē' a (*chiefly, of animals*). Compare EAT. **3.** Faire paître: fār pā'‿trə (*put to grass*).

feeding of, the. **1.** L'alimentation: la"lī"maṅ"ta"sī"‿yoṅ' (*troops*). **2.** La nourriture de: la nūr"‿rī"tür' də. **3.** La pâture de: la pa"tür' də.

feet. Pieds (*n. m.*): pī"‿yē'. See FOOT.—**a depth of ten feet.** Une profondeur de dix pieds: ün pro"foṅ"dūr' də dī pī"‿yē'.—**fifty feet deep.** Cinquante pieds de profondeur: saṅ"-kānt' pī"‿yē' də pro"foṅ"dūr'.—**wet feet.** Pieds mouillés: pī"‿yē' mū"‿i"‿yē'.

feigned, *a.* **1.** Dissimulé: dīs"‿sī"mü"lē'. **2.** Simulé: sī"-mü"lē' (*of illness*). **3.** Déguisé: dē"gī"zē'.

feint, *n.* Attaque simulée (*f.*): at"‿tāk' sī"mü"lē'.

fell, *v.* Abattre: a"bāt'‿trə (*of trees*).

felloe, feller. Jante (*n. f.*): ʒānt (*of a wheel*).

fellow, *n.* **1.** Gaillard (*m.*): gai"‿yār'; camarade (*m.*): ka"ma"rād' (*of persons*). **2.** Pareil: pa"rē'‿yə (*of things*).—**good fellow.** Brave garçon (*n. m.*): brāv gar"soṅ'.—**not fellows or mates.** Pas pareils: pa pa"rē'‿yə (*of shoes, etc.*).

feminine, *a.* Féminin: fē"mī"naṅ'.—**in the feminine gender.** Au féminin: ō fē"mī"naṅ'.

fence, *n.* **1.** Barrière (*f.*): bar"‿rī"‿yār' (*rail-fence*; also *bar or gate at a level crossing*). **2.** Clôture (*f.*): klō"tür'.—**stone fence.** Clôture en pierre: klō"tür' aṅ pī"‿yār'.—**sunken f.** Clôture en fossé: klō"tür' aṅ fōs"‿sē'.—**wire f.** Barrière en fil de fer: bar"‿rī"‿yār' aṅ fīl də fār.

fencing[1], *n.* Matériaux de clôture (*m.*): ma"tē"rī"‿yō' də klō"tür'.

fencing[2], *n.* L'escrime (*f.*): les"krīm' (*with foils*).

ferro-concrete, *n.* **1.** Béton-armé (*m.*): bē"toṅ'‿ar"mē'. **2.** Ciment armé (*m.*): sī"māṅt'‿ar"mē'.

ferry, I. *n.* Bac (*m.*): bāk.—**II.** *v.* **1.** Passer dans un bac: pas"sē' dāṅs‿aṅ bāk. **2.** Traverser: tra"vār"sē'.—**ferry-boat,** *n.* **1.** Bac (*m.*): bāk. **2.** Traille (*f.*): trā'‿yə.

fetch, *v.* Aller chercher: al"‿lē' shār"shē'.

fetlock, *n.* Fanon (*m.*): fa"noṅ'.—**fetlock-joint.** Boulet (*n. m.*): bū"lē'.

fever. Fièvre (*n. f.*): fī"āv'‿rə.—**feverish,** *a.* Fiévreux (*m.*): fī"ēv"rū'; fiévreuse (*f.*): fī"ēv"rūz'.

few, *a.* Peu de: pū də.—**a few.** **1.** Peu de: pū də (*of people*). **2.** Quelque: kel'‿kə; quelques-un (*m.*): kel"kəz‿aṅ"; quelques-une (*f.*): kel"kuz'‿ün (*of things*).

field, *n.* **1.** Champ (*m.*): shaṅ. **2.** Campagne: kaṅ"pā'‿nyə (*campaign*).—**field army.** Armée de campagne (*f.*): ar"mē' də kaṅ"pā'‿nyə.—**f. artillery.** Artillerie de campagne: ar"tī"‿yə-rī' də kaṅ"pā'‿nyə.—**f. bed,** *n.* Lit de camp (*m.*): lī də kaṅ.—**f. cashier.** Payeur d'armée (*n. m.*): pē"‿yūr' dar"mē'.—**f. day.** Jour de revue (*m.*): ʒūr də rə‿vü'.—**f. depot.** Poste de ravitaillement de campagne: pōst də ra"vī"tai"‿yə‿māṅ' də kaṅ"pā'‿nyə.—**f.-exercises.** Exercices de campagne (*m.*): egs"zär"sīs' də kaṅ"pā'‿nyə.—**f.-glasses.** Jumelles de campagne (*f.*): ʒü"mĕl' də kaṅ"pā'‿nyə.—**f.-gun.** Pièce de campagne (*f.*): pī"ĕs' də kaṅ"pā'‿nyə.—**f.-hospital.** Hôpital de camp (*m.*): ō"pī"tāl' də kaṅ.—**f.-marshal.** Maréchal (*m.*): ma"rē"shāl'.—**f. officer of the day.** Officier supérieur de jour: of"‿fī"sī'ē' sü"pē"rī"ūr' də ʒūr.—**f. of action.** Champ d'action: shaṅ dak"sī"‿yeṅ'.—**f. of fire.** Champ de tir: shaṅ də tīr.—**f. of view.** Vues (*n. f.*): vü.—**f. units.** Unités de combat: ü"nī"tē' də keṅ"bā'.—**fieldwork.** Fortification passagère de campagne (*f.*): for"tī"fī"ka"sī"‿yeṅ' pas"‿sa"ʒār' də kaṅ"pā'‿nyə.—**in the field.** En campagne: aṅ kaṅ"pa'‿nyə.—**ploughed f.** Champ labouré (*m.*): shaṅ la"bū"rē'.—**tilled f.** Champ cultivé: shaṅ kül"tī"vē'.—**to take the f.** Se mettre en campagne: sə met'‿trə aṅ kaṅ"pā'‿nyə.

fierce, *a.* Féroce: fē"rēs'; farouche: fa"rūsh'.

fifteen, *a.* & *n.* Quinze (*m.*): kaṅz.—**fifteenth,** *a.* & *n.* Quinzième (*m.*): kaṅ"zī"‿yām'.

fifth, *a.* & *n.* Cinquième (*m.*): saṅ"kī"‿yām'.

fiftieth, *a.* & *n.* Cinquantième (*m.*): saṅ"kaṅ"tī"‿yām'.

fifty, *a.* & *n.* Cinquante: saṅ"kāṅt'.

fig, *n.* Figue (*f.*): fīg.

fight, I. *n.* **1.** Action (*f.*): aks"‿sī"‿yeṅ'. **2.** Combat (*m.*): keṅ"bā'. **II.** *v.* **1.** Combattre: keṅ"bāt'‿trə. **2.** Se battre avec: sə bāt'‿trə a"vek'.—**desultory fight.** Combat décousu: keṅ"bā' dē"ku"sü'.—**f. in the open.** Combat en rase campagne: keṅ"bā' aṅ rāz kaṅ"pā'‿nyə.—**in the thick of the f.** Au fort de l'action: ō fōr də lak"sī"‿yeṅ'.—**to f. a battle.** Livrer une bataille: lī"vrē' ün ba"tai'‿yə.—**to f. hand to hand.** Combattre corps à corps: keṅ"bāt'‿trə kōr a kōr.—**to f. or cut one's way (through).** Frayer un chemin: frā"yē' aṅ shə-maṅ'.

fighting, I. *a.* **1.** Qui combat: kī keṅ"bā' (*of men*). **2.** De combat: də keṅ"bā' (*of things*). **II.** *n.* Combat (*m.*): keṅ"bā'.—**close fighting.** Combat rapproché: keṅ"bā' rap"‿pra"shē'.—**f.-line.** La ligne de feu: la lī'‿nyə də fū.—**f.-men.** Combattants: keṅ"bat"tāṅ'.—**f. unit.** Unité de combat: ü"nī"tē' də keṅ"bā'.

figure, I. *n.* **1.** Tournure (*f.*): tūr"nür' (*of body*). **2.** Taille (*f.*): tai (*of stature*). **3.** Chiffre (*m.*): shīf'‿frə (*in arithmetic*). **II.** *v.* **1.** Figurer: fī"gü"rē'. **2.** Imaginer: ī"ma"ʒī"nē'.—**to figure to oneself.** Se figurer: sə fī"gü"rē'.

filament. Filament (*n. m.*): fī"la"māṅ'.

file, *n.* **1.** File (*f.*): fīl. **2.** Contrôles (*m. pl.*): keṅ"trōl'.—**by files!** Par files! par fīl.—**close file.** File serrée: fīl sār"rē'.—**connecting f.** File de liaison: fīl də lī"ā"zeṅ'.—**left f.!** Par file à gauche! par fīl a gōsh (*left wheel*).—**right f.!** Par file à droite: pār fīl a drwat (*right wheel*).—**single f.!** **1.** En file indienne! aṅ fīl aṅ"dī"‿yen'. **2.** À la file! a la fīl.

fill, *v.* Remplir: raṅ"plīr'.—**to fill a pipe.** Bourrer une pipe: bū"rē' ün pīp.—**to fill up the gaps.** Combler les vides: keṅ"blē' lē vīd.

filly. Pouliche (*n. f.*): pū"līsh'.

film. Pellicule (*n. f.*): pel"‿lī"kül' (*for photography*).

filter, I. *n.* Filtre (*m.*): fīl'‿trə. **II.** *v.* Filtrer: fīl"trē'.—**filtration.** Filtration (*n. f.*): fīl"tra"sī"‿yeṅ'.

find, *v.* **1.** Trouver: trū"vē'. **2.** Prononcer: prō"neṅ"sē' (*a verdict*).—**to find one's bearings.** S'orienter: sō"rī"aṅ"tē'.—**to f. the range.** Constater le pointage: keṅ"sta"tē' lə pwāṅ"tāʒ'.

fine. I. *a.* **1.** Fin (*m.*): faṅ; fine (*f.*): fīn'‿ə. **2.** Délicat (*m.*): dē"lī"kā'; délicate (*f.*): dē"lī"kāt'‿ə. **II.** *n.* Amende (*f.*): a"māṅd'‿ə. **III.** *v.* Mettre à l'amende: met'‿trə a la"māṅd'‿ə.—**liable to a fine.** Passible d'une amende: pas"‿sī'blə dün a"māṅd'‿ə.—**finely,** *adv.* Finement: fīn"māṅ'.

finger. Doigt (*n. m.*): dwā.—**finger-post.** Poteau (*m.*):

pe″tō′ (on maps, *pau.*).—**f.-print.** Empreinte digitale: aṅ″-praṅt′‿ə dĭ″ʒī″tāl′‿ə.

finish. **I.** *n.* **1.** Fini (*m.*): fī″nī′. **2.** Fin (*f.*): faṅ. **3.** Terminaison (*f.*): tār″mī″nā″zoṅ′. **II.** *v.* **1.** Finir: fī″nīr′. **2.** Terminer: tar″mī″nē′.—**a fight to a finish.** Une bataille à outrance: ün ba″tai′‿yə a ū″trāṅ′‿sə.

fir. Sapin (*n. m.*): sa″paṅ′.

fire. **I.** *n.* **1.** Feu (*m.*): fū. **2.** Fusillade (*f.*): fü″zī″yād′‿ə. **II.** *v.* **1.** Tirer: tī″rē′ (*of fire-arms*) **2.** Incendier: aṅ″saṅ″dī″‿yē′ (*set fire to*).—**fire!** Feu! fū (*military order*).—**accurate f.** Justesse de tir: ʒüs″tes′ də tīr.—**covering-f.** Feu couvrant: fū kū″vrāṅ′.—**cross-f.** Feu croisé: fū krwa″zē′.—**curved or high angle f.** Tir indirect: tīr aṅ″dī″rekt′.—**demolition f.**—Tir à démolir: tīr a dē″mō″līr′.—**effective f.** Feu efficace: fū ēf″‿fī″kās′‿ə.—**direct f.** Tir direct: tīr dī″rekt′.—**discontinue f.!** Arrêtez le feu! ar″‿rā″tē′ lə fū (*military order*).—**enfilade f.** Feu d'enfilade: fū daṅ″fī″lād′‿ə.—**f. sector.** Secteur de feu: sek″tūr′ də fū.—**frontal f.** Feu de plein fouet: fū də plaṅ fū″‿ē′.—**grazing f.** Tir rasant: tīr ra″zāṅ′.—**groping f.** Tir progressif: tīr prō″grēs″‿sīf′.—**heavy f.** Feu sévère: fū sē″vār′.—**independent f.** Feu à volonté: fū a vō″loṅ″tē′.—**screen f.** Tir de barrage: tīr də bar″‿rā′‿ʒə.—**searching f.** Tir fouillant: tīr fū″ī″yāṅ′.—**steady f.** Feu régulier: fū rē″gü″lī″‿yē′.—**f.-control post.** Poste d'observation: pōs′‿tə dəb″zār″va″sī″yoṅ′.—**f. trench, front-line trench.** Tranchée sur la ligne du feu: traṅ″shē′ sür la lī′‿nyə dü fū.—**f. at close range.** Tir à courte distance: tīr a kūrt dīs″tāṅ′‿sə.—**f. by salvos at varying ranges.** Tir par salves échelonnées: tīr par sāl′‿və ē″shē″lon″‿nē′.—**f. sweeping an area.** Tir fauchant un terrain: tīr fō″shāṅ′ aṅ tār″‿raṅ′.—**light a f.** Allumer un feu: al″lü″mēr′‿aṅ fū.—**line of fire.** Ligne de tir: lī′‿nyə də tīr.—**to make a f.** Faire du feu: fār dü fū.—**rate of f.** Cadence du tir: ka″dāṅ′‿sə dü tīr.—**volume of f.** L'intensité du feu: laṅ″taṅ″sī″tē′ dü fū.—**to receive f.** Essuyer le feu: es″‿swī″yē′ lə fū.—**reverse f.** Feu à revers: fū a rə-vār′.—**to gain f. superiority.** Obtenir la supériorité du feu: ob″‿tə-nīr′ la sü″pē″rī″or″ī″tē′ dü fū.—**carry him out of f.!** Portez-le hors du feu! pōr″tē′ lə hōr dü fū.—**to open f.** Commencer le feu: kəm″‿maṅ″sē′ lə fū.—**to f. a mine.** Faire sauter une mine: fār sō″tē′ ün mīn′‿ə.

fire engine. Pompe à incendie: pōṅ′‿pə a aṅ″saṅ″dī′.

fireman. Chauffeur (*n. m.*): shōf″‿fūr′.—**firewood.** Bois à feu (*m.*): bwā a fū.

firing charge. Mise de feu: mīz də fū.—**firing** or **gunnery instructions.** Eléments de tir: ē″lē″māṅ′ də tīr.—**firing lever.** Levier d'armement: lə-vī″‿yē′ dar″‿mə-māṅ′.—**firing line.** Ligne de feu: lī′‿nyə də fū.—**firing point.** Stand (*n. m.*): stand.—**firing squad.** Escouade de tir: es″kū″‿ād′ də tīr.—**firing step. 1.** Banquette de tir: baṅ″ket′ də tīr. **2.** Talus intérieur (*m.*): ta″lü′ aṅ″tē″rī″yūr′ (*a ledge in a trench from which soldiers fire at an enemy*).—**cease firing!** Cessez le feu! ses″sē′ lə fū.

firm, *a.* **1.** Ferme (*m. & f.*): fār′‿mə. **2.** Solide (*m. & f.*): so″līd′‿ə.

first, *a.* Premier (*m.*): prə-mī″‿yē′; première (*f.*): prə-mī″-yār′‿ə.—**first of all.** Tout d'abord: tū da″bōr′.—**f.-aid medical packet.** Paquet de pansement (*m.*): pa″kē′ də paṅ″‿sə-māṅ′.—**First of July.** Premier Juillet: prə-mī″‿yē′ ʒü″‿ī″‿yē′ (*The Battle of the Somme, which started on that day*).

fish. Poisson (*n. m.*): pwas″‿soṅ′.—**fishery.** Pêcherie (*n. f.*): pā″shə-rī′ (on maps, *Pechie*).—**fishing.** Pêche (*n. f.*): pā′‿shə.—**fish-pond.** Vivier (*n. m.*): vī″vī″‿yē′.

fistula. Fistule (*n. f.*): fīs″tūl′‿ə.—**fistulous withers.** Mal de garrot (*n. m.*): mal də gar″‿rō′ (*veterinary term*).

fit. **I.** *a.* Apte (*m. & f.*): āpt. **II.** *v.* Ajuster: a″ʒüs″tē′.—**fit for field operations.** Apte aux opérations en rase campagne: āpt ōz‿o″pē′ra″sī″‿yeṅ′ aṅ rāz kaṅ″pā′‿nyə.—**fitted with.** Monté avec: meṅ″tē′ a″vek′.—**fittings.** Installations (*n. f. pl.*): aṅ″stal″la″sī″‿yeṅ′.—**reported fit for duty.** Déclaré bon pour le service: dē″kla″rē′ beṅ pūr lə sār″vīs′.—**the fitting up of wagons for the conveyance.** L'aménagement des wagons pour le transport: la″mē″na″‿ʒə-māṅ′ dē va″geṅ′ pūr lə traṅs″pōr′.—**to be fit to go to.** Être en état de partir: ā′‿trə aṅ ē″tā′ də par″tīr′.—**to fit up.** Monter: meṅ″tē′.

five. **I.** *a.* Cinq: saṅ (*before noun or adjective beginning with consonant or h asp.*); saṅk (*in all other cases*). **II.** *n. m.* Cinq: saṅ and saṅk (*as in case of adjective*).—**five minutes past seven.** Sept heures cinq: set ūr saṅk.—**f. thousand.** Cinq mille (*n. m. pl.*): saṅ mīl′‿ə.

fix, *v.* **1.** Fixer: fīk″sē′. **2.** Attacher: at″‿ta″shē′.—**fixed,** *a.* Fixe: fīks.—**fix bayonets!** Baïonnette au canon! ba″‿yo″net′ ō ka″neṅ′.

flag, *n.* **1.** Pavillon (*m.*): pa″vī″‿yeṅ′. **2.** Drapeau (*m.*): dra″-pō′. **3.** Fanion (*m.*): fa″‿nyeṅ′.—**flag-bearer.** Porte-drapeau (*n. m.*): per′‿tə dra″pō′.—**f. of truce.** **1.** Drapeau blanc: dra″pō′ blaṅ. **2.** Parlementaire (*n. m.*): par″lə-maṅ″tār′.—**f.-ship.** Vaisseau amiral: vēs″sō′ a″mī″rāl′.—**f. signals.** Les signaux: lē sī″nyo′.—**staff-officer's f.** Pavillon d'officier de l'état-major: pa″vī″‿yeṅ′ dof″‿fī″sī″ē′ də lē″tā′ ma″ʒōr′.—**the f. was unfurled.** Le drapeau était déployé: lə dra″pō′ ē″tē′ dē″plwa″yē′.—**to hoist a f.** Arborer un pavillon (*v.*): ar″bō″rē′ aṅ pa″vī″‿yeṅ′.—**white f.** **1.** Le pavillon blanc: lə pa″vī″yeṅ′ blaṅ. **2.** Drapeau blanc (d'un parlementaire): dra″pō′ blaṅ (daṅ par″lə‿maṅ″tār′).

flagstaff. **1.** Hampe (*n. f.*): hāṅp. **2.** Bâton de pavillon: ba″teṅ′ də pa″vī″‿yeṅ′.

flame projector. Projecteur de flammes: pro″ʒēk″tūr′ də [flām.

flank. Flanc (*n. m.*): flaṅ.—**in flank.** Par le flanc: par lə flaṅ.—**to expose the f.** Montrer le flanc: meṅ″trē′ lə flaṅ.

flanker, *n.* **1.** Flanc (*m.*): flaṅ (*fort*). **2.** Flanqueur (*m.*): flaṅ″kūr′ (*one who flanks*).—**the flanks are protected.** Les flancs sont gardés: lē flaṅ seṅ gar″dē′.

flannel, **I.** *n.* Flanelle (*f.*): fla″nēl′. **II.** *a.* De ou en flanelle: də ū aṅ fla″nēl′ (*of* or *in flannel*).

flare, *n.* **1.** Flamme (*f.*): flam; vive clarté (*f.*): vīv klar″tē′. **2.** Flambeau (*m.*), flambeaux (*pl.*): flaṅ″bō′.—**flare-pistol.** Lance-fusée (*n. m.*): laṅs″fü″zē′.—**landing flare.** Feu d'atterrissage (*m.*): fū dat″‿tār″‿rīs″‿sāʒ′ (*used by aviators*).

flash, **I.** *n.* **1.** Lueur (*f.*): lü″ūr′. **2.** Éclair (*m.*): ē″klār′ (*of lightning*). **3.** Éclat (*m.*): ē″klā′. **II.** *v.* Luire: lü″īr′.

flashlight, *n.* Éclair (*m.*): ē″klār′.—**pocket flashlight.** Éclair électrique de poche: ē″klār′ ē″lek″trīk′ də posh.

flat, *a.* **1.** Plat (*m.*): plā; plate (*fem.*): plat. **2.** Camus (*m.*): ka″mü′; camuse (*fem.*): ka″müz′ (*of noses flat or snub*). **3.** Collées: kol″lē′ (*of ears close to the head*).

flavor, *n.* **1.** Saveur (*f.*): sa″vūr′ (*of taste*). **2.** Goût (*m.*): gū (*of meats*). **3.** Arome (*m.*): a″rōm′ (*of tea, coffee, etc.*).

flea. Puce (*n. f.*): püs.—**flea-bitten.** Aubère (*a.*): ō″bār′ (*of horses*).

fleet, *n.* **1.** Flotte (*f.*): flet. **2.** Escadre (*f.*): es″kā′‿drə (*squadron*).

Flemish, *a.* Flamand (*m.*): fla″māṅ′; flamande (*f.*): fla″māṅd′.

flesh, *n.* **1.** Chair (*f.*): shār. **2.** Viande (*f.*): vī″āṅd′ (*meat*).

flight. **1.** Fuite (*n. f.*): fwīt (*rout*). **2.** Vol (*n. m.*): vōl (*of an aviator*).

flinch, *v.* Reculer: rə-kü″lē′.

flint, *n.* **1.** Caillou (*m.*): kai″yū′. **2.** Pierre à fusil (*f.*): pī″‿yār′ a fü″zī′.

flip, *n.* [Aviators' slang.] Flight.

float, *v.* Flotter: flōt″‿tē′.—**floater.** Flotteur: flōt″‿tūr′ (*sustaining plane*).
flood, I. *n.* **1.** Crue (*f.*): krü (*of rising water*). **2.** Inondation (*f.*): ī″noṅ″dạ″sī″‿yeṅ′ (*overflow*). **II.** *v.* Inonder: ī″noṅ″dē′.—**flood=gate.** Écluse de marée (*n. f.*): ē″klüs′ də mạ″rē′.
floor, *n.* Étage (*m.*): ē″tāʒ′.
flooring, *n.* Plancher (*m.*): plạṅ″shē′.
flour, *n.* Farine (*f.*): fạ″rīn′.
fluctuate, *v.* **1.** Balancer: bạ″lạṅ″sē′. **2.** Flotter: flot″‿tē′.
fly, *n.* Mouche (*f.*): mūsh.
fly, *v.* **1.** Voler: vo″lē′ (*in the air*). **2.** Fuir: fwīr (*flee*).—**flying. I.** *n.* Le vol: lə vōl. **II.** *a.* Volant (*m.*): vo″lạṅ′; volante (*f.*): vo″lạṅt′.—**flying colors.** Enseignes déployées: ạṅ″sē′‿nyə dē″plwạ″yē′.—**f.=corps.** Service de l'aéronautique (*m.*): sār″vīs′ də lạ″ē″ro″nō″tīk′.—**f.=column.** Colonne volante: ko″lon′ vo″lạṅt′.—**f.=machine.** Avion (*m.*): ạ″vī″‿yeṅ′.—**f.=squadron.** Escadre d'évolution (*f.*): es″kād′‿rə dē″vo″lü″sī″‿yeṅ′.—**to fly above or over (another).** Survoler (*v.*): sür″vō″lē′.
focus. I. *n.* Foyer (*m.*): fwạ″‿yē′. **II.** *v.* Mettre au foyer, ou au point: met′‿trə ō fwạ″‿yē′, ū ō pwạṅ.
fodder. 1. Fourrage (*n. m.*): fūr″‿rāʒ′. **2.** Pâture (*f.*): pạ″tür′.—**green fodder.** Fourrage en vert: fūr″‿rāʒ′ ạṅ vār.
foe. Ennemi (*n. m.*): en″‿nə-mī′.
fog, *n.* Brouillard (*m.*): brū″‿yār′.—**on account of the fog nothing can be seen.** À cause du brouillard on ne peut rien voir: ạ kōz dü brū″‿yār′ en nə pū rī″‿yạn′ vwār.—**there is too much fog.** Il y a trop de brouillard: īl‿ī yạ trō də brū″‿yār′.
fog=horn. Sirène (*n. f.*): sī″rān′.
fog=signal. Pétard (*n. m.*): pē″tār′.
Fokker. Fokker (*n. m.*): fok″‿kār′ (*German aeroplane*).
follow, *v.* Suivre: swī′‿vrə.—**to f. up.** Poursuivre: pūr″-swī′‿vrə.—**followers.** Domestiques (*n. pl.*): dō″mes″tīk′ (*camp=followers and civilians attached to an army*).
food, *n.* **1.** Nourriture (*f.*): nūr″‿rī″tür′. **2.** Vivres (*m. pl.*): vīv′‿rə (*provisions*).—**give him some food.** Donnez=lui à manger: don″‿nē′ lwī ạ mạṅ″ʒē′.
foolhardy, *a.* Téméraire (*m. & f.*): tē″mē″rār′ (*reckless*).
foot, *n.* Pied (*m.*): pī″‿yē′. Compare FEET.—**foot=board.** Marchepied (*n. m.*): marsh″pī″‿yē′.—**f.=bridge.** Passerelle (*n. f.*): pas′‿sə-rel′.—**f.=soldier.** Fantassin (*n. m.*): fạn″tas″sạṅ′.—**on f.** À pied: ạ pī″‿yē′.
footing. Point d'appui (*n. m.*): pwạṅ dạp″pwī′.
footpath. Sentier (*n. m.*): sạṅ″tī″‿yē′.
footstep. Trace (*n. f.*): trās.
for. I. *prep.* **1.** Pour: pūr (*a person*). **2.** De: də. **II.** *conj.* [Car: kạr.
forage, *n.* Fourrage (*m.*): fūr″‿rāʒ′.—**compressed forage.** Fourrage comprimé: fūr″‿rāʒ′ koṅ″prī″mē′.—**f. shed.** Réserve de fourrage (*n. f.*): rē″zārv′ də fūr″‿rāʒ′.—**f. for horses.** À manger pour les chevaux: ā mạṅ″ʒē′ pūr lē shə-vō′.—**f. stacks.** Meules de foin (*f.*): mūl də fwạṅ.—**to provide with f.** Fourrager (*v.*): fūr″‿rạ″ʒē′.
forager. Fourrageur (*n. m.*): fūr″‿rạ″ʒūr′.
forbid, *v.* Défendre: dē″fạṅ′‿drə.—**forbidden,** *pa.* **1.** Défendu (*m.*): dē″fạṅ″dü′; défendue (*f.*): dē″fạṅ″dü′. **2.** Interdit (*m.*): ạṅ″tār″dī′; interdite (*f.*): ạṅ″tār″dīt′.
force. I. *n.* **1.** Force (*f.*): fōrs. **2.** Troupes (*f. pl.*): trūp. **II.** *v.* Forcer: fōr″sē′.—**to force back.** Faire reculer: fār rə-kü″lē′.
ford. I. *n.* Gué (*m.*): gā. On maps, *Gué.* **II.** *v.* Passer à gué: pas″‿sē′ ạ gā.—**fordable,** *a.* Guéable (*m. & f.*): gē″ā′‿blə.
forearm. Avant=bras (*n. m.*): ạ″vạṅ″brā′.
foreground. Terrain en avant (*n. m.*): tār″‿rạṅ′ ạṅ‿ [ạ″vạṅ′.

forehead, *n.* **1.** Front (*m.*): froṅ. **2.** Chanfrein (*m.*): shaṅ"fraṅ' (*of a horse*).
foreign, *a.* Étranger (*m.*): ē"traṅ"ʒē'; étrangère (*f.*): ē"traṅ"ʒār'.—**Foreign Legion.** Légion Étrangère: lē"ʒī"‿yoṅ' ē"traṅ"ʒār'.
foreman. Contre-maître (*n. m.*): koṅ"‿trə-mā'‿trə.
fore-quarters. Avant-main (*n. m.*): a"vaṅ"maṅ' (*of a horse*).
foresee, *v.* Prévoir: prē"vwār'.
foresight. Prévoyance (*n. f.*): prē"vwa"yāṅs'.
fore sight. Guidon (*n. m.*): gī"doṅ' (*of a rifle, etc.*).
forest. Forêt (*n. f.*): fō"rē'. On maps, *Ft.*—**forester.** Garde forestier (*n. m.*): gārd fō"res"tī"‿yē'.
forge. **I.** *n.* Forge (*f.*): fōrʒ. **II.** *v.* Forger: for"ʒē'.
forger. Faussaire (*n. m. & f.*): fōs"‿sār'.—**forgery,** *n.* **1.** Falsification (*f.*): fal"sī"fī"ka"sī"‿yoṅ'. **2.** (1) Faux (*m.*): fō. (2) Crime de faux (*m.*): krīm də fō.
forget, *v.* Oublier: ū"blī"‿yē'.
fork, *n.* **1.** Fourchette (*f.*): fūr"shet' (*implement*). **2.** Bifurcation (*f.*): bī"fūr"ka"sī"‿yoṅ' (*of roads*). Compare JUNCTION.
form. **I.** *n.* **1.** Forme (*f.*): fōrm. **2.** Figure (*f.*): fī"gūr'. **II.** *v.* Former: fōr"mē'.—**form fours!** Par quatre! par kā'‿trə.—**f. fours, right!** À droite par quatre! a drwāt par kā"‿trə.—**f. line!** En rang! aṅ rāṅ.—**f. squads!** Par groupes! par grūp.—**f. two!** Par deux! par dū.—**handy form.** Maniable: ma"nī"ā'‿blə.—**regulation f.** Modèle réglementaire: mō"dĕl' rē"‿glə-maṅ"tār'.
formation. Formation (*n. f.*): fōr"ma"sī"‿yoṅ'.—**echelon formation.** See ECHELON.
forsake, *v.* Abandonner: a"baṅ"doṅ"‿nē'.
fort. Fort (*n. m.*): fōr. On maps, *Ft.*—**frontier fort.** Fort d'arrêt: fōr dar"‿rē'.—**field-fort.** Fortin (*n. m.*): fōr"taṅ'.—**isolated** or **detached f.** Fort isolé ou détaché: fōr ī"zo"lē' u dē"ta"shē'.—**quadrangular** or **square f.** Fort carré: fōr kar"‿rē'.—**star f.** Fort à étoile: fōr a ē"twal'.
forthwith, *adv.* Sur-le-champ: sür"‿lə-shāṅ'.
fortieth, *a. & n.* Quarantième (*m. & f.*): ka"raṅ"tī"‿yām'.
fortification. Fortification (*n. f.*): for"tī"fī"ka"sī"‿yoṅ'. On maps, *Fortif.*—**permanent f.** Fortification permanente: fōr"tī"fī"ka"sī"‿yoṅ' pār"ma"nāṅt'.
fortify, *v.* Fortifier: fōr"tī"fī"‿yē'.—**fortified,** *a.* Fortifié (*m.*); fortifiée (*f.*): fōr"tī"fī"‿yē'.—**fortified city.** **1.** Place forte (*n. f.*): plās fōrt. **2.** Ville fortifiée (*n. f.*): vīl fōr"tī"fī"‿yē'.—**f. town.** Ville fortifiée: vīl fōr"tī"fī"‿yē'.—**the position is fortified.** La position est fortifiée: la pō"zī"sī"‿yoṅ' ē fōr"tī"fī"‿yē'.
fortnight, *n.* **1.** Quinzaine (*f.*): kaṅ"zān'. **2.** Quinze jours: kaṅz ʒūr.
fortress. Forteresse (*n. f.*): fōr"‿tres'.
forty, *a. & n.* Quarante (*m. & f.*): kar"‿rāṅt'.
forward. **I.** *a. Naut.* À l'avant: a la"vāṅ'. **II.** *adv. Mil.* (1) En avant! aṅ‿a"vāṅ'. (2) En marche! aṅ mārsh.
forward, *v.* **1.** Avancer: a"vaṅ"sē' (*of troops*). **2.** Adresser: a"dres"‿sē' (*of letters*). **3.** Transmettre: traṅs"met'‿trə (*a message*).—**forward, by column of fours, from the right, march!** Par la droite par quatre! par la drwāt par kā'‿trə.—**from forward aft.** De l'avant vers l'arrière (*of a ship*): də la"vāṅ' vār lar"rī"‿yār'.—**forwarding-clerk.** Commis aux expéditions: kom"‿mīz'‿ōz‿eks"pē"dī"sī"‿yoṅ'.
forward, march! En avant! aṅ‿a"vāṅ'.
fougade. Fougasse (*n. f.*): fū"gās'‿sə (*a small mine for blowing up relinquished positions*).—**stone fougasse.** Fougasse-pierrier: fū"gās'‿sə pī"‿yār"‿rī"‿ē'.
found, *pa.* Trouvé (*m.*); trouvée (*f.*): trū"vē'.
foundry. Fonderie (*n. f.*): foṅ"‿də-rī'. On maps, *Frie.*

fountain. Fontaine (*n. f.*): fon″tēn′‿ə. On maps, *Fne.*—**fountain pen.** Porte=plume réservoir: pōr″tə‿plü′‿mə rē″zār″vwār′.—**fountain=pen filler.** Chargeur (*m.*): shar″zūr′.

four, *a.* & *n. m.* Quatre: ka′‿trə.—**a quarter to four.** Quatre heures moins quart: ka′‿tr‿ūr mwan kar.—**"four by two."** A piece of flannel measuring four inches by two used for cleaning the inside of a rifle=barrel.—**four o'clock.** Quatre heures: ka′‿tr‿ūr.—**fourth.** **I.** *a.* Quatrième (*m.* & *f.*): ka″trī″‿yām′. **II.** *n. m.* Quart: kar.—**fourteen.** Quatorze (*a.* & *n. m.*): ka″tor′‿zə.—**fourteenth.** Quatorzième (*a. m.* & *f.*): ka″tōr″zī″ām′.

fowl. Poulet (*n. m.*): pū″lē′.

fracture. Fracture (*n. f.*): frak″tür′.—**compound fracture.** Fracture double: frak″tür′ dū′‿blə.—**open wound f.** Fracture ouverte: frak″tür′ ū″vārt′‿ə.

fraise. Fraise (*n. f.*): frā′‿zə (*a defense of pointed stakes*).

framework. Charpente (*n. f.*): shar″pānt′‿ə.

France, *n. f.* La France: la frān′‿sə.

franc. Franc (*n. m.*): frān.—**that comes to six francs.** Cela fait six francs: sə-la′ fā sī frān.—**twelve francs in change.** Douze francs en petite monnaie: Dūz frān an pə-tīt′ mon″‿nē′.

franc=tireur. Franc=tireur (*n. m.*): fran″tī″rūr′ (*sharpshooter; guerilla*).

frank, *a.* Franc (*m.*): frān; franche (*f.*): frān′‿shə.

freckle. Rousseur (*n. f.*): rūs″‿sūr′.—**to be freckled.** Avoir des rousseurs: a″vwār′ dē rūs″‿sūr′.

free, *a.* Libre (*m.* & *f.*): lī′‿brə.—**to give as free a hand as possible.** Laisser toute l'initiative possible: lās″‿sē′ tūt lin″ī″sī″a″tīv′ pos″‿sī′‿blə.

freedom. Liberté (*n. f.*): lī″bār″tē′.—**to restore to freedom.** Mettre en liberté: met′‿trə an lī″bār″tē′. [(*of persons*).

freeze, *v.* **1.** Geler: ʒə-lē′ (*of the weather*). **2.** Se geler: sə ʒə-lē′

freight. Fret (*n. m.*): frē.—**freight depot.** Gare de marchandises: gār də mar″shan″dīz′‿ə.

French, *a.* Français (*m.*): fran″sā′; française (*f.*): fran″sāz′‿ə.—**a Frenchman.** Un Français (*n. m.*): an fran″sā′.—**are you in the French army?** Êtes vous de l'armée Française? ā′‿tə vū də lar″mē′ fran″sāz′‿ə.—**I speak only a little French.** Je ne parle qu'un peu de français: ʒə nə pār′‿lə kan pū də fran″sā′.—**I understand French better than I speak it.** Je comprends mieux le français que je ne le parle: ʒə kon″prān′ mī″‿ū′ lə fran″sā′ kə ʒə nə lə pār′‿lə.—**the French.** Les Français (*m. pl.*): lē fran″sā′.—**what is it called in French?** Comment cela s'appelle=t=il en français? kom″‿mān′ sə-lā′ sap″‿pel″tīl′ an fran″sā′.

frequent, *a.* Fréquent (*m.*): frē″kan′; fréquente (*f.*): frē″kān′‿tə.—**frequently,** *adv.* Fréquemment: frē″ka″‿mān′.

fresh, *a.* Frais (*m.*): frā; fraîche (*f.*): frā′‿shə.—**freshet.** Inondation subite (*n. f.*): in″on″da″sī″‿yon′ sü″bīt′‿ə.

Friday. Vendredi (*n. m.*): van″‿drə-dī′.

friend. Ami (*n. m.*): a″mī′.—**old friends.** Vieux camarades: vī″‿ū′ ka″ma″rād′‿ə.—**we are good friends.** Nous sommes de bons amis: nū som′‿mə də bonz‿a″mī′.—**friendly,** *a.* Amical (*m.*); amicale (*f.*): a″mī″kāl′.—**friendship.** Amitié (*n. f.*): a″mī″tī″‿ē′.

fright, *n.* **1.** Frayeur (*f.*): frā″yūr′. **2.** Effroi (*m.*): ef″‿frwā′.

frigo, frī″gō′, *n.* [Fr. slang.] Frozen meat: so called by soldiers.

frog, *n.* **1.** Grenouille (*f.*): grə-nū″ī′‿yə (*the animal*). **2.** Porte=sabre (*m.*): pōr″‿tə-sa′‿brə (*support for the sword attached to belt*). **3.** Brandebourg (*m.*): bran″‿də-būr′ (*braided loop on officers' coats*). **4.** Fourchette (*f.*): fūr″shet′‿tə (*of a horse's hoof*).

from, *prep.* **1.** De: də (*of place*). **2.** Depuis: də-pwī′ (*of time*). **3.** Par: pār (*of cause*).

front, *n.* **1.** Front (*m.*): fron (*used also as a word of command*).

2. Devant (*m.*): də-vāñ'.—**at the front.** À la guerre: a la gär.—**battle-front.** Front de bataille: frəñ də ba"tai'‿yə.—**from f. to rear.** De la tête à la queue: də la tē'‿tə a la kū (*of a battalion*).—**in f. of.** 1. En avant de: añ‿a"vāñ' də. 2. Devant: də-vāñ'.—**on a wide front.** Sur un front étendu: sür añ frəñ ē"tañ"dü'.—**to go to the f.** Aller au le front: al"lē' ō lə frəñ.
frontage, *n.* 1. Front (*m.*): frəñ. 2. Façade (*f.*): fa"sād'‿ə (*of a building*).
frontal, *a.* Frontal (*m.*); frontale (*f.*): frəñ"tāl'.
frontier. Frontière (*n. f.*): frəñ"tī"‿yār'‿ə. On maps, *Front^e*.
frost. Gelée (*n. f.*): ʒə‿lē'.
fruit. Fruit (*n. m.*): frwī.—**stewed fruit.** Compote de fruits: kəñ pōt' də frwī.
fry, *v.* Frire: frīr'‿ə.—**frying-pan.** Poêle: pō"ēl'.
fuel, *n.* 1. Chauffage (*m.*): shof"‿fāʒ'. 2. Combustible (*m.*): kəñ"büs"tī'‿blə.
fugitive. Fuyard (*n. m.*): fwī"yar'.
fulfil, *v.* Accomplir: a"kəñ"plīr'.—**to fulfil one's rôle.** Remplir son rôle: rañ"plīr' səñ rōl'‿ə.—**fulfilment.** Accomplissement (*n. m.*): ak"‿kəñ"plīs"‿sə-māñ'.
full, *a.* Plein (*m.*): plañ; pleine (*f.*): plā'‿nə.—**full-blooded.** *a.* Sanguin (*m.*): sañ"gañ'; sanguine (*f.*): sañ"gīn'.—**at full cock.** Au cran de l'armé: ō krañ də lar"mē'.—**full pack.** A soldier carrying all his equipment: slang term.—**to let one have full play.** Laisser faire: lās"‿sē' fār'‿ə.
fully, *adv.* 1. Entièrement: añ"tī"yār"‿ə-māñ'. 2. Complètement: kəñ"plā"‿tə-mañ'.
function. I. *n.* 1. Fonction (*f.*): fəñk"sī"‿yəñ'. 2. Rôle (*m.*): rōl'‿ə. II. *v.* Fonctionner: fəñk"sī"‿yəñ"‿nē'.
fund. Fonds (*n. m.*): fəñ.—**regimental fund.** Masse régimentaire: mās'‿sə rē"ʒī"mañ"tār'‿ə.
funeral. 1. Enterrement (*n. m.*): añ"tār"‿rə-māñ'. 2. Pompes funèbres: pəñp fü"nē'‿brə.—**funeral honors.** Honneurs funèbres (*m.*): əñ"‿nūr' fü"nē'‿brə.
funk. Effroi (*n. m.*): ef"‿frwā'.—**funk hole.** A dugout: soldiers' slang.
[sha-mī"nē'.
funnel, *n.* 1. Tuyau (*n. m.*): twī"‿yō'. 2. Cheminée (*f.*):
furlough. Congé (*n. m.*): kəñ"ʒē'.—**prolongation of furlough.** Prolongation de congé: prō"ləñ"ga"sī"‿yəñ' də kəñ"ʒē'.—**on furlough.** En congé: añ kəñ"ʒē'.
[(*f.*): fūr"nāz'‿ə.
furnace, *n.* 1. Four (*m.*): fūr. On maps, *Fr.* 2. Fournaise
furnish, *v.* 1. Fournir: fūr"nīr'. 2. Constituer: kəñ"stī"tü"‿ē'.—**to furnish information.** Fournir des renseignements: fūr"nīr' dē rañ"sān"‿yə-māñ'.
furrow. Sillon (*n. m.*): sī"yəñ'.
further, *adv.* Plus loin: plü lwañ.—**a little further.** Un peu plus loin: añ pū plü lwañ.
fuse, *n.* 1. Fusée (*f.*): fü"zē'. 2. Mèche (*f.*): mā'‿shə.—**f. hole.** Œil de l'ogive: ū"‿ī' də lō"ʒīv'.—**f. needle.** Rugueux (*m.*): rü"gū'.—**f. punch.** Débouchoir (*m.*): dē"bū"shwār'.—**Bickford fuse.** Mèche lente: mā'‿shə lāñ'‿tə.—**delay f.** Fusée porte-retard: fü"zē' pōr'‿tə rə-tār'.—**double action f.** Fusée à double effet: fü"zē' a dū'‿blə ēf"‿fē'.—**instantaneous f.** Cordon porte-feu: kōr"dəñ' pōr"fū'.—**percussion f.** Fusée percutante: fü"zē' pār"kü"tāñt'‿ə.—**quick f.** Cordeau détonant: kōr"dō' dē"təñ"āñ'.—**slow f.** Cordeau Bickford: kōr"dō' Bīk"fōr'.—**time f.** Fusée fusante: fü"zē' fü"zāñt'‿ə.—**time and percussion f.** Fusée à double effet: fü"zē' a dū'‿blə ef"‿fē'.—**universal f.** Fusée universelle: fü"zē' ün"ī"vār"sel'‿lə.
fuselage. Fuselage (*n. m.*): fü"‿sə-lāʒ' (*light framework of an aeroplane*).—**canvas fuselage.** Fuselage entoilé: fü"‿sə-lāʒ' añ"-twa"yē'.
future. Avenir (*n. m.*): a"‿və-nīr'.

G

gabion. Gabion (*n. m.*): ga″bī″‿yeṅ′.—**gabion revetment, gabionage.** Gabionage (*n. m.*): ga″bī″‿yoṅ″āʒ′.
gage. Réglette (*n. f.*): rē″glet′‿tə (*of artillery*).—**narrow gage.** Voie étroite: vwā ē″trwāt′‿ə.
gain, *v.* Gagner: ga″nyē′.—**to gain ground.** **1.** Gagner du terrain: ga″nyē′ dü tār″‿rāṅ′. **2.** Progresser: prō″grēs′‿sē′.—**to g. a victory.** Remporter une victoire: raṅ″pōr″tē′ ün vīk″twār′‿ə.—**g. time.** See under TIME.
gaiters, *n.* Guêtres (*f. pl.*): gā′‿trə.
gall, *n.* **1.** Fiel (*m.*): fī″yel′. **2.** Bile (*f.*): bīl. **3.** Écorchure (*f.*): ē″kor″shür′. **4.** Blessure (*f.*): bles″‿sür′.—**girth-gall.** Blessure de sangle: bles″‿sür′ də saṅ′‿glə.—**saddle-gall.** Blessure de selle: bles″‿sür′ də sel′‿lə.—**galled withers.** Blessure au garrot: bles″‿sür′ ō gar″‿rō′.
gallant, *a.* Courageux (*m.*): kū″ra″ʒū′; courageuse (*f.*): kū″ra″ʒūz′‿ə.—**gallantry,** *n.* **1.** Galanterie (*f.*): ga″laṅ″‿tə-rī′ (*politeness*). **2.** Bravoure (*f.*): bra″vūr′ (*courage*).—**act of conspicuous gallantry.** Action d'éclat: ak″sī″‿yeṅ′ dē″klā′.
gallery. Galerie (*n. f.*): ga″‿lə-rī′. On maps, *Galie.*—**common gallery.** Grande galerie: grāṅ′‿də ga″‿lə-rī′.—**great g.** Galerie majeure: ga″‿lə-rī′ ma″ʒür′.—**mining g.** Galerie de mine: ga″‿lə-rī′ də mīn′‿ə.—**counter-mine g.** Galerie enveloppe: ga″‿lə-rī′ aṅ″və-lop′.
Galicia. Galicie (*n. f.*): ga″lī″sī′. A division of Austria-Hungary.
gallop. **I.** *n.* Galop (*m.*): ga″lō′. **II.** *v.* Galoper: ga″lo″pē′.—**charging gallop.** Galop de charge: ga″lō′ də shār′‿ʒə.—**full g. 1.** Galop allongé: ga″lōp′‿al″‿leṅ″ʒē′. **2.** Grand galop: grāṅ ga″-lō′.—**forced g.** Galop forcé: ga″lō′ fōr″sē′.—**let us g.** Allons au galop: al″leṅz′‿ō ga″lō′.
galvanized iron. Fer galvanisé: fār gal″va″nī″zē′.
galvanometer. Galvanomètre (*n. m.*): gal″va″no″mā′‿trə.
game, *n.* **1.** Jeu (*m.*): ʒū (*sport*). **2.** Gibier (*m.*): ʒī″bī″‿yē′ (*wild birds*, etc.).—**game-keeper.** Garde-chasse (*n. m.*): gār′‿də shās′‿sə.—**to die g.** Mourir en brave: mū″rīr′ aṅ brā′‿və.—**to make g. of.** Se moquer de: sə mo″kē′ də.
gangrene. Gangrène (*n. f.*): gaṅ″grān′‿ə.
gangway, *n.* **1.** Passerelle (*f.*): pas″‿sə-rel′‿lə (*from a ship to the shore*). **2.** Passavant (*m.*): pas″‿sa″vāṅ′ (*communicating passage on a ship*). **3.** Passage (*m.*): pas″sāʒ′‿ə (*between tents in a camp*).—**horse gangway.** Passerelle à chevaux: pas″‿sə-rel′‿lə a shə-vō′.
gap, *n.* **1.** Brèche (*f.*): brā′‿shə. **2.** Trou (*m.*): trū.
garden. Jardin (*n. m.*): ʒar″dāṅ′. On maps, *Jin.*
gargle. **I.** *n.* Gargarisme (*m.*): gar″ga″rīzm′. **II.** *v.* Gargariser: gar″ga″rī″zē′.
garrison. Garnison (*n. f.*): gar″nī″zoṅ′.
garrot. Garrot (*m.*): gar″‿rō′ (*a temporary tourniquet*).
gas. Gaz (*n. m.*): gāz.—**gas-bomb.** **1.** Bombe asphyxiante (*f.*): boṅ′‿bə as″fīk″sī″‿yāṅt′‿ə. **2.** Bombe suffocante (*f.*): boṅ′‿bə süf″‿fo″kāṅt′‿ə.—**incendiary gas.** Gaz incendiaire: gāz‿aṅ″saṅ″dī″‿yār′‿ə.—**gas-bag.** Enveloppe (*n. f.*): aṅ″‿və-lop′.—**gas cylinder.** Cylindre à gaz: sī″laṅ′‿dre a gāz.—**gas-fumes, gas-clouds.** Nuage de gaz (*m.*): nū″āʒ′‿ə də gāz.—**gas-gong.** An empty shell, which when struck serves as a gong and gives warning of the approach of poisonous gas.—**gas mask.** See GAS-HELMET, under HELMET.—**suffocating gas.** Gaz suffocant: gāz süf″‿fo″kāṅ′.
gash, *n.* **1.** Balafre (*f.*): ba″lā′‿frə. **2.** Estafilade (*f.*): es″ta″-fī″lād′‿ə.
gasoline. Essence (*n. f.*): es″‿sāṅ′‿sə.

gate, *n.* **1.** Porte (*f.*): pōr'‿tə. On maps, *Pte.* **2.** Barrière (*f.*): bar'‿rī"‿yār'‿ə.—**crossing-gate.** Barrière du passage à niveau: bar"‿rī"‿yār'‿ə dü pas"‿sāʒ'‿ə a nī'vō' (*on level railroad crossings*).—**sliding g.** **1.** Barrière à coulisse: bar"‿rī"‿yār'‿ə a kū"-līs'‿sə.—**swinging g.** Barrière roulante: bar"‿rī"‿yār'‿ə rū"-lānt'‿ə.—**two- or three-barred g.** Barrière à deux, trois barres: bar"‿rī"‿yār'‿ə a dū, trwā bār'‿rə.—**through the g.** A travers la grille: a tra"vār' la grī'‿yə.—**gateman** or **g.-keeper.** Garde-barrière (*n. m.*): gārd'ə bar"‿rī"‿yār'‿ə.

gather, *v.* Assembler: as"‿saṅ"blē'.

gauntlet. Gantelet (*n. m.*): gaṅ"‿tə-lē'.

gay, *a.* Gai (*m.*); gaie (*f.*): gā.

gear. **1.** Matériel (*n. m.*): ma"tē"rī"el' (*belongings*). **2.** Engrenage (*n. m.*): aṅ"‿grə-nāʒ'‿ə (*gearing*).—**gear box.** Boite de vitesse: bwāt'‿ə də vī"tēs'‿sə.—**change of g.** Changement de vitesse: shaṅ"‿ʒə-māṅ' də vī"tes'‿sə.—**steering-gear,** *n.* **1.** Gouvernail (*n. m.*): gū"vār"na"‿ī' (as of *boats, ships*, etc.). **2.** Direction: dī"reks"‿yeṅ' (as of *motor vehicles, aeroplanes*, etc.).—**traversing g.** Volant de pointage en direction: vo"lāṅ' də pwaṅ"-tāʒ'‿ə aṅ dī"rek"sī"‿yeṅ'.

gelding. Hongre (*n. m.*): heṅ'‿grə.

general. **I.** *a.* Général (*m.*); générale (*f.*): ʒē"nē"rāl'. **II.** *n.* Général (*m.*): ʒē"nē"rāl'.—**general action.** Action générale: ak"sī"‿yeṅ' ʒē"nē"rāl'.—**g. delivery.** Poste restante (*f.*): pōst res"tāṅ'‿tə.—**g. headquarters.** Quartier général du commandant en chef: kar"tī"‿yē' ʒē"nē"rāl' dü kem"‿maṅ"dāṅ' aṅ shef.—**g. staff.** État-major (*m.*): ē"tā' ma"ʒōr'.—**g. terms.** Termes généraux: tārm ʒē"nē"rō'.—**generally,** *adv.* Généralement: ʒē"-nē"ra"‿lə-māṅ'.

Geneva convention. Convention de Genève (*f.*): keṅ"vaṅ"-sī"‿yeṅ' də ʒə-nāv'‿ə (*agreement entered into 1864–1865 by European powers as to more humane treatment of sick and wounded in war*).

gentle, *a.* Doux (*m.*): dū; douce (*f.*): dūs'‿ə.—**gently,** *adv.* Doucement: dūs"māṅ'.—**carry him gently.** Portez-le doucement: pōr"tē' lə dūs"māṅ'.

gentleman. Monsieur (*n. m.*): mə-sī"‿yū'.—**gentlemanly.** Comme il faut: kem‿īl fō.

German, *a.* & *n.* Allemand (*m.*): al"‿lə-māṅ; allemande (*f.*): al"‿lə-māṅ'‿də.—**the Germans.** Les boches: lē bōsh'‿ə (*name given them by the French soldiers*).—**Germany.** Allemagne (*n. f.*): al"‿lə-mā'nyə.

get, *v.* **1.** Obtenir: ob"‿tə-nīr'. **2.** Procurer: pro"kü"rē'.—**get me.** **1.** Procurez-moi: pro"kü"rē' mwa. **2.** [U. S. slang.] Comprenez-vous? keṅ"pre"nē' vū.—**to get well again.** Se rétablir: sə rē"ta"blīr'.—**to get up.** Se lever: sə lə-vē'.

ghastly. *a.* **1.** Pâle comme la mort: pāl kem la mōr. **2.** Cadavéreux (*m.*): ka"da"vē"rū'.

giant, *n.* Géant (*m.*): ʒē"āṅ'.

gigantic, *a.* Gigantesque: ʒī"gaṅ"tesk'.

gimlet, *n.* **1.** Foret (*m.*): fō"rē'. **2.** Vrille (*f.*): vrī'‿yə.

gin, *n.* Trépied (*m.*): trē"pī"‿yē' (*a three-legged portable hoist*).

ginger, *a.* (*Of hair: used in identification.*) **1.** Roux (*m.*): rū; rousse (*f.*): rūs. **2.** Rouge (*m.* & *f.*): rūʒ. **3.** Rouquin (*m.*): rū"-kaṅ'; rouquine (*f.*): rū"kīn'.

gippo, jip'ō, *n.* [Soldiers' slang.] **1.** Soup. **2.** Bacon grease.

girdle, *n.* Ceinture (*f.*): saṅ"tür'.

girl. Fille (*n. f.*): fī'‿yə.

girth. **I.** *n.* **1.** Sangle (*f.*): saṅ'‿glə. **2.** Contour (*m.*): keṅ"-tūr'. **II.** *v.* Sangler: saṅ"glē'.—**loosen the girth.** Desserrer la sangle: dē"sēr"‿rē' la saṅ'‿glə.

give, *v.* Donner: den"‿nē'.—**give him.** Donnez-lui: den"nē' lwī.—**g. me.** Donnez-moi: den"nē' mwa.—**give me a light,**

artistic; ärt; fat; färe; fast; get; prēy; hit; polīce;
obey; gō; net; ōr; full; rūle; but; būrn; ə = final;

please. Donnez=moi du feu, s'il vous plaît: don"‿nē' mwa dü fu, sīl vū plā.—**to g. one's self away.** Se faire tomber: sə fār toṅ"bē'.—**to g. one's word.** Donner sa parole: don"nē' sa pa"rōl'.—**to g. way.** Fléchir: flē"shīr'.
glacier, *n.* Glacier (*m.*): gla"sī"‿yē'. Abbreviated *Gler.*
glacis, *n.* Glacis (*m.*): gla"sī'.
glad, *a.* **1.** Joyeux (*m.*): ʒwa"yū'; joyeuse (*f.*): ʒwa"yūz'. **2.** Bien aise: bī"yaṅ'‿āz. **3.** Content: koṅ"tūṅ'.—**glad of.** Heureux de: ūr"ū' də.
glade. Clairière (*n. f.*): klā"rī"‿yār'.
glanders. **1.** Mal de garrot (*n. m.*): māl də gar"‿rō'. **2.** Morve (*f.*): mōrv.
glass, *n.* **1.** Verre (*m.*): vār. **2.** Jumelles (*f. pl.*): ʒü"mel' (*field=glass*).—**glass=works.** Verrerie (*n. f.*): vār"‿rə-rī'.
gleet, *n.* **1.** Blennorragie (*f.*): blen"no"ra"ʒī'. **2.** Échauffement (*m.*): ē"shōf"māṅ.
glen, *n.* Vallon (*m.*): val"‿loṅ'; vallée (*f.*): val"‿lē'.
glide, *v.* **1.** Glisser: glīs"‿sē'. **2.** Vol=plané: vōl=pla"nē' (*by aeroplane*).
gloomy, *a.* Sombre: soṅ'‿brə.
glory, *n.* Gloire (*n. f.*): glwār.
gloves. Gants (*n. m.*): gaṅ.
G. M. P., *abbr.* Garrison Military Police. Police (Militaire) de Garnison: pō"līs' (mī'lī"tār') də gar"nī"zoṅ'.
go, *v.* Aller: al"‿lē'. See Appendix.—**go,** *imper.* Allez: al"‿lē'.—**go away.** Allez=vous en: al"‿lē' vūz‿aṅ.—**go slow!** Lentement! laṅ"tə-māṅ'.—**go slowly.** Doucement (*adv.*): dūs"-māṅ'.—**I am sorry to go.** Je suis désolé de partir: ʒə swī dē"sō"lē' də par"tīr'.—**let us go.** Allons: al"‿loṅ'.—**to go away,** *v.* **1.** S'en aller: saṅ al"‿lē'. **2.** Partir: pār"tīr'.—**to go astray.** See astray.—**to go back.** Reculer: rə-kü"lē'.—**to go forward.** Avancer: a"vaṅ"sē'.—**to go on.** Continuer: koṅ"tī"nü"ē'.—**to go on all fours.** Marcher à quatre pattes: mar"shē' a kā'‿trə pāt.—**to let go.** Lacher: la"shē'.
goal, *n.* **1.** But (*m.*): bü. **2.** Terme (*m.*): tārm. **3.** Objectif (*m.*): ob"ʒek"tīf'.
goat, *n.* Chevre (*f.*): shā'‿vrə.
goatee, *n.* Barbe de bouc (*f.*): bār'‿bə də būk.
God, *n.* Dieu (*m.*): dī"‿yū'.
goggles, *n. pl.* **1.** Lunettes (*f.*): lü"nēt'. **2.** Cagoule (*f.*): ka"gūl' (*gas=mask or protected head=piece of canvas with mica=covered eye=holes*).
going, *n.* **1.** Allée (*f.*): al"‿lē'. See aller in Appendix. **2.** Départ (*m.*): dē"pār'. **3.** Marche (*f.*): mār'‿shə.—**are we going?** Allons=nous? al"loṅ' nū.—**g. in.** Entrée (*f.*): aṅ"trē' (*taking over a trench*).—**g. out.** Sortie (*f.*): sōr"tī' (*relief after trench duty*).—**g. over.** Montée (*f.*): moṅ"tē' (*climbing out of a trench to attack*). Contraction of "going over the top."—**g. to.** Allant à: al"‿laṅt'‿a.—**g. up.** Montée (*f.*): moṅ"tē' (*rising*).—**g. west** [soldiers' euphemism]. Dying.—**we are going.** Nous allons: nūz‿al"loṅ'.
goitrous, *a.* Goîtreux (*m.*): gwa"trū'; goîtreuse (*f.*): gwa"trūz'.
gold, *n.* Or (*m.*): ōr.—**goldbeater's=skin.** Baudruche (*n. f.*): bō"drüsh'.—**g.=filled,** *a.* Aurifié (*m.*): o"rī"fī"‿yē'; aurifiée (*f.*): o"rī"fī"‿yē' (*of teeth, in identification*).
golden, *a.* En or (*m.*): aṅ‿ōr.
gone, *pp.* **1.** Allé: al"‿lē'. See aller in Appendix. **2.** Parti (*pp.*): par"tī'.—**he is gone.** **1.** Il est parti: īl‿ē par"tī'. **2.** Il est mort: īl ē mōr (*dead*).—**his money is all g.** Il a dépensé tout son argent: īl a dē"paṅ"sē' tū soṅ ar"ʒāṅ'.—**gone west** [soldiers' euphemism]. Dead.
goniometer. Goniomètre (*n. m.*): go"nī"ō"mē'‿trə (*gun=sighting dial*).

ı = habit; aisle; au = out; oil; iū = feud;
diṅe; chin; go; ŋ = sing; ship; thin; this.

artistic; ārt; fat; fāre; fast; get; prēy; hit; polīce; obey; gō; not; ōr; full; rūle; but; būrn; ə = final;

good, *a.* Bon (*m.*): bon; bonne (*f.*): bon'‿nə.—**good=bye.** Adieu: a"dī"‿yū'.—**g.=bye for a time.** **1.** Au revoir: ō rə-vwār'. **2.** À tantôt: a taṅ"tō'.—**g. day.** Bonjour: boṅ"ʒūr'.—**g. evening.** Bonsoir: boṅ"swār'.—**g. luck!** Bonne chance! bon'‿nə shāṅ'‿sə. —**g. morning!** Bonjour: boṅ"ʒūr'.—**g.=natured,** *a.* Débonnaire (*m. & f.*): dē"bon"‿nār'‿ə.—**goodness.** Bonté (*n. f.*): boṅ"tē'.—**g. night.** Bonne nuit: bon'‿nə nwī.—**goods.** Marchandises (*n. f.*): mar"shaṅ"dīz'‿ə.

goose. Oie (*n. f.*): wā.

gooseberry, *n.* **1.** Groseille (*f.*): grō"sā'‿yə. **2.** A cask=like wooden frame around which barbed wire has been wound: used in wire entanglements.

gorge. Gorge (*n. f.*): gōr'‿ʒə.—**open gorge.** Gorge ouverte: gōrʒ‿ū"vārt'‿ə.—**shut gorge.** Gorge fermée: gōr'‿ʒə fār"mē'.

gout. Goutte (*n. f.*): gūt'‿tə.—**gouty,** *a.* **1.** Goutteux (*m.*): gūt"‿tū'; goutteuse (*f.*): gūt"‿tūz'. **2.** Podagre (*m. & f.*): po"dā'‿grə.

government. Gouvernement (*n. m.*): gū"vār"‿nə-māṅ'.

gradient. Rampe (*n. f.*): rāṅ'‿pə.

grain. Grain (*n. m.*): graṅ.

gramme. Gramme (*n. m.*): grām'‿mə (*one ounce avoirdupois = 28.35 grammes*).

grape, *n.* Raisin (*m.*): rā"zaṅ'.—**grape=shot.** Mitraille (*n. f.*): [mī"tra"‿ī'.

grappling=iron. Grappin (*n. m.*): gra"paṅ'.

grass. Herbe (*n. f.*): ārb'‿ə.

grate. Grille (*n. f.*): grī'‿yə.

grating. Grille (*n. f.*): grī'‿yə.

grave, *n.* **1.** Tombe (*f.*): toṅ'‿bə. **2.** Tombeau (*m.*): toṅ"bō'. On maps, *Tomb.*

gravel. Gravier (*n. m.*): gra"vī"‿yē'.

gravy. Jus (*n. m.*): ʒü.

graze, *v.* **1.** Paître (*act.*): pā'‿trə. **2.** Se paître: sə pā'‿trə (*to eat grass*).—**to graze horses.** Faire paître les chevaux: fār' pā'‿trə lē shə-vō'.

grease. Graisse (*n. f.*): grā'‿sə.—**tin of grease.** Boite de graisse (*f.*): bwā'‿tə də grā'‿sə.

great, *a.* Grand (*m.*): grāṅ; grande (*f.*): grāṅd. Abbreviated [*Gde.*

greatcoat, *n.* **1.** Capote (*f.*): ka"pōt'‿ə. **2.** Capote de garde (*f.*): ka"pōt'‿ə də gār'‿də. **3.** Pardessus (*m.*): par"des"‿sü'.

Greece. Grèce (*n. f.*): grā'‿sə.

green, *a.* Vert (*m.*): vār; verte (*f.*): vār'‿tə.—**light=green.** Vert claire: vār klā'‿rə.

grenade. Grenade (*n. f.*): grə-nā'‿də.—**hand grenade.** Grenade à main: grə-nā'‿də a maṅ.

grey, *a.* Gris (*m.*): grī; grise (*f.*): grī'‿zə.

grind, *v.* Aiguiser: ā"gwī"zē'.—**grinding machine.** Machine à aiguiser (*f.*): ma"shī'‿nə a ā"gwī"zē'.

grocer. Épicier (*n. m.*): ē"pī"sī"‿yē'.—**groceries.** **1.** Épiceries (*f. pl.*): ē"pī"‿sə-rī'. **2.** Produits d'épicerie: pro"dwī' dē"-pī"‿sə-rī'.

grog. Grog (*n. m.*): grōg.

groom. **I.** *n.* **1.** Groom (*m.*): grūm. **2.** Ordonnance (*f.*): or"-don"‿nāṅ'‿sə. **II.** *v.* Panser: paṅ"sē'.—**grooming.** Pansage (*n. m.*): paṅ"sāʒ'‿ə.

groove. Rainure (*n. f.*): rā"nür'‿ə.

grotto. Grotte (*n. f.*): grōt. On maps, *Grte.*

ground. **I.** *n.* **1.** Terrain (*m.*): tār"‿raṅ'. **2.** Terre (*f.*): tār. **II.** *v.* Mettre à terre: mēt'‿trə a tār.—**above g.** En terrain découvert: aṅ tār"‿raṅ' dē"kū"vār'.—**abrupt falls of the g.** Ressauts de terrain (*m.*): res"‿sō' də tār"‿raṅ'.—**amount of g.** Étendue de terrain: ē"taṅ"dü' də tār"‿raṅ'.—**camping g.** Terrain de campement: tār"‿raṅ' də kaṅ"‿pə-māṅ'.—**dead g.** Angle mort: ang'‿lə mər.—**even g.** Terrain uni: tār"‿ran' ü"nī'.—**flat g.** Terrain plat: tār"‿ran' plā.—**folds in the g.** Replis de terrain: rə-plī' də tār"‿ran'.—**ground arms!** Armes à terre! ärms‿a tār.—**hard g.** Terrain dur: tār"‿ran' dür.—**heavy g.** **1.** Terre grasse: tār grās'‿sə. **2.** Terrain lourd: tār"‿ran' lūr. —**kind of g.** Nature du sol: na"tür'‿ə dü sel.—**lie of the g.** Configuration du terrain: kən"fī"gü"ra"sī"‿yen' dü tār"‿ran'.—**light g.** Terrain léger: tār"‿ran' lē"zē'.—**loamy g.** Sol glaiseux: sel glā"zū'.—**medium g.** Terrain moyen: tār"‿ran' mwa"-yan'.—**open g.** Terrain découvert: tār"‿ran' dē"kū"vār'.—**ploughed g.** Terrain labouré: tār"‿ran' la"bū"rē'.—**rough g.** Terrain défoncé: tār"‿ran' dē"fen"sē'.—**soft g.** Terrain mou: tār"‿ran' mū.—**stony g.** Terrain pierreux: tār"‿ran' pi"‿yār"‿rū'.—**to defend every inch of g.** Défendre chaque pouce de terrain: dē"fān'‿drə shā'‿kə pū'‿sə də tār"‿ran'.—**to go to g.** Se terrer: sə tār"‿rē'.—**to make good use of the g.** Savoir utiliser le terrain: sa"vwār' ü"tī"lī"zē' lə tār"‿ran'.—**to take g.** Atterrir: a"tār"‿rīr'.—**training g.** Terrain de manœuvre: tār"‿ran' də man"ū'‿vrə.—**waste g.** Terrain vague: tār"‿ran' vā'‿gə.

group, *n.* **1.** Groupe (*m.*): grū'‿pə. **2.** Massif (*n. m.*): mas"‿sīf' (*of objects in the landscape*).

grousing. Grumbling; discontent: soldiers' slang.

grove. Bosquet (*n. m.*): bes"kē'.

growth. Végétation (*n. f.*): vē"gē"ta"sī"‿yen'.—**growth on top and slope.** Végétation sur hauteur et pente: vē"gē"ta"sī"‿yen' sür hō"tūr' ē pān'‿tə.

gruel, *n.* Gruau (*m.*): grü"ō'.

guard, *n.* **1.** Garde (*f.*): gārd (*a body of men.* Used with the definite article, *la*). **2.** Conducteur: kon"dük"tūr' (*conductor, as of a train*). **3.** Convoi (*m.*): kon"vwā' (*as of a baggage- or supply-train*).—**advance guard.** Avant-garde (*f.*): a"vān"gārd'.—**chain-g.** Garde-chaîne (*m.*): gārd"shān'.—**flank-g.,** *n.* **1.** Flanqueur (*m.*): flan"kūr'. **2.** Flanc-garde (*f.*): flan"gārd'.—**g.-house.** **1.** Corps de garde (*m.*): kər də gārd. Abbreviated *Gde.* **2.** Garde (*n. f.*): gārd.—**g.-room.** **1.** Corps de garde (*m.*): kər də gārd. **2.** Salle de police (*f.*): sāl də po"līs'.—**g., turn out!** Aux armes! ōz‿ārm.—**quarter-g.** Garde du camp: gārd dü kan (*battalion camp-guard*).—**railway g.** Conducteur (*m.*): kon"dük"tūr'.—**rear-g.** Arrière-garde (*f.*): ar"‿rī"‿yār' gārd.—**to call out the g.** Mettre la garde sous les armes: met'‿trə la gārd sū lēz ārm.—**to come off g.** Descendre la garde: dēs"san'‿drə la gārd.—**to mount g.** Monter la garde: mon"tē' la gārd.—**to relieve the g.** Relever la garde: rə-lə-vē' la gārd.

guidance. Conduite (*n. f.*): kon"dwīt'.

guide. **I.** *n.* **1.** Guide (*m.*): gīd. **2.** Conducteur (*m.*): kon"-dük"tūr'. **3.** Indicateur (*m.*): an"dī"ka"tūr' (*railway-signal*). **II.** *v.* **1.** Guider: gī"dē'. **2.** Conduire: kon"dwīr'.—**guide-post.** Poteau indicateur (*n. m.*): pō"tō an"dī"ka"tūr'.—**g.-rope.** Guide-rope (*n. m.*): gīd"rōp'.

guilty, *a.* Coupable (*m. & f.*): kū"pā'‿blə.

gulf. Golfe (*n. m.*): golf.

gully, *n.* **1.** Cassis (*m.*): kas"‿sīs'. **2.** Rigole (*f.*): rī"gol'.

gun, *n.* **1.** Canon (*m.*): ka"non' (*ordnance*). **2.** Fusil (*m.*): fü"zī' (*rifle*).—**gun-carriage.** Affût de canon (*m.*): af'‿fü' də ka"non'.—**gun-cotton.** Coton-poudre: ko"ton' pū'drə; fulmi-coton: fül"mī"ko"ton'.—**gun-fire.** Canonnage (*n. m.*): ka"‿non"‿nāz'.—**gun-layer or pointer.** Maître pointeur (*n. m.*): mā'trə pwan"tūr'.—**gunner,** *n.* **1.** Servant (*m.*): sār"vān'. **2.** Canonnier (*m.*): ka"non"‿nī"‿yē'.—**gun-pit,** *n.* Emplacement de pièce: an"plas"‿ə-mān' də pī"‿yes'.—**gunpowder.** Poudre à canon (*n. f.*): pu'‿drə a ka"non'.—**gunpowder manufactory.** Poudrerie (*n. f.*): pū"drə‿rī'. Abbreviated *Poudie.*—**guns brought into or placed in action.** Canon mise en batterie: ka"non' mīz‿an bat"‿tə-rī'.—**gunshot.** **1.** Portée (*f.*): pōr"tē' (*cannon*= or *r.fle*=*range*). **2.** Coup de feu (*m.*): kū də fū.—**gunshot=wound.** Blessure d'un coup de feu ou fusil (*f.*): bles"‿sür' dañ kū də fū ū fü"zī'.—**machine=g.** Mitrailleuse (*n. f.*): mī"trai"‿yūz'.—**machine=gun ammunition=belt.** Bande de cartouche (*f.*): bãnd də kar"tūsh'.—**siege=g.** Pièce de siège (*f.*): pī"‿yes' də sī"‿āz'.—**quick=firing gun** or **rapid=fire gun.** Canon à tir rapide (*m.*): ka"noñ' a tīr ra"pīd'.—**shield=g.** Canon munis de bouclier: ka"noñ' mü"nī' də bū"klī"ē'.

gunboat, *n.* Chaloupe canonnière (*n. f.*): sha"lūp' ka"non"‿nī"‿yār'.

Gurkha. Gorkha (*n. m.*): gōr"kā', ou Gourkha: gūr"kā' (*Indian soldier*).

gutter. **1.** Rigole (*n. f.*): rī"gol' (*trench, ditch,* or *furrow*). **2.** Caniveau (*n. m.*): ka"nī"vō' (*conduit*). **3.** Ruisseau (*m.*): rwīs"‿sō' (*of a street*).

H

habit, *n.* Habitude (*f.*): a"bī"tüd'.—**bad habits.** Mauvaises habitudes: mō"vēz'‿a"bī"tüd'.

hack, *v.* Hacher: ha"shē'.

haggard, *a.* Hagard (*m.*): ha"gār'; hagarde (*f.*): ha"gārd'‿ə.

Hague, The. La Haye: la hā (*capital of Holland*).—**Hague Tribunal.** Tribunal de la Haye (*m.*): trī"bü"nāl' də la hā (*Permanent Arbitration Court, established 1899*).

hair, *n.* Cheveux (*m. pl.*): shə-vū'.—**hairbrush,** *n.* **1.** Brosse à cheveux (*f.*): bres'‿sə a shə-vū'. **2.** Calendrier: ka"lañ"drī"‿yē' (*a type of hand=grenade*).—**h.=cut.** Coupe de cheveux: kū'‿pə də shə-vū'.—**h.=dresser.** Coiffeur (*n. m.*): kwaf"‿fūr'.—**hairy,** *a.* Poilu (*m.*): pwa"lü' (*popular nickname of French soldier*); poilue (*f.*): pwa"lü'.

half. **I.** *adv.* Demi: də-mī'. **II.** *n.* **1.** Moitié (*f.*): mwa"tī"‿yē'. **2.** Demi (*m.*): də-mī'.—**at half cock.** Au cran de repos: ō krañ də rə-pō'.—**h. an hour.** Une demi=heure (*f.*): ün də-mī' ūr.—**h. a pound.** Une demi livre (*f.*): ün də-mī' līv'‿rə.—**h. past one.** Une heure et demie: ün‿ūr ē də-mī'.—**h. past three.** Trois heures et demie: trwāz‿ūr ē də-mī'.—**h. past twelve.** **1.** Midi et demi: mī"dī' ē də-mī' (*noon*). **2.** Minuit et demi: mī"nū"‿ī' ē də-mī' (*midnight*).

hall, *n.* **1.** Salle (*f.*): sāl'‿lə (*large room*). **2.** Vestibule (*m.*): ves"tī"bül'‿ə (*entrance; passage*).

halt. **I.** *n.* **1.** Halte (*f.*): hālt'‿ə (*stop; resting=place*). **2.** Arrêt (*m.*): ar"‿rē' (*stop; stay*). **3.** Bivouac (*m.*): bī"vū"āk' (*encampment*). **II.** *v.* **1.** S'arrêter: sar"‿rā"tē' (*to halt oneself*). **2.** Faire halte à: far'‿ə hālt'‿ə a (*to halt someone else*).—**h.!** **1.** Halte=là! hālt'‿ə la (*military*). **2.** Arrêtez=vous! ar"‿rā"tē' vū.—**h.! who goes there?** **1.** Qui vive? kī vīv. **2.** Halte! hālt'‿ə.—**halting=place.** Étape (*n. f.*): ē"tāp'‿ə.

halter, *n.* Licou (*m.*): lī"kū".—**halter=cast.** Prise de longe: prī'‿zə də loñ'ʒə.

ham[1]. Jambon (*n. m.*): ʒañ"boñ'.—**ham sandwich.** Sandwich au jambon: sañ"dwītsh' ō ʒañ"boñ'.

ham[2], *n.* Village (*m.*): vīl"lā'‿ʒə (*so called in Flanders*).

hamlet. Hameau (*n. m.*): ha"mo'. On maps, *Hau.*

hammer, *n.* Marteau (*m.*): mar"tō'.—**sledge=hammer.** Marteau à deux mains: mar"tō' a dū mañ.

hammock. Hamac (*n. m.*): ham"āk'.

hamper, *v.* **1.** Embarrasser: añ"bar"‿ras"‿sē'. **2.** Gêner: ʒā"nē'. **3.** Contrarier: koñ"tra"rī"‿yē'.

hand. **I.** *n.* **1.** Main (*f.*): mañ (*in general sense*). **2.** Aiguille (*f.*): ā"gwī'‿yə (*of a clock or watch*). **II.** *v.* Donner: don"‿nē'.—**at hand.** **1.** À portée: a pōr"tē'. **2.** À proximité: a prek"zī"mī"tē'.—**beforehand,** *adv.* D'avance: da"vāñ'‿sə.—**in the hand.** À la main: a la mañ.—**h.=grenade,** *n.* Grenade à main (*f.*): grə-nād′‿a mañ.—**h.=to=h.** Corps à corps: kōrz‿ā kōr.—**hands up!** Haussez les mains! hō″sē′ lē mañ.—**on the other h. 1.** D'un autre côté: dañ‿ō′‿trə kō″tē′. **2.** D'autre part: dō′‿trə pār.—**h.=saw.** Scie à main (*f.*): sī a mañ.—**handbag,** *n.* Sac à main (*m.*): sāk‿a mañ.

handcuffs. Menottes (*n. pl.*): mə-not′‿tə.

handful. Poignée (*n. f.*): pwa″nyē′.

handspike. Anspect (*n. m.*): an″spek′.—**traversing handspike.** Levier de manœuvre: lə-vī″‿yē′ də ma″nū′‿vrə.—**h. ring.** Anneau de pointage: an″‿nō′ də pwañ″tāʒ′‿ə.

handwriting. Écriture (*n. f.*): ē″krī″tür′.—**legible handwriting.** Écriture lisible: ē″krī″tür′ lī″zī′‿blə.

handkerchief. Mouchoir (*n. m.*): mū″shwār′.

handle. I. *n.* **1.** Poignée (*f.*): pwa″nyē′. **2.** Manche (*m.*): māñ′‿shə. **3.** Manivelle (*f.*): ma″nī″vel′‿lə.—**elevation handle.** Manivelle de hausse: ma″nī″vel′lə də hōs′‿sə.

handy. I. *a.* **1.** Commode (*m. & f.*): kəm″‿mōd′‿ə (*of things*). **2.** Habile (*m. & f.*): a″bīl ‿ə (*of persons*). **II.** *adv.* À portée de la main: a pōr″tē′ də la mañ.

hang, *v.* **1.** Pendre: pañ′‿drə. **2.** Suspendre: süs″pañ′‿drə.—**hanging.** Tenture (*n. f.*): tañ″tür′‿ə.

hangar. Hangar (*n. m.*): hañ″gār′ (*shed as for airships*).

happen, *v.* **1.** Arriver: ar″‿rī″vē′. **2.** Se passer: sə pas″‿sē′.

happy, *a.* **1.** Heureux (*m.*): ū″rū′; heureuse (*f.*): ū″rūz′‿ə. **2.** Content (*m.*): koñ″tāñ′; contente (*f.*): koñ″tāñt′‿ə.

harass, *v.* **1.** Contrarier: koñ″tra″rī″‿yē′. **2.** Harceler (*v.*): har″‿sə-lē′.

harbor. Port (*n. m.*): pōr. Abbreviated *Pt.*—**harbor commission.** Commission de port (*f.*): kəm″‿mīs″‿sī″‿yoñ′ də pōr.—**h.=master.** Capitaine de port (*m.*): ka″pī″tān′‿ə də pōr.—**making the h.** Entrée au port (*f.*): añ″trē′ ō pōr.—**h.=watch.** Garde=port (*n. m.*): gar″‿də-pōr′.

hard, *a.* Dur (*m.*); dure (*f.*): dür.—**hard=pressed.** Serré de près: sār″‿rē′ də prā.—**hard tack.** Biscuit de réserve: bīs″kwī′ də rē″zārv′.

hardy, *a.* Audacieux (*m.*): ō″da″sī″‿yū′; audacieuse (*f.*): ō″da″sī″‿yūz′‿ə.

hare. Lièvre (*n. m.*): lī″āv′‿rə.

harken, *v.* Écouter: ē″kū″tē′.

harm. I. *n.* **1.** Mal (*m.*): māl. **2.** Malheur (*m.*): mal″ūr′. **II.** *v.* Nuire à: nwīr a.

harness. I. *n.* **1.** Harnachement (*m.*): har″na″‿shə-māñ′. **2.** Harnais (*m.*): har″nē′. **II.** *v.* Harnacher: har″na″shē′.—**harness=maker.** Bourrelier (*n. m.*): būr″‿rə-lī″‿yē′.—**harnessed,** *pa.* Harnaché (*m.*); harnachée (*f.*): har″na″shē′.

harsh, *a.* Rude (*m. & f.*): rüd.

harvest. I. *n.* **1.** Moisson (*f.*): mwas″‿soñ′. **2.** Récolte (*f.*): rē″kol′‿tə. **II.** *v.* **1.** Moissonner: mwas″‿son″‿nē′. **2.** Récolter: rē″kol″tē′.

has, *v.* A: a.

haste. Hâte (*n. f.*): hā′‿tə.—**hasten,** *v.* Se hâter: sə hā″tē′.

hat. Chapeau (*n. m.*): sha″pō′.

hatch. Écoutille (*n. f.*): ē″kū″tī′‿yə.

hatchet, *n.* **1.** Hache (*f.*): hā′‿shə. **2.** Hachette (*f.*): hash″-ēt′‿tə.

hate. I. *n.* Haine (*f.*): hān′‿ə. **II.** *v.* Haïr: ha″‿īr′.—**full of hate,** *a.* Haineux (*m.*): hā″nū′; haineuse (*f.*): hā″nūz′‿ə.

haughty, *a.* Hautain (*m.*): hō″tañ′; hautaine (*f.*): hō″tā′‿nə.

haul, *v.* Haler: ha″lē′.

haunch. Hanche (*n. f.*): hāñ′‿shə.

have, *v.* Avoir: a″vwār′. [*Note. For parts of this verb see table* *of irregular verbs in Appendix. When used interrogatively the positions of pronoun and verb are reversed, as* ai-je? (ā′‿ʒə) **have I?** Avons nous? (a″voṅ′‿nū) **have we?** Avez-vous? (a″vē′ vū) **have you?**]

haven. Port (*n. m.*): pōr.—**haven of refuge for patrols.** Port de refuge pour les patrouilles: pōr də rə-füʒ′ pūr lē pa″trū″-ī′‿yə.

haversack, *n.* **1.** Havresac (*m.*): ha″‿vrə-sāk′ (*worn on the back*). **2.** Musette (*f.*): mü″zet′‿tə (*worn slung across the shoulders*).

hawser, *n.* **1.** Haussière (*f.*): hōs″sī″‿yār′. **2.** Amarre (*f.*): a″mār′‿rə (*for mooring*).

hay, *n.* **1.** Fourrage sec (*m.*): fūr″‿rāʒ′ sek (*dry fodder*). **2.** Foin (*m.*): fwaṅ.—**bundles of hay.** Foin en bottes: fwaṅ aṅ bōt′‿tə.—**compressed hay.** Foin pressé: fwaṅ prēs″‿sē′.—**hay rack, stable rack.** Ratelier (*m.*): ra″‿tə-lī″‿yē′.—**hay ricks.** Meules de foin (*f.*): mūl də fwaṅ.

haze, *n.* **1.** Brume (*f.*): brüm. **2.** Vapeur (*f.*): va″pūr′.

hazel, *a.* Marron (*m. & f.*): mar″‿roṅ′ (*said of the eyes: a mark of identification*).

he, *pron.* Il: īl (*nominative*); lui: lwī (*objective*).

head, *n.* **1.** Tête (*f.*): tāt′‿ə (*in general sense*). **2.** Chef (*m.*): shef (*chief*).—**administrative head.** Directeur administratif (*m.*): dī″rek″tūr′ ad″mī″nī″stra″tīf′.—**at the head of.** En tête de: aṅ tāt′‿ə də.—**headfast,** *n.* Amarre d'avant: a″mar′ da″vāṅ′ (*hawser holding a vessel's bow*).—**heading.** Titre (*n. m.*): tīt′‿rə.—**headland,** *n.* **1.** Cap (*m.*): kap (*cape*). On maps: *C.* **2.** Promontoire (*m.*): pro″moṅ″twār′‿ə (*promontory*).—**headlight,** *n.* Fanal (*m.*): fa″nāl′.—**head-rope.** Longe (*f.*): loṅ′‿ʒə.—**head-stall.** Têtière (*n. f.*): tē″tī″‿yār′‿ə.—**keep your head down.** Baissez la tête: bās″‿sē′ la tāt′‿ə.

headquarters. Quartier général (*m.*): kar″tī″‿yē′ ʒē″nē″rāl′.—**general headquarters.** Grand quartier général: grāṅ kar″tī″‿yē′ ʒē″nē″rāl′.

heal, *v.* Guérir: gē″rīr′.—**healing.** Guérison (*n. f.*): gē″rī″-soṅ′.

health. Santé (*n. f.*): saṅ″tē′.—**health guard.** Garde de santé: gār′‿də də saṅ″tē′.—**healthy,** *a.* Sain (*m.*): saṅ; saine (*f.*): sān′‿ə.

heap, *n.* **1.** Tas (*m.*): tā. **2.** Monceau (*m.*): moṅ″sō′.

hear, *v.* Entendre: aṅ″tāṅ′‿drə.—**hearing,** *n.* **1.** Ouïe (*f.*): ū″wī′ (*the physical sense*). **2.** Audition (*f.*): ō″dī″sī″‿yoṅ′ (*examination of witnesses*).—**hard of hearing.** Dur d'oreille: dür de″rē′‿yə.—**to have good hearing.** Avoir l'ouïe bonne: a″vwār′ lū″wī′ boṅ′‿nə.

hearsay. Oui-dire (*n. m.*): wī″dīr′.

heart, *n.* **1.** Cœur (*m.*): kūr (*the organ*). **2.** Courage (*m.*): kū″rāʒ′ (*the quality*). **3.** Centre (*m.*): sāṅ′‿trə (*center*).

heat. Chaleur (*m. f.*): sha″lūr′.—**to avoid the heat of the day.** Éviter la chaleur du jour: ē″vī″tē′ la sha″lūr′ dü ʒūr.—**heating.** Échauffement: ē″shōf″‿fə-māṅ′.

heath, *n.* **1.** Lande (*f.*): lāṅ′‿də. **2.** Bruyère (*f.*): brwī″‿yār′‿ə.

heavy, *a.* **1.** Lourd (*m.*): lūr; lourde (*f.*): lūr′‿də. **2.** Fournis (*m.*): fūr″nī′ (*said of the eyebrows: a mark of identification*).—**heavy artillery.** Grosse artillerie: grōs′‿sə ar″tī″‿yə-rī′.

hedge. Haie (*n. f.*): hā. On maps, *Hie.*—**quickset hedge.** Haie vive: hā vīv′‿ə.—**wild h.** Haie forestière: hā fō″res″tī″‿yār′‿ə.—**hedged enclosure.** Clôture en haies: klō″tür′ aṅ hā.

hedgehog. Hérisson (*n. m.*): hē″rīs″‿soṅ′.

heel. Talon (*n. m.*): ta″loṅ′.—**cracked heel.** Crevasse (*n. f.*): krə-vās′‿sə.—**heel rope.** Entrave des pieds de derrière (*f.*): aṅ″trāv′‿ə dē pī″‿yē′ də dār″‿rī″‿yār′‿ə.

height, *n.* **1.** Élévation (*f.*): ē″lē″va″sī″‿yoṅ′. **2.** Hauteur (*f.*): hō″tūr′. **3.** Taille (*f.*): tā′‿yə (*stature*).—**height of burst.** Hauteur d'éclatement: hō″tūr′ dē″kla″‿tə-māṅ′.—**a great h.** Une grande altitude: ūṅ grāṅd′‿ə al″tī″tūd′‿ə.—**the heights on either side are held.** Les hauteurs sont occupées de chaque côté: lē‿hō″tūr′ soṅt‿ok″‿kū″pē′ də shāk′‿ə kō″tē′.

hell, *n.* **1.** Enfer (*m.*): aṅ″fār′. **2.** (*Figuratively.*) Le diable (*m.*): lə dī″ā′‿blə.

helm, *n.* **1.** Barre (*f.*): bār′‿rə (*wheel*). **2.** Timon (*m.*): tī″moṅ′ (*tiller*).—**h. amidships.** Droite la barre: drwā′‿tə la bār′‿rə.—**port the h.** Bâbord la barre: ba″bor′ la bar′‿rə.—**starboard the h.** Tribord la barre: trī″bor′ la bar′‿rə.

helmet. Casque (*n. m.*): kas′‿kə.—**gas** or **smoke helmet.** Cagoule (*n. f.*): ka″gūl′‿ə.

help. **I.** *n.* **1.** Aide (*f.*): ā′‿də. **2.** Secours (*m.*): sə-kūr′. **II.** *v.* Aider: ā″dē′.—**help me.** Aidez-moi: ā″dē′ mwā (*assist me*).—**h.!** **1.** Au secours! ō sə-kūr′. **2.** À l'aide! a lā′‿də (*come to my rescue*).—**helpless,** *a.* **1.** Sans secours: saṅ sə-kūr′. **2.** Faible (*m.* & *f.*): fā′‿blə (*weak*).

helter-skelter. À la débandade: a la dē″baṅ″dād′‿ə.

hem in, *v.* Cerner: sār″nē′.

hemorrhage. Hémorragie (*n. f.*): ē″mōr″‿ra″‿ʒī′.—**arterial h.** Hémorragie artérielle: ē″mōr″‿ra″‿ʒī′ ar″tē″rī″el′‿lə.—**external h.** Hémorragie externe: ē″mōr″‿ra″‿ʒī′ ek″stārn′‿ə.—**internal h.** Hémorragie interne: ē″mōr″‿ra″‿ʒī′ aṅ″tārn′‿ə.—**venous h.** Hémorragie veineuse: ē″mōr″‿ra″‿ʒī′ vā″nūz′‿ə.

hen. Poule (*n. f.*): pūl′‿ə.—**hen-house.** Poulailler (*m.*): pūl″a″‿yē′.—**h.-roost,** *n.* Juchoir (*m.*): ʒū″shwār′.

her, *pron.* Lui: lwī (*objective*); son (*m.*): soṅ; sa (*f.*): sa (*possessive*).

here, *adv.* Ici: i″sī′.—**here is, here are.** Voici: vwa″sī′.—**here he comes.** Le voici: lə vwa″sī′.

hermitage. Ermitage (*n. m.*): ēr″mī″tāʒ′. On maps, *Hermge.*

heroism. Héroïsme (*n. m.*): ē″ro″ism′.

herring. Hareng (*n. m.*): ha″rāṅ′.

herself, *pron.* Elle-même (*f.*): ēl mām.—**by herself.** Seule: sūl.

hesitation. Hésitation (*n. f.*): ē″zī″ta″sī″‿yoṅ′.

Herzegovina. Herzégovine: ār″tsē″gō″vīn′.

hiatus. Brèche (*f.*): brāsh (*breach*).

hickboo, hik″bū′, *n.* [Airmen's slang.] An air-raid.

hide. **I.** *n.* **1.** Peau (*f.*): pō (*skin*). **2.** Cuir (*m.*): kwīr (*leather*). **II.** *v.* Cacher: ka″shē′.—**hidden,** *n.* Caché: ka″shē′.

high, *a.* **1.** Haut (*m.*): ho; haute (*f.*): hōt. On maps, *Ht.* **2.** Élevé (*m.*): élevée (*f.*): ē″lə-vē′. **3.** Découvert (*m.*): dē″kū″vār′; découverte (*f.*): dē″kū″vārt′ (*of a forehead in identification*).—**high road, highway,** *n.* Grand' route (*f.*): grāṅd rūt.—**h.-spirited,** *a.* **1.** Plein de cœur: plaṅ də kūr. **2.** Fougueux (*m.*): fū″gū′; ardent (*m.*): ar″daṅ′.

Highlander, *n.* Écossais (*m.*): ē″kos″‿sē′; écossaise (*f.*): ē″kos″‿sēz′.

hill. Colline (*n. f.*): kol″‿līn′. Abbrev. *Colle.*—**at the top of the h.** En haut de la colline: aṅ hō də la kol″‿līn′.—**to ascend** or **go up the h.** Monter la colline: moṅ″tē′ la kol″‿līn′.—**to descend** or **go down the h.** Descendre la colline: des″saṅ′‿drə la kol″‿līn′.

hillock. Mamelon (*n. m.*): ma″mə-loṅ′. Abbreviated *Mamon.*

hilltop. Sommet (*n. m.*): som″‿mā′ (*summit*).

hilly, *a.* **1.** Montagneux (*m.*): moṅ″ta″‿nyū′; montagneuse (*f.*): moṅ″ta″‿nyūz′. **2.** Accidenté (*m.*): accidentée (*f.*): ak″sī″-daṅ″tē′ (*uneven*).

hilt. Poignée (*n. f.*): pwa″‿nyē′.

him, *pron.* **1.** (*Objective*) Le: lə; celui: sə-lwī′. **2.** (*Dative*) Lui: lwī.—**himself, he himself.** Lui-même: lwī″mām′.
hinder. Empêcher (*v.*): ān″pē″shē′.
hind-quarters. L'arrière-main (*n. m.*): lār″‿rī″‿yār″man′ (*of a horse*).
hinge. Charnière (*n. f.*): shar″nī″‿yār′.
hip, haunch. Hanche (*n. f.*): hansh.
hire. **I.** *n.* **1.** Location (*f.*): lo″ka″sī″‿yon′. **2.** Louage: lū″āʒ′. **3.** Prix de louage ou de location: prī də lū″āʒ′ ū də lo″ka″sī″‿yon′. **II.** *v.* **1.** Louer: lū″ē′. **2.** Soudoyer: sū″dwa″‿yē′.—**hiring.** Louage (*n. m.*): lū″āʒ′.
his, *pron.* **1.** (*Personal*) De lui: də lwī (*of his*). **2.** (*Possessive*) (1) A lui: a lwī (*to him*). (2) Son (*m.*): son (*his*); sa (*f.*): sa (*hers*); ses (*pl.*): sē (*theirs*).—**his or her own.** Le sien (*m.*): lə sī″‿yan′; la sienne (*f.*): la sī″‿yen′.
hit. **I.** *n.* Un coup au but (*m.*): an kū ō bü (*a hit of the objective*). **II.** *v.* **1.** Atteindre: at″‿tan′‿drə. **2.** Frapper: frap″‿pē′ (*shot*). **3.** Toucher: tū″shē′. **4.** Blesser: bles″‿sē′.—**I am hit.** Je suis frappé: ʒə swī frap″‿pē′.
hitch, *n.* Nœud (*m.*): nū.
hobble. **I.** *n.* Entrave (*f.*): an″trāv′. **II.** *v.* Entraver: an″-tra″vē′.—**hobbling,** *a.* Boiteux (*m.*): bwa″tū′; boiteuse (*f.*): bwa″tūz′.
hock, *n.* Jarret (*m.*): ʒar″rē′.
hofstede, *n.* Ferme (*f.*): fārm (so called in Flanders).
hoist. **I.** *n.* **1.** Guindal (*m.*): gan″dal′ (*of a ship*). **2.** Élévateur (*m.*): ē″lē″va″tūr′ (*in mechanics*). **II.** *v.* **1.** Arborer: ar″bo″rē′. **2.** Hisser: hīs″‿sē′ (*haul up*). **3.** Guinder: gan″dē′ (*of masts and sails*). **4.** Hausser: hō″sē′ (*lift up*).—**hoist a flag.** **1.** Arborer un pavillon: ar″bo″rē′ an pa″vī″‿yon′ (*military*). **2.** Hisser un drapeau: hīs″‿sē′ an dra″po′ (*naval*).
hold. **I.** *n.* Prise (*f.*): prīs. **II.** *v.* Tenir: tə-nīr′.
hole, *n.* Trou (*m.*): trū.
Holland. La Hollande (*n. f.*): la hol″land′.
hollow. **I.** *a.* Creux (*m.*): krū; creuse (*f.*): krūz. **II.** *n.* **1.** Fosse (*f.*): fōs. **2.** Cavité (*f.*): kā″vī″tē′.—**hollow-eyed.** Yeux enfoncés: yū an″fon″sē′.—**h. square.** Carré (*m.*): kār″‿rē′.—**h.-way.** Chemin creux (*m.*): shə-man′ krū.
holster. Fonte (*n. f.*): font.
honest, *a.* Honnête (*m. & f.*): on″‿nāt′.
honeycombed, *a.* Chambré (*m.*); chambrée (*f.*): shan″brē′.
hold. **I.** *n.* **1.** Prise (*f.*): prīz (*capture*). **2.** Cale (*n. f.*): kāl. (*of a ship*). **II.** *v.* **1.** Tenir: tə-nīr′. **2.** Occuper: o″kü″pē′.—**hold!** **1.** Tenez! tə-nē′. **2.** Arretez! ar″‿rē″tē′ (*stop*).—**hold-all.** Enveloppe de voyage (*n. f.*): an″‿və-lop′ də vwa″yāʒ′.—**to h. his or its own.** Se maintenir: sə man″‿tə-nīr′.—**to h. off.** **1.** Arrêter: ār″‿rē″tē′. **2.** Tenir éloigné: tə-nīr′ ē″lwa″‿nyē′.—**to h. on.** **1.** Continuer: kon″tī″nü″ē′. **2.** Persévérer: par″sē″vē″rē′.—**to h. the recovered ground.** Retenir le terrain réconquis: rə-tə-nīr′ lə tār″ran′ rē″kon″kī′.
home, *n.* **1.** Chez soi: shē swā (*dwelling*). **2.** Patrie (*f.*): pa″trī′ (*country*).—**homeless,** *a.* Sans demeure: sān də-mūr′.—**homeward,** *adv.* **1.** Vers la maison: vār la ma″zon′. **2.** Vers soi: vār swā. **3.** Au retour: ō rə-tur′ (*of ships bound home*).
honor. Honneur (*n. m.*): on″‿nūr′.—**Legion of Honor.** See LEGION.
hood, *n.* **1.** Capuchon (*m.*): ka″pü″shon′ (*cowl*). **2.** Capote (*f.*): ka″pot′‿ə (*of a vehicle*).
hoof. Sabot (*n. m.*): sa″bō′.
hook. **I.** *n.* **1.** Crochet (*m.*): krō″shē′. **2.** Hameçon (*m.*): a″‿mə-son′ (*fish-hook*). **II.** *v.* **1.** Accrocher: ak″‿krō″shē′. **2.** Agrafer: a″gra″fē′.—**billhook, reap hook.** Serpe (*n. f.*): sār′pə.
horse. Cheval (*n. m.*): shə-vāl′.—**broken-down horse.** Cheval claqué: shə-vāl′ kla″kē′.—**broken-kneed h.** Cheval couronné: shə-vāl′ kū″ron″‿nē′.—**broken-winded h.** Cheval

poussif: shə-väl′ pūs″‿sīf′.—**draught h.** Cheval de trait: shə-väl′ də trā.—**foundered h.** Cheval fourbu: shə-väl′ fūr″bü′.—**half-bred h.** Cheval de demi sang: shə-väl′ də də-mī′ saṅ.—**h. allowance.** Indemnité de monture (*f.*): aṅ″däm″nī″tē′ də moṅ″-tür′.—**h.-box.** Stalle (*n. f.*): stäl′‿lə.—**h.-car.** Tramway à chevaux (*n. m.*): tram″wā′ a shə-vō′.—**horsehair.** Crin (*n. m.*): kraṅ.—**h.-holder.** Garde-chevaux: gärd shə-vō′.—**h.-pick.** Cure-pieds (*n. m.*): kür″pī″‿yē′.—**h.-pond.** Abreuvoir (*n. m.*): a″brū″vwär′.—**h. power.** **1.** Cheval-vapeur (*m.*): shə-väl′ va″pūr′. **2.** Cheval: shə-väl′ (*usually so abbreviated*).—**h.-sling.** Sangle d'embarquement (*f.*): saṅ′‿glə daṅ″bar″‿kə-māṅ′.—**led h.** Cheval de conduite, ou de main: shə-väl′ də koṅ″dwīt′, ū də maṅ.—**my h. has cast a shoe.** Mon cheval a perdu un fer: moṅ shə-väl′ a pār″dü′ aṅ fār.—**my h. is lame.** Mon cheval boite: moṅ shə-väl′ bwät′‿ə.—**my h. is lame on one foot.** Mon cheval boite d'un pied: moṅ shə-väl′ bwät′‿ə daṅ pī″‿yē′.—**my h. ran away.** Mon cheval s'emporta: moṅ shə-väl′ saṅ″pōr″tä′.—**requisitioned h.** Cheval de réquisition: shə-väl′ də rē″kī″zī″-sī″‿yoṅ′.—**restive h.** Cheval rétif: shə-väl′ rē″tīf′.—**saddle-h.** Cheval de selle: shə-väl′ də sēl′‿lə.—**spare h.** Cheval de rechange: shə-väl′ də rə-shaṅ′‿ʒə.—**unsaddled h.** Un cheval dessellé: aṅ shə-väl′ des″‿sel″‿lē′.

horseman. Cavalier (*n. m.*): ka″va″lī″‿yē′.

horses, *n. pl.* Chevaux (*m.*): shə-vō′.—**bring the horses.** Faites venir les chevaux: fāt′‿ə və-nīr′ lē shə-vō′.—**feed the h.** Donnez à manger aux chevaux: don″nē′ a maṅ″ʒē′ ō shə-vō′.—**harness the h.** Harnacher les chevaux: har″na″shē′ lē shə-vō′.—**he is used to h.** Il a l'habitude des chevaux: īl‿a la″bī″tüd′‿ə dē shə-vō′.—**picket the h.** Mettez les chevaux en piquet: met″‿tē′ lē shə-vō′ aṅ pī″kē′.—**saddle the h.** Sellez les chevaux: sel″‿lē′ lē shə-vō′.—**to spare the h.** Ménager les chevaux: mē″na″ʒē′ lē shə-vō′.—**stand by your h.** Restez près de vos chevaux: res″tē′ prā də vō shə-vō′.—**unharness the h.** Déharnachez les chevaux: dē″har″na″shē′ lē shə-vō′.—**water the h.** Donnez à boire aux chevaux: don″‿nē′ a bwär‿ō shə-vō′.

horseshoe, *n.* **1.** Fer à cheval (*m.*): fār a shə-väl′. **2.** Fer (*m.*): fār.—**horseshoe case.** Porte-fers (*n. m.*): pōrt″fār′.—**horseshoe nail.** Clou à ferrer: klū a fār″‿rē′.—**spare horseshoes and nails.** Ferrure de réserve: fār″‿rür′ də rē″sārv′‿ə.

hospital. **1.** Hôpital (*n. m.*): ō″pī″täl′ (*general*). **2.** Lazaret (*m.*): la″za″rē′ (*for contagious diseases*).—**army hospital.** Hôpital militaire: ō″pī″täl′ mī″lī″tār′‿ə.—**auxiliary h.** Hôpital auxiliare: ō″pī″täl′ ōk″sī″lī″ār′‿ə.—**base h.** Hôpital de l'intérieur: ō″pī″täl′ də laṅ″tē″rī″‿yūr′.—**carry him to the h.** Portez-le à l'hôpital: pōr″tē′ lə a lō″pī″täl′.—**clearing h.** Hôpital d'évacuation: ō″pī″täl′ dē″va″kü″a″sī″‿yoṅ′.—**field h.** Hôpital de campagne: ō″pī″täl′ də kaṅ″pä′‿nyə.—**h. attendant.** Infirmier (*n. m.*): aṅ″fār″mī″‿yē′.—**h. for contagious cases.** Hôpital à déstination spéciale: ō″pī″täl′ a dēs″tī″na″sī″‿yoṅ′ spē″sī″‿yäl′.—**h. orderly.** Infirmier: aṅ″fār″mī″‿yē′.—**h. ship.** Navire hôpital (*m.*): na″vīr′ ō″pī″täl′.—**spa h.** Hôpital thermal: ō″pī″täl′ tār″-mäl′.—**stationary h.** Hôpital fixe: ō″pī″täl′ fīk′‿sə.—**temporary h.** Hôpital temporaire: ō″pī″täl′ taṅ″pō″rār′‿ə.—**veterinary h.** Infirmerie vétérinaire (*f.*): aṅ″fār″‿mə-rī′ vē″tē″rī″-nār′‿ə.

hospitality. Hospitalité (*n. f.*): os″pī″tal″ī″tē′.

host, *n.* **1.** Hôte (*m.*): ōt′‿ə (*one who entertains*). **2.** Hôtelier (*m.*): ō″‿tə-lī″‿yē′ (*one who conducts a hotel*). **3.** Foule (*f.*): fūl′‿ə (*multitude*).

hostage. Otage (*n. m.*): ō″tä3′‿ə.—**to take hostages.** Prendre des otages: praṅ′‿drə dēz‿ō″tä3′‿ə.

hosteau, os″tō′, *n.* [Colloq.] A château used as a hospital or convalescent home: so named by French soldiers.

hostess. Hôtesse (*n. f.*): ō″tes′‿sə.

hot, *a.* Chaud (*m.*): shō; chaude (*f.*): shō′‿də.—**he is hot.** Il a chaud: īl‿a shō.—**it is hot.** Il fait chaud: īl fā shō.

hotel. Hôtel (*n. m.*): ō″tel′. Abbreviated *Hel.*

hour. Heure (*n. f.*): ūr.—**hour of starting.** L'heure de départ: lūr də dē″pār′.

house. **I.** *n.* **1.** Maison (*f.*): mā″zoṅ′. **2.** Bâtiment (*m.*): ba″tī″māṅ′ (*building*). **II.** *v.* **1.** Abriter: a″brī″tē′. **2.** Loger: lo″ʒē′. —**country house.** Bastide (*n. f.*): bas″tīd′‿ə. On maps, *Bide.* —**isolated h.** Maison isolée: mā″zoṅ′ ī″zo″lē′.—**to be housed.** Être en grange: ā′‿trə aṅ grāṅ′‿ʒə (*said of animals*).

housewife, *n.* **1.** Ménagère (*f.*): mē″na″ʒār′‿ə (*the mistress of a house*). **2.** Trousse (*f.*): trūs′‿sə (*case containing needles, etc.*).

how, *adv.* Comment: kem″‿māṅ′.—**how are you?** Comment allez-vous? kem″‿māṅt′‿al″‿lē′ vū.—**how far is it from here?** À quelle distance d'ici à . . . ? a kel dīs″tāṅ′‿sə dī″sī′ a. —**how far is it to a town?** À quelle distance sommes-nous d'une ville? a kel dīs″tāṅ′‿sə sem′‿mə nū dün vīl′‿lə.—**how long have you lived here?** Depuis quand êtes-vous ici? də-pwī′ kāṅ āt vūz‿ī″sī′.—**how many?** Combien? keṅ″bī″‿yaṅ′. —**how many miles?** Combien de kilomètres? keṅ″bī″‿yaṅ′ də kī″lō″mē′‿trə.—**how much?** Combien? keṅ″bī″‿yaṅ′.—**how much does it cost a pound?** Combien ça coûte la livre? keṅ″bī″‿yaṅ′ sa kūt la lī′‿vrə.—**how much do they cost?** Combien coûtent-ils? keṅ″bī″‿yaṅ′ kūt‿īl.—**how old are you?** Quel âge avez-vous? kel āʒ a″vē′ vū.

howitzer. Obusier (*n. m.*): ō″bü″zī″‿yē′.—**field-howitzers.** Obusiers de campagne: ō″bü″zī″‿yē′ də kaṅ″pā′‿nyə.—**trench howitzer.** **1.** Crapouillot (*m.*): kra″pū″ī″yō′. **2.** Obusier de tranchée: ō″bü″zī″‿yē′ də traṅ″shē′.

hub. Moyeu (*n. m.*): mwa″yū′.

huffed, *a.* [Soldiers' slang.] Killed: used by aviators.

hull. Coque (*n. f.*): kōk (*of a ship*).

humpback, hunchback, *n.* Bossu (*m.*); bossue (*f.*): bos″‿sü′.

hundred, *a.* & *n.* Cent: saṅ.—**one hundred and one.** Cent un: saṅt‿aṅ.—**hundredth,** *a.* Centième: saṅ″tī″‿yām′.

Hungary, *n.* L'Hongrie (*f.*): leṅ″grī′.

hunger. Faim (*n. f.*): faṅ.—**hungry,** *a.* Affamé: af″‿fā″mē′. —**I am hungry.** J'ai faim: ʒē faṅ.—**to be h.** Avoir faim: a″vwār′ faṅ.

hurdle. **1.** Claie (*n. f.*): klā. **2.** Fascine (*f.*): fa″sīn′.

hurl, *v.* **1.** Jeter: ʒə-tē′. **2.** Lancer: laṅ″sē′.

hurry, *v.* **1.** Se hâter: sə ha″tē′. **2.** Se presser: sə pres″‿sē′.—**hurry up!** **1.** À la hâte: a la hat. **2.** Hâtez-vous: ha″tē′ vū. **3.** Dépêchez-vous: dē″pā″shē′ vū.—**to be in a hurry.** Être pressé: ā′‿trə pres″sē′.

husband, *n.* Mari (*m.*): ma″rī′.

hush, *interj.* Chut: shüt.

hut, *n.* **1.** Baraque (*f.*): ba″rāk′. On maps, *Bqe.* **2.** Cabane (*f.*): ka″bān′. On maps, *Cne.* **3.** Hutte (*f.*): hüt. **4.** Gourbi (*m.*): gūr″bī′ (*improvised shelter*). **5.** Baraquement (*m.*): ba″ra″‿kə-māṅ′ (*collection of huts*).—**hutting.** Baraquement (*n. m.*): ba″ra″‿kə-māṅ′. Abbreviated *Baraqt.*

hussar. Hussard (*n. m.*): hüs″‿sār′.

hydroaeroplane, *n.* **1.** Hydroaéroplane (*m.*): ī″drō″a″ē″rō″-plāṅ′. **2.** Hydravion (*m.*): ī″dra″vī″‿yeṅ′. **3.** Hydroavion (*m.*): ī″dro″a″vī″‿yeṅ′.—**hydroplane,** *n.* Hydroplane (*m.*): ī″drō″-plāṅ′.

hydraulic, *a.* Hydraulique: ī″drō″līk′. On maps, *Hydr.*—**hydraulic-recoil.** Frein hydraulique (*n. m.*): frāṅ ī″drō″līk′.

hydrogen-tube. Tube d'hydrogène (*n. m.*): tüb dī″drō″ʒān′.

hypocritical, *a.* Hypocrite: ī″pō″krīt′.

I

I, *pron.* **1.** Je: ʒə (*contracted to* j' *before a vowel, and used in combination with verbs. It is written with a capital initial letter only at the beginning of a sentence*). **2.** Moi: mwā (*when used alone*). —**I am. 1.** Je suis: ʒə swī. **2.** J'ai: ʒā: used for "I have." See HUNGRY.
ice. Glace (*n. f.*): glā'‿sə.—**ice-axe.** Piolet (*n. m.*): pī"‿yo"lē'.—**iced,** *a.* Frappé (*m.*): frap"‿pē'.—**ice-house.** Glacière (*n. f.*): gla"sī"‿yār'‿ə.
idea. Idée (*n. f.*): ī"dē'.
identical, *a.* Identique (*m. & f.*): ī"daṅ"tīk'.—**identification.** Identification (*n. f.*): ī"daṅ"tī"fī"ka"sī"‿yeṅ'. Compare DESCRIPTION.—**identification** or **identity disk.** See DISK.
idiot. Idiot (*n. m.*): ī"dī"‿yō'; idiote (*n. f.*): ī"dī"yō'‿tə.—**idiotic,** *a.* Idiot (*m.*): ī"dī"‿yō'; idiote (*f.*): ī"dī"yō'‿tə.
if, *prep.* Si: sī.
ignition. Allumage (*n. m.*): al"‿lü"māʒ'‿ə. [rāṅ'‿tə.
ignorant, *a.* Ignorant (*m.*): īn"yo"rāṅ'; ignorante (*f.*): īn"yo"-
ill, *a.* **1.** Malade (*m. & f.*): ma"lād' (*of persons*). **2.** Souffrant (*m.*): sūf"frāṅ'; souffrante (*f.*): sūf"frāṅ'‿tə (*of animals*).—**are you ill?** Etes-vous malade? āt vū ma"lād'.—**I am ill.** Je suis malade: ʒə swī ma"lād'.—**ill-bred.** Mal élevé: mal‿ē"‿lə-vē'.—**illness.** Maladie (*n. f.*): ma"la"dī'.
illiterate, *a.* Illettré (*m.*): illettrée (*f.*): īl"‿lēt"‿trē'.
illustrate, *v.* **1.** Démontrer: dē"meṅ"trē'. **2.** Illustrer: īl"-lüs"trē'.
immigrant. Immigrant (*n. m.*): īm"mī"grāṅ'.
imitate, *v.* Imiter: ī"mī"tē'.
immobilize, *v.* Immobiliser: īm"‿mo"bī"lī"zē'.
impartial, *a.* Impartial (*m.*): impartiale (*f.*): aṅ"par"sī"‿yāl'.
impassable, *a.* **1.** Impraticable (*m. & f.*): aṅ"pra"tī"kā'‿blə. **2.** Impassable (*m. & f.*): aṅ"pas"‿sā'‿blə.
impatient, *a.* Impatient (*m.*): aṅ"pa"sī"‿yāṅ'; impatiente (*f.*): aṅ"pa"sī"‿yāṅ'tə.
implement, *n.* **1.** Ustensile (*m.*): üs"taṅ"sīl'. **2.** Outil (*m.*): ū"tī'.—**portable implements.** Outils portatifs: ū"tī' pōr"ta"tīf'.
implicate, *v.* **1.** Impliquer: aṅ"plī"kē'. **2.** Compromettre: keṅ"prō"met'‿trə.—**to be implicated, implicate oneself.** Se compromettre: sə koṅ"prō"met'‿trə.
imply, *v.* Signifier: sī"‿nyī"fī"‿yē'. [aṅ"pōr"tāṅ'‿tə.
important, *a.* Important (*m.*): aṅ"pōr"tāṅ'; importante (*f.*):
impose, *v.* Imposer: aṅ"pō"zē'.
impossible, *a.* Impossible (*m. & f.*): aṅ"pos"‿sī'‿blə.
impregnable, *a.* Imprenable (*m. & f.*): aṅ"prə-nā'‿blə.
impress, *v.* **1.** Imprimer: aṅ"prī"mē' (*actually*). **2.** Inculquer: aṅ"kül"kē' (*figuratively*).
imprison, *v.* Emprisonner: aṅ"prī"zon"‿nē'.
improve, *v.* Améliorer: a"mē"lī"‿yō"rē'.
in, into, *prep.* **1.** En: aṅ. **2.** Dans: dāṅ. **3.** À: a.
inaccessible, *a.* Inaccessible (*m. & f.*): īn"ak"ses"‿sī'‿blə.
inaccuracy. Inexactitude (*n. f.*): īn"eg"zak"tī"tüd'‿ə.
inactive, *a.* Inactif (*m.*): īn"ak"tīf'; inactive (*f.*): īn"ak"tīv'‿ə.
inadequate, *a.* **1.** Insuffisant (*m.*): aṅ"süf"fī"zāṅ'; insuffisante (*f.*): aṅ"süf"fī"zāṅ'‿tə. **2.** Disproportionné (*m.*): disproportionnée (*f.*): dis"prō"pōr"sī‿yon"‿nē'.
incautious, *a.* Imprudent (*m.*): aṅ"prü"dāṅ'; imprudente (*f.*): aṅ"prü"dāṅ'‿tə.
inch. Pouce (*n. m.*): pū'‿sə.
include, *v.* **1.** Renfermer: raṅ"fār"mē'. **2.** Comprendre: koṅ"-praṅ'‿drə.—**included,** *a.* **1.** Compris (*m.*): koṅ"prī'; comprise (*f.*): koṅ"prīz'‿ə. **2.** Renfermé (*m.*); renfermée (*f.*): raṅ"fār"mē'.

incoming, *a.* Entrant: aṅ"trāṅ' (*of ships*).
increase. I. *n.* **1.** Crue (*f.*): krü. **2.** Augmentation (*f.*): ōg"-maṅ"ta"sī"‿yeṅ'. **II.** *v.* **1.** Augmenter: ōg"maṅ"tē' (*to make larger*). **2.** Croître: krwā'‿trə (*to grow larger*).—**an additional increase.** Une augmentation complémentaire: ün‿ōg"maṅ"-ta"sī"‿yeṅ' keṅ"plē"maṅ"tār'‿ə.
incriminate, *v.* Incriminer: aṅ"krī"mī"nē'.
incur, *v.* **1.** S'exposer à: seks"pō"zē' a. **2.** Contracter: keṅ"-trak"tē'.—**incur expenditure.** Engager des dépenses: aṅ"ga"-ʒē' dē dē"pāṅs'‿ə.—**to i. a heavy responsibility.** Encourir une lourde responsabilité: aṅ"kū"rīr' ün lūrd res"peṅ"sa"bī"lī"tē'.
indeed! Vraiment! vrā"māṅ'.
indemnity. Indemnité (*n. f.*): aṅ"dām"nī"tē'.
indent. Demande (*n. f.*): də-māṅd'‿ə.—**indents for supplies.** Demandes de vivres: də-māṅd' də vīv'‿rə.—**indents for railway transport.** Demandes de transport par voie ferrée: də-māṅd' də troṅs"pōr' par vwā fā"rē'.
independently, *adv.* Indépendamment: aṅ"dē"paṅ"dam"‿māṅ'.
India. Les Indes: lēz‿aṅd'‿ə.—**Indian,** *a.* Indien (*m.*): aṅ"dī"‿yaṅ'; indienne (*f.*): aṅ"dī"‿yeṅ'‿nə.—**Indian corn.** Maïs (*n. m.*): ma"īs'.—**India-rubber.** Caoutchouc (*n. m.*): ka"-ūt"shū'.
indication. Indication (*n. f.*): aṅ"dī"ka"sī"‿yeṅ'.
individual. I. *a.* Individuel (*m.*); individuelle (*f.*): aṅ"dī"-vī"dü"el'. **II.** *n.* **1.** Isolé (*m.*); isolée (*f.*): ī"zō"lē'. **2.** Individu (*m.*): aṅ"dī"vī"dü'.—**individual shelter.** Abri individuel: a"brī' aṅ"dī"vī"dü"el'.
industrial, *a.* Industriel (*m.*); industrielle (*f.*): aṅ"düs"trī"‿yel'.
infantry. Infanterie (*n. f.*): aṅ"faṅ"‿tə-rī'.—**infantry soldier,** *n.* **1.** Fantassin (*m.*): faṅ"tas"‿saṅ'. **2.** Piou-piou (*n. m.*): pī"‿ū' pī"‿ū'.—**i. charge.** Charge d'infanterie: shār'‿ʒə daṅ"faṅ"‿tə-rī'.—**a regiment of i.** Un régiment d'infanterie: aṅ rē"ʒī"māṅ' daṅ"faṅ"‿tə-rī'.—**I am in the i.** Je suis de l'infanterie: ʒə swī də laṅ"faṅ"‿tə-rī'.—**mounted i.** Infanterie montée: aṅ"faṅ"‿tə-rī' meṅ"tē'.
inferior, *a.* Inférieur (*m.*); inférieure (*f.*): aṅ"fē"rī"‿yūr'.
infirmary. Infirmerie (*n. f.*): aṅ"fīr"‿mə-rī'.
infirmity. Infirmité (*n. f.*): aṅ"fīr"mī"tē'.
inflate, *v.* Gonfler: geṅ"flē'.
influence. Influence (*f.*): aṅ"flü"āṅs'.—**moral influences.** Les influences morales: lēz‿aṅ"flü"āṅs' mo"rāl'.
inform. 1. Avertir: a"vār"tīr'. **2.** Informer: aṅ"fōr"mē'. **3.** Déposer: dē"pō"zē' (with *against*).—**information** (*n.*). **1.** Information (*f.*): aṅ"for"ma"sī"‿yeṅ'. **2.** Des renseignements (*m.*): dē raṅ"sē"‿nyə-māṅ'.—**information office.** Bureau de renseignements: bü"rō' də raṅ"sē"‿nyə-māṅ'.—**reliable i.** Renseignements fermes (précis): raṅ"sē"‿nyə-māṅ' ferm (prē"sī').—**supply i.** Fournir des renseignements: fūr"nīr' dē raṅ"sē"‿nyə-māṅ'.—**to give information.** Renseigner (*v.*): raṅ"sē"‿nyē'.—**to lay an i. against.** Dénoncer: dē"neṅ"sē'.—**to publish for i.** Livrer à la publicité: līv"rē' a la pü"blī"sī"tē'.
informer. Délateur (*n. m.*): dē"la"tūr'.
inhabitant, the. L'habitant (*n. m.*): la"bī"tāṅ'.
inherent, *a.* Inhérent (*m.*): in"ā"rāṅ'; inhérente (*f.*): in"-ā"rāṅt'.
initial. I. *n.* Initiale (*f.*): ī"nī"sī'‿yāl'. **II.** *v.* Parafer: pa"-ra"fē'. **III.** *a.* **1.** Initial: ī"nī"sī"‿yāl'. **2.** Premier: prə-mī"‿yē'.
initiate, *v.* Prendre l'initiative: prāṅ'drə lī"nī"sī"‿ya"tīv'.
initiative. Initiative (*n. f.*): ī"nī"sī"‿ya"tīv'.—**to take the initiative.** Prendre l'initiative: prāṅ'‿drə lī"nī"sī"‿ya"tīv'.
injure, *v.* **1.** Endommager: an"dem"‿ma"ʒē'. **2.** Abîmer: a"bī"-mē'. **3.** Faire mal à: fār mal a (*do harm to, animals*). **4.** Blesser: bles"‿sē' (*wound*).

ink, *n.* De l'encre (*f.*): də lāṅ'krə.
inn, *n.* **1.** Auberge (*f.*): ō"bārʒ'. On maps, *Aubge.* **2.** Caravansérail (*m.*): ka"ra"van"sē"rā'yə. On maps, *Carav.*—**village inn.** Cabaret (*n. m.*): ka"ba"rē'. On maps, *Cabat.*—**where is the inn?** Où est l'auberge? ū ē lō"bārʒ'.
inquiry, *n.* Investigation (*n. f.*): aṅ"vēs"tī"ga"sī"‿yəṅ'.—**inquiry office.** **1.** Bureau de renseignements: bü"rō' də raṅ"-sē'‿nyə-māṅ'. **2.** Bureau d'adresses: bü"rō' da"dres'.
insensibility, *n.* Insensibilité (*f.*): aṅ"saṅ"sī"bī"lī"tē'.
inside, *n.* **1.** À l'intérieur: a laṅ"tē"rī"‿yūr'. **2.** Au-dedans de: ō də-dāṅ' də.
insignia, *n. pl.* Insignes (*m.*): aṅ"sī'‿nyə.
inspection, *n.* Inspection (*f.*): aṅ"spek"sī"‿yəṅ'.
instance, *n.* Occasion (*f.*): ək"‿ka"zī"‿yəṅ'.—**for instance.** Par exemple: pār eg"zaṅ'‿plə.
instead, *adv.* À sa place: a sa plas; à la place: a la plas.—**instead of.** Au lieu de: ō lī"‿yū' də.
instruction, *n.* **1.** Instruction (*f.*): aṅ"strük"sī"‿yəṅ' **2.** Ordre (*m.*): ēr'‿drə.—**awaiting i.** En attendant des ordres: aṅ at"‿taṅ"dāṅ' dēz"‿ēr'‿drə.
instrument. Instrument (*n. m.*): aṅ"strü"māṅ'.
insulator. Isolateur (*n. m.*): ī"zō"la"tūr'.
insure, *v.* **1.** S'assurer que: sas"‿sü"rē' kə. **2.** Tenir la main à: tə-nīr' la maṅ a.—**to insure order.** Assurer l'ordre: as"‿sü"rē' lōr'‿drə.
intelligence, *n.* Renseignements (*m. pl.*): raṅ"sē"‿nyə-māṅ'.—**intelligence department,** or **service.** Service des renseignements: sār"vīs' dē raṅ"sē"‿nyə-māṅ'.—**i. personnel.** Le personnel du service des renseignements: lə per"sən"‿nel' dü sār"vīs' dē raṅ"se"‿nyə-māṅ'.
intend, *v. a.* Avoir l'intention de: a"vwār' laṅ"taṅ"sī"‿yəṅ' də.
intention. Intention (*n. f.*): aṅ"taṅ"sī"‿yəṅ'.
intercept, *v.* Intercepter: aṅ"tār"sep"tē'.
intercommunication, *n.* Communications réciproques (*f.*): kəm"‿mü"nī"ka"sī"‿yəṅ' rē"sī"prōk'.
interfere, *v.* Intervenir: aṅ"tār"‿və‿nīr'.—**i. with the operations.** Intervenir dans les opérations: aṅ"tār"‿və-nīr' dāṅ lēz‿o"pē"ra"sī"‿yəṅ'.
interference. Intervention (*n. f.*): aṅ"tār"vaṅ"sī"‿yəṅ'.
intern. **I.** *n.* Interne (*m.*): aṅ"tārn'. **II.** *v.* Interner: aṅ"-tār"nē'.—**all enemy aliens should be interned.** Tous les étrangers ennemis doivent être internés: tū lēz‿ē"traṅ"ʒē' en"‿nə-mī' dwāv‿tāt'‿rə aṅ"tār"nē'.
interpose, *v.* S'intercaler: saṅ"tār"ka"lē' (*place between, as columns*).
interpret, *v.* Interpréter: aṅ"tār"prē"tē'.
interpreter. Interprète (*n. m.*): aṅ"tār"prāt'.
intersect, *v.* Entrecouper: aṅ"‿trə-kū"pē'; croiser: krwa"zē'.
interval. Intervalle (*n. m.*): aṅ"tār"vāl'.—**at intervals.** Par intervalles: par aṅ"tār"vāl'.
interview, *n.* **1.** L'entrevue (*f.*): laṅ"‿trə-vü'. **2.** Interview: aṅ'tār"vī"‿yū' (*journalism*).
intrench, *v.* Faire des tranchées: fār dē traṅ"shē'.
intrenched. Retranché: rə-traṅ"shē'.
intrenching tools. Outils de retranchement (*m.*): ū"tī' də rə-traṅ"‿shə-māṅ'.
intrenchment. Retranchement: rə-traṅ"‿shə-māṅ'.
intricate, *a.* **1.** Embrouillé (*m.*); embrouillée (*f.*): aṅ"brū"‿ī"‿yē'. **2.** Compliqué (*m.*); compliquée (*f.*): koṅ"plī"kē'.
invade, *v.* Envahir: aṅ"va"īr'.
invader. Envahisseur (*n. m.*): aṅ"va"īs"‿sūr'.

invalid. **I.** *n.* Malade (*m.*): ma″lād′. **II.** *v.* Réformer: rē″-fēr″mē′ (*discharge*).
invalided, *pa.* En réforme: aṅ rē″fērm′.—**i. with full allowance.** Réformé avec gratification: rē″fer″mē′ a″vek′ gra″tī″fī″ka″-sī″‿yeṅ′.—**i. without allowance.** Réforme sans gratification: rē″for″mē′ saṅ gra″tī″fī″ka″sī″‿yeṅ′.
invest, *v.* **1.** Bloquer: blō″kē′. **2.** Investir: aṅ″ves″tīr′.—**investigation of claims.** Enquête sur les réclamations: aṅ″kāt′ sür lē rē″kla″ma″sī″‿yeṅ′.
investment, *n.* **1.** Investissement (*n. m.*): aṅ″ves″tīs″‿sə-māṅ′ (*by a military force*). **2.** Placement (*m.*): plas″māṅ′ (*of money*).
invisible, *a.* Invisible (*m.* & *f.*): aṅ″vī″zī′‿blə.—**invisibility.** L'invisibilité (*n. f.*): laṅ″vī″zī″bī″lī″tē′.—**invisibility of works.** L'invisibilité des ouvrages: laṅ″vī″zī″bī″lī″tē′ dēz‿ūv″rāʒ′.
involve, *v.* Impliquer: aṅ″plī″kē′.—**to involve the risk.** Faire courir le risque: fār kū″rīr′ lə rīsk.
irascible, *a.* Irascible (*m.* & *f.*): ī″ra″sī′blə.
Ireland. Irlande (*n. f.*): īr″lānd′.—**the Irish.** Les Irlandais: lēz‿īr″laṅ″dā′.—**an Irishman.** Un Irlandais: aṅ‿īr″laṅ″dā′.
iron. Fer (*n. m.*): fār.—**corrugated iron.** Tôle ondulée (*f.*): tōl eṅ″dü″lē′.—**I. Cross.** Croix de fer (*f.*): krwā də fār.—**i. factory.** Same as IRONWORKS, see below.—**i. grate, i. grating.** Grille (*n. f.*): grī′yə.
ironmonger. Quincaillier (*n. m.*): kaṅ″ka″yē′.
ironworks. Forge (*n. f.*): fērʒ.
irregular, *a.* Irrégulier (*m.*): īr″‿rē″gü″lī″yē′; irrégulière (*f.*): īr″‿rē″gü″lī″yār′.
irrespective, *a.* Sans égard à: sānz‿ē″gārt′‿ā.
irrigation. Irrigation (*n. f.*): īr″rī″ga″sī″‿yeṅ′. On maps, *Irrig.*
is, *v.* Est: ē.—**is it?** Est-il? ēt‿īl.—**is he?** Est-il? ēt‿īl.—**he is.** Il est: īl‿ē.—**is there?** Y a-t-il? ī ā tīl.
island. Île (*n. f.*): īl. On maps, *I.*.
isolated, *a.* Isolé (*m.*); isolée (*f.*): ī″zō″lē′.
issue. **I.** *n.* **1.** Débouché (*m.*): dē″bū″shē′ (*outlet*). **2.** Dénouement (*m.*): dē″nū″māṅ′ (*denouement*, etc.). **3.** Distribution (*f.*): dīs″trī″bü″sī″‿yeṅ′ (*distribution*). **II.** *v.* **1.** Donner: den″‿nē′ (*give*). **2.** Émettre: ē″met′‿trə.—**issue an order.** Donner un ordre: den″‿nē′ aṅ‿ōr′‿drə.—**i. for service.** Mise en service: mīz‿aṅ sār″vīs′.—**register of issues.** Registre des distributions (*n. m.*): rə-ʒīs′‿trə dē dīs″trī″bü″sī″‿yeṅ′.
it, *pron.* **1.** Il: īl (*nominative*). **2.** Le: lə (*objective*). **3.** Cela: sə-lā′.—**it is.** C'est: sē.
Italy. Italie (*n. f.*): ī″ta″lī′.—**Italian,** *a.* & *n.* (*m.* & *f.*). Italien (*m.*): ī″ta″lī″‿yaṅ′; italienne (*f.*): ī″ta″lī″‿yen′‿nə.
itch. **I.** *n.* **1.** Démangeaison (*f.*): dē″maṅ″ʒā″zeṅ′. **2.** Gale (*f.*): gāl (*disease*). **II.** *v.* **1.** Avoir des démangeaisons: a″vwār′ dē dē″maṅ″ʒā″zeṅ′. **2.** Démanger: dē″maṅ″ʒē′.
itself, *pron.* Soi-même (*m.*): swā mām.

J

jack. Cric (*n. m.*); krī (*for lifting*).—**jack-boots,** *n. pl.* Bottes à genouillères (*f.*): bet a ʒə-nū″yār′.
Jack Johnson. A 17-inch German shell.—**j.-knife.** Couteau réglementaire: kū″tō′ rē″‿glə-maṅ″tār′.
jacket, *n.* **1.** Veste (*f.*): vest′‿ə. **2.** Jaquette (*f.*): ʒa″ket′‿tə.—**field-service jacket.** Vareuse d'ordonnance (*f.*): va″rūz′ dōr″don″‿nāṅs′.—**metal j.** Manchon métallique: maṅ″sheṅ′ mē″tal″lik′.—**service j.** Vareuse (*n. f.*): va″rūz′.

jail. Prison (*n. f.*): prī″zoṅ′.
jam. **I.** *n.* Confiture (*n. f.*): koṅ″fī″tür′. **II.** *v.* Enrayer: aṅ″rā″yē′ (*said of cartridges*). See SEIZING.—**jamming,** *a.* Enrayage: aṅ″rā″‿yā′‿ʒə.
January. Janvier (*n. m.*): ʒaṅ″vī″‿yē′.
Japan. Japon (*n. m.*): ʒa″poṅ′.—**Japanese,** *a.* Japonais (*m.*): ʒa″po″‿nē′; japonaise (*f.*): ʒa″po″‿nāz′‿ə.
jaw. Machoire (*n. f.*): mash″wār′.
jealous, *a.* Jaloux (*m.*): ʒa″lū′; jalouse (*f.*): ʒa″lūs′‿ə.
jetty. Jetée (*n. f.*): ʒə-tē′.
job. Travail (*n. m.*): tra″vai′.—**to have an easy job.** Avoir beau jeu: av″wār′ bō ʒū.
Joffre, Joseph J. C., ʒof′‿frə. Marshal of France.
join, *v.* **1.** Réunir: rē″ü″nīr′. **2.** Rallier: ral″‿lī″‿yē′. **3.** Rejoindre: rə-ʒwaṅ′drə.—**joined up,** *pa.* Enrôlé (*m.*): aṅ″rō″lē′. —**joiner.** Menuisier (*n. m.*): mə‿nwī″zī″‿yē′.—**joining,** *a.* Continu (*m.*): continue (*f.*): koṅ″tī″nü′.—**joint,** *n.* **1.** Adjoint (*n. m.*): a′ʒwāṅ′ (*associate*). **2.** Joint (*m.*): ʒwāṅ. **3.** Jointure (*f.*): ʒwaṅ″tür′. **4.** Rôti (*m.*): rō″tī′ (*of meat*).—**universal joint.** **1.** Joint universel: ʒwāṅt‿ü″nī″vār″sel′. **2.** Joint de Cardan: ʒwāṅt də kar′dāṅ′.
joist. Solive (*n. f.*): sol″īv′‿ə.
jolly, *a.* Gai (*m.*); gaie (*f.*): gā.
journey. Voyage (*n. m.*): vwa″yāʒ′‿ə.—**the end of a journey.** La fin d'un voyage: la faṅ daṅ vwa″yāʒ′‿ə.—**it is a long j.** C'est un long voyage: sēt‿aṅ loṅ vwa″yāʒ′‿ə.—**it is a short j.** C'est peu de distance: sē pū də dīs″tāṅs′‿ə.
joy. Joie (*n. f.*): ʒwā.
judge. **I.** *n.* Juge (*m.*): ʒüʒ. **II.** *v.* **1.** Juger: ʒü″ʒē′. **2.** Examiner: eg″za″mī″nē′.—**Judge Advocate General's Office (J. A. G.).** Service judiciaire: sār″vīs′ ʒü″dī″sī″‿yār′‿ə.—**to j. distance.** Apprécier la distance: ap″‿prē″sī″‿yē′ la dīs″tāṅs′‿ə.
jug. Cruche (*n. f.*): krüsh.—**jug of milk.** Pot de lait: pōt də lā.
July. Juillet (*n. m.*): ʒwī″‿yē′.—**the Fourteenth of July.** Le quatorze Juillet: lə ka″tōr′‿zə ʒwī″‿yē′ (*French national holiday*).—**the Fourth of July.** Le quatre Juillet: lə kāt′rə ʒwē″‿yē′ (*United States national holiday*).
jumper. Barre à mine (*n. f.*): bār‿a mīn (*mining-drill*).
jump in, jump up. Monter (*v.*): moṅ″tē′.
junction, *n.* **1.** Jonction (*f.*): ʒoṅk″sī″‿yoṅ′. **2.** Union (*f.*): ü″nī″‿yoṅ′. **3.** Embranchement (*m.*): aṅ″braṅ″‿shə-māṅ′. **4.** Croisement (*m.*): krwa″‿zə-māṅ′ (*of roads*). **5.** Bifurcation (*f.*): bī″für″ka″sī″yoṅ′.—**to effect a junction.** Opérer une jonction: o″pē″rēr′ ün ʒoṅk″sī″‿yoṅ′.
June. Juin (*n. m.*): ʒü″‿aṅ′.
jungle. Jungle (*n. f.*): ʒoṅ′‿glə.
just, *a.* Juste (*m.* & *f.*): ʒüs′‿tə.—**justice.** Justice (*n. f.*): ʒüs″tīs′‿ə.—**department of military justice.** Département de la Justice Militaire: dē″par″‿tə-māṅ′ də la ʒüs″tīs′ mī″lī″tār′‿ə.

K

keep, *v.* **1.** Garder: gar″dē′. **2.** Retenir: rə-tə-nīr′.—**to keep a force in reserve.** Conserver une troupe en main: koṅ″sār″vē′ ün trūp aṅ maṅ.—**to k. aloft.** Tenir l'air: tə-nīr′ lār (*used of aeroplanes*).—**to k. at bay.** Tenir en échec: tə-nīr′ aṅ‿ē″shek′. —**k. away from.** Se tenir loin de: sə tə-nīr′ lwaṅ də.—**k. clear.** Laisser libre: lās″‿sē′ lī′‿brə.—**k. in communication.** Se tenir en communication: sə tə-nīr′ aṅ kom″‿mü″nī″ka″sī″‿yoṅ′.—**to k. informed of.** Tenir au courant de: tə-nīr′‿ō kū″-

rāṅ' də.—**keep off,** *v.* Écarter: ē"kɑr"tē'.—**k. off!** Au large: ō lɑ̄rʒ'‿ə.—**k. quiet!** Restez tranquille: res"tē' traṅ"kīl'.—**k. a sharp lookout.** Surveiller avec soin: sür"vā"‿yē' ɑ̄"vek' swāṅ.—**k. straight on.** Continuez tout droit: køṅ"tī"nü"‿yē' tū drwā.—**k. in touch with.** Être en liaison avec: ā'trə ɑṅ lī"‿yā"zøṅ'‿ɑ"vek'.—**to k. under observation.** Surveiller: sür"vā"yē'.—**k. up a brisk fire.** Entretenir un feu nourri: ɑṅ"‿trə-tə-nīr' aṅ fū nūr"‿rī'.—**k. up to date.** Tenir à jour: tə-nīr' ɑ ʒūr.—**k. up with.** Marcher à la même allure: mar"-shē' ɑ lɑ mām ɑl"‿lür'‿ə.

kepi. Képi (*n. m.*): kē"pī' (*French soldier's cap*).

Kerke, kerk, *n.* [D. & Fl.]. Èglise (*f.*): ē"glīz' (*church*).

kettle, *n.* **1.** Bouilloire (*f.*): bū"‿ī"‿wār'. **2.** Marmite (*f.*): mar"mīt'‿ə.—**camp kettle.** Marmite de campement: mar"mīt' də kɑṅ"‿pə‿mɑ̄ṅ'. Compare MARMITE.

key, *n.* **1.** Clef (*n. f.*): klā. **2.** Manipulateur (*m.*): mɑ"nī"-pü"lɑ"tūr' (*telegraph-key*).

khaki. Kaki (*n. m.*): kɑ"kī'.

kick. **I.** *n.* **1.** Coup de pied (*m.*): kū də pī"‿yē' (*of persons*). **2.** Ruade (*f.*): rü"ɑ̄d'‿ə (*of animals*). **II.** *v.* Ruer: rü"‿ē'.

kidney. Rognon (*n. m.*): røṅ"‿yøṅ'.

kill, *v.* Tuer: tü"ē'.—**killed,** *pa.* Tué (*m.*); tuée (*f.*): tü"ē'.—**killed outright.** Tué raide: tü"ē' rād.

kiln. Fourneau (*n. m.*): fūr"nō'. On maps, *Fneau.*

kilogram. Kilogramme (*n. m.*): kī"lo"grɑ̄m'‿mə (2.15 *lbs.*).—**kilometre.** Kilomètre (*n. m.*): kī"lo"māt'‿rə (⁵/₈ *mile*).

kind, *n.* **1.** Espèce (*f.*): es"pās'‿ə. **2.** Sorte (*f.*): sōr'‿tə.—**in kind.** En nature: ɑṅ nɑ"tür'.—**you are very k.** Vous êtes très gentil: vūz‿āt trē ʒɑṅ"tī'.

king. Roi (*n. m.*): rwā.

kit, *n.* **1.** Effets (*m. pl.*): ef"‿fē'. **2.** Équipement (*m.*): ē"kīp"mɑ̄ṅ'. **3.** Paquetage (*m.*): pɑ"‿kə-tɑ̄ʒ'.—**kit bag.** Havre-sac (*n. m.*): hɑ"‿vrə-sɑ̄k'.—**horse-kit.** Effets de pansage: ef"‿fē' də pɑṅ"sɑ̄ʒ'‿ə.—**personal kit.** Objets personnels (*m. pl.*): øb"ʒē' pār"søn"‿nel'.

kitchen. Cuisine (*n. f.*): kwī"zīn'‿ə.—**field-kitchen.** Cuisine: kwī"zīn'‿ə.—**traveling field-k.** Cuisine roulante: kwī"zīn'‿ə rū"lɑ̄ṅt'‿ə.—**k. garden.** Jardin potager: ʒɑ̄r"daṅ' po"tɑ"ʒē'.—**k. utensils.** Ustensiles de cuisine (*m.*): üs"tɑṅ"sīl' də kwī"zīn'‿ə.

kite. Cerf-volant (*n. m.*): sārf vo"lɑ̄ṅ'.

knapsack, *n.* **1.** Sac (*m.*): sɑ̄k. **2.** Havresac (*n. m.*): hɑ"‿vrə-sɑ̄k'.

knee. Genou (*n. m.*): ʒə-nū'.—**kneel,** *v.* Se mettre à genoux: sə māt'‿trə ɑ ʒə-nū'.—**kneel** (*imperative*). À genoux: ɑ ʒə‿nū'.

knife, *n.* **1.** Couteau (*m.*): kū"tō' (*table*). **2.** Canif (*m.*): kɑ"nīf' (*pen*).—**k., fork and spoon.** Couvert (*m.*): kū"vār'.

knight. Chevalier (*n. m.*): shə-vɑ"lī"‿yē'.—**a Knight of the Legion of Honor.** Chevalier de la Légion d'honneur: shə-vɑ"lī"‿yē' də lɑ lē"ʒī"‿yøṅ' døn"‿nūr'.

knoll, *n.* **1.** Mamelon (*n. m.*): mɑ"‿mə-løṅ'. **2.** Taupinière (*f.*): tō"pī"nī"‿yār'.

knot, *n.* **1.** Nœud (*m.*): nū. **2.** Aiguillette (*f.*): ē"gwī"‿yet'‿tə (*shoulder-knot*).

know, *v.* **1.** Connaître: køṅ"‿nā'‿trə. **2.** Savoir: sɑv"wār'.—**do you know?** **1.** Savez-vous: sɑ"vē" vū. **2.** Connaissez-vous? køn"‿nās"‿sē' vū.—**I do not k. exactly.** Je ne sais pas exactement: ʒə nə sā pɑ̄z‿eg"zɑk"‿tə-mɑ̄ṅ'.—**knowledge.** Savoir (*n. m.*): sɑ"vwār'.—**technical knowledge.** Connaissance technique: køn"‿nās"‿sɑ̄ṅs'‿ə tāk"nīk'‿ə.

knuckle-duster. Same as FRENCH BAYONET (*soldiers' slang*).

kookenette. Lampe à alcool (*n. f.*): lɑ̄ṅp‿ɑ ɑl"køl' (*camp cooker*)

L

label. Étiquette (*f.*): ē″tī″ket′.
labor. Travail (*m.*): tra″vai′.—**labor corps.** Corps d'ouvriers civils (*m.*): kōr dū″vrī″‿yē′ sī″vīl′.—**l. gangs.** Équipes d'ouvriers: ē″kīp′ dū″vrī″‿yē′.
laboratory. Laboratoire (*n. m.*): la″bo″ra″twār′.
lack. **I.** *n.* **1.** Manque (*m.*): mańk. **2.** Défaut (*m.*): dē″fō′ (*defect*). **3.** Besoin (*m.*): bə-zwań′ (*need*). **II.** *v.* **1.** Manquer: mań″kē′. **2.** Avoir besoin de: av″wār′ bə-zwań′ də (*need*).
lad. Garçon (*n. m.*): gar″soń′.
ladder. Échelle (*n. f.*): ē″shel′‿ə.—**collapsible ladder.** Échelle observatoire: ē″shel′‿ə ob″zar″va″twār′.—**scaling l.** Échelle de siège: ē″shel′ də sī″‿āʒ′.
ladle. Louche (*n. f.*): lūsh.
lady. Dame (*n. f.*): dam.
lagoon. Lagune (*n. f.*): la″gün′.
laissez-passer (*n. m.*): lās″‿sē′ pas″‿sē′. A pass; literally, ["permit to pass."]
lake. Lac (*n. m.*): lak.
lamb, *n.* Agneau (*m.*): a″nyō′.—**shorn lamb.** Brebis tondue (*f.*): brə-bī′ toń″dü′.
lame, *a.* & *n.* Boiteux (*m.*): bwa″tū′; boiteuse (*f.*): bwa″tūz′.
lamp. Lampe (*n. f.*): lańp.—**lamp-bracket.** Porte-lanterne (*n. m.*): port″lań″tārn′.
lance. Lance (*n. f.*): lańs.—**lance-bucket.** Porte-lance (*n. m.*): port″lańs′.—**l.-corporal.** **1.** Soldat de première classe: sol″dā′ də prə-mī″‿yār′ klas. **2.** Élève caporal: ē l″āv′ ka″po″rāl′. —**lancer.** Lancier (*n. m.*): lań″sī″‿yē′.—**lancet.** Lancette (*n. f.*): lań″set′.
land. **I.** *n.* **1.** Terre (*f.*): tār (*earth*). **2.** Pays (*m.*): pā″‿yī′ (*country*). **II.** *v.* Débarquer: dē″bar″kē′.—**land-front.** Front de terre (*n. m.*): froń də tār.—**the l. of death.** Pays de mort: pā″‿yī′ də mōr (French name for "No Man's Land").—**the l. of the woods.** Le pays des bois: lə pā″‿yī′ dē bwa.
landing. Débarquement (*n. m.*): dē″bar″‿kə-māń′.—**attempted landings.** Tentatives de débarquement: tań″ta″tīv′ də dē″bar″‿kə-māń′.—**landing appliances.** Appareil de débarquement: ap″‿pa″rē′‿yə də dē″bar″‿kə-māń′.—**l. carriage.** Chariot d'atterrissage: shar″ī″ō′ dat″‿tār″‿rīs″‿sāʒ′ (*of an avion*).—**l. chassis.** Châssis d'atterrissage: shas″‿sī′ dat″‿tār″‿rīs″‿sāʒ′ (*of an avion*).—**l. ground.** Terrain d'atterrissage: tār″rań′ dat″‿tār″‿rīs″‿sāʒ′ (*in aviation*).—**l. place.** Débarcadère (*m.*): dē″bar″ka″dār′.—**l.-sheet,** *n.* Drap d'atterrissage: dra dat″‿tār″‿rīs″‿sāʒ′.—**l.-stage,** *n.* **1.** Appontement (*m.*): ap″‿poń″‿tə-māń′ (*gangway*). **2.** Débarcadère (*f.*): dē″bar″ka″dār′.
landmark, *n.* **1.** Borne (*f.*): born. **2.** Point de repère: pwań də rə-pār′.
language, *n.* **1.** Langue (*f.*): lań′‿gə. **2.** Langage (*m.*): lań″gāʒ′‿ə (*tone: matter of conversation*).
lantern. Lanterne (*n. f.*): lań″tārn′.—**lantern-jaw.** **1.** Mâchoire écartée: ma″shwār′ ē″kar″tē′. **2.** Joue creuse: ʒū krūz.
lanyard. Tire-feu (*n. m.*): tīr″fū′.
larch. Mélèze (*n. m*): mē″lāz′‿ə.
large, *a.* **1.** Grand (*m.*): grāń; grande (*f.*): grāńd′‿ə. On maps, *Grd., Grde.* **2.** Large (*m.* & *f.*): lār′‿ʒə.—**it is not large enough.** Ce n'est pas assez grand: sə nē pāz‿as″‿sē′ grāń.—**it is too l.** C'est trop grand: sē trō grāń.
lash, *v.* Amarrer: a″mar″‿rē′.—**lashing.** Amarre (*n. f.*): a″mar′‿rə.
last. Dernier (*m.*): dār″nī″‿yē′; dernière (*f.*): dār″nī″‿yār′‿ə. —**last post.** Sonnerie funèbre (*f.*): son″‿nə-rī′ fü″nā′‿brə.—**l. week.** La semaine dernière: la sə-māń′‿ə dār″nī″yār′‿ə.

late, *a. & adv.* Tard (*m.*): tār; tarde (*f.*): tār'‿də.—**at the latest.** Au plus tard: ō plü tar.—**to be l.** Être en retard: ā'‿trə aṅ rə-tār'.—**to get late.** Se faire tard: sə fār tār.

lath, *n.* **1.** Latte (*f.*): lat'‿tə. **2.** Lattis (*m.*): lat"‿tī' (*lathing*).

latrine, la"trīn', *n.* [Fr.] **1.** A privy; water-closet. **2.** Feuillées (*n. f. pl.*): fū"‿ī"yē' (*pit dug near a bivouac to serve as a latrine*).

laugh. **I.** *n.* **1.** Rire (*m.*): rīr. **2.** Ris (*m.*): rī. **II.** *v.* Rire: rīr.

launch. **I.** *n. f.* Chaloupe: sha"lūp'‿ə. **II.** *v.* **1.** Lancer: laṅ"sē'. **2.** Mettre à l'eau: māt'‿trə a lō.—**to launch an attack.** Déclencher une attaque: dē"klaṅ"shē' ün‿at"‿tāk'.—**launching.** Lancement (*n. m.*): laṅ"‿sə-māṅ'.

laundry, *n.* **1.** Blanchisserie (*f.*): blaṅ"shīs"‿sə-rī'. **2.** Buanderie (*f.*): bü"aṅ"‿də-rī'.

law. Loi (*n. f.*): lwā.—**international law.** Droit international: drwa aṅ"tār"na"sī"‿yeṅ"āl'.—**martial law.** **1.** Loi martiale: lwā mar"sī"āl'. **2.** État de siège: ē"tā' də sī"ēʒ'.—**lawful,** *a.* Légal (*m.*); légale (*f.*): lē"gāl'.

lay, *v.* Mettre: met'‿trə.—**to lay aside.** Mettre de côté: met'‿trə də kō"tē'.—**lay down.** **1.** Mettre bas: met'‿trə ba. **2.** Déposer: dē"pō"zē' (*said of weapons*). **3.** Spécifier: spē"sī"fī"ē' (*instructing*) **4.** Désigner: dē"zī"‿nyē' (*plans*).—**to lay out a camp.** Établir un camp: ē"tab"līr' aṅ kāṅ.—**to lay the dust.** Abattre la poussière: a"‿bāt'‿trə la pūs"‿sī"‿yār'‿ə.

laying. Pointage (*n.m.*): pwaṅ"tāʒ' (*aiming*).—**laying for direction.** Pointage en direction: pwaṅ"tāʒ'‿aṅ dīr"ek"sī"‿yeṅ'.—**laying for elevation.** Pointage en hauteur: pwaṅ"tāʒ'‿aṅ hō"tūr'.—**indirect laying.** Pointage indirect: pwaṅ"tāʒ'‿aṅ"-dīr"ekt'.

lazy, *a.* Paresseux (*m.*): par"es"‿sū'; paresseuse (*f.*): par"es"‿sūz'‿ə.

lead. **I.** *n.* **1.** Plomb (*m.*): ploṅ (*metal*). **2.** Conduite (*f.*): koṅ"dwīt'‿ə (*advance*). **II.** *v.* **1.** Ouvrir la marche: ū"vrīr' la mārsh'‿ə (*start*). **2.** Mener: mə-nē' (*as a prisoner, horse, etc.*). **3.** Conduire: koṅ"dwī'‿rə (*direct*).—**to lead into ambush.** Attirer dans une embuscade: at"‿tī"rē' daṅz‿ün‿aṅ"büs"kād'‿ə.

leader. Chef (*n. m.*): shef.—**leading.** Conduite (*n. f.*): koṅ"dwīt'‿ə.

leading, *a.* Premier (*m.*): prə-mī"‿yē'; première (*f.*): prə-mī"‿yār'.

lean, *a.* Maigre (*m. & f.*): mā'‿grə (*of the body in identification*).—**to lean on.** S'appuyer sur: sap"‿pwī"‿yē' sür.

learn, *v.* Apprendre: ap"‿prāṅ'‿drə.

leather. Cuir (*n. m.*): kwīr.

leave. **I.** *n.* **1.** Congé (*m.*): koṅ"ʒē'. **2.** Permission (*f.*): pār"-mīs"‿sī"‿yeṅ'. **II.** *v.* Laisser: lās"‿sē'.—**leave on full pay.** Permission avec solde entière: pār"mīs"‿sī"‿yeṅ' a"vek' sold aṅ"tī"‿yār'‿ə.—**sick l.** Congé de convalescence: koṅ"ʒē' də koṅ"va-les"‿sāṅs'.—**to go on leave.** Aller en permission: al"‿lē' aṅ pār"mīs"‿sī"‿yeṅ'.—**to l. the ranks.** Quitter les rangs: kīt"‿tē' lē rāṅ.

leaves. Feuilles (*n. f. pl.*): fū'‿yə.

ledge. Liteau (*n. m.*): lī"tō'.

left. **I.** *n.* Gauche (*f.*): gō'‿shə. **II.** *a.* Gauche (*m. & f.*): gō'‿shə.—**left turn.** Par file à gauche: pār fīl‿a gō'‿shə.—**l. wheel.** À gauche: a gō'‿shə.—**to the l., on the l.** **1.** À gauche: a gō'‿shə. **2.** À la gauche: a la gō'‿shə.

leg. Jambe (*n. f.*): ʒāṅ'‿bə.—**in the l.** À la jambe: a la ʒāṅ'‿bə.—**fore legs.** Membres antérieurs: māṅ'‿brə‿aṅ"tē"-rī"‿yūr'.—**hind legs.** Membres postérieurs: māṅ'‿brə pos"-tē"rī"‿yūr'.—**leg-irons.** Barre de justice: bār də ʒüs"tīs' (*naval use*).—**leg of mutton.** Gigot (*n. m.*): ʒī"gō'.

leggings, *n.* **1.** Jambières (*f. pl.*): ʒaṅ"bī"‿yār'‿ə. **2.** Molletières (*f. pl.*): mol"‿lə-tī"‿yār'‿ə.

Legion of Honor. Légion d'honneur (*n. f.*): lē"ʒī"‿yeṅ' den"‿nūr'.

lemon. Citron (*n. m.*): sī″treṅ′.—**lemon squash. 1.** Citron frappé (*m.*): sī″treṅ′ frăp″‿pē′. **2.** Citronnade (*f.*): sī″treṅ″nād′‿ə.
lend, *v.* Prêter: prē″tē′.—**to lend itself.** Se prêter: sə prē″tē′.—**l. me.** Prêtez-moi: prē″tē′ mwā.
length. Longueur (*n. f.*): leṅ″gūr′.—**horse length.** Longueur de cheval: leṅ″gūr′ də shə-văl′ (*8 feet*).
lens. Lentille (*n. f.*): laṅ″tī′‿yə.
less, *adv.* Moins: mwaṅ.
let. 1. Laisser: lās″‿sē′. **2.** Permettre: pār″met′‿trə. **3.** Louer: lū″‿ē′ (*rent a house*).—**let go!** Lâchez-tout! la″shē′ tū.—**let us go.** See GO.
letter. Lettre (*n. f.*): let′‿trə.—**are there any letters for me?** Y a-t-il des lettres pour moi: ī‿ya tīl dē let′‿trə pūr mwā.—**I must write a letter.** Il faut que j'écrive une lettre: īl fō kə ʒē″krī′‿və ün let′‿trə.—**registered l.** Lettre recommandée: let′‿trə rə-kom″‿maṅ″dē′.—**what is the postage on a letter for the United States?** Quel est le port d'une lettre aux États Unis: kel ē lə pōr dün let′‿trə ōz‿ē″tāz′‿ü″nī′.
lettuce. Laitue (*n. f.*): lā″tü′.
level. I. *a.* Égal (*m.*): Égale (*f.*): ē″gāl′ (*equal*).—**get the level.** Prenez le niveau: prə-nē′ lə nī″vō′. **II.** *n.* Niveau (*m.*): nī″vō′.—**on a l. with.** Au niveau de: ō nī″vō′ də.—**spirit l.** Niveau (*m.*): nī″vō′.—**sea l.** See under SEA.—**to level or place on a l.** Mettre de niveau: met′‿trə də nī″vō′.—**water l.** Niveau des eaux: nī″vō′ dēz′‿ō.
lever. Levier (*n. m.*): lə-vī″‿yē′.—**control lever. 1.** Palonnier (*n. m.*): pa″lon″‿nī″‿yē′. **2.** Levier de commande: lə-vī″‿yē′ də kom″‿māṅd′.
levy, *v.* Lever: lə-vē′.—**levy of money.** Contribution en argent: kōṅ″trī″bü″sī″‿yoṅ′ aṅ‿ar″ʒāṅ′.
liable. Sujet à: sü″ʒē′ a.
liar. Menteur (*n. m.*): man″tūr′.
liberty. Liberté (*n. f.*): lī″bēr″tē′. Liberty, equality, fraternity: Liberté, égalité, fraternité: lī″bār″tē′, ē″ga″lī″tē′, fra″-tār″nī″tē′ (*motto of the French Republic*).—**liberty to manœuvre.** Liberté de manœuvre: lī″bēr″tē′ də ma″nu′‿vrə.
licence, *n.* **1.** Licence (*f.*): lī″sāṅs′. **2.** Autorisation (*f.*): ō″-tō″rī″za″sī″‿yeṅ′.
lie. I. *n.* **1.** Mensonge (*m.*): maṅ″soṅʒ′. **2.** Configuration (*f.*): koṅ″fī″gü″ra″sī″‿yeṅ′ (*of the country*). **II.** *v.* **1.** Mentir: man″-tīr′.—**lie down. 1.** S'étendre: sē″tāṅ′‿drə. **2.** Se coucher: sə kū″shē′. **3.** (*Imper.*) Couchez-vous: kū″shē′ vū.—**lie of the ground.** Configuration du terrain: koṅ″fī″gü″ra″sī″‿yeṅ′ dü tār″raṅ′.
lieutenant. Lieutenant (*n. m.*): lī″‿yū″‿tə-nāṅ′.—**lieutenant-colonel.** Lieutenant-colonel(*n.m.*): lī″‿yū″‿tə-nāṅ′ kol″ə″nel′.
life. Vie (*n. f.*): vī.
lift, *v.* **1.** Lever: lə-vē′. **2.** Hausser: hōs″‿sē′.—**lift him gently.** Haussez-le doucement: hōs″‿sē′ lə dūs″māṅ′—**lifting power.** Pouvoir ascensionnel: pū″vwār′ as″‿saṅ″sī″‿yoṅ″‿nel′.
light. I. *a.* **1.** Clair (*m.*), claire (*f.*): klār (*clear; bright of hair*). **2.** Léger (*m.*): lē″ʒē′; légère (*f.*): lē″ʒār′‿ə (*in weight*). **II.** *n.* **1.** Lumière (*f.*): lü″mī″‿yār′‿ə. **2.** Clarté (*f.*): klār″tē′. **3.** Feu de navire: fū də na″vīr′‿ə (*of a ship*). **III.** *v.* **1.** Allumer: al″‿lü″-mē′. **2.** Éclairer: ē″klā″rē′.—**floating light. 1.** Feu flottant (*m.*): fū flot″‿tāṅ′. **2.** Feu sur bouée (*m.*): fū sür bū″‿ē′.—**l. infantry.** Infanterie légère (*f.*): aṅ″faṅ″‿tə-rī′ lē″ʒār′‿ə.—**l. pistol.** Lance-fusée (*n. f.*): laṅs″ fü″zē′ (*a device used for signaling*).—**lights out.** Extinction des feux (*f.*): eks″taṅk″sī″‿yeṅ′ dē fū (*retiring-time in barracks*).
lighter, *n.* **1.** Allège (*f.*): al″‿lāʒ‿ə. **2.** Gabare (*f.*): ga″būr′‿ə.—**lighterman.** Marinier (*n. m.*): ma″rī″nī″‿yē′.—**pilot.** See under PILOT.

lighthouse. Phare (*n. m.*): fär′‿ə.
lightning, *n.* **1.** Éclair (*n. m.*): ē″klär′‿ə. **2.** Foudre (*n. f.*): fū′‿drə.—**lightning=arrester, l.=conductor.** **1.** Paratonnerre (*m.*): pa″ra″ton″‿när′‿ə. **2.** Parafoudre (*f.*): pa″ra″fū′‿drə.
like. **I.** *a.* **1.** Semblable (*m. & f.*): saṅ″bla′‿blə. **2.** Pareil (*m.*), pareille (*f.*): pa″rā′‿yə. **II.** *adv.* Comme: kom′‿mə. **III.** *v.* Aimer: ā″mē′. Compare LOVE.
likely, *adv.* Probable: pro″ba′‿blə.—**likely to.** Dans le cas [de: daṅ lə ka də.
limb. Membre (*n. m.*): māṅ′‿brə.
limber. Avant=train (*n. m.*): a″vāṅ′ traṅ (*forward part of a gun=carriage*).—**limber=up** (*v.*): Amener les avant=trains: a″‿mə-nē′ lēz‿a″vaṅ′ traṅ.—**l.=box.** Coffre de l'avant=train: kof′‿frə də la″vaṅ′ traṅ.
limit. **I.** *n.* **1.** Limite (*f.*): lī″mīt′‿ə. **2.** Terme (*m.*): tār′mə. **II.** *v.* Limiter: lī″mī″tē′.
limousine. Limousine (*n. f.*): lī″mū″sīn′‿ə.
limping, *a.* Boiteux (*m.*): bwa″tū′; boiteuse (*f.*): bwa″tūz′‿ə (*a mark of identification*).
linden. Tilleul (*n. m.*): tī″‿yūl′.
line. Ligne (*n. f.*): lī′‿nyə.—**blocked line.** Ligne bloquée: lī′‿nyə blo″kē′.—**clear l.** Ligne libre: lī′‿nyə lī′‿brə.—**county l.** Limite d'arrondissement: lī″mī′‿tə dār″‿roṅ″dīs″‿sə-māṅ′.—**crest l.** Ligne de crête: lī′‿nyə de krāt′‿ə.—**department l.** Limite de département: lī″mīt′ də dē″par″‿tə-maṅ′.—**first l.** **1.** Première position: prə-mī″‿yār′ po″zī″sī″‿yeṅ′. **2.** Première ligne: prə-mī″‿yār′ lī′‿nyə.—**in l. of company columns.** En ligne de colonnes de compagnie: aṅ lī′‿nyə də ke″len′ də keṅ″pa″‿nī′.—**l. of advance.** Ligne de marche: lī′‿nyə də mar′‿shə.—**l. of communication.** Ligne de communication: lī′‿nyə də kem″‿mū″nī″ka″sī″‿yeṅ′.—**l. of defense.** Ligne de défense: lī′‿nyə də dē″fāṅs′‿ə.—**l. of flight.** Ligne de vol: lī′‿nyə də vōl.—**l. of resistance.** Ligne de résistance: lī′‿nyə də rē″zīs″-tāṅs′‿ə.—**l. of retreat.** Ligne de retraite: lī′‿nyə də rə-trāt′.—**on the front l.** En première ligne: aṅ prə-mī″‿yār′ lī′‿nyə.—**side l.** Point côté: pwaṅ kō″tē′.—**state l.** Limit d'état: lī″mīt′ dē″tā′.—**to man, to strengthen the l.** Garnir la ligne de feu: gar″nīr′ la lī′‿nyə də fū.—**township l.** Limite de canton: lī″mīt′ də kaṅ″toṅ′.—**trench l.** Ligne de tranchées: lī′‿nyə də traṅ″shē′.—**village l.** Limite de commune: lī″mīt′‿ə də kem″mün′‿ə
linen. Linge (*n. m.*): laṅ′‿ʒə.
link. Maillon (*n. m.*): mai″‿yeṅ′.
lint. Charpie (*n. f.*): shar″pī′.
lips, *n.* Lèvres (*f. pl.*): lā′‿vrə.—**protruding, thick lips.** Lèvres épaisses: lā′vrəz‿ē″pās′‿sə (*used in identification*).—**pursed l.** Lèvres pincées: lā′‿vrə paṅ″sē′ (*used in identification*).—**thin=lipped.** À lèvres minces: a lā′vrə maṅ′‿sə (*used in identification*).
liquid fire. Pétrole enflammé: pē″trol′ aṅ″flam″‿mē′.
list, *n.* **1.** Liste (*f.*): līs′‿tə. **2.** Rôle (*m.*): rōl′‿ə.—**billeting=list.** État de cantonnement (*m.*): ē″tā′ də kaṅ″ton″‿nə-māṅ′.
listen, *v.* Écouter: ē″kū″tē′.—**listen!** Écoutez! ē″kū″tē′.—**listening post.** Poste d'écoute (*n. f.*): pōst dē″kūt′‿ə (*post where soldiers are detailed to listen for mining=operations, etc., or the men detailed to this duty*).
liter. Litre (*n. m.*): lī′‿trə (9/10 *quart*).
litter. **1.** Brancard (*n. m.*): braṅ″kār′. **2.** Litière (*n. f.*): līt″yār′ (*of a stable*).
little, *a.* Petit (*m.*): pə-tī′; petite (*f.*): pə-tīt′‿ə.—**a little,** *adv.* Un peu: aṅ pū.—**little by little.** Peu à peu: pū a pū.
live, *v.* **1.** Demeurer: də-mū″rē′ (*dwell*). **2.** Habiter: a″bī″tē′ (*inhabit*). **3.** Vivre: vī′‿vrə (*exist*).
liver. Foie (*n. m.*): fwā.
livid, *a.* Livide (*m. & f.*): lī″vīd′‿ə (*a mark of identification*).

load. **I.** *n.* Charge (*f.*): shar'‿ʒə. **II.** *v. a.* Charger: shar"ʒē'.
loaf. **I.** *n.* Pain (*m.*): pañ (*of bread*). **II.** *v.* **1.** Flâner: fla"nē'. **2.** Vagabonder: va"ga"boñ"dē'.
loafer. Vagabond (*n. m.*): va"ga"boñ'.
lobster. Homard (*n. m.*): ho"mār'.
local, *a.* Local (*m.*), locale (*f.*): lo"kāl'.
locate. Déterminer l'emplacement: dē"tār"mī"nē' lañ"plas"‿sə-māñ'.
lock, *n.* **1.** Verrou (*m.*): vār"‿rū'. **2.** Serrure (*f.*): sār"‿rūr'. **3.** Écluse (*f.*): ē"klüz' (*of a canal*).—**lock up.** Prison (*n. f.*): prī"zoñ'.
locomotive. Locomotive (*n. f.*): lo"ko"mō"tīv'‿ə.
lodging. Logement (*n. m.*): lō"‿ʒə-māñ'.—**lodging allowance.** Indemnité de logement: añ"dām"nī"tē' də lō"‿ʒə-māñ'.
loft. Grenier (*n. m.*): grə-nī"‿yē'.
log, *n.* **1.** Bûche (*f.*): büsh. **2.** Rondin (*m.*): roñ"dañ'.
loins. Reins (*n. m.*): rañ.—**to sprain** or **strain one's loins.** Se donner un tour de reins: sə doñ"‿nē' añ tūr də rañ.
long. **I.** *a.* Long (*m.*): loñ; longue (*f.*): lōng. **II.** *adv.* Longtemps: loñ"tāñ'.—**long live.** Vive: vīv'‿ə. See VIVE.
longshoremen, *n.* **1.** Ouvriers de port: ūv"rī"‿yē' də por. **2.** Débardeur (*m.*): dē"bar"dūr'.
long-sighted, *a.* **1.** À longue vue (*m.* & *f.*): a lōng vü (*far-sighted*). **2.** Presbyte (*m.* & *f.*): pres"bīt' (*incident to old age*).
look. **I.** *n.* Regard (*m.*): rə-gār'. **II.** *v.* Regarder: rə-gar"dē'. —**l. after him.** Soignez-le: swa"‿nyē' lə.—**l. alive.** See ALIVE. —**l. at.** Voyez: vwa"yē'; regardez: rə-gar"dē'.—**l. here!** Dites donc: dīt doñk.—**l. out!** Garde à vous: gard a vū.
lookout. Surveillance (*n. f.*): sür"vē"‿yāñs'.—**look-out.** Guetteur (*n. m.*): gē"tūr'.
loop. Bride (*n. f.*): brīd.—**looping the l.** Boucler la boucle: bū"klē' la bū'‿klə (*in aviation*).
loophole, *n.* **1.** Meurtrière (*f.*): mūr"trī"‿yār' (*in fortification*). **2.** Créneau (*m.*): krē"nō' (*as at the top of trench*).—**l.-plate.** Plaque de tir à meurtrières: plak də tīr a mūr"trī"‿yār'.—**to l. a wall.** Créneler un mur: krē"nə-lē' añ mūr.
loosen. Relâcher (*v.*): rə-la"shē'.
loot. **I.** *n.* Butin (*m.*): bü"tañ'. **II.** *v.* Piller (*v.*): pī"‿yē'.
looter. Pillard (*n. m.*): pī"‿yār'.
lorry. Camion (*n. m.*): ka"mī"‿yoñ'.—**light lorry.** Camionnette (*n. f.*): ka"mī"‿yoñ"‿net'.
lose. Perdre (*v.*): pēr'drə.—**to lose one's way.** Ségarer: sē"ga"rē'.
loss. Perte (*n. f.*): pērt.—**make good losses.** Combler les pertes: koñ"blē' lē pērt.
lost, *pp.* Perdu: pār"dü'.
lot. Quantité (*n. f.*): kañ"tī"tē'.
love, *v.* Aimer: ā"mē'. See Appendix.—**do you love me.** M'aimez-vous: mā"mē"vū'.—**I l. you.** Je vous aime: ʒə vūz‿ām'.
low, *a.* Bas: ba.
lower, *a.* Bas (*m.*): bā; basse (*f.*): bās.
low-spirited, *a.* Triste (*m.* & *f.*): trīst.
luggage. Bagage (*n. m.*): ba"gāʒ'.—**left luggage office.** Consigne (*n. f.*): koñ"sī'‿nyə.—**l.-room.** Magasin aux bagages: ma"ga"zañ' ō ba"gāʒ'.—**l.-van.** Wagon de bagage: va"goñ' də ba"gāʒ'.
lumber. See TIMBER.
lunch, luncheon. **I.** *n.* **1.** Second déjeuner: sə-goñ' dē"ʒū"nē'. **2.** Goûter (*m.*): gū"tē'. **II.** *v.* Goûter: gū"tē'.
lunette. Lunette (*n. f.*): lü"net'. Abbreviated *Lun.*
lung. Poumon (*n. m.*): pū"moñ'.
lyddite. Lyddite (*n. f.*): līd"‿dīt'.
lying, *a.* Couché (*m.*), couchée (*f.*): kū"shē'.

M

machine. Machine (*n. f.*): ma″shīn′‿ə.—**highly sensitive machine.** Mécanisme extrêmement délicat: mē″kan″ïsm′ eks″-trē″mə‿māṅ′ dē″lī″kā′.—**machine-gun.** Mitrailleuse (*n. f.*): mī″-trai″‿yūz′.—**Machine-Gun Corps, Heavy Section.** British official designation for the "tanks."

"mack." Mackintosh (*soldiers' slang*).

Machonochie. A brand of canned meat or vegetables.

mad, *a.* Fou (*m.*): fū; folle (*f.*): fol′‿le.

made up, *pa.* Composé (*m.*), composée (*f.*): kөṅ″pō″zē′.

magazine. **1.** Magasin (*n. m.*): ma″ga″zaṅ′ (*as of a rifle*). **2.** Revue (*n. f.*): rə-vü′ (*periodical*).—**to charge the magazine.** Charger le magasin: shar″ʒē′ lə ma″ga″zaṅ′.

magneto. Magneto (*n. m.*): ma″‿nyē″to′.

mail, *n.* **1.** Dépêche (*f.*): dē″pāsh′‿ə (*letter*). **2.** Malle-poste (*f.*): mal″pөst′ (*mail-coach*). **3.** Courrier (*m.*): kūr″‿rī″‿yē′ (*courier*).—**when does the mail go out?** Quand va la poste? kaṅ vā la pөst′‿ə.

maim, *v.* **1.** Estropier: es″trō″pī″‿yē′. **2.** Mutiler: mü″tī″lē′.

main. **I.** *a.* Principal (*m.*), principale (*f.*): praṅ″sī″pāl′. **II.** *n.* Principal (*m.*): praṅ″sī″pāl′.—**main body.** **1.** Gros (*n. m.*): grō. **2.** Corps principal: kōr praṅ″sī″pāl′.—**m. point of resistance.** Centre de résistance: saṅ′trə də rē″zīs″tāṅs′.—**m. road.** Grande route: graṅd rūt′‿ə.—**m.-spring.** Grand ressort: graṅ rə-sōr′.—**the m. body of the army.** Le gros de l'armée: lə grō də lar″mē′.

mainly. Principalement: praṅ″sī″pal″māṅ′.

maintenance, *n.* **1.** Moyens de vivre (*m. pl.*): mwa″yaṅ′ də vīv′‿rə. **2.** Entretien (*m.*): aṅ″‿trə‿tī″‿yaṅ′.

maize. Maïs (*n. m.*): ma″īs′ (*Indian corn*).

major. **1.** Major (*n. m.*): ma″ʒōr′. **2.** Chef de bataillon, ou d'escadron: shef də ba″tai″‿yөṅ′, ū des″kad″rөṅ′.—**major-general.** Général de brigade: ʒē″nē″rāl′ də brī″gād′.

make, *v.* Faire: fār.—**m. known.** Faire connaître: fār kөn″-nā′‿trə.—**m. off.** Se sauver (*r.*): sə sō″vē′.—**m. room.** Faire place: fār plās.—**m. sure of.** S'assurer de (*r.*): sas″‿sü″rē′ də.—**m. up his mind.** Prendre son parti: prāṅ′‿drə sөṅ par″tī′.

male, *n.* Mâle (*m.*): mal.—**male nurse.** Infirmier (*n. m.*): aṅ″fīr″mī″‿yē′.

mallet, *n.* **1.** Maillet (*m.*): mai″‿yē′. **2.** Mail (*m.*): mā′‿yə.

man. **I.** *n.* Homme: өm. **II.** *v.* **1.** Garnir d'hommes: gar″nīr′ dөm. **2.** Armer: ar″mē′ (*of a ship*). **3.** Servir: sār″vīr′ (*of a gun*).

manage, *v.* **1.** Manœuvrer: ma″nū″vrē′ (*a machine gun*). **2.** Conduire: kөṅ″dwīr′ (*run, as a business*). **3.** Traiter: trā″tē′ (*animals*).—**management.** Traitement (*n. m.*): trā″‿tə‿māṅ′.—**manager.** Directeur (*n. m.*): dī″rek″tūr′.

mane. Crinière (*n. f.*): krī″‿nyār′ (*of a horse*).

maneuver. Manœuvre (*n. f.*): ma″nū′‿vrə.

mange. Gale (*n. f.*): gal.

manner, *n.* **1.** Manière (*f.*): ma″nī″‿yār′. **2.** Habitude (*f.*): a″bī″tüd′. **3.** Politesse (*f.*): pө″lī″tes′.—**manners,** *n. pl.* Manières polies: ma″nī″‿yār′ pө″lī′ (*behavior*).

man-of-war. Vaisseau de guerre (*m.*): vā″sō′ də gār.

manor. Manoir (*n. m.*): man″war′.

mansion. **1.** Château (*m.*): sha″tō′ (*country place*). **2.** Hôtel (*n. m.*): ō″tel′ (*city residence*).

manual of arms. Manuel d'armes: ma″nü″el′ dārm.

manufactory. **1.** Manufacture (*n. f.*): ma″nü″fak″tür′. Abbreviated *Manufre.* **2.** Fabrique (*f.*): fa″brīk′. **3.** Atelier (*m.*): a″tel″‿yē′ (*workshop*). **4.** Usine (*f.*): ü″zīn′ (*works*).

manufacture, *v.* Fabriquer: fa"bri"kē'.

many, *a.* & *n.* **I.** *a.* **1.** Beaucoup: bō"kū'. **2.** Plusieurs: plü"zī"‿yūr'. **II.** *n.* **1.** Un grand nombre: aṅ gran neṅ'‿brə. **2.** Une multitude: ün mül"tī"tüd'.

map. 1. Carte géographique (*n. f.*): kart ʒē"o"gra"fīk' (*of a continent* or *country*). **2.** Mappemonde (*f.*): map"‿pə-meṅd'‿ə (*of the world*). **3.** Plan (*m.*): plan (*of a city* or *town*).—**map-case,** *n.* Étui (*m.*): ē"twī'.—**from the map.** D'après la carte: da"prē' la kart.—**to map out. 1.** Faire une carte: fār ün kart. **2.** Marquer sur la carte: mar"kē' sür la kart.

marauder. Maraudeur (*n. m.*): ma"rō"dūr'.

March, *n.* Mars (*m.*): mars (*third month of the year*).

march, *n.* Marche (*f.*): mār'‿shə.—**a day's march.** Une journée de marche: ün ʒūr"nē' də mār'‿shə.—**flank or oblique m.** Marche de flanc: mār'‿shə də flaṅ.—**forced m.** Marche forcée: mār'‿shə fer"sē'.—**m. past.** Défilé (*n. m.*): dē"fī"lē'.—**night m.** Marche de nuit: mār'‿shə də nwī.—**quick m., m.!** Pas accéléré, marche! pāz‿āks"‿sē"lē"rē', mār'‿shə.—**route m.** Marche militaire: mār'‿shə mī"lī"tār'.—**on the m.** En marche: aṅ mār'‿shə.

march, *v.* Marcher: mar"shē'.—**to m. abreast.** Marcher de front: mar"shē' də freṅ.—**to m. back.** Revenir (*v.*): rə-və-nīr'.—**to m. down.** Descendre (*v.*): de"sāṅ'‿drə.—**to m. in.** Entrer (*v.*): aṅ"trē'.—**to m. in line.** Marcher en ligne: mar"shē' aṅ lī'‿nyə.—**to m. off.** Se mettre en marche: sə mēt'‿trə aṅ mār'‿shə.—**to m. out.** Sortir (*v.*): sēr"tīr'.—**to m. out of step.** Ne pas marcher au pas: nə pā mar"shē' ō pā.—**to m. up.** Avancer: a"vaṅ"sē'.—**to resume the m.** Reprendre la marche: rə-prāṅ'‿drə la mār'‿shə.

marching orders. 1. Ordre de mission (*n. m.*): ēr'‿drə də mīs"‿sī"‿yeṅ'. **2.** Ordre de marche: ēr'drə də mār'‿shə.—**in marching order.** En tenue de campagne: aṅ tə-nü' də kaṅ"pā'‿nyə.—**m. rate of speed.** Vitesse de marche: vī"tēs' də mār'‿shə.

mare. Jument (*n. f.*): ʒü"māṅ'.

margin, *n.* **1.** Marge (*f.*): mārʒ. **2.** Bord (*m.*): bēr.

marine, *n.* Fusilier marin (*m.*): fü"zī"lī"‿yē' ma"raṅ'.

mark, *n.* **1.** Marque (*f.*): mark (*in general*). **2.** Point de repère: pwaṅ də rə-pār' (*landmark*). **3.** Cible (*n. f.*): sī'‿blə (*firing-objective*).—**mark time!** Marquez le pas! mar"kē' lə pā.

marker. Jalonneur (*n. m.*): ʒa"len"‿nūr'.

market. I. *n.* Marché (*m.*): mar"shē'. Abbreviated *Mché*. **II.** *v.* **1.** Acheter au marché: a"‿shə-tē'.ō mar"shē'. **2.** Vendre au marché: vāṅ'‿drə ō mar"shē'.—**m.-place.** Halle (*n. f.*): hal.

marksman, *n.* **1.** Tireur (*m.*): tī"rūr'. **2.** Bon tireur (*m.*): beṅ tī"rūr'.—**marksmanship.** Adresse au tir: a"dres'‿ō tīr.

marlinespike. Épissoir (*n. m.*): ē"pīs"swār'.

marmalade. Marmelade (*n. f.*): mar"‿mə-lād'.

marmite, mar"mīt', *n.* [Fr. soldiers' slang.] A large shell fired from a "Jack Johnson." Compare KETTLE.

marquis. Marquis (*n. m.*): mar"kī'.

marriage, *n.* **1.** Mariage (*m.*): ma"rī"āʒ'. **2.** *pl.* Les noces (*f.*): lē nōs (*wedding ceremony*).—**marriage contract.** Contrat de mariage: keṅ"trā' də ma"ri"āʒ'.—**m. settlement.** Douaire (*n. m.*): dū"ār'.

marsh. 1. Marais (*n. m.*): ma"rē'. **2.** Marécage (*n. m.*): ma"rē"kāʒ'. Abbreviated *Marge*.—**salt marshes.** Marais salants: ma"rē' sa"lāṅ'.

marshal. Maréchal (*n. m.*): ma"rē"shāl'.

marshy, *a.* Marécageux (*m.*): ma"rē"ka"ʒū'; marécageuse (*f.*): ma"rē"ka"ʒūz'.

martingale. Martingale (*n. f.*): mar"taṅ"gāl'.

mask. I. *n.* A gas-mask. See under GAS. II. *v.* 1. Masquer: mas″kē′ (*put on masks*). 2. Déguiser: dē″gī″zē′ (*disguise*). **—to mask a battery.** Masquer une batterie: mas″kē′ ün bat″‿tə-rī′.

masonry. Maçonnerie (*n. f.*): ma″seṅ″‿nə-rī′.

mass, *n.* 1. Somme (*f.*): sōm. 2. Ensemble (*m.*): aṅ″sāṅ′‿blə. **—mass formation.** Formation en masse: fer″ma″sī″‿yeṅ′ aṅ mās.

master, *n.* 1. Patron (*m.*): pa″treṅ′. 2. Maître (*m.*): mā′trə.

match. Allumette (*n. f.*): al″‿lü″met′.—**matches must not be struck.** Il est défendu de frotter des allumettes: il‿ē dē″-faṅ″dü′ də frot″‿tē′ dēz‿al″‿lü″met′.

mate, *n.* 1. Camarade (*m.*): ka″ma″rād′. 2. *Naut.* Second (*m.*): sə-geṅ′ (*chief officer*).

material. Matériel (*n. m.*): ma″tē″rī″‿yel′.

matron. Infirmière en chef (*n. f.*): aṅ″fīr″mī″‿yār′ aṅ shef (*of a hospital*).

matter, *n.* 1. Matière (*f.*): ma″tī″‿yār′. 2. Sujet (*m.*): sü″ʒē′. 3. Affaire (*f.*): af″‿fār′.—**a matter of taste.** Une affaire de goût: ün af″‿fār′ də gū.—**no m.** N'importe! naṅ″pērt′.—**what is the m.?** Qu'est-ce qu'il y a? kē′‿sə kīl‿ī ā.—**what is the m. with you?** Qu'avez-vous? ka″vē′ vū.

mauser rifle. Fusil mauser: fü″zī′ me″zār′.

May. Mai (*n. m.*): mā (*fifth month of the year*).

may, *v.* [*May* and *might* when auxiliary verbs are the sign of the subjunctive or conditional.] Pouvoir: pū″vwār′.—**he may go.** Il peut sortir: il pū sōr″tīr′.—**it might be.** Cela se pourrait: sə-lā′ sə pūr″‿rē′.—**it might happen that.** Il pourrait se faire que: il pūr″‿rē′ sə fār kə.—**may be.** Peut être: pūt‿ā′‿trə.—**may I?** Puis-je? pwī′‿ʒə.—**you might have gone there.** Vous auriez pu y aller: vūz‿ō″rī″‿yē′ pü ī al″‿lē′.

mayor. Maire (*n. m.*): mār.

me, *pron.* 1. Moi: mwā; as, "give *me*," donnez-moi: den″‿nē′ mwā. 2. Me: mə.—**of** or **from me.** De moi: də mwā.—**for me.** Pour moi: pūr mwā.—**to me.** 1. Moi: mwā. 2. À moi: a mwā. 3. Me: mə.

meadow, *n.* 1. Pré (*m.*): prē. 2. Prairie (*f.*): prā″rī′. Abbreviated *Pr.*

meal. Repas (*n. m.*): rə-pā′.—**at meal-times.** Aux heures des repas: ōz‿ūr dē rə-pā′.—**I shall take my meals.** Je prendrai mes repas: ʒə praṅ″drē′ mē rə-pā′.—**have we time for a meal?** Y a-t-il le temps à manger? ī a tīl lə taṅ a maṅ″ʒē′.—**let us eat!** Mangeons! maṅ″ʒeṅ′.

mean, *a.* 1. Vil (*m.*), vile (*f.*): vīl (*despicable*). 2. Moyen (*m.*): mwa″yaṅ′; moyenne (*f.*): mwa″yen′ (*middle*).—**mean distance.** Distance moyenne: dīs″tāṅs′ mwa″yen′.—**m. width.** Largeur moyenne: lar″ʒūr′ mwa″yen′.

mean, *n.* 1. Milieu (*m.*): mīl″‿yū′. 2. Moyen (*m.*): mwa″-yaṅ′.—**by means of.** Au moyen de: ō mwa″yaṅ′ də.—**by no means.** Par aucun moyen: par ō″kaṅ′ mwa″yaṅ′.—**by this means.** Par ce moyen: par sə mwa″yaṅ′.

meaning. 1. Sens (*m.*): saṅs. 2. Signification (*f.*): sī″‿nyī″-fī″ka″sī″‿yeṅ′.

measles, *n. pl.* Rougeole (*f. sing.*): rū″ʒōl′.

measure. I. *n.* 1. Mesure (*f.*): mə-zür′. 2. Portée (*f.*): per″tē′. II. *v.* 1. Mesurer: mə-zü″rē′ (*in general*). 2. Arpenter: ar″paṅ″tē′ (*land*).

meat. Viande (*n. f.*): vī″āṅd′.—**boiled meat.** Bouilli (*m.*): bū″‿yī′.—**canned, preserved** or **tinned m.** Conserves de viande: keṅ″sārv′ də vī″āṅd′.—**fresh m. supply.** Ravitaillement en viande fraîche: ra″vī″tai″‿yə-māṅ′ aṅ vī″āṅd′ frēsh.—**roast m.** Rôti (*m.*): rō″tī′.—**frozen m.** Viande congelée: vī″āṅd′ koṅ″ʒē″lē′. See FRIGO.

mechanic. Mécanicien (*m.*): mē″ka″nī″sī″‿yaṅ′.—**mechanical,** *a.* Mécanique: mē″ka″nīk′.—**m. transport.** Service automobile: sār″vīs′ ō″tō″mō″bīl′.—**mechanism,** *n.* **1.** Mécanisme (*m.*): mē″ka″nīsm′. **2.** Mécanique (*f.*): mē″ka″nīk′.

medal. Médaille (*n. f.*): mē″dai′‿yə (*decoration*).

medical, *a.* Médical (*m.*), médicale (*f.*): mē″dī″kāl′.—**medical board.** Conseil de santé (*m.*): keṅ″sē′‿yə də saṅ″tē′.—**m. record book.** Cahier de visite: ka″yē′ də vī″sīt′.—**m. service.** Service de santé: sār″vīs′ də san″tē′.

medicine, *n.* **1.** Médecine (*f.*): mē″‿də-sīn′. **2.** Remède (*m.*): [rə-mād′.

meet, *v.* **1.** Rencontrer: raṅ″keṅ″trē′. **2.** Faire face à: fār fas a (*to face*). **3.** (1) S'assembler: sas″‿saṅ″blē′ (*assemble*). (2) Se réunir: sə rē″ü″nīr′.—**advancing to meet them.** S'avançant à leur rencontre: sa″vaṅ″sāṅt′ a lūr raṅ″ken′‿trə.—**m. the attack.** Faire face à l'attaque: far fas a lat″‿tāk′.—**to go to m.** Aller au devant de: al″‿lē′ ō də-vāṅ′ də (*at a station*).—**to m. death.** Affronter la mort: af″‿freṅ″tē′ la mōr.—**when shall we m. again?** À quand notre prochaine réunion? a kaṅ nō′‿trə pro″shēn′ rē″‿yü″nī″‿yeṅ′.

meeting, *n.* **1.** Réunion (*f.*): rē″yü″nī″‿yeṅ′. **2.** Rencontre (*f.*): raṅ″koṅ′trə. **3.** Confluent (*m.*): keṅ″flü″āṅ′ (*of rivers*). **4.** Jonction (*f.*): ʒeṅk″sī″‿yeṅ′ (*of roads*).

megaphone. Porte-voix (*n. m.*): pērt″vwā′.

mêlée. Mêlée (*n. f.*): mā″lē′.

mélinite. Mélinite (*n. f.*): mē″lī″nīt′ (*explosive*).

member, *n.* **1.** Membre (*m.*): maṅ′‿brə. **2.** Député (*m.*): dē″pü″tē′.

memorandum, *n.* **1.** Note (*f.*): nōt. **2.** Bordereau (*m.*): bōr″‿də-rō′.—**to make a memorandum of.** Prendre note de: prāṅ′‿drə nōt də.

men, *n. pl.* **1.** Hommes (*m. pl.*): ōm. **2.** Pièces (*f. pl.*): pī″‿yes′ (*in chess*). **3.** Dames (*f. pl.*): dam (*in drafts* or *checkers*).

menace. **I.** *n.* Menace (*n. f.*): mə-nās. **II.** *v.* Menacer: mə-na″sē′.

mend, *v.* **1.** Raccommoder: rak″‿kem″‿mō″dē′ (*sew*). **2.** Réparer: rē″pa″rē′ (*repair*).—**can you mend my coat?** Pouvez-vous raccommoder mon habit: pū″vē′ vū rak″‿kem″‿mō″dē′ moṅ‿a″bī′. See COAT.

mention, *v.* **1.** Mentionner: maṅ″sī″‿yoṅ″‿nē′. **2.** Désigner: dē″zī″‿nyē′.—**mention in dispatches.** Citation à l'ordre de l'armée: sī″ta″sī″‿yoṅ′ a lōr′drə də lar″mē′.—**to m. in general orders.** Mettre à l'ordre du jour: mēt′‿trə a lōr′drə dü ʒūr.

merchandise. Marchandises (*n. f.*): mar″shaṅ″dīz′.

mercy, *n.* **1.** Grâce (*f.*): gras′‿ə. **2.** Pardon (*m.*): par″deṅ′.

merely, *adv.* **1.** Simplement: saṅ″‿plə‿māṅ′. **2.** Seulement: sūl″‿māṅ′.

merit, *n.* Mérite (*m.*): mē″rīt′.

mess, *n.* **I.** [*Of military officers.*] **1.** Pension: paṅ″sī″‿yoṅ′. **2.** Mess (*m.*): mes. **3.** [*Of non-commissioned officers.*] Table (*f.*): tā′‿blə. **4.** [*Of privates.*] Ordinaire (*m.*): ōr″dī″nār′. **II. 1.** [*Of naval officers.*] Table (*f.*): tā′blə. **2.** [*Of seamen.*] (1) Plat (*m.*): plā. (2) Ordinaire (*m.*): ōr″dī″nār′.—**of the same mess.** Du même ordinaire: dü mām ōr″dī″nār′.

mess, *v.* Manger ensemble: maṅ″ʒē′ aṅ″sāṅ′‿blə.—**m.-box.** Cantine de mess d'officiers: kaṅ″tīn′ də mes dof″‿fī″sī″‿yē′.—**m.-room.** Chambrée (*f.*): shaṅ″brē′.—**m.-sergeant.** Étapier (*n. m.*): ē″tā″pī″‿yē′.—**m.-tin.** Gamelle (*f.*): ga″mel′.—**officers' m.** La pension des officiers: la paṅ″sī″‿yoṅ′ dēz‿of″‿fī″sī″‿yē′.—**m. orderly.** Ordonnance (*n. f.*): ōr″doṅ″‿nāṅs′.

message. **1.** Message (*n. m.*): mes″‿sāʒ′. **2.** Commission (*f.*): kom″‿mī″sī″‿yoṅ′.—**telegraphic message.** Dépêche (*f.*): dē″pāsh′.

met, *pp.* of MEET, *v.* Rencontré: rañ″kəñ″trē′.—**I met no one.** Je n'ai rencontré personne: ʒə nā rañ″kəñ″trē′ pār″sən′.
meter, metre. Mètre (*n. m.*): mē′trə (*3 ft. 3.37 inches*).
M. G., *abbrev.* Machine Gunner.—**M. G. C.,** *abbrev.* Machine Gun Corps.
midday. Midi (*n. m.*): mī″dī′.
middle. I. *a.* **1.** Du milieu: dü mīl″‿yū. **2.** Du centre: dü sāñ′‿trə. **II.** *n.* **1.** Milieu (*m.*): mīl″yū′. **2.** Centre: sāñ′‿trə.
midnight. Minuit (*n. n.*): mīn″‿wī′.
midshipman. Aspirant (*n. m.*): as″pī″rāñ′.
midships, *adv.* Par le travers: par lə tra″vār′.
might, *imp.* of MAY, *v.* Pourrait: pūr″‿rē′.—**that might be.** Cela pourrait être: sə-lā′ pūr″‿rēt′‿ā′trə. See also MAY.
mild, *a.* Doux (*m.*): dū; douce (*f.*): dūs.
mile, *n.* Mille (*m.*): mīl (*1,609.35 meters*).—**milestone,** *n.* Borne (*f.*): bōrn.
military, *a.* Militaire (*m. & f.*): mī″lī″tār′.—**military cross. 1.** La croix militaire: la krwa mī″lī″tār′. **2.** La croix de guerre: la krwa də gār.—**military law.** Code militaire (*m.*): kōd mī″lī″-tār′.—**m. medal.** Médaille militaire (*f.*): mē″dai′‿yə mī″lī″-tār′.—**m. police.** Police militaire (*f.*): pō″līs′ mī″lī″tār′.—**m. service.** Service militaire (*m.*): sār″vīs′ mī″lī″tār′.—**m. terms.** Termes militaires (*m.*): tārm mī″lī″tār′.
milk. I. *n.* Lait (*m.*): lā. **II.** *v.* Traire: trār.—**do you take milk?** Prenez-vous du lait? prə-nē′ vū dü lā.—**some m., please.** Du lait, s'il vous plaît: dü lā, sīl vū plā.—**to milk the line.** Dégarnir la ligne: dē″gar″nīr′ la lī′‿nyə (*secure reinforcements by drawing out battalions here and there*).
mill. I. *n.* **1.** Moulin (*m.*): mū″lañ′. **2.** Usine (*f.*): ü″zīn′ (*factory*). **II.** *v.* Moudre: mū′‿drə (*crush*).—**water-mill.** Moulin à eau: mū″lañ a ō.—**windmill.** Moulin à vent: mū″lañ′ a vañ.
million. Million (*n. m.*): mīl″‿yəñ′. [la mī″‿yen′.
mine[1], *poss. pron.* Le mien (*m.*): lə mī″‿yañ′; la mienne (*f.*):
mine[2]. **I.** *n.* Mine (*f.*): mīn. **II.** *v.* **1.** Miner: mī″nē′. **2.** Creuser: krū″zē′ (*fortifications*).—**counter-mine. I.** *n.* Contre-mine (*f.*): kəñ″‿trə-mīn′. **II.** *v.* Contre-miner: kəñ″trə-mī″nē′.—**floating m.** Mine flottante: mīn flət″‿tāñt′.—**ground m.** Mine immergée: mīn im″‿mār″ʒē′.—**m.-chamber.** Fourneau de mine: fūr″nō′ də mīn.—**m. sweeping.** Enlèvement des mines: añ″lāv″‿māñ′ dē mīn.—**submarine m.** Mine immergée: mīn im″mār″ʒē′.
miner. Sapeur mineur (*n. m.*): sa″pūr′ mī″nūr′.
mineral, *a.* Minéral (*m.*), minérale (*f.*): mī″nē″rāl′.—**artificial mineral water.** Eau minérale artificielle: ō mī″nē″rāl′‿ə ar″tī″fī″sī″‿yel′.—**mineral water.** Eau minérale (*f.*): ō mī″nē″-rāl′‿ə.—**natural mineral water.** Eau minérale naturelle: ō mī″nē″rāl′‿ə na″tü″rel′. See SODA-WATER.
minute, *n.* **1.** Moment (*m.*): mo″māñ′. **2.** Minute (*f.*): mī″nüt′.—**minutes of proceedings.** Procès-verbal: pro″sē′ ver″bāl′.
mire, *n.* **1.** Boue (*f.*): bū. **2.** Bourbe (*f.*): būrb.
mirror, *n.* Miroir (*m.*): mīr″‿wār′.
misguide, *v.* **1.** Donner une fausse direction à: dəñ″‿nē′ ün fōs dī″rek″sī″‿yəñ′ a. **2.** Égarer: ē″gā″rē′.
misinform, *v.* Donner de faux renseignements à: dəñ″nē′ də fō rañ″sē″‿nyə-māñ′ a.
mislead, *v.* Induire en erreur: añ″dwīr′ añ‿ār″‿rūr′.—**mislead the enemy.** Tromper l'ennemi: troñ″pē′ len″‿nə-mī′.
miss, *n.* Mademoiselle (*f.*): ma″də‿mwa″zel′.
miss, *v.* Manquer: mañ″kē′.—**miss fire.** Rater: ra″tē′.
missing, *a.* **1.** Disparu (*pp. m.*), disparue (*f.*): dīs″pa″rü′. **2.** Absent (*m.*): ab″sāñ′: absente (*f.*): ab″sāñt′‿ə. **3.** Égaré (*m.*),

égarée (*f.*): ē″ga″rē′.—**killed, wounded, or missing.** Tués, blessés, ou disparus: tü″ē′, bles″‿sē′, ū dis″pa″rü′.

mist. Brume (*n. f.*): brüm.

mistake. **1.** Méprise (*f.*): mē″prīz′. **2.** Erreur (*f.*): ār″rūr′. **3.** Faute (*n. f.*): fōt.—**correct mistakes.** Corriger les fautes: kor″‿rī″ʒē′ lē fōt.—**make a mistake.** Faire une méprise: fār ün mē″prīz′.

mister. Monsieur (*n. m.*): mū″sī″‿yū′. See Mr.

mistress, *n.* **1.** Maîtresse (*f.*): mā″três′. **2.** Madame (*f.*): ma″dām′.

mistrust, *v.* **1.** Se méfier de: sə mē″fī″‿yē′ də. **2.** Soupçonner: sūp″son″‿nē′.

misunderstanding, *n.* **1.** Malentendu (*m.*): mal″aṅ″taṅ″dü′. **2.** Erreur (*f.*): ār″rūr′.

mitrailleuse. Mitrailleuse (*n. f.*): mī″trai″‿yūz′ (*machine gun*).

moat. Fossé (*n. m.*): fos″‿sē′.

mobilize, *v.* Mobiliser: mo″bī″lī″zē′.—**order to mobilize.** L'ordre de mobilisation: lōr′drə də mo″bī″lī″za″sī″‿yoṅ′.—**mobilization.** Mobilisation (*n. f.*): mo″bī″lī″za″sī″‿yoṅ′.—**on mobilization.** À la mobilisation: a la mo″bī″lī″za″sī″‿yeṅ′.

modification. Modification (*n. f.*): mō″dī″fī″ka″sī″‿yeṅ′.

mole-hill, *n.* Taupinière (*f.*): tō″pī″nī″yār′.

Monday. Lundi (*n. m.*): lun″dī′.

money. **1.** L'argent (*n. m.*): lar″ʒāṅ′. **2.** Monnaie (*n. f.*): mon″‿nē′.—**I have no money.** Je n'ai pas d'argent: ʒə nā pā dar″ʒāṅ′.—**how much is that in French m.?** Combien est-ce en argent français? keṅ″bī″‿yaṅ′ es‿ə aṅ ar″ʒāṅ′ fraṅ″sē′.—**m.-changer.** Changeur (*n. m.*): shaṅ″ʒūr′.—**m.-order.** Mandat (*n. m.*): maṅ″dā′.—**post office money-order.** Mandat de poste: maṅ″dā′ də pōst.—**where can I get m. changed?** Où pourrai-je faire changer de l'argent? ū pūr″‿rē′‿ʒə fār shaṅ″ʒē′ də lar″ʒāṅ′.—**will you give me French m.?** Voulez-vous me donner de l'argent français? vū″lē′ vū mə doṅ″nē′ də lar″ʒāṅ′ fraṅ″sē′.

For English, French and German Money see page 91.

monoplane. Monoplan (*n. m.*): mo″no″plāṅ′.

Montenegro. Monténégro (*m.*): meṅ″tē″nē″grō′.

month. Mois (*n. m.*): mwa.—**last month.** Le mois dernier: lə mwa dār″nī″‿yē′.—**in a month's time.** Dans un mois: dāṅz‿aṅ mwa.

monument. Monument (*n. m.*): moṅ″ü″māṅ′.

moon. Lune (*n. f.*): lün.

moor, *v.* Amarrer: a″mar″‿rē′.

moral. **I.** *a.* Moral (*m.*), morale (*f.*): mo″rāl′. **II.** *n.* Moralité (*f.*): mo″ra″lī″tē′.—**bad morals.** Mauvaises mœurs: mo″vāz′ mūr.—**good m.** Bonnes mœurs: bon mūr.

more, *adv.* & *a.* **1.** Plus: plü. **2.** Encore: aṅ″kōr′.—**m. and m.** De plus en plus: də plüs‿aṅ plü.—**much m.** Beaucoup plus: bo″kū′ plü.

moricaud, mo″rī″kō′. [Fr.] **I.** *a.* Brownish. **II.** *n.* Brown. Applied to Senegalese and other brown troops.

morning. Matin (*n. m.*): ma″taṅ′.—**good morning.** See under Good.—**this m.** Ce matin: sə ma″taṅ′.

Moroccan contingent. Goum. marocain: gūm ma″ro″kaṅ′.

Morocco. Maroc (*n. m.*): ma″rok′.

mortar. Mortier (*n. m.*): mor″tī″‿yē′.

mother. Mère (*n. f.*): mār.

motion, *n.* Mouvement (*m.*): mū″‿və-maṅ′.—**in motion.** En marche: aṅ mār″‿shə.

motor, *n.* Moteur (*m.*): mo″tūr′.—**armored motor.** Automobile cuirassé: ō″tō″mō″bil′ kwī″ras″‿sē′.—**m.-bus.** Autobus (*n. m.*): ō″tō″büs′.—**m.-car.** Automobile (*n. m.*): ō″tō″mo″bil′.—**m.-cycle.** Motocyclette: mo″to″sī″klet′.—**m.-lorry.** Camion

ENGLISH, FRENCH, AND GERMAN MONEY

With the comparative values of the coins, etc., in the currency of the United States

Abbreviations

b = Bronze. *g* = Gold. *n* = Nickel. *p* = Paper. *s* = Silver.

ENGLISH MONEY

Dollars and Cents	
½	Farthing (*b*)
1	Half penny (*ha'penny*) (*b*)
2	Penny (*b*)
4	Two pence (*tuppence*) (*b*)
6	Three " [1] (*thrippence*) (*s*)
12½	Six " [2] (*s*)
25	Shilling[3] (*s*)
50	Two shillings (*s*)
62½	Two " and six pence[4] (*s*)
1.25	Five " [5] (*crown*) (*s*)
2.50	Ten " [6] (*half a sovereign*) (*g* & *p*)
5.00	Twenty " [7] (*sovereign*; *pound*)
5.25	Twenty one shillings (*guinea*[8]) (*g* & *p*)
25.00	Five pounds (*p*)
50.00	Ten " (*p*)
100.00	Twenty " (*p*)

NOTES.—[1] Thrippenny bit (*slang*); [2] A tanner (*slang*); [3] A bob (*slang*); [4] Half a crown (*slang*, half a dollar); [5] Crown (*slang*, a dollar); [6] Half a quid (*slang*); [7] A quid (*slang*); [8] A unit of reckoning though the coin is no longer in circulation.

FRENCH MONEY

Dollars and Cents		
1	One sou:	Un sou (*b*)
2	Two sous:	deux sous (*b*)
5	Five "	cinq " (*n*)
10	Ten "	dix " (*s*)
20	One franc:	un franc (*s*)
40	Two francs:	deux francs (*s*)
1.00	Five "	cinq francs (*s* & *p*)
2.00	Ten "	dix francs (*g* & *p*)
4.00	Twenty "	vingt francs[1] (*g* & *p*)
10.00	Fifty "	cinquante francs (*p*)
20.00	One hundred francs:	cent francs (*p*)
100.00	Five hundred "	cinq cent francs (*p*)
200.00	One thousand francs:	mille francs (*p*)

NOTE.—[1] The gold piece is called also a *Napoleon*.

GERMAN MONEY

Dollars and Cents	
¼	One pfennig (*b*)
½	Two pfennigs (*b*)
1¼	Five " (*n*)
2½	Ten " (*n*)
6¼	Twenty five pfennigs (*n*)
12½	Fifty pfennigs (*s* & *p*)
25	One mark (*s* & *p*)
50	Two marks (*s* & *p*)
75	Three marks[1] (*s* & *p*)
1.25	Five marks (*s* & *p*)
2.50	Ten " (*g* & *p*)
5.00	Twenty marks (*g* & *p*)

NOTE.—[1] Called also *thaler*.

automobile (*m.*): ka″mī″‿yeṅ′ o″to″mo″bīl′.—**m. power.** Force motrice (*f.*): fōrs mō″trīs′.—**m.=truck. m.=wagon.** Camion automobile (*m.*): ka″mī″‿yeṅ′ ō″tō″mo″bīl′.

mount. **I.** *n.* **1.** Monture (*f.*): meṅ″tür′ə (*horses*). **2.** Mont (*m.*): meṅ (*mountain*). **II.** *v.* Monter: meṅ″tē′.—**mount!** Montez! meṅ″tē′ (*order to cavalry*).—**prepare to m.!** À cheval! a shə-vāl′.—**to m. guard.** Monter la garde: moṅ″tē′ la gār′‿də.—**mounted infantry.** Infanterie montée: aṅ″faṅ″‿tə-rī′ moṅ″-tē′.

mountain, *n.* **1.** Mont (*m.*): meṅ. Abbreviated *Mt.* **2.** Montagne (*f.*): meṅ″tā′‿nyə. On maps, *Mgne.*—**mountain=battery.** Batterie de montagne: bat″‿tə-rī′ də moṅ″tā′‿nyə.

mouse. Souris (*n. f.*): sū″rī′.—**mouse=colored, m.=gray.** Gris de souris: grī də sū″rī′.

mouth, *n.* Bouche (*f.*): būsh′‿ə.—**mouth of river.** Embouchure (*f.*): aṅ″bū″shür′. Abbreviated *Embure.*

move, *v.* **1.** Se remuer: sə rə-mü″ē′. **2.** Transporter: traṅs″-pōr″tē′. **3.** Faire marcher: fār mar″shē′. **4.** Faire aller: fār al″‿lē′.—**m. off.** S'en aller: saṅ‿al″‿lē′.—**m. out.** Sortir: sor″tīr′.—**on the m.** En mouvement: aṅ mūv″māṅ′.—**to m. into position.** Prendre position: prāṅ′drə po″zī″sī″‿yeṅ′.—**to m. off.** Quitter (*v.*): kī″tē′.—**to move the points** (*of a railway track*). Aiguiller (*v.*): ā″gwī″yē′ (*switch*).

movement. Mouvement (*n. m.*): mūv″māṅ′.—**converging movement.** Un mouvement convergent: aṅ mūv″māṅ′ keṅ″-vār″ʒāṅ′.—**enveloping m.** Mouvement enveloppant: mūv″māṅ′ aṅ″və-lop″‿pāṅ′.—**forward m.** Mouvement en avant: mūv″-māṅ′ aṅ‿a″vāṅ′.—**retrograde m.** Mouvement rétrograde: mūv″māṅ′ rē″tro″grād′.

mow (*v.*) or **to mow down.** Faucher (*v.*): fō″shē′.

Mr. Monsieur (*n. m.*): mū″sī″‿yū′.—**Mrs., Madam.** Madame (*n. f.*): ma″dām′.

M. T., *abbrev.* Mechanical Transport.

much, *adv.* Beaucoup de: bō″kū′ də.—**as much as.** Autant que: ō″tāṅ′ kə.—**how much?** Combien? koṅ″bī″‿yaṅ′.

mud. Boue (*n. f.*): bū.—**mudguard.** Garde=boue (*n. m.*): gard″bū′.—**muddy,** *a.* Bourbeux (*m.*): būr″bū′; bourbeuse (*f.*): būr″būz′.

muffler, *n.* **1.** Cache=nez (*m.*): kash″nā′. **2.** Silencieux (*m.*): sī″laṅ″sī″‿yū′ (*silencer on a motor*).

mufti. Habit bourgeois: a″bī′ būr″ʒwā′ (*plain clothes*).—**in mufti.** Être en civil: ā′‿trə aṅ sī″vīl′.

mug, *n.* Gobelet (*m.*): gōb″‿ə-lē′.

muggy, *a.* **1.** Lourd: lūr. **2.** Mou: mū.

mule. Mulet (*n. m.*): mü″lē′.—**mule path** or **track.** Sentier (*n. m.*): saṅ″tī″‿yē′.

munitions, *n. pl.* Munitions (*f. pl.*): mü″nī″sī″‿yeṅ′ (*military stores of all kinds*).

music. Musique (*n. f.*): mü″zīk′.—**give us some music.** Faites de la musique: fāt də la mü″zīk′.

musketoon. Mousqueton (*n. m.*): mūs″‿kə-teṅ′.

must, *v.* Falloir: fal″‿lwār′. See Appendix.—**it must be done.** Il faut le faire: īl fō lə fār.—**I must.** Il me faut: īl mə fō.—**I m. eat.** Il me faut manger: īl mə fō maṅ″ʒē′.—**I m. do it.** Il faut que je le fasse: īl fō kə ʒə lə fās.—**must I?** Dois-je: dwā′‿ʒə.

mustard. Moutarde (*n. f.*): mū″tārd′‿ə.

muster. **I.** *n.* Rassemblement: ras″‿saṅ″‿blə-māṅ′. **II.** *v.* **1.** Se rassembler: sə ras″‿saṅ″blē′. **2.** Faire l'appel: fār lap″‿pel′. **3.** Répondre à l'appel: rē″poṅ′‿drə a lap″pel′.—**muster=roll.** Contrôles (*n. pl.*): koṅ″trōl′.

mute, *n.* Muet (*m.*): mü″ē′; muette (*f.*): mü″ēt′.

mutton, *n.* Mouton (*m.*): mū″toṅ′.—**leg of mutton.** Gigot (*n. m.*): ʒī″gō′.—**m.-chop.** Côtelette de mouton: kō″‿tə-let′ də mū″teṅ′.

muzzle. **I.** *n.* **1.** Bouche (*n. f.*): būsh (*of a gun*). **2.** Bout (*m.*): bū (*of a rifle, pistol,* etc.). **II.** *v.* Museler: mü″‿zə-lē′.—**muzzle-plug.** Couvre-bouche (*n. m.*): kū″vrə-būsh′.

my, *poss. pron.* Mon (*m.*): meṅ; ma (*f.*): ma; mes (*pl. m. & f.*): mē.

myself, *pron.* Moi: mwa; (or *emphatic*) moi-même: mwa″mām′.

N

nail. **I.** *n.* Clou (*m.*): klū. **II.** *v.* Clouer: klū″ē′.—**nail in the foot.** Clou de rue: klū də rü (*disease in a horse's foot*).—**planks or boards for nailing.** Planches à clous: plaṅsh a klū.

name. **I.** *n.* Nom (*m.*): neṅ. **II.** *v.* **1.** Appeler: ap″‿pə-lē′. **2.** Nommer: nem″‿mē′.—**my name is.** Je m'appelle: ʒə map″‿pel′‿lə.—**your n. and address.** Votre nom et adresse: vō′‿trə neṅ ē a″‿dres′‿sə.—**what is the n. of this place?** Comment s'appelle cette place: kem″māṅ′ sap″‿pel′‿lə set′‿tə plās′‿ə.—**what is your name?** Quel est votre nom? kel ē vō′‿trə neṅ.—**named.** Nommé: nem″‿mē′.—**namely.** C'est à dire: sēt‿a dīr′‿ə.

nap. Somme (*n. m.*): sem′‿mə.—**to take a nap.** Faire un petit somme: fār aṅ pə-tī′ sem′‿mə.

napper. (*Soldiers' slang for head.*)

narrow. **I.** *a.* Étroit (*m.*): ē″trwā′; étroite (*f.*): ē″trwāt′‿ə. **II.** *v.* **1.** Resserrer: rə-sār″‿rē′. **2.** Rétrécir: rē″trē″sīr′.

nasty, *a.* **1.** Sale (*m. & f.*): sāl′‿ə. **2.** Mauvais (*m.*): mō″vā′; mauvaise (*f.*): mō″vāz′‿ə.

nation, *n.* **1.** Nation (*f.*): na″sī″‿yeṅ′. **2.** Race (*f.*): rās′‿ə.—**national.** **I.** *a.* National (*m.*): na″sī″‿yen″āl′; nationale (*f.*): na″sī″‿yen″āl′‿ə. Abbreviated *Natl., Natle.* **II.** *n.* Citoyen (*m.*): sī″twa″‿yaṅ′; citoyenne (*f.*): sī″twa″‿yen′‿nə.—**nationality,** *n.* Nationalité (*f.*): na″sī″‿yeṅ″a″lī″tē′.

native. **I.** *a.* **1.** Natif (*m.*): na″tīf′; native (*f.*): na″tīv′‿ə. **2.** Natal (*m.*): na″tāl′; natale (*f.*): na″tāl′ə. **II.** *n.* **1.** Habitant (*m.*): a″bī″tāṅ′ (*of a civilized country*). **2.** Indigène (*m.*): aṅ″dī″ʒāṅ′‿ə (*primitive tribes*).—**native land.** **1.** Patrie (*n. f.*): pa″trī′. **2.** Pays (*n. m.*): pā″‿yī′.—**native place.** Lieu de naissance (*m.*): lī″‿yū′ də nās″‿sāṅ′‿sə.

nature. Nature (*n. f.*): na″tür′‿ə.—**natural,** *a.* Naturel (*m.*): na″tü″rel′; naturelle (*f.*): na″tü″rel′‿lə.

naval, *a.* Naval (*m.*); navale (*f.*): na″vāl′.—**naval air service.** Service de l'aviation navale: sār″vīs′ də la″vī″a″sī″‿yeṅ′ na″vāl′.—**n. officer.** Officier de marine: ef″‿fī″sī″‿yē′ də ma″rīn′.—**n. service.** Service navale: sār″vīs′ na″vāl′.—**n. terms.** Termes de marine: tārm′‿ə də ma″rīn′.

nave, *n.* **1.** Moyeu (*m.*): mwa″‿yū′ (*of a wheel*). **2.** Nef (*f.*): nef (*of a church*).

navigable, *a.* Navigable (*m. & f.*): na″vī″gā′‿blə. Abbreviated *Navig.*—**navigable river.** Rivière navigable: rī″vī″‿yār′‿ə na″vī″gā′‿blə.

navigate, *v.* Naviguer: na″vī″gē′.—**navigation.** Navigation (*n. f.*): na″vī″ga″sī″‿yeṅ′.

navy. Marine (*n. f.*): ma″rīn′‿ə.—**cooperation of the navy.** Coopération de la flotte: ko″ep″ār″a″sī″‿yeṅ′ də la flot′‿tə.

N. C. O. Non-commissioned officer. Sous-officier: sūz‿ef″‿fī″sī″‿yē′.

near. **I.** *adv.* Près: prā. **II.** *prep.* Près de: prā də.—**nearly,** *adv.* **1.** Presque: pres′kə. **2.** À peu près: a pū prā.—**near side.** Côté du montoir: kō″tē′ dü mon″twār′. Commonly contracted to *montoir* (*the left hand or mounting side of a horse*).

necessary. **I.** *a.* Nécessaire (*m.* & *f.*): nē″ses″‿sār′. **II.** *n.* Nécessaire (*m.*): nē″ses″‿sār′.—**necessaries.** Objets de petit équipement: ob″ʒē′ də pə-tīt′‿ē″kī″‿pə-māṅ′.
neck, *n.* **1.** Cou (*m.*): kū (*of a person*). **2.** Encolure (*f.*): aṅ″-ko″lūr′‿ə (*of a horse*). **3.** Manche (*m.*): maṅ′‿shə (*of a balloon*).—**necktie.** Cravate (*n. f.*): kra″vāt′‿ə.
need. **I.** *n.* Besoin: bə-zwāṅ′. **II.** *v.* **1.** Avoir besoin de: av″wār′ bə-zwāṅ′ də. **2.** Exiger: eg″zī″ʒē′.—**I need.** Il me faut: īl mə fō.
needle. Aiguille (*n. f.*): ā″gwī′‿yə. Abbreviated *Aigle.*
neglect. **I.** *n.* Négligence (*f.*): nē″glī″‿ʒāṅs′‿ə. **II.** *v.* Négliger: nē″glī″ʒē′.
neigh. **I.** *n.* Hennissement (*m.*): han″‿nīs″‿sə-māṅ′. **II.** *v.* Hennir: han″‿nīr′.
neighbor. Voisin (*n. m.*): vwa″zaṅ′.—**neighboring,** *a.* Voisin (*m.*): vwa″zaṅ′; voisine (*f.*): vwa″zīn′‿ə.—**neighborhood.** **1.** Voisinage (*m.*): vwa″zī″nāʒ′ (*of a person*). **2.** Environs (*m. pl.*): aṅ″vī″reṅ′ (*of a place*).
net, netting, *n.* **1.** Filet (*m.*): fī″lē′. **2.** Bastingage (*m.*): bas″taṅ″gā′‿ʒə (*naval*).—**network.** Réseau (*n. m.*): rē″zō′.
neutral. Neutre (*n. m.*): nū′‿trə.—**neutrality.** Neutralité (*f.*): nū″tra″lī″tē′.—**neutralize.** Neutraliser: nu″tra″lī″zē′.
never, *adv.* Jamais: ʒa″mā′.
new. **1.** Neuf (*m.*): (*before a consonant*) nu, (*before a vowel*) nūf; neuve (*f.*): nūv. **2.** Nouveau (*m.*): nū″vō′; nouvelle (*f.*): nū″vel′‿lə.
news, *n.* Nouvelles (*f. pl.*): nū″vel′‿lə.—**bad news.** De mauvaises nouvelles: də mō″vās′ nū″vel′‿lə.—**good n.** De bonnes nouvelles: də bon′‿nə nū″vel′‿lə.
newspaper. Journal (*n. m.*): ʒūr″nāl′.
newsroom. Salle de lecture: sal də lek″tūr′.
New Zealand. La Nouvelle Zélande: la nū″vel′‿lə zē″lāṅd′.
next. **I.** *a.* **1.** Prochain (*m.*): pro″shaṅ′; prochaine (*f.*): pro″-shān′. **2.** [*Following*] Suivant (*m.*): swī″vāṅ′; suivante (*f.*): swī″-vāṅt′. **3.** [*Neighboring*] Voisin (*m.*): vwa″zaṅ′; voisine (*f.*): vwa″-zīn′. **II.** *adv.* **1.** Après: a″prā′ (*after*). **2.** Ensuite: aṅ″swīt′ (*following*). **III.** *prep.* **1.** Auprès de: ō″prē′ də. **2.** À côté de: a kō″tē′ də.—**next week.** La semaine prochaine: la sə″mān′ pro″shān′.
nice, *a.* **1.** Joli (*m.*), jolie (*f.*): ʒō″lī′ (*to the sight*). **2.** Bon: boṅ; bonne (*f.*): bōn′‿nə (*to the taste*).
night. Nuit (*n. f.*): nwī.—**by n.** **1.** De nuit: də nwī. **2.** Pendant la nuit: paṅ″dāṅ′ la nwī (*during the night*).—**good night.** Bonsoir (*m.*): boṅ″swār′; bonne nuit (*f.*): bōn′nə nwī.—**n. attack.** Attaque de nuit: at″‿tāk′ də nwī.—**n. march.** Marche de nuit: mārsh də nwī.—**to stay overnight.** Passer la nuit: pas″‿sē′ la nwī.
nightfall, *n.* La tombée de la nuit (*f.*): la tōṅ″bē′ də la nwī.
nine, *a.* & *n.* Neuf (*n. m.*): nūf. See NUMBERS.—**nineteen,** *a.* Dix-neuf: dīz″nūf′.—**nineteenth,** *a.* Dix-neuvième: dīz″-nū″vī″‿yām′‿ə.—**ninety,** *a.* Quatre-vingt-dix: ka″trə-vaṅ″-dīs′—**ninth,** *a.* Neuvième: nū″vī″‿yām′‿ə.—**ninetieth.** Quatre-vingt-dixième: ka″trə-vaṅ″dī″zī″‿yām′‿ə.
nippers. Pinces coupantes (*n. f.*): paṅs kū″pāṅ′‿tə (*wire-cutters*).
no, *adv.* Non: noṅ.
nobody. Personne (*n. m.*): pār″son′‿nə.
noise. Bruit (*n. m.*): brwī.
no man's land. **1.** Pays de mort: pā″‿yī′ də mor: French rendering. Literally, the land of the dead. **2.** Pays de personne: pā″‿yī′ də pār″son′‿nə.
non-combatant. Non-combattant (*n. m.*): noṅ koṅ″bat″‿tāṅ′.
non-commissioned officers. Sous-officiers: sūz‿of″fī″sī″‿yē′.

non-compliance. 1. Refus d'acquiescer: rə-fü' da"kī"es"‿sē'. 2. Inexécution (*n. f.*): īn"eg"zē"kü"sī"‿yeṅ'.
non-skid, *a.* Antidérapant (*m.*): an"tī"dē"ra"pāṅ'; antidérapante (*f.*): an"tī"dē"ra"pāṅt'‿ə.
non-transportable, *a.* Intransportable (*m.* & *f.*): aṅ"traṅs"-pōr"tā'‿blə.—**non-transportable patient.** Blessé intransportable: bles"‿sē' aṅ"traṅs"pōr"tā'‿blə. See TAG.
none, *a.* 1. Nul (*m.*): nül; nulle (*f.*): nül'‿lə. 2. Aucun (*m.*): ō"kaṅ'; aucune (*f.*): ō"kü'‿nə.
noon. Midi (*n. m.*): mī"dī'.
normal, *a.* Normal (*m.*), normale (*f.*): nōr"māl'.—**under normal conditions.** Dans des conditions normales: dāṅ dē keṅ"dī"sī"‿yeṅ' nor"māl'.
north. Nord (*n. m.*): nor.—**northeast.** Nord-est: nord"-ēst'.—**northward.** Vers le nord: vār lə nōr.—**northwest.** Nord-ouest: nōrd"west'.
Norway. Norvége (*n. f.*): nor"vē'ʒə.—**Norwegian** (*a.* & *n.*, *m.* & *f.*) Norvégien (*m.*): nōr"vē"ʒī"‿yaṅ'; Norvégienne (*f.*): nōr"vē"ʒī"‿yen'‿nə.
nose, *n.* 1. Nez (*m.*): nē. 2. Bec (*m.*): bek (*of an aeroplane*). —**nose-bag.** Musette (*f.*): mü"zet'‿tə.—**to nose dive** (*Aviation*). 1. Piquer du bec: pī"kē' dü bek. 2. Piquer du nez: pī"kē' dü nē.
nostril, *n.* 1. Narine (*f.*): na"rīn' (*of a person*). 2. Naseau (*n. m.*): na"zo'.
not, *adv.* 1. Ne . . . pas: nə . . . pā. 2. Ne . . . point: nə . . . pwaṅ.—**I do not like him.** Je ne l'aime pas: ʒə nə lām'‿ə pā.—**not at all.** Pas du tout: pā dü tū.—**not at home.** N'y est pas: nī ē pā.—**not guilty.** Non coupable: neṅ ku"pā'‿blə.
notch. Cran (*n. m.*): krāṅ.—**notch of back-sight.** Cran de mire de la hausse: krāṅ də mīr də la hōs'‿sə.
note, *n.* 1. Note (*f.*): nōt'‿ə. 2. Billet de banque (*m.*): bī"yē' də bāṅk.—**change this note for me, please.** Veuillez me changer ce billet de banque, s'il vous plaît: vū"‿ī"yē' mə shaṅ"ʒē' sə bī"yē' də bāṅk, sīl vū plā.
note-book. Calepin (*n. m.*): ka"‿lə-paṅ'.—**attendance n.-book.** Cahier de visite (*m.*): ka"yē' də vī"zīt'‿ə (*of medical visits*, etc.).
note-paper. Papier à lettres (*m.*): pa"pī"‿yē' a let'‿trə.
nothing. Rien (*n. m.*): rī"‿yaṅ'.—**nothing more.** Rien de plus: rī"‿yaṅ' də plü.
notice. I. *n.* 1. Avis (*m.*): a"vī' (*warning*). 2. Connaissance (*f.*): ken"‿nās"sāṅs'‿ə (*consideration*).—**at short notice.** À court délai: a kūr dē"lā'.
November. Novembre (*n. m.*): nō"vāṅ'‿brə.
now, *adv.* 1. Maintenant: maṅ"‿tə-nāṅ'. 2. À présent: a [prē"zāṅ'.
nucleus. Noyau (*n. m.*): nwa"‿yō'.
number. I. *n.* 1. Numéro (*m.*): nü"mē"rō' (*of things in succession, as horses*). Abbreviated *No.* 2. Nombre (*m.*): neṅ'‿brə (*mathematical*). 3. Quantité (*f.*): kan"tī"tē' (*quantity*). II. *v.* 1. Nombrer: neṅ"brē' (*general sense*). 2. Numéroter: nü"mē"rō"tē' (*of things in succession*).—**the army numbered fifty thousand men.** L'armée se composait (*or* montait à: meṅ"tē a) de cinquante mille hommes: lar"mē' sə keṅ"pō"zē' də saṅ"kāṅt' mīl em. —**to n. from the right.** Numéroter à partir de la droite: nü"-mē"rō"tē' a par"tīr' də la drwāt'‿ə.—**my n. is —.** Mon numéro est: meṅ nü"mē"rō' ē.

Cardinal Numbers	Nombres Cardinaux	neṅ'‿brə kar"dī"nō'
1	un,	aṅ.
2	deux,	dū.
3	trois,	trwā.
4	quatre,	kāt'‿rə.
5	cinq.	saṅk.

Cardinal Numbers	Nombres Cardinaux	noṅ'‿brə kar"dī"nō'
6	six,	sīs.
7	sept,	set.
8	huit,	hwīt.
9	neuf,	nuf.
10	dix,	dīs.
11	onze,	eṅz.
12	douze,	dūz.
13	treize,	trāz.
14	quatorze,	ka"tōrz'.
15	quinze,	kaṅz.
16	seize,	sāz.
17	dix-sept,	dīs"‿set'.
18	dix-huit,	dīz"wīt'.
19	dix-neuf,	dīz"nūf'.
20	vingt,	vaṅ.
21	vingt et un,	vaṅ"tē"aṅ'.
22	vingt-deux,	vaṅ"dū'.
23	vingt-trois,	vaṅ"trwā'.
24	vingt-quatre,	vaṅ"kāt'‿rə.
25	vingt-cinq,	vaṅ"saṅk'.
26	vingt-six,	vaṅ"sīs'.
27	vingt-sept,	vaṅ"set'.
28	vingt-huit,	vaṅ"wīt'.
29	vingt-neuf,	vaṅ"nūf'.
30	trente,	trānt.
31	trente et un,	traṅt"‿ē"aṅ'.
32	trente-deux,	trant"dū'.
40	quarante,	kar"ānt'.
50	cinquante,	saṅ"kāṅt'.
60	soixante,	swas"‿sāṅt'.
70	soixante-dix,	swas"‿saut"dīs'.
80	quatre-vingt,	ka"trə-vaṅ'.
90	quatre-vingt-dix,	ka"trə-vaṅ"dīs'.
100	cent,	saṅ.
101	cent un,	sant"‿aṅ'.
200	deux cents,	dū saṅ.
1000	mille,	mīl.
10,000	dix mille,	dī mīl.
1,000,000	un million,	aṅ mil"‿yeṅ'.

numerous, *a.* Nombreux (*m.*): noṅ"brū'; nombreuse (*f.*): noṅ"brūz'‿ə.

nurse. I. *n.* **1.** Infirmier (*m.*): aṅ"fīr"mī"‿yē'; infirmière (*f.*): aṅ"fīr"mī"‿yār ‿ə. **2.** Garde-malade (*m.* & *f.*): gārd ma"lād'‿ə. **II.** *v.* **1.** Soigner: swa"nyē'. **2.** Garder: gar"dē'. (*All the above refer only to the nursing of the sick.*)

nursery. Crèche (*n. f.*): krēsh'‿ə (*for infants*).—**nursery-garden.** Pépinière (*n. f.*): pē"pī"nī"‿yār'‿ə. Abbreviated *Pépre.*

nut, *n.* **1.** Écrou (*m.*): ē"krū' (*mechanical*). **2.** Noix (*f.*): nwā (*tree*). **3.** Noisette (*f.*): nwa"zet'.—**nut-cracker,** *a.* **1.** En galoche: aṅ ga"lōsh'‿ə (*said of the nose and chin*). **2.** Prognathe (*m.* & *f.*): prog"nāt' (*said of the jaw: a mark of identification*).

O

oak. Chêne (*n. m.*): shān.

oar. Rame (*n. f.*): rām'‿ə.

oath. Serment (*n. m.*): sār"māṅ'.—**on** or **under oath.** Sous la foi du serment: sū la fwa dü sār"māṅ'.

oats. Avoine (*n. f.*): av"wān'.

obedience. Obéissance (*n. f.*): o"bē"īs"‿sāṅs'.

obey, *v.* Obéir: o"bē"īr'.—**obey orders!** Obeyez aux ordres! o"bē"‿yēz'‿ōz‿ōr'‿drə.

artistic; ärt; fat; fâre; fast; get; prēy; hit; police; obey; gō; not; ōr; full; rūle; but; būrn; ə = final;

object. But (*n. m.*): bü.
objective. Objectif (*n. m.*): ob″ʒĕk″tīf′.—**the objective to be attained.** L'objectif à atteindre: ləb′ʒek″tīf′ ɑ ɑt″‿tañ′drə.
oblige, *v.* **1.** Obliger: o″blī″ʒē′. **2.** Faire plaisir à: fâr plā″zīr′ ɑ.—**I am very much obliged to you.** Je vous suis bien obligé: ʒə vū swī bī″‿yañ′ o″blī″ʒē′.
oblique, *a.* Oblique (*m. & f.*): ob″līk′.
obliterate, *v.* Effacer: ef″‿fɑ″sē′.
observation. **1.** Observation (*n. f.*): ob″sâr″vɑ″sī″‿yoṅ′. **2.** Surveillance (*n. f.*): sür″vā″‿yāṅs′.—**army observation corps.** Corps d'armée d'observation: kor dɑr″mē′ dob″sâr″vɑ″sī″‿yoṅ′.—**o. balloon.** Ballon d'observation (*n. m.*): bɑl″‿loṅ′ dob″sâr″vɑ″sī″‿yoṅ′.—**o.-car.** **1.** Voiture observatoire: vwɑ″tür′ ob″sâr″vɑ″twär′ (*military*). **2.** Wagon observatoire: vɑ″goṅ′ ob″sâr″vɑ″twär′ (*railway*).—**o. post.** Poste d'observation: pōst dob″sâr″vɑ″sī″‿yoṅ′.—**to take an o.** Faire une observation: fâr ün‿ob″sâr″vɑ″sī″‿yoṅ′.
observatory. Observatoire (*n. m.*): ob″sâr″vɑ″twär′. Abbreviated *Obsre.*
observe, *v.* Observer: ob″sâr″vē′.—**observer.** Observateur (*n. m.*): ob″sâr″vɑ″tūr′.
obstacles. Obstacles (*n. m.*): ob″stā′klə.—**to encounter obstacles.** Rencontrer des obstacles: rañ″koṅ″trē′ dēz‿ob″stā′klə.
obstruct, *v.* **1.** Obstruer: ob″strü″ē′. **2.** Barrer: bɑr″‿rē′. **3.** Fermer: fâr″mē′.
obstructed. **1.** Barré: bɑr″rē′. **2.** Fermé: fâr″mē′.
obtain, *v.* **1.** Obtenir: ob″‿tə-nīr′. **2.** Procurer: pro″kü″rē′.—**easily obtained.** Facile à obtenir: fɑ″sīl′ ɑ ob″‿tə-nīr′.
obturator. Obturateur (*n. m.*): ob″tü″rɑ″tūr′ (*a shutter or check*).
occupation. Occupation (*n. f.*): ok″‿kü″pɑ″sī″‿yoṅ′.—**occupation of a country.** L'occupation d'un pays: lok″‿kü″pɑ″sī″‿yoṅ′ dañ pā″‿yī′.
occupy, *v.* Occuper: ok″kü″pē′.
October. Octobre (*n. m.*): ok″to′brə.
odometer. Odomètre (*n. m.*): o″do″mā′‿trə (*speed indicator*).
of. De: də.—**of it.** En: ɑṅ.—**of them.** En: ɑṅ.—**on the first of January.** Le premier Janvier: lə prə-mī″‿yē′ ʒañ″vī″‿yē′.—**to consist of.** Consister en: koṅ″sīs″tē′ ɑṅ.
off. **I.** *a.* Eloigné (*m.*), éloignée (*f.*): ēl″wɑ″‿nyē′. **II.** *adv.* Loin: lwañ.—**far off.** Très éloignée: trāz″‿ēl″wɑ″‿nyē′.—**off side.** Côté hors montoir: kō″tē′ hōr moṅ″twär′ (*the right hand side of a horse*).—**off with you!** Allez! ɑl″‿lē′.
offender, *n.* **1.** Coupable (*m.*): kū″pā′‿blə. **2.** Délinquant (*m.*): dē″lañ″kāṅ′. **3.** Criminel (*m.*): krī″mī″nel′; criminelle (*f.*): krī″mī″nel′.
offense, *n.* **1.** Crime (*m.*): krīm. **2.** Délit (*m.*): dē″līt′. **3.** Infraction (*f.*) à la loi militaire: añ″frɑk″sī″‿yoṅ′ ɑ lɑ lwɑ mī″lī″târ′.
offensive. **I.** *a.* Offensif (*m.*): of″‿fañ″sīf′; offensive (*f.*): of″‿fañ″sīv′. **II.** *n.* Offensive (*f.*): of″‿fañ″sīv′.—**to act on or assume the offensive.** Prendre l'offensive: prāñ′‿drə lof″‿fañ″sīv′.
office. Bureau (*n. m.*): bü″rō′. Abbreviated *Bau.*
officer. Officier (*n. m.*): of″‿fī″sī″‿yē′.—**field officer.** Officier supérieur: of″‿fī″sī″‿yē′ sü″pē″rī″‿yūr′.—**non-commissioned o.** Sous-officier: sūz‿of″‿fī″sī″‿yē′.—**o. of the day.** Officier de jour: of″‿fī″sī″‿yē′ də ʒūr —**senior o.** Officier supérieur: of″‿fī″sī″‿yē′ sü″pē″rī″‿yūr′.—**staff-o.** Officier d'état-major: of″‿fī″sī″‿yē′ dē″tā′ mɑ″ʒōr′.—**subordinate o.** Un sous-ordre (*n. m.*): añ sūz‿ōr′drə.—**supply o.** **1.** Officier d'approvisionnement: of″‿fī″sī″‿yē′ dɑp″‿pro″vī″zī″‿yon″‿nə-māṅ′. **2.** Intendant, ou sous-intendant: añ″tañ″dāṅ′, ū sūz‿

aṅ″taṅ″dāṅ′.—**warrant-o.** *Military.* 1. Officier breveté (*m.*): brə-və-tē′. 2. Adjudant sous-officier (*m.*): ad″ʒü dāṅ′ sūz‿of″‿fī″-sī″‿yē′. 3. *Naut.* Maître d'équipage (*m.*): mā′‿trə dē″kī″pāʒ′‿ə.
official. I. *a.* Officiel (*m.*), officielle (*f.*): of″‿fī″sī″‿yel′. II. *n.* Fonctionnaire (*m.*): fonk″sī″‿yən″‿nār′.—**official boundary-mark.** Bornes militaires: bər′‿nə mī″lī″tār′.—**o. report.** Procès-verbal (*m.*): pro′sē′ vār″bāl′.
often, *adv.* Souvent: sū″vāṅ′.
ogival, ogive. Ogive (*n. f.*): o″ʒīv′ (*pointed arch at the head of a shot*).—**elongated ogive.** Ogive allongée: o″ʒīv′ al″‿loṅ″ʒē′. —**truncated o.** Ogive tronquée: o″ʒīv′ troṅ″kē′.
oil. I. *n.* Huile (*n. f.*): wīl. II. *v.* 1. Huiler: wī″lē′. 2. Graisser: grās″sē′ (*lubricate a machine*).—**lubricating oil.** 1. Huile lubrifiante: wīl lü″brī″fī″‿yāṅt′. 2. Graisse (*n. f.*): grās (*fat or other lubricator*).—**oil-buffer.** Frein hydraulique (*n. m.*): fraṅ ī″drə″-līk′.—**oil-can.** 1. Bidon à huile (*n. m.*): bī″doṅ′ a wīl. 2. Burette (*n. f.*): bü″ret′.
ointment. Onguent (*n. m.*): oṅ″gāṅ′.—**boracic ointment.** Vaseline boriquée: va″sə-līn′ bo″rī″kē′.
old, *a.* 1. Ancien (*m.*): aṅ″sī″‿yaṅ′; ancienne (*f.*): aṅ″sī″‿yen′. Abbreviated *Ancn.* 2. (1) Vieux (*m.*): vī″‿yū′. Abbreviated *Vx.* (2) Vieille (*f.*): vī″‿yel′. Abbreviated *Vlle.*
"Old Contemptibles." Nickname of the British Expeditionary Force in France in 1914. From the reference of the German Emperor to "England's contemptible little army."
olive, *n.* 1. Olivier (*m.*): o″lī″vī″‿yē′ (*the tree or its wood*). 2. Olive (*f.*): o″līv′ (*fruit*).
omnibus, *n.* 1. Autobus (*m.*): o″tō″büs′. 2. Omnibus (*n. m.*): om″nī″büs′.
on, *adv.* Sur: sür.
once, *adv.* 1. Une fois: ün fwā. 2. Jadis: ʒa″dīs′ (*formerly*). —**once again.** Derechef (*adv.*): də-rə-shef′.—**o. a week.** Une fois par semaine: ün fwā pār sə-māṅ′‿ə.
one. I. *a.* Un (*m.*): aṅ; une (*f.*): ün. II. *pron.* 1. [1]On: oṅ. [2]L'on: loṅ. 2. Celui (*m.*): sə-lwī′; celle (*f.*): sel. 3. Quelqu'un: kel″kaṅ′.—**one another.** L'un l'autre (*m.*): laṅ lō′trə; l'une l'autre (*f.*): lün lō′trə.—**one-armed,** *a.* Manchot (*m.*): maṅ″shō′; manchote (*f.*): maṅ″shōt′.—**one-eyed,** *a.* Borgne (*m.* & *f.*): bōrn′‿yə.—**one-handed,** *a.* Manchot (*m.*): maṅ″shō′; manchote (*f.*): maṅ″shōt′.—**one-legged.** Qui n'a qu'une jambe: kī nā kün ʒaṅb —**one o'clock.** Une heure: ün ūr.
onion. Oignon (*n. m.*): ə″‿nyoṅ′.
only, *adv.* Seulement: sūl″‿māṅ′.
onrush. Poussée (*n. f.*): pūs″‿sē′.
onslaught. Assaut furieux: as″‿so′ fü″rī″ū′.
onward. En avant: aṅ‿a″vāṅ′.
ooze. I. *n.* Vase (*f.*): vāz′‿ə. II. *v.* Suinter: swaṅ″tē′.
open. I. *a.* 1. Ouvert (*m.*): ū″vār′; ouverte (*f.*): ū″vārt′‿ə. 2. Loyal (*m.*), loyale (*f.*): lwa″yāl″ (*said of character*). II. *v.* Ouvrir: ū″vrīr′.—**open!** Ouvrez! ū″vrē′.—**in the o.** En terrain découvert: aṅ tār″‿raṅ′ dē″kū″vār′.—**o. order.** Ordre étendu: ōr′drə ē″taṅ″dü′.—**o. out.** *v.* S'allonger: sal″‿loṅ″ʒē′.— **o. the door.** Ouvrez la porte: ū″vrē′ la pōrt′‿ə.—**to o. the way.** Ouvrir le chemin à: ū″vrīr′ lə shə-maṅ′ a.
opening. Ouverture (*n. f.*): ū″vār″tūr′.
operate, *v.* Opérer: ō″pē″rē′.—**You must be operated on.** Il faut vous opérer: īl fō vūz‿ō″pē″rē′.
operation. Opération (*n. f.*): o″pē″ra″sī″‿yoṅ′.—**impending operations.** Opérations imminentes: o″pē″ra″sī″‿yoṅz′‿īm″‿mī″nāṅt′.—**the theatre of o.** Le théâtre des opérations: lə tē″ā′‿trə dēz‿o″pē″ra″sī″‿yoṅ′.
opinion. Opinion (*n. f.*): o″pī″nī″‿yoṅ′.
opponent. Adversaire (*n. m.*): ad″vār″sār′.
opportunity. Occasion (*n. f.*): ok″‿ka″zī″‿yoṅ′.

oppose, *v.* Opposer: op″‿pō″zē′.—**the opposing forces.** Les forces opposées: lē fer′‿sə op″‿pō″zē′.
opposite. En face: aṅ fas.
optics, *n. pl.* Optique (*f. sing.*): op″tīk′.
or, *conj.* Ou: ū.
orange. Orange (*n. f.*): o″rāṅ′‿ʒə.—**orange-tree.** Oranger (*n. m.*): o″raṅ″ʒē′. Abbreviated *Orer.*
oratory. Oratoire (*n. m.*): o″ra″twār′. Abbreviated *Orat.*
orchard. Verger (*n. m.*): vār″ʒē′.
order. **I.** *n.* **1.** Commande (*f.*): kem″‿māṅd′‿ə. **2.** Ordre (*m.*): ōr′‿drə. **II.** *v.* **1.** Ordonner: ōr″den″‿nē′. **2.** Commander: kem″‿maṅ″dē′.—**admission order.** Billet d'entrée: bī″‿yē′ daṅ″trē′.—**await further orders.** Attendre des ordres ultérieurs: at″‿tāṅ′drə dēz‿ōr′‿drə ül″tē″rī″ūr′.—**close order.** Ordre serré: ōr′‿drə sār″‿rē′.—**discharge o.** Billet de sortie: bī″‿yē′ də sōr″tī′.—**emergency o.** Billet d'urgence: bī″‿yē′ dür″ʒāṅ′‿sə.—**extended o.** Ordre étendu: ōr′‿drə ē″taṅ″dü′.—**formal orders.** Ordres formels: ōr′‿drə fōr″mel′.—**general o.** Ordres généraux: ōr′‿drə ʒē″nē″rō′.—**in order.** En règle: aṅ rē′‿glə.—**open o.** Ordre dispersé: ōr′‿drə dīs″pār″sē′.—**operation orders.** Ordres d'opération: ōr′‿drə de″pē″ra″sī″‿yeṅ′.—**order of the day.** Ordre du jour: ōr′‿drə dü ʒūr.—**o. for drugs.** Bon de médicaments: beṅ də mē″dī″ka″māṅ′.—**o. for food.** Bon d'aliments: beṅ da″lī″māṅ′.—**o. of march.** Ordre de marche: ōr′‿drə də mār′‿shə.—**routine orders.** Ordres du service courant: ōr′‿drə dü sār″vīs′ kū″rāṅ′.—**order of seniority.** Ordre d'ancienneté: ōr′‿drə daṅ″sī″‿yen″‿nə-tē′.—**standing orders.** Ordres permanents: ōr′‿drə pār″ma″nāṅ′.
orderly. **1.** Officier d'ordonnance: of″‿fī″sī″‿yē′ dōr″den″‿nāṅs′. **2.** Planton (*n. m.*): plaṅ″teṅ′ (*room orderly*). **3.** Ordonnance (*n. f.*): ōr″den″‿nāṅs′.—**be on o. duty.** Etre de planton: ā′trə də plaṅ″teṅ′.—**hospital o.** Infirmier (*n. m.*): aṅ″fīr″mī″‿yē′.—**o. officer.** **1.** Officier de jour: of″‿fī″sī″‿yē′ də ʒūr. **2.** Officier d'ordonnance: of″‿fī″sī″‿yē′ dōr″den″‿nāṅs′.—**orderly man.** Garde de camp: gārd də kāṅ.—**o. in waiting.** Planton (*n. m.*): plaṅ″teṅ′.
ordinary. **I.** *a.* Ordinaire (*m. & f.*): ōr″dī″nār′ (*that is common: said of meals, wine, etc.*). **II.** *n.* Ordinaire (*m.*): ōr″dī″nār′ (*private soldiers' mess or allowance of wine*). See MESS.
ordnance. **1.** Matériel de guerre (*m.*): ma″tē″rī″‿yel′ də gār. **2.** Artillerie (*n. f.*): ar″tī″‿yə-rī′.—**ordnance map.** **1.** Carte du dépôt de la guerre: kart dü dē″pō′ də la gār. **2.** Carte d'état-major: kārt dē″tā′ ma″ʒōr′.—**pièce of o.** Pièce d'artillerie: pī″yās′ dar″tī″‿yə-rī′.
organize, *v.* Organiser: er″ga″nī″zē′.
orientation. Orientation (*n. f.*): o″rī″aṅ″ta″sī″‿yeṅ′ (*finding one's bearings*).
osier-ground, o.-land. Oseraie (*n. f.*): ōz″rā′.
other. Autre (*pn.*): ō′‿trə.—**each other.** L'un l'autre: laṅ lō′‿trə.—**no o. than.** Personne autre que: par″sen′‿nə ō′‿trə kə.—**of all others.** Entre tous: aṅ′‿trə tū.—**the other day.** L'autre jour: lō′‿trə ʒūr.
ounce. Once (*n. f.*): eṅs (*28 grammes*).
our, *pron.* Notre (*sing.*): nō′‿trə; nos (*pl.*): nō.
ourselves, *pron.* Nous-même: nū″mām′.
oust, *v.* **1.** Débusquer: dē″büs″kē′. **2.** Déloger: dē″lō″ʒē′.
out, *adv.* **1.** Dehors: də-ōr′ (*outside*). **2.** Sorti: ser″tī′ (*gone out*). **3.** Sur pied: sūr pī″‿yē′ (*military*). **4.** Épuisé: ē″pwī″zē′ (*used up*).—**out of.** **1.** À bout de: a bū də. **2.** Sans: saṅ. **3.** Dans: daṅ (*out of a book*). **4.** Par: par.—**out there.** Là bas: la ba (*a euphemism for No Man's Land or Le Pays des Morts.* See NO MAN'S LAND).—**to be out of.** **1.** Être sans: ā′‿trə saṅ (*be without*). **2.** Manquer de: maṅ″kē′ də (*short of*). **3.** À bout de: a bū də.

outbuilding. Dépendance (*n. f.*): dē″pań″dāńs′.
outfit. Équipement (*n. m.*): ē″kīp″māń′.
outflank, *v.* **1.** Déborder: dē″ber″dē′. **2.** Tourner: tūr″nē′.
outgoing, *a.* Sortant: sēr″tāń′ (*of ships*).
outlet, *n.* **1.** Sortie (*f.*): sēr″tī′. **2.** Débouché (*m.*): dē″bū″-shē′.
outlying, *a.* **1.** Avancé (*m.*), avancée (*f.*): a″vań″sē′. **2.** Éloigné (*m.*), éloignée (*f.*): ēl″wa″‿nyē′.
outmaneuver, *v.* Surpasser en manœuvre: sür″pas″‿sē′ ań ma″nū′‿vrə.
outnumber, *v.* **1.** Dépasser: dē″pas″sē′. **2.** Surpasser en nombre: sür″pas″‿sē′ ań neń′brə.
outpost. Avant-poste (*n. m.*): a″vań″pōst′.—**outpost reserves.** Réserves d'avant-poste: rē″zārv′ da″vań″pōst′.—**o. screen.** Réseau d'avant-poste: rē″zō′ da″vań″pōst′.
outset. Début (*n. m.*): dē″bü′.—**at the outset.** Au début: ō dē″bü′.
outside. **I.** *adv.* **1.** Dehors: də-ēr′. **2.** Hors de: hēr də (*excepting*). **II.** *n.* **1.** Dehors (*m.*): də-ēr′. **2.** L'extérieur: leks″-tē″rī″‿yūr′. **3.** Rissole (*m.*): rīs″‿sol′ (*of roast meat*). **III.** *adv.* **1.** En dehors: ań də-ēr′. **2.** À l'extérieur: a leks″tē″rī″‿yūr′.—**outside Belgium.** Hors la Belgique: hēr la bel″zīk′.
outskirt, *n.* **1.** Bord (*m.*): ber (*general*). **2.** Faubourg (*m.*): fō″būr′ (*of a town*). **3.** Lisière (*f.*): lī″zī″‿yār′ (*of a forest* or *wood*).
outspoken, *a.* Franc (*m.*): frań; franche (*f.*): frāń′‿shə.
outstep, outstrip, *v.* Devancer: də vań″sē′.
outward, *adv.* **1.** À l'extérieur: a leks″tē″rī″‿yūr′. **2.** Au dehors: ō də-hēr′.
outwit, *v.* Surpasser en finesse: sür″pas″‿sē′ ań fī″nēs′.
outworks. Ouvrages avancés: ūv″rāʒ′ a″vań″sē′. Abbreviated *Ouvr.*
oval, *a.* Ovale (*m.* & *f.*): ō″vāl′.
oven, *n.* **1.** Four (*m.*): fūr. **2.** Fourneau (*m.*): fūr″nō′. Abbreviated *Fneau.*—**baking oven.** Four à pain: fūr a pań.—**mobile field-o.** Four roulant de campagne: fūr rū″lāń′ də kań″-pā′‿nyə. Compare CAMP-OVEN under OVEN.
over. **I.** *adv.* **1.** D'un côté à l'autre: dań kō″tē′ a lō′‿trə (*from side to side*). **2.** Par-dessus: par″des″‿sü′ (*on the surface*). **3.** Au-dessus: ō″də-sü′ (*above*). **4.** Passé: pas″‿sē′ (*said of danger*). **II.** *prep.* **1.** Sur: sür. **2.** Par-dessus: See def. 2 above. **3.** Au-dessus: See def. 3 above. **4.** De l'autre côté: də lō′‿trə kō″tē′.—**over again.** Derechef (*adv.*): də-rə-shef′.—**o. there.** Par-là: par″lā′.—**o. the top!** Au-dessus! ō″də-sü′ (*order to British soldiers to climb out of the trenches and attack*).
overcoat. Pardessus (*n. m.*): par″des″‿sü′.
overcome, *v.* **1.** Vaincre: vań′‿krə. **2.** Surmonter: sür″meń″-tē′.
overhead. Au-dessus de la tête: ō″də-sü′ də la tāt.—**overhead firing.** Tir passant au-dessus de la tête: tīr pas″‿sāń′ ō″-də-sü′ də la tāt (*fire over the heads of one's advancing troops*).
overlap, *v.* Envelopper: ań″vlep″‿pē′.
overload, *v.* Surcharger: sür″shar″ʒē′.
overlook, *v.* **1.** Dominer: do″mī″nē′ (*dominate*). **2.** Commander: kom″‿mań″dē′ (*command, as a position*). **3.** Examiner: eg″za″mī″nē′ (*look over*).
overnight, *adv.* **1.** Du soir au lendemain: dü swar ō lań″də-mań′. **2.** Pendant la nuit: pań″dāń′ la nwī. **3.** La veille au soir: la vē′‿yə ō swar.—**he stayed overnight.** Il passa la nuit: īl pas″‿sā′ la nwī.
overpay, *v.* **1.** Payer trop: pā″‿yē′ trō. **2.** Payer trop cher: pā″‿yē′ tro shār (*pay too much for*).
overpopulated, *a.* Trop peuplé: trō pū″plē′.
overpower, *v.* **1.** Subjuguer: süb″ʒü″gē′ (*subjugate*). **2.** Vaincre: vań′‿krə (*conquer*)

overrule, *v.* **1.** Rejeter: rə-ʒə-tē′. **2.** Casser: kas″sē′ (*annul*).
overthrow. **I.** *n.* Défaite (*f.*): dē″fāt′. **II.** *v.* **1.** Mettre en déroute: met′‿trə aṅ dē″rūt′ (*rout*). **2.** Défaire: dē″fār′ (*defeat*). **3.** Culbuter: kül″bü″tē′ (*throw over*).
overwhelm, *v.* **1.** Accabler: ak″‿ka″blē′. **2.** Écraser: ē″kra″-zē′ (*crush*).
owe, *v.* Devoir: də-vwār′.—**owing to.** En raison de: aṅ rā″-ʒəṅ′ də.—**to be owing to.** Être dû à: ā′‿trə dü a.—**you owe me that.** Vous me devez ça: vū mə də-vē′ sa.
owner. Propriétaire (*n. m.*): pro″pri″‿yē″tār′
ox, *n.* [OXEN, *pl.*] Bœuf: būf; bœufs (*pl.*): bū.
oysters. Huîtres (*n. f.*): wī′‿trə.

P

pace. **I.** *n.* **1.** Pas (*m.*): pā (*step*). **2.** Allure (*f.*): al″‿lür′ (*carriage; way of walking*). **II.** *v.* **1.** Marcher au pas: mar″shē′ ō pa. **2.** Aller au pas: al″‿lē′ ō pā.—**double quick pace.** Pas redoublé: pa rə-dū″blē′.—**quicken the p.** Accélérer le pas: ak″sē″lē″rē′ lə pa.—**set the p.** Régler l'allure: rē″glē′ la″lür′.—**pacing.** Amble (*n. m.*): āṅ′‿blə.
pacifist. Pacifiste (*n. m.*): pa″sī″fīst′.
pack. **I.** *n.* **1.** Havresac du fantassin (*m.*): ha″‿vrə-sak′ dü faṅ″tas″‿saṅ′. **2.** Bât (*m.*): bā (*pack-saddle*). **3.** Sac (*m.*): sak. **II.** *v.* Emballer: aṅ″bal″‿lē′.—**pack animals.** Animaux de bât: an″ī″mō′ də bā.—**p.-horse.** Cheval de bât: shə-vāl′ də bā.—**p. of cards.** Jeu de cartes (*m.*): ʒū də kart.
package. Colis (*n. m.*): ko″lī′.
packet. Paquet (*n. m.*): pa″kē′.
packing, *n.* **1.** Chemise (*f.*): shə-mīz′‿ə (*asbestos wrapped around a machine-gun to prevent the water which cools the barrel from leaking*). **2.** Emballage (*m.*): aṅ″bal″‿lāʒ′.
pad. **I.** *n.* **1.** Bourrelet (*m.*): būr″‿rə-lē′. **2.** Tampon (*m.*): taṅ″pəṅ′. **II.** *v.* **1.** Ouater: wa″tē′ (*as with absorbent cotton*).—**cotton-pad.** Tampon de coton: taṅ″pəṅ′ də ko″təṅ′.
paddock, *n.* Pré (*m.*): prē (*small meadow*).
padlock. **I.** *n.* Cadenas (*m.*): ka″‿də-nā′. **II.** *v.* Cadenasser: ka″‿də-nas″‿sē′.
paid. Payé: pā″‿yē′.
pail. Seau (*n. m.*): sō.
pain, *n.* **1.** Douleur (*f.*): dū″lūr′. **2.** Mal (*m.*): mal.—**acute pain.** **1.** Douleur vive: dū″lūr′ vīv. **2.** Mal atroce: mal a″trōs′.—**are you in much pain?** Souffrez-vous beaucoup? sūf″‿frē′-vū bō″kū′.—**he suffers great p.** Il souffre beaucoup: il sūf′‿frə bō″kū′.—**I am in much p.** Je souffre beaucoup: ʒə sūf′‿frə bō″kū′.—**in great p.** Très souffrant: trā sūf″‿frāṅ′.—**internal p.** Mal interne: mal aṅ″tārn′.—**much p.** Beaucoup de mal: bo″kū′ də mal.—**my pains are internal.** Mes douleurs sont internes: mē dū″lūr′ səṅt‿aṅ″tārn′.—**to suffer p.** Souffrir: sūf″‿frīr′.—**where is your p.?** Où est vôtre mal? ū ē vō′‿trə māl.
painful, *a.* Douloureux (*m.*): dū″lū″rū′; douloureuse (*f.*): dū″-lū″rūz′.
pair, *n.* **1.** Paire (*f.*): pār (*as of gloves*). **2.** Couple (*m.*): kū′‿plə (*as of man and wife*).
palace. Palais (*n. m.*): pa″lā′.
pale, *a.* Pâle (*m.* & *f.*): pāl.
paling, palisade. Palissade (*n. f.*): pa″līs″‿sād′.
pannier. Panier (*n. m.*): pa″nī″‿yē′ (*a wicker basket for provisions*).
pants, *n. pl.* Pantalon (*m.*): pan″ta″ləṅ′.
paper, *n.* **1.** Papier (*m.*): pa″pī″‿yē′ (*writing-paper*). **2.** Journal (*m.*): ʒūr″nāl′ (*newspaper*).—**evening paper.** Journal

du soir: ʒūr″nāl′ dü swär.—**morning p.** Journal du matin: ʒūr″nā′ dü ma″taṅ′.—**papers,** *n. pl.* **1.** Papiers (*pl.*): pa″pī″‿yē′ (*personal papers*). **2.** Journaux (*pl.*): ʒūr″nō′ (*newspapers*).

parachute, *n.* Parachute (*m.*): pa″ra″shüt′.

parade, *n.* **1.** Parade (*f.*): pa″rād′. **2.** Place d'armes (*f.*): plas darm (*drill ground*).

parados. Revers (*n. m.*): rə-vār′ (*as of a trench*).

paraffin, *n.* **1.** Paraffine (*f.*): pa″ra″fīn′. **2.** Pétrole (*n. m.*): [pē″trol′.

parallel. **I.** *n.* Parallèle (*n. f.*): pa″ral″‿lāl′. **II.** *v.* Mettre dans une ligne parallèle à: met′‿trə daṅz′‿ün lī′‿nyə pa″ral″‿lāl′ a.

paralyze, *v.* Paralyser: pa″ra″lī″zē′.

parapet. Parapet (*n. m.*): pa″ra″pē′.—**battery-parapet.** Épaulement de batterie (*n. m.*): ē″pōl″māṅ′ də bat″‿tə-rī′.—**glacis or slope of a p.** Plongée (*n. f.*): ploṅ″ʒē′.—**protective p.** Masse couvrante (*f.*): mās′‿sə kū″vrāṅt′. See BREASTWORK.—**top of p.** Crête de feu (*f.*): krāt də fu.

parcel. Paquet (*n. m.*): pa″kē′.—**how much will this parcel cost?** Combien coûtera ce paquet? koṅ″bī″‿yaṅ′ kū″‿tə-rā′ sə pa″kē′.—**p. post.** Poste des colis postaux (*f.*): pōst dē ko″lī′ pos″tō′.—**p.-room.** Consigne (*n. f.*): koṅ″sī′‿nyə.

pardon, pardon me. Pardon (*n. m.*): par″doṅ′.—**I beg your pardon.** **1.** Pardonnez-moi: par″doṅ″nē′ mwa. **2.** Je vous demande pardon: ʒə vū də-māṅd′ par′doṅ′.

Paris. Paris: pa″rī′.—**the City of Paris.** La ville de Paris: [la vīl də pa″rī′.

park. **I.** *n.* Parc (*m.*): park. **II.** *v.* Parquer: par″kē′.—**gun park.** Parc des pièces: park dē pī″‿yās′.—**wagon p.** Parc à voitures (*n. f.*): park a vwa″tür′.

parley. **I.** *n.* Pourparler (*n. m*).: pūr″par″lē′. **II.** *v.* Parlementer: par″‿lə-maṅ″tē′.

parlor. Petit salon (*n. m.*): pə-tī′ sa″loṅ′.

parole. Parole (*n. f.*): pa″rōl′.—**on parole.** Sur parole: sür [pa″rōl′.

part. **I.** *n.* **1.** Partie (*f.*): par″tī′. **2.** Part (*f.*): par. **3.** Rôle (*m.*): rōl. **II.** *v.* **1.** Partager: par″ta″ʒē′. **2.** Séparer: sē″pa″rē′. —**component part.** Partie constitutive: par″tī′ koṅ″stī″tü″tīv′‿ə.—**to play a part.** Jouer un rôle: ʒū″‿ē′ aṅ rōl′‿ə.

parting, *n.* **1.** Séparation (*f.*): sē″pa″ra″sī″‿yoṅ′. **2.** Départ (*m.*): dē″pār′ (*departure*). **3.** Raie (*f.*): rā (*of the hair*).—**with a parting.** Avec la raie: a″vek′ la rā (*said of the hair: a mark of identification*).

party, *n.* **1.** Partie (*f.*): par″tī′. **2.** Détachement (*m.*): dē″-tash″‿ə-māṅ′.—**conducting party.** Cadre de conduite (*m.*): ka′‿drə də koṅ″dwīt′.—**forage p.** Corvée de fourrage: kor″vē′ də fūr″rāʒ′‿ə.—**fuel p.** Corvée de vivres: kor″vē′ də vī′‿vrə. —**storming p.** Détachement pour donner l'assaut: dē″ta″‿shə-māṅ′ pūr don″‿nē′ las″‿sō′.—**working p.** Détachement de travailleurs: dē″ta″‿shə-māṅ′ də tra″vai″‿yūr′.

pass. **I.** *n.* **1.** Permis (*m.*): pār″mī′. **2.** Laissez-passer (*m.*): lās″‿sē′ pas″‿sē′. **3.** Col (*m.*): kol (*mountain*). **4.** Gorge (*f.*): gōr′‿ʒə. Abbrev. *Grge.* **II.** *v.* Passer: pas″‿sē′.—**passable.** Praticable (*a. m. & f.*): pra″tī″kā′‿blə.—**passing not allowed.** Défense de passer: dē″fāṅ′‿sə də pas″‿sē′.—**passing troops.** Troupes qui passent: trūp kī pās′‿sə.—**pass this way.** Passez par ici: pas″‿sē′ pār ī″sī′.—**to p. through the lines.** Franchir les lignes: fraṅ″shīr′ lē lī′nyə.—**without a p.** Sans permis: sāṅ pār″mī′.

passage. Passage (*n. m.*): pas″‿sā′‿ʒə. Abbreviated *Pge*

passenger. Voyageur (*n. m.*): vwa″ya″ʒūr′.

passport. Passeport (*n. m.*): pas″pōr′.

password. Mot d'ordre: mō dōr′‿drə.

pastern. Pâturon (*n. m.*): pa″tü″roṅ′.

pasture. Pâturage (*n. m.*): pa″tü″rāʒ′‿ə.—**highland pasture.** Haut pâturage: hō pa″tü″rāʒ′‿ə.

path, *n.* **1.** Chemin (*m.*): shə-maṅ′ (*in general*). **2.** Sentier (*m.*): saṅ″tī″‿yē′ (*foot path*). **3.** Passage (*m.*): pas″sāʒ′‿ə.—**to make good a path.** Faciliter un passage: fa″sī″lī″tē′ aṅ pas″‿sāʒ′‿ə. [sée (*f.*): bles″‿sē′.
patient, *n.* **1.** Malade (*m.* & *f.*): ma″lād′. **2.** Blessé (*m.*), bles-
patrol. Patrouille (*n. f.*): pa″trū″‿ī′‿yə.—**cavalry patrol.** Patrouille de cavalerie: pa″trū″‿ī′‿yə də kā″vā″‿lə-rī′.—**reconnoitring p.** Patrouille de reconnaissance: pa″trū″‿ī′‿yə də rə-keṅ″‿nās″‿sāṅ′‿sə.—**standing p.** Patrouille permanente: pa″trū″‿ī′‿yə pār″ma″nānt′‿ə.—**to send out patrols.** Envoyer des patrouilles: aṅ″vwa″yē′ dē pa″trū″‿ī′‿yə.
pattern, *n.* **1.** Type (*m.*): tīp. **2.** Modèle (*m.*): mo″dēl′‿ə.
pause. Arrêt (*n. m.*): ar″‿rē′.—**sudden pauses.** Des arrêts subits: dēz‿ar″‿rē′ sü″bī′.
pave, *v.* Paver: pa″vē′.—**to pave the way.** Aplanir le chemin: a″pla″nīr′ lə shə-maṅ′.
pavement. Trottoir (*n. m.*): trot″‿twār′.
pavilion. Pavillon (*n. m.*): pa″vī″‿yeṅ′. Abbreviated *Pon.*
paving. Pavé (*n. m.*): pa″vē′.—**bad paving.** Mauvais pavé: mō″vā′ pa″vē′.—**paving-stone.** Pavé (*n. m.*): pa″vē′.
pay. I. *n.* **1.** Solde (*f.*): sol′‿də. **2.** Paye (*f.*): pā′‿yə. **II.** *v.* **1.** Payer: pā″‿yē′. **2.** Soudoyer: sū″dwa″‿yē′.—**Army Pay Department in the Field.** Service de la Trésorerie (*m.*): sār″-vīs′‿ə də la trē″zō″‿rə-rī′.—**Clerk of the Army Pay Department.** Commis de trésorerie (*m.*): kom″‿mī′ də trē″zō″‿rə-rī′.—**how much have I to pay you?** Combien dois-je vous payer? keṅ″bī″‿yaṅ′ dwā′‿ʒə vū pā″‿yē′.—**I want to pay my bill.** Je veux payer mon compte: ʒə vū pā″‿yē′ meṅ keṅ′‿tə.—**pay and allowances.** Solde et indemnités: sol′‿də ē aṅ″dēm″nī″tē′.—**pay-book.** Livret individuel: lī″vrē′ aṅ″dī″vī″dü″el′.—**extra pay.** Haute paye: hōt pā′‿yə.—**full pay.** Solde entière: sol′‿də aṅ″tī″‿yār′‿ə.—**half pay.** Demi-solde: də-mī′ sol′‿də.—**in the pay of.** À la solde de: a la sol′‿də də.—**on half pay.** En demi-solde: aṅ də-mī′ sol′‿də.—**reduced pay.** Pension proportionnelle (*f.*): paṅ″sī″‿yeṅ′ prō″pēr″sī″‿yen″‿nel′ (*proportional allowance granted to men rendered unfit for service by wounds or sickness contracted while on duty*).—**retired pay.** Pension de réforme (*f.*): paṅ″sī″‿yeṅ′ də rē″fōr′‿mə (*granted to officers after twenty years of service*).
paymaster. Trésorier (*n. m.*): trē″zō″rī″‿yē′.—**assistant paymaster.** Payeur adjoint: pā″‿yūr′ ad″ʒwaṅ′.—**divisional p.** Payeur particulier: pā″‿yūr′ par″tī″kü″lī″‿yē′.
pea. Pois (*n. m.*): pwā.—**green peas.** Petits pois: pə-tī′ pwā.
peace. Paix (*n. f.*): pā.—**on a peace footing.** Sur un pied de paix: sür aṅ pī″‿yē′ də pā.
peajacket, *n.* **1.** Veste (*f.*): vās′‿tə. **2.** Veston (*m.*): vās″teṅ′.
peak, *n.* **1.** Pic (*m.*): pīk. **2.** Piton (*m.*): pī″teṅ′. **3.** Aiguille (*f.*): ā″gwī′‿yə. **4.** Visière (*f.*): vī″zī″‿yār′ (*visor of a cap*).
peal, *n.* **1.** Bruit (*m.*): brwī. **2.** Éclat (*m.*): ē″klā′ (*of thunder*). **3.** Carillon (*m.*): ka″rī″‿yeṅ′ (*of bells*). **4.** Salve (*f.*): sal′‿və (*of cannon*). [rī″‿yē′.
pear. Poire (*n. f.*): pwār.—**pear-tree.** Poirier (*m.*): pwa″-
peasant, *n.* Paysan (*m.*): pā″ī″‿zāṅ′; paysanne (*f.*): pā″ī″‿zān′.
peat-bed. Tourbière (*n. f.*): tūr″bī″yār′.
pebble. Caillou (*n. m.*): kai″‿yū′.
pedal. Pédale (*n. f.*): pē″dāl′‿ə.
peel. I. *n.* **1.** Peau (*f.*): pō. **2.** Pelure (*f.*): pə-lür′. **3.** Écorse (*f.*): ē″kors′ (*of oranges, lemons*). **II.** *v.* Peler: pə-lē′.
peg, *n.* Piquet (*m.*): pī″kē′ (*tent-peg*).—**picketing p.** Piquets à crochets, (or) pointes: pī″kēz′‿a kro″shē′ pwaṅt.—**to fix the pegs.** Planter les piquets: plaṅ″tē′ lē pī″kē′.
pen, *n.* **1.** Plume (*f.*): plüm (*for writing*). **2.** Poulailler (*m.*): pū″lai″‿yē′ (*for poultry*). **3.** Parc (*m.*): park (*for cattle*).

penal, *a.* **1.** Pénal (*m.*), pénale (*f.*): pē″nāl′. **2.** Punissable (*m.* & *f.*): pü″nīs″‿sa′blə.
penalty, *n.* **1.** Amende (*f.*): a″mäṅ′‿də. **2.** Peine (*f.*): pān. **3.** Châtiment (*m.*): sha″tī″mäṅ′.
pencil. Crayon (*n. m.*): krā″yeṅ′.
penetrate, *v.* Pénétrer dans: pē″nē″trē′ däṅ.
peninsula. Presqu'île (*n. f.*): pres″kīl′‿ə. Abbreviated *Pr. I.*
penknife. Canif (*m.*): ka″nīf′.
penny. Sou (*n. m.*): sū.—**it's not worth a penny.** Ça ne vaut pas un sou: sa nə vō paz‿aṅ sū.—**to be without a penny.** N'avoir ni sou ni maille: na″vwär′ nī sū nī mai′‿yə.
pension. Pension (*n. f.*): paṅ″sī″‿yeṅ′.
people, *n.* **1.** Peuple (*m.*): pū′‿plə (*a nation*). **2.** Gens (*m. plur.*): ʒaṅ (*persons in general*).—**people say.** On dit: eṅ dī.—**the p. of.** Les habitants de: lēz‿a″bī″täṅ′ də
pepper. Poivre (*n. m.*): pwā′‿vrə.—**cayenne pepper.** Poivre rouge: pwā′‿vrə rū′‿ʒə.—**pepper and salt.** Poivre et sel: pwā′‿vrə ē sel (*said of hair: a mark of identification*).
perceive, *v.* Apercevoir: a″pār″‿sə-vwār′.
percentage. Pour=cent (*m.*): pūr″säṅ′.
percussion=lock. Platine percutante (*n. f.*): pla″tīn′ pār″kü″-täṅt′‿ə.
perfect, *a.* Parfait (*m.*): par″fā′; parfaite (*f.*): par″fāt′‿ə.
perform, *v.* **1.** Exécuter: eg″zē″kü″tē′ (*carry out*). **2.** S'acquitter de: sa′kīt″‿tē′ də (*accomplish*). **3.** Jouer: ʒū″‿ē′ (*music, acting*, etc.).—**performance.** **1.** Accomplissement (*n. m.*): ak″‿keṅ″plīs″‿sə-mäṅ′. **2.** Exécution (*f.*): eg″zē″kü″sī″‿yeṅ′.
perhaps, *adv.* Peut=être: pūt″‿ā′‿trə.
perimeter. Périmètre (*n. m.*): pē″rī″mā′‿trə.
period, *n.* **1.** Temps (*m.*): täṅ. **2.** Période (*f.*): pē″rī″ōd′‿ə. **3.** Durée (*f.*): dü″rē′ (*duration*).
periscope. Périscope (*n. m.*): pē″rīs″kōp′‿ə.
permanent, *a.* Permanent (*m.*): pār″ma″näṅ′; permanente (*f.*): pār″ma″näṅt′‿ə.
permit. **I.** *n.* Permission (*f.*): pār″mīs″‿sī″‿yeṅ′. **II.** *v.* Permettre: pār″met′‿trə.
perseverance. Persévérance (*n. f.*): pār″sē″vē″räṅs′‿ə.
person. Personne (*n. f.*): pār″sēn′.
personnel. Personnel (*n. m.*): pār″sēn″‿nel′.
petard. Pétard (*n. m.*): pē″tār′.
petrol, *n.* **1.** Essence (*f.*): es″‿säṅs′. **2.** Pétrole (*m.*): pē″-trōl′.—**can you sell me some petrol?** Pouvez-vous me vendre du petrole? pū″vē′ vū mə vaṅ′‿drə dü pē″trōl′.—**the p. tank is leaking.** Le réservoir de pétrole coule: lə rē″sār″vwār′ də pē″trōl′ kūl′‿ə.
petroleum. Pétrole (*n. m.*): pē″trōl′.
phase, *n.* **1.** Phase (*f.*): fāz′‿ə. **2.** Face (*f.*): fās′‿ə.
phlegmon. Phlegmon (*n. m.*): flāg″moṅ′ (*suppurative inflammation*).
photograph. **I.** *n.* Photographie (*n. f.*): fō″tō″gra″fī′. **II.** *v.* Photographier: fō″tō″gra″fī″‿yē′.—**full length photograph.** Photographie en pied: fō″tō″gra″fī′ aṅ pī″‿yē′.—**half length p.** Photographie en buste: fō″tō″gra″fī′ aṅ büs′‿tə.—**photographer.** Photographe (*n. m.*): fō″tō″grāf′‿ə.—**side face photograph.** Photographie en profil: fō″tō″gra″fī′ aṅ prō″fīl′‿ə.—**three quarter p.** Photographie en trois-quarts: fō″tō″gra″fī′ aṅ trwā kār.
physical appearance. Physique (*n. m.*): fī″zīk′.
pick. **I.** *n.* Pic (*m.*): pik. **II.** *v.* Piquer: pī″kē′.—**pickaxe.** Pioche (*n. f.*): pī″ōsh′.
picked men. Hommes d'élite: om dē″līt′.
picket, *n.* **1.** Piquet (*m.*): pī″kē′ (*camp=guard*). **2.** Petit poste

(*m.*): pə-tī' pōst (*outpost*). **3.** Piquet de terre (*m.*): pī"kē' də tār (*stake*).—**on picket duty.** Au piquet: ō pī"kē'.—**p.-line.** Ligne des avant-postes (*f.*): lī'‿nyə dēz‿a"vāṅ' pōst.—**p.-post.** Petit poste (*m.*): pə-tī' pōst.—**p. supports.** **1.** Grand' gardes (*f.*): graṅd gard. **2.** La réserve des avant-postes: la rē"zārv' dēz‿a"vāṅ' pōst.

piebald, *a.* Pie (*m.* & *f.*): pī.

piece, *n.* **1.** Pièce (*f.*): pī"‿yās' (*as of money*). **2.** Morceau (*m.*): mōr"sō' (*as of soap*).—**to take to pieces.** Démonter: dē"-moṅ"tē'.

pier, *n.* **1.** Embarcadère (*m.*): aṅ"bar"ka"dār' (*of a wharf*). Abbreviated *Embre.* **2.** Jetée (*f.*): ʒə-tē' (*of a harbor*). Abbreviated *Jée.* **3.** Pile (*f.*): pīl (*of a bridge*).

pierce, *v.* Percer: pār"sē'.—**piercing,** *adj.* Perçant (*m.*): pār"sāṅ'; perçante (*f.*): pār"sāṅt'.

pig, *n.* **1.** Cochon (*m.*): ko"shoṅ'. **2.** Porc (*m.*): pork (pōr before a consonant).

pigeon. Pigeon (*n. m.*): pī"ʒeṅ'.—**carrier-pigeon.** Pigeon voyageur: pī"ʒeṅ' vwa"‿ya"ʒūr'.—**p. loft,** *n.*, **p. house,** *n.* **1.** Colombier (*m.*): ko"leṅ"bī"‿yē'. Abbreviated *Colombr.* **2.** Pigeonnier (*m.*): pi"ʒon"‿nī ‿yē'.—**p. post specialist.** Sapeur colombophile: sa"pūr' ko"leṅ"bo"fīl'.

pigsty. Porcherie (*n. f.*): pōr"‿shə-rī'.

pile. **I.** *n.* Pile (*f.*): pīl. **II.** *v.* **1.** Entasser: aṅ"tas"‿sē'. **2.** Ranger: raṅ"ʒē'. **3.** Mettre: met'‿trə. See PILE ARMS.—**pile arms.** **1.** Mettez en faisceaux: met"‿tēz'‿aṅ fā"sō'. **2.** Formez les faisceaux: for"mē' lē fā"sō'.—**pile-driver.** Sonnette (*n. f.*): son"‿net'.—**pilework,** *n.* **1.** Palée (*f.*): pa"lē'. **2.** Pilotage (*m.*): pī"lo"tāʒ'.

pillage. **I.** *n. m.* Pillage: pī"‿yāʒ'. **II.** *v.* Piller: pī"‿yē'.—**pillager.** Pillard (*n. m.*): pī"‿yār'.

pillar. Pilier (*n. m.*): pī"lī"‿yē'. Abbreviated *Pilr.*

pillow, *n.* Oreiller (*m.*): o"rē"‿yē'.—**pillowcase.** Taie d'oreiller: tā do"rē"‿yē'.

pilot. **I.** *n.* Pilote (*m.*): pī"lōt'. **II.** *v.* Piloter: pī"lō"tē'.—**pilot light.** Same as "VERY" LIGHT.

pimpled, *a.* **1.** Bourgeonné (*m.*): būr"ʒen"‿nē'. **2.** Pustuleux (*m.*): pūs"tū"lū'; pustuleuse (*f.*): pūs"tū"lūz'.

pin. **I.** *n.* **1.** Épingle (*n. f.*): ē"paṅ'‿glə. **2.** Cran (*m.*): kraṅ (*in machinery*). **II.** *v.* **1.** Attacher: at"‿ta"shē'. **2.** Épingler: ē"paṅ"glē'. **3.** Clouer: klū"ē'.—**safety-pin** or **-check.** **1.** Goupille (*n. f.*): gū"pī'‿yə (*as on a machine-gun*). **2.** Cheville (*n. f.*): shə-vī'‿yə (*bolt*).

pincers, *n. pl.* **1.** Tenailles (*f. pl.*): te"nai'‿yə. **2.** Pince (*n. f.*): paṅs.

pine-tree. Pin (*n. m.*): paṅ.

pinion. **I.** *n.* Pignon (*m.*): pī"nyeṅ' (*gear-wheel*). **II.** *v.* Garrotter: gar"‿rō"tē' (*bind a prisoner*).

pioneer, *n. m.* Sapeur: sa"pūr'.

pioupiou, *n.* pī"‿yū"‿pī"‿yū'. A nickname for a French soldier.

pipe, *n.* **1.** Conduite (*f.*): keṅ"dwīt' (*as for gas*). **2.** Tuyau (*m.*): twī"yō' (*as for water*). **3.** Pipe (*f.*): pīp (*for smoking*).

piquet, *n.* **1.** Piquet (*m.*): pī"kē' (*game*). **2.** See PICKET.

pistol. Pistolet (*n. m.*): pīs"tō"lē'.—**automatic pistol.** Pistolet automatique: pīs"tō"lē' ō"tō"ma"tīk'.

pit, *n.* **1.** Fosse (*f.*): fōs. **2.** Cavité (*f.*): ka"vī"tē'.—**military pit,** or **pit-fall.** Trou de loup (*n. m.*): trū də lū.

pitch, *v.* **1.** Asseoir: as"‿swār' (*as a camp*). **2.** Dresser: drēs"‿sē' (*as a tent*). **3.** Établir: ē"ta"blīr' (*general*).

pity, *n.* Pitié (*f.*): pī"tī"‿yē'.

pivot. **I.** *n.* Pivot (*m.*): pī"vō'. **II.** *v.* **1.** Faire pivoter: fār pī"vo"tē'. **2.** Pivoter: pī"vo"tē'.—**pivot-man.** Guide (*m.*): gīd.

place, *n.* **1.** Place (*f.*): plās. **2.** Endroit (*m.*): aṅ"drwā'.—**what place is this?** Où sommes nous ici? ū sōm nūs‿ī"sī'. Literally, "Where are we here?"

plain. **I.** *n.* Plaine (*f.*): plān. **II.** *a.* **1.** Simple: saṅ'‿plə (*of things*). **2.** Franc: fraṅ (*frank*).—**in plain clothes.** See under CLOTHES.

plan, *n.* Plan (*m.*): plaṅ.

plane. Plan (*n. m.*): plaṅ. Contraction of aero*plane*, bi*plane*, etc. (*an avion*).—**balancing=plane.** Stabilisateur: sta"bī"lī"za"tūr'.—**bombarding=p.** Avion de bombardement: a"vī"‿yōṅ' də bōn"bar"‿də-māṅ'.—**bottom p.,** or **lower p.** Plan inférieur: plaṅ aṅ"fē"rī"‿yūr'.—**range=finding p.** Avion de réglage de tir (*n. f.*): a"vī"‿yōṅ' də rē"glāʒ' də tīr.—**reconnoitering=p.** Avion de reconnaissance: a"vī"‿yōṅ' də rə-kōn"‿nā"sāṅ'‿sə.—**top p., upper p.** Plan supérieur: plaṅ sü"pē"rī"‿yūr'.

plantation. Plantation (*n. f.*): plan"ta"sī"‿yeṅ'.

plaster. Emplâtre (*n. m.*): aṅ"plā'‿trə.—**court=plaster.** Taffetas d'Angleterre: taf"‿fə‿tā' dan"glə-tār'.—**p.=quarry.** Plâtrière (*n. f.*): pla"trī"‿yār'. Abbreviated *Plâtrre.*—**sticking=p.,** *n.* **1.** Diachylum (*m.*): dra"kī"lum'. **2.** Sparadrap (*m.*): spa"ra"drā' (*cerecloth or waterproof covering*).

plate, *n.* **1.** Assiette (*f.*): as"‿sī"‿yet'. **2.** Râtelier (*m.*): ra"‿tə-lī"‿yē' (*for teeth*).—**plate=layer.** Poseur de rails: po"zūr' də ra'‿yə (*one who lays rails on a railway*).

plateau. Plateau (*n. m.*): pla"tō'.

platform, *n.* **1.** Plate=forme (*f.*): plat"fōrm'. **2.** Quai (*m.*): kā. **3.** Terre=plein (*m.*): tār"plaṅ'.

platoon. Peloton (*n. m.*): pə-lō"təṅ'.

play, *v.* Jouer: ʒū"ē'.

plaza. Place (*n. f.*): plas.

pleasant, *a.* Agréable (*m.* & *f.*): a"grē"ā'‿blə.

please, *v.* Plaire à: plār a.—**if you please.** S'il vous plaît: sīl vū plā.—**pleased,** *a.* Content: kəṅ"tāṅ'.

plenty, *a.* Beaucoup (*m.* & *f.*): bō"kū'.

plot. **I.** *n.* Complot (*m.*): koṅ"plō'. **II.** *v.* Comploter: kəṅ"plō"tē'.

plow, plough. Charrue (*n. f.*): shar"‿rü'.—**plowed, ploughed.** Labouré: la"bū"rē' (*of fields*).

pluck. **I.** *n.* Courage (*m.*): kū"rāʒ'. **II.** *v.* **1.** Tirer: tī"rē'. **2.** Cueillir: kū"‿yīr' (*fruit*). **3.** Plumer: plü"‿mē' (*poultry*).—**plucky,** *a.* Courageux (*m.*): kū"ra"ʒū'.

plug, *n.* **1.** Fiche (*f.*): fīsh (*peg*). **2.** (1) [*Spark=plug.*] Tampon (*m.*): taṅ"poṅ'. (2) Bougie: bū"ʒī'.

plum. Prune (*n. f.*): prün.

plunder. **I.** *n.* **1.** Pillage (*m.*): pī"‿yāʒ'. **2.** Butin (*m.*): bü"taṅ'. **II.** *v.* Piller: pī"‿yē'.—**plunderer.** Pillard (*n. m.*): pī"‿yār'.

ply[1], *v.* S'appliquer à: sap"‿plī"kē' a.—**to ply with questions.** Presser de questions: pres"‿sē' də kes"tī"‿yoṅ'.

ply[2], *v.* **1.** S'occuper: sok"‿kü"pē'. **2.** Faire le service: fār lə sār"vīs' (*as vehicles, between two points*).

pneumonia. Pneumonie (*n. f.*): pnu"mō"nī'.

pock=marked, *a.* Grêlé (*m.*); grêlée (*f.*): grā"lē'.

pocket. **I.** *n.* Poche (*f.*): pōsh. **II.** *v.* Empocher: aṅ"pō"shē'.—**pocket=book,** *n.* Porte=monnaie (*m.*): por'tə moṅ"‿nē'.—**to have in one's pocket.** Avoir en poche: a"vwār' aṅ pōsh.

poilu, pwa"lü'. **I.** *n.* A French soldier whose beard has grown while he has served in the trenches. **II.** *a.* Bearded.

Poincaré, Raymond, pwaṅ"ka"rē', rē"moṅ'. President of France since 1913.

point. **I.** *n.* **1.** Pointe (*f.*): pwaṅt (*sharp end*). **2.** Point (*m.*): pwaṅ (*place*). **II.** *v.* **1.** Pointer: pwaṅ"tē' (*as a gun*). **2.** Mettre en joue: met'‿trə aṅ ʒū (*aim*).—**from that point.** À partir de ce point: a par″tïr′ də sə pwaṅ.—**p. of support.** Point d'appui: pwaṅ dap″‿pwī′.—**pointed,** *a.* Pointu (*m.*), pointue (*f.*): pwaṅ″-tü′ (*said of the ears, in identification*).—**to p. out.** **1.** Désigner: dē″zī″nyē′. **2.** Indiquer: aṅ″dī″kē′. [aṅ″pwa″zeṅ″nē′.

poison. **I.** *n.* Poison (*m.*): pwa″zeṅ′. **II.** *v.* Empoisonner:

poisonous, *a.* Venimeux (*m.*): və-nī″mū′; venimeuse (*f.*): və-nī″mūz′.—**a poisonous wound.** Plaie envenimée: plā aṅ″və-nī″-mē′.—**poisoning.** Empoisonnement (*n. m.*): aṅ″pwa″zən″‿nə-māṅ′.

Poland. La Pologne: la po″lēṅ′‿yə.

polder, polderland, *n.* [D.] Polder: pəl″dār′ (*cultivated land reclaimed from the sea*).

pole, *n.* **1.** Timon (*m.*): tī″məṅ′ (*of a vehicle*). **2.** Bâton (*m.*): ba″təṅ′. **3.** Perche (*f.*): pārsh (*measure of length*).

police. Police (*n. f.*): pō″līs′.—**police barracks.** Gendarmerie (*n. f.*): ʒaṅ″dar″‿mə-rī′.—**p.-duty.** Service de police: sār″vīs′ də pō″līs′.—**p. inspector.** Commissaire de police: kəm″‿mīs″‿sār′ də pō″līs′.—**military p.** La prévôté (*n. f.*): la prē″vō″tē′.—**mounted p.** Gendarmerie: ʒaṅ″dar″‿mə-rī′.—**sanitary p.** Police sanitaire: pō″līs′ sa″nī″tār′.—**p. station.** **1.** Bureau de police: bü″rə′ də pō″līs′. **2.** Gendarmerie: ʒaṅ″dar″‿mə-rī′. Abbreviated *Gie.*—**town p.** Police municipale: pō″līs′ mü″nī″sī″pāl′.

policeman. **1.** Gendarme (*n. m.*): ʒaṅ″dārm′. **2.** Sergent de ville: sar″ʒāṅ′ də vīl. **3.** Agent de police: a″ʒāṅ′ də pō″līs′.—**rural policeman.** Garde champêtre: gard shaṅ″pā′‿trə.

polite, *a.* Poli (*m.*): polie (*f.*): pō″lī′.

poll, *n.* **1.** Tête (*f.*): tāt′‿ə (*of men*). **2.** Nuque (*f.*): nük (*of animals*). **3.** Liste (*f.*): līst′‿ə (*election list*).

pommel. Pommeau (*n. m.*): pəm″‿mō′.

pom-pom. Pompom (*n. m.*): pēṅ″pēṅ′ (*heavy cannon*).

poncho, pən″shō′, *n.* A rubber cape used in U. S. Army.

pond, *n.* **1.** Étang (*m.*): ē″tāṅ′. Abbreviated *Etg.* **2.** Mare (*f.*): mār. Abbreviated *Mare.*

pontonier. Pontonnier (*n. m.*): peṅ″tən″‿nī″‿yē′ (*a soldier who has charge of pontoons*).

pontoon. Ponton (*n. m.*): peṅ″teṅ′.—**pontoon bridge.** Pont de ponton (*m.*): peṅ də peṅ″tēṅ′.—**p. train.** Équipage de pont: ē″kī″pāʒ′ də peṅ.

poor, *a.* **1.** Pauvre (*m.* & *f.*): pō′‿vrə. **2.** Mauvais (*m.*): mō″vā′; mauvaise (*f.*): mō″vāz′.

poplar. Peuplier (*n. m.*): pū″plī″‿yē′.

populace. Populace (*n. f.*): pə″pü″lās′‿ə. [nounced pēr.)

pork. Porc (*n. m.*): pērk. (Before a consonant it is pro-

port, *n.* **1.** Port (*m.*): pēr (*harbor*). **2.** Bâbord (*m.*): ba″bēr′ (*left side of a vessel*).—**to enter port.** Prendre port: prān′‿drə pēr.—**to p. the helm.** Mettre la barre à bâbord: met′‿trə la bar a bā″bēr′—**p.-hole.** Hublot (*n. m.*): hü″blō′. [tīv′.

portable, *a.* Portatif (*m.*): pēr″ta″tīf′; portative (*f.*): pēr″ta″-

portcullis. Herse (*n. f.*): hār′‿sə.

porter, *n.* **1.** Porteur (*m.*): pēr″tūr′ (*general*). **2.** Facteur (*m.*): fak″tūr′ (*railway*). **3.** Commissionnaire (*m.*): kəm″‿mīs″‿sī″‿yən″‿nār′‿ə (*licensed messenger*).

portmanteau. Valise (*n. f.*): va″līz′.

position, *n.* **1.** Position (*f.*): pō″zī″sī″‿yeṅ′ (*in general*). **2.** Emplacement (*m.*): aṅ″pla″‿sə-māṅ′ (*in military sense*).—**advanced position.** Position avancée: pō″zī″sī″‿yeṅ′ a″vaṅ″sē′.—**the p. assigned.** L'emplacement assigné: laṅ″pla″‿sə-māṅ′ as″‿sī″‿nyē′.—**p. of readiness.** Position d'attente: pō″zī″sī″‿yeṅ′ dat″‿tāṅt′‿ə.

possible, *a.* Possible (*m.* & *f.*): pəs″‿sī′‿blə.

post, *n.* **1.** Poste (*m.*): pōst (*military station*). **2.** Poste (*f.*): pōst (*post office*). **3.** Poteau (*m.*): pō″tō′ (*for signs*).—**can I**

artistic; ȧrt; fat; fāre; fast; get; prēy; hit; polīce; obey; gō; not; ōr; full; rūle; but; būrn; ə = final;

---

post a letter here? Puis-je mettre une lettre à la poste ici? pwī'‿ʒə met'‿trə ün let'‿trə a la pōst ī"sī'.—**connecting posts.** Postes de liaison: pōst də lī"ā"zoṅ'.—**has the post gone?** La poste a-t-elle parti? la pōst a tel par"tī'.—**how far is it to the p.-office?** Combien y a-t-il d'ici à la poste? koṅ"-bī"yaṅ' ī a tīl dī"sī' a la pōst.—**please p. this letter.** Ayez la bonté de mettre cette lettre à la poste: ā"‿yē' la boṅ"tē' də met'‿trə set let'‿trə a la pōst.

postage. Port de lettre (*n. m.*): pōr də let'‿trə.—**extra postage.** Supplément de port: süp"plē"māṅ' də pōr.—**p.-stamp.** Timbre-poste (*n. m.*): taṅ"‿brə-pōst'.—**to pay the p. of.** Payer le port de: pā"‿yē' lə pōr də.—**what is the p. on this?** Combien de timbres faut-il pour cela? koṅ"bī"‿yaṅ' də taṅ'‿brə fō‿tīl pūr sə-lā'.

postal, *a.* Postal (*m.*), postale (*f.*): pōs"tāl'.—**Army Postal Service in the Field.** Service des Postes: sār"vīs' dē pōst.—**p. card.** Carte postale (*f.*): kārt pōs"tāl'‿ə.—**p. order.** Mandat de poste (*n. m.*): maṅ"da' də pōst.—**to get a p. order cashed.** Faire payer un mandat de poste: fār pa"yē' aṅ maṅ"da' də pōst.

postern. Poterne (*n. f.*): po"tārn'‿ə.

post-office. Bureau de poste (*m.*): bü"rō' də pōst.

pot. Pot (*n. m.*): pō.

potato. Pomme de terre (*n. f.*): pōm də tār.—**mashed potatoes.** Pomme de terre en purée: pōm də tār aṅ pü"rē'.

pouch. Cartouchière (*n. f.*): kar"tū"shī"‿yār'‿ə (*for cartridges*).

poultry. Volaille (*n. f.*): vō"lai'‿yə.—**poultry-yard.** Basse-cour (*n. f.*): bas"kūr'.

pounce, *v.* **1.** Saisir: sā"zīr' (*seize*). **2.** Foncer foṅ"sē' (*rush upon*).

pound. Livre (*n. f.*): lī'‿vrə.—**pound sterling.** Livre sterling: lī'‿vrə stār"laṅ'.

pourparler, pūr"par"lē' (*n. m.*). A preliminary conference.

powder. Poudre (*n. f.*): pū'‿drə.—**powder-magazine.** Poudrière (*n. f.*): pū"drī"‿yār'‿ə. Abbreviated *Poudre.*—**smokeless p.** Poudre sans fumée: pū'‿drə sāṅ fü"mē'.

power, *n.* **1.** Force (*f.*): fōr'‿sə. **2.** Puissance (*f.*): pwīs"‿sāṅs'‿ə.—**p. of endurance.** Force de résistance: fōrs də rē"-zīs"tāṅs'‿ə.—**the allied powers.** Les puissances alliées: lē pwīs"‿sāṅs'‿al"‿lī"‿yē'.—**to develop full power.** Donner le maximum de rendement: don"‿nē' lə max"ī"mom' də raṅ"‿də-māṅ' (*said of an engine*).

powerful, *a.* Puissant (*m.*): pwīs"sāṅ'.

practically, *adv.* En fait: aṅ fā.

practise, *n.* Pratique (*f.*): pra"tīk'.—**in practise.** Dans la pratique: daṅ la pra"tīk'.

precaution. Précaution (*n. f.*): prē"kō"sī"‿yoṅ'.—**sanitary precautions.** Précautions sanitaires: prē"kō"sī"‿yoṅ' sa"nī"-tār'.

precede, *v.* Précéder: prē"sē"dē'.

precipice. Précipice (*n. m.*): prē"sī"pīs'.—**precipitous,** *a.* Escarpé (*m.*), escarpée (*f.*): es"kar"pē'.—**precipitously,** *adv.* **1.** À pic: a pīk: colloquially, "in the nick of time." **2.** Précipitamment: prē"sī"pī"tam"‿maṅ'.

preclude, *v.* Empêcher: aṅ"pā"shē'.

prefer, *v.* Préférer: prē"fē"rē'. See Appendix.

preliminary. Préliminaire: prē"lī"mī"nār'.

premature, *a.* Prématuré (*m.*): prē"ma"tü"rē'.

prescription. Ordonnance (*n. f.*): ōr"don"‿nāṅs'.

present. I. *a.* Présent (*m.*): prē"zāṅ'; présente (*f.*): prē"zāṅt'. **II.** *n.* **1.** Présent: prē"zāṅ' (*of time*). **2.** Cadeau: ka"dō' (*a gift*).

present, *v.* Présenter: prē"zaṅ"tē'.—**present arms!** See under ARMS.

ı = habit; aisle; au = out; oil; iū = feud; diūne; ch̄in; go; ŋ = sing; ship; th̄in; this.

preserved, *a.* Conservé (*m.*), conservée (*f.*): kon"sār"vē'.

press. **I.** *n.* Presse (*f.*): prēs. **II.** *v.* **1.** Presser: prēs"‿sē' (*hurry; squeeze*). **2.** Serrer: ser"rē' (*push hard*).—**press correspondent.** Correspondant de la presse: kor"‿res"poṅ"dāṅ' də la prēs. See WAR.—**p. forward.** Pousser de l'avant: pūs"‿sē' də la"vāṅ'.—**p. the enemy hard.** Serrer l'ennemi de près: ser"‿rē' len"nə‿mī' də prā.

pressure, *n.* **1.** Impulsion (*m.*): aṅ"pül"sī"‿yoṅ'. **2.** Pression (*f.*): prēs"‿sī"‿yoṅ'.—**high, low,** or **medium pressure.** Pression haute, basse ou moyenne: prēs"‿sī"‿yoṅ', hōt, bās ū mwa"yen'.

pretext. Prétexte (*n. m.*): prā"tekst'.—**under any pretext.** Sous aucun prétexte: sūz‿ō"kaṅ' prā"tekst'.

pretty, *a.* Joli (*m.*), jolie (*f.*): ʒō"lī'.

prevent, *v.* Empêcher de: aṅ"pā"shē' də.—**to prevent them from getting the range.** Les empêcher d'obtenir la portée lēz‿āṅ"pā"shē' dob"‿tə-nīr' la pōr"tē'.—**to p. the garrison from withdrawing.** Empêcher la garnison de se retirer: aṅ"pā"shē' la gar"nī"zoṅ' də sə rə-tī"rē'.—**to p. all misunderstanding.** Pour prévenir toute erreur: pūr prē"‿və-nīr' tūt‿er"‿rūr'—**to p. the rattling of one's arms.** Empêcher le cliquetis de ses armes: aṅ"pā"shē' lə klī"tī' də sēz‿arm.

price. Prix (*n. m.*): prī.—**what is the price?** Quel est le prix? kel ē lə prī.—**the price is net.** Le prix est fixe: lə prī ē fīks.

priest, *n.* **1.** Prêtre (*m.*): prā'‿trə. **2.** Curé (*m.*): kü"rē'.

priming. Amorçage (*n. m.*): a"mor"sāʒ'.

principle. Principe (*n. m.*): praṅ"sīp'.—**the principle commonly accepted.** Le principe généralement accepté: lə praṅ"sīp' ʒē"nē"ra"lə‿māṅt'‿ak"sep"tē'.

prismatic, *a.* À prîmes: a prīm (*of field-glasses*).

prison. Prison (*n. f.*): prī"zoṅ'.—**prisoner.** Le prisonnier (*n. m.*): lə prī"zoṅ"‿nyē'.—**take prisoner.** Faire prisonnier: fār prī"zoṅ"‿nyē'.—**p. of war.** Prisonnier de guerre: prī"zon"‿nyē' də gār.

private. **I.** *a.* Privé (*m.*), privée (*f.*): prī"vē'. **II.** *n.* **1.** Soldat de la ligne: sol"dā' də la lī'‿nyə. **2.** Simple soldat: saṅ'‿plə sol"dā'. **3.** Soldat de seconde classe: sol'dā' də sə-goṅd' klās.—**private premises.** Lieux privés (*n. m. pl.*): lī"‿yū' prī"vē'.

prize. **I.** *n.* **1.** Prise (*f.*): prīz. **2.** Prix (*m.*): prī. **II.** *v.* Évaluer: ē"va"lü"ē'.

probationer. Elève infirmier (*n. m.*): e"lāv' aṅ"fīr"mī"‿yē' (*nurse in training*).

proclamation. Proclamation (*n. f.*): prō"kla"ma"sī"‿yoṅ'.—**to issue a proclamation.** Faire une proclamation: fār ün prō"kla"ma"sī"‿yoṅ'.

profession, *n.* **1.** Métier (*m.*): mē"tī"‿yē' (*trade*). **2.** Déclaration (*f.*): dē"kla"ra"sī"‿yoṅ' (*statement*)

professional, *a.* Professionnel (*m.*): prō"fes"‿sī"‿yen"‿nel'.

profile. Profil (*n. m.*): prō"fīl'.

prohibit, *v.* **1.** Défendre à: dē"fāṅ'‿drə a (*forbid*). **2.** Prohiber: prō"ī"bē' (*interdict*).

projectile. Projectile (*n. m.*): prō"ʒek"tīl'.

projector, *n.* **1.** Projecteur (*m.*): prō"ʒek"tūr'. **2.** Pompe projectrice (*f.*): poṅp prō"ʒek"trīs'.

prominent, *a.* Proéminent (*m.*): pro"ē"mī"nāṅ'.

promote, *v.* **1.** Promouvoir: prō"mū"vwār'. **2.** Avancer: a"van"sē'.—**he was promoted to the rank of general.** Il fut promu au grade de général: īl fü pro"mü' ō grād də ʒē"nē"rāl'.—**to be promoted.** **1.** Donner de l'avancement: don"‿nē' də la"vaṅ"‿sə-māṅ'. **2.** Être promu: ā'‿trə prō"mü'.

promotion, *n.* **1.** Avancement (*m.*): a"van"‿sə-māṅ'. **2.** Promotion (*f.*): prō"mō"sī"yōṅ'.—**promotion by selection.** **1.** Avancement au choix: a"vaṅ"‿sə-māṅ' ō shwā. **2.** Nomina-

tion au choix: no″mī″na″sī″‿yoṅ′ ō shwā.—**p. by seniority. 1.** Avancement à l'ancienneté: a″vaṅ″‿sə-māṅ′ a laṅ″sī″‿yen″‿nə-tē′. **2.** Nomination à l'ancienneté: no″mī″na″sī″‿yoṅ′ a laṅ″-sī″‿yen″‿nə-tē′.
promotion-list. Tableau d'avancement (*m.*): ta″blō′ da″‿van″sə-māṅ′.
propeller. Hélice (*n. f.*): ē″līs′.
proper, *a.* **1.** Propre (*m.* & *f.*): pro′‿prə. **2.** Respectif (*m.*): rēs″pek″tīf′; respective (*f.*): rēs″pek″tīv′. **3.** Juste (*m.* & *f.*): ʒüst.
propitious, *a.* **1.** Propice (*m.* & *f.*): pro″pīs′. **2.** Favorable (*m.* & *f.*): fa″vər″ā′‿blə.
proprietor. Propriétaire (*n. m.* & *f.*): pro″prī″ē″tār′‿ə.
prosecute, *v.* Poursuivre: pūr″swī′‿vrə.—**prosecuting counsel.** Commissaire du gouvernement: kəm″‿mīs″‿sār′ dü gū″vār″‿nə‿māṅ′ (*a court-martial*).
prospect. Perspective (*n. f.*): pār″spēk″tīv′.—**prospect of success.** Chance de succès (*f.*): shāṅs də sük″sē′.
protect, *v.* Protéger: prō″tē″ʒē′.—**protection,** *n.* **1.** Protection (*n. f.*): pro″tek″sī″‿yoṅ′. **2.** Sauvegarde (*f.*): sōv″gār′‿də.—**protector.** Couvre-nuque (*n. m.*): kū″‿vrə-nük′ (*flap of cloth or rubber worn at the back of the helmet or cap as a protection from sun and rain*).
protract, *v.* Prolonger: prō″loṅ″ʒē′.—**a protracted resistance.** Une résistance prolongée: ün rē″zīs″tāṅs′ prō″loṅ″ʒē′.
proud, *a.* Fier (*m.*), fière (*f.*): fī″‿yār′.
prove, *v.* Vérifier: vē″rī″fī″‿yē′.
provide, *v.* **1.** Fournir: fūr″nīr′. **2.** Donner: doṅ″‿nē′ (*supply*).—**provide the needs of the army.** Satisfaire les besoins de l'armée: sa″tīs″fār′ lē bə-zwaṅ′ də lar″mē′.—**p. the means of.** Donner les moyens de: don″‿nē′ lē mwa″yaṅ′ də.
provided, *conj.* Pourvu que: pūr″vü′ kə.—**provided with.** Muni de: mü″nī′ də.
province, *n.* **1.** Province (*f.*): prō″vaṅs′ (*general term*). **2.** Ressort (*m.*): rə″sōr′ (*jurisdiction*). **3.** Département (*m.*): dē″-par″tə-māṅ′ (*general*).—**it is not in his province.** Ce n'est pas de sa compétence: sə nē pā də sa koṅ″pē″tāṅ′‿sə.
provision. Provision (*n. f.*): pro″vī″zī″‿yoṅ′.
provisions, *n. pl.* **1.** Vivres (*m.*): vī′‿vrə. **2.** Comestibles (*m.*): kom″es″tī′‿blə.—**provision wagon.** Fourgon de vivres (*n. m.*): fūr″goṅ′ də vī′‿vrə.
proviso. Condition (*n. f.*): koṅ″dī″sī″‿yoṅ′.—**with the above proviso.** Dans les conditions ci-dessus: dāṅ lē koṅ″dī″sī″‿yoṅ′ sī də-sü′.
provoke, *v.* **1.** Provoquer: prō″vō″kē′. **2.** Exciter: ek″sī″tē′.—**to provoke the enemy into action.** Exciter l'ennemi à combattre: ek″sī″tē′ len″‿nə-mī′ a koṅ″bāt′‿trə.
provost. Prévôt (*n. m.*): prē″vō′.—**provost marshal.** Grand prévôt (*n. m.*): grāṅ prē″vō′.—**p. marshal's department.** Service de la prévôté: sār″vīs′ də la prē″vō″tē′.—**p.-sergeant.** Sergent-prévôt: sār″ʒāṅ′ prē″vō′.
prowler. Rôdeur (*n. m.*): rō″dūr′.
proximity. Proximité (*n. f.*): prok″sī″mī″tē′.—**in close proximity.** Tout près de: tū prē də.
Prussia. Prusse (*n. f.*): prüs′‿sə.—**Prussian,** *a.* & *n.* Prussien (*m.*): prüs″‿sī″yaṅ′; Prussienne (*f.*): prüs″‿sī″yen′‿nə.
public, *a.* Public (*m.*), publique (*f.*): püb″līk′.
pudding, *n.* **1.** Entremets sucré (*m.*): aṅ″‿trə-mē′ sü″krē′. **2.** Poudingue (*m.*): pū″daṅg′.
pull, *v.* Tirer: tī″rē′.—**pull-through,** *n.* A weighted cord to one end of which an oiled rag is tied: used to pass through a rifle-barrel in cleaning it.
pulse. Pouls (*n. m.*): pū.—**to feel the pulse.** Tâter le pouls: ta″tē′ lə pū.

pump. I. *n.* Pompe (*n. f.*): poṅ'‿pə. II. *v.* Pomper: poṅ"pē'. **force-p.** Pompe foulante: poṅ'‿pə fū"lāṅt'‿ə.—**lift-and-force-p.** Pompe aspirante et foulante: poṅ'‿pə as"pī"rāṅt'‿ē fū"lāṅt'‿ə.—**suction-p.** Pompe aspirante: poṅ'‿pə as"pī"-rāṅt'‿ə.

punch, *n.* 1. Emporte-pièce (*m.*): aṅ"pōrt' pī"yās' (*tool*). 2. Poinçon (*m.*): pwaṅ"soṅ' (*tool*). 3. Coup de poing: kū də pwaṅ (*blow of the fist*).

puncture, *n.* 1. Crevaison (*m.*): krə-vā"zoṅ' (*of a tire*). 2. Pique (*f.*): pīk (*general*). 3. Piqûre (*f.*): pī"kür' (*general*). 4. Ponction (*f.*): poṅk"sī"‿yoṅ' (*surgical term*).—**to mend a puncture.** Réparer un pneu: rē"pa"rē' aṅ pnū.

punish, *v.* Punir: pü"nīr'.

punishment. Punition (*n. f.*): pü"nī"sī"‿yoṅ'.—**capital punishment.** Peine de mort: pān də mōr.

pupil, *n.* 1. Pupille (*f.*): pü"pīl' (*of the eye*). 2. Élève (*m.*): ē"lāv' (*scholar*).

purchase. I. *n.* Achat (*m.*): a"shā'. II. *v.* Acheter: a"‿shə-tē'.—**purchase by contract.** Achat de gré à gré: a"shā' də grē a grē.—**p. in the open market.** Achat sur le marché: a"shā' sür lə mar"shē'.

purport. Teneur (*n. f.*): tə-nūr' (*of a report*).

purpose. But (*n. m.*): bü.—**for any purpose.** Pour quelque motif que ce soit: pūr kel'‿kə mō"tīf' kə sə swā.—**for this p.** A cet effet: a set ef"‿fē'.—**specific p.** But déterminé: bü dē"-tēr"mī"nē'.

purse. Porte-monnaie (*n. m.*): port"moṅ"‿nā'.

purser. Commissaire (*n. m.*): kom"‿mīs"‿sār'.

pursue, *v.* Poursuivre: pūr"swī'‿vrə.

pursuit. Poursuite (*n. f.*): pūr"swīt'‿ə.—**to take up the pursuit.** Mener la poursuite: mə-nē' la pūr"swī'‿tə.

push, *v.* Pousser: pūs"‿sē'.—**to push the attack home.** Pousser l'attaque à fond: pūs"‿sē' lat"‿tāk' a foṅ.—**to p. back.** Faire reculer: fār rə-kü"lē'.—**p. forward.** Pousser en avant: pūs"‿sē' aṅ‿a"vāṅ'.—**to p. forward an attack.** Presser une attaque: prēs"‿sē' ün‿at"‿tāk'.—**p. straight on.** Pousser droit devant soi: pūs"‿sē' drwā də-vāṅ' swā.

put, *v.* Mettre: met'‿trə.—**put into execution.** Mettre à exécution: met'‿trə a ek"sē"kü"sī"‿yoṅ'.—**to put a gun out of sight.** Défiler une pièce: dē"fī"lē' ün pī"‿yās'.—**put out pickets.** Placer des petits postes: pla"sē' dē pə-tī' pōst.—**to put out of use.** Mettre hors de service: met'‿trə hōr də sār"vīs'.—**to put to the sword.** Passer au fil de l'épée: pas"‿sē' ō fīl də lē"pē'.

puttees. Molletières: mōl"‿lə-tī"‿yār'.

Q

quagmire. Fondrière (*n. f.*): fōn"drī"‿yār'.

quantity. Quantité (*n. f.*): kaṅ"tī"tē'.

quarantine. Quarantaine: ka"raṅ"tān'.—**quarantine (health) officer.** Agent de la santé (*n. m.*): a"zāṅ' də la san"tē'.

quarrel, *v.* 1. Quereller: kə-rē"lē'. 2. Disputer: dīs"pü"tē'.

quarry. Carrière (*n. f.*): ka"rī"yār'. Abbreviated *Carre.*

quart, *n.* 1. Quart (*m.*): kār. 2. Litre (*m.*): lī'trə (*measure*).

quarter, *n.* 1. Quart (*m.*): kār (*of time,* etc.). 2. Quartier (*m.*): kar"tī"yē' (*district*). Abbreviated *Qr.*—**a quarter of an hour.** Un quart d'heure: aṅ kar dūr.—**to give q.** Faire quartier: fār kar"tī"‿yē'.—**to give no q.** Ne pas faire quartier: nə pa fār kar"tī"‿yē'. [WHERE.

quartered. En quartier: aṅ kar"tī"‿yē'. See also under

quartermaster, *n.* 1. Fourrier (*m.*): fūr"‿rī"‿yē'. 2. Officier d'approvisionnement, de casernement, ou d'habillement: of"‿fī"-sī"‿yē' dap"‿prō"vī"zī"ən"‿nə-mān' də ka"zār"‿nə-mān' ū da"-bī"‿yə-mān'. **3.** Maréchal de logis: ma"rē"shāl' də lo"ʒī'.—**assistant quartermaster-general.** Sous-chef d'état-major adjoint: sū"shef' dē"tā' ma"ʒor' ad"ʒwaṅ'.—**q.-general.** Sous-chef d'état-major: sū"shef' dē"tā' ma"ʒōr'.—**q.-general's department.** Direction de l'arrière: dī"rek"sī"‿yeṅ' də lar"‿rī"‿yār'.—**quartermaster's stores.** Le dépôt de l'officier de casernement: lə dē"pō' də lof"‿fī"sī"‿yē' də ka"zār"‿nə-māṅ'.

quarters. Billets de logement: bī"‿yē' də lō"‿ʒə-māṅ'.—**to come to close q.** En venir aux prises: aṅ və-nīr' ō prīz.—**occupy q.** Cantonner: kaṅ"tən"‿nē'.—**supply quarters to.** Faire le logement de: fār lə lō"‿ʒə-māṅ' də.—**I want q. for.** Il me faut des logements pour: īl mə fō dē lō"‿ʒə-māṅ' pūr. See also under WEAR.

quay. Quai (*n. m.*): kā.

queen. Reine (*n. f.*): rē'‿nə.

question. **I.** *n.* Question (*f.*): kēs"tī"‿yeṅ'. **II.** *v.* **1.** Questionner: kēs"tī"‿yen"‿nē'. **2.** Interroger: aṅ"tār"‿rō"ʒē'.

quick. **I.** *a.* **1.** Vif (*m.*): vīf; vive (*f.*): vīv (*lively*). **2.** Ardent (*m.*): ar"dāṅ'; ardente (*f.*): ar"dāṅt' (*brisk*). **II.** *n.* Vif (*m.*): vīf.—**quick march! q. time!** Pas accéléré! paz‿ak"sē"lē"rē'.

quickly. Vite: vīt.—**as quickly as possible.** Le plus tôt possible: lə plü tō pes"‿sī'‿blə.

quid, *n.* **1.** [Slang.] A pound: une livre: ün lī'‿vrə (*English money* = $4.85). **2.** Chique (*f.*): shīk (*of chewing tobacco*).

quiet, *a.* Tranquille: tran"kīl'.—**be quiet.** Taisez-vous: tā"zē' vū.—**keep q.** Restez tranquille: rēs"tē' traṅ"kīl'.

quilt, *n.* Couvre-pied (*m.*): kū"‿vrə-pī"‿yē'.

quit, *v.* Quitter: kī"tē'.

quite, *adv.* **1.** Tout à fait: tūt‿o fā (*completely*). **2.** Parfaitement: par"fā"‿tə-māṅ' (*just so*).—**quite near.** Tout près: tū prā.

R

rabbit. Lapin (*n. m.*): la"paṅ'.—**rabbit hole,** *n.* **1.** Rabouillère (*f.*): ra"bū"ī"‿yār' (*burrow*). **2.** Terrier (*m.*): tār"‿rī"‿yē' (*hole*).—**r.-hutch.** Clapier (*n. m.*): kla"pī"‿yē'. [*petition*).

race, *n.* **1.** Race (*f.*): ras (*breed*). **2.** Course (*f.*): kūrs (*com-*

rack, *n.* Râtelier (*m.*): ra"‿tə-lī"‿yē' (*for arms; also, stable-rack*).—**racking.** Brellage (*n. m.*): brel"‿lāʒ'‿ə (*act of attaching beams to pontoons*).—**rack-stick.** Garrot (*n. m.*): gar"‿rō'.—**rifle-rack.** Râtelier d'armes: ra"‿tə-lī"‿yē' darm.—**to rack down,** *v.* Garrotter: gar"‿rot"‿tē'.

radiator. Radiateur (*n. m.*): ra"dī"a"tūr' (*of a motor-car*).

radius. Rayon (*n. m.*): rā"‿yeṅ'.—**within a radius of.** Dans un rayon de: daṅz‿aṅ rā"‿yoṅ' də.

raft. Radeau (*n. m.*): ra"dō'. Abbreviated *Rau.*—**tow of rafts.** Train de bois: traṅ də bwā.

rafter. Chevron (*n. m.*): shə-vroṅ' (*as of a building*).

rag. Chiffon (*n. m.*): shif"‿feṅ'.

rage. **I.** *n.* **1.** Rage (*f.*): rā'‿ʒə. **2.** Fureur (*f.*): fü"rūr'. **II.** *v.* **1.** Sévir: sē"vīr' (*of war*). **2.** Rager: ra"ʒē'. **3.** S'emporter: saṅ"pōr"tē' (*of persons*).

rail. Rail (*n. m.*): rai'‿yə.—**by rail.** Par voie ferrée: par vwa fār"‿rē'.—**check-r., guard-r.** Contre-rail (*n. m.*): koṅ"trə-rai'‿yə.—**hand-r.** Garde-fou (*n. m.*): gar"‿də-fū'.—**wheel-r.** Garde-roue (*n. m.*): gar"də-rū'.

railhead. Tête de ligne d'étapes (*n. f.*): tāt də lī'‿nyə dē"tāp'.

railroad, railway, *n.* **1.** Chemin de fer (*m.*): shə-maṅ' də fār. **2.** Voie, ou ligne, ferrée (*f.*): vwa, ū lī'‿nyə, fār"‿rē'.—**double track r.** Ligne à double voie: lī'‿nyə a dū'‿blə vwa.—**r.-agent.** Chef de gare: shef də gār (*station-master*). **2.** Agent de chemin de fer: a"ʒāṅ' də shə-māṅ' də fār.—**r.-carriage.** Wagon:

va″geṅ′.—**r.=junction.** Embranchement de chemin de fer: aṅ″-bransh″māṅ′ də shə-māṅ′ də fār.—**r.=line.** Voie ferrée (*f.*): vwa fār″‿rē′.—**r. system within the zone of operations.** Réseau des armées: rē″zō′ dēz‿ar″mē′.—**r.=station.** Gare (*n. f.*): gār.—**r.=ticket.** Billet (*n. m.*): bī″‿yē′. See RETURN.—**r. time=table.** Tableau des heures (*m.*): ta″blō′ dēz‿ūr.—**r. transport service.** Service de transport des chemin de fer: sār″vīs′ də traṅ″-spōr′ dē shə-maṅ′ də fār.—**r.=van.** Wagon (*n. m.*): va″geṅ′.—**r. way=bill.** Feuille de route: fū′‿yə də rūt.—**single track r.** Ligne à voie simple: lī′‿nyə a vwa saṅ′‿plə.—**where is the r. station?** Où est la gare? ū ē la gār. [See Appendix.

rain. **I.** *n.* Pluie (*n. f.*): plwī. **II.** *v.* Pleuvoir: plū″vwār′.

raise. **I.** *n.* Lever (*m.*): lə-vē′. **II.** *v.* **1.** Lever: lə-vē′. **2.** Hausser: hōs″sē′ (*lift*). See Appendix.—**to raise up.** Soulever (*v.*): sū″‿lə-vē′.

rally. **I.** *n.* Ralliement (*m.*): ral″lī″māṅ′ (*concentration*). **II.** Se rallier: sə ral″‿lī″‿yē′ (*reform*).

ram, *v.* **1.** Damer: da″mē′. **2.** Enfoncer: aṅ″feṅ″sē′ (*sink*). **3.** Bourrer: būr″rē′ (*push down, as a charge*).

rammer. Refouloir (*n. m.*): rə-fūl″wār′.

rampart. Rempart (*n. m.*): raṅ″pār′.

range, *n.* **1.** Hausse (*f.*): hōs. **2.** Distance (*f.*): dīs″tāṅs′. **3.** Portée (*f.*): pōr″tē′.—**at close or short range.** À portée courte: a pōr″tē′ kūr′‿tə.—**at long r.** À longue portée: a lōng pōr″tē′.—**effective r.** Portée efficace: pōr″tē′ ēf″‿fī″kās′.—**in range.** À portée: a pōr″tē′.—**out of r.** Hors de la portée: hōr də la pōr″tē′.—**r.=finder.** Télémètre (*n. m.*): tē″lē″mā′‿trə.—**to find the r.** Trouver la portée: trū″vē′ la pōr″tē′.—**within r. of.** À portée de: a pōr″tē′ də.

ranger. Garde=forestier (*n. m.*): gārd fō″res″tī″‿yē′.

rank, *n.* **1.** Rang (*m.*): raṅ. **2.** Grade (*m.*): grad.—**all ranks.** Tous les gradés: tū lē gra″dē′.—**quit the r.** **1.** Quitter les rangs: kīt″‿tē′ lē raṅ. **2.** Se débander: sə dē″baṅ″dē′ (*disband*).—**r. and file.** **1.** La ligne: la lī′‿nyə. **2.** Les rangs: lē raṅ.—**ranker.** Soldat de fortune: sel″dā′ də fōr″tün′.

rapid, *a.* Rapide (*m. & f.*): ra″pīd′.

rate, *n.* **1.** Prix (*m.*): prī (*price*). **2.** Vitesse (*f.*): vī″tēs′ (*speed*). **3.** Proportion (*f.*): pro″pōr″sī″‿yeṅ′. **4.** Tarif (*m.*): ta″rīf′ (*of allowances, pay,* etc.).—**at any rate.** En tous cas: aṅ tū ka.

ration. **I.** *n.* **1.** *pl.* Vivres (*m.*): vī′‿vrə. **2.** Portion (*f.*): pōr″sī″‿yeṅ′. **3.** Ration (*f.*): ra″sī″yeṅ′ (*horse's*). **II.** *v.* **1.** Nourrir: nūr″‿rīr′. **2.** Rationner: ra″sī″‿yeṅ″nē′.—**emergency rations.** Vivres de réserve: vī′vrə də rē″zārv′.—**iron r.** A can of bully beef, two biscuits, and a can that contains sugar, tea, and beef=tea cubes.

rattle. Faire du bruit: fār dü brwī. See under PREVENT.—**rattled,** *a.* **1.** Étourdi (*m.*): ē″tūr″dī′; étourdie (*f.*): ē″tūr″dī′ (*dizzy*). **2.** Embrouillé (*m.*): aṅ″brwa″lē′ (*confused*).

ravine, *n.* **1.** Ravin (*m.*): ra″vaṅ′ (*hollow road*). Abbreviated *Rav.* **2.** Ravine (*f.*): ra″vīn′ (*mountain torrent*).

razor. Rasoir (*n. m.*): ra″zwār′.—**razor=strap.** Cuir à rasoir (*m.*): kwīr a ra″zwār′.

reach. **I.** *n.* Atteinte (*f.*): at″‿taṅt′. **II.** *v.* Atteindre: at″-taṅ′‿drə.—**within reach of.** À portée de: a pōr″tē′ də. Compare RANGE.

read, *v.* Lire: līr.—**can you read English?** Pouvez=vous lire l'anglais? pū″vē″ vū līr laṅ″glā′.—**do you read French?** Lisez=vous le français? lī″sē′ vū lə fraṅ″sā′.

readiness, *a.* Promptitude (*n. f.*): preṅ″tī″tüd′.—**in readiness.** En état prêt: aṅ‿ē″tā′ prā.

ready, *a.* **1.** Prompt (*m.*): preṅ; prompte (*f.*): preṅt (*quick*). **2.** Prêt (*m.*): prā; prête (*f.*): prāt (*prepared, as food*).—**to get ready.** Se tenir prêt: sə tə-nīr′ prā.

real, *a.* Vrai (*m.*): vrā; vraie (*f.*): vrā.
rear. **I.** *n.* L'arrière (*n. m.*): lar"‿rī"‿yār'. **II.** *v.* Se cabrer: sə ka"brē'.—**in the rear.** En arrière: aṅ‿ar"‿rī"‿yār'.—**r.=guard.** Arrière=garde (*n. f.*): ar"‿rī"‿yār'-gārd.—**r.=sight.** Hausse (*n. f.*): hōs.
reason. Raison (*n. f.*): rā"zoṅ'.
rebel, *n.* Un révolté (*m.*): aṅ rē"vol"tē'; une révoltée (*f.*): ūn rē"vol"tē'.
recall. **I.** *n.* Rappel (*m.*): rap"‿pel'. **II.** *v.* Rappeler: rap"‿pə-lē'.
recant, *v.* Rétracter: rē"trak"tē'.
recapture. **I.** *n.* Reprise (*f.*): rə-prīz'. **II.** *v.* Reprendre: rə-prāṅ'‿drə.—**recapture the position one has evacuated.** Reprendre la position qu'on a évacuée: rə-prāṅ'‿drə la po"zī"sī"‿yoṅ' koṅ‿a ē"va"kü"ē'.
recede, *v.* Reculer: rə-kü"lē'.
receipt. Reçu (*n. m.*): rə-sü'.—**take a receipt.** Prendre un reçu: prāṅ'‿drə aṅ rə-sü'.
receive, *v.* Recevoir: rə-sə-vwār'.—**receiver.** Récepteur (*n. m.*): rē"sep"tūr' (*also a receiving instrument*).
recent, *a.* Récent (*m.*): rē"sāṅ'; récente (*f.*): rē"sāṅt'.
reckon, *v.* Calculer: kal"kü"lē'.—**reckoning from to=day.** À partir d'aujourd'hui: a par"tīr' dō"ʒūr"dwī'.—**the reckoning.** Le compte (*n. m.*): lə kōṅt (*amount of a bill* or *the bill itself*).
recognize, *v.* Reconnaître: rə-koṅ"‿nā'‿trə.
recoil. Recul (*n. m.*): rə-kül'.
reconnaissance. Reconnaissance (*n. f.*): rə-koṅ"‿nā"sāṅs'.—**preliminary reconnaissance.** Reconnaissance préliminaire: rə-koṅ"‿nā"sāṅs' prē"lī"mī"nār'.
reconnoiter, *v.* Reconnaître: rə-koṅ"‿nā'‿trə.—**to go reconnoitering.** Aller en reconnaissance: al"‿lē' aṅ rə-koṅ"‿nā"sāṅs'.
record. **I.** *n.* **1.** Registre (*m.*): rə-ʒīs'‿trə. **2.** Souvenir (*m.*): sū"‿və-nīr'. **II.** *v.* Enregistrer: aṅ"‿rə-ʒīs"trē'.—**recorder.** Enregistreur: aṅ"‿rə-ʒīs"trūr'.—**record=card.** Fiche (*n. f.*): fīsh (*indicating condition of wounded after treatment*).—**r.=office,** *n.* **1.** Bureau des archives (*m.*): bü"rō' dēz‿ar"shīv'. **2.** Greffe (*m.*): gref.
recording. Enregistrant: aṅ"‿rə-ʒīs"trāṅ'.—**recording instrument.** Enregistreur (*n. m.*): aṅ"‿rə-ʒīs"trūr'.
recourse. Recours (*n. m.*): rə-kūr'.
recover, *v.* **1.** Reprendre: rə-prāṅ'‿drə. **2.** Retrouver: rə-trū"vē'. **3.** Guérir: gē"rīr' (*health*). **4.** Remettre: rə-met'‿trə.—**recovery.** Guérison (*n. f.*): gā"rī"zoṅ' (*of health*).
recruit, *n.* **1.** Conscrit (*m.*): koṅ"skrī'. **2.** Recrue (*f.*): rə-krü'.
recruiting, recruitment. Recrutement: rə-krü"‿tə-māṅ'.—**recruiting sergeant.** Sergent recruteur: sār"ʒāṅ' rə-krü"tūr'.
red, *a.* Rouge (*m.* & *f.*): rūʒ.—**red cap.** A British staff officer because he wears a red band around his cap.—**the Red Cross.** La Croix Rouge: la krwa rūʒ.—**Red Cross Society.** La Société de la Croix Rouge: la sō"sī"ē"tē' də la krwa rūʒ.—**reddish,** *a.* Roux (*m.*): rū; rousse (*f.*): rūs.
redan. Redan (*n. m.*): rə-dāṅ'. Abbreviated *Red.*
redoubt. Redoute (*n. f.*): rə-dūt'. Abbreviated *Rede.*
reduce, *v.* Réduire: rē"dwīr'.—**to reduce to the ranks.** Casser: kas"‿sē' (*broken: said of non=commissioned officers*).
reference. Référence (*n. f.*): rē"fē"rāṅs'.
refill, *v.* Remplir: raṅ"plīr'.—**refilling points.** Points de ravitaillement: pwaṅ də ra"vī"ta"‿yə-māṅ'.
refined, *a.* Distingué (*m.*), distinguée (*f.*): dīs"taṅ"gē'.
refinery. Raffinerie (*n. f.*): raf"‿fī"‿nə-rī'. Abbreviated *Rafie.*
reform, *v.* Reformer: rə-for"mē' (*form again, as a battalion*).
refreshment=room. Buffet (*n. m.*): büf"‿fē'.—**where is the refreshment=room?** Où est le buffet? ū ē lə büf"‿fē'.

refuge. Refuge (*n. m.*): rə-fūʒ'.—**refugee.** Réfugié (*n. m.*): rē'fü"ʒī"‿yē'.

regard, *n.* **1.** Égard (*m.*): ā"gār' (*respect to*). **2.** Considération (*f.*): koṅ"sī"dē"ra"sī"‿yeṅ'.—**as regards.** Pour ce qui est de: pūr sə kī ē də.—**in regard to.** À l'égard de: a lē"gār' də.—**with r. to.** Quant à: kaṅt‿a.

regiment. Régiment (*n. m.*): rē"ʒī"māṅ'.—**we are looking for our regiment.** Nous cherchons notre régiment: nū shār"sheṅ' nō'‿trə rē"ʒī"māṅ'.—**which is your r.?** Quel est votre régiment? kel ē vō'‿trə rē"ʒī"māṅ'.

register, *v.* Enregistrer: aṅ"‿rə-ʒīs"trē'.—**registered letter.** See LETTER.

registration. Immatriculation (*n. f.*): īm"‿ma"trī"kü"la"sī"‿yeṅ'.

regular, *a.* Régulier (*m.*): rē"gü"lī"‿yē'; régulière (*f.*): rē"gü"lī"‿yār'.

regulate, *v.* **1.** Régler: rē"glē'. **2.** Diriger: dī"rī"ʒē'.—**to regulate the firing.** Régler le tir: rē"glē' lə tīr.

regulation. **1.** Règlement (*n. m.*): rē"‿glə-māṅ'. **2.** Ordonnance (*f.*): ōr"deṅ"‿nāṅs'.

Reims, raṅz, *not* rīms. French city.

reins, *n.* **1.** Brides (*f.*): brīd (*for driving*). **2.** Rênes (*f.*): rāṅ (*for riding*).

reinforcements, *n. pl.* **1.** Renforts (*m.*): raṅ"fōr'. **2.** *sing.* Renforcement (*m.*): raṅ"fōr"‿sə-māṅ'.

relatives. Parents (*n. m.*): pa"rāṅ'.

relay. **I.** *n.* Relais (*m.*): rə-lē'. **II.** *v.* **1.** Replacer: rə-pla"sē'. **2.** Reposer: rə-po"zē' (*set again*).

release, *v.* **1.** (1) Libérer: lī"bē"rē'. (2) Mettre en liberté: met'‿trə aṅ lī"bār"tē'. **2.** Dégager: dē"ga"ʒē' (*disentangle*). **3.** Relâcher: rə-la"shē' (*let go of*).

relegate, *v.* Reléguer: rə-lē"gē'.—**to relegate to the rear.** Reléguer à l'arrière: rə-lē"gē' a lar"‿rī"‿yār'.

reliable, *a.* **1.** Sûr: sür (*of information*). **2.** Sérieux (*m.*): sē"rī"‿yū' (*of persons*); sérieuse (*f.*): sē"rī"‿yūz'.

relief, *n.* **1.** Relève (*f.*): rə-lāv' (*of a sentry*). **2.** Secours (*m.*): sə-kūr' (*help*). **3.** Soulagement (*m.*): sū"la"‿ʒə-māṅ' (*alleviation of pain*).

relieve, *v.* **1.** Relever: rə‿lə‿vē' (*a sentry*). **2.** Venir en aide: və‿nīr' aṅ‿ād'‿ə (*bring help to*). **3.** Soulager: sū"la"ʒē' (*alleviate*).—**be relieved from.** Être délivré de: ā'‿trə dē"lī"vrē' də.—**relieving,** *n.* **1.** Soulagement (*m.*): sū"laʒ"‿ə-māṅ'. **2.** Secours (*m.*): sə-kūr'. **3.** Aide (*f.*): ād'ə.—**relieving-officer.** Commissaire des pauvres: kom"‿mī"sār' dē pō'vrə.

rely, *v.* [Always with *on* or *upon.*] Compter sur: koṅ"tē' sür.

remain, *v.* Rester: res"tē'.—**remain in the field.** Tenir la campagne: tə-nīr' la kaṅ"‿pa'nyə.

remember, *v.* **1.** Se souvenir de: sə sū"‿və-nīr' də. **2.** Se rappeler: sə rap"‿pə-lē'. See Appendix.

remit, *v.* Remettre: rə-met'‿trə.

remount. **I.** *n.* Un cheval de remonte: aṅ shə-vāl' də rə-meṅt'. **II.** *v.* Remonter: rə-meṅ"tē'.—**department of remounts.** Service de la remonte (*m.*): sūr"vīs' də la rə‿meṅt'.—**remount depot.** Dépôt de remonte: dē"pō' də rə-meṅt'.

removal, *n.* **1.** Enlèvement (*m.*): aṅ"lāv"‿ə-māṅ'. **2.** Départ (*m.*): dē"pār'.—**removal of sick and wounded.** L'évacuation des malades et des blessés: lē"va"kü"a"sī"‿yeṅ' dē ma"lād' ē dē blēs"‿sē'.

remove, *v.* **1.** Déloger: dē"lō"ʒē' (*as inhabitants*). **2.** Déplacer: dē"pla"sē' (*as from a position*). **3.** Enlever: aṅ"lə-vē' (*carry or clear away*).—**r. mines.** Enlever les mines: aṅ"‿lə-vē' lē mīn.—**to r. the wounded.** Enlever les blessés: aṅ"‿lə-vē' lē blēs"‿sē'.

rend, *v.* Fendre: fāṅ'drə.

renew, *v.* Renouer: rə-nū"ē'.

rent. **I.** *n.* Loyer (*m.*): lwa″yē′. **II.** *v.* Louer: lū″ē′.—**renting officer.** Officier chargé des locations: ef″‿fī″sī″‿yē′ shar″ʒē′ dē lō″ka″sī″‿yeṅ′.
reopen, *v.* Ouvrir de nouveau: ū″vrīr′ də nū″vō′.
repair. **I.** *n.* Réparation (*f.*): rē″pa″ra″sī″‿yeṅ′. **II.** *v.* **1.** Réparer: rē″pa″rē′ (*mend*). **2.** Raccommoder: rak″‿kem″‿mo″dē′ (*repair, as clothes*).—**out of repair.** En mauvais état: aṅ mō″vāz′‿ē″tā′.—**repairing outfit.** Trousse à réparations: trūs‿ā rē″pa″ra″sī″‿yeṅ′.
repeat, *v.* Répéter: rē″pē″tē′.—**repeat that, please.** Répétez ça, s'il vous plaît: rē″pē″tē′ sa, sīl vū plā.
repel, *v.* **1.** Repousser: rə-pūs″‿sē′. **2.** Refouler: rə-fū″lē′.—**repel the enemy.** Refouler l'ennemi: rə-fū″lē′ len″‿nə-mī′.
repetition. Répétition (*n. f.*): rē″pē″tī″sī″‿yeṅ′.
replace, *v.* Remplacer: raṅ″pla″sē′.—**replacement.** Remplacement (*n. m.*): raṅ″pla″‿sə-māṅ′.
replacing, *n.* **1.** Remise en place (*f.*): rə-mīz′‿aṅ plas. **2.** Remplacement (*m.*): raṅ″pla″‿sə-māṅ′.—**the replacing of ammunition.** La remise en place des munitions: la rə-mīz′‿aṅ plas dē mü″nī″sī″‿yeṅ′.—**replacing of losses.** Le remplacement des pertes: lə raṅ″pla″‿sə-māṅ′ dē pārt.
replenish, *v.* **1.** [Used with *with.*] Remplir de: raṅ″plīr′ də (*fill up afresh*). **2.** Se remplir: sə raṅ″plīr′ (*to fill oneself*).—**replenish ammunition and supplies.** Ravitailler en munitions et vivres: ra″vī″ta″‿yē′ aṅ mü″nī″sī″‿yeṅz′‿ē vī′vrə.
reply, *v.* Répondre: rē″peṅ′‿drə.
report. **I.** *n.* Rapport (*m.*): rap″‿pōr′. **II.** *v.* **1.** Rendre compte: rāṅ′‿drə keṅt. **2.** Se présenter à *or* au: sə prē″zaṅ″tē′ a *or* ō (*report to*).—**the report has not been confirmed.** On n'a pas vérifié le rapport: eṅ na pa vār″ī″fī″‿yē′ lə rap″‿pōr′.—**they will r. to the commander.** Ils se présenteront au commandant: īl sə prē″zaṅ″‿tə-roṅ′ ō kem″‿maṅ″dāṅ′.
representative. Représentant (*n. m.*): rə-prē″zaṅ″tāṅ′.
reprimand. Réprimande (*n. f.*): rē″prī″māṅd′.
reprisals. Représailles (*n. f.*): rə-prē″zai′‿yə.—**to have recourse to** (or **make**) **reprisals.** User des représailles: ü″zē′ dē rə-prē″zai′‿yə.
republic. République (*n. f.*): rē″pü″blīk′.
repulse. **I.** *n.* **1.** Refoulement (*m.*): rə-fūl″‿māṅ′. **2.** Echec (*m.*): ē″shek′. **II.** *v.* Repousser: rə-pūs″‿sē′.—**repulsed.** Repoussé: rə-pūs″‿sē′.
requirement. Exigence (*n. f.*): eg″zī″ʒāṅs′.
requisite, *a.* Requis (*m.*): rə-kī′; requise (*f.*): rə-kīz′. Exigé (*m.*), exigée (*f.*): eg″zī″ʒē′.
requisition. Réquisition (*n. f.*): rē″kī″zī″sī″‿yeṅ′.—**assistant director of requisition service.** Directeur-adjoint du service des réquisitions: dī″rek″tūr′ ad″ʒwaṅ′ dü sār″vīs′ dē rē″kī″zī″sī″‿yeṅ′.—**fill a requisition.** Exécuter une réquisition: eg″zē″kü″tē′ ün rē″kī″zī″sī″‿yeṅ′.—**r.-office.** Bureau de règlement des réquisitions: bü″rō′ də rā″‿glə-māṅ′ dē rē″kī″zī″sī″‿yeṅ′.—**r.-officer.** Officier chargé des réquisitions: ef″‿fī″sī″‿yē′ shar″ʒē′ dē rē″kī″zī″sī″‿yeṅ′.—**r. of manual labor.** Réquisition de travail de manœuvre: rē″kī″zī″sī″‿yeṅ′ də tra″vā′‿yə də ma″nū′vrə.—**r. of supplies.** Réquisition de vivres: rē″kī″zī″sī″‿yeṅ′ də vī′‿vrə.—**requisitioning.** Réquisition (*n. f.*): rē″kī″zī″sī″‿yeṅ′.
rescue, *v.* **1.** Sauver: sō″vē′. **2.** Secourir: sə-kū″rīr′.—**to the rescue!** Au secours! ō sə-kūr′.
réseau, rē″zō′, *n. m.* [Fr.] **1.** A network. **2.** A system of cross-lines as of railroads or of telegraph wires.
reserve, *n.* **1.** Réserve (*f.*): rē″zārv′. **2.** Réserve d'avants postes: rē″zārv′ da″vāṅ′ pōst.—**reservist.** Réserviste (*n. m.*): rē″zār″vīst′.
resignation. Démission (*n. f.*): dē″mīs″‿sī″‿yeṅ′.—**to send**

in one's resignation. Donner sa démission: dən"‿nē' sa dē"-mĭs"‿sĭ"yəṅ'.

resist, *v.* Résister: rē"zĭs"tē'.—**resistance.** Résistance (*n. f.*): rē"zĭs"täṅs'.—**a desperate resistance.** Une résistance acharnée: ün rē"zĭs"täṅs'‿ä"shar"nē'.

resolute, *a.* Résolu (*m.*), résolue (*f.*): rē"zo"lü'.

resort. Recours (*n. m.*): rə-kūr'.—**in the last resort.** En dernier ressort: aṅ där"nĭ"‿yē' rə-sōr'.—**r. to.** Avoir recours à: av"wär' rə-kūr' a.

resources, *n. pl.* Ressources (*f.*): res"‿sūrs'.

respect, *n.* **1.** Respect (*m.*): res"pē'. **2.** Rapport (*m.*): rap"‿pōr'.—**in other respects.** Sous d'autres rapports: sū dō'‿trə rap"‿pōr'.—**in respect to.** Par rapport à: pär rap"‿pōrt'‿a.—**in some r.** En quelque sorte: aṅ kel'kə sōrt.—**in some respects.** Sous quelques rapports: sū kel'kə rap"‿pōr'.—**with respect to.** Quant à: kaṅt‿a.

respirator. Masque respirateur (*n. m.*): mäsk res"pĭ"ra"tūr'.

respite. Répit (*n. m.*): rē"pĭ'.—**give no respite.** Donner aucun répit: don"‿nē' ō"kaṅ' rē"pĭ'.

responsible, *a.* Responsable (*m.* & *f.*): res"peṅ"sä'‿blə.—**responsibility.** Responsabilité (*n. f.*): res"pəṅ"sa"bĭ"lĭ"te'.—**on my own responsibility.** Sous ma propre responsibilité: sū ma prō'‿prə res"pəṅ"sa"bĭ"lĭ"tē'.

rest[1], *n.* **1.** Reste (*m.*): rest (*remainder*). **2.** Les autres (*m. pl.*): lēz‿ō'‿trə.—**among the rest.** Entre autres: aṅ'‿trə ō'‿trə (*among the others*).

rest[2]. **I.** *n.* Repos (*m.*): rə-pō'. **II.** *v.* Se reposer: sə rə-pō"zē'.—**at rest.** **1.** En station: aṅ sta"sĭ"‿yəṅ'. **2.** Sur place: sür pläs. **3.** En arrêt: aṅ‿ar"‿rē' (*of a lance*).

restore, *v.* Rendre: räṅ'‿drə.

result. Résultat (*n. m.*): rē"zül"tä'.—**without endeavoring to obtain a decisive result.** Sans chercher à obtenir un résultat décisif: saṅ shär"shē' a ob"‿tə-nĭr' aṅ rē"zül"tä' dē"sĭ"zĭf'.

resume, *v.* **1.** Reprendre: rə-präṅ'‿drə. **2.** Continuer: kəṅ"-tĭ"nü"ē'.—**resume the advance.** Reprendre la marche en avant: rə-präṅ'‿drə la märsh aṅ‿a"väṅ'.

resumption, *n.* **1.** Reprise (*f.*): rə-prīz'. **2.** Continuation (*f.*): kəṅ"tĭ"nü"a"sĭ"‿yəṅ'.

retake, *v.* Reprendre: rə-präṅ'‿drə. See RECAPTURE.

retaliate, *v.* User des représailles: ü"zē' dē rə-prē"zai'‿yə (*make reprisals*).

retaliation. Représailles (*n. f.*): rə-prē"zai'‿yə.

retire, *v.* **1.** Se retirer: sə rə-tĭ"rē' (*fall back*). **2.** Reculer: rə-kü"lē'.—**retired, or on the retired list.** En retraite: aṅ rə-trāt' (*said of officers*).—**to put on the retired list.** Mettre à la retraite: met'‿trə a la rə-trāt'.

retirement, *n.* **1.** Retraite (*f.*): rə-trāt' (*under age limit*). **2.** Évacuation (*f.*): ē"va"kü"a"sĭ"‿yəṅ' (*withdrawal*).

retract, *v.* **1.** Se rétracter: sə rē"trak"tē'. **2.** Se dédire: sə dē"-dĭr'. See Appendix.

retreat. **I.** *n.* Retraite (*f.*): rə-trāt'. **II.** *v.* Battre en retraite: bät'‿trə aṅ rə-trāt'.—**line of retreat.** See under LINE.—**to cover the r.** Couvrir la retraite: kū"vrĭr' la rə-trāt'.

retrenchment. Retranchement (*n. m.*): rə-traṅ"‿shə-mäṅ'.

retrograde, *a.* **1.** Rétrograde: rē"tro"gräd'. **2.** En arrière: aṅ‿ar"‿rĭ"‿yär'.—**retrograde movement.** Mouvement rétrograde: mū"‿və-mäṅ' rē"tro"gräd'.

return. **I.** *n.* **1.** Retour (*m.*): rə-tūr'. **2.** Rapport (*m.*): rap"-pōr'. **3.** Compte rendu: kəṅt raṅ"dü'. **II.** *v.* **1.** Retourner: rə-tūr"nē'. **2.** Revenir: rə-və-nĭr'.

reveille, *n.* Réveil (*m.*): rē"vē'‿yə.

revetting. Matériel de revêtement: ma"tē"rĭ"el' də rə-vā"‿tə-mäṅ'.

revetment. Revêtement (*n. m.*): rə-vā"‿tə-mān'.
revictual, *v.* Ravitailler: ra"vī"tai"‿yē'.—**revictualling.** Ravitaillement (*n. m.*): ra"vī"tai"‿yə-mān'.
review. **I.** *n.* Revue (*f.*): rə‿vü'. **II.** *v.* **1.** Revoir: rə-vwār' (*examine*). **2.** Passer en revue: pas"‿sē' aṅ rə-vü' (*pass in review*).—**in review order.** En grande tenue: aṅ grand tə‿nü'.—**to take a r. of** or **survey the situation.** Examiner la situation: eg"za"mī"nē' la sī"tü"a"sī"‿yoṅ'.
revive, *v.* Ressusciter: res"‿sü"sī"tē'.
revolver. Revolver (*n. m.*): rē"vol"vār'.—**revolver-case.** Etui de revolver: ē"twī' də rē"vol"vār'.
rheumatism. Rhumatisme (*n. m.*): rü"ma"tīsm'.
rib, *n.* **1.** Côte (*f.*): kōt. **2.** Nervure (*f.*): nār"vür' (*in architecture a side-rib of a groined vault*).
rice. Riz (*n. m.*): rī.
rich, *a.* Riche (*m. & f.*): rīsh.
ricochet. **I.** *n.* Ricochet (*m.*): rī"ko"shē'. **II.** *v.* Ricocher: rī"ko"shē'.
riddle, *v.* Cribler: krī"‿blē'.—**to be riddled with bullets.** Être criblé de balles: ā'‿trə krī"blē' də bal.
ride, *v.* Monter à cheval: mon"tē' a shə-vāl'.—**rider,** *n.* **1.** Cavalier (*m.*): ka"va"lī"‿yē'. **2.** Écuyer (*m.*): ē"kwī"‿yē'.
ridge, *n.* **1.** Crête (*f.*): krāt (*of a mountain*). **2.** Rebord (*m.*): rə-bōr' (*a ledge*).—**shelving ridge.** Dos d'âne: dō dān.—**mountain ridge.** **1.** Chaîne (*n. f.*): shān. **2.** Ligne de crête: lī'nyə də krāt.
rifle. Fusil (*n. m.*): fü"zī'.—**automatic rifle.** Fusil automatique: fü"zī' ō"to"ma"tīk'.—**r.-barrel.** Canon de fusil: ka"noṅ' də fü"zī'. See BARREL.—**r.-grenade.** Grenade à fusil: gre"nād' a fü"zī'.—**r.-pit.** Trou de tirailleur: trū də tī"rai"‿yūr'.
rifled. Rayé: rā"‿yē'.—**rifled gun.** Canon rayé (*m.*): ka"noṅ' rā"yē'.
rifling. Rayure (*n. f.*): rā"‿yür'.
rifleman, *n.* **1.** Tireur (*m.*): tī"rūr'. **2.** Chasseur (*m.*): shas"‿sūr'.
right. **I.** *a.* **1.** Droit (*m.*): drwa; droite (*f.*): drwat. **2.** Juste (*m. & f.*): ʒüst. **II.** *adv.* Bien: bī"‿yaṅ'.—**on the right.** À droite: a drwāt.—**on the r., close.** Appuyez à droite: ap"‿pwī"‿yēz'‿a drwat.—**on the r.-hand side.** Du côté droit: dü kō"tē' drwa.—**right about.** See under ABOUT.—**r., dress!** Alignez, à droite! a"lī"‿nyē' a drwat.—**r. flank.** Flanc droit: flaṅ drwa.—**right turn.** **1.** Par fil à droite: pār fīl a drwat. **2.** Demi à droite: də-mī' a drwat.—**r. wheel.** À droite: a drwat.—**r. wing.** Aile droite (*n. f.*): āl drwat.—**to the r.** À droite: a drwat.
rigidity. Rigidité (*n. f.*): rī"ʒī"dī"tē'.
rim. Jante (*n. f.*): ʒāṅt.—**detachable rim.** Jante amovible: ʒāṅt a"mo"vī'‿blə.
riot, *n.* Émeute (*f.*): ē"mūt'.
rise. **I.** *n.* **1.** Origine (*f.*): ō"rī"ʒīn' (*source*). **2.** Élévation (*f.*): ē"lē"va"sī"‿yoṅ'. **3.** Montée (*f.*): moṅ"tē' (*of a hill*). **II.** *v.* **1.** Se lever: sə lə-vē' (*get up*). **2.** Monter: moṅ"tē' (*as a balloon*). **3.** Se soulever: sə sū'‿lə-vē' (*in rebellion*).—**I must rise early to-morrow morning.** Il me faut lever de bonne heure demain matin: īl mə fō lə-vē' də bōn‿nūr də-maṅ' ma"taṅ'.—**gentle rise.** Montée douce: moṅ"tē' dūs.—**rough r.** Montée rude: moṅ"tē' rüd.—**sharp r.** Montée raide: moṅ"tē' rād.
rising. Soulèvement (*n. m.*): sū"lā"‿və-mān' (*insurrection*).
river, *n.* **1.** Rivière (*f.*): rī"vī"‿yār'. Abbreviated *R.* **2.** Fleuve (*m.*): flūv. Abbreviated *Fl.*—**the r. has overflowed.** La rivière est débordée: la rī"vī"‿yār' ē dē"bōr"dē'.—**to ford the r.** Traverser la rivière à gué: tra"vār"sē' la rī"vī"‿yār' a

gē.—**rivulet.** **1.** Ruisseau (*n. m.*): rwīs″‿sō′. **2.** Ruisselet (*n. m.*): rwīs″‿sə-lē′. **3.** Rivierette (*f.*): rī″vī″‿yār″et′.

road, *n.* **1.** Route (*f.*): rūt. **2.** Chemin (*m.*): shə-man′. **3.** Chaussée (*f.*): shōs″‿sē′. Abbreviated *Chée.* **4.** Rue (*f.*): rü. **5.** Ligne d'étapes: lī′‿nyə dē″tāp′ (*transport*).—**across the road, or street.** Au travers de la route, ou rue: ō tra″vār′ də la rūt, ū rü.—**branch r.** Embranchement de route: an″bran″‿shə-mān′ də rūt.—**branching r.** Bifurcation (*n. f.*): bī″für′ka″sī″‿yen′.—**by=r.,** or **lane.** Chemin de moyenne communication: shə-man′ də mwa″yen′ kom″‿mü″nī″ka″sī″‿yen′.—**clear r.** Route libre: rūt lī′‿brə.—**county=r.** Chemin communal: shə-man′ kom″‿mü″nāl′.—**cross=r.** **1.** Chemin de traverse: shə-man′ də tra″vārs′‿ə. **2.** Carrefour: kar″‿rə-fūr′.—**departmental r.** Route départementale: rūt dē″par″‿tə-man″tāl′.—**dusty r.** Route poussiereuse: rūt pūs″‿sī″‿yā″rūz′.—**forked r.** Route bifurquée: rūt bī″für″kē′.—**heavy r.** **1.** Route grasse: rūt grās. **2.** Chemin rompu: shə-man′ ren″pü′.—**hilly r.** Route montueuse: rūt men″tü″ūz′.—**high r.** See under HIGH.—**hollow or sunken r.** Route encaissée: rūt an″kās″‿sē′.—**level r.** Route plate: rūt plat.—**local r.** Chemin communal: shə-man′ kom″‿mü″nāl′.—**main r.** Chemin de grande communication: shə-man′ də grand kom″‿mü″nī″ka″sī″‿yen′.—**metal r.** Route cailloutée: rūt kai″‿yū″tē′.—**national r.** Route nationale: rūt na″sī″‿yō″nāl′.—**on the r.** **1.** En route: an rūt. **2.** Sur la route de: sür la rūt də (used with *to*).—**picketed r.** Route enfermée de piquet: rūt an″-fār″mē′ də pī″kē′. See PICKET.—**passable r.** Route viable: rūt vī″ā′‿blə.—**raised r.** Route en chaussée: rūt an shōs″‿sē′.—**r. junction.** **1.** Croisement de route: krwa″‿zə-mān′ də rūt. **2.** Embranchement de route: an″bran″‿shə-mān′ də rūt (*cf railroads*).—**Roman r.** Voie romaine: vwa ro″mān′.—**state r.** Route départementale: rūt dē″par″‿tə-man″tāl′.—**stony r.** Route pierreuse: rūt pī″‿yā″rūz′.—**the r. to follow.** La route à suivre: la rūt a swī′‿vrə.—**what is the condition of the r.?** Comment est l'état de viabilité? kom″‿mān′ ē lē″tā′ də vī″a″bī″lī″tē′.—**roadhead,** *n.* Tête d'étape: tāt dē″tāp′.—**where does this r. lead?** Où mène cette route? ū mān set rūt.

roadside. Bas côté (*n. m.*): bā kō″tē′.

roadstead. Rade (*n. f.*): rād.

roadway, *n.* **1.** Chemin (*m.*): shə-man′. **2.** Chemin de fer (*m.*): shə-man′ də fār (*railway*). **3.** Chaussée (*f.*): shōs″‿sē′.

roan, *a.* Rouan: rū″ān′.

roast. Rôti (*n. m.*): rō″tī′.—**roast beef.** Rosbif (*n. m.*): res″-bīf′.

rob, *v.* Voler: vō″lē′.—**robber.** Voleur (*n. m.*): vo″lūr′.

rock, *n.* **1.** Roche (*f.*): rōsh. **2.** Rocher (*m.*): rō″shē′.—**rock=drill.** Barre à mine (*n. f.*): bar‿a mīn.—**rocky,** *a.* Rocheux (*m.*): ro″shū′; rocheuse (*f.*): ro″shūz′.

rocket, *n.* Fusée (*f.*): fü″zē′.—**flare=rocket.** Fusée éclairante: fü″zē′ ē″klā″rānt′.

rod, *n.* **1.** Perche (*f.*): pār′shə (*5.029 meters*). **2.** Verge (*f.*): vār′ʒə (*wand*). **3.** Canne à pêcher (*f.*): kan a pā″shē′ (*fishing=rod*).

roll. Appel (*n. m.*): ap″‿pel′.—**check=roll.** Contre=appel (*n. m.*): ken′trə ap″‿pel′.—**r. call.** L'appel: lap″‿pel′.—**to call the r.** Faire l'appel: fār lap″‿pel′.—**r. of honor.** Rôle d'honneur (*n. m.*): rōl don″‿nūr′.

roller=bridge. Pont roulant: pon rū″lān′.

rolling=stock. Matériel roulant: ma″tē″rī″‿yel′ rū″lān′.

roof. Toit (*n. m.*): twa (*also, house=top, hence, the top, as of a mine*).—**roofing.** Toiture (*n. f.*): twa″tür′.

room. Chambre (*n. f.*): shān′‿brə.

root. **I.** *n.* Racine (*f.*): ra″sīn′. **II.** *v.* Enraciner: an″ra″sī″nē′.—**to root out.** Découvrir (*v.*): dē″kū″vrīr′ (*drive out of*).

rooty, rū′ti, *n.* [Soldiers' slang.] Bread.

rope, *n.* **1.** Corde (*f.*): kōrd. **2.** Cordage (*m.*): kōr″dāʒ′.

rough, *a.* **1.** Grossier (*m.*): gros″‿sī″‿yē′; grossière (*f.*): gros″‿sī″‿yār′. **2.** Ébauché (*m.*), ébauchée (*f.*): ē″bō″shē′.
rough-shoe, *v.* Ferrer à glace: fār″rē′ a glās.
roughly, *adv.* Approximativement: ap″‿prok″sī″ma″tī″‿və-mān′.
round, *n.* **1.** Ronde (*f.*): rənd (*inspection: usually in the plural*). **2.** Cartouche (*f.*): kar″tūsh′ (*ammunition*).
round, *adv.* Autour: ō″tūr′.—**grand r.** Ronde major: rōnd ma″zōr′.—**night r.** Ronde de nuit: rōnd də nwī.—**number of r. fired.** Le nombre de cartouches tirées: lə nen′brə də kar″-tūsh′ tī″rē′.
rout. Mettre en déroute: mēt′‿trə an dē″rūt′.
route, rūt, *n.* [Eng. & Fr.] **1.** A course, road, or way by which one may travel. **2.** An itinerary, as of a march, indicating the way to be taken and the location of headquarters for each evening. —**route-order.** Feuille de route (*n. f.*): fū′‿yə də rūt.—**transport r.** Routes d'étapes: rūt dē″tāp′.
rub, *v.* Frotter: frot″‿tē′.—**a rub down. 1.** Un coup de bouchon: an kū də bū″shen′ (*as a horse, with a wisp of straw*). **2.** Un coup de torchon: an kū də tor″shon′ (*when done with a cloth*). —**to rub down.** Bouchonner: bū″shon″‿nē′ (*as horses, with a wisp of straw*).
rubber. Caoutchouc (*n. m.*): ka″ūt″shū′.
rudder. Gouvernail (*n. m.*): gū″vēr″nā′‿yə.
rude, *a.* Impoli (*m.*), impolie (*f.*): an″po″lī′.
ruin. Ruine (*n. f.*): rü″īn′.
rule. Règle (*n. f.*): rā′‿glə.—**as a rule.** En général: an zē″nē″rāl′.
rum. Rhum (*n. m.*): rem (*liquor*).
rumor. Rumeur (*n. f.*): rü″mūr′.
rump. La croupe d'un cheval: la krūp dan shə-vāl′.
run. I. *n.* Course (*f.*): kūr′‿sə. **II.** *v.* **1.** Courir: kū″rīr′. **2.** *Imper.* Courez! kū″rē′.
runaway. Fuyard (*n. m.*): fwī″yār′.—**runaway horse.** Cheval emporté: shə-vāl′ an″pōr″tē′.
runner, *n.* **1.** Coureur (*m.*): kū″rūr′. **2.** Courrier (*m.*): kū″-rī″‿yē′. **3.** Estafette (*f.*): ēs″ta″fēt′ (*an officer's orderly in the trenches*).
running, *a.* Courant (*m.*): kū″rān′; courante (*f.*): kū″rānt′. —**running fight.** Escarmouche de route (*f.*): es″kar″mūsh′ də rūt.
rush. I. *n.* **1.** Mouvement précipité (*m.*): mū″‿və-mān′ prē″sī″pī″tē′. **2.** Élan (*m.*): ē″lān′ (*dash*). **II.** *v.* Enlever par un coup de main: an″‿lə-vē′ pār an kū də man.—**rush with the bayonet.** S'élancer à la baionnette: sē″lan″sē′ a la ba″‿yō″net′.—**to r. forward.** S'élancer en avant: sē″lan″sē′ an‿a″vān′.—**to r. the position,** *v.* Se précipiter sur la position: sə prē″sī″pī″tē′ sür la pō″zī″sī″‿yon′.—**short r.** Un bond rapide: an ben ra″pīd′.
Russia. Russie (*n. f.*): rüs″‿sī′.—**Russian,** *n.* Un Russe: an rüs.
rye. Seigle (*n. m.*): sā′‿glə.

S

S. A. A., *abbrev.* Small Arms Ammunition.
saber. Sabre (*n. m.*): sā′‿brə.
sack. I. *n.* Sac (*m.*): sak. **II.** *v.* Saccager: sak″‿ka″zē′.
sad, *a.* Triste (*m. & f.*): trist.
saddle. I. *n.* Selle (*f.*): sel. **II.** *v.* Seller: sel″‿lē′.—**saddle-bag,** *n.* **1.** Sacoche (*f.*): sa″kōsh′. **2.** Bissac (*m.*): bis″‿sāk′.—**saddle-cloth,** *n.* **1.** Couverture (*f.*): kū″vār″tür′. **2.** Housse (*f.*): hūs′‿sə.—**s.-shaped.** Dos d'âne: dō dān.
saddler, *n.* **1.** Bourrelier (*m.*): būr″‿rə-lī″‿yē′. **2.** Sellier (*m.*): sel″‿lī″‿yē′.—**saddler-sergeant,** *n.* Maître bourrelier: mā′‿trə būr″‿rə‿lī″‿yē′.

saddlery. Sellerie (*n. f.*): sel″‿lə-rī′.
safe, *a.* **1.** Sauf (*m.*): sōf; sauve (*f.*): sōv. **2.** Prudent (*m.*): prü″dāṅ′; prudente (*f.*): prü″dāṅt′.—**safe from.** À l'abri de: a la″brī′ də.—**safeguarding.** Mise en sûreté: mīz‿aṅ sü″‿rə-tē′.—**safety.** Sûreté (*n. f.*): sü″‿rə-tē′.—**safety-catch.** Cran de sûreté: kraṅ də sü″‿rə-tē′.
sail. **I.** *n.* Voile (*f.*): vwal. **II.** *v.* Naviguer: na″vī″gē′.
sailor. Marin (*n. m.*): ma″raṅ′.
St. Vitus dance. Danse de St.-Guy: daṅs də saṅ gī.
salient. Saillant (*n. m.*): sai″‿yāṅ′.
sallow, *a.* **1.** Jaunâtre: ʒō″nā′‿trə. **2.** Blême: blām.
sally. **I.** *n.* Sortie (*f.*): sər″tī′. **II.** *v.* Sortir: sər″tīr′.
saloon. Estaminet (*n. m.*): es″ta″mī″nē′.
salt. Sel (*n. m.*): sel.—**salt-pit.** Saline (*n. f.*): sā″līn′.—**rock s.** Sel gemme: sel ʒem′‿mə.—**Epsom salts.** Sel anglais: sel aṅ″glā′.—**some salt.** Du sel: dü sel.
salute. **I.** *n.* Salut (*m.*): sa″lü′. **II.** *v.* Saluer: sa″lü″ē′.—**fire a salute.** Tirer une salve: tī″rē′ ün salv.—**to salute the colors.** Saluer le drapeau: sa″lü″ē′ lə dra″pō′.
salvo. Salve (*n. f.*): salv.
"Sam Brown." A heavy leather, web, or cloth surcingle, with light strap running diagonally over the right shoulder.
same, *a.* & *adv.* Même: mām.
sand. Sable (*n. m.*): sa′‿blə. Abbr. *Se.*—**sand-bag.** Sac à terre: sak a tār.—**s.-dunes, s.-hills.** Dunes (*n. f.*): dün.—**s.-pit.** Sablière (*n. f.*): sa″blī″‿yār′. Abbreviated *Sablre.*—**s. plain.** Lande (*n. f.*): laṅd.—**sandy,** *a.* Sablonneux (*m.*): sa″-blen″‿nū′; sablonneuse (*f.*): sa″blen″‿nūz′.
sandwich. Sandwich (*n. m.*): saṅ″dwītsh′. See CHEESE; HAM.
sangar. Parapet en pierres: pa″ra″pē′ aṅ pī″‿yār′ə (*breast-work*).
sanitary, *a.* Sanitaire (*m.* & *f.*): sa″nī″tār′.—**sanitary measures.** Mesures sanitaires: mə-zür′ sa″nī″tār′.—**s. service.** Service sanitaire: sār″vīs′ sa″nī″tār′.—**sanitation.** Hygiène (*n. f.*): ī″ʒī″ān′.
sap. **I.** *n.* Sape (*f.*): sap (*ditch*). **II.** *v.* Saper: sa″pē′ (*undermine* or *approach by trenches*).—**counter-sap.** Contre-sape: keṅ′‿trə sap.—**covered sap.** Sape couverte: sap kū″vārt′.—**double sap.** Sape double: sap dū′‿blə.—**flying sap.** Sape volante: sap vō″lāṅt′.—**sap and mine works.** Travaux de sape et de mine: tra″vō′ də sap ē də mīn.—**sap-fork.** Fourche de sap: fūrsh də sap.—**sap-shield.** Bouclier de mineur: bū″klī″‿yē′ də mī″nūr′.
saphead. Tête de sape: tāt də sap.
sapper. Sapeur (*n. m.*): sa″pūr′.
satisfy. Satisfaire: sa″tīs″fār′.—**to satisfy oneself,** *v.* S'assurer: sas″‿sür″ē′.
Saturday. Samedi (*n. m.*): sa″‿mə-dī′.
sauce. Sauce (*n. f.*): sōs.
saucer. Soucoupe (*n. f.*): sū″kūp′.
saucepan. Casserole (*n. f.*): kas″‿sə-rōl′.
sausage, *n.* **1.** [Small.] Saucisse (*f.*): sō″sīs′. **2.** [Large.] Saucisson (*m.*): sō″sīs″‿seṅ′ (*name applied to kite balloons*).
save, *v.* **1.** Sauver: sō″vē′. **2.** Préserver: prē″zār″vē′. **3.** Éviter: ē″vī″tē′. **4.** Gagner: ga″‿nyē′.—**God save the king!** Vive le roi! vīv lə rwa.—**s. delay, s. time.** Gagner du temps: ga″‿nyē′ dü taṅ (*gain time*).
saw. **I.** *n.* Scie (*f.*): sī. **II.** *v.* Scier: sī″‿yē′.—**chain-** or **jointed saw.** Scie articulée: sī ar″tī″kü″lē′.—**cross-cut saw.** Scie à doubles dents: sī a dū′‿blə daṅ.—**folding saw.** Scie articulée: sī ar″tī″kü″lē′.
sawmill. Scierie (*n. f.*): sī″‿ə-rī′. Abbreviated *Scie.*
say, *v.* Dire: dīr.—**so to say.** Pour ainsi dire: pūr aṅ″sī′ dīr.

scab, *n.* **1.** Croûte (*f.*): krūt (*in medicine*). **2.** Gale (*f.*): gal (*in veterinary science*).
scabbard. Fourreau de sabre (*n. m.*): fūr″‿rō′ də sa′‿brə.
scaffolding. Échafaudage (*n. m.*): ē″sha″fō″dāʒ′.
scald, *v.* Échauder: ē″shō″dē′.
scale. **I.** *n.* **1.** Tarif (*m.*): ta″rīf′ (*of prices*). **2.** Échelle (*f.*): ē″shel′ (*of a map*). **II.** *v.* Escalader: es″ka″la″dē′.—**deflection scale.** Planchette des dérives: plaṅ″shet′ dē dē″rīv′.—**scale (or climb) a hill.** Gravir une colline: gra″vīr′ ün kel″‿līn′.—**scale of rations.** Taux des rations: tō dē ra″sī″‿yoṅ′.
scaling. Escalade (*n. f.*): es″ka″lād′.—**scaling=ladder.** Échelle de siège (*f.*): ē″shel′ də sī″āʒ′.
scales. Balance (*n. f.*): bal″āṅs′ (*for weighing*).
scant, *a.* **1.** Claire (*m. & f.*): klār (*of the hair, in identification*). **2.** Insuffisant (*m.*): aṅ″süf″‿fī″zāṅ′; insuffisante (*f.*): aṅ″süf″‿fī″zāṅt′.—**scanty,** *adv.* **1.** Insuffisant. See SCANT, *a.* 2. **2.** Clairsemé: klār″‿sə-mē′ (*of the hair*).
scar. Cicatrice (*n. f.*): sī″ka″trīs′.
scarf, *n.* **1.** Écharpe (*f.*): ē″shārp′. **2.** Cravate (*f.*): kra″vāt′.
scarp. Escarpe (*n. f.*): es″kārp′.—**scarp=gallery.** Galerie d'escarpe (*f.*): ga″‿lə-rī′ des″kārp′.—**s.=recess.** Coffre d'escarpe (*n. m.*): kef′‿frə des″kārp′.
scatter, *v.* **1.** Disperser: dis″pār″sē′. **2.** Éparpiller: ē″par″pī″‿yē′.
scheme, *n.* **1.** Projet (*m.*): pro″ʒē′. **2.** Plan (*m.*): plaṅ.
school, *n.* École (*f.*): ē″kōl′.—**s. of musketry.** École de tir: ē″kōl′ də tīr.
scissors, *n.* Ciseaux (*m. pl.*): sīs″zō′.
scope, *n.* **1.** Espace (*f.*): es″pās′. **2.** Place (*f.*): plās.
score. Vingtaine (*n. f.*): vaṅ″tān′ (*twenty*).
Scotch, Scottish, *a.* Écossais (*m.*): ē″kos″‿sā′; écossaise (*f.*): ē″kos″‿sāz′.—**Scotsman.** Écossais: ē″kos″‿sā′.—**Scotland.** Écosse (*n. f.*): ē″kos′‿sə.
scout. **I.** *n.* Éclaireur (*m.*): ē″klā″rūr′. **II.** *v.* Éclairer: ē″klā″rē′.—**mounted scout.** Éclaireur à cheval, ou monté: ē″klā″rūr′ a shə-vāl′, ū moṅ″tē′.—**s.=duty.** Service d'éclaireur: sār″vīs′ dē″klā″rūr′.
screen. **I.** *n.* **1.** Écran (*m.*): ē″krāṅ′. **2.** Rideau (*m.*): rī″dō′. **II.** *v.* **1.** Mettre à l'abri: met′‿trə a la″brī′. **2.** Défiler: dē″fī″lē′ (*protect*). **3.** Dissimuler: dīs″‿sī″mü″lē′ (*conceal; hide*).—**outpost screen.** Réseau des avant=postes: rē″zō′ dēz‿av″āṅ′ pōst (*system of outposts*).—**s. of troops.** Rideau de troupes: rī″dō′ də trūp.—**screened communication.** Communication défilée: kom″‿mü″nī″ka″sī″‿yoṅ′ dē″fī″lē′ (*sheltered from enemy fire*).—**to be screened from the enemy's fire.** Être défilé du feu de l'ennemi: ā′‿trə dē″fī″lē′ dü fū də len″‿nə-mī′.—**to screen the artillery.** Dissimuler l'artillerie: dīs″‿sī″mü″lē′ lar″tī″‿yə-rī′.—**to s. oneself.** Se dissimuler: sə dīs″‿sī″mü″lē′.
screw. Vis (*n. f.*): vīs.—**adjusting=screw.** Vis de commande: vīs də kom″‿mānd′.—**breech=s.** Vis de culasse: vīs də kü″lās′.—**s.=driver.** Tournevis (*n. m.*): tūrn″vīs′. [3. Rixe (*f.*): riks.
scrimmage, *n.* **1.** Lutte (*f.*): lüt. **2.** Bagarre (*f.*): ba″gār′.
scrub. **I.** *n.* **1.** Fourrés (*m. pl.*): fūr″‿rē′ (*thicket*). **2.** Broussailles (*f. pl.*): brūs″‿sal′‿yə (*brushwood*). **II.** *v.* **1.** Laver: la″vē′. **2.** Écurer: ē″kü″rē′ (*pots, pans, etc.*).
sea. Mer (*n. f.*): mār.—**seaboard.** Littoral (*n. m.*): līt″‿to″rāl′.—**seaboard=bluffs.** Rochers plats dans la mer: ro″shē′ plā dāṅ la mār.—**sea level.** Niveau de la mer (*m.*): nī″vō′ də la mār.
seaplane. Hydro=avion (*n. m.*): ī″drō′ a″vī″‿yoṅ′.
seaport. Port maritime: pōr ma″rī″tīm′.
seashore. Plage (*n. f.*): plaʒ.

sear, *v.* Brûler: brü″lē′.
search. **I.** *n.* **1.** Recherche (*f.*): rə-shārsh′. **2.** Exploration (*f.*): eks″plo″ra″sī″‿yeṅ′. **II.** *v.* **1.** Explorer: eks″plo″rē′. **2.** Fouiller: fū″yē′. **3.** Chercher: shār″shē′.—**to search the country.** Fouiller le terrain: fū″yē′ lə tār″raṅ′.
searching, *a.* Perçant (*m.*): pār″sāṅ′; perçante (*f.*): pār″sāṅt′ (*said of a look, the wind, etc.*).
searchlight. Projecteur (*n. m.*): prē″ʒek″tūr′.
season. **I.** *n.* Saison (*f.*): sā″zeṅ′. **II.** *v.* **1.** Assaisoner: as″‿sā″zo″nē′ (*of food*). **2.** Acclimater: ak″‿klī″ma″tē′ (*acclimate*).
seat. **I.** *n.* **1.** Siège (*m.*): sī″āʒ′. **2.** Place (*f.*): plās. **II.** *v.* **1.** Faire asseoir: fār as″swār′. **2.** Accommoder: ak″‿kem″‿mō″dē′.—**seat of war.** Le théâtre de la guerre: lə tē″ā′‿trə də la gār.
second. Second (*n. m.*): sə-geṅ′.
secrecy. Secret (*n. m.*): sə-krē′.
secret. **I.** *a.* Secret (*m.*): sə-krē′; secrète (*f.*): sə-krēt′. **II.** *n.* Secret (*m.*): sə-krē′.—**s. service.** Service de renseignements: sār″vīs′ də raṅ″sē″‿nyə-māṅ′.—**agent of the secret service.** Agent secret: a″ʒāṅ′ sə-krē′.
secretary. Secrétaire: sə-krē″tār′.—**secretary of state for war.** Ministre de la guerre: mī″nīs′‿trə də la gār.
section. Section (*n. f.*): sek″sī″‿yeṅ′.
sector. Secteur (*n. m*).: sek″tūr′.
secure, *v.* **1.** Mettre en sûreté: met′‿trə aṅ sür″‿ə-tē′. **2.** S'emparer de: saṅ″pa″rē′ də.
see, *v.* Voir: vwar. See Appendix.—**see there!** Voilà! vwa″-lā′.—**we are glad to see you.** Nous sommes heureux de vous voir: nū somz‿ūr″ū′ də vū vwar.
see-saw. **I.** *n.* **1.** Bascule (*f.*): bas″kül′. **2.** Va-et-vient (*f.*): vā ē vī″aṅ′. **II.** *v.* Basculer: bas″kü″lē′.
seek, *v.* Chercher: shār″shē′.—**to seek out the enemy.** Rechercher l'ennemi: rə-shār″shē′ len″‿nə-mī′.
seem, *v.* **1.** Sembler: saṅ″blē′ (*give the impression*). **2.** Paraître: pa″rā′‿trə (*appear*).—**it seems to me.** Il me semble: īl mə sāṅ′‿blə.
seen, *pa.* Vu (*m.*), vue (*f.*): vü.—**have you seen —?** Avez-vous vu —? a″vē′ vū vü.
seize, *v.* **1.** Saisir: sā″zīr′. **2.** S'emparer de: saṅ″pa″rē′ də. **3.** Enlever: aṅ″‿lə-vē′.—**seize a position.** Enlever une position: aṅ″‿lə-vē′ ün po″zī″sī″‿yeṅ′.
seizing. Enrayage (*n. m.*): aṅ″rā″‿yāʒ′ (*sticking fast, owing to excessive heat, as a cartridge in a magazine rifle*).
seizure, *n.* **1.** Prise (*f.*): prīz. **2.** Saisie (*f.*): sā″zī′. **3.** Mainmise (*f.*): maṅ″mīz′.
seldom, *adv.* Rarement: ra″‿rə-māṅ′.
self, *pron.* Soi-même: swa″mām′.—**self-reliance.** Confiance en soi-même: keṅ″fī″āṅs′‿aṅ swa″mām′.
self-starter. **1.** Mise en marche: mīz‿aṅ mārsh. **2.** Démarreur automatique: dē″mar″‿rūr′ ō″tō″ma″tīk′.
sell, *v.* Vendre: vāṅ′‿drə.—**do you sell —?** Vendez-vous —? vaṅ″dē′ vū.—**seller,** *n.* Vendeur (*m.*): vaṅ″dūr′; vendeuse (*f.*): vaṅ″dūz′.
semaphore, *n.* Sémaphore (*m.*): sē″ma″fēr′.
seminary. Séminaire (*n. m.*): sē″mī″nār′.
send, *v.* Envoyer: aṅ″vwa″‿yē′.—**to send a cable ashore.** Jeter, ou lancer, l'amarre: ʒə-tē′, ū laṅ″sē′, la″mār′.—**s. on.** Envoyer en avant: aṅ″vwa″‿yē′‿aṅ‿a″vāṅ′.—**s. out patrols.** Envoyer des patrouilles: aṅ″vwa″‿yē′ dē pa″trū″ī′‿yə.
senior, *a.* **1.** Aîné (*m.*), aînée (*f.*): ā″nē′. **2.** Plus élevé: plüs‿ē″‿lə-vē′. **3.** Plus ancien (*m.*): plüs‿aṅ″sī″‿yaṅ′; plus ancienne (*f.*): plüs‿aṅ″sī″yēn′‿nə (*of persons in office*).—**senior officer.** L'officier le plus élevé: lef″‿fī″sī‿yē′ lə plüs‿ē″‿lə-vē′.—**seniority.** Ancienneté (*n. f.*): aṅ″sī″yēn″‿nə-tē′.

sense. Sens (*n. m.*): saṅs.—**common sense.** Bon sens: boṅ saṅs.
sentence. Jugement (*m.*): ʒü″‿ʒə-māṅ′.
sentinel. Same as SENTRY.
sentry. Sentinelle (*n. f.*): saṅ″tī″nel′.—**sentry-box.** Guérite (*n. f.*): gā″rīt.—**mounted s.** Vedette (*n. f.*): və-det′.—**protected s.-post. 1.** Chemin couvert: shə-maṅ′ kū″vār′. **2.** Ronde (*n. f.*): roṅd.—**s.-post.** L'emplacement d'une sentinelle: laṅ″pla″‿sə-māṅ′ dün saṅ″tī″nel′.—**to be on s.** Être en sentinelle: ā′‿trə aṅ saṅ″tī″nel′.—**to obey the s.** Obéir à la sentinelle: o″bē″īr′ a la saṅ″tī″nel′.—**to post a s.** Mettre en sentinelle: met′‿trə aṅ saṅ″tī″nel′.—**to relieve the sentries.** Relever les sentinelles: rə-lə-vē′ lē saṅ″tī″nel′.—**to stand s.** Faire sentinelle: fār saṅ″tī″nel′.—**to supply sentries.** Fournir des sentinelles: fūr″nīr′ dē saṅ″tī″nel′.
September. Septembre (*n. m.*): sep″tāṅ′‿brə.
septic, *a.* Septique (*m. & f.*): sep″tīk′.
Serbia, Servia. Serbie (*n. f.*): sār″bī′.—**Serbian, Servian.** Serbe (*m. & f.*): sārb.
sergeant, *n.* **1.** Sergent (*m.*): sār″ʒāṅ′ (*infantry*). **2.** Maréchal des logis (*m.*): ma″rē″shāl′ dē lo″ʒī′ (*cavalry*).—**sergeant-major,** *n.* **1.** Sergent-major (*m.*): sār″ʒāṅ′ ma″ʒōr′ (*of infantry*). **2.** Maréchal des logis chef (*m.*): ma″rē″shāl′ dē lo″ʒī′ shef (*of cavalry*).
serious, *a.* **1.** Sérieux (*m.*): sē″rī″ū′; sérieuse (*f.*): sē″rī″ūz′. **2.** Grave (*m. & f.*): grāv.
servant, *n.* **1.** Domestique (*m. & f.*): do″mēs″tīk′ (*household*). **2.** Brosseur (*m.*): bros″‿sūr′. Compare ORDERLY.
service. Service (*n. m.*): sār″vīs′.—**army service corps.** Commissariat (*n. m.*): kem″‿mīs″‿sa″rī″ā′.—**auxiliary s.** Service auxiliaire: sār″vīs′‿ok″sī″lī″‿yār′.—**on active s. 1.** En campagne (*during war*): aṅ kaṅ″pā′‿nyə. **2.** Service actif: sār″vīs′ ak″tīf′ (*during peace time passed with the colors*).—**personal s.** État de services: ē″tā′ də sār″vīs′ (*chart recording individual service*).
servile, *a.* Servile (*m. & f.*): sār″vīl′.
set, *v.* **1.** Placer: pla″sē′. **2.** Poser: po″zē′. **3.** Mettre: met′‿trə (*put*). **4.** Régler: rē″glē′ (*regulate*).
setting, *n.* **1.** Mise (*f.*): mīz. **2.** Pose (*f.*): pōz. **3.** Placement (*m.*): plas″māṅ′.—**setting-up exercises.** Exercices d'assouplissement: eg″zār″sīs′ das″‿sū″plīs″‿sə-māṅ′.
settle, *v.* **1.** Établir: ē″ta″blīr′. **2.** Fixer: fīk″sē′.
seven, *a. & n.* Sept: set.—**seventh,** *a. & n.* Septième (*m. & f.*): set″yām′.—**seventeen,** *a. & n.* Dix-sept: dī″set′.—**seventeenth,** *a. & n. m.* Dix-septième: dī″set″yām′.—**seventieth,** *a. & n. m.* Soixante-dixième: swas″‿sāṅt′ dīz″yām′.—**seventy,** *a. & n. m.* Soixante-dix: swas″‿sāṅt′ dīs.—**seventy-one,** *a. & n. m.* Soixante et onze: swas″‿sāṅt′‿ē oṅz.
seventy-fives. Les soixante-quinzes: lē swas″‿sāṅt′ kaṅz (*75-centimeter guns, which fire the "flying pigs"*).
sew, *v.* Coudre: kū′‿drə.
sewing-case or **kit.** Nécessaire à coudre (*m.*): nē″ses″sār′ a kū′‿drə.
sewing-cotton. Coton (*n. m.*): kō″toṅ′.
shade. Ombre (*n. f.*): ōṅ′‿brə.
shaft, *n.* **1.** Brancard (*m.*): braṅ″kār′. **2.** Timon (*m.*): tī″moṅ′.
shaggy, *a.* **1.** Poilu (*m.*), poilue (*f.*): pwa″lü′. **2.** Touffu (*m.*), touffue (*f.*): tūf″‿fü′. Compare POILU.
shake, *v.* Secouer: sə-kū″ē′.—**shake hands with.** Serrer la main à: sār″‿rē′ la maṅ a.
shall, *v.* **1.** Devoir: də-vwār′. **2.** Vouloir: vūl″wār′.—**I shall go.** J'irai: ʒī″rā′.—**shall I go?** Irai-je? ī″rā′‿ʒə.
shallows, *n. pl.* Bas-fonds (*m.*): ba″foṅ′.
sham fight. Petite guerre: pə-tīt′ gār.

shape, *n.* Forme (*f.*): fōrm.
sharp, *a.* **1.** Pointu (*m.*), pointue (*f.*): pwañ″tü′. **2.** Aigu (*m.*), aigue (*f.*): ā″gü′ (*said of the chin in identification*).
sharpshooter. Tirailleur (*n. m.*): tī″rai″‿yūr′.
shatter, *v.* **1.** Briser: brī″zē′. **2.** Fracasser: fra″kas″‿sē′.
shave, *v.* Raser: ra″zē′.—**shaved,** *a.* Rasé: ra″zē′.—**to get shaved.** Se faire raser: sə fār ra″zē′.
shaving=brush. Blaireau (*n. m.*): blā″rō′.
she, *pron.* Elle (*f.*): el.
shears, *n. pl.* **1.** Cisailles (*f.*): sī″zai′‿yə. **2.** Ciseaux (*m.*): sī″zō′.—**hand=shears.** Cisailles à main: sī″zai′‿yə a mañ.
sheath, *n.* **1.** Étui (*n. m.*): ē″twī′. **2.** Fourreau (*n. m.*): fūr″‿rō′.
shed, *n.* **1.** Hangar (*n. m.*): hañ″gār′. **2.** Étable (*f.*): ē″tā′‿blə.
sheep, *n. sing. & pl.* Mouton (*n. m. sing.*): mū″toñ′.—**sheep-fold,** *n.* **1.** Bercail (*m.*): bēr″kai′. **2.** Bergerie (*f.*): bār″‿ʒə-rī′.—**sheep=pen.** Parc à moutons (*m.*): park a mū″toñ′.
sheer=line hawser. Cincenelle (*n. f.*): sañ″‿sə-nel′.
sheers, *n. pl.* Bigue (*n. f.*): bīg (*spars and tackle for hoisting*).
sheet, *n.* Drap (*n. m.*): dra.—**ground=sheet,** *n.* Toile vernie: twal vār″nī′ (*rubber=sheet*).
sheeting or **timbering,** *n.* **1.** Blindage (*m.*): blañ″dāʒ′. **2.** Boisage (*m.*): bwa″zāʒ′ (*timbering*). **3.** Coffrage (*m.*): kof″‿frāʒ′ (*coffering*).
shell, *n.* Obus (*m.*): ō″bü′.—**green=cross shell.** Obus asphyxiant: ō″bü′ as″fīks″sī″yāñ′ (*gas=shell*).—**H. E. S.,** *abbr.* High explosive shell commonly called "*H. E.*" Obus détonant: ō″bü′ dē″to″nāñ′.—**illuminating s.** Obus éclairant: ō″büz′‿ēk″lā″rāñ′.—**percussion s.** Obus percutant: ō″bü′ pār″kü″tāñ′.—**segment s.** Obus à mitraille: ō″büz′‿a mī″trai′‿yə.—**shell=base,** *n.* Culot d'un obus: kü″lō′ dañ ō″‿bü′.—**shell=body.** Corps d'un obus: kōr dañ ō″‿bü′.—**s.=hole.** Trou d'obus: trū dō″bü′.—**shrapnel s.** Obus à balles: ō″büz′‿a bāl.—**straw=s.** Obus à étoiles éclairantes: ō″büz′‿a ē″twāl′ ē″klār″āñt′ (*for illuminating an enemy's position as they explode*).—**time=s.** Obus fusant: ō″bü′ fü″zāñ′.
shell, *v.* **1.** Bombarder: boñ″bar″dē′. **2.** Canonner: ka″noñ″‿nē′. **3.** Lancer des obus sur: lañ″sē′ dēz‿ō″bü′ sür.
shelter, *n.* **1.** Abri (*m.*): a″brī′. **2.** Refuge (*m.*): rə-füʒ′. On maps, *Rge.*—**shelter=tent.** Tente=abri (*n. f.*): tant″a″brī′.—**s.=trench.** Tranchée de refuge: trañ″shē′ də rə-füʒ′.—**splinter=proof s.** Pare=éclat (*n. m.*): par″ē″klā′.
shelter, *v.* **1.** Abriter: a″brī″tē′. **2.** Protéger: prō″tē″ʒē′.
shepherd, *n.* Berger (*n. m.*): bār″ʒē′.—**shepherd's=hut. 1.** Buron (*n. m.*): bü″roñ′. **2.** Cortail: kor″tai′. Abbreviated *Ctal.*
shield. Bouclier (*n. m.*): bū″klī″‿yē′.—**portable=shield.** Bouclier portatif: bū″klī″‿yē′ pōr″ta″tīf′.—**s.=apron.** Bouclier de canon (*n. m.*): bū″klī″‿yē′ də ka″noñ′.
shilling. Shelling: shə-lañ′. See MONEY.
shining, *a.* Brillant (*m.*): brī″‿yāñ′; brillante (*f.*): brī″‿yāñt′.
ship, *n.* **1.** Vaisseau (*m.*): vās″‿sō′. **2.** Navire (*m.*): na″vīr′. **3.** Bâtiment (*m.*): ba″tī″māñ′.—**ship=broker,** *n.* Courtier maritime (*m.*): kūr″tī″‿yē′ ma″rī″tīm′.—**s.=chandler,** *n.* Fournisseur de la marine (*m.*): fūr″nīs″‿sūr′ də la ma″rīn′.—**s. of war.** Vaisseau de guerre: vās″sō′ də gār.—**ship's company.** Équipage (*n. m.*): ē″kī″pāʒ′ (*crew*).—**troop=s.** Transport militaire (*m.*): trañs″pōr′ mī″lī″tār′ (*transport*).
shipmaster. Capitaine de navire (*m.*): ka″pī″tān′ də na″vīr′ (*merchant marine*).
shirk, *v.* **1.** Éviter: ē″vī″tē′. **2.** Éluder: ē″lü″dē′.
shirt, *n.* Chemise (*n. f.*): shə-mīz′.
shock, *n.* Choc (*n. m.*): shōk.—**shock=absorber.** Amortisseur (*n. m.*): a″mōr″tīs″‿sūr′.

shod, *imp.* & *pp.* of SHOE, *v.* **1.** Chaussé: shōs″‿sē′ (*of persons*). **2.** Ferré: fãr″‿rē′ (*of horses, etc.*).—**properly shod.** Ferré convenablement: fãr″‿rē′ koṅ″‿və-na″‿blə-mūṅ′.

shoe. **I.** *n.* **1.** (1) Soulier (*m.*): sū″lī″‿yē′. (2) *pl.* Chaussures: shōs″‿sūr′. **2.** Pneu (*m.*): pnū (*motor=wheel tire*). **3.** Fer (*m.*): fãr (*horse*). **II.** *v.* **1.** Chausser: shōs″‿sē′. **2.** Ferrer: fãr″‿rē′ (*of animals*). **3.** Saboter: sa″bō″tē′ (*of machinery*).—**locking=shoe.** Sabot d'enrayage: sa″bō′ daṅ″rā″‿yūʒ′.—**s.=lace,** *n.* Lacet de chaussures: la″sē′ də shōs″‿sūr′.—**these shoes are too small.** Ces souliers sont trop petits: sē sū″lī″yē′ soṅ trō pə-tī′.—**to shoe a horse.** Ferrer un cheval: fēr″‿rē′ aṅ shə-vāl′.

shoeing, *n.* Le ferrage (*n. m.*): lə fãr″‿rāʒ′ (*of horses*).—**shoeing=smith,** *n.* Maréchal ferrant (*n. m.*): ma″rē″shāl′ fãr″‿rāṅ′ (*farrier*).

shoot, *v.* Tirer: tī″rē′.—**to shoot down.** Abattre d'un coup de feu: a″bāt′‿trə daṅ kū də fū.

shop, *n.* **1.** Magasin (*m.*): ma″ga″zaṅ′. **2.** Boutique (*f.*): bū″tīk′.—**where is the best shop?** Où est le meilleur magazin? ū ē lə mē″‿yūr′ ma″ga″zaṅ′.—**where is the cheapest s.?** Où est le magazin de plus bon marché? ū ē lə ma″ga″zaṅ′ də plū boṅ mar″shē′.

short, *a.* **1.** Court (*m.*): kūr; courte (*f.*): kūrt. **2.** Petit (*m.*): pə-tī′; petite (*f.*): pə-tīt′. **3.** Brusque (*m.* & *f.*): brūsk (*abrupt*).—**be short of.** Manquer de (*v.*): maṅ″kē′ də.—**s. circuit.** Cour=circuit (*n. m.*): kūr″sīr″kwī′.—**s. cut.** Raccourci (*n. m.*): rak″‿kūr″sī′.

short=sighted, *a.* Myope: mī″ō′‿pə.—**be short=sighted.** Avoir la vue courte: av″wār′ la vü kūrt.

shot. **I.** *n.* **1.** (1) Balle (*f.*): bāl (*bullet of a rifle*). (2) Boulet (*m.*): bū″lē′ (*ball of a cannon*). **2.** Coup (*m.*): kū (*discharge of a firearm*). **3.** Tireur (*m.*): tī″rūr′ (*marksman*). **II.** *imp.* & *pp.* of SHOOT, *v.* Frappé: frap″‿pē′ (*hit*). See HIT.—**good shot.** Un bon tireur: aṅ boṅ tī″rūr′.—**I am s.** Je suis frappé: ʒə swī frap″‿pē′.—**poor s.** Un mauvais tireur: aṅ mo″vā′ tī″rūr′.—**to be s.** Être fusillé: ā′‿trə fū″zī″‿yē′.

should, *imp.* of SHALL.—**I should like.** Je voudrais: ʒə vū″drā′.

shoulder, *n.* Épaule (*n. f.*): ē″pōl′.—**shoulder arms.** See under ARMS.—**s.=strap.** Patte d'épaule (*n. f.*): pat dē″pōl′.

shout, *v.* Crier: krī″‿yē′.

shovel. **I.** *n.* Pelle (*n. f.*): pēl. **II.** *v.* Pelleter: pel″‿lə-tē′.—**shovel and spade.** Pelle=bêche (*n. f.*): pēl″bāsh′ (*combination trench tool*).

show, *v.* **1.** Montrer: moṅ″trē′. **2.** Indiquer: aṅ″dī″kē′.—**show me some.** Faites=moi voir de: fāt mwa vwar də.—**show me that.** Montrez=moi ça: moṅ″trē′ mwa sa.

shrapnel. Obus à balles (*m.*): ō″büz′‿a bal.

shrouds, *n. pl.* Haubans (*m.*): hō″bāṅ′.

"shun!" Contraction of "Attention": used as a word of command.

shut, *a.* Fermé (*m.*), fermée (*f.*): fēr″mē′.

shutter, *n.* **1.** Volet (*m.*): vo″lē′. **2.** Obturateur (*m.*): ōb″tü″ra″tūr′ (*in ordnance*).

shy. **I.** *a.* **1.** Timide (*m.* & *f.*): tī″mīd′ (*of persons*). **2.** Ombrageux: oṅ″bra″ʒū′ (*of horses*). **II.** *v.* **1.** Faire un écart: fār aṅ ē″kār′ (*of horses*). **2.** Être ombrageux: ā′‿trə oṅ″bra″ʒū′ (*of horses*).

sick. **I.** *a.* Malade (*m.* & *f.*): ma″lād′. **II.** *n. pl.* Malades (*m.* & *f.*): ma″lād′ (*of troops*).—**sick=leave.** Congé de convalescence: koṅ″ʒē′ də koṅ″va″les″‿sāṅs′. In French soldiers' argot, la convalo (*n. f.*): la koṅ″va″lo′.—**sickness.** Maladie (*n. f.*): ma″la″dī′.

side, *n.* Côté (*n. m.*): kō″tē′.—**toward the side.** Vers le côté: vãr lə kō″tē′.

sidewalk, *n.* Trottoir (*n. m.*): trot″‿twār′.

sideways, *adv.* De côté: də kō″tē′.

siding, *n.* **1.** Voie de garage (*f.*): vwa də ga″rāʒ′ (*main or double track line*). **2.** Gare d'évitement: gar dē″vī″‿tə-mān′ (*single track line*).
siege, *n.* Siège (*n. m.*): sī″āʒ′.—**siege=howitzer.** Obusier (*n. m.*): ō″bü″zī″‿yē′.—**s. operations.** Opérations de siège: o″pē″ra″sī″‿yen′ də sī″āʒ′.
sift, *v.* **1.** Cribler: krī″blē′ (*with a sieve*). **2.** Examiner: eg″-za″mī″nē′ (*mentally*).
sight. **I.** *n.* **1.** Vue (*f.*): vü (*general*). **2.** Hausse (*f.*): hōs (*of a gun*). **3.** Visée (*f.*): vī″zē′ (*line of vision*). **II.** *v.* **1.** Voir: vwar. **2.** Apercevoir: a″pār″‿sə-vwār′.—**at first sight.** À première vue: a prə-mī″‿yār′ vü.—**back=s.** Cran de mire: kran də mīr.—**fore=s.** Guidon, *m.*: gī″den′.—**independent s.** Hausse indépendante: hōs an″dē″pan″dānt′.—**keen s.** Bonne vue: bōn′‿nə vü.—**line of sight.** Ligne de mire: lī′‿nyə də mīr.—**telescope s.** Hausse à lunette: hōs a lü″net′.—**to set the s.** Régler la hausse: rē″glē′ la hōs.
sign, *n.* Signe (*n. m.*): sī′‿nyə.—**sign=board.** Poteau indicateur (*n. m.*): po″tō′ an″dī″ka″tūr′.—**s.=post,** *n.* Poteau d'enseigne: po″tō′ dan″sē′‿nyə.
signal, *n.* Signal (*n. m.*): sī″‿nyāl′. Abbreviated *Sal.*—**prearranged signal.** Signal convenu d'avance: sī″‿nyāl′ ken″‿və-nü′ da″vāns′.—**signal=box,** *n.* Cabine de signaleur (*f.*): ka″bīn′ də sī″‿nya″lūr′.—**s.=corps,** *n.* Sapeurs télégraphistes: sa″pūr′ tē″lē″gra″fīst′—**s.=mast,** *n.* Mât de signaux (*m.*): mā də sī″‿nyō′.—**to s. the train.** Signaler le train: sī″‿nya″lē′ lə tran.
Sikh, *n.* Sikh (*m.*): sīk; sikhe (*f.*): sī′‿kə.
silence. **I.** *n.* Silence (*m.*): sī″lāns′. **II.** *v.* Éteindre: ē″tan′-drə (*said of gun=fire*).
silencer, *n.* Silencieux (*n. m.*): sī″lan″sī″‿yū′. See MUFFLER.
Silent Land. Le Pays sourd: lə pā″‿yī′ sūr. ("The configuration of a part of Picardy muffles sound and the country folk call it *Silent Land*." JOHN BUCHAN. *Battle of the Somme*, p. 30.)
Silesia, *n.* Silésie (*n. f.*): sī″lē″sī′‿ə.
silver, *n.* Argent (*n. m.*): ar″ʒān′. See MONEY.
simultaneous, *a.* Simultané (*m.*), simultanée (*f.*): sī″mül″-ta″nē′.
since, *prep.* Depuis: də-pwī′.
sing, *v.* Chanter: shan″tē′.
single, *a.* Seul (*m.*), seule (*f.*): sūl.
sink, *v.* **1.** Tomber au fond: ten″bē′ ō fen. **2.** Couler à fond: kū″lē′ a fen (*of a ship*).
sip, *v.* Boire à petits coups: bwar a pə-tī′ kū.
Sir, *n.* **1.** Mon (*a. m.*): men (as a title of address, "*mon* capitaine," my captain). **2.** Monsieur (*n. m.*): mū-sī″‿yū′.
siren, *n.* Sirène (*n. f.*): sī″rā′‿nə.
sister, *n.* **1.** Sœur (*n. f.*): sūr. **2.** [Slang.] La frangine (*n. f.*): la fran″ʒīn′. Used also as a nickname for Red Cross nurse.—**ward=sister.** Infirmière=major: an″fīr″mī″‿yār′ ma″ʒōr′.
site, *n.* Emplacement (*n. m.*): an″pla″‿sə-mān′.
sitting, *pa.* Assis (*m.*): as″‿sī′; assise (*f.*): as″‿sīz′ (*describing condition of hospital patient*).
situation, *n.* Situation (*n. f.*): sī″tü″a″sī″‿yen′.
six, *a.* & *n.* Six (before a consonant): sī; (before a vowel): sīz; (at the end of a phrase): sīs.—**six=foot way.** Entrevoie (*n. f.*): an″‿trə-vwā′.—**sixth,** *a.* & *n.* Sixième (*m.* & *f.*): sī″zī″‿yām′.
sixteen, *a.* & *n.* Seize (*m.*): sēz.—**sixteenth,** *a.* & *n.* Seizième (*m.* & *f.*): sē″zī″‿yām′.—**sixtieth,** *a.* & *n.* Soixantième (*m.* & *f.*): swas″‿san″tī″‿yām′.—**sixty,** *a.* & *n.* Soixante (*m.*): swas″‿sānt′.
size, *n.* **1.** Grandeur (*f.*): gran″dūr′. **2.** Taille (*f.*): tai′‿yə. **3.** Dimension (*f.*): dī″man″sī″‿yen′.

sketch. I. *n.* Croquis (*m.*): kro″kī′. II. *v.* Esquisser: es″-kīs″‿sē′.
skid, *v.* Déraper: dē″ra″pē′.
skim, *v.* 1. Effleurer: ef″‿flū″rē′ (*general*). 2. Raser: ra″zē′ (*raze the ground*). 3. Écrêter: ē″krā″tē′ (*sweep the top of the battlements*).
skin. I. *n.* 1. Peau (*f.*): pō. 2. Cuir (*m.*): kwīr (*hide*). II. *v.* 1. Écorcher: ē″kor″shē′. 2. Peler: pə-lē′ (*peel, as potatoes, etc.*).
skirmish. I. *n.* Escarmouche (*n. f.*): es″kar″mūsh′. II. *v.* Escarmoucher: es″kar″mū″shē′.—**in skirmishing order.** 1. À l'escarmouche: a les″kar″mūsh′. 2. En tirailleurs: aṅ tīr″ai″‿yūr′. —**skirmishers.** Tirailleurs (*m. pl.*): tīr″ai″‿yūr′.
skirts, *n.* (*f.*) *pl.* Lisières: lī″zī″‿yār′ (*of a forest, wood, etc.*).
skirting=wall, *n.* Mur d'enceinte (*n. f.*): mür daṅ″saṅt′.
skull, *n.* Crâne (*n. m.*): krān.—**broad=skulled.** À pariétaux écartés: a pa″rī″ē″tōz′‿ē″kar″tē′.
Skupshtina, skup′shti-na, *n.* 1. The Serbian parliament. 2. The Montenegrin national assembly.
sky, *n.* Ciel (*n. m.*): sī″‿yel′.
slacken, *v.* Relâcher: rə-la″shē′.
slacker, *n.* Insoumi (*n. m.*): aṅ″sū″mī′.
slacks, *n. pl.* Pantalon (*n. m.*): paṅ″ta″loṅ.
slash. I. *n.* 1. Coupure (*f.*): kū″pür′ (*of the body*). 2. Balafre (*f.*): ba″lā′‿frə (*of the face*). II. *v.* 1. Sabrer: sa″brē′ (*saber*). 2. Balafrer: ba″la″frē′ (*the face*).—**to slash right and left.** Taillader à droite et à gauche: tai″‿ya″dē′ a drwat ē a gōsh.
slate, *n.* Ardoise (*n. f.*): ar″dwāz′.—**slate=quarry.** Ardoisière (*n. f.*): ar″dwa″zī″‿yār′. Abbreviated *Ardre.*
slaughter. I. *n.* 1. Massacre (*m.*): mas″‿sā′‿krə. 2. Abattage (*m.*): a″ba″tāʒ′ (*of animals*). II. *v.* 1. Égorger: ē″gor″ʒē′. 2. Massacrer: mas″‿sa″krē′. 3. Abattre: a″bāt′‿trə (*of animals*). —**slaughter=house.** Abattoir (*n. m.*): a″bat″‿twār′. Abbreviated *Abat.*
sleep. I. *n.* Sommeil (*m.*): som″‿mē′‿yə. II. *v.* Dormir: dōr″mīr′.—**I slept well.** J'ai dormi comme un sabot: ʒā dōr″mī′ kem aṅ sa″bō′.—**sleep well!** 1. Bon repos: boṅ rə-pō′. 2. Dormez bien: dōr″mē′ bī″‿yaṅ′.
sleeper, *n.* Traverse (*f.*). tra″vārs′ (*for railroad rails*).
sleeping=draught, *n.* Potion calmante (*n. f.*): po″sī″‿yeṅ′ kal″-māṅt′.—**sleeping=suits.** Vêtements de nuit: vā″‿tə-māṅ′ də nwī.
sleepless. Sans sommeil: saṅ som″‿mē′‿yə.—**sleeplessness.** Insomnie (*f.*): aṅ″som″nī′.—**sleepless night.** Nuit blanche: nwī blaṅsh.
slender, *a.* Élancé (*m.*), élancée (*f.*): ē″laṅ″sē′.
slight, *a.* 1. Mince (*m.* & *f.*): maṅs (*of a human figure*). 2. Faible (*m.* & *f.*): fā′blə (*weak*). 3. Peu important (*m.*): pu aṅ″-por″tāṅ′; peu importante (*f.*): pu aṅ″por″tāṅt′ (*of no importance*). —**a s. wound.** Une blessure légère: ün bles″‿sür′ lē″ʒār′.—**there is slight chance of danger.** Il y a peu de hasard: il‿ī a pu də ha″zār′.
slim, *a.* Svelte (*m.* & *f.*): svelt.
slime. Vase (*n. f.*): vāz.
sling. I. *n.* 1. Écharpe (*f.*): ē″shārp′ (*for a broken limb*). 2. Élingue (*f.*): ē″laṅg′ (*nautical use*). 3. Sangle (*f.*): sāṅ′‿glə (*for horses*). 4. Bretelle (*f.*): brə-tel′ (*rifle-strap*). II. *v.* 1. Lancer: laṅ″sē′ (*throw*). 2. Suspendre: süs″pāṅ′‿drə (*hang*). 3. Élinguer: ē″laṅ″gē′ (*in nautical use*).—**sling arms!** En bandoulière! aṅ baṅ″dū″lī″‿yār′.—**s. the nets!** Gréez les filets! grē″ē′ lē fī″lē′.
slip. I. *n.* 1. Faux pas (*m.*): fō pā (*mistake*). 2. Cale (*f.*): kāl (*of a harbor*). II. *v.* Glisser: glīs″‿sē′.
slippery, *a.* Glissant (*m.*): glīs″‿sāṅ′; glissante (*f.*): glīs″‿sāṅt′.

slope. I. *n.* 1. Pente (*f.*): pant. 2. Talus (*m.*): ta"lü'. 3. Coteau (*m.*): kō"tō' (*declivity*). Abbreviated *Cot.* 4. Versant (*m.*): vār"sān' (*of a pass or mountain*). II. *v.* 1. Pencher: pan"shē'. 2. Incliner: an"klī"nē'.—**gentle slope.** Pente douce: pant dūs.—**midway up a s.** À mi-pente: a mī pant.—**s. arms!** Armes à volonté! ārmz‿a vol"en"tē'.—**sloping-ground.** Terrain en pente: tār"ran' an pant.—**steep slope.** Pente raide: pant rād.

slot, *n.* Fente (*n. f.*): fant —**cartridge-belt slot.** Couloir d'alimentation: kūl"wār' da"lī"man"ta"sī"‿yen'.

slow, *a.* Lent (*m.*): lan; lente (*f.*): lant.—**slowly.** Lentement: lan"‿tə‿mān'.

sluice, *n.* Écluse (*n. f.*): ē"klüz'.

sly, *a.* Sournois (*m.*): sūr"nwā'; sournoise (*f.*): sūr"nwāz'.

small, *a.* Petit (*m.*): pə-tī'; petite (*f.*): pə-t t'.

smash, *v.* 1. Écraser: ē"kra"zē' (*crush*) 2. Briser: brī"zē' (*break*).

smell, *v.* Sentir: san"tīr'.

smith, *n.* Forgeron (*n. m.*): fōr"‿ʒə-ren'.

smithy, *n.* Forge (*n. f.*): fōr'‿ʒə. Abbreviated *Fge.*

smoke. I. *n.* Fumée (*n. f.*): fü"mē' Not to be confused with *fumier* (fü"mī"‿yē'), manure. II. *v.* Fumer: fü"mē'.—**let us smoke.** Fumons: fü"mōn'.—**no smoking allowed.** Il est défendu de fumer: īl ē dē"fan"dü' də. fü"mē'.—**something to smoke.** Quelque chose à fumer: kel'‿kə shōʒ‿a fü"mē'.—**smoking tobacco.** Tabac à fumer (*n. m.*): ta"bā' a fü"mē'.

smoke-bomb, *n.* Same as GAS-BOMB, see under GAS.

smoker, *n.* Fumeur (*m.*): fü"mūr'; fumeuse (*f.*): fü"mūz'.

smoke-helmet, *n.* See under HELMET.

snaffle, *n.* Filet (*m.*): fī"lē'.

snare, *n.* 1. Piège (*m.*): pī"yāʒ'. 2. Guet-apens (*m.*): gē"ta"-pān' (*ambush*).

sneeze. I. *n.* Éternuement (*m.*): ē"tār"nü"mān'. II. *v.* Éternuer: ē"tār"nü"ē'.

snipe, *v.* Canarder: ka"nar"dē'.—**snipe-hole, sniping-hole,** *n.* Créneau de canardeur (*m.*): krē"nō' də ka"nar"dūr'.

sniper, *n.* Canardeur (*m.*): ka"nar"dūr'.

snow, *n.* Neige (*n. f.*): nā'‿ʒə.—**snow-bound.** Arrêté par la neige: ar"‿rē"tē' par la nā'‿ʒə.—**s.-line.** Limite des neiges: lī"mīt' dē nā'‿ʒə.—**s.-plow.** Chasse-neige (*n. m.*): shas nā'‿ʒə.

snub-nose. Nez camus (*n. m.*): nē ka"mü'.—**snub-nosed.** Au nez camus: ō nē ka"mü'.

so, *conj.* 1. Ainsi: an"sī' (*thus*). 2. (1) Si: sī. (2) Tellement: tel"‿lə-mān'. (3) Tant: tan (*in such a degree*).—**so that.** De façon que: də fa"sen' kə.

soak, *v.* Tremper: tran"pē'.—**I am soaked through.** Je suis tout trempé: ʒə swī tū tran"pē'.

soap. I. *n.* Savon (*m.*): sa"ven'. II. *v.* Savonner: sa"ven"nē'.

sober, *a.* 1. Sérieux (*m.*): sē"rī"‿yū' (*serious*); sérieuse (*f.*): sē"rī"yūz'. 2. Pas ivre: paz‿ī'‿vrə (*not drunk*).

socks, *n pl.* Chaussettes (*f.*): shōs"‿set'.

sod, *n.* Motte de gazon (*f.*): mot də ga"ʒen'.

soda, *n.* Soude (*n. f.*): sūd (*for washing*).—**soda-water.** Eau de Seltz: ō də selz.—**soda-water and milk.** Lait et siphon: lē ē sī"fen'.

soft, *a.* 1. Doux (*m.*): dū; douce (*f.*): dūs. 2. Tendre (*m. & f.*): tān'‿drə. 3. Mou (*m.*): mū; molle (*f.*): mol.

soil. I. *n.* 1. Terrain (*m.*): tār"‿ran' (*land*) 2. Fumier (*m.*): fü"mī"‿yē' (*manure*). 3. (1) Terre (*f.*): tār. (2) Sol (*m.*): sel (*earth*).—**soil easy to work.** Terrain facile à remuer: tār"ran' fa"sīl' a rə-mü"ē'.

sold, *v.* Vendu: van"dü'.

soldier, *n.* Soldat (*n. m.*): sel"dā'. Compare INFANTRY.

sole, *n.* **1.** Semelle (*f.*): sə-mel′ (*of a shoe*). **2.** Plante (*f.*): plān′‿tə (*of the foot*). **3.** Sole (*n. f.*): sōl (*of a horse's hoof*).
some, *a.* **1.** Du (*m.*): dü; de la (*f.*): də la; des (*pl*): dē. **2.** Quelque (*m.*): kel′‿kə.—**some more.** Encore (*adv.*): aṅ″kōr′.
somebody, *n.* Quelqu'un (*m.*): kel″‿kaṅ′; quelqu'une (*f.*): kel″‿küṅ′.
somehow, *adv.* D'une façon ou d'une autre: dün fa″səṅ′ ū dün ō′‿trə.
something, *a.* Quelque chose: kel′kə shōz.
sometime, *adv.* Un de ces jours: aṅ də sē ʒūr.
somewhere, *adv.* Quelque part: kel′‿kə par.—**"somewhere in France."** Un endroit quelconque en France: aṅ‿aṅ″drwā′ kel″keṅk′ aṅ fraṅs.
so much. Tant (*adv.*): taṅ.
son, *n.* Fils (*n. m.*): fīs.
song, *n.* Chanson (*n. f.*): shaṅ″səṅ′.
soon, *adv.* Bientôt: bī″‿yaṅ″tō′.—**we shall be too soon.** Nous serons de trop tôt: nū sə-rəṅ′ də trō tō.
sore, *n.* Plaie (*n. f.*): plā.—**sore back.** Blessure au dos: bles″sür′ ō dō.—**sore throat.** Mal de gorge: mal də gōrʒ.—**to have sore eyes, ears.** Avoir mal aux yeux, aux oreilles: a″vwār′ mal ōz‿yū, ōz‿o″rē′‿yə. See also EARACHE.
sorrow, *n.* **1.** Douleur (*f.*): dū″lūr′. **2.** Chagrin (*m.*): sha″-graṅ′.
soul, *n.* Âme (*n. f.*): ām.
sound. **I.** *n.* **1.** Son (*m.*): səṅ. **2.** Bruit (*m.*): brwī. **II.** *v.* Sonner: sən″‿nē′.—**bugle s.** Sonnerie de clairon (*f.*): sən″‿nə-rī′ də klā″rəṅ′.—**sounds of battle.** Bruit de combat: brwī də kəṅ″bā′.—**sound the advance, alarm.** See under ADVANCE, ALARM.
soup, *n.* **1.** Consommé (*m.*): kəṅ″səm″‿mē′ (*clear*). **2.** Pot-au-feu (*m.*): pōt″‿ō″fū′ (*ordinary*). **3.** Potage (*m.*): pō″tāʒ′ (*thick*). **4.** Soupe (*f.*): sūp.—**soup-tablet.** Potage condensé: po″tāʒ′ kəṅ″daṅ″sē′.
source, *n.* Source (*n. f.*): sūrs.
south, *n.* Sud (*n. m.*): süd.—**southeast.** Sud-est (*n. m.*): süd″‿ēst′.—**southward,** *adv.* Vers le sud: vār lə süd.—**southwest.** Sud-ouest (*n. m.*): süd″west′.
space, *n.* Espace (*n. m.*): ēs″pās′.
spade, *n.* Bêche (*n. f.*): bāsh.—**trail-s.** Bêche de crosse: bāsh də krōs.
Spain, *n.* Espagne (*n. f.*): es″pā′‿nyə.
span, *n.* Portée (*n. f.*): pōr″tē′.
spanner, *n.* **1.** Clef à boulon (*f.*): klē a bū″ləṅ′. **2.** Clef à levier (*f.*): klē a lə-vī″‿yē′. See WRENCH.
spar, *n.* Levier en bois: lə-vī″‿yē′ aṅ bwa (*wooden lever*).
spare, *v.* **1.** Épargner: ē″par″nyē′ (*lay by, save*). **2.** Économiser: ē″kəṅ″o″mī″zē′ (*economize*). **3.** Dispenser de: dī″spaṅ″sē′ də (*go without*). **4.** Donner: don″‿nē′ (*to let have*). **5.** S'abstenir de: sab″‿stə-nīr′ də (*to forbear from*).
spare, *a.* **1.** Maigre (*m. & f.*): mā′grə (*lean of body*). **2.** Au delà du nécessaire: ō də-lā′ dü nē″ses″‿sār′ (*more than necessary*). **3.** De rechange: də rə-shāṅʒ′ (*of animals and mechanical parts*).—**s. parts.** Pièces de rechange (*f.*): pī″‿yās′ də rə-shāṅʒ′.—**s. wheel.** Roue de rechange: rū də rə-shāṅʒ′.
spark, *n.* Étincelle (*n. f.*): ē″taṅ″sēl′.—**spark-plug, sparking-plug.** **1.** Tampon (*n. m.*): taṅ″poṅ′. **2.** Bougie (*n. f.*): bū″ʒī′.
sparkling-water. Eau de seltz: ō də seltz.
spasmodic, *a.* Spasmodique (*m. & f.*): spas″mō″dīk′.
spats, *n. pl.* Guêtres (*f*): gā′‿trə.
speak, *v* Parler: par″lē′.—**do not speak so fast.** Ne parlez pas si vite: nə par″lē′ pa sī vīt.—**do you s. English?** Parlez-

vous anglais: par″lē′ vūz‿an″glā′.—**generally speaking.** Parlant d'une façon générale: par″lān′ dün fa″sōn′ ʒē″nē″rāl′.—**I do not speak French.** Je ne parle pas français: ʒə nə parl pa fran″sā′.—**speak!** (*imperative*). Parlez! par″lē′.—**s. more slowly.** Parlez plus lentement: par″lē′ plū lan″‿tə-mān′.

spectacles, *n. pl.* Lunettes (*n. f.*): lü″net′.

speed, *n.* Vitesse (*n. f.*): vī″tēs′.—**at full speed.** 1. À franc étrier: a fran ē″trī″‿yē′ (*of horses*). 2. À grande vitesse: a grand vī″tēs′ (*of goods, etc., to be forwarded by express train*). See EXPRESS.—**s.-indicator.** Enregistreur de vitesse: an″‿rə-ʒis″trūr′ də vī″tēs′.

sphere, *n.* Sphère (*n. f.*): sfār.

spica, *n.* Spica (*n. m.*): spī″kā′ (*a spiral bandage*).

spike, *n.* 1. Pointe (*f.*): pwant. 2. Clou (*m.*): klū (*a nail*). 3. Cheville (*f.*): shə-vī′‿yə (*wooden peg*).—**spiked stick.** Bâton ferré (*n. m.*): ba″ton′ fār″rē′.—**to spike a gun.** Enclouer un canon: an″klū″ē′ an ka″non′.

spill, *v.* Verser: vār″sē′ (*as water*).

spin, *v.* Faire tourner: fār tūr″nē′ (*twist around*).

spindle, *n.* 1. Fuseau (*m.*): fü″zō′. 2. Pivot (*m.*): pī″vō′ (*rod on which something turns*).

spire, *n.* Flèche (*n. f.*): flāsh (*of a steeple*).

spirit, *n.* 1. Esprit (*m.*): es″prī′. 2. Morale (*f.*): mo″rāl′. 3. Ardeur (*f.*): ar″dūr′. 4. Énergie (*f.*): ē″nār″ʒī′.—**spirited,** *a.* 1. Fort (*m.*): fōr; forte (*f.*): fōrt. 2. Animé (*m.*): animée (*f.*): a″nī″mē′. 3. Vigoureux (*m.*): vī″gū″rū′; vigoureuse (*f.*): vī″gū″rūz′.—**spirits,** *n. pl.* Cognac (*m.*): ko″‿nyāk′.

spit, *v.* Cracher: kra″shē′.—**spittle.** Salive (*n. f.*): sa″līv′.

splice. I. *n.* Épissure (*f.*): ē″pīs″‿sür′. II. *v.* 1. Épisser: ē″pīs″‿sē′ (*nautical*). 2. Joindre à onglet: ʒwan′‿drə a on″glē′ (*carpentry*).

splint, *n.* 1. Éclisse (*f.*): ē″klīs′. 2. Planchette (*f.*): plan″shet′. 3. Attelle (*f.*): at″‿tel′.

splinter, *n.* Éclat (*n. m.*): ē″klā′ (*of a shell*).

split, *v.* 1. Fendre: fān′‿drə (*separate*). 2. Diviser: dī″vī″ʒē′ (*divide*). 3. Partager: par″ta″ʒē′ (*share*). 4. Crever: krə-vē′ (*burst*). 5. Déchirer: dē″shī″rē′ (*tear*). 6. Briser: brī″zē′ (*break, shatter*).

splutter, *v.* Crachoter: kra″shō″tē′.

spoiled, *a.* Gâté (*m*), gâtée (*f.*): ga″tē′.

spoke, *n.* Rayon (*n. m.*): rā″yon′.

sponge, *n.* 1. Éponge (*n. f.*): ē″ponʒ′. 2. Écouvillon (*n. m.*): ē″kū″vī″‿yon′.

spoon, *n.* Cuiller *or* cuillère (*n. f.*): kwī″‿yār′.—**spoonful.** Cuillerée (*n. f.*): kwī″‿yə-rē′.

sporran, *n.* Bourse (*n. f.*): būrs.

spot, *n.* 1. (1) Endroit (*m.*): an″drwā′. (2) Lieu (*m*): lī″‿yu′ (*place*). 2. Tache (*f.*): tash (*stain*).—**dead on the spot.** Raide mort: rād mōr.—**killed on the s.** Tué raide: tü″ē′ rād.—**on the s.** 1. Sur-le-champ: sür lə shan (*immediately*). 2. Sur la place: sür la plas.

sprain. I. *n.* 1. Foulure (*f.*): fū″lür. 2. Entorse (*f.*): an″tōrs′. II. *v.* 1. Donner une entorse à: don″‿nē′ ün an″tōrs′‿a. 2. Se fouler: sə fū″lē′.—**he has sprained his ankle.** Il s'est donné une entorse à la cheville: il sē don″‿nē′ ün an″tōrs′ a la shə-vī′‿yə.—**I have sprained my wrist.** Je me suis foulé le poignet: ʒə mə swī fū″lē′ lə pwa″‿nyē′.—**spraining.** Luxation (*n. f.*): lük″‿sa″sī″‿yon′ (*dislocation*).

spread, *v.* 1. (1) Étendre: ē″tān′‿drə. (2) Déployer: dē″plwa″‿yē′ (*as a sail*). 2. Propager: pro″pa″ʒē′ (*as a disease*). 3. Se propager: sə pro″pa″ʒē′.

spring, *n* 1. Source (*f.*): sūrs (*of water*). Abbreviated *Sce.* 2.

Ressort (*m.*): rə-sōr′ (*elasticity*). **3.** Printemps (*m.*): prañ″tāñ′ (*the season*).—**buffer-spring.** Ressort plat: rə-sōr′ plā.—**clip-s.** Ressort à pinces: rə-sōr′ a pañs.—**coiled s.** Ressort à boudin: rə-sōr′ a bū″dañ′.—**percussion-s.** Ressort de percussion: rə-sōr′ də pār″kü″sī″‿yoñ′.—**spring-catch.** Same as CLIP SPRING.

spruce. **I.** *n.* Sapin (*m.*): sa″pañ′. **II.** *v.* Se faire beau: sə fār bō.—**to spruce up.** Se bichonner: sə bī″shon″‿nē′.

spur. **I.** *n.* **1.** Éperon (*m.*): ē″‿pə-roñ′. **2.** Contrefort (*m.*): koñ″‿trə-fōr′ (*buttress*). **II.** *v.* Éperonner: ē″‿pə-roñ″‿nē′.—**jack-spur.** Éperon à la chevalière: ē″‿pə-roñ′ a la shə-va″-lī″‿yār′ (*fastened with a strap*).—**screw-s.** Éperon à vis: ē″‿pə-roñ′ a vīs.—**s.-strap.** Courrole d'éperon: kūr″‿rwā′ dē″‿pə-roñ′.—**set spurs to one's horse.** Piquer des deux: pī″kē′ dē dū.

spy. **I.** *n.* Espion (*m.*): ēs″pī″‿yoñ′; espionne (*f.*): ēs″pī″‿yōn′. **II.** *v.* Espionner: ēs″pī″‿yoñ″‿nē′.—**spy duty.** Être aux aguets: ā′trə ōz‿a″gā′ (*on the watch*).—**spy-glass.** **1.** Longue-vue (*f.*): lōñ″‿gə-vü′. **2.** *pl.* Jumelles (*f.*): ʒü″mel′.

spying, *n.* Espionnage (*n. m.*): es″pī″‿yoñ″‿nāʒ′.—**spying-post.** Abri de guetteur: a″brī′ də gāt″‿tūr′.

squad, *n.* Escouade (*n. f.*): es″kū″ād′.—**squad-drill.** École de peloton (*f.*): ē″kōl′ də pə-lo″toñ′.

squadron, *n.* **1.** Escadron (*m.*): es″ka″droñ′ (*of cavalry*). **2.** Escadre (*f.*): es″kā′‿drə (*of ships*). **3.** Escadrille (*f.*): es″ka″-drī′‿yə (*of aeroplanes*).

square, *n.* **1.** Place (*f.*): plās. **2.** Carré (*m.*): kar″‿rē′.—**form squares!** En carré! añ kar″‿rē′.

squint, *v.* Loucher: lū″shē′.—**squinter,** *n.* Loucheur (*m.*): lū″shūr′.

stabiliser, *n.* Stabilisateur (*m.*): sta″bī″lī″za″tūr′ (*for maintaining balance in aeroplanes and for checking spontaneous discharge in explosives*).

stable, *n.* Écurie (*n. f.*): ē″kü″rī′. Abbreviated *Ecie.*—**stable-rack,** *n.* Râtelier (*n. m.*): ra″‿tə-lī″‿yē′.

stack, *v.* Mettre en faisceaux: met′‿trə añ fās″‿sō′ (*of arms*).—**stack arms!** Formez les faisceaux! fōr″mē′ lē fās″‿sō′. Compare ARMS.

staff, *n.* L'état-major (*n. m.*): lē″tā′ ma″ʒōr′.—**general staff.** État-major général: ē″tā′ ma″ʒōr′ ʒē″nē″rāl′.—**staff-clerk.** Archiviste d'état-major: ar″shī″vīst′ dē″tā′ ma″ʒōr′.—**s.-college.** École de guerre: ē″kōl′ də gār.—**s.-officer.** See under OFFICER.

stage, *n.* Phase (*n. f.*): fāz (*of a military operation*).

stake, *n.* **1.** Piquet de terre (*n. m.*): pī″kē′ də tār (*peg*). **2.** Enjeu (*m.*): añ″ʒū′ (*prize*).

stallion, *n.* Étalon (*n m*): ē″ta″loñ′.

stamina, *n.* Force vitale (*f.*): fōrs vī″tāl.

stamp, *v.* Affranchir: af″‿frañ″shīr′ (*as a letter*).—**postage-stamp,** *n.* See under POSTAGE.

stampede, *n.* Fuite précipitée (*n. f.*): fwīt prē″sī″pī″tē′

stand, *v.* **1.** Se tenir debout: sə tə-nīr′ də-bū′ (*stand up*). **2.** S'arrêter: sar″‿rā″tē′ (*stop*). **3.** Faire halte: fār hāl′‿tə (*halt*).—**s. at ease!** Repos! rə-pō′.—**s. down.** Descendez: des″‿sañ″dē′ (*order to step down from the firing step*).—**s. to!** **1.** Aux armes! ōz‿ārm. **2.** Tenez-y! tə-nēz′‿ī (*hold fast*).—**to make a firm s.** Se tenir bon: sə tə-nīr′ boñ.—**to stand fast.** Se tenir ferme: sə tə-nīr′ fārm.

standing orders. See under ORDERS

stanchion *n.* **1.** Étançon (*m.*): ē″tañ″soñ′ (*stay, prop*). **2.** Épontille (*f.*): ē″poñ″tī′‿yə (*nautical*).

standard, *n.* Étendard (*m.*): ē″tañ″dār′.

starboard, *n.* Tribord (*m.*): trī″bōr′.

start. **I.** *n.* Départ (*m.*): dē″pār′. **II.** *v.* **1.** Partir: par″tīr′. **2.** Se mettre en route: sə met′‿trə añ rūt.—**to s. the engine.**

artistic; ärt; fat; fāre; fast; get; prēy; hit; police;
obey; gō; not; ōr; full; rūle; but; būrn; ə = final;

straits, *n. pl.* Détroit (*n. m. sing.*): de″trwā′. Abbreviated Det[t] (*geographical*).
strange, *a.* Étrange (*a. f.*): ē″trāṅ′‿ʒə.
stranger, *n.* **1.** Étranger (*m.*): ē″trañ″ʒē′; étrangère (*f.*): ē″trañ″ʒār′. **2.** Inconnu (*m.*), inconnue (*f.*): añ″ken″‿nü′ (*unknown*).—**he is a stranger to me.** Il m'est inconnu: il mēt‿añ″ken″‿nü′.
strangles, *n. pl.* Gourme (*n. f. sing.*): gūrm (*a disease of horses*).
strap. **I.** *n.* Courroie (*f.*): kūr″‿wā′. **II.** *v.* **1.** Attacher avec une courroie: at″‿ta″shē′ a″vek′‿ün kūr″‿wā′. **2.** Boucler: bū″-klē′ (*buckle*). **3.** Repasser: rə-pas″‿sē′ (*of a razor*). See STROP.—**straps and belt.** Buffleterie (*n. f.*): büf″‿flə-tə-rī′.—**supporting-straps.** Courroies de support: kūr″wā′ də süp″‿pēr′.
stratagem. Stratagème (*n. m.*): stra″ta″ʒām′.—**strategic,** *a.* Stratégique (*m. & f.*): stra″tē″ʒik′.—**strategy.** Stratégie (*n. f.*): stra″tē″ʒī′.
straw. Paille (*n. f.*): pai′‿yə.
strawberry. Fraise (*n. f.*): frāz.
stray, *v.* S'égarer: sē″ga″rē′.
stream, *n.* **1.** Courant (*m.*): kū″rāñ′ (*current*). **2.** Cours d'eau (*m.*): kūr dō (*water course.*) **3.** Fleuve (*m.*): flūv (*river*).—**down stream.** See DOWN.—**up s.** See under UP.
streamer. See POSTILION.
street. Rue (*n. f.*): rü.
strength, *n.* **1.** Force (*f.*): fērs. **2.** Effectif (*m.*): ef″fek″tīf′ (*of numbers*).—**at full strength.** Au complet: ō keñ″plē′.—**strengthen,** *v.* Renforcer: rañ″fer″sē′.
stretcher. Brancard (*n. m.*): brañ″kār′.—**stretcher-bearer.** Brancardier (*n. m.*): brañ″kar″di″‿yē′.—**wheeled-s.** Brouette à porte-brancard: brū″ēt′ a pert″brañ″kār′.
strike, *v.* **1.** Frapper: frap″‿pē′ (*hit*). (1) Amener: a″‿mə-nē′ (*haul down, as a flag*). (2) Baisser: bās″‿sē′ (*lower*). **2.** Sonner: señ″‿nē′ (*ring, as a clock*).—**to strike tents.** Lever le camp: lə-vē′ lə kañ.
striker, *n.* **1.** Marteau (*m.*): mar″tō′. **2.** Percuteur (de fusil) (*m.*): pār″kü″tūr′ (də fü″zī′).—**within striking distance.** À bonne portée de: a bōn per″tē′ də. See also under DISTANCE.
string. Ficelle (*n. f.*): fī″sel′.
stringer, *n.* Longeron (*n. m.*): leñ″‿ʒə-reñ′ (*lengthwise timber for rails*).
strip. **I.** *n.* Lambeau (*m.*): lañ″bō′ (*as of land*). **II.** *v.* Dépouiller: dē″pū″yē′.
stripe, *n.* **1.** Galon (*m.*): ga″leñ′. **2.** Chevron (*m.*): shə-vreñ′.
stroke (of a piston), *n.* Course (*f.*): kūrs; coup (*m.*): kū; mouvement (*m.*): mū″‿və-māñ′.
strong, *a.* **1.** Fort (*m.*): fer; forte (*f.*): fert. **2.** Formidable (*m. & f.*): fēr″mī″dā′‿blə.—**to muster strong.** Se rassembler en grand nombre: sə ras″‿sañ″blē′ añ grañ neñ′‿brə.
stronghold. **1.** Place forte (*f.*): plas fērt. **2.** Forteresse (*n. f.*): fer″‿tə-res′.
strop, *v.* Repasser sur le cuir: rə-pas″‿sē′ sür lə kwīr.
struggle. **I.** *n.* Lutte (*f.*): lüt. **II.** *v.* Lutter: lüt″‿tē′.
stubble. Chaume (*n. m.*): shōm.
stud, *n.* **1.** Tenon (*m.*): tə-neñ′ (*bolt of fire-arms*). **2.** Bouton de chemise (*n. m.*): bū″toñ′ də shə-mīz′.
style. **I.** *n.* **1.** Style (*m.*): stīl. **2.** Genre (*m.*): ʒāñ′‿rə. **II.** *v.* Appeler: ap″‿pə-lē′.
subaltern, *n.* Sous-lieutenant (*m.*): sū″lī″‿yū″‿tə-nāñ′.
sub-district. Sous-préfecture (*n. m.*): sū″prē″fek″tür′.
subdue, *v.* Maîtriser: mā″trī″zē′.—**a subdued voice.** Une voix étouffée: ün vwa ē″tūf″‿fē′.—**in a s. tone.** **1.** En baissant la voix: añ bās″‿sāñ′ la vwa (*lowering the voice*). **2.** D'un ton soumis: dañ teñ sū″mī′ (*subdued tone*).

ı = habit; aisle; au = *out*; oil; iū = *feud*;
diūne; chin; go; ŋ = sing; ship; thin; this.

subject. **I.** *a.* Sujet à: sü″ʒē′ a (with *to*). **II.** *v.* Soumettre à: sū″met′‿trə a.—**subject to other orders.** Sous réserve d'autres ordres: sū rē″zārv′ dō′‿trə ērd′‿rə.—**to subject oneself to.** S'exposer à: seks″pō″zē′ a.
sublimate. Sublimé (*n. m.*): süb″lī″mē′.
submarine. Sous-marin (*n. m.*): sū″ma″raṅ′.
submission. Soumission (*n. f.*): sū″mīs″‿sī″‿yeṅ′.
subordinate. Sous-ordre (*n. m.*): sūz″ēr′‿drə.
subsistence, *n.* **1.** Vivres (*m. pl.*): vī′‿vrə. **2.** Alimentation (*f.*): a″lī″maṅ″ta″sī″‿yeṅ′.
suburb. Faubourg (*n. m.*): fō″būr′. Abbreviated *Fbg.*
subway, *n.* **1.** Passage souterrain: pas″‿sāʒ′ sū″tār″raṅ′. **2.** [Paris.] Métro: mē″trō′.
succeed, *v.* Réussir: rē″üs″‿sīr′.
succeeded, *pa.* Réussi: rē″ü″sī′.
success, *n.* **1.** Succès (*m.*): sük″‿sē′. **2.** Bonne chance (*f.*): bōn′‿nə shaṅs (*good luck*).
succession, *n.* **1.** Succession (*f.*): sük″ses″‿sī″‿yeṅ′. **2.** Suite (*f.*): swīt.
such, *a.* **1.** Tel (*m.*), telle (*f.*): tel. **2.** Certain (*m.*): sār″taṅ′; certaine (*f.*): sār″tān′.—**give me such things as . . .** Donnez-moi des choses telles que . . . : deṅ″nē′ mwa dē shōz tel kə . . . .—**s. a one.** Un tel (*m.*): aṅ tel; une telle (*f.*): ün tel.—**s. as you.** Tel que vous: tel kə vū.
sudden, *a.* Soudain (*m.*): sū″daṅ′; soudaine (*f.*): sū″dān′.—**all of a sudden.** Tout d'un coup: tū daṅ kū.—**s. death.** Mort subite (*f.*): mōr sü″bīt′.
suffer, *v.* Souffrir: sūf″‿frīr′.—**do you suffer?** Souffrez-vous? sūf″‿frē′ vū. Compare PAIN.
sufficient, *a.* Suffisant (*m.*): süf″fī″zāṅ′; suffisante (*f.*): süf″-fī″zāṅ′‿tə.—**sufficient for.** Suffisant pour: süf″fī″zāṅ′ pūr.—**that is s.** Cela suffit: sə-lā′ süf″‿fī′.
sugar. Sucre (*n. m.*): sü′‿krə.—**some sugar, please.** Du sucre, s'il vous plaît: dü sü′‿krə, sīl vū plā.
suit, *v.* Convenir: keṅ″‿və-nīr′.
suit. **I.** *n.* **1.** Collection (*f.*): kel″‿lek″sī″‿yeṅ′. **2.** Nombre complet (*m.*): neṅ′‿brə keṅ″plē′ (*a complete set*). **II.** *v.* **1.** Adapter: a″dap″tē′. **2.** Convenir à: keṅ″‿və-nīr′ a (*be becoming to*).—**that just suits me.** **1.** Cela me convient: sə-lā′ mə keṅ″vī″‿yaṅ′. **2.** Cela fait mon affaire: sə-lā′ fā meṅ‿af″‿fār′ (*helps my interests*).—**suit of clothes.** Habillement complet: a″bī″‿yə-māṅ′ keṅ″plē′.
suitable. Approprié: ap″‿pro″prī″‿yē′. — **suitable to.** Adapté à: a″dap″tē′ a.
suitcase. Valise (*n. f.*): va″līz′.
suite (of rooms). Apartement (*n. m.*): ap″‿par″‿tə-māṅ′.
sultry, *a.* **1.** D'une chaleur brûlante: dün sha″lūr′ brü″lāṅt′‿ə. **2.** Étouffant (*m.*): ē″tūf″‿fāṅ′; étouffante (*f.*): ē″tūf″fāṅt′‿ə.
sum. **I.** *n.* Somme (*f.*): sōm. **II.** *v.* Additioner: ad″‿dī″sī″-yeṅ″‿nē′.—**to sum up the case.** Résumer les débats: rē″zü″-mē′ lē dē″bā′.
summer. **I.** *n.* Été (*m.*): ē″tē′. **II.** *v.* Passer l'été: pas″sē′ lē″tē′.
summit, *n.* **1.** Sommet (*m.*): som″mē′. **2.** Crête (*f.*): krāt.
summon, *v.* Sommer: som″‿mē′.—**summon the enemy to surrender.** Sommer l'ennemi de se rendre: som″mē′ len″‿nə-mī′ də sə rāṅ′‿drə.—**summons.** Sommation (*n. f.*): som″‿ma″sī″‿yeṅ′.
sump. Puisard (*n. m.*): pwī″zār′ (*mining*).
sun. Soleil (*n. m.*): so″lē′‿yə.
Sunday. Dimanche (*n. m.*): dī″māṅsh′.
sunken, *a.* Enfoncé (*m.*), enfoncée (*f.*): aṅ″feṅ″sē′ (*deep-set, said of the eyes in identification*).

artistic; ārt; fat; fāre; fast; get; prēy; hit; polīce; obey; gō; not; ōr; full; rūle; but; būrn; ə = final;

sunrise, *n.* Lever du soleil (*m.*): lə-vē′ dü sō″lē′‿yə.
sunset, *n.* Coucher du soleil (*m.*): kū″shē′ dü sō″lē′‿yə.
sunshine, *n.* Clarté du soleil (*f.*): klar″tē′ dü sō″lē′‿yə.—**broad sunshine.** Grand soleil: grañ sō″lē′‿yə.—**in the s.** Au soleil: ō sō″lē′‿yə.
sunstroke, *n.* **1.** Coup de soleil (*m.*): kū də sō″lē′‿yə. **2.** Insolation (*f.*): añ″so″la″sī″‿yoñ′.—**suffering from sunstroke.** Frappé d'insolation: frap″‿pē′ dañ″so″la″sī″‿yoñ′.
sup, *v.* Souper: sū″pē′.
superdreadnought, *n.* Cuirassé de première classe (*m.*): kwī″ras″‿sē′ də prə-mī″‿yār′ klās.
superintend, *v.* Surveiller: sür″vē″‿yē′.
superintendent, *n.* Surintendant (*m.*): sür″añ″tañ″dāñ′.—**superintendent of police.** Commissaire de police: kəm″mīs″‿sār′ də pō″līs′.
superior, *a.* Supérieur (*m.*), supérieure (*f.*): sü″pē″rī″‿yūr′.
superiority, *n.* Supériorité (*f.*): sü″pē″rī″ō″rī″tē′.
supersede, *v.* Remplacer: rañ″pla″sē′.
supervise, *v.* Surveiller: sür″vē″‿yē′.—**supervision.** Surveillance (*n. f.*): sür″vē″‿yāñs′.
supper. Souper (*n. m.*): sū″pē′.—**supper time.** L'heure de souper: lūr də sū″pē′.
supplement, *v.* Compléter: koñ″plē″tē′.
supplies, *n.* **1.** Approvisionnements: ap″prō″vī″zī″‿yoñ″‿nə-māñ′. **2.** Provisions (*f. pl.*): pro″vī″zī″‿yoñ′. **3.** Vivres (*m. pl.*): vī′‿vrə (*victuals*). **4.** Subsistances (*f. pl.*): süb″sīs″tāñs′. **5.** Renforts (*m. pl.*): rañ″fōr′.—**director of supplies.** Directeur d'étapes et des services (*n. m.*): dī″rek″tūr′ dē″tāp′ ē dē sār″vīs′.—**regimental s.** Vivres régimentaires: vī′vrə rē″ʒī″mañ″tār′.
supply. **I.** *n.* Approvisionnement (*n. m.*): ap″prō″vī″zī″‿yoñ″-nə-māñ′. See SUPPLIES. **II.** *v.* Fournir: fūr″nīr′.—**artillery supply service.** Service de l'artillerie: sār″vīs′ də lar″tī″‿yə-rī′.—**daily s.** Approvisionnement quotidien: ap″‿prō″vī″zī″‿yoñ″‿nə-māñ′ ko″tī″dī″‿yañ′.—**occasional s.** Approvisionnement d'occasion: ap″‿prō″vī″zī″yoñ″‿nə-māñ′ dək″‿ka″zī″‿yoñ′.—**s. column. 1.** Colonne de ravitaillement: ko″lōn′ də ra″vī″ta″‿yə-māñ′ (*revictualing*). **2.** Colonne d'approvisionnement: ko″lōn′ dap″‿prō″-vī″zī″‿yoñ″‿nə-māñ′.—**s. department.** Service de l'intendance: sār″vīs′ də lañ″tañ″dāñs′ (*commissariat*).—**s. officers.** Officiers de l'intendance: of″‿fī″sī″‿yē′ də lañ″tañ″dāñs′.—**supply-ship.** Vaisseau d'approvisionnement (*n. m.*): vēs″‿sō′ dap″‿prō″vī″zī″‿yoñ″‿nə-māñ′.
support. **I.** *n.* **1.** Action de supporter, ou soutenir: ak″sī″‿yoñ′ də süp″‿pōr″tē′, ū sū″‿tə-nīr′. **2.** (1) Soutien (*m.*): sū″tī″‿yañ′ (*maintenance*). (2) Support (*m.*): süp″‿pōr′ (*prop*). **3.** Appui (*m.*): a″pwī′ (*base of support*). **4.** *pl.* Les grand' gardes: lē grañ gard (*outposts*). **II.** *v.* **1.** Soutenir: sū″‿tə-nīr′ (*uphold, sustain*). **2.** Appuyer: ap″‿pwī″yē′ (*back up*). **3.** Supporter: süp″-pōr″tē′ (*tolerate, endure*). **4.** Entretenir: añ″‿trə-tə-nīr′ (*provide the necessaries of life*).—**support an attack.** Appuyer une attaque: ap″‿pwī″yē′ ün‿at″‿tāk′.—**supporting point.** Point d'appui: pwañ dap″‿pwī′.—**to support the infantry advance.** Soutenir la marche en avant de l'infanterie: sū″‿tə‿nīr′ la marsh añ a″vāñ′ də lañ″fañ″‿tə-rī′.
suppress, *v.* **1.** Réprimer: rē″prī″mē′. **2.** Contenir: koñ″tə-nīr′ (*check*).
surcingle, *n.* **1.** Surfaix (*m.*): sür″fē′. **2.** Sangle (*f.*): sāŋ′‿[glə.
sure, *a.* **1.** Sûr: sür. **2.** Assuré (*m.*), assurée (*f.*): as″sü″rē′.
surface, *n.* Surface (*f.*): sür″fās′.
surgeon. **1.** *Milit.* Médecin: mē″də-sañ′. **2.** Chirurgien (*n. m.*): shī″rür″ʒī″‿yañ′.—**assistant surgeon.** Médecin aide-major: mē″də-sañ′ ād″ma″ʒōr′.—**field s.** Médecin d'ambulance: mē″də-sañ′ dañ″bü″lāñs′.—**military s.** Médecin militaire: mē″-

ı = habit; aisle; au = out; oil; iū = feud; düne; chin; go; ŋ = sing; ship; thin; this.

də-saṅ' mī"lī"tār'.—**s.-colonel.** Médecin principal de première classe: mē"də-saṅ' praṅ"sī"pāl' də prə-mī"‿yār' klās'‿sə.—**s.-general.** Médecin inspecteur général: mē"də-saṅ' aṅ"spek"tūr' ʒē"nē"rāl'.—**s. lieutenant-colonel.** Médecin principal de deuxième classe: mē"də-saṅ' praṅ"sī"pāl' də du"zī"‿yām' klās'‿sə.—**s.-major.** Médecin-major de première classe: mē"də-saṅ' ma"ʒōr' də prə-mī"yār' klās'‿sə.—**s. major-general.** Médecin inspecteur: mē"də-saṅ' aṅ"spek"tūr'.

surgical, *a.* Chirurgical (*m.*), chirurgicale (*f.*): shī"rür"ʒī"kāl'.—**surgical ambulance motor-car.** Ambulance chirurgicale automobile: aṅ"bü"lāṅs' shī"rür"ʒī"kāl' ē"to"mō"bīl'.

surname, *n.* Nom de famille (*m.*): neṅ də fa"mī'‿yə.

surprize. I. *n.* **1.** Surprise (*f.*): sür"prīz'. **2.** Coup de main: kū də maṅ (*unexpected attack*). **3.** Étonnement (*m.*): ē"ten"‿nə-māṅ' (*astonishment*). **II.** *v.* Surprendre: sür"prāṅ'‿drə.—**to take by surprize.** Surprendre: sür"prāṅ'‿drə.—**to take one by s.** Prendre au dépourvu: prāṅ'‿drə ō dē"pūr"vü'.

surrender. I. *n.* **1.** Reddition (*f.*): red"‿dī"sī"‿yeṅ' (*military*). **2.** Renonciation (*f.*): rə-neṅ"sī"a"sī"‿yeṅ' (*of a claim*). **II.** *v.* **1.** Se rendre: sə rāṅ'‿drə. **2.** Se livrer: sə līv"rē'.

surround, *v.* **1.** Cerner: sār"nē' (*invest*). **2.** Entourer: aṅ"-tū"rē' (*encompass*). **3.** Encercler: aṅ"sār"klē' (*encircle*). **4.** Environner: aṅ"vī"reṅ"‿nē'.—**surrounded,** *a.* Entouré: aṅ"tū"rē'.—**surrounding,** *a.* Environnant (*m.*): aṅ"vī"reṅ"‿nāṅ'; environnante (*f.*): aṅ"vī"reṅ"‿nāṅt'.—**surrounding country.** Terrain environnant: tār"raṅ' aṅ"vī"reṅ"‿nāṅ'.

survey. I. *n.* **1.** Vue (*f.*): vü. **2.** Arpentage (*m.*): ar"paṅ"tāʒ' (*land survey*). **II.** *v.* **1.** Examiner: eg"za"mī"nē'. **2.** Arpenter: ar"paṅ"tē'.—**surveyed,** *pp.* Tracé (*m.*), tracée (*f.*): tra"sē'.

suspect, *v.* Soupçonner: sūp"seṅ"‿nē'.

suspicion, *n.* Soupçon (*m.*): sūp"seṅ'.

suspicious, *a.* Suspect (*m.*), suspecte (*f.*): süs"pekt'.

sutler. 1. Cantinier (*m.*): kaṅ"tī"nī"‿yē'. **2.** Vivandier (*m.*): vī"vaṅ"dī"‿yē'; vivandière (*f.*): vī"vaṅ"dī"yār'.

S. W., *abbr.* Shell-wound. Blessure d'obus: bles"‿sür' dō"bü'.

swallow. I. *n.* Hirondelle (*f.*): ī"reṅ"del' (*bird*). **II.** *v.* Avaler: a"va"lē' (*food or drink*).

swamp, *n.* **1.** Lette (*f.*): lēt. **2.** Marais (*m.*): ma"rā'.

swank, swaŋk, *v.* & *n.* Swagger; bluster.

swear, *v.* Jurer: ʒü"rē'.

sweat. I. *n.* Sueur (*f.*): sü"ūr'. **II.** *v.* Suer: sü"ē'.

sweater, *n.* **1.** Tricot (*m.*): trī"kō'. **2.** Vareuse (*f.*): va"rūz'. **3.** Chandail (*m.*): shaṅ"dā'‿yə.

Sweden, *n.* La Suède: la swād.

sweep, *v.* Balayer: ba"lā"‿yē'.—**sweep the approaches.** Balayer les approches: ba"lā"‿yē' lēz‿ap"‿prōsh'.

sweet, *a.* Doux (*m.*): dū; douce (*f.*): dūs.—**you're a sweet youth!** Vous êtes un joli garçon! vūs‿āt aṅ ʒō"lī' gar"soṅ'.

sweetbread, *n.* Ris de veau (*m.*): rī də vō.

swim, *v.* Nager: na"ʒē'.—**to swim across.** Traverser à la nage: tra"vār"sē' a la nāʒ.—**to s. over.** Passer à la nage: pas"‿sē' a la nāʒ.

swindle, *n.* Escroquerie (*f.*): es"kro"‿kə-rī'.—**swindler,** *n.* Chevalier d'industrie (*m.*): shə-va"lī"‿yē' daṅ"düs"trī'.

swingle-tree. Palonnier (*n. m.*): pa"leṅ"‿nyē'.

switch. Aiguille (*n. f.*): ā"gwīl' (*points of a railway-track*).—**to switch off.** Couper l'allumage: kū"pē' lal"‿lü"māʒ'.—**to s. on.** Mettre l'allumage: mēt'‿trə lal"‿lü"māʒ'.—**switchman.** Aiguilleur (*n. m.*): ā"gwī"‿yūr'.

Switzerland, *n.* La Suisse: la swīs'‿sə.

swivel, *n.* **1.** Mousqueton (*m.*): mūs"‿kə-teṅ'. **2.** Pierrier (*m.*): pī"‿yār"‿rī"‿yē'. Called also **swivel-gun.**

swooning. Évanouissement (*n. m.*): ē"van"ū"īs"‿sə-māṅ'.

sword (saber), *n.* **1.** Épée (*f.*): ē″pē′. **2.** Sabre (*m.*): sā′‿brə. —**draw swords!** Sabre main! sā′‿brə man.—**present swords!** Présentez sabre! prē″zan″tē′ sā′‿brə.—**return s.!** Remettez sabre: rə‿met″‿tē′ sā′‿brə.—**slope s.** Portez sabre: pōr″tē′ sā′‿brə.—**sword-cut,** *n.*, **s.-thrust,** *n.* Coup d'épée (*f.*): kū dē″pē′. —**s.-knot.** Dragonne (*n. f.*): dra″gōn′.

sworn, *pa.* Assermenté: as″‿sār″man″tē′.

sympathize (with), *v.* Sympathiser avec: san″pa″tī″zē′ a″vek′.

sympathy. Sympathie (*n. f.*): san″pa″tī′.

synagogue. Synagogue (*n. f.*): sī″na″gōg′. Abbreviated *Syne.*

syncope. Syncope (*n. f.*): san″kōp′ (*faintness*).

syringe. I. *n.* Seringue (*f.*): sə-raŋ′. **II.** *v.* **1.** Seringuer: sə-ran″gē′. **2.** Injecter: an″ʒek″tē′.—**hypodermic syringe.** Seringue hypodermique: sə-raŋ′ ī″po″dār″mīk′.

system, *n.* **1.** Système (*m.*): sīs″tām′. **2.** Réseau (*m.*): rē″zō′ (*as of railways*). **3.** Régime (*m.*): rē″ʒīm′.

T

table, *n.* Table (*f.*): tā′‿blə.—**table-land.** Plateau (*n. m.*): pla″tō′. Abbreviated *Plau.*—**table of mobilization stores.** Tableaux d'approvisionnements de mobilisation: ta″blō′ dap″‿pro″-vī″zī″ən″‿nə-mān′ də mo″bī″lī″za″sī″‿yen′.

tackle. Attirail (*n. m.*): at″‿tī″rai′ (*blocks and ropes*).

tactics, *n. pl.* Tactique (*n. f. sing.*): tak″tīk′.

tag, *n.* Fiche (*f.*): fīsh. In army hospital service a **red tag** (*fiche rouge*) is attached to a patient whose case is transferable and a **white tag** (*fiche blanche*) to one whose case is not transferable.—**transit tag.** Fiche d'évacuation (*f.*): fīsh dē″va″kü″a″-sī″‿yen′.

tail. Queue (*n. f.*): kū.—**tail-skid,** *n.* **1.** Crosse de queue (*f.*): krōs də kū. **2.** Patin de queue (*m.*): pa″tan′ də kū.

tailor. Tailleur (*n. m.*): tai″‿yūr′.

take, *v.* Prendre: prān′‿drə. In the imperative **prenez!** prə-nē′.—**take advantage of.** Profiter de: pro″fī″tē′ də.—**t. arms.** Rompez les faisceaux: ron″pē′ lē fes″‿so′.—**t. by surprize.** Surprendre: sür″prān′‿drə.—**t. care!** Veillez! vē″‿yē′.—**t. care of (someone).** Soignez-le: swa″‿nyē′ lə.—**t. down. 1.** Faire descendre: fār dē″sān′‿drə (*an object*). **2.** Coucher par écrit: kū″shē′ pār ē″krī′ (*in writing*).—**to t. in coal.** Faire du charbon: fār dü shar″ben′.—**to t. in water.** Faire de l'eau: fār də lō.—**take me to.** Conduisez-moi à: ken″dwī″zē′ mwa a.—**t. notes.** Prendre des notes: prān′‿drə dē nōt.—**t. off,** *v.* **1.** Ôter: ō″tē′. **2.** Enlever: an″‿lə-vē′.—**t. over. 1.** Prendre en main: prān′‿drə an man. **2.** Se charger de: sə shar″ʒē′ də.—**t. part in.** Prendre part à: prān″drə pārt‿a.

talk, *v.* Parler: par″lē′. See SPEAK.

talker, *n.* **1.** Causeur (*m.*): kō″zūr′; causeuse (*f.*): kō″zūz′. **2.** Vantard (*m.*): van″tār′ (*blow hard*).

talking, *n.* Conversation (*f.*): ken″vār″sa″sī″‿yen′.

tall, *a.* Haut (*m.*): hō; haute (*f.*): hōt.

tam-o-shanter. Béret (*n. m.*): bē″rē′.

tamping. Bourrage (*n. m.*): būr″‿rāʒ′.

tank, *n.* **1.** Réservoir (*m.*): rē″zēr″vwār′ (*water, or gas-tank*). Abbreviated *Rroir.* **2.** Tank (*m.*): tank (*armored vehicle*).—**tank-wagon.** Wagon réservoir (*m.*): va″gen′ rē″zēr″vwār′.

tap. I. *n.* Robinet (*m.*): ro″bī″nē′ (*faucet*). **II.** *v.* **1.** Taper: ta″pē′ (*cut in*). **2.** Frapper: frap″‿pē′ (*hit*). **3.** Faire la ponction, le branchement: fār la penk″sī″‿yen′, lə bran″‿shə-mān′.—**to tap a wire.** (*Teleg.*) **1.** Taper un fil: ta″pē′ an fīl. **2.** Intercepter une communication: an″tār″sep″tē′ ün kem″mü″nī″kā″sī″yen′.

taproom. Estaminet (*n. m.*): es″ta″mī″nē′.

taps. Same as LIGHTS OUT. See under LIGHT.

artistic; ārt; fat; fāre; fast; get; prēy; hit; polīce; obey; gō; not; ōr; full; rūle; but; būrn; ə = final;

target. **1.** Objectif (*n. m.*): ob″ʒek″tīf′. **2.** Cible (*n. f.*): sī′‿blə.—**bull's-eye target.** Cible réglementaire: sī′blə rē″‿glə-mañ″tār′.—**disappearing t.** Cible à éclipse: sī′‿blə a ē″klīp′sə.—**figure t.** Cible silhouette: sī′‿blə sī″lū″āt′.—**moving** or **running t.** Cible mobile: sī′‿blə mō″bīl′.—**stationary t.** Cible fixe: sī′‿blə fīks.—**target practice.** Tirer à la cible: tī″rē′ a la sī′‿blə.

tarpaulin. **1.** Toile goudronnée (*n. f.*): twāl gū″dron″nē′. **2.** Prélart (*n. m.*): prē″lār′. **3.** Bâche (*n. f.*): bā′shə (*of a wagon*).

tart, *n.* Tarte (*f.*): tārt′‿ə.

task, *n.* **1.** Travail (*m.*): tra″vai′ (*labor*). **2.** Ouvrage (*m.*): ū″vrā′‿ʒə (*work*). **3.** Devoir (*m.*): də-vwār′ (*duty*). **4.** Rôle (*m.*): rōl (*part*).

taste. **I.** *n.* Goût (*n. m.*): gū. **II.** *v.* Goûter: gū″tē′.

tattoo. **I.** *n.* Retraite (*f.*): rə-trāt′. **II.** *v.* Tatouer: ta″tū″ē′.

tattooing. Tatouage (*n. m.*): ta″tū″āʒ′.

taube. Taube (*n. m.*): tō′‿bə (*German aeroplane*).

tcha, tshā, *n.* [Rus.] Tea.

tea, *n.* Thé (*n. m.*): tē.—**make tea.** Faire le thé: fār lə tē.—**teacup.** Tasse à thé: tas‿a tē.

teach, *v.* **1.** Instruire: añ″strwīr′ (*instruct*). **2.** Enseigner: añ″sē″‿nyē′ (*inform*).

team, *n.* **1.** Attelage (*m.*): at″‿tə-lāʒ′ (*of horses*). **2.** Camp (*m.*): kañ (*of games*).—**unhitch the team.** Dételer l'attelage: dē″‿tə-lē′ lat″‿tə-lāʒ′.

teapot. Théière (*n. f.*): tē″‿yār′.—**tea-time.** L'heure de thé: lūr də tē.

tear. **I.** *n.* **1.** Déchirure: dē″shī″rür′ (*of clothes,* etc.). **2.** Larme (*n. f.*): lārm (*of weeping*). **II.** *v.* Déchirer: dē″shī″rē′.—**to tear up a railway.** Enlever les rails d'un chemin de fer: añ″-lə-vē′ lē rai dañ shə-mañ′ də fār.

teeth. Dents (*n. f. pl.*): dañ.—**filled teeth.** Dents plombées: dañ plon″bē′.

telegram. Dépêche (*n. f.*): dē″pāsh′.

telegraph. **I.** *n.* Télégraphe (*m.*): tē″lē″grāf′. Abbreviated *Télége.* **II.** *v.* Télégraphier: tē″lē″gra″fī″‿yē′.—**telegraphing apparatus.** Appareil télégraphique: ap″pa″rē′‿ya tē″lē″gra″fīk′.—**telegraph-junction.** Poste de jonction télégraphique: pōst də ʒoṅk″sī″‿yoṅ′ tē″lē″gra″fīk′.—**t.-post,** *n.* Poteau télégraphique (*m.*): pō″tō′ tē″lē″gra″fīk′.—**t.-wire,** *n.* **1.** Fil télégraphique (*m.*): fīl tē″lē″gra″fīk′ (*specific use*). **2.** Télégraphe (*m.*): tē″lē″-grāf′ (*in general use*).—**to lay a t. line.** Installer une ligne télégraphique: añ″stal″‿lē′ ün lī′‿nyə tē″lē″gra″fīk′.

telegraphist. Télégraphiste (*n. m.*): tē″lē″gra″fīst′.

telegraphy. Télégraphie (*n. f.*): tē″lē″gra″fī′.—**air-line telegraphy.** Télégraphie aérienne: tē″lē″gra″fī′ a″ē″rī″‿yen′.—**cable** or **underground t.** Télégraphie souterraine: tē″lē″gra″fī′ sū″tār″rān′.—**wireless t.** Télégraphie sans fil: tē″lē″gra″fī′ sañ fīl.

telemetrist. Télémétriste (*n. m.*): tē″lē″mē″trīst′ (*one who gages distance for artillery*).

telephone. Téléphone (*n. m.*): tē″lē″fōn′.—**telephone message.** Message téléphonique: mes″sāʒ′ tē″lē″fo″nīk′.

telescope, *n.* **1.** Télescope (*m.*): tē″les″kōp′ (*specific*). **2.** Lunette (*f.*): lü″net′ (*any glass used to look through or with*).

tell, *v.* Dire: dīr.—**tell me, please . . .** Dites-moi s'il vous plaît . . . : dīt mwa, sīl vū plā.—**to t. off.** **1.** Énumérer (*v.*): ē″nü″mē″rē′ (*of articles*). **2.** Désigner (*v.*): dē″zī″‿nyē′ (*of men*). **3.** Détacher (*v.*): dē″ta″shē′ (*of troops*).

temper, *n.* Colère (*f.*): ko″lār′ (*anger*).—**bad temper.** Mauvaise humeur (*f.*): mō″vāz′ ü″mūr′.—**good t.** Bonne humeur: bōn‿ü″mūr′.

temperature. Température (*f.*): tañ″pē″ra″tür′.—**temperature-chart,** *n.* Feuille de température (*f.*): fū‿yə də tañ″pē″ra″-tür′.

i = habit; aisle; au = *out*; oil; iū = feud; dūne; chin; go; ŋ = si*ng*; ship; thin; this.

temple. Temple (*n. m.*): tăn'‿plə.
temporary. Temporaire: taṅ"po"rār'.
ten, *a.* Dix: dīs. When used before a consonant, pronounced dī; when before a vowel or silent *h*, dīz; when occurring at the end of a clause, dīs.—**ten o'clock.** Dix heures: dīz‿ūr.—**ten thousand.** Dix mille: dī mīl.—**tenth,** *a.* Dixième: dī"zī"‿yām'.
tender. **I.** *a.* **1.** Tendre: tăn'‿drə. **2.** Délicat: dē"lī"kā' (*effeminate*). **II.** *n.* Soumission (*f.*): sū"mīs"‿sī"‿yəṅ'.
tendon. Tendon (*n. m.*): taṅ"dəṅ'.
tent, *n.* **1.** Tente (*f.*): taṅt. **2.** Pavillon (*m.*): pa"vī"‿yəṅ'. —**ambulance=tent.** Tente tourtoise: taṅt tūr"twāz'.—**bell= or circular t.** Tente conique: taṅt ko"nīk'.—**field=t.** Tente de marche: taṅt də mār'‿shə.—**hospital=t.** Tente d'ambulance: taṅt daṅ"bü"lāṅs'.—**ridge=tent.** Tente à traverse: taṅt a tra"vārs'.—**shelter t.** Tente=abri (*f.*): taṅt‿a"brī'.—**t.=ditch** or **furrow.** Rigole (*n. f.*): rī"gōl'.—**t.=flooring.** Plancher de tente: plaṅ"shē' də taṅt.—**t.=peg.** Piquet (*m.*): pī"kē'.—**t.=pole.** Montant (*m.*): məṅ"tāṅ'.—**t.=rope.** Corde de tente: kōrd də taṅt.—**to pitch one's tent.** Dresser sa tente: dres"‿sē' sa taṅt.—**to strike t.** Lever les tentes: lə-vē' lē taṅt.—**wall t.** Tente à parois, ou pentes: taṅt a pa"rwā', u paṅt.
term. Expression (*n. f.*): eks"prēs"‿sī"‿yəṅ'.
terminal, *n.* **1.** Fin (*f.*): faṅ. **2.** Borne (*f.*): bōrn (*in electricity*). See also BOUNDARY; LANDMARK.
terrain, *n.* Terrain (*m.*): tār"‿raṅ'.
territorial, *a.* Territorial (*m.*): tār"‿rī"tō"rī"‿yāl'.
test, *v.* **1.** Faire l'épreuve de: fār lē"prūv' də. **2.** Éprouver: ē"prū"vē'.—**to put to the test.** Mettre à l'épreuve: met'‿trə a lē"prūv'.
testicle. Testicule (*n. m.*): tes"tī"kül'.
testimonial. Certificat (*n. m.*): sār"tī"fī"kā'.
testimony. Déposition (*n. f.*): dē"pō"zī"sī"‿yəṅ'.
thank, *v.* **1.** Remercier de: rə-mār"sī"‿yē' də (*for or of a thing*). **2.** Remercier pour: rə-mār"sī"‿yē' pūr (*for or of a person*). —**I thank you.** Je vous remercie: ʒə vū rə-mār"sī'.—**many thanks.** Mille remercîments: mīl rə-mār"sī"māṅ'.—**thank you.** Merci: mār"sī'.
that. **I.** *a.* **1.** Ce (*m.*): sə; cette (*f.*): set. **2.** Ce là (*m.*): sə la; cet là (*m.*): set la; cette lā (*f.*): set la. **II.** *conj.* Que: kə; as, **I have heard that you . . .** J'ai appris que vous . . . : ʒā ap"‿prī' kə vū. **III.** *pron.* **1.** Celui=là (*m.*): sə-lwī"lā' (*that one*); celle=là (*f.*): sel"lā'. **2.** Lequel (*m.*): lə-kel'; laquelle (*f.*): la"kel'. **3.** Qui (*m. & f.*): kī.—**that is to say.** C'est=à=dire: sāt‿a-dīr.
thatch. Chaume (*n. m.*): shōm.
thaw. **I.** *n.* Dégel (*m.*): dē"ʒēl'. **II.** *v.* Dégeler: dē"ʒə‿lē'.
the. Le (*m.*): lə; la (*f.*): la; when stressed, lā. Both abbreviated *l'* before vowels. In the *plural* (*m. & f.*) les: lē.—**at the.** **1.** Au (*m.*): ō. **2.** À la (*f.*): a la.—**from the.** Du (*m.*): dü. *Plural* des: dē.—**of the.** De la (*f.*): də la. *Plural* des: dē.—**to the.** **1.** Au (*m.*): ō. **2.** À la (*f.*): a la.
theater. Théâtre (*n. m.*): tē"ā'‿trə.—**theater of war.** Théâtre de la guerre: tē"ā'‿trə də la gār.
thee, *pron.* Toi: twa; te: tə.
their, *pron.* Leur (*sing.*), leurs (*pl.*): lūr.
theirs, *pron.* À eux (*m. pl.*): a ū; à elles (*f. pl.*): a el (*to them*).
them, *pron.* **1.** Eux (*m. pl.*): ū; elles (*f. pl.*): el. **2.** Les (*m. & f. pl.*): lē.—**to them.** Same as THEIRS.—**themselves,** *pron.* Eux=mêmes (*m. pl.*): ū"mām'; elles=mêmes (*f. pl.*): el"mām'.
then. **I.** *adv.* **1.** Alors: a"lōr'. **2.** Ensuite: aṅ"swīt'. **II.** *conj.* Donc: dəṅk.
thence, *adv.* **1.** De là: də la (*from there* or *that place*). **2.** Par l.: par la (*through there* or *that place*).
theory. Théorie (*n. f.*): tē"ō"rī'.

there, *adv.* Là: lä (*place*).—**here and there.** Par-ci par-là: par″sī′ par″lä′.—**t. is, t. are.** 1. Voilà: vwa″lä′. 2. Il y a: il‿ī a.—**t. are no.** Il n'y a pas de: il nī a pa də.—**t. is no.** Il n'y a pas de: il nī a pa də.—**t. he is.** Le voilà: lə vwa″lä′.
thereby. Par ce moyen: par sə mwa″yañ′.
therefore. Donc: deñk.
thermal. Thermal: tēr″māl′.
thermometer. Thermomètre (*n. m.*): tār″mo″mā′‿trə.
these, *pron.* 1. Ces (*m. & f. pl.*): sē. 2. Ceux-ci (*m. pl.*): sū″-sī′; celles-ci (*f. pl.*): sel″sī′.
they, *pron.* Ils (*m. pl.*): īl; elles (*f. pl.*): ēl. *Followed by a relative:* ceux (*m. pl.*): sū; celles (*f. pl.*): sel.—**they say.** On dit: eñ dī.—**t. have.** Ils ont: īlz‿eñ.—**t. have not.** Ils n'ont pas: īl neñ pū.—**t. were.** Ils étaient: īlz‿ē″tē′.
thick, *a.* 1. Épais (*m.*): ē″pā′; épaisse (*f.*): ē″pās′. 2. Gros (*m.*): grō; grosse (*f.*): grōs.—**in the thick of the fight.** Au plus fort de la mêlée: ō plü fōr də la mā″lē′.—**thick-set,** *a.* Trapu (*m.*), trapue (*f.*): tra″pü′ (*of persons*).
thicket, *n.* 1. Buisson (*m.*): bwī″señ′. 2. Bosquet (*m.*): bos″kē′.
thigh. Cuisse (*n. f.*): kwīs.
thin, *a.* 1. Maigre (*m. & f.*): mā′‿grə (*of the body*). 2. Mince (*m. & f.*): mañs (*slender, as of the waist*).
thing. Chose (*n. f.*): shōz.
think, *v.* 1. Penser: pañ″sē′. 2. Croire: krwar (*guess, imagine, suppose*).
third, *a. & n.* Troisième: trwa″zī″‿yām′.
thirst. Soif (*n. f.*): swaf.—**to be thirsty or feel thirst.** Avoir soif: a″vwār′ swaf.—**we are very thirsty.** Nous avons grand' soif: nūz‿a″veñ′ grañd swaf.
thirteen, *a. & n.* Treize: trāz.—**thirteenth,** *a. & n.* Treizième: trā″zī″‿yām′.—**thirtieth,** *a. & n.* Trentième: trañ″tī″‿yām′.
thirty, *a. & n.* Trente: trañt.—**thirty-one.** Trente et un: trañt‿ē añ.—**t.-two.** Trente-deux: trañt dū.
this, *a.* (*demonst.*). Ce (*m.*): sə; cet (*m.*): set; cette (*f.*): set.
thoroughbred. De pur sang: də pür sañ.
thoroughfare. Chemin: shə-mañ′.—**no thoroughfare.** 1. Rue barrée (*n. f.*): rü bar″‿rē′. 2. Passage interdit au public: pas″‿sāʒ′ añ″tār″dī′ ō pü″blīk′.—**main t.** Chemin de grande communication: shə-mañ′ də grañd kem″‿mü″nī″ka″sī″‿yeñ′.
those, *a. & pron.* Ces (*m. pl.*): sé; celles (*f. pl.*): sel.
thought, *n.* 1. Pensée (*f.*): pañ″sē′. 2. Idée (*f.*): ī″dē′.
thousand, *a. & n.* Mille: mīl.—**thousandth,** *a. & n.* Millième: mīl″‿yām′.
thread. I. *n.* Fil (*m.*): fīl. II. *v.* Enfiler: añ″fī″lē′ (*pass through*).
threaten, *v.* Menacer: mə-na″sē′.—**threatened,** *pa.* Menacé (*m.*), menacée (*f.*): mə-na″sē′.
three, *a. & n.* Trois: trwa.—**a quarter to three.** Trois heures moins quart: trwaz‿ūr mwañ kar (*time*).
thresh, *v.* Battre: būt′‿trə (*of grain*).
threshold, *n.* Seuil (*m.*): sū′‿yə.
thrice, *adv.* Trois fois: trwa fwa.
throat. Gorge (*n. f.*): gōrʒ.
through. I. *a.* Direct (*m.*), directe (*f.*): dī″rek′‿tə. II. *adv.* D'un bout à l'autre: dañ bū a lō′‿trə. III. *prep.* 1. À travers: a tra″vār′. 2. Par: par.—**through train.** Train direct: trañ dī″rekt′.
throw, *v.* Lancer: lañ″sē′.—**to throw a bomb.** Jeter une bombe: ʒə-tē′ ün boñb. See also DROP.—**t. out.** Pousser en avant: pūs″‿sē′ añ‿a″vāñ′.
thrush. 1. Teigne (*n. f.*): tā′‿nyə (*a disease of a horse's foot, etc.*). 2. Mal de fourchette: mal də fūr″shet′.

thrust, *n.* Coup de pointe (*m.*): kū də pwant.—**to thrust back.** Repousser: rə-pūs″‿sē′.
thumb, *n.* Pouce (*m.*): pūs.
thunder. I. *n.* Tonnerre (*m.*): ten″‿nār′. **II.** *v.* Tonner: ten″nē′.
Thursday. Jeudi (*n. m.*): ʒū″dī′.
thus, *adv.* Ainsi: an″sī′.
ticket. I. *n.* **1.** Fiche (*f.*): fīsh. See TAG. **2.** Billet (*n. m.*): bī″‿yē′. **II.** *v.* **1.** Étiqueter: ē″tī″‿kə-tē′. **2.** Numéroter: nü″mē″ro″tē′.—**give up your ticket.** Rendez votre billet: ran″dē′ vō′‿trə bī″‿yē′.—**please give me a ticket to . . .** Donnez-moi un billet pour . . ., s'il vous plaît: don″‿nē′ mwa an bī″‿yē′ pūr . . . sīl vū plā.—**ticket-clerk.** Buraliste (*n. m.*): bü″ra″līst′ (*station agent*).—**t.-collector.** Contrôleur (*n. m.*): ken″trōl″‿lūr′.
tide, *n.* **1.** Marée (*f.*): ma″rē′ (*sea*). **2.** Cours (*m.*): kūr (*events*).
tie. I. *n.* **1.** Traverse (*f.*): tra″vārs′ (*railway-sleeper*). **2.** Cravate (*f.*): kra″vāt′ (*neck scarf*). **II.** *v.* Attacher: at″‿ta″shē′.
tile. I. *n.* Tuile (*f.*): twīl. **II.** *v.* Carreler: kar″‿rə-lē′.—**tile-kiln.** Four à tuiles: fūr a twīl.
till, *prep.* **1.** Jusqu'à: ʒüs″kā′. **2.** Jusqu'à ce que: ʒüs″kā′ sə kə.—**till to-morrow.** À demain: a də-man′.
timber. Bois (*n. m.*): bwa.—**timbering,** *n.* **1.** Coffrage (*m.*): kef″‿frāʒ′ (*of trench and mine supports*). **2.** Boisage (*m.*): bwa″sāʒ′ (*of woodwork in general*).—**timber-work.** Charpente (*n. f.*): shar″pānt′.—**t. yard.** Chantier de bois de construction: shan″tī″‿yē′ də bwa də ken″strük″sī″‿yen′.
time. I. *n.* **1.** Temps (*m.*): tan (*specified space of time*). **2.** Terme (*m.*): tārm (*period, term*). **3.** Fois (*f.*): fwa (*multiplied or repeated*). **II.** *v.* Régler: rē″glē′.—**at any time.** À tout moment: a tū mō″mān′.—**at such times.** À de tels moments: a də tel mo″mān′.—**double time.** See DOUBLE.—**for some t.** Pour quelque temps: pūr kel′‿kə tan.—**from t. to t.** De temps en temps: də tanz‿an tan.—**in opportune t.** En temps opportun: an tans‿ep″‿pēr″tun′.—**mark t.** See MARK.—**so timed as.** Réglé tellement que: rē″glē′ tel″mān′ kə.—**there is no time to lose.** Il n'y a pas de temps à perdre: īl nī a pa də tans‿a pār′‿drə.—**the right t. 1.** L'heure juste (*f.*): lūr ʒüst′‿ə. **2.** Le vrai moment: lə vrā mē″mān′.—**t. of departure.** Heure de départ: ūr də dē″pār′.—**to gain t.** Gagner du temps: ga″‿nyē′ dü tan.—**what time is it?** Quelle heure est-il? kel‿ūr‿et‿īl.
time-table, *n.* **1.** Indicateur des chemins de fer (*m.*): an″dī″ka″tūr′ dē shə-man′ də fār. **2.** Horaire (*m.*): ēr″ār′. **3.** Liste des heures de départ et d'arrivée (*f.*): līst dēz‿ūr də dē″pār′ ē dar″‿rī″vē′.
timely. I. *a.* **1.** Juste (*m. & f.*): ʒüst. **2.** Convenable (*m. & f.*): ken″‿və-nā′‿blə. **II.** *adv.* **1.** À propos: a pro″pō′. **2.** En temps opportun: an tans‿op″‿per″tun′.
tin. Bidon (*n. m.*): bī″den′ (*can* or *tin cup*).
tincture of iodine. Teinture d'iode (*f.*): tan″tür′ dī″ōd′.
tire, *n.* **1.** Jante (*f.*): ʒant (*felly*). **2.** Bandage (*m.*): ban″dāʒ′ (*metal wheel*). **3.** Pneumatique (*m.*): nū″ma″tīk′ (*motor-car wheel*). See BURST, DEFLATE, INFLATE, etc.—**spare t.** Pneu de rechange (*n. m.*): nū də rə-shānʒ′.
tired, *pa.* Fatigué (*m.*), fatiguée (*f.*): fa″tī″gē′.
to, *prep.* À: a.—**to the.** Au (*m.*): ō; à la (*f.*): a la.
toast, *n.* Pain grillé (*m.*): pan grī″‿yē′.
tobacco. Tabac (*n. m.*): ta″bā′.—**some tobacco.** Du tabac: dü ta″bā′.—**tobacconist.** Marchand de tabac (*m.*): mar″shān′ də ta″bā′.—**t.-pouch.** Blague (*f.*): blāg.
to-day, *adv.* Aujourd'hui: ō″ʒūr″dwī′.
toe, *n.* **1.** Orteil (*m.*): or″tā′‿yə. **2.** Doigt du pied (*m.*): dwa dü pī″‿yē′.
together, *adv.* Ensemble: an″sān′‿blə.
toilet, *n.* Toilette (*f.*): twa″let′.

told, *pa.* Dit: dī.—**I told him.** Je lui ai dit: ʒə lwī ā dī.—**told off.** Désigné (*pa. m.*): dē″zī″‿nyē′.

to-morrow, *adv.* Demain: də-māṅ′.

tongue. Langue (*n. f.*): lāṅ′‿gə.—**hold your tongue.** Taisez-vous: tā″zē′ vū.

to-night, *adv.* **1.** Ce soir: sə swar. **2.** Cette nuit: set nwī.

tonnage. Tonnage (*n. m.*): ton″‿nāʒ′.

too, *adv.* Aussi: ō″sī′.—**too little.** Trop peu: tro pū.—**too much.** Trop: trō.

tool. Outil (*n. m.*): ū″tī′.—**intrenching tool.** See under INTRENCH.—**t.-bag.** Sacoche à outils (*n. f.*): sa″kōsh′ a ū″tī′.—**t.-box or chest.** Boîte (*f.*), ou coffre (*m.*), à outils: bwāt, ū kof′‿frə a ū″tī′.

tooth. Dent (*n. f.*): daṅ.—**tooth-brush.** Brosse à dents: bros‿a daṅ.—**toothless,** *a.* Sans dents: saṅ daṅ.

top, *n.* **1.** Haut (*m.*): hō (*in general*). **2.** Cime (*f.*): sīm (*of a mountain, rock* or *tree*). **3.** Dessus (*m.*): də-sü′ (*of a table*).

torch, *n.* **1.** Torche (*f.*): tōr′‿shə. **2.** Flambeau (*m.*): flaṅ″-bō′.

torpedo. Torpille (*n. f.*): tor″pī′‿yə.—**aerial torpedo.** Torpille aérienne: tor″pī′‿yə a″ē″rī″‿yen′.—**fire a t.** Lancer une torpille: laṅ″sē′ ün tor″pī′‿yə.—**t.-boat.** Torpilleur (*n. m.*): tor″pī″‿yūr′.—**t.-boat destroyer.** Contre-torpilleur (*n. m.*): koṅ′‿trə tor″pī″‿yūr′.

torrent. Torrent (*n. m.*): tor″‿rāṅ′. Abbreviated *Tnt.*

touch, *n.* **1.** Liaison (*f.*): lī″ā″zoṅ′. **2.** Contact (*m.*): koṅ″-tākt′.—**be in touch with.** Être en contact avec: ā′‿trə aṅ koṅ″tākt′ a″vek′.—**to lose t. with.** Perdre contact avec: pēr′‿drə koṅ″tākt′ a″vek′.

tourniquet. Tourniquet (*n. m.*): tūr″nī″kē′.—**emergency tourniquet.** Garrot (*n. m.*): gar″‿rō′.

tough, *a.* **1.** Dur (*m.*), dure (*f.*): dür (*of meat*). **2.** Raide (*m. & f.*): rād (*of things*).

tow, *v.* Remorquer: rə-mor″kē′.—**tow-line, tow-rope.** Remorque (*f.*): rə-mōrk′.

towards, *prep.* Vers: vār.

towel, *n.* **1.** Essuie-mains (*m.*): es″‿swī′ māṅ. **2.** Serviette (*f.*): sār″vī″‿yet′.

tower, *n.* **1.** Tour (*f.*): tūr. **2.** Citadelle (*f.*): sī″ta″del′.—**conning-tower.** Kiosk du commandant: kī″osk′ dü kom″‿maṅ″-dāṅ′.

town. Ville (*n. f.*): vīl.—**fortified t.** Ville fortifiée: vīl for″tī″-fī″‿yē′.—**t.-hall,** *n.* Hôtel de ville (*m.*): ō″tel′ də vīl.—**unfortified t.** Ville ouverte: vīl ū″vārt′.—**walled t.** Ville fermée: vīl fār″mē′.—**what is the nearest town?** Quelle est la ville la plus proche? kel ē la vīl la plü prōsh.—**what t. is this?** Quel est le nom de cette ville-ci? kel ē lə noṅ də set vīl sī.

township, *n.* **1.** Bourg (*m.*): būr. **2.** Village (*m.*): vīl″‿lāʒ′.

tow-path. Chemin de halage: shə-maṅ′ də ha″lāʒ′.

trace. **I.** *n.* **1.** Trace (*f.*): tras (*indication*). **2.** Trait (*m.*): trā (*harness*). **3.** Vestige (*m.*): ves″tī′‿ʒə (*remains*). **II.** *v.* **1.** Tracer: tra″sē′. **2.** Calquer: kal″kē′ (*in drawing*). **3.** Suivre à la trace: swī′‿vrə a la tras (*track*).—**fasten or fix the traces.** Attacher les traits: at″‿ta″shē′ lē trā.

track, *n.* **1.** Sentier (*m.*): saṅ″tī″‿yē′. **2.** Voie (*f.*): vwa.—**double track.** Voie double: vwa dū′‿blə. See under RAILROAD.—**side t.** Voie de garage: vwa də ga″rāʒ′.—**single t.** Voie simple: vwa saṅ′‿plə. See under RAILROAD.—**t.-watchman,** *n.* Garde-voies (*m.*): gar″‿də-vwā′.

tractor, *n.* **1.** Tracteur (*m.*): trak″tūr′. **2.** Hélice tractive aérienne (*f.*): ē″līs′ trak″tīv′ a″ē″rī″‿yen′ (*of an aeroplane*).—**military motor tractor.** Tracteur militaire automobile: trak″-tūr′ mī″lī″tār′ ō″tō″mō″bīl′.

artistic; ärt; fat; färe; fast; get; prēy; hit; polïce;
obey; gō; net; ōr; full; rüle; but; bürn; ə = final;

traffic, *n.* **1.** Circulation (*f.*): sïr"kü"la"sï"‿yeṅ' (*coming and going*). **2.** Roulage (*m.*): rü"lä'‿ʒə (*freight traffic*). **3.** Mouvement (*m.*): mū"‿və-māṅ' (*life*).—**heavy traffic.** Grand mouvement: graṅ mū"‿və-māṅ'.—**light t.** Mouvement léger: mū"‿və-māṅ' lē"ʒē'.

trail. Crosse d'affût (*n. f.*): krōs daf"‿fü' (*stock of a gun-carriage*).—**trail-hook.** Cheville ouvrière (*f.*): ʃhə-vī'‿yə ū"vrī"‿yār'.

train. **I.** *n.* Train (*m.*): traṅ. **II.** *v.* **1.** Exercer: eg"zār"sē'. **2.** Dresser: dres"‿sē'.—**ambulance train.** Train sanitaire: traṅ sa"nī"tār'.—**armored t.** See under ARMORED.—**breakdown-t.** See WRECKING-TRAIN, below.—**express t.** See under EXPRESS.—**fast t.** **1.** Train éclair: traṅ ē"klār'. **2.** Train rapide: traṅ ra"pīd'.—**field-t.** Train de combat: traṅ də keṅ"bā' (*company wagons, victuals, canteen and ambulance*, etc.).—**freight** or **goods t.** Train de marchandises: traṅ də mar"ʃhaṅ"dīz'.—**hospital t.** Train sanitaire: traṅ sa"nī"tār'.—**limited t.** Train à places limitées: traṅ a plās lī"mī"tē'.—**local t.** Train omnibus: traṅ om"nī"büs'.—**passenger-t.** Train de voyageurs: traṅ də vwa"‿ya"ʒūr'.—**passenger and goods t.** Train mixte: traṅ mīkst.—**regimental t.** Train régimentaire: traṅ rē"ʒī"maṅ"tār' (*baggage, supplies*, etc.).—**slow t.** Train omnibus: traṅ om"nī"büs'.—**t.-dispatcher.** **1.** Chef de dépôt: ʃhef də dē"po'. **2.** Chef du mouvement: ʃhef dü mūv"māṅ'.—**when will the t. start?** Quand ira le train? kaṅ ī"rā' lə traṅ.—**wrecking-t.** Train de secours: traṅ də sə-kūr'.

trained, *a.* Exercé: eg"zār"sē'.—**fully trained.** Complètement exercé: keṅ"plē"‿tə-māṅ' eg"‿zār"sē'.—**ill-trained.** Mal exercé: mal eg"‿zār"sē'.

training. Instruction (*n. f.*): aṅ"strük"sī"‿yeṅ'.—**training-manual.** Manuel d'instruction (*m.*): ma"nü"el' daṅ"strük"sī"‿yeṅ'.

trajectory. Trajectoire (*n. f.*): tra"ʒek"twār'.

trample, *v.* Piétiner: pī"yē"tī"nē'.—**trampled on.** Piétiné (*pa.*): pī"‿yē"tī"nē'.

tramway. Tramway (*n. m.*): tram"wā'. Abbreviated *Tram.*

transfer. **I.** *n.* **1.** Transport (*m.*): traṅs"pōr'. **2.** Évacuation (*f.*): ē"va"kü"a"sī"‿yeṅ'. **3.** Transfert (*m.*): traṅs"fār' (*in law*). **II.** *v.* **1.** Transférer: traṅs"fē"rē'. **2.** Transporter: traṅs"pōr"tē'. **3.** Évacuer: ē"va"kü"ē (*of sick and wounded* or *prisoners*).—**transfer of prisoners.** Évacuation des prisonniers: ē"va"kü"a"sī"‿yeṅ' dē prī"zen"‿nī"‿yē'.—**t. of sick and wounded.** Évacuation des malades et des blessés: ē"va"kü"a"sī"‿yeṅ' dē ma"lād' ē dē bles"‿sē'.

transferable, *a.* **1.** Transportable: traṅs"pōr"tā'‿blə. **2.** Évacuable: ē"va"kü"ā'‿blə.—**not transferable.** Personnel: pār"sen"‿nel' (*of tickets*).

transit-tag. Fiche d'évacuation (*f.*): fīʃh dē"va"kü"a"sī"yeṅ'.

transmission gear. Organe de transmission (*m.*): er"gān' də traṅs"mīs"‿sī"‿yeṅ'.

transmit, *v.* Transmettre: trans"mēt'‿trə.—**transmitter.** Transmetteur (*n. m.*): traṅs"met"tūr'.—**transmitting apparatus.** Appareil de transmission: ap"‿pa"rā'‿yə də traṅs"mīs"‿sī"‿yeṅ'.

transport, *n.* **1.** Transport (*m.*): traṅs"pōr'. **2.** Convoi (*m.*): keṅ"vwā'.—**director of railway transport.** Directeur de transport des chemins de fer: dī"rek"tūr' də traṅs"pōr' dē ʃhə-maṅ' də fār.—**first line t.** Train de combat: traṅ də keṅ"bā'. See FIELD-TRAIN, under TRAIN.—**inland water t.** Service de la navigation fluviale: sār"vīs' də la na"vī"ga"sī"‿yeṅ' flü"vī"‿yāl'‿ə.—**material transport service.** Service du transport de matériel de guerre: sār"vīs' dü traṅs"pōr' də ma"tē"rī"‿yel' də gār.—**personnel transport service.** Service de transport de personnel: sār"vīs' də traṅs"pōr' də pēr"sen"‿nel'.—**railway t. service.** See under RAILWAY.—**road t.** Service des étapes: sār"vīs' dēz‿ē"-

tāp'.—**sea-t.** Transport de mer: traṅs"pōr' də mār.—**t. service.** Service du transport: sār"vīs' dü traṅs"pōr'.—**t. wagon.** Fourgon de transport: fūr"goṅ' də traṅs"pōr'.

trap. **I.** *n.* Piège (*m.*): pī"‿ā'‿ʒə. **II.** *v.* Attraper: at"‿tra"pē'.

travel, *v.* Voyager: vwa"‿ya"ʒē'.—**traveler.** Voyageur (*n. m.*): vwa"‿ya"ʒūr'.—**traveling,** *a.* Voyageur: vwa"‿ya"ʒūr'.

traverse. **I.** *n.* Tranchée pare-éclats (*f.*): traṅ"shē' par ē"klā' (*protective work against bursting shells*). See ALL AROUND TRAVERSE. **II.** *v.* Traverser: tra"vēr"sē'.—**traversing-jack.** Levier de pointage: lə-vī"‿yē' də pwaṅ"tāʒ' (*for artillery*).

treachery. Trahison (*n. f.*): tra"‿ī"zoṅ'.

treason. Trahison (*n. f.*): tra"‿ī"zoṅ'.

treasury department. Département de la trésorerie aux armées: dē"par"‿tə-māṅ' də la trē"zō"‿rə-rī' ōz‿ar"mē'.

treat, *v.* Traiter: trā"tē'.—**be treated.** Être traité: ā'‿trə trā"tē'.

treatment. Traitement (*n. m.*): trā"‿tə-māṅ' (*of illness*).—**treatment of the sick and wounded.** Le traitement des malades et des blessés: lə trā"‿tə-māṅ' dē ma"lād' ē dē bles"‿sē'.

treaty. Traité (*n. m.*): trā"tē'.—**negotiate a treaty.** Négocier un traité: nē"gō"sī"‿yē' aṅ trā"tē'.

tree. Arbre (*n. m.*): ār'‿brə.

trench. Tranchée (*n. f.*): traṅ"shē'.—**approach trench.** Cheminement (*n. m.*): shə-mīn"māṅ'.—**branch-t.** Boyau de tranchée (*m.*): bwa"yō' də traṅ"shē'.—**communication-t.** Boyau de communication: bwa"‿yō' də kom"‿mü"nī"ka"sī"‿yoṅ'.—**fire t.** See under FIRE.—**first t.** **1.** Tranchée de départ: traṅ"shē' də dē"pār' (*point from which siege operations begin*). **2.** La parallèle: la pa"ral"‿lāl' (*first trench or parallel dug before a place to be attacked*).—**to map out a t.** Ébaucher une tranchée: ē"bō"shē' ün traṅ"shē'.—**t.-mortar,** *n.* **1.** Obusier de tranchée (*m.*): ō"bü"zī"‿yē' də traṅ"shē'. **2.** Crapouillot (*m.*): kra"pū"ī"‿yō'. **3.** Lance-bombe (*f.*): laṅs"boṅb'. **4.** Mortier de tranchée (*m.*): mor"tī"‿yē' də traṅ"shē'.—**reserve t.** Tranchée de réserve: traṅ"shē' də rē"zārv'.—**shelter-t.** Tranchée-abri: traṅ"shē'-a"brī'.—**supply-t.** Voie de ravitaillement: vwa də ra"vī"tai"‿yə-māṅ'.—**support t.** Tranchée d'appui: traṅ"shē' dap"‿pwī' (*of the supports*).

trestle. Chevalet (*n. m.*): shə-va"lē'.

trial. **1.** Essai (*n. m.*): es"‿sā'. **2.** Mise en jugement (*f.*): mīz‿aṅ ʒü"‿ʒə-māṅ'.—**on t.** À l'essai: a les"‿sā'.

trigger, *n.* **1.** Détente (*f.*): dē"tāṅt'. **2.** Gâchette (*f.*): ga"-shet'.—**pull the trigger.** Tirer la détente: tī"rē' la dē"tāṅt'.

trimmer. Arrimeur (*n. m.*): ar"‿rī"mūr'.

trip. **I.** *n.* **1.** Voyage (*m.*): vwa"‿ya'‿ʒə. **2.** Visite (*f.*): vī"-zīt'. **3.** Randonnée (*f.*): raṅ"dōn"nē' (*round trip*). **II.** *v.* **1.** Trébucher: trē"bü"shē'. **2.** Faire trébucher: fār trē"bü"shē' (*cause to trip*).

triplane. Triplane (*n. m.*): trī"plān'.

triple entente. See ENTENTE.

tripod. Trépied (*n. m.*): trē"pī"‿yē'.—**aiming-tripod.** Chevalet de pointage (*n. m.*): shə-va"lē' də pwaṅ"tāʒ'.

triumph. Triomphe (*n. m.*): trī"oṅf'.—**triumph over.** Triompher de: trī"oṅ"fē' də.

troop. **1.** Troupe (*n. f.*): trūp. **2.** Détachement (*n. m.*): dē"-tash"māṅ'.—**to repatriate or send troops home.** Rapatrier des troupes: ra"pa"trī"‿yē' dē trūp.—**troopship,** *n.* **1.** Transport (*n.*): traṅs"pōr'. **2.** Bâtiment de transport (*m.*): ba"tī"māṅ' də traṅs"pōr'.—**troop of horse.** Détachement de cavalerie: dē"-tash"māṅ' də ka"va"‿lə-rī'.—**troop-train.** Train de troupes: traṅ də trūp.—**where are the troops?** Où sont les troupes?

ū sen lē trūp.—**where have the troops gone?** Où sont allées les troupes? ū sent‿al″lē′ lē trūp.
trooper, *n.* **1.** Cavalier (*m.*): ka″va″lī″‿yē′ (*mounted*). **2.** Troupier (*m.*): trū″pī″‿yē′ (*soldier in general*).
trophy. Trophée (*n. m.*): tro″fē′.
tropical, *a.* Tropical (*m.*), tropicale (*f.*): tro″pī″kāl′.
trot. **I.** *n.* Trot (*m.*): trō. **II.** *v.* **1.** Trotter: tret″‿tē′. **2.** Aller au trot: al″‿lē′ ō trō.—**at full t.** Au grand trot: ō gran trō.—**at gentle or slow trot.** Au petit trot: ō pə-tī′ trō.
trotting. Au trot: ō trō.
trouble. **I.** *n.* Trouble (*m.*): trū′‿blə. **II.** *v.* Troubler: trū″blē′.
trough. Auge (*n. f.*): ō′ʒə.
trousers. Pantalon (*n. m.*): pan″ta″len′.
truce, *n.* **1.** Trève (*f.*): trāv′‿ə (*long*). **2.** Armistice (*m.*): ar″mīs″tīs′ (*short*).
truck, *n.* **1.** Truc (*m.*): trük (*railway*). **2.** Camion (*m.*): ca″-mī″‿yen′ (*street*).—**open truck.** Tombereau (*m.*): ten″bə-rō′ (*railway*).
true, *a.* Vrai (*m.*), vraie (*f.*): vrā.—**is that true?** Est-ce vrai? es′‿sə vrā.
trumpet. Trompette (*n. f.*): tren″pēt′. Compare BUGLE.—**trumpeter.** Trompette (*n. m.*): tren″pēt′.
trunk, *n.* **1.** Malle (*f.*): māl′‿lə (*clothes*). **2.** Tronc (*m.*): tren (*tree*). **3.** Trompe (*f.*): tren′‿pə (*elephant*).
trunnion. Tourillon (*n. m.*): tū″rī″‿yen′.—**trunnion-cradle.** Berceau à tourillons (*m.*): bār″sō′ a tu″rī″‿yen′.
truss. **1.** Bandage (*n. m.*): ban″dāʒ′ (*surgical*). **2.** Botte (*f.*): bet (*of straw*).
trust, *v.* **1.** Mettre sa confiance en: met′‿trə sa ken″fī″‿yāns′ an. **2.** Se fier à: sə fī″‿yē′ a.
trustworthy, *a.* **1.** Digne de confiance: dī′‿nyə də ken″fī″‿yāns′. **2.** Exact (*m.*): eg″zākt′.
trusty, *a.* **1.** Fidèle (*m. & f.*): fī″dēl′. **2.** Loyal (*m.*), loyale (*f.*): lwa″‿yāl′.
try, *v.* **1.** Essayer: es″‿sā″‿yē′. **2.** Tâcher: tā″shē′.—**to try to come out.** Chercher à sortir: shār″shē′ a sēr″tīr′.
tub, *n.* **1.** Cuve (*f.*): küv. **2.** Baril (*m.*): ba″rī′.
tube, *n.* **1.** Tube (*m.*): tüb (*general*). **2.** Âme (*f.*): ām (*cannon*). **3.** Métro (*m.*): mē″tro′ (*railway*). See SUBWAY.—**inner tube.** Chambre à air (*n. f.*): shān′‿brə a ār.—**priming tube.** Tube de mise de feu: tüb də mīz də fū (*of a shrapnel-shell*).
Tuesday. Mardi (*n. m.*): mar″dī′.
tug, *v.* Remorquer: rə-mēr″kē′ (*tow*).
tug-boat. Remorqueur (*n. m.*): rə-mēr″kūr′.
tumble, *v.* Tomber: ten″bē′.
tumbler, *n.* **1.** Gâchette (*f.*): ga″shet′ (*of a firearm*). **2.** Grand verre (*m.*): gran vār (*drinking-glass*).
tune, *n.* Air (*m.*): ār.
tuned up. Resté conforme: res″tē′ ken″fērm′.
tunic. Tunique (*n. f.*): tü″nīk′.
tunnel. **I.** *n.* Tunnel (*n. m.*): tün″‿nel′. Abbreviated *Tel.* **II.** *v.* Faire un souterrain: fār an sū″tār″ran′.
Turk, *n.* Turc (*m.*), Turque (*f.*): türk.
Turco (*n. m.*): tür″ko′ (*French African troops*).
Turkey, *n.* La Turquie (*f.*): la tür″kī′.
turkey, *n.* Dindon (*m.*): dan″den′; dinde (*f.*): dand (*poultry*).
turn, *v.* Tourner: tūr″nē′.—**by turns.** À tour de rôle: a tūr də rōl.—**downhill turn.** Virage avec descente (*m*): vī″rāʒ′ a″vek′ des″‿sānt′.—**in one's t.** À son tour: a sen tūr.—**in turns.** Tour à tour: tūr a tūr.—**turn about!** Same as FACE ABOUT, see under FACE.—**t. out!** Aux armes! ōz‿ārm′‿ə (*military com-*

mand).—**t. to.** **1.** S'appliquer: sap"‿plī"kē'. **2.** Se mettre à: sə met'‿trə a.—**turn to the left.** Tournez à gauche: tūr"nēz'‿a gōsh.—**t. turtle.** **1.** Culbuter (*v.*): kül"bü"tē'. **2.** Faire la culbute: fār la kül"büt' (*cause to turn turtle*).—**uphill t.** Virage avec montée: vī"rāʒ' a"vek' mēn"tē'. [(*said of the nose*).

turned up. Retroussé (*a. m.*), retroussée (*f.*): rə-trūs"‿sē'

turning, *n.* **1.** Tournant (*m.*): tūr"nāñ'. **2.** Virage (*m.*): vī"rāʒ'. **3.** Coude (*m.*): kūd (*elbow-like*).—**t. to the left,** or **right.** **1.** Virage à gauche, ou droite: vī"rāʒ' a gōsh, ū drwāt. **2.** Tournant à droite: tūr"nāñt'‿a drwāt.—**sharp t.** **1.** Coude brusque: kūd brüsk. **2.** Virage hardi: vī"rāʒ' har"dī'.

turnip. Navet (*n. m.*): na"vē'.

turntable. Plaque tournante (*n. f.*): plāk tūr"nāñt'.

turpinite. Turpinite (*n. f.*): tür"pī"nīt' (*high explosive*).

turret. Tourelle (*n. f.*): tū"rel'‿lə.

turtle. Tortue (*n. f.*): tēr"tü'. Compare TURN TURTLE, under TURN.

twelfth, *a.* & *n.* Douzième: dū"zī"‿yām'.—**twelve,** *a.* & *n.* Douze: dūz.—**twelve o'clock.** Midi: mī"dī'.—**ten minutes to t.** Midi moins dix: mī"dī' mwañ dīs.

twentieth, *a.* & *n.* Vingtième: vañ"tī"‿yām'.

twenty, *a.* & *n.* Vingt: vañ.—**twenty-one.** Vingt et un: vañt"‿ē"‿añ'.—**t.-first.** **I.** *a.* Vingt-et-unième: vañt"‿ē"‿ün"‿yām'. **II.** *n.* Vingt et un: vañt"‿ē"‿añ' (*of the month*, etc.).—**t.-second.** **I.** *a.* Vingt-deuxième: vañ" ‿dū"‿zī"‿yām', etc. **II.** *n.* Vingt-deux: vañ"dū'.—**t. to six.** Six heures moins vingt: sīz‿ūr mwañ vañ.—**t.-two.** Vingt-deux: vañ"dū', etc. See CARDINAL NUMBERS, under NUMBER.

twice, *adv.* Deux fois: dū fwa.

twilight. Crépuscule (*n. m.*): krē"püs"kül'.

twist. **I.** *n.* Entorse (*f.*): añ"tērs' (*sprain*). **II.** *v.* Tordre: tēr'‿drə.

two. Deux: dū.—**it is two o'clock.** Il est deux heures: īl‿ē dūz‿ūr.—**two hundred.** Deux cents: dū sañ. See CARDINAL NUMBERS, under NUMBER.

twofold, *a.* Double: dū'‿blə.

typewriter, *n.* [Soldiers' slang.] A machine-gun.

typhoid, *a.* Typhoïde (*m.* & *f.*): tī"fo"ī'‿də.

typhoid fever. Fièvre typhoïde (*n. f.*): fī"ā'‿vrə tī"fō"ī'‿də.

typhus. Typhus (*n. m.*): tī"fü'.

U

uhlan. Uhlan (*n. m.*): ü"lāñ'.

umbrella. Parapluie (*n. m.*): pa"ra"plwī'.

umpire. Arbitre (*n. m.*): ar"bī'‿trə.

unable, *a.* Incapable: añ"ka"pā'‿blə.

unauthorized, *a.* Non autorisé: neñ ō"to"rī"zē'.

unavoidable, *a.* Inévitable (*m.* & *f.*): in"ē"vī"tā'‿blə.

unbiased, *a.* Impartial (*m.*), impartiale (*f.*): añ"par"sī"āl'.

unbridle, *v.* Débrider: dē"brī"dē'.

uncaught, *a.* Non pris: neñ prī.

uncertain, *a.* Incertain: añ"sār"tañ'.—**uncertainty.** Incertitude (*n. f.*): añ"sēr"tī"tüd'.

unconscious, *a.* Sans connaissance: sañ koñ"‿nās"‿sāñs' (*insensible*).—**to be unconscious.** Avoir perdu connaissance: a"vwār' pār"dü' koñ"‿nās"‿sāñs'.

uncork, *v.* Déboucher: dē"bū"shē'.

under. **I.** *adv.* En dessous: añ də-sū'. **II.** *prefix.* **1.** Sous: sū. **2.** Aide: ād. **III.** *prep.* **1.** Sous: sū. **2.** En: añ (*in a state of*).—**u. repair.** En état de réparation: añ ē"tā' də rē"pa"ra"sī"‿yoñ'.

underbrush. Sous-bois (*n. m.*): sū"bwā'.

underdone, *a.* Saignant (*m.*): sē"‿nyāṅ'; saignante (*f.*): sē"‿nyāṅt' (*of rare meat*).
undershirt, undervest. Gilet: ʒī"lē'. Applied also to a *vest* or *waistcoat*.
understand, *v.* Comprendre: koṅ"prāṅ'‿drə.—**do you u.?** Comprenez-vous? keṅ"pre"nē' vū.—**I do not u. you.** Je ne vous comprends pas: ʒə nə vū keṅ"prāṅ' pā.—**I u.** Je comprends: ʒə keṅ"prāṅ'.—**you u. me.** Vous me comprenez: vū mə keṅ"-pre"nē'.
undertake, *v.* Entreprendre: aṅ"‿trə-prāṅ'‿drə.
undervest. Gilet: ʒī"lē'. See also UNDERSHIRT, VEST, WAISTCOAT.
undesirable. Non désirable: neṅ dē"zī"rā'‿blə.
undress. I. *n.* Petite tenue (*f.*): pə-tīt' tə-nü'. **II.** *v.* Déshabiller: dē"za"bī"‿yē'. See Appendix.—**to undress a wound.** Lever l'appareil de: lə-vē' lap"‿pa"rē'‿yə də.
undulating, *a.* Accidenté: ak"‿sī"daṅ"tē' (*of ground*).
unequal, *a.* **1.** Inégale: īn"‿ē"gāl'. **2.** Inférieur (*m.*), inférieure (*f.*): aṅ"fē"rī"yūr'.
unexpected, *a.* **1.** Imprévu (*m.*), imprévue (*f.*): aṅ"prē"vü'. **2.** Inattendu (*m.*), inattendue (*f.*): īn"at"‿taṅ"dü'.—**unexpectedly,** *a.* **1.** Soudainement: sū"dān"‿māṅ'.
unfaithful, *a.* Infidèle (*m.* & *f.*): aṅ"fī"dāl'.
unfavorable, *a.* Défavorable (*m.* & *f.*): dē"fa"vo"rā'‿blə.
unfix bayonets! Remettez les baïonnettes! rə-mēt"tē' lē ba"‿yeṅ"‿net'.
unfordable, *a.* Inguéable: aṅ"gē"ā'‿blə.
unfortified, *a.* Non fortifié: neṅ fōr"tī"fī"‿yē'.
unfurl, *v.* **1.** Déferler: dē"fār"lē'. **2.** Déployer: dē"plwa"yē' (*deploy*).
unguarded, *a.* **1.** Non gardé: neṅ gar"dē'. **2.** Sans garde: [saṅ gard.
unhappy, *a.* Malheureux (*m.*): ma"lū"rū'; malheureuse (*f.*): ma"lū"rūz'.
uniform. I. *a.* Uniforme (*m.* & *f.*): ü"nī"form'. **II.** *n.* Uniforme (*m.*): ü"nī"fərm'.—**in dress uniform.** See IN FULL DRESS, under DRESS.
uninjured, *a.* Sans blessure: saṅ bles"‿sür'.
Union of South Africa. L'Union Sud-Africaine (*n. f.*): lü"nī"‿yeṅ' süd af"rī"kān'.
Union-jack. Pavillon anglais: pa"vī"‿yeṅ' aṅ"glē'.
unharness, unhook, *v.* Dételer: dē"‿tə-lē'.
United States (the). Les États-Unis: lēz‿ē"tāz'‿ü"nī'.
unit. Unité (*n. f.*): ü"nī"tē'.
unload, *v.* Décharger: dē"ʃar"ʒē'.
unlucky, *a.* Malheureux (*m.*): ma"lū"rū'; malheureuse (*f.*): ma"lū"rūz'.
unmarried, *a.* Non marié: neṅ ma"rī"‿yē'.
unmask, *v.* Démasquer: dē"mas"kē'.
unoccupied, *a.* **1.** Pas occupé: pas‿ok"‿kü"pē' (*of persons*). **2.** Inhabitée (*f.*): īn"a"bī"tē' (*of houses*).
unpack, *v.* **1.** Dépaqueter: dē"pa"‿kə-tē' (*of packages*). **2.** Déballer: dē"bal"‿lē' (*of goods*).
unpile arms! Rompez les faisceaux! reṅ"pē' lē fās"sō'.
unprepared, *a.* Non préparé: noṅ prē"pa"rē'.
unprotected, *a.* Sans protection: saṅ pro"tek"sī"‿yeṅ'.
unprovided, *a.* Dépourvu de: dē"pūr"vü' də.—**unprovided with.** Pas muni de: pa mü"nī' də.
unrecognizable, *a.* Méconnaissable: mē"ken"‿nās"‿sā'blə.
unreliable, *a.* Sur qui on ne peut pas compter: sür kī eṅ nə pū pa keṅ"tē'.
unrelievable, *a.* Qu'on ne peut secourir: keṅ nə pū sə-kū"rīr'.
unscrew, *v.* Dévisser: dē"vīs"sē'.
unseen, *a.* Inaperçu: īn"a"pār"sü'.

unserviceable, *a.* **1.** Inutile: ī″nü″tīl′. **2.** Hors de service: hər də sār″vīs′.
unstrung, *a.* Détendu: dē″taṅ″dü′.
unsupported, *a.* Non soutenu: nəṅ sū″‿tə-nü′.
untenable. Pas tenable: pa tə-nā′‿blə.
until. **1.** Jusque: ʒüs′‿kə. Spelt *jusqu'* before a vowel. **2.** Jusqu'à ce que: ʒüs′kə sə kə. **3.** Qu'après: ka″prē′ (*until after*). **4.** Ne que: nə kə; as, "I shall not go out until the afternoon": je (ʒə) *ne* (nə) sortirai (sōr″tī″rā′) *que* (kə) l'après-midi (la″prē′ mī″dī′). **5.** Jusqu'au moment où: ʒüs′kō mo″māṅ′ ū.
untrustworthy, *a.* Inexact (*m.*), inexacte (*f.*): īn″eg″zāk′‿tə (*of news, reports*).
unwounded, *a.* Non blessé: nəṅ bles″sē′.
up, *adv.* **1.** Levé: lə-vē′ (*out of bed*). **2.** Debout: də-bū′ (*standing*). **3.** Sur pied: sür pī″‿yē′ (*afoot*). **4.** En haut: aṅ hō (*above*).—**up-hill.** En montant: aṅ məṅ″tāṅ′ (*of motion*).—**up-stream.** En amont: aṅ‿a″məṅ′ (*against the stream*).
upon, *prep.* Sur: sür.
upset, *v.* **1.** Renverser: raṅ″vār″sē′. **2.** Verser: vār″sē′ (*of vehicles*). **3.** Chavirer: sha″vī″rē′ (*of boats*).
upside-down, *adv.* Sens dessus dessous: saṅs də-sü′ də-sū′.—**to be turned upside-down.** Être bouleverser: ā′trə būl″vār″sē′.
upward. **1.** Vers le haut: vēr lə hō. **2.** Au-delà: ō″‿də-lā′ (*over, more than*).
urgent, *a.* **1.** Urgent (*m.*): ür″ʒāṅ′; urgente (*f.*): ür″ʒāṅt′. **2.** Pressant (*m.*): pres″‿sāṅ′; pressante (*f.*): pres″‿sāṅt′. **3.** Pressé (*m.*), pressée (*f.*): pres″‿sē′ (*of letters*).
us. Nous: nū.
use. **I.** *n.* **1.** Usage (*m.*): ü″zāʒ′. **2.** Emploi (*m.*): aṅ″plwā′. **II.** *v.* Se servir de: sə sār″vīr′ də.—**of great use.** Très utile: trāz‿ü″tīl′.—**useful,** *a.* Utile (*m.* & *f.*): ü″tīl′—**user,** *n.* Quelqu'un qui se sert de: kel″kaṅ′ kī sə sār də.
usual, *a.* **1.** Commun (*m.*): kəm″maṅ′; commune (*f.*): kəm″-mün′. **2.** Habituel (*m.*), habituelle (*f.*): a″bī″tü″el′.—**usually.** **1.** D'habitude: da″bī″tüd′. **2.** Ordinairement: ər″dī″nār″‿ə-māṅ′.
utilize, *v.* Utiliser: ü″tī″lī″zē′.
utmost, *a.* **1.** Extrême (*m.* & *f.*): eks″trām′. **2.** Dernier (*m.*): dēr″nī″‿yē′; dernière (*f.*): dər″nī″‿yār′ (*last*).
uvula. Luette (*n. f.*): lü″‿et′.

V

vague, *a.* Vague (*m.* & *f.*): vag.—**vaguely,** *adv.* Vaguement: vag″māṅ′.
vale. Vallée (*f.*): val″‿lē′.
valise, *n.* **1.** Valise (*f.*): va″līs′. **2.** Portemanteau (*m.*): pērt″-maṅ″tō′. **3.** Sac de couchage: sak də kū″shā′‿ʒə (*military sleeping-bag*).
valley. Vallée (*n. f.*): val″‿lē′. Abbreviated *Vée.*
valor, *n.* **1.** Mérite (*m.*): mē″rīt′. **2.** Vaillance (*f.*): vai″‿yāṅs′. **3.** Bravoure (*f.*): bra″vūr′.—**for valor.** Pour le mérite: pūr lə mē″rīt′.
value. Valeur (*n. f.*): va″lūr′.—**valuable,** *a.* De valeur: də va″lūr′.
valve, *n.* **1.** Soupape (*f.*): sū″pāp′. **2.** Valve (*f.*): vāl′‿və.—**valve-gear.** Appareil de soupape (*m.*): ap″pa″rē′‿yə də sū″pāp′.
van, *n.* **1.** Fourgon (*m.*): fūr″gəṅ′ (*military*). **2.** Wagon (*m.*): va″gəṅ′ (*railway*). **3.** Same as VANGUARD.—**brake-van.** Fourgon à frein: fūr″gəṅ′ a fraṅ.—**guard's van.** Wagon du chef de train: va″gəṅ′ dü shef də traṅ.—**luggage van.** See under LUGGAGE and BAGGAGE.—**mail-van.** Wagon-poste: va″gəṅ′ pōst.
vanguard. Avant-garde (*n. f.*): a″vaṅ″gārd′.

vanquish, *v.* Vaincre: vaṅ'‿krə.
varicose veins. Varice (*n. f.*): va"rīs'.
veal. Veau (*n. m.*): vō.
vegetable. Légume (*n. m.*): lē"güm': commonly used in the plural *légumes* but pronounced the same way.
vehicle. Voiture (*n. f.*): vwa"tür'.
ventilate, *v.* Aérer: a"ē"rē'.—**ventilating shaft.** Gaine d'aérage: gān da"ē"rā'‿ʒə.—**ventilation,** *n.* Aérage (*m.*): a"ē"rāʒ'.—**ventilator,** *n.* Ventilateur (*m.*): vaṅ"tī"la"tūr'.
verdict. Jugement (*n. m.*): ʒü"‿ʒə-māṅ'.
Verdun, vār"daṅ', *not* ver"dūn'. Fortified French city.
version. Version (*n. f.*): vār"sī"‿yeṅ'.
very, *adv.* **1.** Très: trā. **2.** Fort: fōr.—**in the very act.** En flagrant délit: aṅ fla"grāṅ' dē"lī'.—**v. much.** Beaucoup (*a.*): bō"kū'.
"Very" light, ver"ı-lait', *n.* A star shell used in lighting "No Man's Land" and enemy territory at night. Named for its inventor.
vessel, *n.* **1.** Vaisseau (*m.*): vās"‿so' (*receptacle;* also, *a ship*). **2.** Navire (*m.*): na"vīr' (*ship*).
vest. **I.** *n.* **1.** Gilet (*m.*): ʒī"lē'. **2.** Veste (*f.*): vest. **3.** Tricot (*m.*): trī"ko'. **II.** *v.* Investir de: aṅ"ves"tīr'.
veterinarian (*n.*), **veterinary** (*a.* & *n.*), or **veterinary surgeon.** Vétérinaire (*n. m.*): vē"tē"rī"nār'.—**veterinary department service.** Service vétérinaire: sār"vīs' vē"tē"rī"nār'.—**veterinary captain.** Vétérinaire en premier: vē"tē"rī"nār' aṅ prə-mī"‿yē'.—**v. equipment.** Matériel vétérinaire: ma"tē"rī"el' vē"tē"rī"nār'.—**v. lieutenant.** Vétérinaire en seconde: vē"tē"rī"nār' aṅ sə-goṅd'.—**v. lieutenant-colonel.** Vétérinaire de première classe: vē"tē"rī"nār' də prə-mī"‿yār' klas.—**v. major.** Vétérinaire principal de seconde classe: vē"tē"rī"nār' praṅ"sī"pāl' də sə-goṅd' klas.—**v. second lieutenant.** Aide-vétérinaire: ād vē"tē"rī"nār'.
via, *adv.* Par voie de: par vwa də (*by way of*).
viaduct. Viaduc (*n. m.*): vī"a"dük'. Abbrev. *Vduc.*
viaticum, *n.* Provisions de route (*f. pl.*): pro"vī"zī"yeṅ' də rūt.
vice. **I.** *adv.* Vice: vīs; as, *vice* admiral (*vice-amiral*), *vice* consul (*vice-consul*). **II.** *n.* Défaut (*m.*): dē"fō' (*immorality*).
vice-versa. Vice-versa: vī"sē' vār"sā'.
vicious, *a.* Vicieux (*m.*): vī"sī"‿yū'; vicieuse (*f.*): vī"sī"yūz'.
victory. Victoire (*n. f.*): vīk"twār'.
victual, *v.* **1.** Avitailler: a"vī"tai"‿yē'. **2.** Approvisionner: ap"-pro"vī"zī"‿yeṅ"‿nē'.
victualing, *n.* Avitaillement (*m.*): a"vī"tai"‿yə-māṅ'.
victuals, *n.* **1.** Vivres (*m. pl.*): vī'‿vrə (*food supplies*). **2.** Provisions (*f. pl.*): pro"vī"zī"‿yeṅ'. **3.** Manger (*m.*): maṅ"ʒē' (*table food*).
view. Vue (*n. f.*): vü.—**field of view.** Champ (*n. m.*): ŝhaṅ (*through a field-glass*, etc.).—**in v.** En vue: aṅ vü.—**object in v.** Le but: lə bü.—**point of v.** Point de vue: pwaṅ də vü.—**with a v. to making use of.** En vue d'utiliser: aṅ vü dü"tī"lī"zē'.
vigilance, *n.* **1.** Surveillance attentive (*f.*): sür"vē"yaṅs' at"‿taṅ"tīv'. **2.** Vigilance (*n. f.*): vī"ʒī"lāṅs'.—**vigilant,** *a.* **1.** Vigilant (*m.*): vī"ʒī"lāṅ'; vigilante (*f.*): vī"ʒī"lāṅ'‿tə. **2.** Éveillé (*m.*), éveillée (*f.*): ē"vē"‿yē'.
vigor. Énergie (*n. f.*): ē"nār"ʒī'.
village, *n.* **1.** Village (*m.*): vīl"‿lāʒ'. Abbreviated *Vage.* **2.** Hameau (*m.*): ha"mō' (*hamlet*). Abbreviated *Hau.*
villain. Gredin (*n. m.*): grə-daṅ'.
vine. Vigne (*n. f.*): vī'‿nyə.
vinegar. Vinaigre (*n. m.*): vī"nā'‿grə.
vineyard. **1.** Vigne (*n. f.*): vī'‿nyə. **2.** Vignoble (*n. m.*): vī"‿nyō'‿blə.

violate, *v.* Violer: vī″ō″lē′.—**violence.** Violence (*n. f.*): vī″o″-lāṅs′.—**to use violence.** Employer la force: aṅ″plwa″‿yē′ la fōrs.
violent, *a.* Violent (*m.*): vī″o″lāṅ′; violente (*f.*): vī″o″lāṅt′.
virgin. Vierge (*n. f.*): vī″ērȝ′. Abbreviated *Vge.*
virtue. Vertu (*n. f.*): vār″tü′.—**by virtue of.** En vertu de: aṅ vār″tü′ də.
vise, *n.* Étau (*m.*): ē″tō′ (*tool*).
visit. Visite (*n. f.*): vī″zīt′.
vive, vīv, *interj.* Long live!
vivid, *a.* Vif: vīf.
voice. Voix (*n. f.*): vwa.
voilà, vwa″lā′, *prep.* [Fr.] **1.** See there. **2.** Behold.
volley, *n.* **1.** Décharge (*f.*): dē″shār′‿ȝə (*of rifles*). **2.** Volée (*f.*): vo″lē′ (*of artillery*). **3.** Salve (*f.*): sāl′‿və (*in salute*).—**volley firing.** **1.** Feu de peloton: fū də pə-lo″teṅ′ (*by platoon*). **2.** Feu de bataillon: fū də ba″tai″‿yeṅ′ (*by battalion*).
volplane, *v.* Vol-planer: vel″pla″nē′.—**to land by volplaning.** Atterrir en volplanant: at″‿tār″‿rīr′ aṅ vel″pla″nāṅ′.
voltmeter. Voltmètre (*n. m.*): volt″mē′‿trə.
volunteer. **I.** *n.* Volontaire (*m.*): vo″leṅ″tār′. **II.** *v.* S'offrir volontairement: sof″‿frīr′ vo″leṅ″tār″‿ə-māṅ′.
vomit, *v.* **1.** Vomir: vo″mīr′. **2.** Rendre: rāṅ′‿drə.
vomiting. **1.** Vomissement (*m.*): vo″mīs″‿sə-māṅ′ (*the act*). **2.** Vomitif (*m.*): vo″mī″tīf′ (*the matter ejected*).
voucher, *n.* **1.** Garantie (*f.*): ga″raṅ″tī′ (*guarantee*). **2.** Preuve (*f.*): prūv (*proof*). **3.** Laissez-passer (*m.*): lās″‿sē′ pas″‿sē′ (*pass*).
voyage. Voyage (*n. m.*): vwa″yā′‿ȝə.—**home voyage.** Voyage de retour: vwa″yā′‿ȝə də rə-tūr′.—**outward v.** Voyage d'aller: vwa″yā′‿ȝə dal″lē′.
vulgar, *a.* Grossier (*m.*): grōs″sī″‿yē′; grossière (*f.*): grōs″-sī″yār′.
vulture. Vautour (*n. m.*): vō″tūr′.

W

wad, *n.* **1.** Bourre (*f.*): būr (*of cartridge*). **2.** Touffe (*f.*): tūf (*as of cotton*).
waffle. Gaufre (*n. f.*): gō′‿frə.
wagon, *n.* **1.** Wagon (*m.*): va″geṅ′. **2.** Chariot (*m.*): sha″rī″‿yō′. **3.** Caisson (*m.*): kās″‿seṅ′. **4.** Fourgon (*m.*): fūr″goṅ′.—**baggage-wagon.** **1.** Fourgon à bagage: fūr″geṅ′ a ba″gāȝ′ (*military*). **2.** Wagon à bagage: va″geṅ′ a ba″gāȝ′ (*railroad*).—**battery-w.** Caisson de batterie: kās″‿soṅ′ də bat″‿tə-rī′.—**supply-wagon.** Fourgons à vivres: fūr″geṅs′‿a vī′‿vrə.
waistbelt. Ceinturon (*n. m.*): saṅ″tü″roṅ′.
waistcoat. Gilet (*n. m.*): ȝī″lē′. See also UNDERVEST and VEST.
wait, *v.* Attendre: at″‿tāṅ′‿drə.
waiting. Attente (*n. f.*): at″‿tāṅt′.—**waiting-room.** Salle d'attente (*n. f.*): sal dat″tāṅt′.
wake, *v.* **1.** Éveiller: ē″vē″‿yē′. **2.** Réveiller: rē″vē″‿yē′.
walk. **I.** *n.* **1.** Marche (*f.*): mārsh. **2.** Promenade (*f.*): pro″-mə-nād′. **II.** *v.* **1.** Marcher: mar″shē′. **2.** Aller à pied: al″‿lē′ a pī″‿yē′.—**walk!** Au pas! ō pa (*order for cavalry*).—**I can no longer w.** Je ne puis plus marcher: ȝə nə pwī plü mar″shē′.
wall, *n.* **1.** Mur (*m.*): mūr. **2.** Muraille (*f.*): mū″ra″‿yə.
wan, *a.* Pâle (*m. & f.*): pāl.
want. **I.** *n.* Besoin (*m.*): bə-zwaṅ′. **II.** *v.* **1.** Vouloir: vūl″-wār′. **2.** Désirer: dē″zī″rē′. **3.** Avoir besoin de: a″vwār′ bə-swaṅ′ də.—**I want.** **1.** Je veux: ȝə vū. **2.** Je désire: ȝə dē″zīr′ (*desire*). **3.** Il me faut: īl mə fō (*need*).

war. Guerre (*n. f.*): găr.—**on a war footing.** Sur un pied de guerre: sür aṅ pī″yē′ də găr.—**state of war.** État de guerre (*m.*): e″tā′ də găr.—**to be at war.** Être en guerre: ā′‿trə aṅ găr.—**war establishments.** Établissements de guerre: ē″ta″-blīs″‿sə-māṅ′ də găr.—**war levy.** Contribution de guerre (*f.*): keṅ″trī″bü″sī″‿yeṅ′ də găr.—**war office.** Ministère de la guerre (*m.*): mī″nīs″tār′ də la găr.

war=biscuit. Biscuit de réserve: bīs″kwī′ də rē″zārv′.

war=correspondent. Correspondant de guerre (*m.*): ker″‿res″-peṅ″dāṅ′ də găr.

ward, *n.* **1.** Salle (*n. f.*): sal (*of a hospital*). **2.** Arrondissement (*m.*): ar″‿reṅ″dīs″‿sə-māṅ′ (*of a town*).

ward, ward off, *v.* Parer: pa″rē′ (*of blows*).

warehouse, *n.* **1.** Hangar (*m.*): haṅ″găr′. **2.** Entrepôt (*m.*): aṅ″‿trə-pō′.—**warehouse=keeper, warehouseman.** Garde=magasin (*n. m.*): gard ma″ga″zaṅ′.

warfare. Guerre (*n. f.*): găr.

warm. **I.** *a.* Chaud (*m.*): shō; chaude (*f.*): shōd. **II.** *v.* Chauffer: shō″fē′.—**things are warming up.** Çà chauffe: sa shōf.

warn, *v.* **1.** Prévenir: prē″‿və-nīr′. **2.** Avertir: a″văr″tīr′.—**warning.** Avertissement (*n. m.*): a″văr″tīs″‿sə-māṅ′.—**to give warning.** Avertir: a″văr″tīr′ (*done, as by striking an empty shell in case of a gas=attack*).

warp, *v.* Gauchir: gō″shīr′.—**warping.** Gauchissement (*n. m.*): gō″shīs″‿sə-māṅ′.

war=plane. Avion de combat (*n. m.*): a″vī″‿yeṅ′ də keṅ″bā′.

warrant=officer. Maître d'équipage (*n. m.*): mā′‿trə dē″kī″-pāʒ′ (*naval service*). See also under OFFICER.

warren. Garenne (*n. f.*): ga″reṅ′. Abbreviated *Gar*[ne].

war=tax. Impôt de guerre (*n. m.*): aṅ″pō′ də găr.

was, *v.* A defective verb used to supply the imperfect of the verb *be.* See Appendix.—**he was.** Il était (*m.*): īl‿ē″tā′.—**I was.** J'étais: ʒē″tā′.—**she was.** Elle était (*f.*): el‿ē″tā′.

wash. **I.** *n.* **1.** Lavage (*m.*): la″vā′‿ʒə. **2.** Blanchissage (*m.*): blaṅ″shīs″‿sā′‿ʒə (*laundry*). **II.** *v.* **1.** Laver: la″vē′. **2.** Blanchir: blaṅ″shīr′.—**I would like a wash.** Je voudrais me laver: ʒə vū″drā′ mə la″vē′.—**wash=house.** Lavoir (*n. m.*): lav″wār′. Abbreviated *Lr.*

washer. Rondelle (*n. f.*): reṅ″del′ (*for machinery*).

wastage. Gaspillage (*n. m.*): gas″pī″‿yāʒ′.

waste. **I.** *n.* Gaspillage (*m.*): gas″pī″‿yāʒ′. **II.** *v* Gaspiller: gas″pī″‿yē′.—**to prevent waste.** Éviter le gaspillage: ē″vī″tē′ lə gas″pī″‿yāʒ′.—**w. no time over it.** Ne perdez pas de temps là=dessus: nə pār″dē′ pa də taṅ la də-sü′.

watch. **I.** *n.* **1.** Guet (*m.*): gē (*military*). **2.** Montre (*f.*): mōṅ′‿trə (*timepiece*). **3.** Quart (*m.*): kar (*on shipboard*). **II.** *v.* **1.** Faire le guet: fār lə gē (*patrol*). **2.** Veiller: vē″‿yē′ (*attend without sleep, as an invalid*). **3.** Surveiller: sür″vē″‿yē′ (*exercise surveillance over*).—**be on the watch.** **1.** Être à l'affût: ā′‿trə a laf″‿fü′. **2.** Être aux aguets: ā′‿trə ōz‿a″gā′.—**set the watch carefully.** Régler le guet avec soin: rē″glē′ lə gē a″vek′ swaṅ.

watchful, *a.* **1.** Vigilant (*m.*): vī″ʒī″lāṅ′; vigilante (*f.*): vī″ʒī″-lāṅt′. **2.** Attentif (*m.*): at″‿taṅ″tīf′; attentive (*f.*): at″‿taṅ″tīv′.

watchman. Garde (*n. m.*): gard.—**track=watchman.** Garde=voie (*n. m.*): gard″vwā′.

watchword. Mot d'ordre (*n. m.*): mō dēr′‿drə.

water. **I.** *n.* Eau (*f.*): ō. Abbreviated *E.* **II.** *v.* Donner à boire: den″‿nē′ a bwar.—**boil the w.** Faire bouillir l'eau: fār bū″‿yīr′ lō.—**clear w.** Eau claire: ō klār.—**cold w.** De l'eau froide: də lō frwad.—**draw w.** Puiser de l'eau: pwī″zē′ də lō.—**drinkable** or **drinking w.** Eau potable: ō pō″tā′‿blə.—

fresh w. Eau douce: ō dūs (*not salt*).—**get some w.** Allez chercher de l'eau: al″lē′ shār″shē′ də lō.—**hard w.** Eau crue: ō krū.—**hot w.** De l'eau chaude: də lō shōd.—**ice=water.** Eau glacée (*n. f.*): ō gla″sē′.—**is the w. drinkable?** L'eau est-elle potable? lō ēt‿el pō″tā′‿blə.—**mineral w.** See under MINERAL.—**muddy w.** Eau troublée: ō trū″blē′.—**running w.** Eau courante: ō kū″rānt′.—**salt w.** Eau salée: ō sa″lē′.—**sea w.** Eau de mer: ō də mār.—**some w. for my horse.** De l'eau pour mon cheval: də lō pūr meṅ shə-vāl′.—**some w. to drink.** De l'eau à boire: də lō a bwar.—**spring w.** Eau de source: ō də sūrs.—**stagnant w.** Eau dormante: ō dōr″māṅt′.—**w.=bailiff.** Garde=pêche (*n. m.*): gard″pāsh′.—**w.=bottle.** Bidon (*n. m.*): bī″deṅ′.—**w.=bottle strap.** Courroie de bidon (*f.*): kūr″wā′ də bī″deṅ′.—**w.=closet.** Latrines (*n. f. pl.*): la″trīn′.—**water-course.** **1.** Cours d'eau (*n. m.*): kūr dō. **2.** Chute d'eau (*n. f.*): shüt dō.—**watergand,** *n.* [Fl.] Fossé (*m.*): fos″sē′ (*foss or ditch*).—**w.=jacket.** Chemise d'eau (*f.*): shə-mīz′ dō.—**w.=mill.** Moulin à eau (*m.*): mū″laṅ′ a ō.—**w.=plane.** Hydroplane (*n. m.*): ī″drō″plāṅ′.—**w. supply.** **1.** Approvisionnement d'eau (*m.*): ap″pro″vī″zī″yeṅ″‿nə-māṅ′ dō. **2.** La distribution d'eau: la dīs″trī″bü″sī″‿yeṅ′ dō (*of towns*).—**w.=tank.** Réservoir à l'eau (*m.*): rē″zār″vwār′ a lō.—**w. unfit to drink.** Eau non potable: ō neṅ pō″tā′‿blə.—**where can I get water?** Où puis=je trouver de l'eau? ū pwī′‿ʒə trū″vē′ də lō.—**where can we water our horses?** Où pouvons=nous abreuver nos chevaux? ū pū″veṅ′ nūz‿a″brū″vē′ nō shə-vō′.—**will you please w. my horse?** Voulez=vous donner à boire à mon cheval, s'il vous plait? vū″lē′ vū den″‿nē′ a bwar a meṅ shə-vāl′, sīl vū plā.

watercress. Cresson (*n. m.*): kres″‿seṅ′.

waterfall, *n.* **1.** Cascade (*f.*): kas″kād′ə. **2.** Chute d'eau (*f.*): shüt dō.

watering place, w.=trough. Abreuvoir (*n. m.*): a″bru″vwār′ (*for animals*).

waterproof, *a.* Imperméable (*m. & f.*): aṅ″pēr″mē″ā′‿blə.—**waterproof=coat.** Manteau imperméable (*n. m.*): maṅ″tō′ aṅ″pār″mē″ā′‿blə.—**w. sheet.** **1.** Toile vernie (*f.*): twal vār″nī′. **2.** Drap imperméable (*m.*): dra aṅ″pēr″mē″ā′‿blə.

waterway. **1.** Voie d'eau (*f.*): vwa dō. **2.** Cours d'eau navigable (*m.*): kūr dō na″vī″gā′‿blə.

wave, *n.* **1.** Onde (*f.*): ōṅd (*surge*). **2.** Vague (*f.*): vāg (*of the sea*).

waverer. Un indécis (*n. m.*): aṅ aṅ″dē″sī′ (*one who is undecided*).

way, *n.* **1.** Chemin (*m.*): shə-maṅ′ (*path, etc.*). **2.** Route (*f.*): rūt (*road*). **3.** Voie (*f.*): vwa (*of railroad*).—**can you tell me the way to . . . ?** Pouvez=vous me diriger vers . . . ? pū″vē′ vū mə dī″rī″ʒē′ vār.—**come this way.** Venez par ici: və-nē′ par ī″sī′.—**covert way.** Chemin couvert: shə-maṅ′ kū″vār′.—**I have lost the way.** J'ai perdu mon chemin: ʒā pār″dü′ meṅ shə-maṅ′.—**permanent way.** **1.** La voie ferrée: la vwa fār″rē′ (*railroad*). **2.** Réseau permanent (*m.*): rē″zō′ pār″ma″nāṅ′ (*railway system*).—**that way.** **1.** Par là: par lā (*through there*). **2.** De ce côté: də sə kō″tē′ (*by this side*).—**the way in.** L'entrée (*n. f.*): laṅ″trē′.—**the way out.** La sortie (*n. f.*): la sōr″tī′.—**which is the way to . . . ?** Quel chemin faut=il prendre pour aller à . . . ? kel shə-maṅ′ fōt‿il prāṅ′drə pūr al″lē′ a (literally, "What road must one take to go to . . .?").—**which way?** **1.** Par où? par ū. **2.** De quel côté? də kel kō″tē′.—**which way did you come?** Par quel chemin êtes=vous venu? par kel shə-maṅ′ ā′‿tə vū və-nü′.

waybill. Feuille de route (*n. f.*): fū′‿yə də rūt.

wayside. Au bord de la route: ō bōr də la rūt.—**wayside=cross.** Calvaire (*n. m.*): kal″vār′.

we, *pron.* **1.** Nous: nū (*definite*). **2.** On: eṅ (*indefinite,* "one").

—**we are.** Nous sommes: nū sōm.—**we are going to . . .** Nous allons à . . .: nūz‿al″‿leṅz′‿a.—**we can not.** Nous ne pouvons pas: nū nə pū″veṅ′ pa. See CAN.—**we have.** Nous avons: nūz‿a″veṅ′.—**we were.** Nous étions: nūz‿ē″tī″‿yeṅ′.

weak, *a.* Faible (*m.* & *f.*): fā′‿blə.—**weaken,** *v.* **1.** Affaiblir: af″‿fā″blīr′. **2.** Diminuer: dī″mī″nü″ē′.—**weakening.** Affaiblissement (*n. m.*): af″‿fā″blīs″māṅ′.—**weakly,** *a.* Chétif (*m.*): shē″tīf′; chétive (*f.*): shē″tīv′ (*puny*).—**weakness.** Faiblesse (*n. f.*): fā″bles′.

weapons. Armes (*n. f. pl.*): arm (*in general*).

wear, *v.* **1.** Porter: pōr″tē′ (*of clothes,* etc.). **2.** User: ü″zē′ (*use by wear*).—**wear down,** *v.* **1.** User: ü″zē′. **2.** Épuiser: ē″pwī″zē′.

weather. Temps (*n. m.*): taṅ.—**misty weather.** Temps brumeux: taṅ brü″mū′.—**stormy w.** Temps d'orage: taṅ dō″rā′‿ʒə.

Wednesday. Mercredi (*n. m.*): mār″‿krə-dī′.

week. Semaine (*n. f.*): sə-mān′.—**from to-morrow week.** De demain en huit: də də-maṅ′ aṅ hwīt.—**in a w.** Dans huit jours: daṅ hwī ʒūr.—**last w.** La semaine dernière: la sə-mān′ dār″nī″‿yār′.

weigh, *v.* Peser: pə-zē′.

weight. Poids (*n. m.*): pwa.

weir. **1.** Barrage (*n. m.*): bar″‿rāʒ′ (*dam*). **2.** Déversoir (*m.*): dē″vār″swār′ (*spill-water*).

welfare, *n.* **1.** Bonheur (*m.*): bəṅ″‿nūr′. **2.** Bien-être (*m.*): bī″‿yaṅ′‿ā′‿trə.

well, *n.* Puits (*n. m.*): pwī. Abbreviated *Pts.*

well, *adv.* Bien: bī″‿yaṅ′.—**all's well.** Tout va bien: tū va bī″‿yaṅ′.—**w.-bred,** *a.* **1.** Bien élevé: bī″‿yaṅ′ ē″lə-vē′. **2.** Poli: pō″lī′ (*polite*).—**w. done!** Bien fait! bī″‿yaṅ′ fā.

Welsh (the). Les Gallois (*n. m.*): lē gal″wā′.

were you? Étiez-vous? ē″tī″‿yē′ vū.

west. Ouest (*n. m.*): ū″‿est′.—**in the west.** À l'ouest: a lū″‿est′.—**to go w.** To die: British soldiers' euphemism.

western, *a.* Occidental (*m.*), occidentale (*f.*): ək″‿sī″daṅ″tāl′.

westward. Vers l'ouest: vēr lū″‿est′.

wet, *a.* Mouillé (*m.*), mouillée (*f.*): mū″‿yē′.—**wet through.** Trempé (*a. m.*), trempée (*f.*): traṅ″pē′.—**wet to the bone** or **skin.** Mouillé jusqu'aux os: mū″‿yē′ ʒüs″kōz′‿ō.

wharf, *n.* **1.** Quai (*m.*): kā. **2.** Débarcadère (*m.*): dē″bar″ka″dār′. Abbreviated *Débre.* **3.** Entrepôt (*m.*): aṅ″‿trə-pō′.

what, *pron.* **1.** Quoi? kwa (*as subject*). **2.** Que: kə (*as object*). **3.** Qu'est-ce que: kes′ə kə.—**what is it?** Qu'est-ce que c'est? kes′-kə sē (*interrogatively*).—**what is the date?** Quelle date sommes-nous? kel dat som nū.—**w. is your calling, trade** or **profession?** Quel est votre métier? kel‿ē vō′‿trə mē″tī″‿yē′.—**w. is your name?** Comment vous appelez-vous? kəm″‿māṅ′ vūz‿ap″‿pə-lē′ vū.—**w. is your nationality?** Quelle est votre nationalité? kel‿ē vō′‿trə na″sī″‿yeṅ″a″lī″tē′.—**w. is your number?** Quel est votre numéro? kel‿ē vō′‿trə nü″mē″rō′.—**w. is your regiment?** Quel est votre régiment? kel‿ē vō′‿trə rē″ʒī″māṅ′. —**w. it is.** Ce que c'est: sə kə sē.—**w. place is this?** Où sommes-nous ici? ū sōm nūz‿ī″sī′.—**w. troops are those?** Quelles sont ces troupes-là? kel seṅ sē trūp la.—**w. were you doing?** Que faisiez-vous? kə fā″zī″‿yē′ vū.

wheat, *n.* **1.** Froment (*m.*): frō″māṅ′. **2.** Blé (*m.*): blē.

wheel. **I.** *n.* **1.** Roue (*f.*): rū. **2.** Volant (*m.*): vo″lāṅ′ (*fly-wheel*). **II.** *v.* **1.** Faire une conversion: fār ün keṅ″vār″sī″‿yeṅ′. **2.** Faire demi-tour: fār də-mī′ tūr (*take a half-turn*).—**elevating wheel.** Volant de pointage en hauteur (*m.*): vo″lāṅ′ də pwaṅ″tāʒ′‿aṅ hō″tūr′.—**fly-w.** Volant (*m.*): vo″lāṅ′.—**steering-w.** **1.** Volant de direction (*m.*): vo″lāṅ′ də dī″rek″sī″‿yeṅ′. **2.** Roue de gouvernail (*f.*): rū də gū"vār"nai'.—**traversing roller** or **w.** Volant de pointage en direction (*m.*): vo"lāṅ' də pwaṅ"tāʒ'‿aṅ dī"rek"sī"‿yeṅ'.—**w. to the right.** Appuyer à droite: ap"‿pwī"‿yē' a drwat.

wheelbarrow. Brouette (*f.*): brū"et'.

wheelwright. Charron (*n. m.*): shar"‿reṅ'.

when. **I.** *conj.* Lorsque: lōrs'‿kə. **II.** *adv.* Quand: kaṅ.—**when were you retired? or declared unfit?** Quand étiez=vous mis à la réforme? kaṅ ē"tī"‿yē' vū mīz‿a la rē"fērm'.

where. Où (*adv.*): ū.—**where are . . . ?** Où sont . . . ? ū seṅ.—**w. are the officers quartered?** Où sont cantonnés les officiers? ū seṅ kaṅ"teṅ"‿nē' lēz‿of"‿fī"sī"‿yē'.—**w. are our quarters?** Où sont nos logements? ū seṅ nō lo"‿ʒə-māṅ'.—**w. are we?** Où sommes=nous? ū sōm nū.—**w. can the kitchens be set?** Où peut=on établir les cuisines? ū pūt‿eṅ ē"ta"-blīr' lē kwī"zīn'.—**w. can we fill our water=bottles?** Où pouvons=nous remplir nos bidons? ū pū"veṅ' nū raṅ"plīr' nō bī"deṅ'.—**w. can we get food?** Où pouvons=nous trouver à manger? ū pū"veṅ' nū trū"vē' a maṅ"ʒē'.—**w. have you come from?** D'où êtes=vous venu? dū āt"vū' və-nü'.—**w. do you live?** Où demeurez=vous? ū də-mū"rē' vū.—**w. do you want to go?** Où voulez=vous aller? ū vū"lē' vūz‿al"‿lē'.—**w. is . . . ?** Où est . . . ? ū ē.—**w. is he?** Où est=il? ū ē"‿tīl.—**w. were you hit?** Où avez=vous été blessé? ū a"vē' vūz‿ē"tē' bles"‿sē'.

whereas, *adv.* **1.** Tandis que: taṅ"dī' kə. **2.** D'un autre côté: daṅ‿ō'‿trə ko"tē'.

which, *adj.* Quel (*m.*), quelle (*f.*): kel.

whiffle=tree. Palonnier (*n. m.*): pa"lon"‿nī"‿yē'. See SWINGLE=TREE.

whip, *n.* Fouet (*m.*): fū"ē'.

whiskers, *n.* **1.** Favoris (*m. pl.*): fa"vō"rī'. **2.** Côtelettes (*f. pl.*): kō"‿tə-let' (*short side whiskers*).

whistle. Sifflet (*n. m.*): sīf"‿flē'.—**whistle=blast.** Coup de sifflet (*m.*): kū də sīf"‿flē'.

white, *a.* Blanc (*m.*): blaṅ; blanche (*f.*): blaṅsh.—**white=feather,** *n.* Lâche (*n. m.*): lāsh. Literally, "plume blanche": plüm blaṅsh.

who, *pron.* Qui: kī.—**who are you?** Qui êtes=vous? kī āt vū.—**who goes there?** **1.** Qui vive? kī vīv. **2.** Qui va là? kī va la.

whole. **I.** *a.* Entier (*m.*): aṅ"tī"‿yē'; entière (*f.*): aṅ"tī"‿yār'. **II.** *n.* Tout (*m.*): tū.—**as a whole.** **1.** En totalité: aṅ to"ta"lī"tē'. **2.** En bloc: aṅ blok.

why. Pourquoi (*adv.*): pūr"kwā'.

wick. Mèche (*n. f.*): māsh.

wicker. Osier (*n. m.*): ō"zī"‿yē'.

wide, *a.* Large (*m.* & *f.*): larʒ.—**width.** Largeur (*n. f.*): lar"ʒūr'.

wife. Femme (*n. f.*): fam.

wig. Perruque (*n. f.*): pār"‿rük'.

wigwag. **1.** Signaux à bras (*m.*): sī"‿nyō' a bra. **2.** La transmission de signaux à bras (*f.*): la traṅs"mīs"‿sī"‿yeṅ' də sī"‿nyō' a bra.

wilfully. Volontairement (*adv.*): vō"leṅ"tār"māṅ'.

will. Volonté (*n. f.*): vō"leṅ"tē'.—**will you?** Voulez=vous? vū"-lē' vū.

willow, *n.* Saule (*m.*): sōl.

win, *v.* Gagner: ga"‿nyē'.

winch. Treuil (*n. m.*): trū'‿yə.—**winchman.** Homme du treuil (*m.*): om dü trū'‿yə.

wind. Vent (*n. m.*): vaṅ.

windlass. Treuil (*n. m.*): trū'‿yə. Abbreviated *Trl.*

windmill, *n.* Moulin à vent (*m.*): mū"laṅ' a vaṅ.

wind=screen. Pare=brise (*n. m.*): par"brīs'.

wind, *v.* Tourner: tūr″nē′.—**to wind up.** Remonter le mouvement: rə-mon″tē′ lə mūv″mān′ (*of watches, clocks*).
window. Fenêtre (*n. f.*): fə-nā′‿trə.
windy, *a.* Venteux: van″tū′.—**it is too windy.** Il fait trop de vent: īl fā trō də van.
wine. Vin (*n. m.*): van.—**a bottle of red wine.** Une bouteille de vin rouge: ün bū″tē′‿yə də van rū′‿ʒə.—**w. list.** Carte des vins (*n. f.*): kart dē van.—**wine-shop.** Cabaret (*m.*): ka″ba″rē′.
wing. Aile (*n. f.*): āl.—**left wing.** Aile gauche: āl gōsh.—**wing-spread.** Empennage (*n. m.*): an″‿pen″‿nāʒ′—**wing-tip.** 1. Bout d'aile (*n. m.*): bū dāl. 2. Aileron (*n. m.*): ā″‿lə-ron′.
winning, *a.* Gagnant: ga″nyān′. See WIN.
winter. Hiver (*n. m.*): ī″vār′.
"Wipers," wai′pərs. Brit. soldiers' slang for YPRES.
wire, *n.* 1. Fil (*m.*): fīl. 2. Fil de fer (*m.*): fīl də fār.—**barbed wire.** See under BARBED.—**brass w.** Fil de laiton: fīl də lā″ton′.—**copper w.** Fil de cuivre: fīl də kwī′‿vrə.—**w.-cutter.** Pince coupante (*n. f.*): pans kū″pan′‿tə.—**w. entanglement.** Réseau de fil de fer (*m.*): rē″zō′ də fīl də fār.—**w.-netting.** Grillage de fil de fer (*m.*): grī″‿yāʒ′ də fīl də fār.—**w.-tapping.** L'interception des dépêches (*f.*): lan″tār″sep″sī″‿yon′ dē dē″pāsh′.
wireless. 1. Télégraphie sans fil (*f.*): tē″lē″gra″fī′ san fīl. 2. Radiotélégraphie (*f.*): ra″dī″ō″tē″lē″gra″fī′.—**wireless telegram.** Radiotélégramme (*n. m.*): ra″dī″ō″tē″lē″grām′.
wisdom. Sagesse (*n. f.*): sa″ʒes′.
wish. Désir (*n. m.*): dē″zīr′.
with, *prep.* Avec: a″vek′.
withdraw, *v.* 1. Retirer: rə-tī″rē′ (*take away*). 2. Se retirer: sə rə-tī″rē′ (*leave*).—**withdrawal.** Retraite (*n. f.*): rə-trāt′.
withers. Garrot (*n. m.*): gar″‿rō′.
withhold, *v.* 1. Retenir: rə-tə-nīr′. 2. S'abstenir de: sabs″‿tə-nīr′ də (*withhold from*).
within. I. *adv.* 1. En: an. 2. Dedans: də-dan′. II. *prep.* 1. En: an. 2. Dans: dan.
without. I. *adv.* En dehors: an də-ōr′. II. *conj.* 1. À moins que: a mwan kə. 2. Sans que: san kə. III. *prep.* Sans: san.
witness. Témoin (*n. m.*): tē″mwan′.—**eye-witness.** Témoin oculaire: tē″mwan′ o″kü″lār′.
woman. Femme (*n. f.*): fam.
wood. Bois (*n. m.*): bwa. Abbreviated *B.*—**wooded,** *a.* Boisé (*m.*), boisée (*f.*): bwa″zē′.—**wooded ground.** Terrain boisé (*m.*): tar″‿ran′ bwa″zē′.—**wooden,** *a.* 1. De bois: də bwa. 2. En bois: an bwa.—**woods,** *n.* 1. Bois (*m.*): bwa. 2. Forêt (*f.*): fo″rē′.—**woodwork.** Charpente (*n. f.*): shar″pān′‿tə.—**wood-yard.** Chantier (*n. m.*): shan″tī″‿yē′. See TIMBER-YARD.
wool, *n.* 1. Laine (*f.*): lān. 2. Ouate (*f.*): ū″‿āt′ (*absorbent cotton-wool*).
word. Mot (*n. m.*): mō.
work. I. *n.* 1. Travail (*m.*): tra″vai′‿yə. 2. Ouvrage (*m.*): ū″vrāʒ′. II. *v.* Travailler: tra″vai″‿yē′.—**working.** Fonctionnement (*n. m.*): fonk″sī″‿yon″‿nə-mān′ (*of machines*).—**works,** *n.* 1. Ouvrages (*m.*): ū″vrāʒ′. 2. Travaux: tra″vō′.—**field works.** Fort (or) ouvrages, de campagne: fōr (or) ū″vrāʒ′, də kan″pā′‿nyə.—**permanent works.** Ouvrages de fortification: ū″vrāʒ′ də fōr″tī″fī″ka″sī″‿yon′. 3. Fabrique (*f.*): fa″brīk′ (*building*). Abbreviated *Fabe.* 4. Usine (*f.*): ü″zīn′ (*factory*). Abbreviated *Use.*—**advanced works.** Ouvrages avancés: ū″vrāʒ′ a″van″sē′.—**defence w.** Ouvrages de défense: ū″vrāʒ′ də dē″fāns′.—**flanking w.** Ouvrages de flanquement: ū″vrāʒ′ də flan″‿kə-mān′.—**intermediate w.** Ouvrages intermédiaires: ū″vrāʒ′ an″tār″mē″dī″‿yār′.—**irregular w.** Ouvrages en ligne brisée: ū″vrāʒ′ an lī′‿nyə brī″zē′.—**regular w.** Ouvrages en ligne droite: ū″vrāʒ′ an lī′‿nyə

drwat.—**supporting w.** Ouvrages d'appui: ū"vrāʒ' dap"pwī'.—**temporary w.** Fortifications passagères: fōr"tī"fī"ka"sī"‿yeṅ' pas"sa"ʒār'.
workshop. Atelier (*n. m.*): a"tel"‿yē'.
worse. **I.** *a.* **1.** Pire: pīr. **2.** Plus mauvais: plü mō"vā'. **II.** *adv.* **1.** Pis: pī. **2.** Plus mal: plü mal.
worth. Valeur (*n. f.*): va"lūr'.
wound, *n.* **1.** Blessure (*f.*): bles"‿sür'. **2.** Plaie (*f.*): plā.—**bruised** or **contused w.** Plaie contuse: plā keṅ"tüz'.—**lacerated w.** Plaie par déchirure: plā par dē"shī"rür'.—**shot w.** Blessure par coup de feu: bles"‿sür' par kū də fū.—**stab w.** Plaie pénétrante: plā pē"nē"trāṅt'.—**superficial w.** Plaie superficielle: plā sü"pēr"-fī"sī"‿yel'.—**to cleanse a wound.** Nettoyer, (or) purifier une blessure: net"‿twa"‿yē', (or) pü"rī"fī"yē' ün bles"‿sür'.—**to clip a w.** Débrider une plaie (*m.*): dē"brī"dē' ün plā.—**to dress a w.** Panser une blessure: paṅ"sē' ün bles"‿sür'.
wounded, *pa.* Blessé (*m.*), blessée (*f.*): bles"‿sē'.—**to be w.** Être blessé: ā'‿trə bles"‿sē'.—**to bring in the w.** Relever les blessés: rə-lə-vē' lē bles"‿sē'.—**where are you w.?** Où êtes-vous blessé? ū ēt vū bles"‿sē'.—**w. in the arm, foot.** Blessé au bras, pied: bles"‿se' ō bra, pī"‿yē'.—**w. in the shoulder.** Blessé à l'épaule: bles"‿sē' a lē"pōl'.
wreath. Couronne (*n. f.*): kū"ren'.
wreathe, *v.* Enrouler: aṅ"rū"lē'.
wrench, *n.* Clef (*f.*): klē.—**monkey-wrench.** Clef anglaise (*n. f.*): klē aṅ"glāz'.
wrinkled, *a.* **1.** Plissé (*m.*), plissée (*f.*): plīs"‿sē' (*of clothes, etc.*). **2.** Ridé (*m.*), ridée (*f.*): rī"dē' (*of the face*).
wrist. Poignet (*n. m.*): pwa"nyē'.—**wrist-watch.** Montre à poignet (*n. f.*): meṅ'‿trə a pwa"nyē'.—**wristlet.** Bracelet (*n. m.*): bra"‿sə-lē'.
write, *v.* Écrire: ē"krīr'.—**w. your name.** Écrivez votre nom: ē"krī"vē' vō'‿trə neṅ.—**in writing.** Par écrit: par ē"krī'.—**writing-paper.** **1.** Papier à lettres (*n. m.*): pa"pī"yē' a let'‿trə. **2.** Papier à écrire (*n. m.*): pa"pī"‿yē' a ē"krīr'.
wrong. **I.** *a.* Faux (*m.*), fō; fausse (*f.*): fōs. **II.** *n.* **1.** Mal (*m.*): mal. **2.** Tort (*m.*): tōr. **III.** *v.* Faire tort à: fār tōr a.—**to be wrong.** Avoir tort: a"vwār' tōr.

X

x-rays, *n. pl.* Rayons X (*m.*): rā"yeṅ' eks.

Y

yacht. Yacht (*n. m.*): ī"‿yāk'.
yard. Cour (*n. f.*): kūr.—**yard,** or **yard-arm.** Vergue (*n. f.*): vārg.
year. **1.** An (*n. m.*): aṅ (*dates only*). **2.** Année (*n. f.*): an"‿nē' (*descriptive in general*).—**to be ten years old.** Avoir dix ans: a"vwār' dīz‿aṅ.—**yearly,** *adv.* Par an: par aṅ.
yellow, *a.* Jaune (*m. & f.*): ʒōn.—**yellowish,** *a.* Jaunâtre: ʒō"nā'‿trə.—**yellowish-white,** *a.* Blanc sale: blaṅ"sal'.
yes, *adv.* Oui: wī.
yesterday, *adv.* Hier: ī"‿yār'.
yet. **I.** *adv.* Encore: aṅ"kōr'. **II.** *conj.* **1.** Cependant: sə-paṅ"dāṅ'. **2.** Pourtant: pūr"tāṅ'.—**as yet.** **1.** Jusqu'ici: ʒüsk"‿ī"sī'. **2.** Jusqu'à présent: ʒüsk"‿a' prē"zāṅ'.—**not yet,** or **not as yet.** Pas encore: paz‿aṅ"kōr'.
yield, *v.* Produire: pro"dwīr'.
Y. M. C. A. Young Men's Christian Association. Union Chrétienne de Jeunes Gens: ü"nī"‿yoṅ' krē"tī"‿yen' [illegible] ʒün ʒaṅ.
you, *pron.* Vous: vū.

young, *a.* Jeune (*m.* & *f.*): ʒŭn.
your, *a. m.* & *f.* Votre (*sing.*): vō'‿trə; vos (*pl.*): vō.
yours, *pron.* **1.** Le vôtre (*m. sing.*): lə vō'‿trə. **2.** La vôtre (*f. sing.*): la vō'‿trə. **3.** Les vôtres (*pl. m.* & *f.*): lē vō'‿trə.
yourself, *pron.* Vous-même (*sing.*): vū"mām'. Also, vous: vū, for "you, yourself."
yourselves, *pron.* Vous-mêmes (*pl.*): vū"mām'.
Ypres, ī'prə. Belgian town.

Z

zebra. Zèbre (*n. m.*): zā'‿brə.
zero, *n.* **1.** Zéro (*m.*): zē"rō'. **2.** Rien (*m.*): rī"‿yaṅ'.
zig-zag, *a.* En zigzags: aṅ zīg"zāg'.
zinc. Zinc (*n. m.*): zaṅk.
zither. Cithare (*f.*): sī"‿tār'.
zone. **1.** Zone (*n. f.*): zōn. **2.** Ceinture (*f.*): saṅ"tür' (*girdle*). —**army zone.** Zone des armées: zōn dēz‿ar"mē'.—**collecting zone.** Zone où l'on ramasse les blessés: zōn ū loṅ ra"mās' lē bles"‿sē'.—**danger z.** Zone dangereuse: zōn daṅ"ʒə-rūz'.—**distribution z.** Zone de répartition: zōn də rē"par"tī"sī"‿yoṅ'. —**evacuating z.** Zone d'évacuation: zōn dē"va"kü"a"sī"‿yoṅ'. —**home z.** Zone de l'intérieur: zōn də laṅ"tē"rī"‿yūr'.—**military z.** Zone militaire: zōn mī"lī"tār'.—**z. of fire.** Champ de tir: shaṅ də tīr.
Zouave. Zouave (*n. m.*): zū"āv' (*light-armed French infantryman*).

APPENDIX

SOME ELEMENTS OF FRENCH GRAMMAR

The Article
The Adjective
The Noun
The Pronoun
The Verb
The Adverb
The Preposition
The Conjunction
The Interjection

MEASURES AND WEIGHTS

Capacity
Distance
Length
Square
Thermometric
Weights

SOME ELEMENTS OF FRENCH GRAMMAR

There are in French nine parts of speech, namely: article, adjective, noun, pronoun, verb, adverb, preposition, conjunction, and interjection.

ARTICLE. There are three sorts of articles, the definite, the indefinite, and the partitive.

The **definite article** *the* is *le* before a masculine noun, *la* before a feminine noun, and *les* for both genders in the plural (*le livre*, lə lī′‿vrə, the book; *la pomme*, la pem, the apple; *les livres*, lē lī′vrə, *les pommes*, lē pem, the books, the apples). The **indefinite article** *a*, *an*, is *un* before a masculine noun, and *une* before a feminine noun (*un manteau*, aṅ man″tō′, a cloak; *une table*, ün tā′‿blə, a table). Hence it may be deduced that *both articles always agree in gender and number with the nouns to which they relate.*

When the article *le* or *la* is to be used before a noun or adjective beginning with a vowel or an *h* not aspirate, an apostrophe is put in the place of *e* or *a*, so that the article and the noun or adjective form one word (*l'or* [lōr] for *le or*, the gold; *l'histoire* [līs″twār′] for *la histoire*, the history; *l'ancien* [laṅ″-sī″‿yaṅ′] for *le ancien*, the senior or elder). When there is occasion to use the article *le* immediately after the preposition *de*, of, from, by, with, in, upon, out of, some, any, for, at, to, both are contracted into *du*, of the, from the, by the, some, any; the same contraction occurs in *des*, of, instead of *de les; au*, to the, instead of *à le*, *aux* instead of *à les;* but it does not take place when *le* is followed by a noun or adjective beginning with a vowel or an *h* not aspirate (*de l'or* [də lōr], of the gold; *de l'homme* [də lem], of the man; *de l'ancien monde* [də laṅ″sī″‿yaṅ′ mōnd], of the ancient world).

The **partitive article** is *du*, *de la*, *de l'* (before a vowel or an *h* not aspirate), *des*, according to the gender and number of the noun (*du pain* [dü paṅ], some *or* any bread; *de la haine* [də la hān], some *or* any hatred; *de l'hôtel* [də lō″tel′], of the hotel; *de l'or* [də lōr], some of the gold; *des poires* [dē pwar], some of the pears); but after a negation, or before an adjective followed by a noun, *de* alone is used without any distinction of gender or number (*il ne mange pas de pain* [īl nə mān′‿ʒə pa də paṅ], he eats no bread; *nous avons de bon vin et de belles figues* [nūz‿a″veṅ′ də beṅ vaṅ ē də bel fīg′ə], we have good wine and fine figs).

ADJECTIVE. The adjective *agrees in gender and number with the noun to which it relates*, and this difference of gender and number is generally marked by the termination of the adjective (*un beau cheval*, a fine horse; *une poire mûre*, a ripe pear; *les beaux arts*, the fine arts).

Adjectives ending in *e* are of both genders (*homme aimable*, amiable man; *femme aimable*, amiable woman). Adjectives ending in *d*, *é*, *eur*, *i*, *t*, *u*, form their *feminine* by the addition of an *e* (*grand*, *grande*, great, large; *sensé*, *sensée*, sensible; *intérieur*, *intérieure*, interior; *poli*, *polie*, polite; *gratuit*, *gratuite*, gratuitous; *tortu*, *tortue*, crooked, twisted); the same addition is made to those ending in *ais*, *as*, *eil*, *el*, *es*, *et*, *ien*, *il*, *on*, *os*, *ot*, *ul*, but the final consonant is doubled (*épais*, *épaisse*, thick; *pareil*, *pareille*, alike; *net*, *nette*, clean, neat; *bon*, *bonne*, good; *sot*, *sotte*, foolish). Adjectives ending in *f* change it into *ve* (*naïf*, *naïve*, simple, unaffected), and those ending in *x* change it into *se* (*jaloux*, *jalouse*, jealous). About thirty adjectives ending in *au*, *c*, *g*, *ou*, *x*, have quite irregular plurals which are indicated by the French dictionaries (*beau*, *belle*, beautiful; *blanc*, *blanche*, white; *long, longue*, long; *bénin, bénigne*, benign; *fou, folle*, foolish; *doux, douce*, soft; *faux, fausse*, false; *vieux, vieille*, old); others ending in *r* (*cher, chère*, dear), and eight others ending in *et* form their feminine by adding *e*, and require a grave accent on the penultimate *e* (*inquiet, inquiète*, anxious, uneasy).

Adjectives ending in *c, d, e, é, f, g, i, n, t, u*, form their *plural* by the addition of an *s* (*grand, grands; poli, polis; intelligent, intelligents*). Adjectives ending in *s* or *x* do not change their termination in the plural (*gros*, big; *hideux*, hideous); those ending in *au* take *x* in the plural (*beau, beaux*); some of those in *al* take *s*, as *fatal, fatals, final, finals, naval, navals;* others change their termination into *aux* (*égal, égaux*, equal; *amical, amicaux*, amicable); but most of them have no plural masculine (*frugal*, frugal, etc.).

Of the three degrees of comparison, the positive is the adjective in its simple state. The **comparative of superiority** is formed by putting *plus* (plü), more, before the adjective (*plus joli*, finer; *plus illustre*, more illustrious); the **comparative of inferiority,** by prefixing *moins* (mwaṅ), less, to the adjective (*moins belle*, mwaṅ bel, less beautiful), and the **comparative of equality,** by putting *aussi* (ōs″‿sī′) before the adjective in affirmative, and *si* (sī) in negative phrases; the terms of comparison, when expressed, are connected with the comparative by the conjunction *que* (*aussi instruit que* [ōs″‿sī′ aṅ″strwī′ kə], as learned as; *il n'est pas si âgé qu'elle* [īl nē pɑ sī ā″‿ʒē′ kel], he is not so old as she). The comparatives of *bon*, beṅ, *mauvais*, mō″vā′, *petit*, pə-tī′, are *meilleur*, mā″‿yūr′, *pire*, pīr, *moindre*, mwaṅ′‿drə.

The **superlative absolute** is formed by putting *très*, trā, *fort*, fōr, or *bien*, bī″‿yaṅ′, very, before the adjective, and the **superlative relative,** by prefixing the article *le, la, les*, according to the gender and number required, to the comparative (*une très belle ville* [ün trā bel vīl], a very fine city; *la plus belle des villes* [lɑ plü bel dē vīl], the finest of cities). When a possessive pronoun is to be used before the comparative, the article is left out (*mon meilleur ami* [meṅ mā″‿yūr′ ɑ″mī′], my best friend).

When the adjective relates to two nouns singular, of the same gender, it must be put in the plural and agree with them in gender (*ma mère et ma sœur sont contentes* [mɑ mār ē mɑ sūr seṅ keṅ″tānt′‿ə], my mother and sister are satisfied); but when the two nouns to which the adjective relates are of different genders, the adjective must be put in the masculine plural (*mon père et ma mère sont contents* [meṅ pār ē mɑ mār seṅ keṅ″tāṅ′], my father and mother are satisfied).

In French qualifying adjectives are placed indifferently before or after the nouns they qualify. The ear and the taste determine their positions. Certain adjectives, however, change in sense according to their positions; such are *brave* (brav), *grand* (graṅ), *bon* (beṅ), *commun* (kem″‿maṅ′), *petit* (pə-tī′). For example: "Un homme bon" is a good, charitable man, but "un bon homme" is a simple, credulous man. Most adjectives are placed after the noun—a magnificent palace: *Un palais magnifique* (aṅ pɑ″lā′ mɑ″nyī″fīk′); a wise man: *Un homme sage* (aṅ‿em sā′‿ʒə); an industrious woman: *Une femme industrieuse* (ün fām aṅ″düs″trī″‿yūz′). The following come before them:

Beau, cher (denoting affection), *gros, jeune, mauvais, méchant, petit*—a handsome horse: *Un beau cheval* (aṅ bō shə-vāl′); my dear boy: *mon cher garçon* (moṅ shār gɑr″soṅ′); the fat man: *le gros bonhomme* (lə grō beṅ″em′); the young girl: *la jeune fille* (lɑ ʒūn fī′‿yə); in bad taste: *de mauvais goût* (də mō″vā′ gū); the naughty boy: *le méchant garçon* (lə mē″shāṅ′ gɑr″soṅ′); the small hat: *le petit chapeau* (lə pə-tī′ shɑ″pō′).

NOUN. There are two sorts of nouns: the **proper noun,** which is applied to a particular person or thing (*César* [sē″zār′], Cæsar; *les Alpes* [lēz alp], Alps), and the **common noun,** which belongs to a whole class of objects (*homme* [əm], man; *forêt* [fō″rē′], forest).

To nouns belong gender and number. *There are two genders,* the *masculine* (*un homme* [aṅ əm], a man; *un livre* [aṅ lī′‿vrə], a book; *le courage* [lə kū″rāʒ′‿ə], courage), and the *feminine* (*une femme* [ün fām], a woman; *une forêt* [ün fō″rā], a forest; *la victoire* [la vīk″twār′], victory). The French dictionary is the only guide to follow to ascertain the gender of inanimate objects. Nouns are of two numbers, the singular (*arbre* [ār′‿brə], tree; *tour* [tūr], tower), and the plural (*arbres* [ār′‿brə], trees; *tours* [tūr], towers); some nouns are used only in the singular (*le courage* [lə kū″rā′‿ʒə], courage; *l'or* [lēr], gold), and others only in the plural (*les mouchettes* [lē mū″shet′], snuffers; *des épinards* [dēz‿ē″pī″nār′], spinach).

The *plural* is formed by adding *s* to the singular (*homme* [əm], man, *hommes* [əm], men; *livre* [lī′‿vrə], book, *livres* [lī′‿vrə], books). But nouns ending in *s, x, z* in the singular, remain the same in the plural (*fils* [fīs], son, *fils* [fīs], sons; *voix* [vwa], voice, *voix* [vwa], voices; *nez* [nē], nose, *nez* [nē], noses); nouns ending in *au, eu, ou* are rendered plural by adding an *x* (*bateau* [ba″tō′], boat, *bateaux* [ba″tō′], boats; *vœu* [vū], vow, *vœux* [vū], vows; *bijou* [bī″‿ʒū′], jewel, *bijoux* [bī″‿ʒū′], jewels); nouns ending in *al, ail,* change it into *aux* in the plural (*cheval* [shə-vāl′], horse, *chevaux* [sh ə-vō′], horses; *travail* [tra″vai′], work, *travaux* [tra″vō′], works), except *bal* (bal), ball; *détail* (də-tai′), detail, and some others which follow the general rule.

PRONOUN. There are five kinds of pronouns.

1. Personal pronouns.

SINGULAR.—*1st person*

Subject	*Je,*	ʒə. . . I
Object	*Me,*	mə. . me
	Moi,	mwa. me
	Me,	mə. . to me
	Moi,	mwa. to me

2d person

Subject	*Tu,*	tü. . . thou
Object	*Te,*	tə. . . thee
	Toi,	twa. . thee
	Te,	tə. . . to thee
	Toi,	twa. . to thee

3d person

Subject	*Il,*	īl. . . . . he
	Elle,	el. . . . . she
Object	*Le, lui,*	lə, lwī. . him, it
	La, elle,	la, el. . . her
	Lui,	lwī. . . . to him, to it
	Lui,	lwī. . . . to her

PLURAL.—*1st person*

Subject	*Nous,*	nū. . we
Object	*Nous,*	nū. . us
	Nous,	nū. . to us

2d person

Subject	*Vous,*	vū. . you
Object	*Vous,*	vū. . you
	Vous,	vū. . to you

3d person

Subject	*Ils, elles,*	il, el. . . . they
Object	*Les, eux, elles,*	lē, ū, el. . them
	Leur,	lūr. . . . . to them

REFLECTED AND RECIPROCAL PRONOUN.—*3d person*

Sing. { *Se,* sə, himself, herself, one's self.
Se, sə, to himself, to herself, to one's self.

Plur. { *Se,* sə, themselves, one another.
Se, sə, to themselves, to one another.

Soi, swa, himself, to himself, oneself, to oneself.

PERSONAL AND RELATIVE PRONOUNS

En, aṅ, of him, of her, of it, of them, some of them, of that, thence, hence.

Y, ī, to him, to her, to it, to them, there, here, thither.

2. Possessive pronouns.

CONJUNCTIVE.—*1st person*

Sing.	*Mon* (məṅ), m. *Ma* (ma), f.	my
Plur.	*Mes* (mē), m. f.	my
Sing.	*Nôtre* (nō'‿trə), m. f.	our
Plur.	*Nos* (nō), m. f.	our

2d person

Sing.	*Ton* (təṅ), m. *Ta* (ta), f.	thy
Plur.	*Tes* (tē), m. f.	thy
	Vôtre (vō'‿trə), m. f. *Vos* (vō), m. f.	your

3d person

Sing.	*Son* (səṅ), m. *Sa* (sa), f. *Ses* (sē), m. f.	his her its
Plur.	*Leur* (lūr), m. f. *Leurs* (lūr), m. f.	their

RELATIVE.—*1st person*

Sing.	*Le mien* (lə mī"‿yaṅ'), m. *La mienne* (la mī"‿yen'), f.	mine
Plur.	*Les miens* (lē mī"‿yaṅ'), m. *Les miennes* (lē mī"‿yen'), f.	mine
Sing.	*Le nôtre* (lə nō'‿trə), m. *La nôtre* (la nō'‿trə), f.	ours
Plur.	*Les nôtres* (lē nō'‿trə), m. f.	ours

2d person

Sing.	*Le tien* (lə tī"‿yaṅ'), m. *La tienne* (la tī"‿yen'), f.	thine
Plur.	*Les tiens* (lē tī"‿yaṅ'), m. *Les tiennes* (lē tī"‿yen'), f.	thine
Sing.	*Le vôtre* (lə vō'‿trə), m. *La vôtre* (la vō'‿trə), f.	yours
Plur.	*Les vôtres* (lē vō'‿trə), m. f.	yours

3d person

Sing.	*Le sien* (lə sī"‿yaṅ'), m. *La sienne* (la sī"‿yen'), f.	his hers its
Plur.	*Les siens* (lē sī"‿yaṅ'), m. *Les siennes* (lē sī"‿yen'), f.	his hers its
Sing.	*Le leur* (lə lūr), m. *La leur* (la lūr), f.	theirs
Plur.	*Les leurs* (lē lūr), m. f.	theirs

Mon, *ton*, *son*, are used before a noun feminine, when beginning with a vowel or *h* mute (*mon âme*, my soul; *ton humeur*, thy humor). For pronunciations see under CONJUNCTIVE, above.

3. Demonstrative pronouns.

CONJUNCTIVE

Sing.	*Ce* (sə), masc. before a consonant or an *h* aspirate. *Cet* (set), masc. before a vowel or an *h* mute. *Cette* (set), fem. in all cases.
Plur.	*Ces* (sē), m. f.

EXAMPLE. *Ce livre* (sa lī'‿vrə), this book; *ce héros* (sə hē"rō'), that hero; *cet enfant* (set‿aṅ"fāṅ'), this child; *cet homme* (set‿om), that man; *cette fille* (set fī'‿yə), that girl; *cette âme* (set‿ām), this soul; *ces livres* (sē lī'‿vrə), those books; *ces hommes* (sēz‿om), these men; *ces enfants* (sēz‿aṅ"fāṅ'), those children.

RELATIVE

Singular		Plural	
Celui-ci (sə-lwī″sī′), m. *Celle-ci* (sel″sī′), f. *Ceci* (sə-sī′)	this	*Ceux-ci* (sū″sī′), m. *Celles-ci* (sel″sī′), f.	these
Celui-là (sə-lwī″lā′), m. *Celle-là* (sel″‿lā′), f. *Cela* (sə-la′)	that	*Ceux-là* (sū″lā′), m. *Celles-là* (sel″‿lā′), f.	those

4. Relative pronouns.

Subject:
- *Qui* (kī) (common to persons and things), who, which.
- *Quoi* (kwa), what.
- *Quel* (kel), *quelle* (kel), *quels* (kel), *quelles* (kel), which, what.
- *Lequel* (lə-kel′(, *laquelle* (la″kel′), *lesquels* (lē″kel′), *lesquelles* (lē″kel′) (common to persons and things), who, which, what.

Object:
- *Qui* (kī) (referring to persons), whom.
- *Que* (kə) (common to persons and things), whom, which.
- *Quoi* (kwa), what.
- *De qui* (də kī) (said of persons only), of whom, from whom, of which, from which.
- *Dont* (dəṅ) (common to persons and things), of whom, whose, of which.
- *À qui* (a kī) (said of persons only), to whom.
- *Lequel* (lə-kel′), *laquelle* (la″kel′), *lesquels* (lē″kel′), *lesquelles* (lē″kel′) (common to persons and things), whom, which.
- *Duquel* (dü″kel′), *de laquelle* (də la″kel′), *desquels* (dē″-kel′), *desquelles* (dē″kel′) (common to persons and things), of whom, of which, from whom, from which.
- *Auquel* (ō″kel′), *a laquelle* (a la″kel′), *auxquels* (ō″kel′), *auxquelles* (ō″kel′) (common to persons and things), to whom, to which.
- *D'où* (dū), from which.
- *Où* (ū), to which.

5. Indefinite pronouns: *on* (əṅ), one; *quelqu'un* (kel″kaṅ′), some one; *quelque* (kel′‿kə), some; *chaque* (śhak), each; *l'un et l'autre* (laṅ ē lō′‿trə), the one and the other; *quiconque* (kī″-kəṅ′‿kə), whoever, etc.

VERB. A verb **active** expresses an action and implies an agent and an object acted upon (*elle aime son père* [el ām səṅ pār], she loves her father). A verb **passive** expresses a passion and the receiving of an action (*elle est aimée de son père* [el ēt‿ā″mē′ də səṅ pār], she is loved by her father). A verb **neuter** expresses being or a state of being (*je suis* [ʒə swī], I am; *je dors* [ʒə dōr], I sleep; *je vais à Londres* [ʒə vā a ləṅ′‿drə], I go to London). A verb **pronominal,** or conjugated with two pronouns, is reflective, when the action it implies falls upon the subject (*je me flatte* [ʒə mə flat], I flatter myself); neuter, when it marks only a state of the subject (*elle se repent* [el sə rə-pāṅ′], she repents; *il s'enfuit* [īl san″fwī′], he ran away), and reciprocal, when there is a reciprocity of action between two or more subjects (*ils s'entr'aident* [īl saṅ″trā′‿də], they help one another); it is also used impersonally (*il se bâtit* [īl sə ba″tī′], there is building; *il s'est dit* [īl sē dī], it has been said). **Impersonal** verbs are only used in the third person singular (*il neige* [īl nā′‿ʒə], it snows), and neuter verbs frequently assume the same form (*il vint un homme* [īl vaṅt‿an‿em], there came a man).

FRENCH VERBS OF REGULAR CONJUGATION

There are three regular conjugations of French verbs: (1) *donner* (don″‿nē′), give; (2) *finir* (fī″nīr′), finish; (3) *vendre* (vūn′‿drə), sell. From the principal parts of the verbs, (1) the infinitive, (2) the present participle, (3) the past participle, (4) the present indicative, (5) and the preterit indicative, all forms of regular verbs may be inferred. See Tables of Regular Verbs, below.

Most of the French verbs are of the first regular conjugation, in which the infinitive ends in *-er*.

Eng.	*Infinitive Present and Past Participle*	*Indic. Present*	*Imperfect*	*Preterit*	*Future*	*Notes*
	FIRST REGULAR CONJUGATION. Infinitive ending in *-er*, as *donner* (give)					
give giving given	donner (*inf.*) donnant (*pr.*) donné (*pp.*)	(*I give*) je donne* tu donnes il donne n. donnons* v. donnez* i. donnent	(*I did give*) je donnais tu donnais il donnait n. donnions v. donniez i. donnaient	(*I gave*) je donnai tu donnas il donna n. donnâmes v. donnâtes i. donnèrent	(*I shall give*) je donnerai tu donneras il donnera n. donnerons v. donnerez i. donneront	* For the Imperative singular and plural omit the pronouns *je*, *nous*, *vous*: donne (*give*); donnons (*let us give*); donnez (*give ye*). The Present Subjunctive, formed by adding the conjunction *que* to the Indicative Present: *que je donne* (that I may give), and the Imperfect Subjunctive, *que je donnasse* (that I might give), are omitted for lack of space.
	SECOND REGULAR CONJUGATION. Infinitive ending in *-ir*, as *finir* (finish).					
finish finishing finished	finir (*inf.*) finissant (*pr.*) fini (*pp.*)	(*I finish*) je finis tu finis il finit n. finissons v. finissez i. finissent	(*I was finishing*) je finissais tu finissais il finissait n. finissions v. finissiez i. finissaient	(*I finished*) je finis tu finis il finit n. finîmes v. finîtes i. finirent	(*I shall finish*) je finirai tu finiras il finira n. finirons v. finirez i. finiront	
	THIRD REGULAR CONJUGATION. Infinitive ending in *-re*, as *vendre* (sell).					
sell selling sold	vendre (*inf.*) vendant (*pr.*) vendu (*pp.*)	(*I sell*) je vends tu vends il vend n. vendons v. vendez i. vendent	(*I was selling*) je vendais tu vendais il vendait n. vendions v. vendiez i. vendaient	(*I sold*) je vendis tu vendis il vendit n. vendîmes v. vendîtes i. vendirent	(*I shall sell*) je vendrai tu vendras il vendra n. vendrons v. vendrez i. vendront	ABBREVIATIONS: *n.* = nous (*we*); *v.* = vous (*you*); *i.* = ils (*they*). For the feminine (*elle*, *elles*), see under PRONOUN.

FRENCH IRREGULAR AND DEFECTIVE VERBS.

In the following table (1) the Imperfect Indicative, (2) the Conditional, (3) the Imperative, (4) the Present Subjunctive, and (5) Imperfect Subjunctive are omitted. These tenses are formed: (1) the *Imperfect Indicative*, from the present participle by changing *-ant* into *-ais;* thus, *all-ant j'all-ais, batt-ant, je batt-ais.* (2) The *Conditional* is formed by adding *s* to the Future Tense; thus, *je chanterai, je chanterais; je parlerai, je parlerais.* (3) The *Imperative* is formed from the Indicative Present by omitting the pronoun (except in *aller*, where it is *va*). Thus, *je parle* (indic. pres.); *parle* (imperative), and so on. There are three exceptions, and these are the verbs *avoir* (have), *être* (be), and *savoir* (know). (4) The *Present Subjunctive* is formed very irregularly, but may be easily ascertained from a French grammar. (5) The *Imperfect Subjunctive* is formed from the preterit indicative by the addition of *-se*, etc., to the second person singular; as, *tu parlas, que je parlas-se.**

Compound forms for all parts of a French verb, excepting the imperative and the past participle, are formed, as in English, by adding the past participle to the various forms of the auxiliary verb, which is usually *avoir* (have), but sometimes *être* (be). For example: (1) Past participle, *allé;* perfect infinitive, *être allé.* (2) Past participle, *envoyé;* perfect infinitive, *avoir envoyé*, etc.

Eng.	*Inf. Ppr. & Pp.*	*Indic. Present*	*Preterit*	*Future*
		FIRST CONJUGATION		
go	aller	je vais	j'allai	j'irai
	allant	tu vas	allas	iras
	allé	il va	alla	ira
		n. allons	allâmes	irons
		v. allez	allâtes	irez
		i. vont	allèrent	iront
send	envoyer	j'envoie	j'envoyai	j'enverrai
	envoyant	envoies		
	envoyé	envoie		
		envoyons		
		envoyez		
		envoient		
		SECOND CONJUGATION		
acquire	acquérir	j'acquiers	j'acquis	j'acquerrai
	acquérant	tu acquiers	acquis	acquerras
	acquis	il acquiert	acquit	acquerra
		n. acquérons	acquîmes	acquerrons
		v. acquérez	acquîtes	acquerrez
		i. acquièrent	acquîrent	acquerront
assault	assaillir	j'assaille	j'assaillis	j'assaillirai
	assaillant	assailles		
	assailli	assaille		
		assaillons		
		assaillez		
		assaillent		
boil	bouillir[1]	je bous	je bouillis	je bouillerai
	bouillant	bous		
	bouilli	bout		
		bouillons		
		bouillez		
		bouillent		
boil away	ébouillir			
	ébouilli			
clothe	vêtir	je vêts	je vêtis	je vêtirai
	vêtant	vêts		
	vêtu	vêt		
		vêtons		
		vêtez		
		vêtent		

Second Conjugation Continued

Eng.	*Inf. Ppr. & Pp.*	*Indic. Present*	*Preterit*	*Future*
die	mourir mourant mort	je meurs meurs meurt mourons mourez meurent	je mourus	je mourrai
fail	faillir[2] faillant failli	je faux faux faut faillons faillez faillent	je faillis	je faudrai
faint	défaillir[3] défailli	n. défaillons v. défaillez i. défaillent	je défaillis ils défailli- rent	
feel, smell	sentir sentant senti	je sens sens sent sentons sentez sentent	je sentis	je sentirai
fetch	quérir[4]			
flee	fuir fuyant fui	je fuis fuis fuit fuyons fuyez fuient	je fuis	je fuirai
flourish, prosper	fleurir fleurissant florissant fleuri	je fleuris fleuris fleurit fleurissons fleurissez fleurissent	je fleuris	je fleurirai
gather	cueillir cueillant cueilli	je cueille cueilles cueille cueillons cueille cueillent	je cueillis	je cueillerai
happen	advenir advenant advenu	il advient	il advint	il adviendra
hold	tenir tenant tenu	je tiens tiens tient tenons tenez tiennent	je tins	je tiendrai
lie (ill or dead)	gésir[5] gisant	gît gisons gisez gisent		
open	ouvrir ouvrant ouvert	j'ouvre ouvres ouvre ouvrons ouvrez ouvrent	j'ouvris	j'ouvrirai
run	courir courant couru	je cours cours court courons courez courent	je courus	je courrai

Second Conjugation Continued

Eng.	*Inf. Ppr. & Pp.*	*Indic. Present*	*Preterit*	*Future*
serve	servir servant servi	je sers sers sert servons servez servent	je servis	je servirai
sleep	dormir dormant dormi	je dors dors dort dormons dormez dorment	je dormis	je dormirai
strike	férir[6] féru			

Third Conjugation

Eng.	*Inf. Ppr. & Pp.*	*Indic. Present*	*Preterit*	*Future*
be able	pouvoir pouvant pu	je peux *or* je peux [puis peut pouvons pouvez peuvent	je pus pus put pûmes pûtes purent	je pourrai pourras pourra pourrons pourrez pourront
become, befit	seoir[7] séant	il sied ils siéent		il siéra ils siéront
fall, lose	déchoir[8] déchu	je déchois déchois déchoit déchoyons déchoyez déchoient	je déchus	je décherrai
fall due, expire	échoir[9] échéant échu	il échoit *or* il échet	il échut	il écherra
foresee	prévoir prévoyant prévu	je prévois prévois prévoit prévoyons prévoyez prévoient	je prévis	je prévoirai
have	avoir ayant eu	j'ai as a avons avez ont	j'eus	j'aurai
know	savoir[10] sachant su	je sais sais sait savons savez savent	je sus	je saurai
move	mouvoir mouvant mu	je meus meus meut mouvons mouvez meuvent	je mus	je mouvrai
be necessary	falloir[11] fallu	il faut	il fallut	il faudra
prevail	prévaloir prévalant prévalu	je prévaux prévaux prévaut prévalons prévalez prévalent	je prévalus	je prévaudrai

Third Conjugation Continued

Eng.	*Inf. Ppr. & Pp.*	*Indic. Present*	*Preterit*	*Future*
promote	promouvoir[12] promu			
provide	pourvoir pourvoyant pourvu	je pourvois pourvois pourvoit pourvoyons pourvoyez pourvoient	je pourvus	je pourvoirai
put off, suspend	surseoir sursoyant sursis	je sursois sursois sursoit sursoyons sursoyez sursoient	je sursis	je surseoirai
rain	pleuvoir pleuvant plu	il pleut	il plut	il pleuvra
recover, have again	ravoir[13]			
see	voir voyant vu	je vois vois voit voyons voyez voient	je vis	je verrai
set	asseoir asseyant assis	j'assieds assieds assied asseyons asseyez asseient	j'assis	j'assiérai *or* j'assoirai
sit,	seoir[14]			
be willing, will, be inclined	vouloir[15] voulant voulu	je veux veux veut voulons voulez veulent	je voulus	je voudrai
be worth	valoir[16] valant valu	je vaux vaux vaut valons valez valent	je valus	je vaudrai

Fourth Conjugation

Eng.	*Inf. Ppr. & Pp.*	*Indic. Present*	*Preterit*	*Future*
absolve	absoudre absolvant absous (*m.*) absoute (*f.*)	j'absous absous absout absolvons absolvez absolvent	*wanting*	j'absoudrai absoudras absoudra absoudrons absoudrez absoudront
abstract	abstraire abstrayant abstrait	j'abstrais abstrais abstrait abstrayons abstrayez abstraient	*wanting*	j'abstrairai
appear	paraître paraissant paru	je parais parais parait paraissons paraissez paraissent	je parus	je paraîtrai

FOURTH CONJUGATION CONTINUED

Eng.	*Inf. Ppr. & Pp.*	*Indic. Present*	*Preterit*	*Future*
be	être étant été	je suis es est sommes êtes sont	je fus	je serai
beat	battre battant battu	je bats bats bat battons battez battent	je battis	je battrai
believe	croire croyant cru	je crois crois croit croyons croyez croient	je crus	je croirai
be born	naître naissant né	je nais nais naît naissons naissez naissent	je naquis	je naîtrai
bray	braire	il brait		il braira
break	rompre rompant rompu	je romps romps rompt rompons rompez rompent	je rompis	je romprai
circumcise	circoncire circoncisant circoncis	je circoncis circoncis circoncit circonci-sons circoncisez circonci-sent	je circoncis	je circoncirai
close	clore[17] clos	je clos tu clos il clôt		je clorai
conclude	conclure concluant conclu	je conclus conclus conclut concluons concluez concluent	je conclus	je conclurai
conquer	vaincre vairquant vaincu	je vaincs vaincs vainc vainquons vainquez vainquent	je vainquis	je vaincrai
curse	maudire maudissant maudit	je maudis maudis maudit maudissons maudissez maudissent	je maudis	je maudirai
dawn; sting	poindre	il point		il poindra

FOURTH CONJUGATION CONTINUED

Eng.	*Inf. Ppr. & Pp.*	*Indic. Present*	*Preterit*	*Future*
drink	boire buvant bu	je bois bois boit buvons buvez boivent	je bus	je boirai
feed	repaître repaissant repu	je repais repais repaît repaissons repaissez repaissent	je repus	je repaîtrai
follow	suivre suivant suivi	je suis suis suit suivons suivez suivent	je suivis	je suivrai
forfeit, trespass be false to	forfaire à[18]			
(make) fry	frire (faire)[19] frit	je fris tu fris il frit		je frirai
graze	paître paissant pu	je pais pais paît paissons paissez paissent		je paîtrai
grind	moudre moulant moulu	je mouds mouds moud moulons moulez moulent	je moulus	je moudrai
grow	croître croissant crû	je crois crois croît croissons croissez croissent	je crûs	je croîtrai
hatch blow (*of flowers*)	éclore eclos	il éclôt ils éclosent		il éclôra ils éclôront
hurt, to injure	nuire à nuisant nui	je nuis nuis nuit nuisons nuisez nuisent	je nuisis	je nuirai
join	joindre joignant joint	je joins joins joint joignons joignez joignent	je joignis	je joindrai
laugh	rire de riant ri	je ris ris rit rions riez rient	je ris	je rirai

FOURTH CONJUGATION CONTINUED

Eng.	*Inf. Ppr. & Pp.*	*Indic. Present*	*Preterit*	*Future*
live (on or upon)	vivre de vivant vécu	je vis vis vit vivons vivez vivent	je vécus	je vivrai
make, do	faire faisant fait	je fais fais fait faisons faites font	je fis	je ferai
make one believe	accroire[20] *i. e.* faire accroire à			
pickle, preserve	confire confisant confit	je confis confis confit confisons confisez confisent	je confis	je confirai
please	plaire plaisant plu	je plais plais plaît plaisons plaisez plaisent	je plus	je plairai
put	mettre mettant mis	je mets mets met mettons mettez mettent	je mis	je mettrai
read	lire lisant lu	je lis lis lit lisons lisez lisent	je lus	je lirai
reduce	réduire réduisant réduit	je réduis réduis réduit réduisons réduisez réduisent	je reduisis	je reduirai
resolve	résoudre résolvant résolu *or* résous	je résous résous résout résolvons résolvez résolvent	je résolus	je résoudrai
result from	s'ensuivre ensuivant ensuivi	il s'ensuit	il s'ensuivit	il s'ensuivra
roar, to rustle	bruire[21] bruyant			
say	dire disant dit	je dis dis dit disons dites disent	je dis	je dirai

FOURTH CONJUGATION CONTINUED

Eng.	*Inf. Ppr. & Pp.*	*Indic. Present*	*Preterit*	*Future*
sew	coudre cousant cousu	je couds couds coud cousons cousez cousent	je cousis	je coudrai
shine	luire luisant lui	je luis luis luit luisons luisez luisent		je luirai
slander	médire de médisant médit	je médis médis médit médisons médisez médisent	je médis	je médirai
suffice	suffire (à) suffisant suffi	je suffis suffis suffit suffisons suffisez suffisent	je suffis	je suffirai
take	prendre prenant pris	je prends prends prend prenons prenez prennent	je pris	je prendrai
write	écrire écrivant écrit	j'écris écris écrit écrivons écrivez écrivent	j'écrivis	j'écrirai

* The subjunctive present of *aller* is *que j'aille, que tu ailles, qu'il aille, que nous allions, que vous alliez, qu'ils allient*. The subjunctive imperfect is *que j'allasse, que tu allasses, qu'il allât, que nous allassions, que vous allassiez, qu'ils allassent*.

NOTES:—[1]The verb *faire* (make, do) is commonly used to conjugate this verb; as, *faire bouillir*, etc., except when used directly in the 3d person singular and plural. [2]Is used infrequently but in the preterit, the compound tenses, and in the infinitive, after another verb. [3]The imperfect indicative is used: *je défaillais*. The Academy states, however, that the verb is seldom used except in the plural. [4]Used only in familiar speech and in the infinitive after *aller, envoyer, venir*. [5]Imperfect indicative is used: *je gisais*, etc. [6]Infinitive used only in the phrase *sans coup férir*, "without striking a blow." [7]Is used only in the 3d person. Has no compound tenses. [8]Indicative imperfect: *je déchoyais*, etc. [9]Commonly used only in the 3d person. [10]Imperative: *sache, sachons, sachez*. Indicative imperfect is *je savais*, etc. [11]Imperative wanting. *Il fallait* is used. [12]Used only in the infinitive, in the compound tenses, and in the imperfect of the subjunctive. [13]Used only in the infinitive. [14]Used only in the two participles: *séant; sis*. [15]Imperative 2d person plural is *veuillez*, please to. [16]Imperative wanting. [17]Used in all the compound tenses. [18]Used only in the infinitive and compound tenses. [19]To supply the tenses and persons lacking the verb *faire* is used. [20]Always used with the verb *faire* and only in the infinitive. [21]Indicative imperfect: *il bruyait* (sing.), *ils bruyaient* (plural).

IRREGULAR AND DEFECTIVE VERBS

Conjugated in the same way as the verbs in the preceding table. For explanation of symbols used to indicate pronunciation, see PRONUNCIATION, pages viii–xii.

First Conjugation

English	French		See
go away	s'en aller	saṅ‿al″‿lē′	go
send back	renvoyer	raṅ″vwa″‿yē′	send

Second Conjugation

English	French		See
abstain	s'abstenir	sabs″‿tə-nīr′	hold
agree	consentir	keṅ″saṅ″tīr′	feel
agree (in compound tenses with *être*)	convenir	keṅ″‿və-nīr′	hold
arrive	parvenir	par″‿və-nīr′	"
befall	survenir	sür″‿və-nīr′	"
become	devenir	də-və-nīr′	"
become again	redevenir	rə-də-və-nīr′	"
belie	démentir	dē″maṅ″tīr′	feel
belong to	appartenir	ap″‿par″‿tə-nīr′	hold
boil again	rebouillir	rə-bū″‿yīr′	boil
circumvent	circonvenir	sīr″keṅ″‿və-nīr′	hold
clear (a table)	desservir	des″sār″vīr′	serve
clothe oneself	se vêtir	sə-vā″tīr′	clothe
clothe again	revêtir	rə-vā″tīr′	"
collect oneself	se recueillir	sə rə-kū″yīr′	gather
come	venir	və-nīr′	hold
come back	revenir	rə-və-nīr′	"
concur	concourir	keṅ″kū″rīr′	run
conquer	conquérir	keṅ″kē″rīr′	acquire
contain	contenir	keṅ″‿tə-nīr′	hold
cover	couvrir	kū″vrīr′	open
cover again	recouvrir	rə-kū″vrīr′	"
deny	disconvenir	dīs″keṅ″‿və-nīr′	hold
desist	se départir de	sə dē″par″tīr′ də	feel
discover	découvrir	dē″kū″vrīr′	open
distribute	répartir	rē″par″tīr′	feel
divest of (prejudice)	déprévenir	dē″prē″‿və-nīr′	hold
vest oneself	se révêtir	sə rē″vē″tīr′	clothe
dress again	revêtir	rə-vē″tīr′	"
entertain	entretenir	aṅ″‿trə-tə-nīr′	hold
fall asleep	s'endormir	saṅ″dēr″mīr′	sleep
fall asleep again	se rendormir	sə raṅ″dēr″mīr′	"
feel	ressentir	rə-saṅ″tīr′	feel
feel effects of	se ressentir de	sə rə-saṅ″tīr′ də	"
forbear	se retenir	sə rə-tə-nīr′	hold
foresee	pressentir	pres″‿saṅ″tīr′	feel
forewarn	prévenir	prē″və-nīr′	hold
gather together	recueillir	rə-kū″‿yīr′	gather
go out	sortir	sēr″tīr′	feel
go out again	ressortir	rə-sēr″tīr′	"
happen	survenir	sür″‿və-nīr′	hold
hasten to	accourir	ak″‿kū″‿rīr′	run
have recourse to	recourir à	rə-kū″rīr′ a	"
ill-treat	desservir	des″‿sār″vīr′	serve
incur	encourir	aṅ″kū″rīr′	run
infringe	contrevenir	koṅ″‿trə-və-nīr′	hold
inquire	s'enquérir	saṅ″kē″rīr′	acquire
intervene	intervenir	aṅ″tār″və-nīr′	hold
lie	mentir	maṅ″tīr′	feel
lull to sleep	endormir	aṅ″dēr″mīr′	sleep

English	French		*See*
maintain[1]	maintenir	mañ″tə-nīr′	hold
maintain[2]	soutenir	sū″tə-nīr′	"
make use of	se servir	sə sār″vīr′	serve
maltreat	desservir	des″‿sār″vīr′	"
obtain	obtenir	ob″‿tə-nīr′	hold
offer	offrir	of″‿frīr′	open
open	ouvrir	ū″vrīr′	"
open again	rouvrir	rū″vrīr′	"
prepossess	prévenir	prē″‿və-nīr′	hold
proceed from	provenir	pro″‿və-nīr′	"
provide for	subvenir à	süb″və-nīr′ a	"
recollect	se souvenir de	sə sū″‿və-nīr′ də	"
reconquer	reconquérir	rə-koñ″kē″rīr′	acquire
refrain from	se contenir	sə koñ″tə-nīr′	hold
remember	se ressouvenir	sə rə-sū″‿və-nīr′	"
repent	se repentir	sə rə-pañ″tīr′	feel
request	requérir	rə-kē″rīr′	acquire
retain	retenir	rə-tə-nīr′	hold
run away	s'enfuir	sañ″fwīr′	flee
run over	parcourir	par″kū″rīr′	run
set off again	repartir	rə-par″tīr′	feel
set out	partir	par″tīr′	"
sleep again	se rendormir	sə rañ″dōr″mīr′	sleep
start up	tressaillir	tres″‿sai″‿yīr′	assault
succor	secourir	sə-kū″rīr′	run
suffer	souffrir	sūf″‿frīr′	open
suit	convenir	koñ″və-nīr′	hold
swerve from	se départir de	sə dē″par″tīr′ də	feel
talk about	discourir de	dīs″kū″rīr′ də	run
uncover	découvrir	dē″kū″vrīr′	open
underbid	mésoffrir	mē″zof″‿frīr′	"
undress	dévêtir	dē″vā″tīr′	clothe
welcome	acceuillir	ak″kū″‿yīr′	gather

Third Conjugation

be concerned	s'émouvoir	sē″mū″vwār′	move
be equivalent	équivaloir	ē″kī″val″wār′	prevail
be moved	s'émouvoir	sē″mū″vwār′	move
be unbecoming	messeoir	mes″‿swār′	become
fall again	rechoir	rə-shwār′	fall
glimpse (get a)	entrevoir	añ″trə-vwār′	see
leave unprovided	dépourvoir	dē″pūr″vwār′	provide
move	émouvoir	ē″mū″vwār′	move
pay back, return, like for like	revaloir	rə-val″wār′	prevail
replace, reset, reseat	rasseoir	ras″‿swār′	sit
resee, see again	revoir	rə-vwār′	see
see each other	s'entrevoir	sañ″trə‿vwār′	"
sit down	s'asseoir	sas″‿swār′	set
stir up	émouvoir	ē″mū″vwār′	move
take advantage of	se prévaloir de	sə prē″val″wār′ də	prevail

Fourth Conjugation

abate	rabattre	ra″bāt′‿trə	beat
abstract	abstraire	abs″trār′	milk
acknowledge	reconnaître	rə-kon″‿nā′‿trə	appear
adjoin	adjoindre	ad″ʒwañ′‿drə	join
admit	admettre	ad″met′‿trə	put
allow	permettre	pēr″met′‿trə	"
anoint	oindre	wañ′‿drə	join

English	French		*See*
appear to sight	apparaître	ɑp″‿pɑ″rā′‿trə	appear
appear before court	comparaître	kəṅ″pɑ″rā′‿trə	“
appear again	reparaître	rə-pɑ″rā′‿trə	“
ask too much	surfaire	sür″fār′	make
astonish	surprendre	sür″prɑ̄ṅ′‿drə	take
avoid	se soustraire (à)	sə sūs″trār′ (ɑ)	milk
back	se rabattre	sə rɑ″bāt′‿trə	beat
bake	cuire	kwīr	reduce
bake again	recuire	rə-kwīr′	“
beacquainted with	connaître	kon″nā′‿trə	appear
be afraid	craindre	krāṅ′‿drə	join
be born again	renaitre	rə-nā′‿trə	born
be displeased with	se déplaire	sə dē″plār′	please
be lost by limitation	se prescrire	pres″krīr′	write
beat again	rebattre	rə-bāt′‿trə	beat
belie	dédire	dē″dīr′	slander
bow out	éconduire	ē″kəṅ″dwīr′	reduce
bribe	séduire	sē″dwīr′	“
bring down	rabattre	rɑ″bāt′‿trə	beat
build	construire	kəṅ″strwīr′	reduce
build again	reconstruire	rə-kəṅ″strwīr′	“
chide	reprendre	rə-prɑ̄ṅ′‿drə	take
choose	élire	ē″līr′	read
circumscribe	circonscrire	sīr″kəṅ″skrīr′	write
clasp	étreindre	ē″traṅ′‿drə	join
color	teindre	taṅ′drə	“
combat	combattre	kəṅ″bāt′‿trə	beat
commit	commettre	ko″mēt′‿trə	put
complain	se plaindre	sə plaṅ′‿drə	join
compromise	compromettre	kəṅ″pro″met′‿trə	put
compromise oneself	se compromettre	se kəṅ″pro″met′‿trə	“
conceal	taire	tār	please
conduct	conduire	kəṅ″dwīr′	reduce
conduct again	reconduire	rə-kəṅ″dwīr′	“
confine	restreindre	res″traṅ′‿drə	join
confine oneself	s'astreindre	sɑs″traṅ′‿drə	“
conjoin	conjoindre	kəṅ″ʒwan′‿drə	“
constrain	contraindre	kəṅ″tran′‿drə	“
contradict	contredire	kəṅ″trə-dīr′	slander
construct	construire	kəṅ″strwīr′	reduce
convince	convaincre	kəṅ″vaṅ′‿krə	conquer
cook	cuire	kwīr	reduce
cook again	recuire	rə-kwīr′	“
correct oneself	se reprendre	sə rə-prɑ̄ṅ′‿drə	take
corrupt	corrompre	kər″rəṅ′‿prə	break
debate	débattre	dē″bāt′‿trə	beat
decay	se détruire	sə dē″trwīr′	reduce
decrease	decroitre	dē″krwā‿trə	grow
deduct	déduire	dē″dwīr′	reduce
“	soustraire	sūs″trār′	milk
delight	se complaire	sə kəṅ″plār′	please
delight in	se repaître	sə rə-pā′‿trə	feed
describe	décrire	dē″krīr′	write
“	dépeindre	dē″paṅ′drə	join
destroy	détruire	dē″trwīr′	reduce
disappear	disparaître	dīs″pɑ″rā′‿trə	appear
disbelieve	mécroire	mē″krwār′	believe
discolor	déteindre	dē″taṅ′‿drə	join
disengage	déprendre	dē″prɑ̄ṅ′drə	take
disjoin	déjoindre	dē″ʒwaṅ′drə	join
“	disjoindre	dīs″ʒwaṅ′‿drə	“
dislocate	démettre	dē″met′trə	put

English	French		*See*
disown	dédire	dē″dīr′	slander
“	méconnaître	mē″keṅ″ā′‿trə	appear
displease	déplaire	dē″plār′	please
dissolve	dissoudre	dīs″sū′‿drə	absolve
distract	distraire	dīs″trār′	milk
divert	“	“	“
do over	enduire	ɑṅ″dwīr′	reduce
drink again	reboire	rə-bwār′	drink
dye	teindre	taṅ′‿drə	join
elect	élire	ē″līr′	read
elect again	réélire	rē″ē″līr′	“
emit	émettre	ē″met′‿trə	put
enclose	enceindre	ɑṅ″saṅ′‿drə	join
“	enclore	ɑṅ″klōr′	close
encompass	ceindre	saṅ′‿drə	join
enjoin	enjoindre	ɑṅ″ʒwaṅ′‿drə	“
enter one's name	s'inscrire	saṅs″‿krīr′	write
escape	se soustraire (à)	sə sūs″trār′ (ɑ)	milk
exclude	exclure	eks″klür′	conclude
expose	compromettre	keṅ″pro″met′‿trə	put
extinguish	éteindre	ē″taṅ′‿drə	join
extract	extraire	eks″trār′	milk
fall back upon	se rabattre	sə rɑ″bɑ̄t′‿trə	beat
fall down	s'abattre	sɑ″bɑt′‿trə	“
fear	craindre	kraṅ′‿drə	join
feign	feindre	faṅ′‿drə	“
fetch	aveindre	ɑ″vaṅ′‿drə	“
fight	se battre	sə bɑ̄t′‿trə	beat
fight	combattre	keṅ″bɑ̄t′‿trə	“
fine-draw	rentraire	rɑṅ″trār′	milk
forbid	interdire	aṅ″tēr″dīr′	slander
foreclose	forclore	fer″klōr′	close
foretell	prédire	prē″dīr′	slander
forget oneself	se méconnaître	sə mē″keṅ″nā′‿trə	appear
fry again	refrire	rə-frīr′	fry
get rid	se défaire	sə dē″fār′	make
gird	ceindre	saṅ′‿drə	join
glitter	reluire	rə-lü″wīr′	shine
grind over again	remoudre	rə-mū′‿drə	grind
grow again	recroître	rə-krwā′‿trə	grow
grow out	surcroître	sür″krwā′‿trə	“
hear of	apprendre	ɑp″‿prɑ̄ṅ′‿drə	take
humor	complaire	keṅ″plār′	please
imitate	contrefaire	keṅ″trə-fār′	make
imprint	empreindre	ɑṅ″praṅ′‿drə	join
include	comprendre	koṅ″prɑṅ′‿drə	take
increase	accroître	ak″krwā′‿trə	grow
induce	induire	aṅ″dwīr′	reduce
infringe	enfreindre	ɑṅ″fraṅ′drə	join
inscribe	inscrire	aṅs″krīr′	write
instruct	instruire	aṅs″trwīr′	reduce
interdict	interdire	aṅ″tār″dīr′	slander
interpose	s'entremettre	sɑṅ″‿trə-met′‿trə	put
interrupt	interrompre	aṅ″tēr″‿reṅ′‿prə	break
introduce	introduire	aṅ″tro″dwīr′	reduce
issue	émettre	ē″met′‿trə	put
join again	rejoindre	rə-ʒwaṅ′‿drə	join
keep secret	taire	tār	please
kill oneself	se détruire	sa dē″trwīr′	reduce
know	connaître	keṅ″nā′‿trə	appear
laugh at	se rire	sa rīr	laugh
lay the tire of a wheel	embattre	ɑṅ″bɑ̄t′trə	beat
lead	conduire	koṅ″dwīr′	reduce

English	French		See
learn	apprendre	ap″‿prän′‿drə	take
learn again	rapprendre	rap″prän′‿drə	"
loosen	déprendre	dē″prän′‿drə	"
make again	refaire	rə-fār′	make
meddle	s'entremettre	sań″‿trə-met′‿trə	put
melt	dissoudre	dis″‿sū′‿drə	absolve
mistake	se méprendre	sə mē″prän′drə	take
moan	geindre	ʒań′‿drə	join
not to know	méconnaître	mē″kəń″‿nā′‿trə	appear
outlaw	proscrire	pros″krīr′	write
outlive	survivre (à)	sür″vī′‿vrə (a)	live
omit	omettre	ō″met′trə	put
overtake	atteindre	at″tań′‿drə	join
overtake again	ratteindre	rat″tań′‿drə	"
paint	peindre	pań′‿drə	"
paint again	repeindre	rə-pań′‿drə	"
perfect	parfaire	par″fār′	make
permit	permettre	pār″met′trə	put
pursue	suivre	swī′‿vrə	follow
pity	plaindre	plań′‿drə	join
plaster	enduire	ań″dwīr′	reduce
plaster anew	renduire	rań″dwīr′	"
please to humor	complaire	kəń″plār′	please
predict	prédire	prē″dīr′	slander
prescribe	prescrire	pres″krīr′	write
produce	produire	pro″dwīr′	reduce
promise	promettre	pro″met′‿trə	put
prosecute	poursuivre	pūr″swī′vrə	follow
proscribe	proscrire	pros″krīr′	write
pull down	abattre	a″bāt′trə	beat
reach	atteindre	at″‿tań′‿drə	join
read again	relire	rə-līr′	read
read over previously	prélire	prē″līr′	"
recant	se dédire	sə dē″dīr′	slander
recognize	reconnaître	rə-kəń″‿nā′‿trə	appear
recover	se refaire	sə rə-fār′	make
redeem an estate	retraire	rə-trār′	milk
refuse	éconduir	ē″kəń″dwīr′	reduce
remain silent	se taire	sa tār	please
reproduce	reproduire	rə-pro″dwīr′	reduce
replace	remettre	rə-met′‿trə	put
resign	se démettre de	sa dē″met′‿trə də	"
restrain	restreindre	res″trań′‿drə	join
retract	se dédire	sa dē″dīr′	slander
revive	renaître	rə-nā′‿trə	born
"	revivre	rə-vī′‿vrə	live
satisfy	satisfaire	sa″tis″fār′	make
say again	redire	rə-dīr′	say
seduce	séduire	sē″dwīr′	reduce
set again	remettre	rə-met′‿trə	put
set forth	émettre	ē″met′‿trə	"
sharpen	émoudre	ē″mū drə	grind
sharpen again	rémoudre	rē″mū′‿drə	"
shine (to glitter)	reluire	rə-lwīr′	shine
shine a little	entre-luire	ań″trə-lwīr′	"
shut up	reclure	rə-klūr′	conclude
smile	sourire	sū″rīr′	laugh
squeeze out	épreindre	ē″prań′‿drə	join
struggle	se débattre	sə dē″bāt′‿trə	beat
subdue	soumettre	sū″met′‿trə	put
subject	astreindre	as″trań′‿drə	join
submit	soumettre	sū″met′‿trə	put

English	French		See
subscribe	souscrire	sūs″krīr′	write
subtract	soustraire	sūs″trār′	milk
surprize	surprendre	sür″prāṅ′‿drə	take
survive	survivre (à)	sür″vī′‿vrə	live
take again	reprendre	rə-prαṅ′‿drə	take
take from	aveindre	α″vaṅ′‿drə	join
take one's pleasure	s'ébattre	sē″bāt′‿trə	beat
take out	aveindre	α″vaṅ′‿drə	join
take to pieces	déconstruire	dē″kəṅ″strwīr′	reduce
thin (syrups, etc.)	décuire	dē″kwīr′	"
thirst after	se repaître	sə rə-pā′‿trə	feed
tie close	étreindre	ē″trāṅ′‿drə	join
transcribe	transcrire	trαṅs″krīr′	write
transgress	enfreindre	αṅ″fraṅ′‿drə	join
translate	traduire	trα″dwīr′	reduce
transmit	transmettre	trαṅs″met′‿trə	put
turn	se rabattre	sə rα″bāt′‿trə	beat
turn off	" "	" "	"
understand	comprendre	kəṅ″prāṅ′‿drə	take
undertake	entreprendre	αṅ″‿trə-prāṅ′drə	"
unclose	déclore	dē″‿klər′	close
undo	défaire	dē″fār′	make
undo again	redéfaire	rə-dē″fār′	"
unlearn	désapprendre	dē″zα″prāṅ′‿drə	take
unsay	dédire	dē″dīr′	slander
unsew	découdre	dē″kū′‿drə	coudre
whet	émoudre	ē″mū′‿drə	grind
whine	geindre	ʒaṅ′‿drə	join
write again	récrire	rē″krīr′	write

ADVERB. So called because it most frequently accompanies the verb. There are in French several kinds of adverbs of which the following are the principal: (1) Place (*ailleurs* [αi″‿yūr′], elsewhere); (2) Time (*aujourd'hui* [ō″ʒūr″‿dwī′], to-day); (3) Quantity (*assez* [αs″sē′], enough); (4) Manner or Comparison (*ensemble* [αṅ″sāṅ′‿blə], altogether); (5) Affirmation or Doubt (*certainement* [sār″tān″māṅ′], certainly); (6) Negation (*non* [noṅ], no).

Adverbs are generally formed by adding *-ment* to the adjective in its feminine form: *parfait* (pαr″fā′), masculine; *parfaite* (pαr″fāt′), feminine; adverb, *parfaitement* (pαr″fā″tə-māṅ′).

Several adverbs are employed interrogatively, as: *Quand partez-vous?* [kαṅ pαr″tē′ vū], when are you going? They form their degrees of comparison like the adjectives, with the exception of the following three which are irregular in the comparative degree: *bien*, bī″‿yaṅ′ (well); *mieux*, mī″‿yū′ (better); *mal*, mal (badly); *pis*, pī (worse); and *peu*, pū (little); *moins*, mwaṅ (less). The superlative relative of these three adverbs is respectively: *le mieux*, *le pis* and *le moins*, and the superlative absolute—*très* (trā) *bien*, *très mal* and *très peu*.

Adverbs are *placed immediately after the verb in French*, not before, as in English.

I never saw him. *Je ne l'ai jamais vu*: ʒə nə lā ʒα″mā′ vü.

He often comes here. *Il vient souvent ici*: īl vī″‿yaṅ′ sū″vāṅ′ ī″sī′.

I always speak French. *Je parle toujours français*: ʒə pαr′‿lə tū″ʒūr′ frαn″sā′.

They seldom go out. *Ils sortent rarement*: īl sōrt rα″‿rə-māṅ′.

Adverbs of quantity require *de* before the next noun.

He has money enough. *Il a assez d'argent*: īl α αs″sē′ dαr″ʒāṅ′.

They have much wit. *Ils ont beaucoup d'esprit*: īls‿oṅ bō″kū′ des″prī′.

Few people think. *Peu de gens pensent*: pū də ʒaṅ paṅs.
He never has money. *Il n'a jamais d'argent*: īl na ʒa″mā′ dar″ʒāṅ′.

PREPOSITION. A particle that denotes the relation of an object to an action or thing. In French some have been formed from nouns, as *malgré* (mal″grē′), notwithstanding; from adjectives, as *sauf* (sōf), except; from imperatives, as *voici = vois ici* (vwa″sī′), here is; from present participles, as *durant* (dü″rāṅ′), during; *pendant* (paṅ″dāṅ′), while; *touchant* (tū″shāṅ′), concerning, etc.; or from past participles, as *vu* (vü), considering; *attendu que* (at″taṅ″dü′ kə), seeing that; *excepté* (ek″sep″tē′), except, save; *hormis* (ēr″mī′), saving, etc.
The relations expressed are (1) *of position;* as, *à* (a), at; *contre* (keṅ′trə), against; *jusque* (ʒüs′kə), as far as, until; (2) *of starting point;* as, *de* (də), of, from; *par* (par), by; (3) *of direction;* as, *vers* (vār), toward; (4) *of manner;* as, *avec* (a″vek′), with; *par* (par), through; *sans* (saṅ), without; (5) *of time;* as, *avant* (a″vāṅ′), before; *après* (a″prē′), after; *dès* (dā), since; *pendant* (paṅ″dāṅ′), while, etc.; (6) *of place;* as, *dans* (daṅ), in; *en* (aṅ), in, within, on, to, at, like, as a, out of, by, for; *chez* (shē), at the house of, at, to, in, the native place of; *devant* (də-vāṅ′), before; *derrière* (dār″‿rī″yār′), behind; *sur* (sür), on; *sous* (sū), under; *entre* (āṅ′‿trə), between; *parmi* (par″mī′), among.
Almost every French grammar points out the fact that the correct use of prepositions can be taught by practise alone. The chief difficulty arises from the fact that there are about 400 words—adjectives, verbs, and participles—that must be connected with the infinitive that follows sometimes by aid of a preposition, often without this aid; as, "Il ambitionne *de* conquérir" (īl aṅ″bī″sī″yeṅ′‿nə də keṅ″kē″rīr′): "He is earnestly desirous of conquering," or "He desires earnestly to conquer;" "Il veut conquérir" (īl vū keṅ″kē″rīr′): "He wishes to conquer."
Sometimes prepositions must be introduced in French when there are none in the English sentence one wishes to utter; as, "Je doute *de* cela" (ʒə dūt də sə-lā′): "I doubt that"; "Il a nui à mon frère" (īl a nwī a meṅ frār): "He has injured my brother."
Likewise, sometimes, *but infrequently*, the preposition in an English sentence is suppressed in French:—We listen *to* the chaplain: Nous écoutons le chapelain (nūz‿ē″kū″teṅ′ lə sha″-pə-lāṅ′).

CONJUNCTION. A part of speech which serves to connect words or sentences. In French they are classified as: (1) *Copulative conjunctions*, conjunctions expressing addition or expansion; as, *et* (ē), and; *aussi* (ōs″sī′), also. (2) *Alternative conjunctions*, or those that introduce an alternative; as, *ou* (ū), or; *ni* (nī), nor. (3) *Coordinate conjunctions*, or those that join coordinate clauses in compound sentences; as, *mais* (mā), but; *néanmoins* (nē″aṅ″mwaṅ′), notwithstanding. (4) *Subordinate conjunctions*, or those that join subordinate to principal clauses; as, *quoique* (kwā′kə), altho.
The principal conjunctions are: *ainsi* (aṅ″sī′), thus; *aussi* (ōs″sī′), also; *car* (kar), for; *cependant* (sə-paṅ″dāṅ′), yet; *comme* (kem), as; *donc* (deṅk), therefore; *et* (ē), and; *lorsque* (lērs′kə), when; *mais* (mā), but; *néanmoins* (nē″āṅ″mwaṅ′), notwithstanding; *ni* (nī), nor; *ou* (ū), or; *or* (ēr), but, now; *pourquoi* (pūr″kwā′), why; *puisque* (pwīs′kə), since; *quand* (kaṅ), altho; *que* (kə), that; *quoique* (kwā′kə), whatever, altho; *si* (sī), if; *sinon* (sī″neṅ′), if not, otherwise; *soit* (swa), either, whether, or; *toutefois* (tūt″fwā′), nevertheless.

INTERJECTION. A part of speech which is used to express sudden emotion, excitement, or feeling. The following are the chief interjections in French: *Ah! Aïe* (ā″yī′); *Bah! Bravo! Eh! Fi!* (fī: English, *Fie!*); *Gare* (gar); that is, Make way! beware! *Ha! He!* (he); *Hélas* (ē″lās′: English, *Alas!*): *Ho! O! Oh! Sus* (süs: English, At them!); *Zest* (zest: English, *Pshaw!*).

There are, however, certain words that have interjectional force; as, *Alerte* (a″lärt′): Look out! *Allons* (al″leṅ′): Come on! *Bon* (beṅ): Good! Well! *Ciel* (sī″yel′): Heaven! *Courage* (kū″rā′‿ʒə): Courage! *Ferme* (fārm): Stand firm! Cheer up! *Halte* (hāl′‿tə): Halt! *Paix* (pā): Peace! *Preste* (pres′‿tə): Quick! Look alive! *Silence* (sī″lāṅs′): Silence! *Tenez* (tə-nē)! Hold! See! *Tiens* (tī″‿yaṅ′): Look!

MEASURES AND WEIGHTS

Capacity

1 pint	=	0.5679 litres (lĭ′‿trə).
1 quart (2 pints)	=	1.1359 "
1 gallon (4 quarts)	=	4.5434 "
1 peck (2 gallons)	=	9.0869 "
1 bushel (8 gallons)	=	36.348 "
1 quarter (8 bushels)	=	290.781 "

1 litre	= 0.22 gallons	or	$1\frac{3}{4}$ pints.
2 litres	= 0.44 "	"	1 qt. $1\frac{1}{2}$ pints.
3 "	= 0.66 "	"	2 qts. $1\frac{1}{2}$ pints.
4 "	= 0.88 "	"	3 qts. 1 pint.
5 "	= 1.10 "	"	1 gal. 0 qts. $\frac{3}{4}$ pint.
10 "	= 2.20 "	"	2 gal. 0 qts. $1\frac{1}{2}$ pints.

Distance

1 kilomètre (kĭ″lō″mā′trə)	= $^{5}/_{8}$ mile.	15 kilomètre (kĭ″lō″mā′trə)	= $9^{1}/_{3}$ miles.
2 "	= $1^{1}/_{4}$ "	16 "	= 10 "
3 "	= $1^{7}/_{8}$ "	17 "	= $10^{5}/_{8}$ "
4 "	= $2^{1}/_{2}$ "	18 "	= $11^{1}/_{4}$ "
5 "	= $3^{1}/_{10}$ "	19 "	= $11^{7}/_{8}$ "
6 "	= $3^{3}/_{4}$ "	20 "	= $12^{1}/_{2}$ "
7 "	= $4^{1}/_{3}$ "	30 "	= $18^{5}/_{8}$ "
8 "	= 5 "	40 "	= $24^{7}/_{8}$ "
9 "	= $5^{5}/_{8}$ "	50 "	= 31 "
10 "	= $6^{1}/_{4}$ "	60 "	= $37^{1}/_{4}$ "
11 "	= $6^{7}/_{8}$ "	70 "	= $43^{1}/_{2}$ "
12 "	= $7^{1}/_{2}$ "	80 "	= $49^{3}/_{4}$ "
13 "	= 8 "	90 "	= 56 "
14 "	= $8^{3}/_{4}$ "	100 "	= $62^{1}/_{8}$ "

For means of conversion see under LENGTH, below.

Length

1 inch = 0.0254 mètres (mā′trə) or 2.54 centimètres (saṅ″tĭ″mā′trə).
1 foot = 0.3048 " " 30.48 "
1 yard = 0.9144 " " 91.44 "
1 mile = 1609 mètres (1 kilom. 609 mètres).
Millimètre (1000th of a mètre) = 0.03937 (about $^{1}/_{25}$) inch.
Centimètre (100th of a mètre) = 0.393708 (about $^{2}/_{5}$) inch.
Décimètre (10th of a mètre) = 3.937079 (about $3^{19}/_{20}$) inches.
Mètre = 3.2808992 ft., roughly 1 yd. $3\frac{1}{2}$ in.
Kilomètre (1000 mètres) = 1093.633 yds., or about $^{5}/_{8}$ of a mile.

CONVERSION. To convert kilomètres into miles multiply by 5 and divide by 8; and miles into kilomètres multiply by 8 and divide by 5. See also illustration comparing inches and centimètres on the following page.

Square or Superficial

1 square inch = 0.0006451 mètres carrés (mā′trə kar″rē′) or 6.451 ($6^{9}/_{20}$) centimètres carrés.
1 square foot = 0.0929 mètres carrés or 929 centimètres carrés.
1 square yard = 0.8361 mètres carrés or 8361 centimètres carrés.
1 acre = 0.404671 hectares (ek″tär′) (4047 mètres carrés).
1 mètre carré = { 1550 square inches. / 10.764 (about $10^{3}/_{4}$) square feet. / 1.196 (about $1^{1}/_{5}$) square yards.
1 hectare (10,000 mètres carrés) = 2.471143 (about $2\frac{1}{2}$) acres.

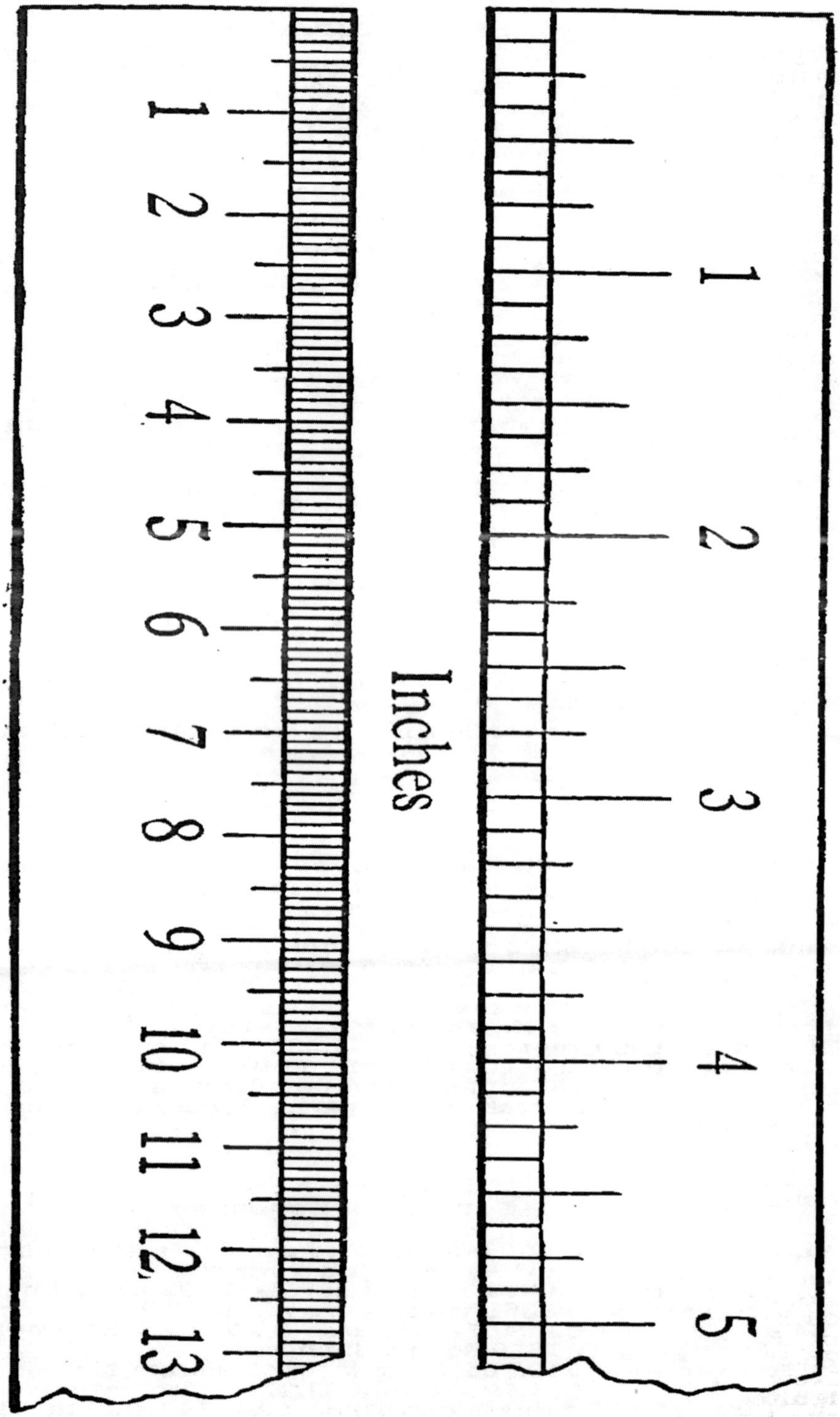

COMPARATIVE RELATION OF CENTIMETERS TO INCHES

THERMOMETRIC

The thermometric scale used in the United States and in Great Britain is that of Fahrenheit. On the Continent, that of Celsius, the Centigrade scale, is employed.

Freezing point Fahr., 32°
" " Cent., 0
Boiling point Fahr., 212°
" " Cent., 100°

Blood heat, that is the normal temperature of the human body, is 98½° Fahr. or 37° Cent. Any rise above this temperature indicates fever heat.

In cases of fever temperatures of 99.5° to 100.5° Fahrenheit are considered as mild; 100.5° to 101.5° Fahr. as slight; up to 103° Fahr. as moderate; up to 105° Fahr. as considerable; above 105° Fahr. as high fever. The highest fever temperature within the limits of life (excluding exceptionally rare cases) is, on an average, 107.6° to 108.5° Fahr. The normal temperature of a sick-room is 65° Fahr.

By the Centigrade scale, oil of turpentine solidifies at 27° below zero; cyanogen boils at 20° below, sulfur dioxid at 20° below, and tetrylene at 4° below zero; 0° is the freezing-point of water, and 4° its point of greatest density; acetic acid melts at 17°, cæsium at 26.5°, butter at 33°; ether boils at 34.9°; rubidium melts at 38.5°; carbon disulfid boils at 46°; stearin melts at 55°; white wax melts at 65°; ethyl acetate boils at 74.3°; alcohol boils at 78.4°; water boils at 100°; Dead Sea water boils at 105°. By the Fahrenheit scale, 79° below zero represents the greatest natural cold (reported by Captain Amundsen from Boothia in 1905); bromin solidifies at 20° below zero; methyl chlorid boils at 9° below; 0° represents the temperature of a mixture of ice and salt; 30° is the point at which olive-oil solidifies. The average temperature of Berlin is 48.5°, of London 50.3°, of New York 53.8°, of San Francisco 56.6°, of Rome 59.7°, of Sydney 63°, of New Orleans 68.6°, of Calcutta 78.3°. 130° represents highest shade temperature (recorded from New South Wales); 600° is the melting-point of lead; at 762° coal ignites; at 1981° gold melts; at 2500° steel melts; 4000° represents the heat of a Bessemer furnace.

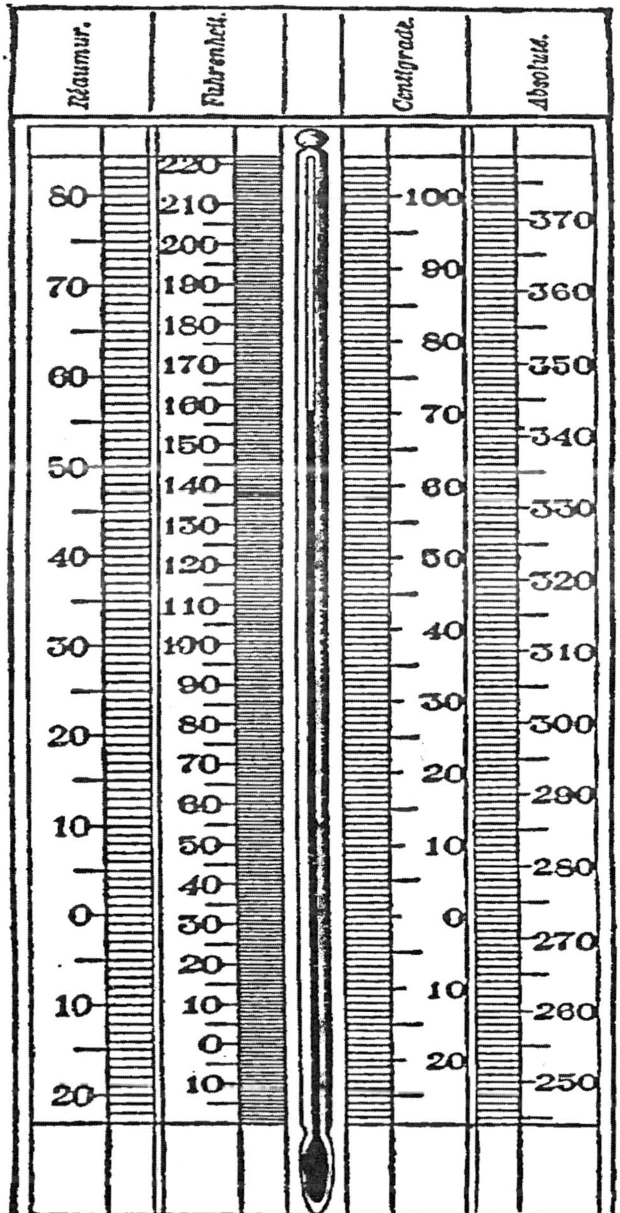

The Four Principal Thermometers Compared

Table for Conversion

Fahr. degrees may be converted to Cent. by subtracting 32 and multiplying by $^5/_9$; for instance, 77 degrees Fahr. = (77-32) × $^5/_9$ = 25 degrees Cent.

Cent. degrees may be converted to Fahr. by multiplying by $^9/_5$ths and adding 32; for instance, 25 degrees Cent. = (25 × $^9/_5$ + 32) = 77 degrees Fahr.

55 Fahr.	=	12.7 Cent.	80 Fahr.	=	26.6 Cent.
60 "	=	15.5 "	85 "	=	29.4 "
65 "	=	18.3 "	90 "	=	32.2 "
70 "	=	21.1 "	95 "	=	35 "
75 "	=	23.8 "	100 "	=	37.7 "

WEIGHT

Avoirdupois

1 ounce	= 0.02835 kilos. (28.35 grammes).
1 pound (16 ozs.)	= 0.454 kilos. (454 grammes).
1 quarter (28 lbs.)	= 12.7 kilos.
1 hundredweight (112 lbs.)	= 50.8 kilos.
1 ton (20 cwt.)	= 1016.046 kilos.
1 kilogramme (1000 grs.)	= 2.2055 lbs. or 2 lbs. 3¼ oz.
2 "	= 4.4110 lbs. or 4 lbs. 6½ oz.
3 "	= 6.6165 lbs. or 6 lbs. 9¾ oz.
4 "	= 8.8220 lbs. or 8 lbs. 13 oz.
5 "	= 11.0275 lbs. or 11 lbs. ½ oz.
1 livre (½ kilogramme)	= 1.1028 lbs. or 1 lb. 1½ oz.

To convert kilos. to pounds (roughly) multiply by 2¼.